AMERICAN INTERVENTION IN GREECE, 1943–1949

Contemporary American History Series
William E. Leuchtenburg, General Editor

AMERICAN INTERVENTION IN GREECE, 1943–1949

Lawrence S. Wittner

1982
COLUMBIA UNIVERSITY PRESS
NEW YORK

Clothbound editions of Columbia University Press books are Smyth-sewn and printed on permanent and durable acid-free paper.

Copyright © 1982 Columbia University Press
All rights reserved.
Printed in the United States of America

Columbia University Press
New York   Guildford, Surrey

Library of Congress Cataloging in Publication Data

Wittner, Lawrence S.
  American Intervention in Greece, 1943–1949.

  (Contemporary American history series)
  Bibliography: p.
  Includes index.
  1. United States—Foreign relations—Greece.
2. Greece—Foreign relations—United States.
3. Greece—History—1944–1949.   4. United
States—Foreign relations—1945–1953.   I. Title.
II. Series.
E183.8.G8W57   327.730495   81–38521
ISBN 0–231–04196–9   AACR2

TO JULIA

CONTENTS

PREFACE

In recent decades, scholars have spent a great deal of time writing about the origins and development of the Cold War. Surveying the panorama of a world in conflict, they have produced an abundant literature marked by sharply divergent interpretations. Although the debate has grown heated, at times overheated, it has been fruitful, prodding many inside the scholarly community and some outside to reassess positions that once seemed axiomatic. Even so, at present the debate seems to be producing diminishing returns, with much the same data rearranged and reassessed. As a result, a sense of exhaustion may be setting in. This is unfortunate, for the Cold War remains a problem of great magnitude and the debate on its origins and development, while stalled, has never been resolved satisfactorily.

If new substance is to be injected into our understanding of the Cold War, it will probably emerge through the case study method—the gathering of new evidence on a country-by-country basis. Of course, in world affairs, the microcosm is never completely typical of the macrocosm; it cannot tell us all we want to know about the global picture. Nevertheless, some lines of investigation are clearly very important and should be pursued with greater vigor. Furthermore, gathered together, case studies can provide a new and richer basis for generalization; at the very least, they will give scholars concrete examples with which to support their favorite interpretations.

I began my research on American policy toward Greece with this in mind. The Truman Doctrine of March 1947 was one of the best-known and most frequently cited items of postwar American diplomacy. Yet most scholarly writing on the subject consisted of little more than a pastiche of platitudes lifted from the President's address. Behind the doctrine lay a bitter political conflict in Greece that, as early as 1943, had begun laying the groundwork for the disastrous and bloody Greek civil war. The international implications of this civil war attracted the intervention of the British and, later, of the Americans, who commenced a massive program of military and economic aid to the right-wing Greek government. After late 1949, when an American-directed counter-insurgency program had succeeded in restoring stability, Greece became a Cold War ally of the United States and a prototype for subsequent U.S. intervention in small, under-developed nations. An in-depth study of American policy toward Greece, then, promised to yield important findings concerning the nature and practice of recent American foreign policy.

Unfortunately, it is one thing to recommend that scholars embark on in-depth studies and quite another to undertake them. In this case, at least, the task proved formidable. To do the job properly, one must consult a great many documents, particularly government records—so many that I feared for a time that no individual could possibly read them all. Yet, ironically, some of the most vital sources are simply not available. Important U.S. government records still remain classified (e.g., most materials originating with the CIA), although I have managed to obtain a small portion of them through the Freedom of Information Act. Virtually all Greek records—with the exception of Greek diplomatic correspondence located in British and American archives—are also closed to researchers. This would be a better book if I (or anyone) had access to the Greek government's files or, for that matter, to those of the Soviet Union. But government secrecy is a perennial dilemma of foreign policy scholars, who have learned to do the best they can with what is available.

The absence of accessible Greek government sources, in combination with my own interest in American diplomacy, has led me to focus my account upon the American role in Greece. In discussing Greece's internal affairs, I have sought to draw on the best scholarly studies available, as well as on the advice of some of the foremost writers on modern Greece. Accordingly, I lay no claim to breakthroughs in the area of modern Greek history. In fact, I will be content if I summarize accurately the existing scholarly knowledge in this area. I do think I have unearthed new material on U.S. policies and programs—material with important ramifications for diplomatic history, Greek politics, and American public policy.

Those acquainted with the debate over the origins of the Cold War may have some difficulty categorizing this study and its conclusions. In general, it bolsters the "revisionist" case, for it emphasizes the "Open Door" concerns of American officials and the limited ambitions of Soviet diplomacy. Yet, in certain respects, its findings should bring some comfort to scholars with a more traditional approach, for it demonstrates that Washington policymakers genuinely feared the extension of Soviet power, viewed the Greek left as a catspaw for masterminds in the Kremlin, and had little interest in exploiting Greece economically.

Whatever their theoretical predispositions, however, readers will probably find this a startling, even jarring, account of U.S. government behavior. America's dealings with wartime and postwar Greece are not very pretty, and any attempt to relate them accurately leads, inevitably, to the exposure of official lying, cynicism, and cruelty. It may be useful to keep in mind the fact that the story presented here is probably biased *toward* the Americans, for I have relied primarily upon their records and those of their British allies. (What they chose not to retain in their files or what the leftist insurgents thought of them was undoubtedly more damning.) Naturally, the United States is not unique in villainy, and a detailed study of France's treatment of its African colonies or of the Soviet Union's behavior toward its East European client states would also make grim reading. Nevertheless, the nastiness of numerous "great powers" in world affairs—their wars, their secret police, and their bullying of smaller nations—does not strike me as sufficient justification for tidying up this nation's record in accordance with patriotic norms. Quite the contrary, the sooner we remove our nationalistic blinders, the sooner we will be able to understand the world and provide a decent life for its people.

In a number of respects, this book has been a cooperative venture. I would like to thank the Research Foundation of the State University of New York, the Truman Library, and the Eleanor Roosevelt Institute of the Roosevelt Library for generous financial assistance that greatly facilitated my research. I am also grateful to numerous librarians and archivists who located and duplicated research materials, and to those persons who assisted me in typing the manuscript, most notably Angeliki Aretakis and Billie Albrecht. Many scholars and researchers were kind enough to provide me with copies of relevant documents uncovered through their own research, among them George Alexander, Lars Baerentzen, Henry Berger, Robert Griffith, William Loveland, Stanley Max, Yiannis Roubatis, and Howard Schonberger. Elias Vlanton was of particular assistance along these lines. I am also indebted to those scholars who read portions of the manuscript and gave me helpful comments or criticism. Their number includes many of the above, as well as G. J. Barker-Benfield, Barton Bernstein, Harry and Anne Cliadakis, Blanche Wiesen Cook, Arthur Ekirch, George Frangos, John Iatrides, H. Peter Krosby, William E. Leuchtenburg, William H. McNeill, Martin Sherwin, L. S. Stavrianos, and Joseph Zacek. In the last stage of the project, Stanley Max prepared the index, while Bernard Gronert and Karen Mitchell of Columbia University Press steered the work toward publication.

Finally, this book is dedicated to my daughter, Julia Wittner, in the hope that she and other children will inherit a world whose national leaders are wiser and more compassionate.

Lawrence S. Wittner

Albany, New York

In this world, he thought, you're either a lamb or a wolf. If you're a lamb, you're eaten up; if you're a wolf, you do the eating. My God, is there no third animal, a stronger, kinder one?

Nikos Kazantzakis,
The Fratricides, p. 86

1.
CONTAINING THE WARTIME RESISTANCE
1943–1945

Subversive social forces are continuing to operate powerfully in
Greece today. . . . The new growth of class-consciousness and
proletarianism has altered the . . . problem of maintaining British
control.

Lincoln MacVeagh, October 15, 1944[1]

American relations with Greece predated the establishment
of the United States, but acquired significance for U.S. policymakers only with the onset of World War II. Before the
war, America's interest in that land had been based primarily
on a respect for classical civilization, sympathy for the Greek
independence struggle, absorption of several hundred thousand Greek immigrants, modest trading ventures, and sponsorship of charitable activities—features which American
statesmen regarded as of limited importance.[2] With the outbreak of the Second World War, then, it was Great Britain—
long the dominant power in the eastern Mediterranean—
which assumed responsibility for the defense of Greece and,
later, for its liberation. The war, however, set new forces in
motion: in Greece, the collapse of the old order and the
emergence of a broadly based, left-wing resistance movement;
in Europe and the Near East, the decline of British power
and the extension of Soviet influence; and, in the world, a
scramble for petroleum resources. These added a new dimension to the situation—one which left American officials
far less disinterested than in the past. As a result, they grew
anxious at the turbulent situation in Greece and became ever
more deeply involved in efforts to control it.

Situated in the southeastern corner of Europe, athwart the sea routes to Asia and the Middle East, the small, impoverished nation of Greece was long coveted by the world's "great powers." The Greeks had barely broken free from Turkish rule in the early nineteenth century when the dominant powers of Europe began clashing for control of the new nation. Territorial settlements, royal dynasties, and even political parties came under the influence of what Greeks called "the foreign factor."[3] By World War I, Great Britain had emerged as the major external force in Greek affairs, but in the 1930s it was challenged by Benito Mussolini's Italy and Adolf Hitler's Germany. The Axis powers received an apparent windfall in 1936 when, assisted by Greece's King George II, General John Metaxas assumed dictatorial power in Athens, instituting the Greek version of a fascist state. Yet, though Metaxas borrowed from Nazi programs, he was also a fierce nationalist; consequently, he refused to submit to an Italian ultimatum in 1940.[4] Called to arms to defend their nation against foreign aggression, the Greek people responded with such fervor that they drove the marauding Italians back deep into Albania. As a result, Hitler found it necessary to send in crack German units. Meanwhile, the British dug in for what they hoped would be a prolonged defense. But the death of Metaxas, coupled with the defeatism (verging on collaborationism) of his surviving colleagues, led in early 1941 to the collapse of the Anglo-Greek war effort. Together with their Italian and Bulgarian allies, the Germans fastened upon Greece a grim and brutal occupation regime.[5]

In the midst of widespread suffering and repression, a vigorous resistance movement arose within Greece to contest the Axis occupation. Although the first acts of defiance were isolated and spontaneous, perhaps 90 percent of the resistance eventually came under the direction of the National Liberation Front (better known by its Greek acronym, EAM). Organized in September 1941 by the Greek Communist Party (KKE) and initially staffed by party militants, EAM remained thereafter largely under Communist control, particularly at the upper levels of power. Nevertheless, EAM was never a narrow, sectarian affair, but an unorthodox, predominantly non-Communist organization, with a membership by 1944 of perhaps 1½ million people (out of Greece's 7½ million) and armed forces (ELAS) of about 50,000 guerrilla fighters. Thousands of republican officers, large numbers of women and peasants, virtually the entire labor movement, and a surprising array of clergymen and intellectuals took up the resistance cause. In the course of the war, EAM pinned down 300,000 enemy troops; accounted for enemy casualties in the tens of thousands; frustrated fascist plans for labor conscription; sabotaged German transportation, supply, and communications networks; and rescued thousands of prisoners of war, Jews, and Allied airmen from the occupation forces.[6] Large areas of the countryside freed themselves entirely from the fascist yoke, establishing radical political, social, and cultural institutions which resistance ideologues promised were only the beginning of *laokratia*, "people's rule," in Greece. Along the way, EAM also made many enemies, particularly among those whom it attacked, sometimes violently, as collaborators or rivals, or those who blamed it for the savage German reprisals which followed EAM raids. Even so, EAM enjoyed immense popularity within Greece and, despite the Axis occupation, became the dominant force in much of the country.[7]

The development of a left-wing resistance movement was watched with foreboding by more traditional sectors of Greek society. Many former royalists flocked to a succession of Quisling governments in Athens, while thousands of zealous anti-Communists joined the right-wing Security Battalions, participating in German-led counterinsurgency campaigns.[8] Most of the old-line political party leaders, while not collaborators, either remained inactive in Athens or departed for Cairo, where the Greek government-in-exile regrouped under the British wing. In early 1943, the Cairo government had no plans for guerrilla warfare and even warned loyal army officers in Greece against cooperation with EAM or its much smaller, conservative competitor, EDES, the National Republican Greek League. The leader of the latter organization, General Napoleon Zervas, took to the field only after the disgusted

British tired of funding him without results and threatened to denounce him to the Gestapo. Not surprisingly, Zervas ended up secretly cooperating with the Germans.[9] Although the Greek King opposed the German invasion and cooperated, in exile, with the British, his reputation was hardly much better than that of the collaborators among most Greeks. Having helped to install the hated Metaxas regime and worked with it loyally thereafter, the King was stigmatized by years of cruel, right-wing dictatorship. Indeed, he was the very symbol of the old order that EAM vowed to destroy.[10]

The British, who had inherited the Mediterranean as their theater of wartime operations, hardly knew how to cope with this situation. After all, Britain was at war, and military considerations necessitated the maximum possible resistance to German power. To stimulate and coordinate this resistance, the first detachment of officers from Britain's Strategic Operations Executive (SOE), led by Colonel Eddie Myers, parachuted into Greece in late September 1942. Although the SOE mission discovered, to its dismay, that EAM was Communist-led, it maintained close if chilly relations with the leftist resistance, supplying it for a time with small quantities of arms and sizable allotments of gold sovereigns.[11] On the other hand, immediate military imperatives clashed with longer-term political objectives. Ever since the nineteenth century, the British Foreign Office had viewed British control of Greece as vital to protecting the "imperial lifeline," particularly the sea routes to India and to the oil of the Middle East.[12] Winston Churchill and the Foreign Office believed that Britain's postwar supremacy in Greece could best be secured by working through the Greek monarchy, an institution to which they also felt a strong sentimental attachment.[13] In this context, the growing strength of the leftist resistance movement represented a significant danger. British Foreign Secretary Anthony Eden thus initially opposed any aid to EAM,[14] while Churchill issued the following directive on April 18, 1943: "Subject to special operational necessity, S.O.E. should always veer in the direction of groups willing to support the King."[15]

But SOE officials pressed for a compromise, convinced by their experience in wartime Greece that London's commitment to a discredited monarchy would only undermine British influence. By announcing that the King would not return until he had received a popular mandate in a postwar plebiscite, Myers argued, the British would "knock the bottom out of EAM's anti-Royalist propaganda." In August 1943, Myers flew with six resistance leaders (four of them from EAM) to Cairo, where they met with the cabinet ministers of the Greek government-in-exile. Agreement was unanimous: a plebiscite on the monarchy must precede the King's return. Shocked by this militant republicanism, British authorities peremptorily ordered the resistance leaders to leave Cairo, dismissed Myers from his post in disgrace, and laid plans for a violent confrontation.[16] On September 29, 1943, Churchill cabled his chiefs of staff to ready British troops, armored cars, and Bren gun carriers for the occupation of Athens after the withdrawal of the Germans.[17] Responding to an armed attack on EDES by EAM the following month, the British cut off all supplies to EAM, reinforced EDES, and girded themselves for a total break with the Greek left—a break postponed only by the temporary necessity of some cooperation against the Germans.[18]

The situation remained explosive. In April 1944, the official Greek armed forces in Egypt mutinied, demanding the resignation of the government-in-exile and the establishment of a republic. Many looked fondly on EAM's government in the mountains. Complaining that the troops had been "contaminated by revolutionary and Communist elements," Churchill ordered the rebellion crushed and 10,000 suspect soldiers—about half of the Greek armed forces—confined to African concentration camps for the duration of the war. He cabled the British ambassador, Sir Reginald Leeper, that "the King . . . cannot be discarded to suit a momentary surge of appetite among ambitious *émigré* nonentities" or replaced by a government based upon "particular sets of guerrillas, in many cases indistinguishable from banditti."[19] On April 24, the British appointed a bitter foe of EAM, George Papandreou, as the Greek prime minister, pressing him to bring

EAM into the Cairo government on a minority basis and to place its armed forces under direct British military control.[20] Leeper "need not be in the least afraid of the charge that England is intervening in the affairs of Greece," Churchill told Eden. "You cannot be too stiff in handling this situation and making them feel" that Britain was "capable of giving any of them a good smack over the head."[21]

Anxious to mobilize the support of his Russian ally for British policy, Churchill instructed Eden on May 4, 1944 to draft a paper for the cabinet setting forth "the brute issues between us and the Soviet Government which are developing in Italy, in Roumania, in Bulgaria, in Yugoslavia and above all in Greece."[22] The following day, Eden initiated conversations with the Soviet ambassador in London, thus beginning exchanges among the "great powers" which culminated in an agreement that Russia would exercise predominance in Romania while Britain would maintain hegemony in Greece.[23] Nevertheless, despite the complete cooperation of Soviet Premier Joseph Stalin, Churchill remained distraught. His mind was "full of forebodings about what will happen when the Germans leave Athens," the Prime Minister's physician entered in his diary. "Winston never talks of Hitler these days; he is always harping on the dangers of Communism."[24] In October 1944, Churchill and Eden journeyed to Moscow to firm up the Anglo-Soviet understanding—"in order to have the freedom to save Greece," as Churchill explained to Roosevelt.[25] Ushered into a private meeting with Stalin on October 9, Churchill immediately unveiled his designs. He recalled:

The moment was apt for business, so I said, "Let us settle about our affairs in the Balkans. . . . I wrote out on a half sheet of paper:

Roumania	
Russia	90%
The others	10%
Greece	
Great Britain	90%
(in accord with U.S.A.)	
Russia	10%
Yugoslavia	50–50%

Hungary	50–50%
Bulgaria	
Russia	75%
The others	25%

Churchill pushed the paper across to Stalin who, after a slight pause, "took his blue pencil and made a large tick upon it, and passed it back to us. . . . It was all settled in no more time than it takes time to set down."[26]

Stalin's willingness to carve up the Balkans reflected not only his satisfaction at his share of the spoils but his relative indifference to Greece. Despite the Communist leadership of EAM, the Russians had no direct contact in wartime with the leftist resistance movement or with the Greek Communist Party until the summer of 1944.[27] In late 1943, Soviet Foreign Minister V. M. Molotov reassured the British of Russian disinterest in Greece, and in early January of the following year, at the prodding of the British, the Russians joined them in urging the guerrillas to unite under the leadership of the Cairo government.[28] In March, U.S. Army intelligence reported that, despite claims to the contrary, "the Soviet Legation in Cairo is lending no support to the E.A.M. Movement here." Indeed, the Soviet ambassador, Nikolai Novikov, told a former Greek Communist deputy "that internal Greek politics was of no interest to the Russian Legation."[29] Nonetheless, when the armed forces mutinies began in the spring of 1944, the embarrassed British could not resist the temptation to blame Moscow. "The Russians could stop the trouble in a minute if they would," Leeper complained. But as evidence of Soviet mendacity the British could do no more than point to Novikov's privately voiced criticism of British conduct and several unflattering stories in the Soviet press. Although the Russians had little sympathy for British backing of the King and the Cairo government, which they considered tainted by fascism, their diplomatic conduct remained quite proper.[30]

The same could not be said of the neighboring Yugoslav partisans, organized by the veteran Communist leader, Josip Broz Tito. A Marxist-Leninist militant whose wartime independence and successful armed struggle irked Stalin and intrigued Churchill,[31] Tito felt little besides contempt for the old order in Greece. Indeed, he and other Yugoslav Communist leaders clashed even with the KKE, which they considered insufficiently revolutionary.[32] As Tito's fortunes rose, he appears to have developed a desire to add Greek Macedonia to its counterparts in Yugoslavia and Bulgaria, thus forming a Macedonian republic within a federated Yugoslavia. This attitude disturbed EAM's leadership, which in 1943 pointedly rejected Yugoslav pressures for a joint "Balkan command" with Tito's forces, and in 1944 attacked and dispersed pro-Yugoslav armed bands in Greek Macedonia. Tito's regional lieutenant, the imperious Svetozar Vukmanovic-Tempo, warned Greek Communists that, if they did not change their attitudes, "KKE together with [the] British will find themselves up against the new Yugoslavia and the Soviet Union."[33] Although the two guerrilla movements exchanged information on German troop deployment after January 1944, when they established wireless contact, military cooperation proved more difficult. General Stefanos Sarafis, the non-Communist military commander of ELAS, recalled with some bitterness that although the Greek *andartes* repeatedly requested arms and supplies from the Yugoslav partisans and the Russian army, "we never received any."[34]

Russian indifference to the fate of the Greek left was formally confirmed in the summer of 1944. On the night of July 25, a ten-member Soviet military mission landed on an airfield near EAM headquarters. Although the Foreign Office feared (and General Sarafis hoped) that the mission presaged Soviet military aid, U.S. intelligence agents reported that "moderates" in EAM's mountain government believed that the mission would "pacify extremists and guide EAM towards participation in a unity government."[35] This belief proved to be well-founded. Headed by Colonel Gregori Popov, the mission questioned EAM leaders, coolly surveyed ELAS strength, and (as U.S. intelligence noted) "told EAM to agree to any demands of the National Government."[36] It was a stunning blow to Greek revolutionaries. Combined with Novikov's pressure in Cairo and with the demands of the "moderates," led by Alexander Svolos, the highly respected non-Communist president of the mountain government, it led that August to EAM's acceptance of participation in the Papandreou cabinet.[37] In September, EAM placed ELAS under formal Greek cabinet control.[38] Svolos, noted Eden, told British officials "that the attitude of the Russians showed complete solidarity with the other Allies and that they took the line that Greece was a British commitment."[39]

From the standpoint of the British government, the results should have been quite satisfactory. In early October, as the German occupation forces withdrew from Greece, ELAS tamely garrisoned the nation, awaiting the arrival of the British. Ordered by British General Ronald Scobie to remain clear of Athens, ELAS did not enter the city after the departure of the Germans on October 12. Six days later, when British troops and the Papandreou government reached the Greek capital, they found no sign of the much-feared revolutionary government but only a vast welcoming crowd, including thousands of EAM supporters. Hailing "the brave children of Great Britain, our freedom-loving ally," the KKE loyally promised the restoration of order. "If EAM had wished to seize control of Athens as the Germans withdrew, nothing could have prevented them," recalled Myers' successor, C. M. Woodhouse. "By no conceivable calculation could a better opportunity be expected to recur."[40] Instead, like its left-wing counterparts in France and Italy, EAM plunged actively into conventional politics. To the disgust of Yugoslav and EAM militants, who championed a more revolutionary approach, EAM leader (and KKE chairman) George Siantos told the press that the Communist Party strongly supported "the people's government" and the "normal development of political life."[41] As the British reinforced the thinly garrisoned capital,[42] the Papandreou cabinet moved to tackle the difficult problem of disarming the resistance forces.

Convinced of EAM's unregenerate villainy, British leaders remained nervous. "We might as well admit it," Britain's Resident Minister in the Middle East, Harold Macmillan, declared with considerable emotion. "All the rest of the Balkans are gone. This is our last chance of avoiding the establishment of a Communist society." Noting Papandreou's optimism, Eden reported: "I am not too sanguine myself about the political situation." EAM remained "active and we should be unwise in my judgment to underestimate its strength." Indeed, it was "the only really organized party" in liberated Greece.[43] Despite the peaceful setting, Churchill was convinced that a military confrontation with his former guerrilla allies was necessary and desirable. Carefully he readied British soldiers and the royalist rump of the Greek armed forces for action. "Having paid the price we have to Russia for freedom in Greece, we should not hesitate to use British troops," he told Eden on November 7. "I hope the Greek Brigade will soon arrive, and will not hesitate to shoot when necessary. . . . I fully expect a clash with E.A.M., and we must not shrink from it."[44] At other times, he fretted that, through foolhardy compromises, Papandreou would deliver a peaceful victory to the left. "Everything is degenerating in the Greek Government, and we must make up our minds whether we will assert our will by armed force, or clear out altogether," he wrote to Eden. "One begins to ask oneself the question, 'Are we getting any good out of this old fool at all?'"[45]

America's President, Franklin D. Roosevelt, shared Churchill's stubborn attachment to the old order in Greece.[46] Noting that the U.S. Navy was scheduled to give a sub-chaser to the Greek armed forces, Assistant Secretary of State Adolf A. Berle suggested in March 1943 that it *not* be named after the King. "Most American Greeks are republican," he explained, and "it is probable that most Greek Greeks are, too." When Roosevelt replied that he wanted the vessel named the "King George II," Under Secretary of State Sumner Welles put that matter more forcefully. Remarking that most Greek-Americans disliked the monarchy, that "their principal organization, Ahepa, has consistently opposed King George on the ground that he is imbued with Metaxist theories," and that "there have been overt indications of anti-monarchist sentiment in the Greek Army," Welles strongly urged Roosevelt to change course. Two days later, Roosevelt retorted that "the King of Greece is still the head of their nation," and in view of the fact that other ships had been named for royalty and "of the fact that the Greek Navy is known as the 'Royal Greek Navy,' the ship should be named 'King George II.'"[47] Three months later, the British embassy in Cairo reported happily that "from the tone of the President's speech" upon delivery of the warship, it inferred that the U.S. government was "generally following the same policy as H.M.G."[48]

Roosevelt's commitment to the Greek monarchy became evident later that year. On August 18, 1943, the King cabled Roosevelt and Churchill appealing for their support against the unanimous demand of the resistance leaders and Greek cabinet ministers that he postpone his return to Greece until after a plebiscite.[49] Four days later, Roosevelt, Churchill, and other top Anglo-American officials took up the matter at their meeting in Quebec. According to the official minutes, it was decided that Britain and the United States "should continue to support the governments and regimes now recognized by them." Furthermore, "it was agreed between the President and Prime Minister that the British Foreign Office should reply to the King's telegram, supporting his contention that he was prepared to return to Greece as soon as possible."[50]

Even when the British, briefly, reversed course, Roosevelt clung to this position. In late November 1943, the Foreign Office—worried that it lacked the troop strength to enforce its will—suddenly urged the King to forgo an immediate return, contenting himself with a regency until a plebiscite could be held.[51] Arriving in Cairo in early December, Roosevelt took a prominent role in opposition. The Greek and Yugoslav resistance movements were "problem children," he told British General Henry Wilson.[52] As for the King, Roosevelt found him "stupid," but liked him "very much." Accordingly, the President insisted that "Georgie" (as he called him) "should go back to his country with his troops." Shortly afterward, George II met privately with Roosevelt, charging that he was being "railroaded" and "blackmailed" by the British.[53] Eden recalled that, after Roosevelt's tête-à-tête with the Greek monarch, the President "was cold towards me and complained of the way I had been treating the King." The following day, Roosevelt "complained bitterly to Mr. Churchill of my conduct," saying "that I was trying to deprive the King of his crown and that I had no right to do this." Churchill noted that the President "had been much wrought up on the subject"—a fact attested to by U.S. Ambassador Lincoln MacVeagh, whom Roosevelt warned to dissociate himself from any effort to force the King "to a course of action against his will."[54] Disinclined to press the matter any further, the British reverted to their earlier position. Privately, Roosevelt informed MacVeagh that "a tiny spot in the Mediterranean, like Greece, has its reputation enhanced if it has a constitutional monarch."[55]

As Churchill and the Foreign Office grew more intransigently hostile to the Greek left, the President made no effort to pursue an independent course. When the antiroyalist mutinies struck the Greek armed forces in April 1944, Roosevelt issued a statement of support for British policy, urging Greeks to "set aside pettiness" and "think of their glorious past." MacVeagh reported that the Greeks in Cairo viewed Roosevelt's letter "as a sign that the United States is backing Great Britain in her policy of interference in Greek affairs."[56] On August 17, Churchill outlined to Roosevelt his plans for dealing with EAM. "We have always marched together in complete agreement about the Greek policy," wrote the Prime Minister. Therefore, he was bringing to the President's attention the danger which "seems very likely" to follow the German evacuation of Greece: a seizure of Athens by "EAM and Communist extremists." "I do not expect you will relish more than I do the prospect either of chaos and street fighting or of a tyrannical Communist Government being set up." Therefore, would the President kindly approve his plans for "a British force, not exceeding 10,000 men, which could be sent by the most expeditious means into the capital when the time is ripe"? The President's reply, on August 26, was totally supportive: "I have no objection to your making preparations to have a sufficient British Force to preserve order in Greece. . . . There is also no objection to the use . . . of American transport airplanes." In a meeting with Roosevelt two days earlier, MacVeagh caught the drift of things: "As far as the Balkans are concerned, he has told Mr. Churchill to go right ahead and run the show."[57]

Although Roosevelt cooperated fully, the U.S. State Department proved more discriminating. In June 1942, the department's Adviser on Political Relations, Wallace Murray, wrote a long memo to his superiors outlining George II's chronic unpopularity in Greece, his close association with the Metaxas dictatorship, and the skepticism among Greeks about "the King's seeming conversion to democratic ways."[58] Later that year, Murray and the Near East division teamed up to assail Britain's apparent commitment "to a restoration of King George II to the Greek throne whether the Greek people want him back or not. The declared aim of the British Government is to bring the Greeks together 'and to "sell" the King . . . to them.'"[59] In early January 1943, Foy Kohler of the Near East division warned that, if the United States assisted in the reestablishment of the King and his government in Greece, "we are just asking for internal disturbances in that country."[60] That March, Kohler and Murray presented a memorandum to Secretary of State Cordell Hull for use in his dealings with Eden. "If the King can 'sell' himself to the Greek people, despite having let them down several times before, well and good," they argued. "The selling job should not, however, be undertaken by a foreign power." Moreover, "the British conclusion that only a monarchical regime will assure stable government in Greece seems to us to be warranted neither by the facts of recent Greek history nor by a reasonable analysis of the present temper of the Greek people." Indeed, the return of the King "might well involve serious internal disorders" and a "turn to Soviet Russia."[61]

The State Department, then, had discerned the major flaw in Churchill's policy. It was impossible both to restore the King *and* to stave off a left-wing rebellion. Like SOE, the State Department worried that British restoration of the monarchy was likely to trigger a civil war and a radical victory. In a memorandum of August 25, 1943, Berle warned that he and other State Department officials thought that the immediate return of the King "would be disruptive." Privately, he noted in his diary: "Our specialists think it means political upheaval and even civil war." Consequently, Berle and others pressed hard to modify Britain's stubborn commitment to the King or, at the least, to dissociate American policy from the British.[62] The Foreign Office, though, rejected what it termed "the non-committal attitude suggested by the United States Government," while Roosevelt faithfully followed Churchill's lead. For the State Department, the result was frustration.[63]

The State Department official closest to events in Greece and Cairo, Ambassador MacVeagh, felt this frustration keenly. To MacVeagh, a patrician devotée of classical civilization and friend of the President's, the British appeared "unnecessarily stupid" in their handling of the Greek situation. In a letter of February 17, 1944, MacVeagh warned Roosevelt of "the likelihood that if Great Britain remains in the forefront here, playing her old game of power politics with inadequate means, while we remain aloof, the whole area will eventually fall under the dominating influence of . . . Russia."[64] Fearing EAM's popular appeal, he wrote in his diary that the resistance organization was "communist and thoroughly non-Greek essentially." When the armed forces mutiny occurred in Egypt, he advised Roosevelt that it was fundamentally different from all previous Greek upheavals, for "beneath all its traditional Greek trappings, it was inspired and maintained by an ideology especially associated with Russia." In view of the movement "of the extreme left into the national Greek councils," he predicted that "when Athens is restored we may look to see a diplomatic game there . . . between Great Britain . . . and the Union of Soviet Socialist Republics." The situation in Greece, he wrote in his diary, "is today part of a world situation, and . . . we shall not be looking after our own interests if we ignore it. . . . We all see grave possibilities of trouble ahead in the unchecked advance of Russian interests and influence across the British Imperial life-line."[65]

In MacVeagh's opinion, British policies in both Greece and Yugoslavia were sadly misguided, for, despite quite differing approaches, they would establish the preconditions for Communist victories. Britain's support of Tito would result in "the disappearance of the ruling class in Yugoslavia" and the establishment of "a communist, Gestapo-like regime." In Greece, the same result would follow from Britain's heavy-handed reimposition of the monarchy.[66] Like the State Department, then, MacVeagh favored concessions to Greek republicanism. In the absence of such concessions, MacVeagh had no objections to British plans to garrison Athens after liberation. As early as December 1943 he wrote that "the British will have to send in a substantial force if anarchy, or even a reign of terror, is to be avoided."[67] Even after the peaceful return of the exile government to Athens, MacVeagh fretted that while "for the moment danger of a red terror seems to have been removed," hunger and disorganization "may bring it right back again."[68]

Though alienated by British policy toward Greece, MacVeagh and the State Department never quite reached the level of bad feeling with the British government attained by America's Office of Strategic Services. After August 1943, about three hundred OSS officers worked in occupied Greece; others connected with Greek affairs were stationed in Cairo and Washington. Although some formed close ties with their British counterparts, many—particularly within the large contingent of Greek-Americans—were quite critical of British personnel and policy. They complained of anti-Greek prejudices, right-wing political biases, and plans to restore the King.[69] "Our Government is justified in looking behind the fiction that is called the Greek Government," one OSS officer told a White House aide. "An American mission should be sent into Greece to pacify the country by giving them the assurance they want—that the King will not return prior to a plebiscite."[70] The British, in turn, reacted most unfavorably to OSS. A British intelligence report contended that OSS was "becoming increasingly mischievous. In Cairo they are confined . . . to the circulation . . . of the most puerile and false political gossip," while in Greece "they are giving arms to ELAS."[71]

In July 1944, when the British ordered the withdrawal of OSS personnel from Greece in preparation for an anticipated showdown with EAM, the OSS director, General William Donovan, refused to comply. He explained to Secretary Hull that withdrawal would disrupt U.S. intelligence and put the United States "in a false position of acquiescence" with Britain's "political decisions."[72] By September, the British were irate. Leeper charged that OSS was behind local criticism of Britain's Greek policy, "a whispering campaign against Papandreou," and efforts to establish a center-left coalition. Churchill complained directly to Roosevelt, "expressing dissatisfaction with Donovan's activities in Egypt, Greece and Yugoslavia."[73]

Despite British charges that OSS was siding with EAM, attitudes within the U.S. intelligence agency varied widely. Many junior officers—particularly in the Research and Analysis Branch and in the field—did identify, at least initially, with the left-wing resistance movement. Especially at the grass-roots level of OSS, EAM commanded considerable sympathy and respect.[74] Yet, even here, criticism of British tactics did not necessarily imply support for the left. "As matters stand at present," warned an OSS report of August 1943, "there is a real possibility of serious troubles in postwar Greece in which the Communists . . . can, if they choose, play a leading role." Splitting the Communists from their "numerous non-Communist followers . . . could almost certainly be accomplished by assuring the Greek people that the Allies guarantee them the right to establish their own government after the war."[75] At the higher levels of power, in Cairo and Washington, this attitude was clearly predominant. That October, Donovan advised Roosevelt that "insisting that the King return prior to the holding of elections will only provoke incidents and consolidate the opposition."[76] Symptomatically, the Pericles Mission, the one OSS group established at EAM headquarters, found its efforts at closer relations with EAM frustrated by higher authority. In June 1944, calling attention to "the complete cooperation of EAM," Pericles strongly recommended a major expansion of U.S. intelligence operations within EAM territory but met with opposition from Donovan and other top OSS officials.[77] Britain's ambassador, reporting from Washington that September, observed perceptively: "O.S.S. are obviously not enamoured with EAM owing to Communist predomination. . . . On the other hand they think we are playing into the hands of the extreme left by not wanting to face squarely the constitutional question."[78]

Differences over tactics became evident when Churchill initiated plans for Balkan spheres of influence in 1944. Rebuffed by the State Department,[79] Churchill appealed directly to Roosevelt on June 11. "The Russians are ready to let us take the lead in the Greek business," he declared, "which means that EAM and all its malice can be controlled." Appealing for a three-month trial period, he asked: "Why can you and I not keep this in our own hands considering how we see eye to eye about so much of it?" The following day, without informing the State Department, Roosevelt accepted Churchill's Balkan proposal.[80] When MacVeagh learned of the agreement later that month, he apparently retaliated by leaking the news to C. L. Sulzberger of the *New York Times*. The British succeeded in quashing Sulzberger's story,[81] but they were unable to silence the objections of the State Department. Chastened by the State Department reaction, the Russians apparently sidetracked the agreement,[82] although they expressed no objection to British plans to send troops into Greece or any intention to dispatch their own.[83] Churchill and Eden flew to Moscow in October to firm up the arrangement, much to the State Department's distress. By contrast, Roosevelt remained unperturbed at the Moscow meeting and the ensuing Anglo-Soviet understanding on the Balkans.[84]

Behind the American government's growing preoccupation with Greece lay a heightened appreciation of the importance of the Near and Middle East. During World War II, vast new military demands for petroleum products, coupled with a longer-term shift in energy consumption to oil and natural gas, produced oil shortages. These shortages stirred deep fears among U.S. government and corporate officials that dwindling domestic oil supplies were no longer adequate to meet

American needs.[85] The United States had always been the world's largest consumer and exporter of petroleum products, and had recently averaged about 60 percent of world production. But during the war, government and industry officials came to the realization that domestic holdings represented but a small and shrinking percentage of world petroleum reserves; officials of Standard Oil of New Jersey estimated that less than 15 percent of world oil reserves were located within the United States. The State Department's Economic Adviser, Herbert Feis, doubted "whether future discoveries of oil within the United States will keep pace with our consumption." Anxious about the ability of the United States to "oil another war," Secretary of the Interior Harold Ickes argued that "nothing must be left undone" to extend U.S. oil holdings overseas.[86] "The United States must look to foreign petroleum reserves for an assured continuation of its supplies," agreed the Navy Department. "American holdings should be protected in the interest of both national security and normal commercial life." Investigating the defense program, the Senate's Truman Committee had reached a similar conclusion: "The acquisition of foreign oil rights has become affected with a strong national interest."[87] And "in all surveys of the situation," Feis recalled, "the pencil came to an awed pause at one point and place—the Middle East."[88]

The American focus upon the Middle East as the answer to the petroleum dilemma was hardly surprising. During the war, U.S. officials remarked on the fact that this region contained more than half the known petroleum reserves outside the United States and pointed to indications that further exploration might considerably expand that share. They also noted that the yield per well was "enormously higher" in the Middle East than in more exploited regions, and that anticipated costs of production were relatively low. In 1944, after a trip to the Middle East, the chairman of the U.S. petroleum commission stated emphatically that "the center of gravity of world oil production is shifting until it is firmly established in that area."[89] Furthermore, five of America's largest corporations already maintained sizable holdings in the Middle

East. Standard Oil of New Jersey and Socony-Vacuum controlled 23.8 percent of the oil of Iraq and the Arabian coastal sheikhdoms, while Gulf Oil controlled 50 percent of the oil of Kuwait. The oil of Bahrain and of Saudi Arabia was controlled entirely by two American firms, Standard Oil of California and the Texas Company.[90] Their Saudi Arabiam holdings alone, which constituted the largest exclusive concession in the world, covered an area equivalent to about one-sixth of the United States and were already viewed by American officials as of immense importance. "In Saudi Arabia," the State Department's Chief of Near Eastern Affairs advised his superiors, "the oil resources constitute a stupendous source of strategic power, and one of the greatest material prizes in world history."[91]

Eager to retain this prize, the Texas and California companies (linked in Saudi Arabia as Aramco) pressured the American government to strengthen the U.S. position in Saudi Arabia. Ickes listened sympathetically to Aramco's tales of instability and impending oil shortages but reached a conclusion which corporate spokesmen found shocking: if Mideast oil was vital to America's future, then the U.S. government should assume the task of obtaining, owning, and managing it! In 1943, Ickes convinced the President to form a public firm under his direction, the Petroleum Reserves Corporation (PRC), to purchase Aramco's stock. The PRC's efforts along these lines encountered fierce opposition from Aramco's parent companies, other oil industry titans, and the State Department. Consequently, they met with defeat, as did later plans by Ickes to have the U.S. government build a Middle East oil refinery and a pipeline from the Persian Gulf to the Mediterranean.[92] By late 1944, all that remained of the U.S. government initiative was a direct annual subsidy to King Ibn Saud through the lend-lease program.[93] Accordingly, in December 1944, the Secretaries of State, War, and the Navy urged the President to safeguard and develop "the vast oil resources of Saudi Arabia, now in American hands," through a long-term aid program. The following month, Roosevelt gave such a program his approval.[94]

As all the "great powers" appreciated the growing significance of Mideast petroleum, wartime friction was inevitable.
On February 20, 1944, Churchill informed Roosevelt of British "apprehension . . . that the United States has a desire to
deprive us of our oil assets in the Middle East." Roosevelt
assured him that "we are not making sheep's eyes at your oil
fields in Iraq or Iran," but noted that he was "disturbed by
the rumor that the British wish to horn in on [our] Saudi
Arabian oil reserves."[95] That October, William Langer, chief
of the Research and Analysis Branch of the OSS, claimed
that the "broader strategic importance" of the Near East had
"increased steadily. . . . Britain, the USSR, and more recently
France, have all been mending fences or staking out claims."
"In this region," he predicted, "our Allies of today will be our
rivals of tomorrow." Reporting to the State Department's policy committee that fall, Berle warned that "the British attempt
to exclude the United States from the Middle East will continue," while "the Soviet Union proposes to extend her influence south to the Persian Gulf throughout its entire length."
An effective American policy for the region would thus "require a modification of the ruthlessness of British commer-
cialism and the ruthlessness of Soviet nationalism."[96]

Despite their competitive outlook, however, American officials did not adopt an entirely even-handed approach to the
advances of their rivals. Britain and the United States both
formally accepted the Open Door principle in their dealings
with petroleum resources, Feis observed in 1944, but "the
record clearly indicates . . . that the U.S.S.R. feels no need
of, and sees no benefit in, permitting foreign private oil enterprises to share in the development of its oil resources."[97]
A State Department report on Mideast economic policy, endorsed by Assistant Secretary of State Joseph Grew in May
1945, outlined a similar contrast: "Throughout most of this
region the western democratic, free enterprise system, represented in the main by the British, is now in competition
with the authoritarian, closed economic system represented
by Soviet Russia." For its part, the U.S. government desired
to "encourage the removal of trade restrictions and controls

and all forms of discriminatory treatment," to "give constructive aid to traders engaged in commerce between these countries and the United States," and to "participate in the development of local economic life." The "end in view would be the creation of conditions favorable to the orderly development of the area's resources." Although Soviet influence in the Middle East remained slight, American officials were turning increasingly from their historic resentment at British exclusivity to an anxiety over Soviet advances in the region.[98]

The first sign of an accommodation with the British over Mideast oil emerged in August 1944. After the collapse of Ickes' plan for direct U.S. government participation in the development of Mideast petroleum resources, some arrangement seemed necessary to safeguard the vast private U.S. oil concessions in the region, already rivaling those of Great Britain, and to secure recognition of the Open Door principle for future ventures. The Anglo-American Petroleum Agreement of August 8, 1944 fulfilled these conditions and was welcomed, accordingly, by U.S. officials. Ironically, it was opposed by the U.S. oil industry, which remained suspicious of government motives and concerned that it presaged another attack upon corporate prerogatives. To allay such anxieties, the agreement was renegotiated and an amended version signed on September 22, 1945. This version, too, failed to win Senate approval, largely owing to the opposition of those elements of the oil industry that feared competition from Arabian oil in the domestic market, government regulation, and an agreement that might benefit only the major companies.[99] Even so, to American policymakers, the Anglo-American Petroleum Agreement symbolized the beginning of a modus vivendi with Great Britain on the oil question. As Feis noted, it indicated the willingness of the British and the Americans to establish "order in oil." On June 1, 1945, the chief of the State Departments's Petroleum Division informed his British counterpart that "our petroleum policy toward the United Kingdom is predicated on a mutual recognition of a very extensive joint interest and upon a control . . . of the great bulk of the free petroleum resources of the world."[100]

Increasingly concerned about the future of Mideast oil, U.S. policymakers naturally developed a growing sympathy for Great Britain's traditional defense policy for the region. Since the nineteenth century, British diplomats had used the Near Eastern nations of Greece, Turkey, and Persia as a strategic barrier against Russian penetration of the Middle East. Churchill's wartime handling of Greece contined this well-worn "northern tier" strategy and Roosevelt saw no reason to object—particularly when both his British and his Soviet allies accepted it. Had most other U.S. government officials been as sanguine about the outcome as Roosevelt, they would not have objected either. But the State Department, particularly, considered British tactics in Greece—and especially London's support for the return of the King—ill-suited to Anglo-American goals for the region. The influential MacVeagh, whose reports were more widely read than those of any other State Department official in the field, brooded in October 1944 that, given Britain's arrogant treatment of the Greeks, "it won't be at all wonderful if they turn en masse against the western allies . . . and fall into Russia's arms." The following month, he predicted gloomily that "Great Britain, and the U.S. too, will . . . pay in the long run . . . when Russia inherits the Near and Middle East."[101]

As the State Department and OSS had predicted, Britain's handling of the Greek situation led to a crisis, in December 1944. Fearing the restoration of a right-wing dictatorship, EAM refused Papandreou's order to disarm without the corresponding disarmament of the royalist segment of the Greek armed forces.[102] When Papandreou forced the issue, at Churchill's insistence,[103] the EAM ministers resigned from the cabinet. The following day, December 3, the police opened fire on a massive EAM demonstration, killing or wounding many, all civilians. Shortly afterward, EAM irregulars began attacking Athens police stations. As Greece slid toward civil war, Papandreou attempted to resign and clear the way for political compromise. But Churchill cabled Leeper: "You must force Papandreou to stand to his duty. . . .

Should he resign, he should be locked up till he comes to his senses."[104] As the Greek Prime Minister reluctantly resumed office, Churchill ordered General Scobie's troops "to intervene and fire upon the treacherous aggressors." Scobie was to act as if he were "in a conquered city where a local rebellion is in progress." Three days later, with street fighting raging throughout Athens, Churchill delivered a truculent defense of his policies before a stormy session of the House of Commons. "I trust the people," he insisted, "but . . . not a gang of bandits."[105] In the following days, he informed British and American officials that his maxim was "No peace without victory."[106]

To the consternation of the British, the U.S. reaction to the crisis appeared to be a public rebuke. Leeper recalled that the Americans in Athens "went out of their way to declare themselves neutral," while C. M. Woodhouse, the local SOE commander, complained that this neutrality cloaked "a benevolent bias in favor of EAM."[107] Even worse from the British standpoint was the fact that in the midst of a clamor in most of the British and American press against Churchill's actions—particularly among Labourites and liberals—the new U.S. Secretary of State, Edward R. Stettinius, Jr. issued a press release on December 5 that was widely interpreted as a blanket condemnation of British policy in Greece. Referring to Churchill's recent veto of Count Carlo Sforza as Italian Foreign Minister, Stettinius declared that U.S. policy was that "the composition of the Italian government is purely an Italian affair," and "this policy would apply in an even more pronounced degree with regard to governments of the United Nations in their liberated territories."[108] Enraged by the American statement, Churchill sent an angry rejoinder to Roosevelt: "I do not remember anything that the State Department has ever said about Russia or any other Allied state comparable to this document." Eden informed the British ambassador in Washington that the Prime Minister was "naturally deeply hurt by it," and that America's attitude was "all the more wounding in that the Soviet Government have so far scrupulously abstained from any similar conduct or comment." He instructed him to "see Mr. Stettinius tomorrow and speak to him in this sense as roughly as you like."[109]

The British, however, had overreacted, for the State Department's dissatisfaction with their conduct of Greek affairs was far less sweeping than they—or the public—assumed. As Kohler noted, Stettinius's statement was "occasioned primarily by the Italian situation."[110] In the Italian controversy, British policy was pitted not against a leftist guerrilla movement but against a well-known Italian liberal with considerable influence in the United States. Still smarting from the criticism that its intrigues with Vichy France had provoked among liberals, the State Department felt it necessary, the British ambassador observed, to appease domestic opinion by publicly supporting liberal, antifascist causes. The British reported that in their conversations with Stettinius, "it became clear that the American statement had been drafted hastily in West European Division as a result of press enquiries critical of the State Department. Stettinius had felt that he had to say something and had approved the statement without sufficient reflection."[111] Thereafter, in fact, he hastened to issue a new declaration intended as an expression of support for Churchill's Greek policy. Privately, the Secretary of State *was* irked by British handling of affairs in Greece and Italy; yet (as he confided to American officials) this was primarily because the British acted unilaterally in these situations. "If you had consulted us," Stettinius informed the British, "this incident would never have occurred."[112]

Given the fact that British military forces spent the next two months bombing, strafing, and shooting thousands of EAM resistance fighters with whom the U.S. government presumably sympathized, the State Department did little to alleviate their plight. On December 6, Kohler and William Baxter of the Near East division drafted a memo to the President critical of British support for the monarchy and the royalist army, but it was never sent. In Athens, Ambassador MacVeagh urged his British counterpart to request more British troops.[113] Although Greece's leftist press printed a story claiming that MacVeagh had protested to Leeper against British interference in Greek affairs, MacVeagh issued a public denial, with the State Department's approval. "Confused propaganda in Greece has misinterpreted certain United States statements and fundamental policy," Stettinius privately reassured him.[114] On December 8, MacVeagh wrote to Roosevelt that the British "have not been either deft enough or understanding enough" to give the Greeks the impression of political freedom, "and I greatly fear that the opportunity which their attitude gives the communists . . . will last for years." Unless the United States took the lead, he warned, "communism will continue to exploit its present marvelous opportunities for still further collapsing the social order and creating a 'Greek problem' to plague Britain, and us too." Back in Washington, Murray told the Secretary of State that the opinions expressed in MacVeagh's letter were "very similar to our own."[115]

Although Roosevelt never issued an endorsement of Churchill's actions, he also showed little distress at the fate of the Greek resistance. Convalescing in Warm Springs, Georgia when the crisis broke, Roosevelt played no role in issuing the State Department's presumed rebuke of December 5 and, in general, felt detached from the situation.[116] Roosevelt's own circle of foreign policy advisers—men like Harry Hopkins, James Forrestal, and Joseph Davies—applauded British actions, including Churchill's truculent speech to Commons of December 8. Davies noted in his journal on December 6 that there was "no question" that "Britain was within its rights." On December 18, he was still arguing that Churchill had acted "to prevent chaos and disorder."[117] When U.S. Admiral Ernest King issued an order preventing the use of American LSTs to land British reinforcements in Greece, this did not reflect any lack of White House sympathy for the British. Irritated by the prospective weakening of the Italian front, King had acted on his own. Moreover, when Hopkins learned of the action, he moved quickly to reverse it.[118] Roosevelt cabled Churchill on December 13 as "a loyal friend and ally," who was "as deeply concerned as you have [been] yourself in regard to the tragic difficulties you have encountered in

Greece." The President expressed not a word of criticism about British actions past or present, although—in line with the State Department's position—he now inquired if British pacification efforts "might not be greatly facilitated" by a regency and a plebiscite on the monarchy. Churchill remarked that this was "a very kindly worded telegram." On January 6, 1945, in his annual message to Congress, Roosevelt noted his "concern about many situations—the Greek and Polish, for example." But he quickly added that "these situations are not as easy or as simple to deal with as some spokesmen . . . would have us believe." Such statements could provide scant comfort to supporters of the Greek left; as for Churchill, he concluded that "in the main the President was with me."[119]

The response of the Soviet Union proved even less equivocal. "I am increasingly impressed . . . with the loyalty with which . . . Stalin has kept off Greece in accordance with our agreement," Churchill informed Eden on December 11. Unable to cite publicly Roosevelt's support for British intervention, Churchill did not face the same difficulty with respect to Stalin, and boasted of Soviet backing during meetings with Greek leaders. In later years, Churchill claimed that the Russian dictator had "adhered strictly and faithfully to our agreement of October, and . . . not one word of reproach came from *Pravda* or *Izvestia*."[120] Papandreou reached a similar conclusion. "The U.S.S.R. played the part of a neutral during the whole of December," he wrote, "and went to the extent of announcing . . . the appointment of an Ambassador while the battles were raging in Athens."[121] Publicly, Russian conduct could hardly have been more proper. During the revolt, Colonel Popov resided with the British and was "the very image of non-intervention," recalled English journalist Kenneth Matthews. Assistant U.S. military attaché William McNeill reported on December 26 that the deportment of Russian officers "has been impeccable," and that they apparently had had no contact with ELAS since their arrival in October. Even the anti-Soviet MacVeagh reported that, throughout the confrontation, "Russia maintained a correct attitude towards Greek internal affairs."[122]

Behind the scenes, Stalin's response to the EAM uprising was even chillier. Petros Roussos, a member of the KKE central committee, was en route to Moscow in a bid for Soviet support when he was arrested on December 18 by the Russians, who dumped him unceremoniously back across the Greek frontier three days later. U.S. intelligence reports noted that, on January 13, 1945, the KKE received a telegram "informing it that the Russians categorically disapproved its policy and action."[123] According to the minutes of the Yalta conference, on February 8 Stalin remarked disdainfully "that the Greeks had not yet become used to discussion and therefore they were cutting each other's throats." Churchill stated that the British "were very much obliged to Marshal Stalin for not having taken too great an interest in Greek affairs," to which Stalin responded "that he had no intention of criticizing British actions there." The following day, to Churchill's satisfaction, Stalin reiterated that "he had complete confidence in British policy in Greece."[124] Bubbling with good humor, the British Prime Minister remarked to his physician: "Stalin isn't going to butt in. . . . He'll let his people be beaten up in Greece for the sake of his larger plans. . . . Once he says something, he sticks to it."[125] A British intelligence report noted that at Yalta, "ELAS' attempt to obtain support from certain of the great Allies on the Greek question was decidedly snubbed in precisely those quarters in which ELAS placed their greatest faith."[126]

Tito and other Yugoslav leaders showed greater revolutionary consistency, although in the end they did little more to help the Greek left. On November 30 the Yugoslavs, in contrast to the Russians, had encouraged the KKE to resist orders for disarmament.[127] Thereafter, they had watched the outbreak of fighting in Athens with mounting excitement, directing bitter attacks against British intervention in speeches and radio broadcasts. The latter grew so fierce that, as Stettinius noted, the British government "had occasion to warn Tito of the possible serious consequences of any specific action."[128] Unwilling to proceed further in these circumstances without Soviet support, Tito had encouraged Roussos' disastrous journey to Moscow as well as the dispatch of an EAM mission to France and England via Yugoslavia. By the time the latter reached Belgrade, however, the international configuration had become clear. Consequently, not only did Tito refuse to receive the mission, but it obtained no help reaching France or acquiring Yugoslav papers. Tito, despite his disgust at British policy, apparently dared venture no further than inflammatory rhetoric in the face of the displeasure of the "great powers." On January 15, 1945, when overeager Yugoslav partisans demonstrated at Skoplje in favor of a march on Salonika, participants were arrested and sentenced to death.[129]

Ultimately, it was not external Communist pressure but the fierce course of the fighting, hostile public opinion in Britain and the United States, and dissent within the British government that led to a modification of what Harold Macmillan termed "Winston's king mania."[130] On December 10, Leeper cabled London that the only way to calm the situation in Greece was to appoint Archbishop Damaskinos as Regent. Dispatched to Athens, Macmillan strongly concurred. "Many of those who were enrolled among the rebels were not really Communists," he recalled. "They connected the King with the Metaxas dictatorship and they genuinely believed that the King's return would be the signal for widespread action against the popular forces."[131] Churchill grumbled that he had "heard mixed accounts of the Archbishop, who is said to be very much in touch with E.A.M." Increasingly exasperated, Macmillan cabled from Athens that "there is a large amount of sympathy with EAM in Greece," and "a moderate, reasonable, progressive policy could detach the vague radical element from the hard Communist core." Churchill, however, remained obstreperous, quarreling with Eden and upbraiding Leeper and Macmillan as Britain's two "fuzzy wuzzies."[132] Even so, with virtually the entire British and American governments calling for a regency,[133] Churchill flew to Athens to investigate the situation. Here he met with Damaskinos and found it "impossible to doubt that he greatly feared the Communist . . . combination in Greek affairs." Convinced at last that a distinction could be drawn between Communism and republicanism,[134] Churchill drew on Roosevelt's assistance in finally establishing the regency.[135]

With the question of the monarchy resolved, the way lay open to a compromise peace settlement. The left, at least, had little to gain by prolonging the conflict. Thanks to the arrival of substantial British military reinforcements and to EAM's preoccupation with destroying the rival forces of Zervas in northern Greece, the British had defeated EAM decisively in the "Battle of Athens." At the same time, they had removed the hated Papandreou and installed the government of General Nicholas Plastiras, a well-known stalwart of the republican center in Greek politics. Nor could the British see much sense in further hostilities. Routing EAM in the rest of the nation would require a long, bloody struggle, under the continued opprobrium of Anglo-American opinion. Hence, in early 1945, negotiating sessions began between the British and the leaders of the rebellion. On February 12, the Varkiza agreement rewarded their efforts. In accordance with its provisions, EAM demobilized ELAS, surrendered large quantities of arms,[136] and abandoned its control of three-quarters of Greece in return for promises of legal recognition, free elections, a constitutional plebiscite, freedom of combatants from prosecution for political crimes, and a purge of Axis collaborators from the army and police.[137] Had such an agreement been concluded during the German occupation, Greece might well have been spared what are usually termed the first two "rounds" of its civil war. Even now, the impartial enforcement of the Varkiza agreement would determine whether the nation would begin a period of political and economic reconstruction or would plunge into a third and more horrible round of destruction.

The portents were not entirely reassuring. During the fierce fighting of the preceding months, EAM's forces had taken captives on forced marches and had evened old scores with wartime political enemies, sometimes through summary executions—practices which enflamed hatreds and increased the nation's political polarization.[138] Furthermore, to Wash-

ington's dismay, in the spring of 1945 the British ousted the
Plastiras government and installed a more conservative successor, headed by Petros Voulgaris, a naval admiral known
for his suppression of the April 1944 armed forces mutinies.[139]
"It is difficult for Greece to be run on democratic lines when
all the neighbouring countries are being run on authoritarian
lines," Leeper warned London. Another British official conceded that the King might "have to reintroduce some form
of semi-authoritarian regime," although "he would no doubt
endeavor to avoid following the Metaxas example too closely."[140]
Economic reconstruction also seemed blocked by familiar
British shibboleths. On March 21, 1945, President Roosevelt
proposed sending a tripartite economic mission to Greece
consisting of representatives from the United States, Great
Britain, and the Soviet Union. Anxious to secure American
funding but unwilling to encourage Soviet participation,
Churchill suggested an exclusively Anglo-American mission.
This, in turn, was found unacceptable by the State Department. Roosevelt's reply, which State drafted, argued that
sponsorship of a bilateral commission might make it appear
that the Americans and the British "were disregarding the
Yalta decision for tripartite action in liberated areas." For the
time being, plans for American aid lapsed, while the British
clung to their traditional prerogatives. That April, Macmillan
informed Eden: "It is of great strategic importance for us to
maintain our position in Greece."[141]

And yet, the regency solution and the subsequent Varkiza
agreement indicated that British and American policy were
beginning to converge, a development given new impetus by
the departure of both heads of state in 1945. Roosevelt's death
in April was followed several months later by the defeat of
Churchill's Tories at the polls. Initially, Ambassador Mac-
Veagh feared that Labour's accession to power in Britain
would facilitate a left victory in Greece. He cabled the Secretary of State on August 2: "Should the Labor Government
in England adopt a policy based on the assumption that the
Communist-controlled EAM represents a 'democratic' movement—as seems possible . . . —Moscow's efforts toward es-

tablishing *de facto* ascendancy in Greece . . . would be in-
calculably aided. . . . Great Britain would do well to consider
carefully before pursuing a policy of starry-eyed liberalism."[142]
Repeatedly, MacVeagh warned British officials of the "disruptive strategy as well as the ultimate aims of the Communist
Party and their puppets"; if the British failed to hold the line,
he said, Greece would "sooner or later pass into the Russian
sphere."[143] Actually, the American ambassador need not have
worried, for the new British Foreign Secretary, Ernest Bevin,
was not only a traditional foe of left-wing policies but a
staunch advocate of retaining British control in the Mediterranean and the Middle East. Shortly after the Potsdam conference, Bevin stated his fear of Russia's cutting "right across
. . . the throat of the British Commonwealth." The following
year, in a memorandum to the cabinet, he wrote: "The fundamental assumption of our policy has always been that
. . . Greece must be retained within the British sphere."[144]
The real alteration in British policy lay in the Labour government's unwillingness to jeopardize British control by promoting the Greek right. Instead, it championed free elections,
economic reconstruction, and "moderation."[145]

Ironically, this middle-of-the-road approach—advocated
for so long by the State Department and OSS—had no stable
basis in postwar Greece. Britain's defeat of EAM in December
1944 shattered the hegemony of the left, emboldened the
right, and opened the way for a royalist takeover of the organs
of state power: the police, the army, and the administration.
Macmillan confessed in March 1945 "that a wave of reaction
was sweeping the country and now that the Right felt the
Government was firmly installed with British backing, they
were out for revenge." Throughout the countryside, right-
wing mobs brutalized or killed leftists, republicans, and their
families. National guardsmen attacked left-wing editors and
smashed their printshops. Given the rightist control of the
state, as Woodhouse noted, "an ex-guerrilla was as likely as
not to be found in gaol, and an ex-member of the Security
Battalions as likely as not to be found in the uniformed services."[146] Still clinging to their fragile legality, the remnants of

EAM protested ineffectually and called for reconciliation; increasingly, however, their constituency resorted to violent retaliation, fled to the hills for safety, or dissolved under government persecution.[147]

In the ensuing confrontation and bitterness, the civil war might have resumed immediately had not the KKE acted as a brake on left-wing militance. At Varkiza, the OSS commander in Greece noted, Communist leaders had "decided to make every concession . . . compatible with the continued existence of their party and the possibility of their own political activity in the future." Thereafter, KKE leader George Siantos, genuinely committed to a parliamentary role, sought to reconstruct the Popular Front coalition of wartime in an electoral setting. To some extent, this meant conciliating Svolos and other Socialists, who, offended by the recent resort to arms and concurrent excesses, had withdrawn from EAM in March 1945. An elderly, home-grown party stalwart and leader of the resistance movement, Siantos seemed well-suited for the job. In May 1945, however, he was succeeded as party chieftain by Nikos Zachariades, a younger, doctrinaire, Moscow-trained *apparatchik* who had just returned to Greece after four years in Dachau concentration camp.[148] Suspicious of the relatively loose structure and unorthodox policies of EAM, but cognizant of Russia's emphasis on Allied cooperation, Zachariades initially followed a policy similar to that of Siantos, mobilizing the KKE behind the Varkiza agreement and "national unity." "A real revival of ELAS as a fighting force is not contemplated," an OSS operative reported from Salonika after conversations with several of its former officers.[149] When Ares Velouchiotis, perhaps the best-known and most colorful leader of the wartime resistance, defied party policy and returned to the mountains, he was hounded by government troops and denounced by Zachariades and the KKE. Angry and disheartened, Ares committed suicide that June. His severed head, exhibited by the government at Trikkala, was a telling symbol of rightist violence and leftist passivity.[150]

As usual, the Russians accepted such developments with

a cynical equanimity. "This war is not as in the past," Stalin told visiting Yugoslav leaders in the spring of 1945. "Whoever occupies a territory also imposes on it his own social system." To be sure, in the months after the Varkiza agreement, the Soviet press printed harrowing tales of disorder and terror in Greece, but these appear to have been designed to soften criticism of ruthless Soviet occupation policies elsewhere. As MacVeagh observed: "If . . . world public opinion could be sufficiently aroused over real or imaginary conditions in 'British-dominated' Greece, it might be more tolerant of Soviet activities in other parts of liberated Europe."[151] Stalin frequently sought to extend the pattern of the Anglo-Soviet understanding on the Balkans by fostering new trade-offs. Arguing for a "friendly" Poland, the Russian leader cabled Churchill that "Poland is to the security of the Soviet Union what Belgium and Greece are to the security of Great Britain." He did not want to rake up the Greek unpleasantness, he implied; why, then, did the British pester him about Poland?[152]

At the Potsdam conference of July 1945, when American officials called for the reorganization of the Romanian and Bulgarian governments, Molotov retorted "that there were no excesses in Bulgaria or Romania comparable to those taking place in Greece." Soviet officials now suddenly called for the establishment of a Greek government "in the spirit of the agreement reached at Varkiza." The following day, as U.S. Secretary of State James Byrnes recalled, the Russians brought forth a second series of charges against the Greek government, "in obvious retaliation for a British paper directed against Yugoslavia." Understanding the game, Bevin signaled a retreat by proposing that all three items be dropped from the agenda. Stalin promptly replied: "Yes, welcome."[153] Unlike the Yugoslavs, who continued to denounce the Greek regime as one of "reaction,"[154] Stalin remained eager to strike a bargain.

Yet because they clashed with deep-seated fears of Communist revolution, signs of Soviet cynicism and KKE caution failed to reassure American observers. Within days of the Varkiza agreement, MacVeagh was claiming that "while

Communist controlled EAM may now be expected to collaborate ostensibly with the Government," movements were already afoot for "subversion of the Greek Armed Forces, the obstruction of Greek Government authority, and preservation of the revolutionary machine in all its aspects."[155] In July, he conceded that neither British nor American intelligence had been able to find "direct evidence" of "financial connection between the Soviets and the KKE," but the following month he insisted that Greek Communists were "supported by Russian sympathy if not by Russian gold."[156] A long-standing, if paternalistic philhellene, MacVeagh was distressed by the plague of brutality that had descended upon what he termed "a childlike people."[157] Calling attention to "continued excesses by extreme right-wing organizations and irresponsible elements of the National Guard and Gendarmerie," MacVeagh was genuinely dismayed. Yet he argued that right-wing violence had "actually been of a much less serious character than might have been expected in a country . . . which has just experienced a bloody uprising by the Left." Indeed, thanks to EAM, Greece had "emerged in a modern if less delectable world, where class warfare colors everything, and too often colors it red."[158]

By the end of World War II, then, American policymakers were ready for the counterrevolutionary initiatives of subsequent years. At the time, few recognized this fact, for many Americans, and even EAM, cherished a vision of U.S. foreign policy as sympathetic to the new forces of upheaval unleashed by the war. "The intervention of the United States and Russia was eagerly desired" by EAM activists, noted an OSS intelligence report during the fighting of December 1944. "There was a mystic faith . . . that those two countries would not see EAM's cause collapse." As late as July 1946, the Greek left was still calling for American intervention on its behalf.[159] But such faith in the intentions of American policymakers was sadly misplaced—a product of illusions ranging from the belief in American exceptionalism, to the adoration of Roosevelt, to naive dreams of the Popular Front.[160] Such illusions, of course, were nourished by the well-publicized disagreements between the United States and Great Britain. But in reality these disagreements developed over tactics rather than fundamental policy. Behind American policy, as behind that of Britain and Russia, lay the goal of containing the Greek left. EAM's stubborn disregard of this fact was, from its own standpoint, a tragic miscalculation.

2.
THE GATHERING CRISIS
August 1945–February 1947

We consider it important to the security and prosperity of the
world as well as of the Near and Middle East that the doctrine of
the open door be fully applicable to that part of the world. We
would, therefore, be opposed to any trend in the direction of
preventing that area from enjoying untrammeled economic
relations with the rest of the world.

Loy W. Henderson, September 19, 1946[1]

In the aftermath of the war, American policymakers faced a
congeries of disturbing developments. Throughout Eastern
Europe, the influence of the Soviet Union was spreading,
thanks to the creation of "friendly" governments or the imposition of Communist regimes. The situation in the Balkans
was particularly alarming, for Yugoslavia, Bulgaria, and Albania seemed to provide a channel for the extension of Soviet
power to the Mediterranean and the oil-rich Middle East. In
wartime, American influence had been growing rapidly in this
region, just as British power had been waning. At least potentially, this placed the United States at loggerheads with
the Soviet Union. By the postwar era, only Greece, Turkey,
and Iran separated the Russians from the "black gold" of the
Persian Gulf, and each of these nations, in the eyes of U.S.
policymakers, appeared dangerously susceptible to Soviet influence and control. In Greece, particularly, the situation
became increasingly threatening—all too ripe for the Red
revolution that American officials feared would herald the
fatal breakthrough.

Despite the belated British call for "moderation," governing
authority in postwar Greece lay in the hands of the right,
which did much to encourage the wave of terror and political

persecution that washed over Greek society. Collaborators returned rapidly to positions of power, desperately needed relief supplies became political weapons, and violent retributions against the veterans of EAM flared throughout the countryside. Woodhouse recalled that the police and army "were used to oppress Greeks associated with the resistance movement by official means; armed bandits supplemented the oppression by unofficial means." Caught up in the cycle of revenge, leftists sometimes responded in kind. A major difference, however, was that the right now commanded the full power of the state. In December 1945, the Minister of Justice revealed that charges were pending against nearly 50,000 members of EAM and ELAS.[2] Pointing to the Yalta accords, which pledged the Big Three "to form interim governmental authorities broadly representative of all democratic elements," EAM leaders demanded the creation of an all-party cabinet. But American officials regarded the prospect of EAM participation in the Athens government with unremitting hostility. "While a coalition government including all major parties might more literally approach [the] Yalta formula and overcome some present criticism," Secretary Byrnes admitted on September 1, the State Department believed that efforts to broaden the Greek government "would be disruptive." As in the past, American officials considered the leadership of the left too dangerous and that of the right too provocative. Instead, as MacVeagh noted, they preferred a "middle of the road government."[3]

Unlike his Tory predecessors, Bevin favored this approach and sought, not totally successfully, to implement it. In late November 1945, he engineered the formation of a center government headed by the leader of Greece's Liberal Party, Themistocles Sophoulis.[4] Both the Greeks and the Americans initially perceived this cabinet liberalization as more substantial than it actually was. For a few weeks, EAM and the Communist Party sought to woo the new government,[5] while rightists in the Greek military laid plans for a coup.[6] Once again, MacVeagh brooded on the fickleness of Anglo-American policy. On December 15, he asked the Secretary of State what assurance Greeks had "that British Labour Party preoccupation with Socialist dogma, or an American lapse of interest in Balkan affairs, may not deliver Greece to Communism?"[7] Gradually, however, it became clear that the cabinet reorganization had limited political significance. Sophoulis was 83 years old and relatively ineffective in the sharply polarized circumstances. Rebuffed by the British in his plans for administrative changes and himself unwilling to appoint veterans of ELAS to the armed forces, Sophoulis met little success in blunting the power of the right within the officer corps. The security police and the Metaxist administrators, as he later conceded, remained beyond his control.[8] With the nation slipping toward civil war between left and right, the center's political power dwindled. "We shall be forced in the end to do the best we can with one of the extreme wings," predicted a Foreign Office official, adding: "Obviously the Right in present circumstances."[9]

In this charged atmosphere, U.S. policymakers looked to Allied-supervised elections as a means of restoring stability. Ever since the December 1944 crisis MacVeagh had championed such a plan, arguing that leftist suspicions of the British would be allayed by American and Soviet electoral participation.[10] Anxious to draw on American prestige in Greece but chary of enhancing Soviet influence, the British had accepted the American proposal with reluctance.[11] To London's relief, the Russians refused to play any role in the Greek elections, probably because they feared setting a precedent for British and American supervision of elections in Eastern Europe.[12] A more serious obstacle to elections lay in the objections of the Greek right. Conscious of the considerable advantages afforded them by their control of the administrative apparatus, royalists demanded an immediate plebiscite on the monarchy. In support of their position, they could cite not only the Varkiza agreement but the insistence of Churchill and British conservatives upon holding the plebiscite before beginning general elections.[13] But U.S. policymakers argued that a hasty return to the "constitutional question" would surely inflame an already incendiary situation. Byrnes thought

that a "better method of assuring Greek political stability
. . . would be for elections to precede [the] plebiscite in order
that there might be installed as soon as possible [a] representative govt."[14] Siding with the Americans, Bevin chose to
proceed with the elections.[15] Consequently, an election date
of March 31, 1946 was set, and teams from France, Britain,
and the United States were dispatched to Greece as official
observers.[16]

It soon became apparent, however, that a turn to the ballot
box would do little to restore order. In October 1945, when
elections were first announced, all sectors of Greek political
opinion threatened to boycott them. The right, smoldering
from the rejection of its demand for an immediate plebiscite,
announced its intention of abstaining, while the center and
the left declared their lack of confidence in the fairness of the
then-conservative government.[17] In the following months, as
portents appeared of a right-wing victory, the royalists grew
more enthusiastic.[18] Centrist and leftist interest in participation also gathered strength after the formation of the Sophoulis government.[19] But the inability of Sophoulis and his
Liberal colleagues to curb right-wing vigilantism or to purge
the administration led to renewed hesitation. Charging that
free elections could not take place in a climate of political
terror, the left and most of center demanded that the elections
be postponed until some measure of tranquillity was restored.[20] With most of the cabinet in agreement, Sophoulis
appealed strongly and repeatedly to Bevin for a delay. "The
whole machinery of state" is "in the hands of the extreme
monarchist right," Sophoulis cabled the British Foreign Secretary on February 15, 1946. Coupled with "psychological
pressure and violence" on the part of armed groups, this would
render impossible "a genuine expression of the popular will"
and lead to "disaster and destruction for Greece."[21]

Despite the repeated pleas from the Greek government,
Anglo-American policymakers remained unmoved. Bevin,
particularly, proved implacable, refusing to accept either a
delay or Sophoulis's resignation. "My whole policy would be
undermined if elections were now to be postponed," he cabled

Leeper. "It would at once be suspected that the object of the postponement was to prolong the period for which British troops are to remain in Greece. It would also be said that this delay proved that we were not yet able to maintain law and order."[22] Less concerned with British prestige, ten Greek cabinet ministers, all centrists, resigned in protest. On February 21, 1946, Leeper reported that "the Prime Minister finds himself in conflict [with] most of his supporters. . . . It is only our pressure which keeps him to the mark."[23] A similar assessment came from the U.S. chargé d'affaires in Athens, Karl Rankin, who reported that "75% of present Govt wants postponement." Like Bevin, Rankin felt little sympathy with calls for delay. The "Leftist campaign for delay is ordered from abroad in order to sabotage the elections, gain time to build up Leftist strength and when ready seize power," he contended, while the "Center . . . wishes postponement to gain time . . . to salvage something for their party and themselves by political trading with EAM." Conversely, Anglo-American officials agreed that elections would result in the dominance of anti-Soviet forces in Greek politics.[24] In these circumstances, Washington threw its weight behind the British. At Bevin's urging,[25] the State Department pressured Sophoulis to brook no delay in elections and to see to it that "the entire Greek electorate participate."[26]

Bowing to these demands, Sophoulis and the remnants of his cabinet grimly proceeded to organize parliamentary elections. A center victory would be "the result which would suit us best," noted a member of the Foreign Office, just as "a victory for the E.A.M. . . . would suit us worst"; neither, however, seemed likely.[27] Accepting the shrill royalist contention that the only "real" choices were Communism or the King, many normally centrist voters rallied to the right-wing Populist Party. Others were intimidated by rightist armed bands which repeatedly disrupted leftist political rallies and threatened entire villages with retaliation. Still other electoral distortions seemed probable through rightist manipulation of the voting rolls.[28] American and British observers thought that, in a fair election with broad participation, the right (primarily the Populists) would command the largest vote, although probably less than a majority; they put the voting strength of the left (primarily EAM) at about 33 percent, and of the center (primarily the Liberals) at somewhat less.[29] Although most elements of the center, rather grudgingly, agreed at last to participate in the elections, the left clung stubbornly to plans for a boycott, despite pressures to the contrary from the Russian, French, and Italian Communist leadership.[30] On election day, only 49 percent of registered Greek voters went to the polls, handing the right a resounding if somewhat tarnished victory. The Allied observer mission concluded that while the elections were "on the whole free and fair," there had been "serious intimidation" of leftists "in some localities," as well as a sizable number of abstentions. The result was the election of an overwhelmingly royalist parliament, far to the right of much of the country.[31]

Taking office that April, the new, exclusively right-wing cabinet, headed by the Populist leader Constantine Tsaldaris, acted to consolidate the right's political victory. U.S. intelligence reported "the wholesale acquittal or discharge of accused [Nazi] collaborationists, in which Greek official government agencies or personalities must be acquiescing."[32] Over the bitter objections of the center and the left, the Tsaldaris government passed a draconic Security Law, empowering it to arrest and imprison persons indefinitely without trial. Government-appointed "security committees" exiled thousands of ELAS veterans, Communists, radicals, and republicans (including their spouses and children) to barren islands in the Aegean. Among the exiles were well-known heroes of the resistance, among them the republican officers Stefanos Sarafis, the former ELAS military commander, and Euripidis Bakirdzis, the first head of EAM's wartime "government in the mountains." (Sarafis remained incarcerated for years; Bakirdzis committed suicide.)[33] Meanwhile, armed right-wing bands operated "with the utmost audacity," as a visiting British parliamentary delegation reported. "These armed bands are apparently tolerated by the authorities and no attempt is made to suppress them. Although it is claimed

. . . that their object is to prevent the spread of communism, the fact is that they . . . devote themselves to terrorising the villages and exacting blackmail."[34]

Though not entirely comfortable with this state of affairs, American officials were determined to make the best of it. The "facts seem unquestionnable that government measures for 'law and order' [are] now largely in hands of unscrupulous reactionaries," MacVeagh reported in the summer of 1946. The American ambassador outlined the "growing official tendency (1) to consider all persons Communists unless Royalists, (2) to protect former Metaxists and collaborators and (3) to accept armed assistance from disreputable elements professing royalism." Whatever its guise, he declared, the program of the Greek right "actually approximates Fascism."[35] Yet, characteristically, MacVeagh never questioned his assumption that more serious dangers lay to the left. Writing to the Secretary of State about the exile of former ELAS officers to "the islands," MacVeagh expressed his satisfaction that they were "temporarily out of harm's way." "Neither Sarafis nor Bakirdzis would appear to be communistically inclined," he conceded, "but both are tainted with socialism" and might be "made use of by the present very clever communist leadership." That summer, he reassured the Secretary of State: "No 'terrorism' can possibly exist in a country under Anglo-Saxon hegemony which can be equated with that which accompanies Russian-supported Communism wherever it goes."[36]

Confident of support from Anglo-American officials and of the temporary advantages which political polarization and control of the state apparatus afforded it, the Greek right moved rapidly toward restoration of the monarchy. In early April 1946, the Tsaldaris government pressed to modify Anglo-American objections to an early plebiscite. At the same time, the King intrigued with Bevin in London. Although Bevin had initially favored a postponement of the plebiscite until March 1948, he was now impressed by the King's argument that it not be delayed beyond September of 1946.[37] Convinced that the presence of British troops was necessary to forestall electoral fraud by the right (and a subsequent revolt by the left), Bevin was determined to retain them in Greece until a plebiscite had been completed. On the other hand, he was anxious to encourage withdrawal of Soviet troops from Eastern Europe and hence wanted to remove British forces from Greece as soon as possible. An early plebiscite would resolve this dilemma, giving Bevin the opportunity to withdraw British troops at the earliest possible moment.[38] Withdrawal of British troops would also satisfy the British Labour Party's restive left wing, which had long clamored for an end to British involvement in Greece, although for quite different reasons from Bevin's. Indeed, resigned to the weakness of the Greek center and unalterably opposed to the left, the British Foreign Office, in reality, was consciously if none too happily delivering Greece to the right.[39]

Superficially, British policy's rightward shift in 1946 seemed to reopen the conflict over tactics that had divided the Americans from the British in 1943–44. As if to confirm the return to earlier positions, Churchill reemerged that spring in the thick of Greek politics, singing the praises of monarchism. By contrast, as late as the Potsdam conference the State Department had cited its "belief that a republican form of government offers more possibilities for a peaceful future than the return of a monarchy already stigmatized by totalitarianism."[40] Even after the monarchist right's landslide victory in the Greek elections, Byrnes notified the U.S. embassy in Athens of the State Department's belief that "an early plebiscite on the King's return would be most undesirable." This advice was quite acceptable to MacVeagh, whose observations replicated those of 1944. "The danger of social revolution," he reported, "is only likely to be enhanced by hasty political action." If the royalist government attempted to "rush" the plebiscite, it would be "courting disaster."[41] Even so, with the Cold War heightening on a global basis, American policymakers were ready for a showdown with the left and, by 1946, had lost whatever qualms they might once have felt at supporting the right. This became evident in late April 1946, during the meeting of the Council of Foreign Ministers in

Paris. When Bevin made a strong plea at that meeting for a plebiscite in September, the American Secretary of State provided his endorsement. "He thought we were in a better position to assess the situation," noted the British leader. "Byrnes said that it was essential that the Communists should not get into power in Greece. This must be avoided at all costs. He did not mind how it was done."[42]

Obtaining the approval of British and American officials in early May 1946, the Tsaldaris government announced plans for a plebiscite on the monarchy that September. The Sophoulis Liberals decried this as a "breach of faith" by the British, but remained ineffectual. The left responded with great bitterness, although it was determined not to isolate itself again by a futile boycott.[43] On May 12, the royalist newspaper *Kathimerini* kicked off the monarchist campaign with the now familiar charge that a republic was "the antechamber to Communist dictatorship." Given the febrile state of public opinion in Greece, it seemed quite possible that the monarchy, so unpopular only a few years before, would rally majority support. Nevertheless, a new surge of right-wing violence and intimidation followed. By the summer, MacVeagh was reporting: "Not only thousands of communists . . . but thousands of centrists and republicans as well, who are being equally terrorized by what I have called 'disreputable' royalist elements in effective if not open alliance with the Government . . . will either go to the polls in jeopardy or will not go at all."[44] In September, when the monarchy received a resounding vote of approval, the observer mission reported numerous instances of fraud and harassment by government officials, as well as a 94 percent level of participation, which it regarded as "unreal." Rather embarrassed by the whole thing, Under Secretary of State Dean Acheson confided to MacVeagh that, while the State Department considered the royalist victory legitimate, "the percentage in favor of the King was increased by falsification and unfair practices of [the] Govt."[45]

During 1946, with Greek politics moving rapidly rightward, Communist Party leader Zachariades found his program of legality and "national unity" increasingly untenable. The

KKE, of course, like other Communist parties, was not a democratically structured organization. Nevertheless, the mass base it had acquired during the wartime occupation and the severe reverses the left had suffered since the Varkiza agreement ripened the prospects for dissension. In May, a bitter revolt broke out within the KKE, led by veterans of the wartime resistance, who denounced the policy of conciliation and demanded the formation of a new ELAS in the mountains. Counterattacking, Zachariades assailed the dissidents as adventurers and purged several of their spokesmen from the KKE.[46] But revolutionary militancy could not be disposed of this easily, nor did Zachariades desire to repudiate it completely. Since 1945, thousands of desperate or impatient leftists had been gathering in refugee camps across the Yugoslav, Bulgarian, and Albanian borders. Armed left-wing bands were also coalescing in the Greek mountains. To mollify his critics within the party and to ensure KKE control of the incipient rebellion, Zachariades began to adopt a more militant rhetoric. Moreover, in July 1946, he gave the first orders for low-key military operations to the impatient ELAS veteran, Markos Vafiades, who left for the mountains the following month.[47]

Yet, while many leftists were eager to embark upon a revolutionary struggle for power, the KKE leadership still hesitated. Anxious to retain the comparitive freedom provided by legality, distrustful of Markos and of rural-based insurrections, and mindful of Soviet injunctions to follow a respectable, parliamentary course, Zachariades, Siantos, and most other members of the central committee remained unwilling to commit their party fully to an armed uprising. The KKE chief thus rejected mobilization of ELAS veterans, the peasantry, and the urban working class in 1946, when it was still possible. As Woodhouse notes, the object of the orders to Markos "was only to bring pressure to bear on the Government, not to promote a Communist revolution." Not until the end of October 1946 was a headquarters established in the mountains for the rebels' "Democratic Army"; and even then, the KKE's leaders tarried in Athens, dreaming of government ministries. Torn between conflicting conceptions of the KKE as a revolutionary and a legal entity, a national and an "international" movement, a vanguard and a mass-based party, Greece's Communist leaders faced the crisis of 1946 with the same fatal indecision they had shown in 1944. Indeed, on July 31, when an EAM delegation headed by Siantos called upon MacVeagh, it lamented the Athens government's persecution of the left and delivered what the American ambassador termed a "formal appeal for US intervention."[48]

By late 1946, however, U.S. officials had less interest in defending the Greek left than in isolating it. On October 11, MacVeagh had a "long conversation" with the King in which he pressed him to "insist on the political leaders getting together to form a broadly representative government." He explained that this should be a center-right coalition, excluding the left.(The one right-wing leader MacVeagh thought it best to omit was Petros Mavromichalis, the Defense Minister, whom MacVeagh described as "tending toward Fascism.")[49] Yet, although U.S. officials urged the creation of a center-right cabinet throughout late 1946 and most of 1947, they met with little success, for many Greek Liberals were appalled by the right-wing extremism of the ruling Populist Party and convinced that only a policy of moderation could halt the drift toward civil war.[50] Committed to the right as a legitimate bulwark against the left, U.S. officials considered these centrist holdouts dangerously independent. MacVeagh complained, unfairly, to the State Department that the "Sophoulis branch of the Liberal party . . . not only continues to refuse to meet the Populists on any other terms then its own, but has for a long time pursued a policy of flirting with the Communists." In November, citing the desire of Sophoulis's confidante, the Liberal publisher Dimitrios Lambrakis, for "the formation of a Center to moderate Left Govt," MacVeagh warned of the "probability of any new Sophoulis Govt being actively 'fellow traveller' in character."[51] The American Secretary of State instructed MacVeagh on January 21, 1947 that "groups prepared to cooperate with the communists should be regarded as disloyal, contaminated, or politically immature elements," unworthy of participating in the governing coalition. Referring to Sophoulis, he contended that it would "manifestly be unfair to call upon [the] Greek people to support [a] leader who has not [the] courage to take steps to isolate [the] communists and communist-contaminated groups."[52]

To their dismay, American officials found the royalist government almost as exasperating. Particularly irritating were the repeated demands for territorial concessions at the expense of the Balkan Communist states to the north. "Greek territorial claims appear in most cases exaggerated and invalid," noted a secret State Department policy statement. "We should encourage the Greek Government . . . to be satisfied with the 1941 frontiers." U.S. policymakers worried that expansionism would both sidetrack measures for economic recovery in Greece and embroil that nation in a war with its already hostile Balkan neighbors. "Elementary common sense if not morality would seem to indicate that this is not the time for the Greeks to press for territorial changes," MacVeagh told Washington.[53] Nevertheless, at the Paris peace conference beginning in late July 1946, the Greek government insisted upon its right to southern Albania (which the Greeks termed Northern Epirus) in any peace settlement. Though supported by the Greek left, the Athens government found itself abandoned by its American and British allies. Eventually, therefore, Greek expansionist hopes went unfulfilled, and the Americans settled down to lecturing Greek leaders on the need to be realistic.[54]

The Athens government's economic policies also appeared counterproductive. Greece's economic recovery came under the jurisdiction of the United Nations Relief and Rehabilitation Administration, which found it an impossible task. On April 12, 1945, the UNRRA director in Athens reported that a "successful relief and rehabilitation program requires [the] ability of [a] government to organize and utilize its own resources." Unfortunately, he observed, Greece lacked a government with such capabilities.[55] As the official history of UNRRA delicately noted, in Greece "the Government was

frequently one of the obstacles which UNRRA had to overcome." Inertia, venality, political biases, and corruption were
rife in the Athens administration, much to the disgust of U.N.
officials.[56] In an effort to remedy this situation, the Minister
of Supply, Kyriakos Varvaressos, introduced in June 1945 a
bold program of economic reform—regulating prices and
wages, applying direct taxation, and promoting measures to
control distribution and crack down on the black market. On
September 1, he resigned in despair, blaming a "systematically
organized campaign" by Greek business interests.[57] That October, calling attention to "the absence of a competent and
effective administrative machine" and "the decisive influence" on all Greek governments of a few people "whose main
object is to make money quickly," UNRRA's Deputy Director
General warned of "an approaching economic breakdown."[58]

Although deeply disturbed by Greece's economic disintegration, American officials were unsure how to combat it.
Given the incompetence and corruption of the Greek government, they feared that American economic aid would
prove as useless in stabilizing the situation as had the vast
sums expended by the British and UNRRA. In May 1945,
Under Secretary of State Will Clayton told the Greek ambassador that U.S. reconstruction loans would have to be
based upon "detailed information as to the projects contemplated and the expected sources of funds for the repayment."
Furthermore, "external financial assistance . . . would not,
of course, provide the solution to the inflation and general
financial breakdown threatening Greece. Only stringest internal measures by the Greek government" would be effective.[59] In August, Byrnes complained of the Greeks' "astro-
nomical expectations" of U.S. funding, while in November
he noted the "impression gaining ground abroad" that Greece
might be "incapable of running herself and solving [her] immediate economic problems." Although the U.S. government
would "give sympathetic consideration" to a "Greek request
for loans these must be made on [a] sound economic basis."
There was "little likelihood" of "credits being made available
to [a] country offering as little financial and economic stability
as Greece."[60]

Ironically, then, the economic caution of American policymakers conflicted with their political goals. Even the overwrought MacVeagh, although inclined to take a sanguine view of Greek businessmen and their political allies and to blame Greece's economic difficulties upon allegedly leftist UNRRA and British planners,[61] argued at first against large-scale American economic assistance. Noting that Greek capitalists had traditionally invested heavily overseas, leaving Greece a backward and unprofitable market, MacVeagh contended that "if Greece were now advised that further foreign loans must be dependent on her contributing her own share by investing her foreign capital in her own rehabilitation, this might . . . bring about a stronger state here both politically and economically and one from which any additional foreign capital might at least hope to reap some other profit than further defalcations and renewed requests. . . . It might make this country more attractive to foreign industrial enterprise than it can ever be under a continuation of the old system of helping those who will not help themselves." His recommendations, "which would of course involve giving full support to the continuance of [the] capitalist economy in Greece," entailed "the limiting of further credits to specific uses, in reasonable amounts and for definite periods." America's "association with Greek capital" should be "kept on a conservative, business-like basis."[62]

As the Greek economy moved toward collapse, however, not even conservatives proved willing to consign Greece's fate to the vagaries of the free market. On November 10, 1945, Loy Henderson, Director of the State Department's Office of Near Eastern and African Affairs, informed Byrnes that "present conditions in Greece are so alarming" that the British military had recommended that the United States "share British responsibilities." Henderson thought a U.S. military commitment inadvisable, but he did argue that the situation was "critical enough to justify active steps on our part to improve [economic] conditions." The United States, however, must "make it clear that further assistance to Greece is conditional" on "internal economic reforms," among them: price, wage, export/import, and monetary controls; effective distribution of relief supplies; "stringent taxation"; drastic cutbacks in government expenditures; and "positive action" to restore agricultural and industrial production.[63] Having obtained presidential approval, Byrnes notified MacVeagh later that month of plans for a $25 million Export-Import Bank loan to Greece.[64] To the distress of the department, the President thought the accompanying note "rather harsh" and ordered it reworded;[65] at the same time, officials of the Treasury Department and the State Department's Economic Division questioned the loan on economic grounds.[66] In a panic, MacVeagh pleaded for rapid action, arguing that Greece was the only remaining Balkan nation "attempting [to] retain orthodox ideas [of] private property and free enterprise along American lines."[67] At last, on January 11, 1946, Byrnes announced the loan to the press, remarking that an accompanying note called upon the Athens government to take "energetic steps to put its internal house in order."[68]

"Energetic steps," however, remained elusive. Loath to take measures that might anger its wealthy supporters, convinced of the fidelity of its Anglo-American patrons, and incompetent as ever, the Athens administration avoided sponsorship of all new programs—all new programs, that is, except for further efforts to obtain economic assistance.[69] And in May 1946, the U.S. government did grant Greece a $10 million surplus property credit. But later that month, in connection with rumors of a Greek request for a $200 million Export-Import Bank loan, Byrnes told the American embassy that it "should take every opportunity informally to call [the] attention of Greek Govt officials to [the] fact that none of the 25 million dollar Eximbank loan has been utilized." The following month, Acheson informed Rankin that the State Department was "disturbed by [the] reported Greek attitude that additional financial aid can be expected regardless of Greek inertia in meeting [their] own problems." Tsaldaris, in fact, was told in June that his proposed visit to Washington to obtain further U.S. aid would not be welcome.[70] Undaunted, Tsaldaris met with Byrnes in Paris in early July 1946, requesting $6 billion in U.S. economic assistance. Byrnes responded irritably that such an amount was not within the realm of possibility. Over drinks, he complained to C. L. Sulzberger that he was "a little fed up with the Greeks."[71] Meanwhile, in Washington, at the prodding of Greek-Americans, Secretary of Commerce Henry Wallace sounded out Export-Import Bank officials about further loans to Greece, only to be told "that the Greek leadership was not doing a good job of preventing the flight of Greek capital . . . ; that they were a reactionary outfit; that money furnished them would be wasted."[72]

Consequently, by the summer of 1946, the Athens government appeared in jeopardy of losing the foreign assistance that kept it afloat. In spite of the fact that UNRRA aid was scheduled to terminate at the end of the year, the British Chancellor of the Exchequer, Hugh Dalton, pressed his cabinet colleagues, on financial grounds, to end British funding in Greece. Although Dalton suggested to Athens officials that they turn to the Americans and to U.S.-controlled international lending institutions for assistance,[73] the State Department's response was cold. Indeed, it agreed to receive a visiting Greek economic mission only on the condition that the Greeks forswear discussion of American aid. Meeting with officials from State, Treasury, Commerce, and Agriculture, as well as from UNRRA and the Export-Import Bank, the Greek delegates promptly forgot their promises and launched new appeals for economic assistance. American officials were disgusted. "It is the feeling of the Department," Acheson informed the President on August 7, "that it would be unwise for this Government to commit itself to extend any additional Export-Import credits to Greece until the Greek Government has shown that it is taking the measures within its own power to deal with its economic problems." Under the circumstances, "a new loan would do little, if anything, to solve the basic economic or political difficulties of Greece." To the consternation of the Greek delegation, the President and all other U.S. officials reiterated this point.[74]

But Washington's hard line on economic assistance proved short lived. On September 20, 1946, the Americans granted a credit of $10 million to the Greek government to enable it to bid on maritime equipment, and five days later gave the Greeks an additional credit of $25 million for the purchase of surplus property.[75] The amounts, of course, were still relatively small; yet, behind the scenes, the American commitment was growing. On September 24, 1946, Byrnes cabled Clayton that, though some months before it had been natural enough that economic considerations should largely determine assistance to foreign lands, "the situation has so hardened that the time has now come . . . when the implementation of our general policies requires the closest coordination." The Secretary of State had "in mind particularly two countries which it is of the highest importance for us to assist, Turkey and Greece."[76] On October 15, Byrnes met with the British Defence Minister, A. V. Alexander, telling him (in the words of the latter) that the U.S. government was "anxious about the position" of Greece and Turkey. These two countries, said Byrnes, "might become outposts of great importance and . . . we should do what we could to help them." Byrnes thought it best for the British to continue military aid, while the United States would do what it could "to help the two countries economically."[77] To facilitate U.S. economic assistance, as well as to bypass the inertia and corruption of the Athens administration, the State Department arranged for a U.S. economic mission to visit Greece and make specific recommendations.[78] Although the economic side of the State Department remained uneasy about an open-ended U.S. economic commitment,[79] the political side rejoiced at the turn of events. MacVeagh confided to Henderson: "I feel now as Cassandra might, had anyone suddenly agreed with her!"[80]

Underlying the expanded U.S. aid commitment lay a solidifying belief that Anglo-American difficulties in Greece could be traced directly to what the State Department termed the "maneuvers and machinations" of the Kremlin.[81] After all, Russia was the major enemy of American ambitions in much of the postwar world. Why not then in Greece? According to a State Department policy paper of July 1946, the Soviet goal in Greece was clearly "the transfer of power into

EAM's hands." EAM was "not a 'friend' or ally of the USSR; it is an instrument of Soviet policy." Although discomforting complexities abounded, "it remains true that the paramount factor in the Greek political scene is the international rivalry and that all other questions . . . are subsumed in and assimilated to this larger question."[82] Queried about the difficulties along Greece's northern frontier, MacVeagh pinned the blame on those he called "Soviet puppets": Yugoslavia, Albania, and Bulgaria. "Add continued anti-Greek propaganda and secret Soviet control of [the] Greek Communist party," said MacVeagh, and the "conclusion seems inevitable that [the] Soviet Government . . . must be 'assigned responsibility.'" Russia's strategy, claimed the War Department's intelligence division, was to provide "substantial material as well as moral support to the Communist subversive movement in Greece" through the channel of "Yugoslavia, Bulgaria, and Albania, all completely subservient to Soviet policy." The goal? "To gain complete control of Greece."[83]

Greece continued to be viewed as merely one aspect of a considerably more elaborate picture, involving the future of the Near and Middle East.[84] A draft memorandum to the President by the State Department's Division of Near Eastern Affairs reported that the region had become "a highly dangerous trouble spot." The British and French positions had been "greatly weakened as a result of the two world wars," and there was "danger that the Near Eastern peoples . . . will look to Soviet Russia for a cure of their economic and social ills and as the mainspring of power." There was a critical need "to place sufficient American impress on the region to win and hold it for the Western World." In late 1945, Loy Henderson reported that "the Soviet Union seems to be determined to break down" Britain's "great dam" restraining "the flow of Russian power towards the south" and sweep through to the Mediterranean, the Persian Gulf, and the Indian Ocean. By June 1946, Henderson was arguing forcefully for "at least $120,000,000" in U.S. loans "to bolster our deplorable position in the Near East area." He did not see "how we can justify our failure to employ such loans," for "the Near East is now a major political battlefield."[85] The following month, the U.S. Chief of Naval Operations warned the Secretary of the Navy and the President of new Soviet "footholds in the Mediterranean" and of Russian efforts to undermine "the British position in Greece, Egypt and the Middle East."[86]

When controversies involving Greece, Turkey, Yugoslavia, and Iran flared up in 1946, U.S. officials had little difficulty categorizing them. The War Department's intelligence bureau claimed that the Russians wanted Greece "in order to dominate the Eastern Mediterranean, isolate Turkey . . . and thus facilitate eventual Soviet domination over the Near and Middle East."[87] Russian "encroachments in the Middle East are steadily weakening the British and American positions and strengthening Soviet political and military influence," White House aide Clark Clifford informed the President in a report synthesizing the views of top U.S. civilian and military officials. Incidents in Greece, Turkey, and Iran constituted part of a deliberate Soviet attempt to achieve "the economic, military, and political domination of the entire Middle East."[88] In his account of this period, Joseph Jones, special assistant to the Assistant Secretary of State for Public Affairs, recalled that Soviet leaders "deployed their diplomacy, propaganda, military pressures and economic weapons in persistent efforts to break through the Iran-Turkey-Greece barrier to the south and establish Soviet power in the eastern Mediterranean, the Middle East, and the Indian Ocean." And Soviet hegemony in this region, the Secretary of War informed the President, "would be most prejudicial to the long-range security of the United States."[89]

Convinced of the need to buttress the ramparts of the Middle East,[90] American policymakers adopted increasingly bellicose positions in 1946. On February 28, Secretary of the Navy James Forrestal asked Byrnes if he "was agreeable to the Navy preparing plans for a task force in the Mediterranean." Delighted with the idea, Byrnes suggested that the U.S. naval force accompany the U.S.S. *Missouri*, probably the strongest battleship afloat, to Turkey, where it would deliver the body of the Turkish ambassador, who had recently died in Washington. In his memoirs, Byrnes noted delicately that he and Forrestal thought the gesture "would give encouragement to Turkey and Greece." Returning from Fulton, Missouri after his "iron curtain" address, Churchill learned of the plan from Truman and promptly reported to London that the action was "calculated to make Russia understand that she must come to reasonable terms."[91] During the next year, in addition to the *Missouri*, two U.S. aircraft carriers, seven cruisers, eighteen destroyers, and four auxiliary vessels paid calls at Mediterranean ports, providing an impressive exhibition of U.S. military might. When the *Missouri* touched in Athens, the royalist newspaper *Embros* greeted it ecstatically, claiming that this "glorious giant" represented "the power, the spirit, and the disposition of that colossal universal Titan called United States of America."[92] Later that year, Forrestal announced that the American government would maintain a permanent naval presence in the Mediterranean.[93]

"Showing the flag" in the Mediterranean seemed particularly important with respect to Turkey. On August 7, 1946, the Russians had requested revision of the Montreux convention to allow joint Russian-Turkish defense of the Dardanelles. From the standpoint of U.S. policymakers, this represented an aggressive move, opening the prospects for everything from Soviet bases to direct control of the Turkish nation.[94] On August 15, Acheson warned a gathering of U.S. officials that Soviet pressures upon Turkey "reflected a desire to control and dominate that country." Acceptance of these demands "would be followed next by infiltration and domination of Greece by Russia with the obvious consequences in the Middle East." The State Department, he concluded, believed that Soviet pressures on Turkey should be "resisted" by the United States, "with the full realization that . . . it might lead to armed conflict." Remarking that "we might as well find out whether the Russians . . . [are] bent on world conquest now as in five or ten years," President Truman called for "a firm position."[95] Accordingly, the State Department pressed the Turks to resist Soviet demands, the Navy dispatched U.S. warships to the region, and the Joint Chiefs of

Staff laid plans to sell the Turks U.S. military supplies and send them technicians, including U.S. military officers.[96]

As Acheson later observed, the President's decision to stand firm on Turkey provided "the signal for the administration to go ahead" on Greece.[97] On September 5, 1946, Colonel James McCormack of the U.S. Army submitted a memorandum to the Near and Middle East subcommittee of the State-War-Navy Coordinating Committee (SWNCC) arguing that American security hinged upon support of Greece, for that nation "stands alone in the Balkans as a barrier between the USSR and the Mediterranean."[98] Writing to Byrnes a week later on behalf of SWNCC, Clayton cited difficulties in Greece, Turkey, and Iran and called for development of a policy to "enable us . . . to supply military-type equipment to countries such as those in the Near and Middle East." On September 25, Clayton read Byrnes's dramatic memo of the preceding day on U.S. aid to Secretary of War Robert Patterson and Secretary of the Navy Forrestal, who endorsed it emphatically and urged the loosening of restrictions on U.S. military assistance.[99] On October 15, the day Byrnes broached U.S. aid plans to the British, Acheson notified MacVeagh that the State Department felt "that strained international relations focusing on Greece may result in [an] early major crisis which may be a deciding factor in [the] future orientation of [the] Near and Middle Eastern countries. . . . We are prepared to take suitable measures." These measures, outlined in a memorandum of November 1, 1946, included: public and private statements of support for Greece; U.S. arms sales, if necessary, to the Greek government; recommendations to the Export-Import Bank and the International Bank to resume economic assistance to the Athens regime; and "the immediate dispatch to Greece of an American economic mission."[100]

Ironically, the grim specter of Soviet expansionism that haunted American policymakers was contradicted by the reality of Soviet policy toward Greece. At international conferences, of course, the Russians frequently raised the Greek issue, but it remained a *riposte* to Western attacks on Russian policies elsewhere rather than a serious effort to put the Greek left in power. At the London Council of Foreign Ministers meeting in September 1945, Bevin confidentially assured Archbishop Damaskinos that Soviet criticims of the lack of democracy in Greece were simply rejoinders to comparable Anglo-American charges against Romania and Bulgaria. Within a short time Molotov informed Bevin that the Russians would drop the matter, which they did.[101] The game was renewed on January 21, 1946 when, in retaliation for a complaint about the presence of Soviet troops in northern Iran, the Russians raised the issue of the presence of British troops in Greece at the U.N. Security Council. Within a week, Soviet Deputy Foreign Minister Andrey Vyshinsky offered to drop the Russian charges if the British would recognize the governments of Romania and Bulgaria. Bevin rejected this particular quid pro quo, but a few days later, after a compromise agreement on Iran, the Russian diplomat mellowed and withdrew his complaint about Greece.[102]

For those Greek leftists who looked expectantly to the Soviet Union for support, Moscow's indifference must have been frustrating, if not embittering. On January 16, 1946, an EAM delegation arrived in the Soviet capital, where it commenced weeks of fruitless efforts to meet with Russian leaders. British diplomatic observers reported that, when it departed on February 8, it had seen no one more important than a local trade union functionary. So irritated was the EAM mission that it secretly complained of its treatment to the Greek ambassador![103] By contrast, Tsaldaris enjoyed an extremely cordial meeting with Molotov that July, and both expressed their desire for peaceful and friendly relations between their respective countries. In late August 1946, to be sure, both the Russian and Yugoslav ambassadors were recalled from their posts in Athens, in an apparent gesture of displeasure at the impending restoration of George II. But the farewell meeting of the Soviet ambassador with Greek officials was "very polite and amiable," the British noted, while the Yugoslav ambassador "had been very rude."[104]

This distinction between Soviet and Yugoslav behavior—which totally escaped the comprehension of American officials—reflected the underlying reality of Communist policy toward Greece. Tito apparently felt a sincere sense of political solidarity with the Greek left. Furthermore, although the KKE probably never offered Tito explicit territorial concessions in return for his support, Tito most certainly had territorial ambitions, principally in Macedonia, and these seemed more likely to be realized in a Greece ruled by Markos or Zachariades than in one dominated by the traditionally Slavophobic right. To a lesser extent, Bulgaria and Albania—the latter little more than a puppet of Yugoslavia—shared these motives. In addition, Albania's very survival as a nation was threatened by the irredentism of the Athens government.[105] Consequently, during 1945–46, relations between Greece and its three Balkan neighbors steadily deteriorated, with the first signs of external Communist assistance appearing in Greece. At the same time, the thousands of Greek leftist refugees in Yugoslavia, Bulgaria, and Albania began to receive military training, small quantities of arms, and supplies from their Balkan hosts.[106] Such aid was important to the Greek guerrilla bands, although it represented only a small fraction of the assistance channeled to the Athens government by Great Britain and the United States. No aid came from the Soviet Union—a fact which, it appears, did not result, as Washington thought, from Moscow's satisfaction with Belgrade's policy but rather from Moscow's total lack of sympathy with it.[107]

In subsequent years, Yugoslav leaders made no secret of their aid to the Greek left, nor of Russian hostility to it. Yugoslavia "rendered assistance to the Greek Liberation movement from its very inception . . . despite Stalin's attitude that Greece was in the Western sphere of influence and not to be tampered with," wrote the prominent Yugoslav journalist Vladimir Dedijer. "The leadership of the Soviet Union had no interest whatsoever in a victory of the people's revolutionary movement in Greece," claimed Tito's associate, Vukmanovic-Tempo, "because Greece was 'geographically' remote from the Soviet Union . . . and because it was outside the [Russian] 'sphere of interest.'"[108] Milovan Djilas, Yugoslavia's vice-president during this period and a man who later underwent many years of imprisonment rather than compromise his integrity, recalled that "the Soviet Government took no direct action" to aid the Greek left. Speculating on "the motives that caused Stalin to be against the uprising in Greece," Djilas remarked: "Perhaps he reasoned that the creation in the Balkans of still another Communist state . . . in circumstances when not even the others were reliable and subservient, would hardly have been in his interest, not to speak of possible international complications, which . . . could . . . endanger his already-won positions."[109]

A rift between Yugoslav and Soviet policy in the Balkans does much to explain an apparent anomaly: Soviet support for a U.N. investigation of Greek border violations. In September 1946, the Russians had vetoed an American proposal of this type—a move which merely confirmed to American officials the Kremlin's responsibility for Anglo-American difficulties in Greece.[110] But in December of that year, when the United States again proposed a border investigation, the Russians startled observers by agreeing with the Americans. "To my surprise," recalled Byrnes, Molotov "instructed his representative on the Security Council to support the resolution." Moreover, it would be an investigation on both sides of the border, thus providing a unique instance of U.N. inspection within Communist nations.[111] To be sure, the investigation (in which Russia would participate) could be expected to highlight the repressive policies of the Athens government, thus furnishing Moscow with numerous opportunities for propaganda against that government's British and American patrons. But it was also bound to embarrass Balkan Communist leaders and place them at odds with the West. Djilas recalled that the Soviet government "looked with satisfaction" at Yugoslavia's confrontation with the United States and left that nation "to face the music alone at the United Nations." At the same time, in Greece, such an investigation would inevitably hamper the supply program for the insurgents and oblige the left to maintain reasonably legitimate

behavior. This may account for the fact that the KKE newspaper *Rizospastis* followed the Security Council move by
three days of silence on the subject.[112]

The American defense of the Middle East and its Greek
portal should not be regarded as disinterested. After World
War II, the value of Anglo-American control of Mideast oil
grew to colossal proportions. Between 1938 and 1947, daily
petroleum production in Saudi Arabia rose from 1,400 to
246,000 barrels and in Kuwait from 0 to 45,000 barrels; significant, albeit less spectacular, increases took place in the oil
production of Bahrain, Iran, and Iraq.[113] Mideast oil became
the most cheaply produced in the world, thanks to the vast
size of the concessions, the impoverished living standards of
the people, the supineness of the political leaders, the shal-
lowness of the wells, and the vast abundance of the oil. U.S.
officials reported that, as of January 1, 1947, domestic oil
holdings produced 11 barrels daily per well; the comparable
figure for the Mideast was 3,931. In 1946, oil from Bahrain,
which was estimated to cost $0.25 per barrel to produce, was
selling for $1.05 per barrel and more at the Persian Gulf.[114]
Meanwhile, U.S. dependence upon Mideast oil grew apace
as U.S. imports of crude and refined petroleum products
steadily climbed; in 1946, they were more than twice the prewar level. By 1948, the United States had become a net im-
porter of petroleum for the first time in its history.[115] Given
its sizable domestic production, however, the United States
was less important as a market for American oil companies
than was Europe, whose consumption of oil grew dramatically
in the postwar era. The Persian Gulf, which provided Europe
with 25 percent of its oil in 1938, supplied it with 50 percent
by 1949.[116] With their eyes on a glorious present and an even
brighter future, U.S. oilmen rapidly expanded their investments in the Middle East. By 1946, Aramco alone had poured
in $120 million and had laid plans to augment this by several
hundred million dollars.[117]

Relations with the British, while less than cozy, proved
friendly enough to facilitate the development of the new

American oil empire. In the aftermath of the war, British officials encouraged the Americans to expand their oil operations in the Middle East, provided that they did not conflict with those of Great Britain,[118] and U.S. corporations were quick to comply. In February 1946, Standard Oil of New Jersey, the giant of the industry, together with Socony, began negotiations to purchase 40 percent of Aramco's stock; Aramco's parent companies lacked adequate marketing facilities for Saudi Arabia's oil resources, while Standard and Socony possessed worldwide marketing facilities but lacked an appropriately large share of Mideast oil. Standard also began efforts that year to buy vast quantities of crude oil from the Anglo-Iranian Oil Company. Finally, Aramco announced plans in late 1946 for a thousand-mile Trans-Arabian Pipeline, from the Persian Gulf to the Mediterranean.[119] All three projects required British cooperation: the first, because it violated the British-enforced Red Line Agreement, which prohibited partners in the Iraq Petroleum Corporation from acquiring independent concessions in an area roughly contiguous with the old Ottoman Empire; the second, because the Anglo-Iranian Oil Company was a British-owned firm; and the third because British political influence in the Middle East could potentially block the pipeline transit agreements.[120] Promising "to support the position of the US oil companies," the State Department took action. The Red Line Agreement, Byrnes informed London, "in so far as it restricts the commercial liberties of the parties to it," was "incompatible with the United States' views on restrictive business practices." Acheson instructed the American chargé in London to "press on appropriate officials that [the] US Govt feels very strongly the importance of liberalizing concession arrangements . . . in [the] Middle Eastern area in order to stabilize and secure [the] American oil position."[121] By late 1946, the British had indicated their cooperation in all areas.[122]

The ability of American oil companies to mobilize the State Department behind their postwar ventures reflected the Truman administration's firm commitment to maintaining and extending America's stake in Mideast oil. "For the sake of the

American economy and of future American security, nothing should be left undone to promote full participation by American interests in the development of these areas," an administration spokesman told Congress in late 1945.[123] James Forrestal, Will Clayton, and other top officials lobbied for the Anglo-American Petroleum Agreement, courted Arab leaders of oil-rich nations, and argued the crucial importance of overseas petroleum resources.[124] In a speech delivered on September 19, 1946, Loy Henderson observed that the United States was "actively promoting our commercial and business interests and . . . extractive projects" in the Middle East on the basis of "the doctrine of the open door."[125] Indeed, even in secret planning sessions, State Department officials contended that the U.S. "Open Door policy" provided the foundation of America's program in the region.[126] In an address delivered on July 30, 1946, the director of the State Department's Petroleum Division, John A. Loftus, observed that U.S. policy toward foreign oil operations was marked by:

1. Insistence upon nondiscriminatory commercial treatment of American oil marketers. . . .
2. Insistence upon the "open door" principle of equal commercial opportunity . . . with respect to the granting of rights to explore for and develop oil reserves.
3. Insistence on the principle of just and adequate compensation in circumstances where a foreign government . . . nationalize[s] the oil industry.
4. Diplomatic assistance to and support of American oil companies . . . such assistance and support being more or less routine.

The goal of the U.S. government in these matters, he observed, was "to facilitate and encourage the participation of American capital and enterprise in the development of Eastern Hemisphere" oil reserves, "particularly in the oil rich areas of the Middle East."[127]

The Truman administration's growing appetite for Mideast oil sharpened its obsession with expanding American influence in the region and with containing the influence of others. Juxtaposing the "great mineral wealth" of the Near and Middle East against the "disintegrating effect of many groups of dissatisfied citizens," Henderson warned of the "temptation to powers outside the area." Presumably, the United States was not an "outside" power, and certainly the Soviet Union was. "By penetration and extension of their influence in the Middle East," reported the Joint Chiefs of Staff, the Russians were "threatening the access of the Western powers to the important oil reserves in the area." In September 1946, Clifford warned the President that "our continued access to oil in the Middle East is especially threatened by Soviet penetration into Iran."[128] Indeed, the Iranian crisis of 1946 sent a tremor of fear through the American policymaking establishment. From Teheran, Ambassador Wallace Murray predicted a disastrous domino effect, which would lead to the cancellation of Western oil concessions in Iran, Kuwait, Iraq, and Saudi Arabia and end in "giving Russia control of [the] richest oil fields in the Middle East, possibly the world's greatest." In his *Memoirs*, Truman recalled that if the Russians attained control of Iran's oil, "the raw material balance of the world would undergo a serious change, and it would be a serious loss for the economy of the Western world."[129] If American officials overestimated the temptation of "outside" powers to control the oil-rich Middle East,[130] it was at least partly because they felt the full dimensions of their own.

These lineaments of desire were neatly complemented by a genuine hostility toward Russia. By late 1946, the State Department's chain of command—from Ambassador MacVeagh, to NEA director Henderson, to Under Secretary Acheson—was absolutely convinced of Soviet mendacity and ready to proceed with tougher measures in Greece.[131] Others in the State Department, most notably Secretary Byrnes, while no less anti-Soviet, remained a shade less certain that Greece provided the most appropriate place for America to take a stand.[132] Byrnes, however, was already in eclipse; and his successor, George C. Marshall, leaned heavily upon Acheson for advice, as did Truman.[133] Outside the State Department, U.S. military spokesmen—and particularly the bitterly anti-Soviet Secretary of the Navy James Forrestal—were eager for a confrontation with Soviet power along the Greece-Turkey-Iran barrier.[134] The only figure in the Truman administration who favored a cooperative approach toward Russia was the Secretary of Commerce, Henry Wallace, about whom Acheson warned a Greek government delegation in August 1946;[135] that September, however, Truman fired Wallace in a public dispute over American foreign policy. By late 1946, therefore, the Truman administration was ready for a showdown with Russia over Greece—even if the Russians, in accordance with their putative Machiavellian cunning, were nowhere to be seen.

As American policymakers prepared for an international confrontation, their British counterparts were growing increasingly divided over the wisdom of maintaining their financial commitments in Greece. Ever since mid-1946, Dalton had been seeking to rally his colleagues to end all British funding to the Greek government.[136] By the latter part of the year, with Great Britain facing enormous economic difficulties, the Chancellor of the Exchequer was making headway toward an aid cutoff.[137] Even so, the military and the Foreign Office remained obdurate. On November 13, the British Chiefs of Staff reported that it was imperative for Great Britain "to prevent Greece from falling into the Russian sphere of influence." Informed while overseas of the "very great reluctance here to contemplate a continuation of our military, financial and political commitments in Greece," Bevin fired back on December 5: "The policy of the Government has been based hitherto on the assumption that Greece and Turkey are essential to our political and strategical position in the world. . . . Am I to understand that we may now abandon this position? I really do not know where I stand."[138] Of course, if the Americans could be enticed into taking on the British responsibility in Greece—which would entail U.S. military aid to supplement the economic assistance promised by Byrnes on October 15—both Dalton's and Bevin's goals could be secured. Accordingly, the British intensified their efforts to obtain additional U.S. aid in late 1946 and early

1947, although without much confidence.[139] Meanwhile, the two ministers prepared for a head-on confrontation over British policy toward Greece at the cabinet level.[140]

Bevin clearly won the first round. On January 25, 1947, he recommended to the cabinet that the Greek army be expanded and that the U.S. government be approached regarding "sharing" the costs of the Greek armed forces after March 31. "Having undertaken to try and put Greece on a stable basis," he declared, "we must . . . now see it through."[141] At the cabinet meeting of January 30, he proffered these proposals, whereupon Dalton, according to the minutes, opposed the armed forces increases as extravagant and "said that . . . we should avoid any financial commitment to Greece after the end of the current financial year." Confronted with this clash of opinions, the cabinet made no decision on terminating British funding. Instead, it "agreed in principle that the Greek Armed Forces should be placed in a position to undertake operations . . . in the spring" and established a committee (composed of Foreign Office, Defence, and Treasury) to consider the financial implications of these Greek military operations and to plan "what proposals should be put to the United States Government with regard to long-term financial, economic and military help for Greece."[142] The Foreign Office cabled the British ambassador in Athens: "No decision was taken as to what should happen after the 31st March; this must await the result of discussions with the Americans."[143]

But Dalton had an important impact on London's approach to Washington. Having failed to win his point on the cabinet level, he continued to campaign among his colleagues for "cutting off the Greeks."[144] When the Foreign Office drew up an appeal to the Americans for funding, Dalton redrafted it in a manner which implied a definite aid cutoff. On February 15, 1947, Bevin informed Dalton of his reluctance "to state categorically . . . that we should under no circumstances be prepared to make any further contribution . . . as is proposed in your redraft of my telegram to Washington." Instead, he wanted "to leave the final decision on this point to the

Cabinet after we know what contribution the Americans are prepared to make."[145] On February 18, the two British leaders held a final meeting in an effort to resolve their differences. According to Bevin's notes, Dalton agreed to raise no objection "to going to the Cabinet after the discussion with America" if this proved necessary. In turn, Bevin accepted "a strong telegram to the United States . . . for the sole purpose of bringing matters to a head."[146] Thus, although in reality British officials had made no decision to pull out of Greece, they found it expedient to imply that they had. Hinting at this rather deceptive approach, Prime Minister Clement Attlee later bragged: "We made the Americans face up to the facts in the eastern Mediterranean."[147]

In actuality, American policymakers were hardly the innocents abroad that the British imagined them. When dealing with Greece, they accepted many of the same erroneous "facts," drew similar conclusions, and exhibited a definite eagerness to assume the "burdens of power." Although Tsaldaris fretted about the meaning of the cool response to his repeated entreaties for U.S. aid,[148] the State Department was, in fact, temporarily hamstrung by Export-Import Bank restrictions on further loans to Greece. On the other hand, State expected the U.S. economic mission to Greece, headed by former Office of Price Administration director Paul Porter, to develop a flourishing U.S. economic assistance program in early 1947.[149] Nor were American officials reluctant to enter the military realm. "Ambassador MacVeagh considers it extremely important that the army receive adequate supplies by spring . . . to control the leftist uprisings," Byrnes reported to Truman on December 20, 1946. The British should continue "primary responsibility for supply," Byrnes contended, but the U.S. government was prepared, in turn, to provide the appropriate weaponry to the British.[150] If anything, American officials in the field were inclined to believe the British overly complacent about the future of Greece. On February 11, 1947, MacVeagh and Mark Ethridge, the U.S. representative on the U.N. investigating commission, reported that "economic deterioration here must soon cause revolution on a nationwide scale." Six days later, Ethridge cabled that the Russians regarded Greece as a "ripe plum ready to fall into their hands." On February 19, Porter informed the State Department that this was "the real thing and we cannot hope for economic or political stability in [the] absence of [an] all out effort on our part."[151] Alarmed by these reports, Henderson drew up a dramatic memorandum which Acheson took to Secretary of State Marshall on February 21. "Unless urgent and immediate support is given to Greece," he stated, it appeared "probable" that the Greek government would "be overthrown," a leftist regime would assume power, and the United States would face the "loss of the whole Near and Middle East." Marshall immediately instructed Acheson "to prepare the necessary steps for sending economic and military aid."[152]

Later that same day—Friday, February 21—the British delivered to the State Department two lengthy documents requesting U.S. aid. As Marshall had already left town for the weekend, Henderson received them and brought them immediately to Acheson. "His Majesty's Government, in view of their own situation, find it impossible to grant further financial assistance" after March 31, read the key section, and "trust that the United States may find it possible to afford financial assistance to Greece on a scale sufficient to meet her minimum needs, both civil and military." Acheson immediately instructed Henderson and his counterpart in the European division, John Hickerson, to confer that evening with their staffs in preparation for rapid action on the British request. Still later that evening, Acheson recalled, he talked by telephone with Marshall and Truman, outlining developments and asking "for further orders. They had none."[153] Acheson and his subordinates considered but rejected the notion that the British were "not entirely sincere" and that "the notes had been presented with the idea of pushing the United States Government out in front" to assume Britain's economic, political, and military burdens in the region. Marshall told Forrestal a few days later that the British notes were "tantamount to British abdication from the Middle East with obvious implications as to their successor."[154]

Presented with this long-awaited opportunity, U.S. policymakers moved with alacrity. All that weekend, State Department and military officials rushed about, drawing up memoranda stating what they long had assumed: without external assistance, Greece and Turkey would collapse, and "they and the rest of the Middle East will fall under Russian control." Joseph Jones, who left the most detailed and accurate record of these events, recalled that, underneath "the virtual unanimity of view," the relevant officials "were quite openly elated over the possibility that the United States might now take action . . . to prevent the Soviet Union from breaking through the Greece-Turkey-Iran barrier." On Sunday, February 23, according to Acheson, "Henderson asked me whether we were still working on . . . a decision or the execution of one." Acheson replied that "under the circumstances there could be only one decision. At that we drank a martini or two." Another participant in the hectic planning of that weekend recalled that, despite the importance of the question, "the answer was never really in doubt."[155] On the morning of February 24, Marshall stopped by the State Department offices, read the British notes and Acheson's memoranda, talked briefly with the British ambassador, and proceeded to a meeting with the President on the matter. Advised of the solid support for their position at all levels, Acheson and Henderson worked later that day preparing recommendations for congressional action. On the morning of February 26, the Secretaries of State, War, and the Navy swiftly approved the recommendations, which were immediately endorsed, in principle, by the President.[156] A White House aide recalled that Truman "accepted without question" the assessments of "our own State Department and military departments."[157] And with Truman's support, the policy was set.

Yet below the exhilarating unanimity lurked a variety of dangers. Even in these first days of planning, Acheson was concerned that pressure might build up for referring the issue to the United Nations, which was then conducting its investigation of Greece's frontier disputes. For this reason, he kept the British aid request secret from the State Department's Office of Special Political Affairs, which handled U.N. matters.[158] In Athens, Paul Porter drafted a cable directly to the President, imploring him to demand an armistice in Greece as a precondition for American economic aid. "You are aware of [the] complete reactionary nature of [the] present Government," he told Truman. "But one must work with them as I have to understand how incredibly weak, stupid, and venal they really are. Their principal asset is [the] wide fear in Greece of Communist excesses," he noted; yet this was offset by "their own policies of violence and exploitation." Only through the search for a "peaceful solution" could the United States "offer [the] people of Greece something more than bloodshed and tyranny." Greatly distressed by Porter's outlook, MacVeagh and Ethridge sought to "convince him . . . that the problem must be seen on a wider scale, that in our own interests we must stop Russia." According to the ambassador, he told the "naif" head of the economic mission that "omelets are not made without breaking eggs." But Porter remained "soft-hearted," a "'new deal' liberal," although "it is not his fault." MacVeagh urged the State Department to keep Porter quiet in the future, perhaps by offering him a regular government job.[159] Even more frightening was the question, if relative insiders like Porter could not work up much enthusiasm for rescuing the Greek right, what about the American people? Could they be mobilized to accept the State Department's new venture? Within the Truman administration, this question—and not that of intervention—was the salient one.

3.

THE TRUMAN DOCTRINE
February–June 1947

Congress and the people of this country are not sufficiently aware of the character and dimensions of the crisis that impends, and of the measures that must be taken. . . .

The State Department knows. Congress and the people do not know.

Joseph M. Jones, February 26, 1947[1]

Having swiftly reached agreement on the desirability of American intervention in Greece, the administration now faced a more complex problem: mobilizing public support. As Joseph Jones observed: "The President had been concerned from the beginning not so much about the decision he had to make regarding Greece and Turkey as about the extent to which Congress and the American people could be convinced that a program of aid was necessary."[2] Truman and the State Department had good reason for concern. Thanks to a GOP sweep in the 1946 elections, conservative Republicans dominated Congress and had embarked on a campaign to slash the federal budget; many, moreover, were veteran isolationists. Nor were the Democrats entirely reliable. Despite the administration's repeated confrontations with the Soviet Union, many liberal Democrats clung stubbornly to the wartime notion of Big Three cooperation under the umbrella of the United Nations. The public seemed relatively indifferent to foreign affairs, when not positively hostile to the administration's early Cold War ventures.[3] "The United States must take world leadership and quickly," Clayton wrote on March 5, 1947. "But the United States will not take world leadership effectively unless the people of the United States are shocked into doing so." The State Department's program for Greece, contended the head of the European division, would have to "be presented to Congress in such a fashion as to electrify the American people."[4]

Given the administration's "precarious" relationship with Congress, Truman recalled, "it seemed desirable . . . to advise the congressional leadership as soon as possible" about the situation. Consequently, on the morning of February 27, 1947, Senators Styles Bridges, Arthur Vandenberg, Alben Barkley, and Tom Connally and Congressmen Joseph Martin, Charles Eaton, Sol Bloom, and Sam Rayburn were ushered into the White House for the first administration pep talk. Truman told the legislators that he had "decided to extend aid to Greece and Turkey," while Marshall outlined the crisis in the region, the withdrawal of the British, and his hope that appropriate legislation would receive "bi-partisan support . . . without protracted controversy."[5] From the administration's viewpoint, the response was disconcerting: "How much is this going to cost?" "Isn't this pulling British chestnuts out of the fire?" Acheson was aghast at the legislators' naiveté: "These Congressmen had no conception of what challenged them; it was my task to bring it home," with "no time . . . left for measured appraisal." The situation in the eastern Mediterranean had come to a point, Acheson explained, "where a highly possible Soviet breakthrough might open three continents to Soviet penetration. Like apples in a barrel infected by one rotten one, the corruption of Greece would affect Iran and all to the East." The United States had "arrived at a position which has not been paralleled since ancient history. . . . Not since Athens and Sparta, not since Rome and Carthage have we had such a polarization of power." This was no question of "pulling British chestnuts out of the fire. . . . It is a question of whether two-thirds of the area of the world . . . is to be controlled by Communists."[6]

Now here was a menace that conservative legislators could appreciate! According to Jones's notes, "most of the Congressional leaders were greatly shaken and impressed with this analysis and promised to support whatever measures should be necessary."[7] And, in fairness to Acheson, Marshall, and Truman, Acheson's statement, while hyperbolic, did reflect their underlying fears of global Communist advances. The novelty of the moment lay in the fact that, while such analyses underlay the State Department's early Cold War planning, the administration had not yet talked in such terms to Congress and the public. Realizing the obstacles the administration would encounter in winning passage of a Greek aid bill, as well as their own difficulties in justifying their support of it, the legislators insisted that the "program be presented to the public in terms almost as frank" as those used to explain it to them. Vandenberg, the Republican chairman of the Senate Foreign Relations Committee, urged the President "to make a personal appearance before Congress and scare hell out of the country."[8] Although another meeting with congressional leaders, on March 10, proved less successful in rallying support, anti-Communism was clearly the strongest formula the administration possessed for mobilizing conservatives. Certainly it mobilized Vandenberg. "My private opinion," he told Congressman John Bennett, "is that we are rapidly approaching a point where we must honestly pose this question to ourselves: can the United States survive in a Communist-dominated world?"[9]

Cautioned by their discussion with congressional leaders, administration officials immediately began the public relations program that they recognized as crucial. That evening, Acheson briefed twenty reporters covering the State Department in an off-the-record session. The following morning, he met with Henderson, Hickerson, and other key State Department officials to organize a public information campaign. It was agreed that this program should be headed by Francis Russell, director of the State Department's Office of Public Affairs, and augmented by the SWNCC Subcommittee on Foreign Policy Information.[10] But the content of the public relations campaign remained uncertain. Forrestal argued that "the world could only be brought back to order by the restoration of commerce, trade and business, and that would have to be done by businessmen." The "central problem" facing the United States, he told Clark Clifford, was: "Which of the two systems currently offered the world is to survive?" On the other hand, a capitalism versus communism approach held little appeal for liberals. From Greece, Porter and Ethridge, joined by MacVeagh, warned that the "greatest care should be taken to avoid giving [the] impression that [the] US aim at . . . maintaining in power an essentially reactionary govt. . . . Perhaps [the] aim might be stated [as] to insure [an] opportunity for [a] broader democratic govt and greater implementation of political, social and economic responsibility." Accordingly, the information program should stress that American policies would "be directed towards liberal changes here."[11]

Virtually everyone, however, agreed that to avoid charges of great power intervention it was necessary to skip lightly over the British role in precipitating the crisis and to display a request for aid from the Greek government.[12] Thus, on February 28, the Greek chargé d'affaires, Paul Economou-Gouras, was brought into the State Department and received by Henderson, who smiled, the Greek diplomat recalled, as if from a glowing inner satisfaction. Henderson outlined for Economou-Gouras the U.S. plans for economic and military assistance and presented him with a copy of a request for aid which he wanted signed and delivered by the Greek government. Drafted by the State Department,[13] the aid request had a humanitarian tone, stressing the wartime devastation of Greece and the urgent need for American assistance. Marshall also dispatched a copy of the aid request to MacVeagh, with instructions to have the Greek government submit it to the State Department "without delay." The Greek government should "withhold publicity . . . and allow us to reveal it first," the department added; "this would dramatize [the] matter and enlist popular and Congressional support." By March 3, the Athens government had accepted the American draft and returned it to Washington in the form of a Greek appeal for U.S. aid. The following day, Marshall announced to the press that the Truman administration was considering assistance to Greece. Avoiding any mention of the British notes of February 21, he cited the Greek aid appeal, whose text was released later that day.[14]

For their part, the British saw no reason to interfere with the State Department's careful cultivation of U.S. public opinion. On February 28, when Acheson remonstrated with the British ambassador about the difficulties attendant upon the "short and arbitrary deadlines" provided by Britain's announcement of withdrawal from Greece, the British agreed, Acheson recalled, "to keep the troops on for a while longer and to advance a little more cash for the Greek army provided our aid was moving smartly along."[15] The British also played an important part in facilitating the Greek government's acceptance of the American-drafted aid request. Noting that the State Department draft provided for U.S. advisers with executive powers, Tsaldaris had asked his British patrons what they thought of this "fateful" decision. Sir Clifford Norton, the British ambassador, responded that the "position of Greece" was "desperate," and Britain "could not possibly cope"; he urged Tsaldaris to "make no difficulties." When Tsaldaris came back with a suggestion of "accepting conditions for a period of years," Norton replied that "Greece would be ill-advised to quibble." Indeed, from the British standpoint, it would be foolish to jeopardize American initiatives. "All things considered," Lord Inverchapel cabled the Foreign Office, "we can be gratified with the manner in which [the Truman] administration has set about assuming the task with which they have been confronted . . . and have girded themselves to tackle Congress."[16]

The administration's public relations campaign accelerated after March 7, when Truman brought the Greek-Turkish issue to the attention of his cabinet. At the meeting, the President announced his decision to provide U.S. military and economic aid to the two nations, while Acheson (according to Secretary of War Patterson) "made a general presentation of the case, showing the movements of Soviet aggression in the Middle East." Everyone expressed approval of the President's decision, but a number of cabinet members noted their misgivings about the character of the Greek government and, in particular, about public willingness to support such a venture. "The general consensus," recalled Forrestal, "was that we should support Greece to the extent that we can persuade Congress and the country of the necessity." Seizing the opportunity, Forrestal declared that the situation represented "a fundamental struggle between our kind of society and the Russians." To win that struggle, the United States "would have to turn to business," encouraging it through "the full-out support of Government." Taken by the idea, the President, Acheson noted, appointed a cabinet committee composed of Forrestal, Patterson, Treasury Secretary John Snyder, Commerce Secretary Averell Harriman, Agriculture Secretary Clinton Anderson, Labor Secretary Lewis Schwellenbach, and himself to "call together . . . some financial, business, and labor people, both to get their energetic support . . . and to provide recruits for missions . . . to Greece."[17]

Meeting over the next few days, the cabinet committee, chaired by Snyder, formulated ambitious plans for winning public approval. It recommended that the President, to emphasize the gravity of the situation, deliver a message in person before a joint session of Congress. Although Acheson met secretly with a group of top labor leaders to gather their support, the committee concentrated upon reaching "influential business leaders." By March 13, Acheson was able to report to Marshall: "We have spoken to meetings of bankers and businessmen and will [soon] address a meeting of publishers."[18] The last venture probably was the outcome of Forrestal's efforts, for the preceding day he had submitted a list of nine key publishers for lobbying purposes. He informed *New York Times* columnist James Reston: "I told Dean and Snyder that . . . we should . . . get the publishers like Arthur Sulzberger and Ep Hoyt and Paul Smith and Luce" and "make them aware that this . . . will need sustained educational effort." Then it would be necessary to organize "the radio people" on a nationwide basis. In discussions of the Greek aid program with his network of business and newspaper associates, Forrestal was frank enough. He told the publisher of the San Francisco *Chronicle* that "about 73%" of U.S. imports were raw material "necessities"; currently, the United States required "about three times the volume of basic materials that we chewed up in 1938 and 1939," and the country was "partway" to becoming a "have-not" nation. "We've had a lot of high-level, penthouse economic free trade," he told Reston, "but the guts of it is, can a little guy buy silk in Japan and sell it in New York and make a dollar?"[19]

As Forrestal's remarks imply, in the context of the Greek crisis the administration and business were natural allies. The President hinted at this in an address on March 6 at Baylor University. Peace and freedom, he argued, were "bound up completely with a third objective—reestablishment of world trade." If the dangerous trend toward state-directed economies "is not reversed . . . the Government of the United States will be under pressure, sooner or later, to . . . fight for markets and raw materials."[20] Privately, American policymakers were even more candid. Discussing "this line on Greece and Turkey" with one of his big business acquaintances, Forrestal turned immediately to the question of oil. Estimated reserves in the Middle East "are now up to 27 billion" barrels, he said. "Our total oil in the ground is 21 ½ billion. The economy of Europe is going to be oil. . . . What we are talking about is raw materials and we haven't got them." His businessman friend interjected: "That definitely is something to go to war about." If intervention in Greece were a matter of political or social organization, "the hell with it. But if it is a question of the survival of our economy through procuring materials in those countries, then that to me is the answer." Forrestal responded: "That is the only thing that makes any impression on me at all. That [other] stuff is over my head."[21] In Greece, MacVeagh confided to the South African chargé that the American program was designed to arrest "the spread of Soviet imperialism" and thereby assure "the protection of American interests in the Near East, for example oil."[22]

The appeal to the nation, of course, would require something more spiritually uplifting. At the February 27 meeting with congressional leaders, it appeared that the appropriate inspiration would be supplied by an American-led crusade against Soviet Communism. But the following morning, when Acheson met with his staff to map out the public relations strategy, the Under Secretary unexpectedly vetoed this line of argument and suggested another. As Jones recalled:

Acheson advanced . . . one caution. Although we should be vigorous and forthright, we must not be belligerent or provocative. Our policy was not directed against any country or even any movement, but was a positive policy directed toward helping free nations strengthen their democracy and their independence and thereby protecting the liberties of the individual citizen.[23]

Later that day, when Russell met with the SWNCC Subcommittee on Foreign Policy Information, this hardened into the new orthodoxy. The records of the meeting indicate that "Russell asked if [they] should emphasize the world Communistic revolution picture." "Not in official pronouncements," came the reply. Another participant added that they would "have to draw [the] line on what [the] administration can say [and] what supporters can say." Yet another noted that "there are ways of making [the] situation perfectly clear without specifically mentioning Russia." Then perhaps the administration "should couch it in terms of [a] new policy of this government to go to the assistance of free governments everywhere," Russell suggested. Everyone agreed that it would be useful to "relate military aid to [the] principle of supporting Democracy." As Major General A. V. Arnold put it, the "only thing that can sell [the] public" would be to emphasize the threat to democracy.[24]

The decision to focus upon the defense of democracy was curious in the context of the proposed aid program. Neither the Greek nor the Turkish regime appeared to be a paragon of representative government. Jones recalled: "That the Greek government was corrupt, reactionary, inefficient, and indulged in extremist practices was well known and incontestable; that Turkey . . . had not achieved full democratic self-government was also patent." At the SWNCC subcommittee meeting, participants agreed that the Athens government was a rotten one, although "not basically fascist."[25] Furthermore, postwar U.S. policymakers had hitherto shown no particular interest in defending democracy in Greece or elsewhere. Indeed, even after the decision to emphasize democracy in public relations pronouncements, State Department officials meeting to draft the Greek-Turkish aid legislation rejected defense of "a democratic form of government" as the basis for the program; instead, they approved a draft which came much closer to their actual concerns: "The President is authorized to furnish assistance to any country for the purpose of promoting its stability and independence whenever he finds such assistance is in the interest of the national security." Eventually, however, the public relations men prevailed, and the Truman Doctrine, as it was soon labeled, focused upon "alternative ways of life." As Louis Halle, another State Department official, recalled: "It was still not possible to tell the American people what the real issue was."[26]

Why not? Why did Acheson signal a retreat to warmed-over World War I platitudes? As indicated at the February 27 meeting with congressional leaders, the administration needed a stirring set of principles in which it could couch both the Greek-Turkish aid program and its broader commitment to overseas intervention. Indeed, Vandenberg and the others had made this the price of their support. Truman understood the need very well and objected to early drafts that "made the whole thing sound like an investment prospectus." Even afterward, the President insisted on heightening the rhetoric. "I wanted no hedging in this speech," he insisted.[27] Acheson, too, showed little patience with administration thinking that lacked popular appeal. On the afternoon of March 10, Clifford showed the Under Secretary a draft of the President's speech that he and another White House aide, George Elsey, had prepared; it stressed Greece's strategic importance in defense of the Middle East, called attention to the "great natural resources" of the area, and warned that "there has been a worldwide trend away from the system of free enterprise." If "we permit free enterprise to disappear in the other nations of the world, the very existence of our own economy and our own democracy will be gravely threatened," it read. Important as this line of thinking was within the administration, Acheson considered it inappropriate in the President's speech, and successfully secured its deletion.[28]

On the other hand, there were also good reasons for restraining the anti-Soviet rhetoric. Although Marshall had told the SWNCC subcommittee to disregard his departure for the Council of Foreign Ministers meeting in Moscow as it planned the public relations program,[29] the conference probably played some role in administration thinking. Symptomatically, Marshall and Charles Bohlen, receiving the text of the message en route, objected to "the extent to which the anti-Communist element of this speech was stressed."[30] Not only was an overtly anti-Soviet speech likely to embarrass the Secretary of State in Moscow, but it provided a possible incitement to war. George Kennan, chairman of the State Department's policy planning staff, worried that the Russians might well view the President's address as a *casus belli*. Jones, who drafted the speech, modified sections to reduce that possibility and to avoid alarming Americans about it. Acheson, particularly, feared that announcing too dramatic a departure from past American practice would cause the administration difficulties with Congress. Although desirous of expanding the administration's options for overseas intervention, both Kennan and (to a lesser extent) Acheson worried that the President's address might commit the United States to conflicts which could not be won (e.g., the Chinese civil war). According to Jones: "The administration recognized that taking a stand against Soviet expansion might touch off a jingoistic crusade. At least partly for that reason the President's message avoided mention of the Soviet Union and pitched United States policy on a pro-freedom rather than an anti-Communist plane."[31]

On March 12, 1947, after two weeks of careful press buildup, President Truman delivered his much-touted message to Congress. Noting that the United States had "received from the Greek Government an urgent appeal for financial and economic assistance," Truman went on to describe the economic disintegration in Greece as well as "the terrorist activities of several thousand armed men, led by Communists." As indicated by this reference, however brief, to the menace of Red revolution, the speech did provide occasional glimpses of administration thinking. "It is necessary only to glance at a map," Truman declared, to see that if Greece should fall to the rebels, "confusion and disorder might well spread throughout the entire Middle East." Nevertheless, as Acheson and the public relations men had agreed, the focus of the speech was upon a worldwide struggle between "alternative ways of life": the "free" and the totalitarian. After some heady rhetoric, the President concluded that "it must be the policy of the United States to support free peoples who are resisting attempted subjugation by armed minorities or by outside pressures." Greece and Turkey, the President maintained, were entitled to such support, and should receive an immediate appropriation totaling $400 million for economic and military assistance. American help would be "primarily through economic and financial aid," superintended by "experienced American administrators." The latter, explained the President, had been "asked for" by the Greek government.[32]

Despite the adminstration's attention to public opinion, the response to the President's address was less than enthusiastic. In his *Memoirs*, Truman recalled that opposition to his doctrine came primarily from "Communists and their fellow travelers," but this is belied by the record. As the President completed his remarks, applause in the House chamber was notably restrained,[33] and soon after, legislators began voicing their discontent. Senator Robert Taft of Ohio objected to "the policy of dividing the world into zones of political influence, Communist and anti-Communist"; furthermore, he did "not want war with Russia." Senator Harry Byrd of Virginia expressed concern about bypassing the United Nations and about the expenditures necessary to implement the Truman Doctrine. Senators Claude Pepper of Florida, Allan Ellender of Louisiana, and Glen Taylor of Idaho criticized the Truman Doctrine as warlike and provocative.[34] Even figures close to the foreign policy establishment showed a distinct coolness, among them Bernard Baruch, James Byrnes, and John Foster Dulles.[35] Although an overwhelming majority of the nation's press supported aid to Greece,[36] influential commentators raised embarrassing questions about it. Walter Lippmann wondered if maintenance of the status quo in Greece was in fact the most effective way to combat Soviet expansion. The United States, he warned, was "not rich enough to subsidize reaction all over the world or strong enough to maintain it in power."[37] That March, a Gallup poll found approval of Truman's Greek aid program at only 56 percent, while a Roper poll placed it at 51.9 percent. These and other opinion surveys also reported that a majority of Americans were critical of circumventing the United Nations and of sending U.S. military assistance to Greece.[38]

In general, liberal magazines and organizations were the most eloquent and consistent critics of the Truman Doctrine. Discounting the President' explanations of his program, the *Nation* claimed that the U.S. government was intent on "propping up a rotten, reactionary oligarchy in Greece" as "part of a broad plan to contain Russia." The editor, Freda Kirchwey, decried Truman's references to democracy as "unctuous" and his thinking as based on a series of "false assumptions": that the Greek rebels were Soviet puppets; that a popular revolution could be suppressed easily by an outside power; and that the United Nations was not an appropriate agency for economic reconstruction.[39] James G. Patton, president of the National Farmers Union, told Truman of his organization's "fear that the United States is setting out upon a career of unilateral, imperialistic action" that would destroy the United Nations. At congressional hearings, Charles Bolte of the American Veterans Committee strongly opposed U.S. military aid to Greece, contending that "we cannot stop the spread of Communist ideology by bolstering a corrupt and reactionary regime." Prominent black Americans pointed to the curious discrepancy between the President's eagerness to defend "democracy" in Greece and his reluctance to foster it in the American South.[40] Henry J. Cadbury, chairman of the American Friends Service Committee, noted that the

President had rejected any resort to the United Nations,[41] while the Progressive Citizens of America, the nation's largest liberal organization, attacked the Truman Doctrine for dividing the world into two armed camps.[42]

Particularly disturbing to the administration was the opposition the Truman Doctrine generated among prominent New Dealers. Henry Wallace, editor of the *New Republic* since his forced departure from the cabinet, used his magazine columns, radio addresses, and public speeches to assail the President's program. Once the United States took on the responsibility for funding the Greek and Turkish governments, he told an overflow crowd at Madison Square Garden, "every fascist dictator will know that he has credit in our bank." The real crisis was not one "of the Greek economy, but of the American spirit."[43] Fiorello LaGuardia, testifying against the aid program before the Senate Foreign Relations Committee, used his experience as director of UNRRA to paint a grim picture of corruption and repression in Greece. If the United States intervened, he warned, "we are going in there for a long time."[44] In her newspaper column, Eleanor Roosevelt wondered how the Greek government could be as representative as the President had claimed "and still require military bolstering from the outside." Although Acheson sent a special State Department officer to meet with her in an effort to bring her around, Mrs. Roosevelt remained unmoved. She told the President that she did not believe "that taking over Mr. Churchill's policies in the Near East, in the name of democracy, is the way to really create a barrier to communism or promote democracy."[45]

Overseas, too, opposition to the Truman Doctrine spread considerably beyond the ranks of the Communists. In Great Britain, where the President's message was viewed with great satisfaction by the Foreign Office and by Churchill, who proclaimed that Truman had adopted the "exact policy" he had once pursued,[46] the left wing of the British Labour Party vehemently denounced it as the proclamation of an American empire, carved out with particular attention to the oil-rich Middle East.[47] Indeed, European political leaders generally viewed the President's March 12 address as an announcement of the extension of American frontiers worldwide, and differed principally about the desirability of such a policy. Groups leaning toward the developing American Cold War camp— the center-right in much of Western and Eastern Europe— welcomed the Truman Doctrine.[48] But, in addition to the Communists, the French and Italian Socialists tended to be critical of the American program, as were the governing parties in Sweden, Denmark, Norway, and Switzerland. Surveying the European reaction, one Foreign Office official reported: "The Swedish Social Democrat press . . . deplores this 'challenge to Moscow' on the grounds that it lessens the chance of a peace settlement between the Great Powers." Furthermore, "the French Communists and Socialists deplore it in varying degree; many French commentators regret that France must now lose the mediating role which she thought to play at Moscow. . . . The [Italian] Left in general dislike it" and "fear that Italy will emerge as a colony or protectorate of the United States."[49]

In Greece, where the situation remained alarming from almost any perspective, plans for U.S. intervention received a somewhat more sympathetic response. MacVeagh reported "jubilation" on the right. Marching in the streets, right-wing groups sang joyously of using the atom bomb to "make dust" of the Communists. The center, too, as MacVeagh noted, showed its "satisfaction" at the proposed aid program, although the Liberal press "expressed some reserve re its consequences and implications." Apparently, the Liberals believed that the Americans would help them to pry the control of the state out of right-wing hands. Sophoulis proclaimed his hope that by "condemning the extremes of the Right and Left and recommending a policy of toleration," the United States would contribute to "the internal pacification of Greece without further bloodshed."[50] Ironically, even EAM, while criticizing "arbitrary American intervention," was not totally hostile to the American initiative. An official delegation from the left-wing coalition told MacVeagh that EAM favored American economic aid but opposed the presence of foreign troops or the imposition of foreign control on Greece; instead, it desired the "neutralization" of the nation under United Nations auspices. MacVeagh told Marshall that this idea might well appeal to "large sections of uninformed liberal opinion in Great Britain and the United States," but should, of course, be rejected as merely a component of "a Moscow directed strategy."[51]

The masterminds in Moscow, however, appeared to treat the Greek situation with relative detachment. Despite the heated debate which the Truman Doctrine inspired in the United States and Western Europe, the Russians barely seemed to notice it. After March 13, when *Izvestia* directed some temperate criticism at the President's congressional message, Soviet attacks quickly sputtered out. Ten days later, the British ambassador in Moscow reported to the Foreign Office that "apart from the subsequent *Pravda* rehash of [the] *Izvestia* leader, there has been no further Soviet editorial comment and it does not look as though Soviet authorities intend to make this the subject of a major propaganda campaign." In fact, "by Soviet standards, even the original *Izvestia* leader was mild." By April 1, Acheson, too, had become aware of the puzzling Soviet response. Asked during closed congressional hearings about the effects of the Truman Doctrine on Soviet-American relations, he replied:

There has been no outward effect of any sort so far as the official Russian policy is concerned. It has not been mentioned. Nor has it affected [the Moscow] negotiations in any way, so far as we can see. The inspired newspaper comment in Russia is regarded by all observers as being unusually cautious instead of the rather tremendous blast which they have usually given out.[52]

By contrast, in a speech to the Yugoslav parliament on March 31, Tito denounced "American imperialism" as "openly threatening with war countries that will not submit to its financial and imperialistic dictatorship." In characteristic fashion, he assailed the Greek government's "unlawful terror over the democratic masses in Greece and over the Macedonians in Aegean Macedonia."[53]

The comparative mildness of the Soviet response did nothing to reassure American policymakers. In open congressional hearings, Acheson vigorously denied that the aid measure meant "a joining of issue with the spread of Russian influence and communism in this part of the world" and clung to the administration line about defending "free institutions"; but in hearings held in executive session, American officials were considerably more candid. Testifying before the House Committee on Foreign Affairs, MacVeagh cited Stalin's *Foundations of Leninism* (1924) as the basis of "what is going on in Greece." "It is all there," he stated; "their actions follow out the program." Asked by Chairman Eaton if the whole situation did not represent "a movement on the part of Russia to take over Greece," MacVeagh responded: "Yes, sir. . . . I do not think there is any other statement that fits the facts." A few days later, he told the Senate Foreign Relations Committee that "Greece and Turkey are a strategic line." If the Russians "break that down, the whole Near East falls." The U.S. ambassador to Turkey, Edwin Wilson, also emphasized the strategic factors which had led to the American decision to intervene, adding: "We would do it regardless of what regime was in Turkey or in Greece." Contravening his public statements, Acheson took a similar position. Several supporters of the Greek-Turkish aid bill, including Senator Vandenberg, suggested that its passage might provide the occasion to negotiate a settlement with the Russians on Greece and other issues, but Acheson demurred: "I think it is a mistake to believe that you can, at any time, sit down with the Russians and solve questions." Was there no possibility of a meeting with the Russians to iron things out? "You cannot sit down with them," Acheson insisted.[54]

In closed-door sessions, the administration also revealed that it had discovered the deception of American officials by the Foreign Office over the alleged British decision to withdraw from Greece. On April 1, in closed hearings of the Senate Foreign Relations Committee, Senator Walter F. George grilled Acheson in a fashion that indicated suspicion of the curious circumstances underlying the sudden transfer of power. After ineffectual efforts by Acheson to parry George's questions, the legislator exploded: "You say they are getting out, Mr. Secretary. You have only their note for that." At this point, when Acheson presumably spoke, discussion suddenly went "off the record." But Senator Carl Hatch returned to the Acheson-George colloquy later that day, and in the process summarized some deleted information:

Senator George went into one matter that has puzzled, I think, all of us greatly, and that is the suddenness with which this crisis arose. I gathered from your remarks this morning that the division between the British Foreign Office and the Treasury might have precipitated a situation where the British themselves did not have a definite policy.

This discussion, too, immediately moved "off the record." It did little to mollify Senator George, who continued to criticize the administration for its failure to challenge British conduct in this regard.[55] Soon afterward, Acheson complained to the British ambassador of the enormous "strain he has been put to" by congressional questioning. And in later months, Marshall emphasized the "acute embarrassment caused this Government" by British handling of the situation.[56]

During congressional hearings, the administration encountered few challenges to its depiction of events in Greece, although its performance on this score was not particularly enlightening. MacVeagh and the legislators confused Greek political leaders, mistook cabinet offices, and (apparently in line with their fears) created a Russian name, "Markov," for the Greek guerrilla leader. During World War II, MacVeagh testified, Greece was "destroyed morally, and the country today . . . is full of people who have not got any sense of responsibility. . . . They care only about themselves"; indeed, murder and theft were now "universal. . . . You cannot leave a car for a minute on the street. You just turn around and it is gone. They are expert thieves." MacVeagh trivialized the accomplishments of "the so-called resistance movement," assailed the Varkiza agreement as "a victory for the Communists" (since "the nigger in the woodpile was still there"), misrepresented left-wing strength at 9.3 percent of the electorate, claimed that only Communist-controlled groups abstained during the 1946 elections, and described Markos, inaccurately, as a man with "a long record of being in jail for various crimes he has committed." Many members of the "bandit groups," said MacVeagh, "are just bandits, that is all, just out to loot, but they are gradually becoming unified . . . into a subversive army." Reminded that "the so-called liberals in the United States" had been sharply critical of the Greek government, MacVeagh retorted that "the Greek Government does reactionary and Fascist things from time to time," but "wants to follow our policies as closely as it possibly can." Thus, it was "not a Fascist government. To say so is to follow the Communists' line."[57]

Given their assumption that the difficulty in Greece flowed from a small group of Moscow agents and criminal elements, American officials were naturally optimistic about their ability to overcome it. Queried at committee hearings about the prospects for defeating the Greek left, MacVeagh responded: "They are already on the run, Senator, with just this statement by the President." If "you break down their organization and you chase out or capture the fellows who are organizing them," you could successfully eradicate this "subversive political movement." Despite the President's public assurances that most U.S. aid would be civilian, Clayton told the House Committee on Foreign Affairs that "approximately half" of U.S. funding would go toward arming the Greek military.[58] Colonel Allen Miller, the assistant military attaché at the U.S. embassy in Athens, testified that he was "quite sure that the Greek Army could go in there and clean them up in plus or minus 6 months from the time the supplies arrive." "The most patriotic officials in Greece," he told the committee, "are the high-ranking army and navy officers. The irresponsible people are the politicians." In what would prove to be a serious underestimate, Secretary of War Patterson repeatedly assured American legislators that U.S. military personnel dispatched to Greece would number between 10 and 40. According to Acheson, they would be "chiefly concerned with seeing that the military equipment reaches its proper destination and that estimates and requests are properly checked and in good order." Who could resist this surge of Yankee commitment, efficiency, and power? The Russians, claimed MacVeagh, "are putting up a big bluff. . . . If we say, 'Stop now', they will stop. There is no question in my mind of that, and they have already shown signs that they are scared to death."[59]

Despite the best efforts of the administration, key legislators were irritated by the Truman Doctrine. In closed hearings of the Senate Foreign Relations Committee, members complained about the administration's promotion of the Greek-Turkish aid measure as a defense of freedom, which they considered both dishonest and ridiculous. "The American people are not as dumb as we sometimes assume they are," Senator Alexander Wiley bluntly told Acheson; "I think you ought to call a spade a spade." Even Vandenberg, the pro-administration committee chairman, expressed regret over the decision to emphasize "ideological" factors in the President's March 12 address, rather than explain the nation's "intelligent self-interest" in the program. About the only concurrence with the administration's public relations line came in the form of an amendment to the bill, offered by Senator Henry Cabot Lodge, Jr., declaring that the U.S. intent was not to support totalitarianism. Lodge claimed that this would enable the American government to "take the ideological offensive." Senator Alben Barkley responded that many people already considered the Greek government totalitarian, and that, in his view, the United States should "accept whatever government is there." Although Lodge protested that "this fascist government through which we have to work is incidental," other committee members thought its presence would make any public commitment to freedom at least potentially embarrassing. "If you do not help either the totalitarians of the communistic breed or the totalitarians of the other, you are not going to help anybody in Greece," Connally remarked. Vandenberg insisted that "we are going to use whatever instrumentalities are available to our hands before we get through." Consequently, the committee killed the Lodge amendment.[60]

Furthermore, there was considerable objection to the open-ended commitment implied by the doctrine, particularly among Republicans. In 1947, Congress retained a considerable measure of 1930s-style isolationism. Senators Kenneth Wherry, Wayland Brooks, William Langer, and George Malone argued that the Truman Doctrine would lead to war or America's economic collapse.[61] Dissenting from the favorable report on the bill by the House Committee on Foreign Affairs, Congressman Lawrence Smith of Wisconsin contended that "it is the certain course of imperialism." He warned that the measure would eventually result in international conflict, bankruptcy, and Communism at home. Even the comments of supporters of the bill reflected the concerns of traditional GOP conservatives. "We are the greatest spenders and the most extravagant people in the world, and we can spend ourselves into a revolution," Senator Wiley observed during Senate committee hearings. "After this thing is done we will have a bill of goods sold us by practically every country in Europe where Communism is coming in: 'Boys, you had better come in and look after us.'" Consequently, in their congressional testimony, administration witnesses sought to downplay the notion that the Greek-Turkish aid bill established "a pattern for all future requests for American assistance."[62]

The administration's need to restrict the meaning of the Truman Doctrine became more urgent after the doctrine emerged as a convenient weapon for the powerful China Lobby. On March 15, for example, *Business Week* assured its readers that the administration was preparing to support a broad array of "governments now threatened by Communist minorities," and that China was "likely to fall into this group" in the near future. In Congress, legislators such as Congressman Walter Judd drew upon the promises of the Truman Doctrine to press the administration for a commitment to bail out Chiang Kai-shek's embattled Kuomintang government. Anxiously retreating, Acheson attempted to narrow the implications of the President's address. "You must approach each situation as it occurs," he declared, "in light of the facts of that situation."[63] Secretly, the State Department's policy planning staff recommended removing the "damaging impression" that "the Truman Doctrine is a blank check to give economic and military aid to any area of the world where the Communists show signs of being successful." In the case of Greece and Turkey, the area was "critical," successful results would be "far-reaching," and the "overall cost was relatively small." By contrast, Jones noted, China did not meet "the test of practicability."[64]

Other congressional criticism, while less conservative, was no less incisive. Pointing to the fact that the Truman Doctrine pledged American intervention against revolts by armed minorities, Senator Edwin Johnson wondered if the United States should automatically be placed at odds with all revolutions. Senator Glen Taylor predicted that the passage of the Greek-Turkish aid bill would set "the pattern all over the world. The Royalists, the dictators, the Fascists, and just plain exploiters will cry out that they are threatened by communism, and move up to the trough." Senator Pepper joined Taylor in introducing a resolution to establish an international fund for Greece under U.N. auspices; military aid, however, would be forbidden. "While civil war is bad, while it is terrible," Pepper told the Senate Foreign Relations Committee, "yet we had one and survived it, and in the long run it was better that we were let alone." Perhaps the most damaging of the lot were the barbs of Walter George, long a member of the Senate's inner circle. He did not object to "a challenge to the expansionist movement of Russia," but did not see how "this is going to affect Russia." Speaking on April 2, he observed that Marshall had "got nowhere at all" at the Moscow conference. "No single step has been taken that indicates that the Russians have paid any attention to this." There was no "emergency in the Greco-Turkish situation," he concluded, "except such as Great Britain herself is voluntarily bringing about."[65]

The most telling criticism of the aid program—and the one

which the polls found reflected the sentiment of an overwhelming majority of Americans—was that it bypassed the
United Nations. With a storm of angry letters descending
upon Congress and the administration, some from influential
political figures,[66] supporters of the legislation sought means
of neutralizing this line of attack. The staff of the House
Committee on Foreign Affairs prepared a memorandum
stressing the differences between the Iranian crisis of 1946,
when the United States had asked the United Nations to play
a major role, and the Greek-Turkish crisis of 1947, when there
were no treaty violations or signs of Russian involvement to
justify U.N. action. Answering the repeated criticisms of
unilateral action by the United States, Acheson emphasized
U.N. impotence in the current circumstances, adding en-
couragingly (albeit untruthfully): "We are giving serious study
and consideration to ways in which the United Nations may
take hold of this problem after the emergency is past."[67] Recognizing the extent of public dissatisfaction on the point,
Vandenberg proposed an ingenious solution: an amendment
to the bill that promised U.S. termination of the program in
the event that the Security Council or General Assembly
found "that action taken or assistance furnished by the United
Nations makes the continuance of such assistance unneces-
sary or undesirable."[68]

Advised by pollsters and others that acceptance of Vandenberg's language would transform the "bare majority" enjoyed by the measure into comfortable support, the administration grudgingly endorsed the committee chairman's ritual
bow to the United Nations. Acheson recalled: "This, of
course, was window dressing and must have seemed either
silly or cynical or both in London, Paris, and Moscow. Nevertheless, it was a cheap price for Vandenberg's patronage."[69]
Vandenberg, it might be noted, had no intention of turning
the issue over to the United Nations but, like Acheson, considered a gesture to the world body a useful propaganda ploy.
By formally deferring to the United Nations, he explained
privately to his committee, he would "dramatize" its weakness;
at the same time, the move "would substantially satisfy a great

deal of our anxious public opinion." Senator Wiley, however, objected that demonstrating the impotence of the United Nations would contribute to its demise, while Senator George argued that inviting the United Nations to object to U.S. action was absurd; the United Nations should not be confronted with a fait accompli but given "a chance to say what they want to do." Unnerved by such criticism, which punctured the myth of his commitment to the world organization, Vandenberg retorted angrily that the United States was preserving "the peace of the world," and "if our obligations to the United Nations do not cover the peace of the world, I do not know what the hell they do cover." In the end, Vandenberg succeeded in keeping the committee in line, and his amendment, as Acheson noted, "won over the bulk of the doubters."[70]

Less noticed but significant was the support the President's program attracted within the American business community. According to a study by the Roper polling organization, the level of satisfaction with the Truman Doctrine was directly proportional to wealth.[71] Although the labor movement remained fairly indifferent to the Greek-Turkish aid legislation, Forrestal, Acheson, and other administration spokesmen made greater headway in the nation's boardrooms. "The loud talk was all of Greece and Turkey," *Time* reported, "but the whispers behind the talk were of the ocean of oil to the south"—what the Luce publication termed the "fabulous wealth of the Arabian Nights." *Fortune*, too, ran a long, optimistic story on plans for U.S. control of the region's resources, arguing that "the development of Middle Eastern oil is a matter of supreme importance." "The primary line of defense," it added, "depends on the maintenance of Greece and Turkey as going concerns." *Business Week* considered the U.S. government's new task to be nothing less than "keeping capitalism afloat in the Mediterranean—and in Europe"; U.S. corporate holdings in the Mideast were immense, and "it is already certain that business has an enormous stake in whatever role the United States is to play." W. E. Knox, president of the Westinghouse Electric International Company, informed Truman that "it has been truly gratifying to those of us whose main preoccupation is with international affairs to witness your political offensive for the establishment of a 'Truman Doctrine.'" And Thomas E. Dewey, leader of the Eastern corporate wing of the Republican Party, became a prominent and influential supporter of the Greek-Turkish aid program.[72]

Furthermore, the Eightieth Congress, elected in the Republican sweep of 1946, furnished the administration with a more sympathetic constituency than was originally anticipated. The left wing of the Democratic Party, generally critical of early Cold War moves, had been decimated in that election, much to the delight of top officials. Forrestal considered the liberal disaster of 1946 "a healthy thing" and cited with favor the observation of Mississippi Congressman John Rankin that the "Democrats were not defeated last November but were de-loused."[73] At the same time, many—although far from all—GOP isolationists eventually supported the Greek-Turkish aid legislation because of anti-Communism, then trumpeted by the mass media and congressional leaders (who had fewer worries on this score than the administration) as the underlying basis of White House policy.[74] Republicans "are going to support it," Congressman Carl Vinson assured Forrestal on the day after the President's address. "They don't like Russia. They don't like Communism." And though they disliked having "to do anything to stop it," they were "all put on the spot now and they all have [to] come clean." Eventually, most did, including Senator Taft and other original critics of the Greek-Turkish bill. House Majority Leader Joseph Martin recalled: "To us the Communist menace looked more alarming than had the Hitler menace. . . . Republicans were quick to sense that in militant, imperialistic Communism the United States faced a deadly enemy."[75] In line with this view, many conservatives worried that congressional failure to back a foreign policy initiative by the President would lead to international disaster.[76]

A sizable number of Americans who were not conservatives also proved ready to follow the President's lead. Though uneasy about particular aspects of the Truman Doctrine, many were convinced that the Russians were on the march and had to be stopped. A later congressional study found it noteworthy that "at no time" during House committee hearings on the Greek-Turkish aid bill "were any of the descriptions of Russian behavior or motivation subjected to rigorous questioning"; instead, there was broad "ideological agreement between the committee and the administration."[77] Even among liberal activists, anti-Communism was emerging as a major force. Americans for Democratic Action, the new anti-Communist liberal organization, endorsed the Truman Doctrine and lobbied for it, although not without dissent from a substantial minority.[78] In addition, during the postwar period, for reasons which have yet to be adequately explained, Congress and the public showed an unprecedented willingness to give the President room to maneuver in foreign affairs.[79]

Consequently, despite the criticism and delays encountered by the Greek-Turkish aid bill in Congress, supporters eventually passed the measure by the lopsided vote of 67 to 23 in the Senate and 287 to 107 in the House. With the exception of the earlier vote on the British loan, this represented the most substantial show of opposition to a major Truman administration foreign policy venture from 1945 to 1953. Nevertheless, it came almost entirely from the dwindling bands of liberal-left democrats and GOP isolationists. By contrast, the bill enjoyed hefty majorities within the congressional delegations of both major parties. In the Senate, it won approval by 32 to 7 among Democrats and 35 to 16 among Republicans. In the House, it passed by 160 to 13 among Democrats and 127 to 93 among Republicans.[80] For the administration, it was a hard-fought and important victory. Never again would opponents of the President's Greek policy have so good an opportunity to expose it to public scrutiny or to block its implementation. On May 22, 1947, Truman signed the bill into law in a public ceremony, observing tactfully that in extending assistance to Greece and Turkey, "the United States is helping to further aims and purposes identical with those of the United Nations."[81]

Although the President implied that the Greek-Turkish aid bill served the world community, in reality the reverse came closer to the truth: the U.S. government used the United Nations to justify its program. To be sure, the Soviet Union's veto power in the U.N. Security Council constituted what was thought to be a serious impediment to effective international action. Nevertheless, meaningful action by the United Nations was never seriously considered by American policymakers, who thought the world organization irrelevant. "Neither during the week of decision (February 21–28) nor during the drafting of the President's message," Jones recalled, "was any suggestion made that a recommendation to Congress . . . be delayed or circumscribed in any way on the grounds that it would by-pass the United Nations." Vandenberg and Connally observed that, during the White House meetings with congressional leaders, no one suggested referring the problem of Greece and Turkey to the world organization. It soon became obvious, though, that bypassing the United Nations flouted public opinion. Thus, "practically in the last hour" before delivery of the presidential message to Congress, George Elsey recalled, he "begged" the State Department to "get over to us a few sentences on the United Nations that . . . would help placate the critics."[82] Accordingly, two sentences on the subject found their way into the President's address.[83] Another "step in neutralizing the United Nations issue," Jones wrote, "was the summoning to Washington of [American delegate to the United Nations] Warren R. Austin . . . and the preparation of a statement on United States aid to Greece." On March 28 and April 10, 1947, in appearances before the U.N. Security Council, Austin claimed that the U.S. program was "consistent with the purposes and principles of the United Nations Charter"; to support this point, he called attention to the U.N. investigation of border difficulties between Greece and its northern neighbors.[84]

Austin's line of argument lost some of its force, however, when juxtaposed against the fact that the administration had introduced its Greek aid program into Congress before the United Nations had concluded its investigation or presented its findings. In fact, the U.N. commission report was not signed until the day after the President signed the Greek-Turkish aid legislation, and was not submitted to the U.N. Security Council until five weeks later. Moreover, the report was hardly an impartial assessment, for it was at least in part a reflection of State Department desires. On May 7, for example, Marshall warned Ethridge, the U.S. delegate on the U.N. commission, of the department's "anxiety" that the report might take "into account internal conditions in Greece" to a greater extent than the department wished. Ethridge responded plaintively that, thanks to the Greek government's "discriminatory and gangster-like methods," approximately 25,000 refugees from Greece had fled into Yugoslavia and Bulgaria, where they provided a basis for the guerrilla movement. He did not understand "why sanctity is given to a proposed recommendation formulated by the Department in mid-February before the Commission had uncovered any facts." Appropriate findings were important, however, and the State Department did not want to stumble over embarrassing complexities. On May 16, complaining to Ethridge that the U.N. commission's draft conclusions were not sufficiently "unequivocal," Marshall instructed him to make specific changes in content and phrasing. The exact measure of U.S. influence over the commission's findings is impossible to determine, but certainly it was substantial. "Friendly countries wait on [the] American Delegation for leadership," Ethridge assured Marshall; "we have initiated every major proposal which [the] Commission has so far adopted."[85]

Given the influence of the United States within the eleven-member commission, as well as the noticeable external aid received by the Greek guerrilla movement, the commission's report inevitably bolstered the American position. What caused some concern among policymakers in Athens and Washington was that it did so only in part. From the American standpoint, the most valuable section of the report was clearly the conclusion by the majority—Australia, Belgium, Brazil, China, Colombia, Great Britain, Syria, and the United States—that "Yugoslavia, and to a lesser extent, Albania and

Bulgaria, have supported the guerrilla warfare in Greece."
But the majority also contended—to the irritation of the Athens government and, presumably, of its American patrons as
well—that "the discrimination and persecution to which minorities and political opposition groups were subjected by the
Greek Government" had contributed to the flight of the refugees to the north and to formation of the guerrilla bands.
As might be expected, Russia and Poland refused to sign the
majority statement; instead, they submitted their own minority position, which focused upon the villainy of the Greek
government. More disturbing, however, was the fact that
France also refused to sign the majority statement; instead,
it abstained. Even the majority report was curiously inconclusive, for it indicated reservations by the Belgians and the
Colombians, called attention to "a large number of [frontier]
violations on each side," and found no proof of "any policy
of systematic provocation" by the contending nations. Finally,
nowhere was there so much as an allegation of a Russian role
in the conflict.[86] If the investigation could be said to have
bolstered the State Department's contention of interference
from the north, it nonetheless fell short of vindicating the
Truman Doctrine.

Thereafter, the administration drew on the United Nations
in a highly selective fashion. As guerrilla transit across
Greece's northern frontier provided the strongest point in the
American case, the State Department focused attention on
it through further U.N. boundary investigations and resolu-
tions.[87] On the other hand, the American government worked
to keep the United Nations away from any observation of its
own activities in Greece. On April 9, Andrei Gromyko, the
Soviet delegate to the United Nations, proposed establishing
a U.N. commission to ensure that the projected U.S. aid went
for the benefit of the Greek people. This would have been
one way to implement the Vandenberg amendment, had it
been taken seriously by the Truman administration. Acheson's response, however, was to tell Austin that, if he could
not use indefinite postponements to scotch the measure, "it
is essential that it be defeated." U.S. policymakers reacted

with equal hostility to other suggestions of U.N. action. Asking a U.N. liaison officer to cooperate with the American mission in Greece "might prove dangerous," noted an NEA official in May 1947, for this "might be an open wedge for . . . extensive . . . observation." Henderson noted marginally on the memo: "It would be unfortunate for us to make any move to encourage UN observers to watch over our activities in Greece. The mere presence of such observers might encourage the Communists and their sympathizers to sabotage our efforts." That June, and again in July, Marshall instructed Austin to prevent future U.N. commissions from concerning themselves in any way with America's role in Greece.[88]

The American desire for control also manifested itself in plans for the future Greek-American relationship. During congressional debates, of course, the State Department operated under the constraint of domestic and foreign public opinion; therefore, it announced that it would "scrupulously . . . respect the sovereignty" of Greece and Turkey "with respect to the conduct of their internal as well as their external affairs."[89] Secretly, however, official thinking was already moving along very different lines. At the February 28 meeting of the SWNCC Subcommittee on Foreign Policy Information, the question was raised whether the United States should "take a passive political attitude or whether it should exert internal influence." According to the official minutes, John D. Jernegan, the assistant chief of the Division of Near Eastern Affairs, responded "that the U.S. would exert influence." U.S. officials had "told Greek leaders in [the] past what we thought would improve the political set-up," and in the future would "have more leverage." After all, American administrators would "have effective control of money lent by the U.S. and virtually all resources of the Greek state." Llewellyn Thompson of the Office of European Affairs "said that the U.S. will exert every political influence but we cannot say much about it," for the "Soviet Union might bring the matter up before the UN."[90] On the same day, in the conversation that revealed the American aid program to the Greeks, Henderson stated explicitly to Economou-Gouras that the U.S.

government planned to intervene in Greek internal affairs. "We do this," the American official added in an apparent effort at reassurance, "open-heartedly and open-mindedly. We are not going to get economic benefits." Consequently, the Greek chargé reported to Athens that the U.S. program would entail definite limitations upon Greek sovereignty.[91]

The assumption of the need for American control in Greece was widespread among U.S. officials, and ranged across the political spectrum. MacVeagh cabled Washington on March 4 that he, Ethridge, and Porter agreed that American assistance "should be clearly conditioned" on the Greek government's "acceptance and implementation of specific economic policies." Furthermore, "provisions for supervision by American experts . . . should be broad and inclusive." Porter informed the State Department that same day: "Assurance [of] generous unconditional aid over [a] long period may result [in the] continued gross misconduct of [the] government, pauperization of [the] people, and recurrence [of the] present situation at [the] end [of the] aid period." Noting that he had deliberately toned down his observations about the Greek government in the report of the American economic mission, Porter advised Acheson privately on April 22 that "the Greek venture is destined to failure unless there is determined and active intervention by the United States in Greek affairs." He explained that the Greek government had "no policy except to solicit foreign aid on the basis of Greece's wartime catastrophes and their commitment to resist Communist aggression." It had "no economic program," resisted "obvious measures of reform and control," had "no genuine interest in the masses of the Greek people and intends, if permitted," to use "foreign aid to perpetuate the privileges of exploitation by a small banking and trading cabal which constitutes the real power behind this government."[92]

In their secret testimony before congressional committees, American officials shied away from so mordant a critique of their Greek counterparts but were frank about the need for American intervention. The Greek government would have to "be watched to see that they are actually doing what they

should, and that the money is not wasted," MacVeagh told
the House Foreign Affairs Committee; "if you pour it into the
Ministry of Finance and the Ministry of War, it will go down
a rat hole." MacVeagh stressed the need for American administrative direction of Greek public policies, as did Clayton,
who told the committee: "We must see to it that competent
persons are sent to Greece to ensure the development of
controls at key points and to supervise their application.
. . . We must be assured that sound policies will be adopted
and effectively administered." On April 1, Acheson told the
Senate Foreign Relations Committee of plans to place Americans in "the essential key Ministries. . . . Those people have
to perform control functions" and to "have authority to say
to Greece, 'Stop doing this!'" If U.S. stipulations were written
directly into the aid legislation, Acheson cautioned the Senate
Foreign Relations Committee, the United States would "face
the charge . . . that this is American imperialism." Consequently, "we must do a lot of this thing quite unobtrusively,"
by "persuasion and by holding back if they do not do it. We
must say, 'That is up to you, but if you want this thing you
must come across.'" Naturally, "we must make them agree
that there will be Americans in key positions . . . and that the
whole business will be under control." Some aspects of this
understanding would "be in the [aid] agreement" and others
would be enforced through administrative practices.[93]

After enactment of the Greek aid legislation, the administration developed final plans for implementation. Continuing their cultivation of American public opinion, State Department officials ordered Tsaldaris to stay out of town, since
his presence would be "embarrassing to [the] Dept at this
time,"[94] and drew up a thank-you note to themselves for presentation by the Greek government. ("The hearts of the Greek
people are profoundly touched by the generosity and goodwill
of the American people and by the benevolent interest of a
great and friendly nation in the welfare of Greece.") The
thank-you note would also "lay a basis for American assistance," Acheson explained to the President, by suggesting the
policies already outlined in an American-drafted aid agree-

ment. This agreement represented a compromise between the U.S. Treasury and State Departments, the former pressing for written guarantees of American control and the latter preferring subtler assurances of domination. Article IV, a key section, read:

The Chief of the American Mission will determine, in consultation with representatives of the Government of Greece, the terms and conditions upon which specified assistance shall from time to time be furnished under this Agreement. Under the direction of the Chief, the mission will provide such advisory assistance and will exercise such functions as are necessary and proper to assist the Government of Greece to make the most effective use of any assistance furnished to Greece by the United States and of Greece's own resources.

On May 31, Marshall sent MacVeagh the thank-you note and aid agreement for transmission to Greek authorities, observing that although the State Department did not insist upon the "exact wording" of the former, "any variance" would have to be cleared with Washington. As the Athens government proved predictably docile, the note was dispatched with fanfare on June 15, and the formal signing of the agreement occurred in Athens on June 20, 1947.[95]

By this time, the search for appropriate American administrators had been completed. The White House staff, taking charge of appointing a U.S. mission chief, solicited the views of Forrestal, Patterson, Marshall, Acheson, Harriman, Snyder, and Anderson. Porter and Ethridge, despite their expertise, were quickly ruled out of consideration. Instead, the field was thrown open to a group of big business acquaintances and Republicans, who would presumably enjoy good relations with the Republican Eightieth Congress. One of them, Paul Hoffman, the president of the Studebaker Corporation, was apparently offered the post but declined. Eventually, on June 10, the President announced the appointment of Dwight Griswold, the former governor of Nebraska. A liberal Republican, Griswold was then employed in the U.S. military government of Germany.[96] From a number of standpoints, Griswold seemed an excellent choice. His record as a Republican administrator would smooth the path for approval of his appointment and appropriation of funds by Congress. Furthermore, he was an old World War I buddy of the President's, and had been on close terms with him for two decades. "We soldiered together—we loafed together," Griswold had told a radio audience in 1945; "between real friends . . . party lines are forgotten."[97] Yet Griswold's relative independence of the State Department and his relative liberalism could also create difficulties. And they would. For the time being, however, American policymakers were happy enough. Having surmounted the obstacle of public opinion, they could turn at last to restoring stability in Greece.

4.
CONTROLLING GREEK POLITICS 1947–1949

If it had not been for Greek dependence on the American Aid
Program, there would have been no club with which to force the
Greek political leaders into a program of unity. When some of
these leaders were made to realize that the spending of American
money would be restricted if they went ahead with their partisan
plans, they hesitated and withdrew them. . . . Most of the Greek
political leaders are too tough to penetrate with reason only.

Dwight Griswold, September 15, 1947[1]

The Greek political arena presented American officials with
serious difficulties. Throughout the 1940s, U.S. policymakers
had grown increasingly disturbed about the direction of Greek
politics. Frightened by the growth and militance of the left,
particularly that of the Communist Party, they had sought to
check its influence and establish the supremacy of more conservative forces in Greek political life. By 1947 this had become a formidable task. The heroism of the wartime resistance and the crude brutality of postwar reaction had provided
the Greek left with a large and devoted following. Although
many other Greeks were outraged by leftist excesses or opposed to Communism, they were far from united as to party
or policy. Furthermore, their leaders—whom Americans
often considered short-sighted or incompetent—seemed unwilling to forsake traditional practices of political intrigue and
parliamentary maneuver. Greece had enjoyed parliamentary
government since 1843, and, although punctuated by occasional coups, it did not come to a halt until the Metaxas
dictatorship.[2] Greece's political parties, often weak and evanescent, were nonetheless gradually taking on modern ideological overtones. By 1947, the Greek right had largely re-

grouped around the Populists of Tsaldaris, the center around the Liberals of Sophoulis, and the left around the remnants of EAM. If American officials were to cut through political obstacles and smash leftist influence, they would need to intervene to an unprecedented degree in Greek political life.

Dwight Griswold, appointed chief of the American Mission for Aid to Greece (AMAG) on June 10, 1947, quickly began meeting with State Department officials and organizing his staff, drawn largely from business and government. He arrived in Athens on July 15 and by the end of September was directing 206 American personnel. Within a year, AMAG swelled to 1,216 employees; nearly half were Americans, and more than two-thirds of these were military men. The Americans had "great advantages" over their predecessors, recalled C. M. Woodhouse. "They came fresh to the job, without the staleness and disillusionment which characterised the British. . . . They were vigorous, resourceful and immensely efficient." Yet these admirable features had their less pleasant aspects. The Americans were "apt to assume that history began when they first came on the scene," Woodhouse remarked. "The Greeks also found them harder to deal with than the British: more inflexible, less adaptable . . . more inclined to impose American methods regardless of national characteristics."[3] Of course, British officials like Woodhouse, representing a declining imperial power, tended to regard their American successors with a tinge of jealousy. Even so, there was some justice to their complaints, particularly in the realm of Greek politics.

From the outset, AMAG's intervention in Greek politics was limited only by the need to maintain a proper public relations image. On July 9, 1947, shortly before his departure for Greece, Griswold attended a meeting in Washington with the U.S. Secretaries of State, War, the Navy, and the Treasury and with many of their top aides. Citing the sweeping authority which General Douglas MacArthur exercised in Japan, Griswold declared, according to the minutes of the meeting, that he believed "his immediate task should be to change or reorganize the Greek Government." In his opinion, that government was corrupt, inefficient, and increasingly unpopular. In reply, Henderson said that the State Department "agreed entirely with Governor Griswold in his feeling that certain changes might be necessary" and that "certain officials . . . would have to be eliminated." But it would be "necessary to proceed discreetly, in order to avoid creating resentment. . . . For this purpose it would probably be advisable to establish regular channels of discussion at a high level." Marshall affirmed Henderson's emphasis upon discretion, "pointing out that all of our activities in Greece would be under close scrutiny," while Dean Rusk, who handled the State Department's U.N. liaison, added that the American record should "be designed to avoid charges of imperialism."[4]

That these caveats were confined to the instrumentalities of American intervention rather than to its substance was apparent in the detailed instructions Marshall presented to Griswold two days later. "We desire to see in Greece a government whose members are . . . primarily interested in keeping their country from falling under Communist control or Soviet domination," he told the AMAG chieftain. "Ideally, members of the government should be drawn from the political parties of the left, the center, and the right, but not so far to the left that they are disposed to make concessions to, or deals with, the Communists or so far to the right that they would refuse to cooperate with non-Communists" in a "single-minded" opposition to "the subversive forces." If Griswold and MacVeagh concluded that AMAG's effectiveness would be strengthened through "reorganization of the Greek Government," the State Department "hoped that you and the Ambassador will be able to bring about such a reorganization indirectly through discreet suggestion." Such discretion would avoid the "charge before the United Nations that the United States is interfering in the internal affairs of Greece." Furthermore, the Secretary of State maintained that, in reshaping Greek politics, Griswold should work closely with MacVeagh. "The responsibilities of the Ambassador," Marshall noted, "include in particular the problem of bringing about changes in the Greek Government."[5] Thus, the State Department expected Griswold to secure specific objectives in Greek politics, albeit behind the scenes and in coordination with the regular State Department chain of command.

Marshall's instructions to Griswold reflected the State Department's still-unsuccessful attempt to isolate the Greek left politically through a center-right coalition. To the American government's dismay, the bulk of the centrist Liberals, led by Sophoulis, showed no interest in sharing power with the right-wing Populists, whom they blamed for polarizing the nation and exacerbating the civil war. The best that MacVeagh could do was to engineer a modest cabinet reorganization in January 1947. From the standpoint of American officials, the most promising aspect of the shift was the elevation to the prime ministership of Demetrios Maximos, an elderly Populist banker whom MacVeagh considered the "most non-partisan, moderate and cooperative personality in Government." By contrast, MacVeagh bewailed the "stupidity" of Maximos's predecessor, Tsaldaris, the Populist leader whom MacVeagh feared might also prove his successor, "with consequent difficulties for our mission which anyone who met him in Washington will understand."[6] According to British diplomats, Tsaldaris knew that he was "disliked by the Americans," and "indicated that his first loyalty was still to Great Britain."[7] Although the government reorganization also broadened the cabinet slightly by admitting a few pliant Liberals, the latter proved distressingly fickle. In late March 1947, in the midst of congressional hearings, MacVeagh found it necessary to cable Thomas Karamessines, the Central Intelligence Group's operative on the U.S. embassy staff, that he should inform his "contact" that "it would greatly impede our efforts . . . if Liberal members of [the Greek] Govt. should resign." One of their number, Eleftherios Venizelos, replied that he and his Liberal colleague, Panayiotis Canellopoulos, would abide by the ambassador's advice, for they were "desirous of following the instructions of the US Govt." But although the token Liberals remained in the cabinet, few observers were impressed. Commenting on his trip to Greece in mid-1947, the European representative of the American Federation of

Labor, Irving Brown, reported scathingly that the Greek government was "manned by people who are merely giving lip service to democracy."[8]

Despite the right-wing complexion of the Athens government, the KKE retained hopes that Greece's political climate could be altered short of full-scale civil war. To be sure, from March to July 1947 the guerrilla forces of General Markos grew from 13,000 to 23,000, severing large areas of Greece from government control and accelerating the nation's economic disintegration. As McNeill noted, however, until July "the Communists used them to discredit and demoralize the government, and as a lever for bargaining with Sophoulis." Markos found it so difficult to obtain weapons and supplies from the Balkan Communist states that he was forced to curtail recruiting.[9] At the same time, the KKE leadership remained in the open in Athens, engaged in feverish political maneuvering. U.S. intelligence reports reveal that, until his death by natural causes in May 1947, Siantos, now the number two figure in the party, argued for "a normal political solution" and criticized insurrectionary tactics. Accordingly, he opposed the establishment of a rebel government, as did Markos, who despite his greater militancy, feared that it would entail a shift from guerrilla to positional warfare. Zachariades, the party leader, seemed more intrigued by the concept, apparently as a means of securing more aid from the Balkan governments.[10] In June, at a Communist conference in Strasbourg, France, a KKE delegate did broach the idea of a "free democratic government." Nevertheless, until mid-July 1947, even Zachariades refused to endorse it; instead, he continued his fruitless efforts to secure a reorganization of the Athens government. Writing of the KKE, McNeill observed that while the guerrilla bands escalated their operations "under the leadership of subordinate and therefore relatively inconspicuous Communists," the "men at the top hoped political negotiation might bring them into a Greek Cabinet."[11]

In July 1947, Greek political leaders made what might have been their last serious effort at political compromise. Still calling for a political settlement, Sophoulis spoke with the

King on July 11, requesting that he be asked to form a new government. Predictably, the King refused to cooperate, questioning "whether one so stupid could be sincere" and claiming that Sophoulis would become "another Kerensky." The following day, a KKE representative met with Sophoulis and, according to MacVeagh, "gave him verbally what they called final terms for calling off the civil war." These were:

1. Resignation of [the] present government
2. Dissolution of Parliament
3. Formation of a "pure center government" under Sophoulis with [the] cooperation [of] such leaders as [Emmanuel] Tsouderos, Plastiras, and [Alexander] Mylonas. . . .
4. Agreement between [the] new government and [the] KKE on [the] basis of "Sophoulis's policy of appeasement," i.e. general amnesty, guarantee of security to those laying down arms, and promise of new elections soonest on [the] basis [of] revised electoral lists.

MacVeagh added that he had not been informed of this directly by Liberal leaders, but rather by British officials to whom they had turned for advice. This raised the question of whether Sophoulis was "playing square" with Prime Minister Maximos or, as MacVeagh believed, "following, at least to some extent, [the] well-known Communist tactics of trying to use [the] UK against [the] US."[12]

As MacVeagh's remarks indicated, U.S. officials looked askance at such compromise efforts and, eventually, helped bring about their collapse. On July 18, Marshall informed MacVeagh that, although Bevin favored opening discussions with Sophoulis and Tsouderos on the implementation of specific points, "we should prefer more bluntly informing them that we consider [the] KKE's fair-sounding proposals to be insincere and dangerous, and that any serious discussion of them could only strengthen [the] Communists' hand." Marshall wanted this message transmitted to the Liberal leaders either through the British or, if they demurred, "independently." As things turned out, the British embassy was cooperative, and through it MacVeagh succeeded in conveying

Marshall's warning to the center politicians. Thereafter, relations between the Greek Communists and the Liberals were broken off. The collapse of such negotiations was welcome news to MacVeagh, who, echoing the King, depicted Sophoulis as a "possible Kerensky."[13] From the KKE's vantage point, the political route had come to a dead end. McNeill recalled: "Upon meeting this check, Communist policy hardened for war." U.S. diplomatic and intelligence sources reported large-scale military movements across the northern frontiers and the rapid escalation of guerrilla conflict. In late August, MacVeagh cabled that the situation in Greece was "deteriorating—steadily and dangerously."[14]

Indeed, the country now plunged fully into the third and most destructive phase of its civil war. Previously guerrilla bands had been active in the mountains—harassing government authorities, disrupting transportation and communications, and exacting vengeance on those they called "monarcho-fascists." Rightist bands, too, had roamed the countryside, bent on violent reprisal. But after the summer of 1947, with the breakdown of political compromise, the ferocity of the struggle increased. Rebel military units, larger and better armed than before, carried out dramatic raids upon towns and villages—shelling buildings, sacking homes and shops, executing their enemies, and conscripting the young for service in the mountains. Army and national guard units, initially dilatory and ineffective, became more aggressive—engaging in gory clashes with the "bandits," driving thousands of civilians from rebel territory, and packing off guerrillas and their presumed sympathizers to prisons, concentration camps, or firing squads. Court-martials, political assassinations, and napalm bombing became prominent features of Greek life. Whatever the ideals of the combatants, brutality had become commonplace all across the political spectrum.[15]

Despite the bloody conflict in much of the countryside, conventional political maneuvering continued in Athens, albeit in a truncated form. Opposed, as before, to a purely center government, American officials were still concerned that an overwhelmingly Populist cabinet was too narrow to rally public opinion. Pointing to the skewed nature of the 1946 election results, MacVeagh cabled on July 28, 1947 that a center-right coalition "would go much farther to satisfy [the] public at large than unilateral . . . rule by [the] Populists alone." This coalition could "restore security" and then hold new elections, in which he saw "no apparent necessity [to] include [the] Communists." On August 5, Griswold reported that "every impartial American observer here feels [that] change in [the] political complexion of [the] government is necessary." America "need give no thought to avoidance of [the] accusation of intervention," he added; the "only question is whether good results can be obtained." Although MacVeagh's apparent caution made Griswold "fearful that the present opportunity will not be grasped," the U.S. ambassador was perfectly ready to act. On August 20, he informed the State Department that he was "not fearful of [the] accusation of interference if [it is] handled tactfully and discreetly." The "Greeks know that their salvation depends upon American aid and [I] believe we should use our present prestige to . . . broaden [the] government."[16]

That task, however, proved easier said than done. Tsaldaris was pressing for the formation of a purely Populist cabinet under his leadership. Sophoulis, in turn, insisted that the post of Prime Minister remained his price for participation in the government. On August 21, in exasperation, MacVeagh told Constantine Rendis, one of Sophoulis's Liberal Party lieutenants, that "if Sophoulis remains unwilling [to] collaborate, those of his party who put loyalty to country ahead of party loyalty should break away from him and join patriotic ranks." Meanwhile, the three token Liberals in the cabinet, taking their cues from Griswold, demanded the dismissal of the right-wing General Napoleon Zervas, Minister of Public Order. When Tsaldaris refused to accept their demand, the Maximos government fell on August 23, inspiring a fierce power struggle between Tsaldaris and Sophoulis to head up its successor. On August 25, MacVeagh brought the two party chiefs together at his house but proved unable to convince them to form "a joint government."[17] That same day, Griswold warned one of Tsaldaris's party lieutenants that a Populist government would be "inadmissible." Griswold threatened to cut off American aid in the event of its formation, providing him with a signed memorandum to this effect.[18] The following evening, Tsaldaris stormed before MacVeagh, alternately raging and weeping, and demanded: "Does this mean you declare war on us?" Embarrassed by the crudeness of Griswold's tactics, already cause for talk throughout the Athens political world, MacVeagh sought to placate the hysterical Populist leader. He stated that "inadmissible" meant "inadvisable," and put this in the form of a conciliatory letter. Tsaldaris, having extracted this concession from the U.S. ambassador, proceeded to organize a purely Populist government, designating himself Prime Minister.[19]

From the standpoint of Anglo-American officials, this outcome was most unfortunate. According to U.S. diplomatic sources, the British Foreign Office considered the new government "deplorable," regarding Tsaldaris as a " 'fool' and one of the worst possible Prime Ministers." The American view was at least as unflattering. In the following days, wielding what he termed the "club" of the American aid program, Griswold managed to persuade a number of leading Populists and other rightists to withdraw their support from the Tsaldaris government. At the same time, neither he nor Mac-Veagh, despite their best efforts, proved able to reinstitute a broader government. Finally, Loy Henderson flew in from Washington to take charge of the situation.[20] Shunting aside Griswold, whom they both considered inept at political maneuvering and overly sympathetic to the Liberals, Henderson and MacVeagh began a round of meetings with Greek political leaders. MacVeagh reported that, in their interview with Tsaldaris on September 1, they "emphasized" that if the Greeks did not establish a "government having wide support," the United States "might well refuse [to] expend further energies and resources on aid to Greece." That evening, meeting with Venizelos and Canellopoulos, Henderson explained that the State Department desired a "National Government" that would incorporate the center and the right. He and Mac-Veagh also hinted at their preference for Maximos as Prime Minister. Sophoulis, MacVeagh complained, "won't come in without controlling everything." Attempting to break the impasse, the U.S. officials turned to the King on September 3, informing him that the Populist government "imperilled the development of American aid" and urging him to call a crisis meeting of Greek political leaders. At the King's request, MacVeagh gave him a statement calling for a center-right coalition, which the "King proposed to read as his own."[21]

Ultimately, however, the Americans proved unable to ignore Tsaldaris and Sophoulis who, whatever their flaws, happened to be the leaders of Greece's two major parties on the center-right. Later that day the King telephoned MacVeagh to announce that "our little plan has been torpedoed." Tsaldaris had taken it as a personal affront, and Sophoulis was threatening to attack the King's procedure as unconstitutional. Consequently, on the morning of September 4, Henderson and MacVeagh met with Sophoulis, who immediately announced that he had "good news" for them: Tsaldaris had agreed to the formation of a Populist-Liberal cabinet, with Sophoulis as the Prime Minister. Although this gave the Americans their center-right coalition, they remained reluctant to turn over the top post to a Liberal leader. According to the meeting records, "MacVeagh asked at this point if, aside from the question of the premiership, there would not be other problems to be solved as well." Sophoulis sought to reassure him by declaring that "it was not a question of who the personalities of the new government would be, but rather a matter of making it felt . . . that a radical change had come over Greece's policy." Increasingly distressed, Henderson demanded to know what he meant by a "radical change." Sophoulis was a political veteran, however, and quickly took his measure of the Americans. His program was well-known, he responded soothingly, and "its main lines would be 'wildly anti-Communist.' "[22]

The Americans were not willing to accept this statement at face value; they proceeded to put the octagenarian Liberal

Party leader through a combination of anti-Communist lectures and catechism. According to the meeting records, Henderson asked "the point blank question as to whether, if Mr. Sophoulis were Prime Minister, he believed the Russians and their satellites would let up on their pressure on Greece." When Sophoulis replied that "the tension might lighten," Henderson retorted that "Sophoulis was not well-informed in international matters," for "Soviet Russia had decided that she had to have Greece." Sophoulis explained that his amnesty program for the guerrillas might lead to some measure of pacification, for "all the bandits were not Communists; very many had been mobilized by sheer force [and] a large number had to take to the hills because they were persecuted by the authorities." In obvious irritation, Henderson asked Sophoulis "if he thought that the Greek problem was merely an internal one." Sophoulis replied "categorically" that it was not, although "it certainly was one in its genesis." Gradually, Sophoulis's responses calmed the American officials, particularly his promises to "go slowly" on changes of personnel, to limit the extent of his amnesty program, and to push for a "military solution." He also gave Henderson a memorandum supporting his claim to have always been an anti-Communist. Eventually, then, Henderson agreed to have Sophoulis form a center-right government, warning him not to appoint any "Communists or Communist sympathizers."[23] It was agreed that "individual ministers would be removed at US suggestion if they are uncooperative." On September 7, 1947, a Liberal-Populist coalition took office, and three days later Marshall publicly welcomed this "government of national unity."[24]

American officials found Sophoulis's leadership of the new government acceptable not only because it gave substance to their ideal of a center-right coalition but because they understood that the Liberals had been left little room for maneuver. Although Sophoulis would be Prime Minister, the Liberals would hold only a minority of cabinet posts, with their independence of action circumscribed still further by overwhelming rightist control of parliament, the armed forces, and the administrative apparatus.[25] As David Balfour of the

British Foreign Office noted: "For a few weeks or months the advent of Sophoulis . . . may keep foreign criticism a little less acrimonious; arrests may become less indiscriminate, deportations rarer and trials juster." Nevertheless, Sophoulis' " 'appeasement' venture . . . has as good as failed already by the mere fact that the majority of Ministers are Populists." What, for example, were the guerrillas and the KKE to think of the new Minister of the Interior, Mavromichalis, described by U.S. intelligence as a former Nazi collaborator who had subsequently become "active in channeling armaments to right-wing paramilitary groups"? The British considered him a "second Zervas, only probably worse." U.S. intelligence reported that the new Minister of the Navy, Admiral Alexander Sakellariou, had been "one of the major figures" assisting Metaxas to remodel the Greek navy on "German military lines" and that he was "inclined to use totalitarian solutions." As Balfour noted, Sophoulis had done "what he always used to say he would not do: apply his 'appeasement' policy in the company of ministerial colleagues compromised in his eyes and in the eyes of the KKE by their partiality and their indiscriminate use of 'dynamic' methods."[26] Indeed, within months, Sophoulis began to complain that he was a figurehead for a rightist regime—"a captive Liberal."[27]

In fact, most U.S. officials wanted the politicians of the center restrained by the power of the right. Griswold, to be sure, argued that, "to fight communism" successfully, it was necessary "to build up the leadership of moderate and intelligent liberals." But this was not the view of the U.S. embassy or the State Department, which continued to view the Liberals with suspicion. "We have no assurance that the Liberal party would not again move leftward if it could shake off the leavening influence of the Populists," Rankin argued in February 1948. Therefore, "the best interests of Greece and of the United States would be served by continuation of the coalition government . . . with each of the two parties operating as a brake on the other." In August, Marshall warned of the "danger that Liberals and centrists," in new elections, might "seek support of Greek leftists and 'liberal' world opinion by again espousing [an] appeasement policy toward fellow-travelers and communists." In this context, it would be a "mistake to give Liberals [the] impression that . . . they may . . . indulge in any extravagance with [the] assurance of US support." The "best means" of avoiding "Liberal flirtation with [the] Left would, of course, be [to] urge them [to] remain in [the] present Coalition." Yet, "in view of this danger," if the coalition did break down, U.S. officials should be wary of forming a "combination in which [the] Liberals would have [the] upper hand."[28]

Given these considerations, U.S. officials worked diligently to keep the Populist-Liberal coalition afloat. On September 29, 1947, Griswold told Sophoulis that it was of "utmost importance" that Sophoulis continue as Prime Minister, that "it would be [a] catastrophe for Greece and also for [the U.S.] Mission if your Government should fall." American officials headed off threats by Sophoulis to resign and blocked attempts by Tsaldaris to force Liberal ministers from office. In January 1948, Rankin cabled the State Department that "Sophoulis and Tsaldaris are restless bedfellows whose marriage is unlikely to be either enduring or fruitful without an occasional brandishing of the American shotgun that originally brought it about."[29] Some of Sophoulis's younger party lieutenants, irritated by the Populist stranglehold on the adminstrative apparatus and local governments, called for the dissolution of the coalition. According to Griswold, Venizelos complained bitterly to him in June 1948 that, despite the sentiments of the people, "Greece today was a 'Populist' state." And, in fact, as late as 1949 the U.S. embassy admitted that 95 percent of local officials were Populists, "many serving in Liberal areas." Nevertheless, American officials worked hard and successfuly to fend off these and other challenges to the center-right coalition.[30] In late 1949, one U.S. official suggested "an outright merger" of the Populist and Liberal parties, claiming that "a solid centrist bloc might thus be constituted" between the Metaxist right and the labor left.[31]

As might be expected, then, the advent of the Sophoulis cabinet produced only cosmetic changes. "Behind the government is a small mercantile and banking cabal," Paul Porter reiterated in late September 1947. "This cabal is determined above all to protect its financial prerogatives, at whatever expense to the economic health of the country."[32] Greek governments "are mere figureheads," concluded the chief European correspondent for CBS, Howard K. Smith, in early 1949. "They pass tax laws but cannot collect the taxes. They declare amnesties but cannot enforce them. Real power lies in the bureaucracy, the army and the police, and nothing has been done to purge these instruments even of the most vengeful pro-Nazis not to mention the reactionary monarchists." In territory under their control, the rebels ignored the authority of the center-right coalition and established, in rudimentary form, all the apparatus of a parallel state. Captured by the guerrillas in late 1948 in the Peloponnesus, BBC correspondent Kenneth Matthews found the entire countryside dominated by the rebels, who had established schools, courts, newspapers, military training centers, hospitals, and hundreds of "people's councils." Smith concluded: "'Democracy' in Greece is a paper facade, and beyond a quarter-mile radius of the hotel district of Athens and Salonika, where the foreigners live, not even the facade exists."[33]

Anglo-American officials recognized that the Greek political situation left much to be desired. On February 12, 1948, the U.S. National Security Council secretly adopted NSC 5/2, which declared that "the Greek Government rests on a weak foundation and Greece is in a deplorable economic state." In addition to the "general fear and a feeling of insecurity among the people," there existed "friction among short-sighted political factions, selfishness and corruption in Government, and a dearth of effective leaders." British observers were particularly pessimistic. Reporting to Bevin on November 18, 1948, Ambassador Norton doubted "whether any Greek Government, however constituted, is capable of rising above the demands of selfish and sectional political interests and of confronting the fundamental problems facing the nation." There existed "an all too prevalent attitude, not only that Greece has a right to practically unlimited foreign aid, but that" Greece itself was absolved "from the obligation of making determined efforts or real sacrifices." The task of Greece's foreign advisers, he maintained, was "comparable to those of Hercules or Sisyphus." Indeed, Greece would never amount to very much. "Republic or monarchy," he contended, "modern Greece is not designed to be better than a poor but gay and happy-go-lucky Mediterranean country." Paradoxically, though, the poverty of Greek politics pointed "to the conclusion that the salvation of this country can now only be achieved by an even more radical intervention by the Americans."[34]

U.S. officials drew much the same conclusion. As one AMAG staff member recalled: "To a considerable degree the mission became a super-government of Greece. Americans moved into every sector of Greek governmental affairs." Shortly after Sophoulis took office, AMAG officials urged him to deliver an address to the nation that would present AMAG programs as those of the Greek government. When Sophoulis agreed, Griswold reported, "the mission . . . drafted an extensive radio address to be given by the Prime Minister." Sophoulis delivered the speech, in slightly modified form, much to the satisfaction of the Americans.[35] In May 1948, George McGhee, the coordinator of the Greek-Turkish aid program, privately informed the Under Secretary of State that AMAG "exercises advisory functions . . . in relation to almost all phases of the economy as well as governmental administration and military operations." The "decisions by the mission as to utilization of American aid do in fact determine most important decisions of the Greek Government." Griswold told McGhee that he obtained results "by speaking firmly. . . . The British ambassador says he could never speak to the Greeks as I do." It was not the KKE but the U.S. embassy's Karl Rankin who charged that there had been a "widespread failure among Americans and British" to understand that the Greeks would "not respond cooperatively to 'colonial' treatment."[36]

Rankin's criticism, it should be noted, was raised in the context of a growing rift between AMAG and the U.S. embassy. The formation of the Sophoulis government in September 1947 had brought a number of tensions to the surface. Both MacVeagh and Griswold accepted the need for some form of center-right coalition, but they favored different coalition leadership—MacVeagh the Populists and Griswold the Liberals. In addition, MacVeagh objected strongly to the brusque tactics that Griswold had employed. Finally, the men were bureaucratic rivals, insofar as each claimed jurisdiction over Greek politics. Although the State Department called MacVeagh back to Washington in the fall of 1947, it reserved its sharpest comments for Griswold. Pointing to a *New York Times* story that labeled the AMAG chieftain the "most powerful man in Greece," Under Secretary of State Robert Lovett warned Griswold on October 17, 1947 about appearing to be deeply involved in "details of Greek internal politics." Griswold responded that "it would be wrong for AMAG or for [the] US Government to attempt to represent to world opinion that AMAG . . . is not involved in Greek internal affairs"; indeed, "cables arriving regularly from [the] State Department ask AMAG . . . to involve itself." In exasperation, Marshall replied that the State Department agreed that the U.S. government "is in fact and necessarily involved [in] certain aspects [of] Greek internal affairs" but "it is our policy . . . that American influence be exercised as discreetly as possible."[37]

In an effort to heal the AMAG-embassy rift over Greek politics, the State Department sought, not altogether successfully, to clarify lines of jurisdiction. On November 7, 1947, it sent Griswold new instructions that pointedly reserved "matters of high policy" to the ambassador. Griswold, however, vigorously objected, threatened to resign, and exercised his muscle in American politics. As a result, after some prodding from President Truman, the State Department reversed itself later that month and assured the AMAG chief that it would accept the earlier division of responsibility. Meanwhile, MacVeagh was removed from office and reassigned to the U.S. embassy in Lisbon, with no successor appointed. Griswold's victory was only temporary, however, for the National Security Council insisted on uniting the two roles in the person of a new ambassador. As McGhee later explained, at the time of AMAG's establishment, "it was felt that political responsibilities . . . could be satisfactorily segregated from the economic and military responsibilities." Eventually, though, it became clear that it was "highly desirable to concentrate responsibility for all aspects in one Administrator in order to achieve coordination of United States efforts in Greece and concentration of United States bargaining power vis-a-vis the Greek Government."[38] Griswold resigned—to the relief of the Greek right, which continued to look to the U.S. embassy for assistance—and was succeeded in July 1948 by Henry F. Grady, an American businessman who had been serving as U.S. ambassador to India. Ironically, however, despite the dissolution of AMAG, the concomitant establishment of the Economic Cooperation Administration (ECA) in Greece created a new and relatively independent U.S. diplomatic establishment in Athens.[39]

In their day-to-day dealings in Greek politics, American officials found themselves increasingly drawn into the orbit of the monarchy. George II, who had returned to Greece in the fall of 1946, had remained relatively clear of political intrigue, both because of the intense controversy surrounding his past political ventures and because of his aloof personal style. With his death on April 1, 1947, however, the crown was assumed by Paul I, a younger brother who was both considerably more personable and politically active. As Crown Prince during the 1930s, Paul had become known for his keen interest in sports, especially yachting, and had directed the neofascist National Youth Organization of General Metaxas. His wife, Princess Frederika, a granddaughter of the German Kaiser, had headed up the girls' section, a post to which she brought some expertise thanks to her past membership in the Hitler Youth. While predicting that the new king would probably be more popular than his predecessor, the British ambassador commented that he was "somewhat lacking in brains and in practical grasp of affairs" and that "the simplicity of his character may lay him open, to a greater extent than his predecessor, to the influence of Right-wing extremists."[40] The U.S. embassy agreed that Paul would prove "somewhat less astute" than his brother, and predicted that "Frederika is likely to play [a] decisive role due to her intelligence, energy, strength of character, emotional disposition and intense interest in politics." James Keeley, the embassy counselor, noted that the "royal family, especially Frederika and entourage, have made [a] notable effort [to] cultivate [the] friendship of Americans and Embassy officers by entertainment and special attentions." Not only did the royal family hold some very fine parties on its $480,000 a year government stipend, but it drew upon the Queen's considerable charm, vivacity, and attractiveness to further its ambitions. Frederika "has a way with the men," remarked C. L. Sulzberger, "from Smuts and Marshall on down."[41]

Although formally engaged in "charitable" activities and meetings of the Royal Yacht Club, Paul and Frederika actually spent a good deal of time lobbying for right-wing causes. At a government reception, noted Keeley, "Paul discussed [the] labor situation at length" with a U.S. official, "expressing skepticism respecting [the] value of trade unionism in Greece." In January 1948, the King sought to draw the embassy chargé, Karl Rankin, into criticism of Griswold,[42] while the following month both the King and the Queen pressed for the appointment of the right-wing General Alexander Papagos, architect of the 1940 Albanian campaign and now Paul's military adviser, as commander-in-chief of the armed forces. When Rankin replied that the general's name "was being linked with various schemes to replace the present [coalition] government," Frederika professed to have no interest in establishing a government headed by Papagos. Nevertheless, her other remarks indicated plans for some extraordinary political maneuvers. "She had been very favorably impressed with Mr. Henderson during his visit," Rankin reported, and contended that, "although it was not generally known, Mr. Henderson had assured the King of American support if it were necessary to seek a 'radical solution.' "[43] As conversations along these lines grew more common in Athens, the American press picked up the "talk about the need for a 'strong man.' " At a luncheon that July, the King spoke out in favor of placing Papagos in "a more important position." Ambassador Grady thought that this probably meant the post of commander-in-chief, but noted that Spyros Markezinis, the close political confidante of the King and Papagos, "hinted broadly" that "what was needed at this time to save Greece was a Rightist Dictatorship."[44]

The Greek monarchy's growing interest in a military dictatorship raised some delicate issues for U.S. officials. Not only had American policymakers promoted the Truman Doctrine as a defense of democracy, but—in the absence of other considerations—most probably disliked the imposition of dictatorship. There were, however, other considerations, notably the determination of U.S. officials to defeat the Communist-led revolution. Thus, in October 1947, the first commander of the U.S. Army detachment in Greece reported to his superiors that "a government comparable to that formed by Metaxas . . . is needed in Greece today. A democratic form of government as we know it is too mild to counteract the power methods employed by enemies of the government." Writing to Marshall in February 1948, George McGhee suggested that "the effectiveness of the Greek people" as "an instrument of our policy" could "be increased if certain further steps were taken, much as we might dislike taking them. This includes bringing about the creation of a more authoritarian government."[45] By the fall of 1948, American officials were inclined to blame the disturbing lack of success of the Greek armed forces upon disunity in Greek politics. According to the U.S. military commander, General James Van Fleet, "the political situation in Greece . . . is having a very detrimental effect upon the army." He complained of "the lack of unity" and "wholehearted" support for the armed forces, "adverse criticism and political bickerings."[46] Few American officials could ignore the growing tensions. Complaining of Greece's "ineffective political leadership," Grady cabled on October 22, 1948 that the State Department was "of course aware of [the] dilemma created by [the] desire [to] establish [an] effective government and yet maintain . . . [a] democratic parliamentary system."[47]

In November 1948, when a new period of political instability commenced—aggravated by lack of progress in the war and the illness of Prime Minister Sophoulis—American officials began to gravitate toward authoritarian measures. Although Grady and Van Fleet had approved the appointment of Papagos as commander-in-chief, pressure continued to mount thereafter for a "Papagos solution": the appointment of a cabinet, headed by Papagos and dominated by Markezinis, which, lacking support from parliament, would rule in the name of the King.[48] On November 20, the King told Grady that if Sophoulis and Tsaldaris failed to form a new coalition, he would implement this plan. The American ambassador gave his approval. As he cabled the State Department:

I told [the] King we would support him in his proposal but would expect [the] Papagos Government to consist of effective and efficient ministers and that [the] King would prevent Papagos or similar government from becoming [a] dictatorship. I said [that the] gravity of [the] situation is such that an efficient government for Greece is more important than preserving all traditional democratic forms.

Grady added hopefully that the King thought Papagos might "receive [a] vote of confidence if armed with [a] decree dissolving Parliament, which decree would then not have to be implemented."[49]

In Washington, the State Department's director of Greek, Turkish, and Iranian Affairs, John Jernegan, expressed no qualms about this approach; he merely thought Grady a bit naive. "While I agree with Ambassador Grady that we should 'support' the King's proposal," he wrote, "we should be under no illusions as to the probable character of a Papagos-Markezinis government or take too much stock in any pledge by the King to prevent such a Government from becoming a disguised dictatorship." In assessing the virtues and defects of the Papagos solution, Jernegan showed no interest whatsoever in democracy. Instead, he concluded:

The advantage of such a regime is that it would give promise of providing Greece with the dynamic, efficient, and inspired political leadership which the country so sorely needs. The disadvantage is that such a regime would probably be less responsive to American influence and desires than its more pliable, weaker predecessors . . . and that failure of the regime might well entail [the] collapse of the whole Greek structure, including the throne.[50]

Although the Sophoulis-Tsaldaris coalition still held by a narrow margin, the Papagos "solution" continued to intrigue American officials. On December 1, Rankin provided the State Department with a seven-page memorandum discussing "The Political Position of Spyros Markezinis" and "an eventual Papagos Government." An ardent nationalist, "Markezinis could not be expected to be submissive to foreign direction"; nevertheless, "as he has stated, no intelligent Greek can . . . reject American advice." While Markezinis talked of "democratic methods," his personality contained "strong tendencies toward the assumption of dictatorial power and some of his proposed measures might well require authoritarian methods." Rankin expressed uncertainty about how to evaluate Markezinis and his "New Party," but concluded that "he has something to contribute to Greece in the critical days that lie ahead." Within the State Department, Leonard Cromie—formerly of the U.S. embassy in Athens and now in the Office of Greek, Turkish, and Iranian Affairs—used this dispatch to argue that Markezinis had been "seriously underrated." The New Party leader, he explained, had "been most active in entertaining and otherwise cultivating Embassy officers"—a fact which "at least . . . indicates his zeal." On December 22, Rankin reported that, while he and the British ambassador believed that the establishment of a Papagos-Markezinis government "should not be sponsored by [the] US," this opinion was not shared "by various other Americans and Britons here." The U.S. chargé thought that a "semi-dictatorship may develop however our efforts [are] directed," but believed that the United States "should exercise extreme care to avoid any appearance of having brought it into power unless and until no alternative remains."[51]

The movement for the "Papagos solution" crested in the first weeks of 1949. On January 1, while Grady was out of the country, Averell Harriman, the Special Representative in Europe for ECA, met in Athens with the King and Markezinis. According to C. L. Sulzberger, who talked with the King two days later, Paul was planning to "throw out the present Greek government," demand an all-party cabinet, and, if it were not formed, call upon Papagos to form an extraparliamentary government; if parliament refused to accept the latter, he would dissolve the legislature "indefinitely." Paul said that "he told all this to Ambassador Harriman . . . and that Harriman approved." Having returned to Athens, Grady met with the King on January 4, and, as he informed Washington, was "surprised to learn his opinion that [the] Papagos-Markezinis 'solution' should be tried as soon as possible." Paul "stated [that] he understood [that the] Americans agreed." Grady responded that they did not. He anxiously cabled Marshall that while the "situation may so change as to require our acceptance [of] an extra-parliamentary solution," for the time being "US encouragement" along these lines would be inappropriate.[52] With considerable irritation, Grady cabled Harriman that the King's "position . . . has shifted materially since I last saw him . . . as his plan was to install [a] Papagos government only as [a] last resort," while now he favored an "immediate Papagos-Markezinis government." Although the State Department concurred with Grady's recommendation that the "abandonment of [the] parliamentary system in favor of some form or other of dictatorship" be regarded as a "last resort," the ambassador had great difficulty impressing this point upon the King. Paul and Frederika "still seem to feel that influential American governmental opinion" is "behind [a] drastic solution," Grady cabled on January 18.[53] Finally, after considerable pressure from Grady, the British ambassador, and Britain's Vice-Admiral Lord Mountbatten, the King abandoned the Papagos solution and a new center-right coalition was formed. "Had it not been for Mountbatten," Grady reported, "I am afraid the King would have followed what he regarded as the wishes of ECA."[54]

In retrospect, it seems possible that the King let his eagerness to install a Papagos dictatorship outrun his veracity. Responding to Grady's inquiries, Harriman stated that, at the January meeting with the King, "I listened attentively as he expressed his ideas," but "expressed no views except to urge him to take no steps without full discussion with you and to point out the obvious dangers of adverse reaction at home." Thus, "there is no justification for his considering that I endorsed his proposals." To highlight the King's duplicity, Harriman added that Paul had told Sulzberger that not only Harriman, but Grady as well, "would support his program." Sulzberger vouched for the latter point. Finally, only a few days before the crucial meeting in Athens, Paul Hoffman, the director of ECA, sent Harriman and John Nuveen—the ECA director for Greece—a telegram declaring that the United States "cannot take [the] initiative in overthrowing [the] parliamentary governmeиt" and installing a "dictatorship" or "authoritarian regime." Though it was "recognized that such [a] regime may ultimately come due to conditions over which we have no control," the "ECA will not agitate for powerful pressure by [the] US Mission to reconstitute [the] present government by drastic steps."[55]

On the other hand, the King's version of events has much to commend it. The dispatch of Hoffman's cable, for example, is difficult to explain without at least some suspicion of an ECA plan to use U.S. economic assistance to force drastic political changes. Moreover, it seems at least possible that Paul was not duplicitous when citing Grady's approval of the "Papagos solution," but merely confusing the U.S. ambassador's generally favorable comments of November 1948 with a green light for immediate action the following January. Furthermore, Sulzberger's account of his discussion with Harriman on January 3 not only established a motive for the ECA representative but indicated that Harriman went considerably further in recommending political changes than his cable to Grady implied. According to Sulzberger, although Harriman denied approving the Papagos solution, he thought "the Greek situation was very critical and urgent steps were required. The change in government depends entirely on Ambassador Grady. He doubts if Grady, who is sixty-eight years old, has the ability or drive." Harriman "said he . . . had merely agreed with Paul [that] it was necessary to do something immediately to obtain efficient leadership." Apparently, Sulzberger was not entirely reassured by this explanation, for he took the opportunity to lecture Harriman on democracy. "I gave him as my opinion," Sulzberger recalled, "that it would be disastrous for the United States to permit Paul to exceed his constitutional powers because we would be sacrificing principle for the expedient of efficiency."[56]

Grady, in particular, never doubted that Harriman and Nuveen had given Paul the go-ahead for undemocratic measures. On January 17, for example, he notified McGhee:

I have seen minutes of [the] conversation between Harriman and the King and Nuveen and the King (three days later) in which both are reported to have pressed their well known . . . views. Both are reported to have insisted on [a] drastic solution (along [the] lines of their views) if aid to Greece was to continue.[57]

In his unpublished memoirs, drafted years later from diplomatic correspondence he had retained, Grady developed this theme at greater length. "Nuveen persuaded Averell Harriman . . . that unless we adopted a 'tough policy' our ECA efforts could not succeed," he wrote. "When I arrived in Athens, I found that Ambassador Harriman had talked with the King and had arranged for Nuveen also to see the King and persuade him that what was needed in Greece was a semi-dictatorship under General Papagos. . . . The King was very much impressed with this statement because he felt that it came from those who controlled the purse strings." When he questioned Harriman and Nuveen, Grady observed, "they both stated that they had . . . discussed . . . nothing in the way of political matters. This was not true. I learned what the conversations had been . . . from the memoranda of conversations which the King dictated after these interviews." Such conversations, he recalled, bolstered by the enthusiasm of Van Fleet and his British counterpart for a Papagos government, came very close to triggering an authoritarian "solution." Grady remained "convinced that had our government, through Harriman and Nuveen, been successful, the American people would have been shocked."[58]

Although Grady emphasized the victory of democratic institutions, they continued to rest upon a shaky foundation. The political crisis of January 1949 had been surmounted only after the King summoned the leaders of the political parties to the palace and announced that if a "united government of national salvation" were not organized within twenty-four hours, he would be forced to "find another solution." For the Greek political leadership, as the U.S. ambassador noted, this produced a "shock" and the "fear that this may be [the] last chance to work out [a] parliamentary solution."[59] Furthermore, the New Party of Markezinis entered the cabinet, and General Papagos became commander-in-chief of the armed forces, exercising the new and extraordinary powers he had demanded: martial law, "preventive" censorship, and freedom from cabinet control. As if to underscore the fragility of representative institutions, parliament was suspended for more than four months, leaving politics and the war to the cabinet and Papagos.[60] "Politically, the situation has deteriorated," two high-level U.S. embassy officials warned Grady. "While we should continue to encourage democratic and parliamentary solutions . . . we should not oppose an extra-parliamentary solution as a last resort and as a natural evolution." Harriman complained to Acheson in late February 1949 that "we continue to encounter much the same difficulties in achieving concerted policies" and that Sophoulis and his Deputy Prime Minister "are recognizably too old and weary to pull their colleagues together effectively." The U.S. government, he stated, should "exercise strong discreet pressure" toward "better leadership, greater efficiency, and real coordination." Acheson seemed uneasy about Harriman's implication, for he replied that, while he agreed with him on a number of points, "the attempt to put into power a leader by extra-constitutional means would do more harm than good."[61]

Eventually it took a combination of Markezinis' political downfall and a military breakthrough to arrest the drift toward dictatorship. In March 1949, a controversy developed over the New Party chief's links to a currency scandal. Viewing Markezinis as a dangerous rival for leadership of the Greek right, Tsaldaris mobilized the Populists and, ultimately, Sophoulis, to force Markezinis' removal from the cabinet. Angered by the affair, the King plotted a counterattack.[62] On May 5, the U.S. chargé, Harold Minor, reported that Paul planned to accept Sophoulis's resignation and install a new government. If parliament did not accept it, the King would dissolve that body and call for new elections—although "undoubtedly not within [the] 45 day limit prescribed by [the] constitution." Initially, Minor recommended that "we inform the King [that] we will not stand in [his] way." In the following days, however, he thought better of it, urging that "in replying to [the] King we place emphasis on [the] need for restraint and patience and suggest that [the] present hopeful time when termination [of the] Greek travail may be brought about through force of arms . . . would hardly seem [the] time for [a] radical solution." Acheson agreed that such emergency action now seemed uncalled for; it was also dangerous in light of approaching congressional hearings. Informed of this, the King, according to Minor, "made rather pointed inquiry as to when Congressional hearings . . . might reasonably be expected [to] terminate"; eventually, though, he once again scrapped his plans. Thereafter, although Markezinis agitated for the postponement of elections and the appointment of a "service government" under Papagos, the State Department replied coldly. "I said I did not believe in the idea of being too flexible about the holding of elections," reported George McGhee, and "that I could not see the necessity for having such an Interim Government." Shortly after the war came to an end, Grady felt confident enough about Greece's political future to demand the dismissal of Van Fleet, whom he accused of intriguing with Papagos and the King, and to press forward with plans for the first general elections since the ill-fated ones of March 1946.[63]

The American government's ambivalence toward rightist "solutions" in Greece was exemplified by its treatment of

General Napoleon Zervas. Once the "gambling king" of Athens, Zervas had become commander of EDES during World War II and afterward a right-wing pillar of the Populist governments.[64] Citing the "recent summary arrests and deportations"—actions which might be "characterized as dictatorial" in forthcoming U.S. congressional hearings—MacVeagh urged Maximos on March 7, 1947 to "debarrass himself of General Zervas" as Minister of Public Order. Marshall added his own message along similar lines in May, while in August the British also pressed for his removal, complaining that the general's anti-Communism "lacks finesse."[65] During the cabinet crisis of August–September 1947, triggered by Liberal opposition to Zervas, the latter appealed to the U.S. ambassador to declare that the Americans did not demand his ouster. Refusing to issue such a statement, MacVeagh reported, he told Zervas that "both press and public in the United States are, rightly or wrongly, overwhelmingly of the opinion that he has dictatorial and fascistic tendencies"; therefore, "he does not inspire confidence as a member of any Government proposing to collaborate closely with the United States."[66] Dropped from the cabinet, Zervas regained popularity among American officials soon afterward. Rankin reported in January 1948 that, "although sulking a little and voicing the complaint that he was being unjustifiably neglected by the Americans, Zervas has been earnestly endeavoring to be a 'good boy.'" In early 1948, Lovett noted, the general received a "careful hearing" in Washington, and later that year explained his program at length to a U.S. embassy official in Athens. The Acting Secretary of State wrote in November 1948 that Zervas's views "seem realistic and sensible in many respects." He "should not be left with [the] impression that [the] US is irreconcilably opposed to his further participation in Greek public life." Indeed, there should be "frequent re-evaluation by [the] Embassy of [the] potential contribution of this rather special Greek personality in [the] highly special Greek situation."[67]

A right-wing zealot like Zervas received a considerably more favorable reception among American officials than did the Socialist Party of Greece. Although the Socialist Party had never been a major force in Greek politics, several factors contributed to its postwar importance: (1) the leadership of the distinguished constitutional lawyer, Alexander Svolos, former president of the wartime resistance "government"; (2) recognition of the party by the Socialist International, the coordinating body for democratic socialist parties around the world; and (3) its existence throughout the civil war as a legal political entity. Although the Socialists withdrew from EAM after the uprising of December 1944, they refused to condemn (or to support) the Markos insurrection. MacVeagh contended that the Socialist Party's program was "militantly anti-American and pro-Soviet"; it had so identified itself with the Communists and their fronts "as to become almost indistinguishable therefrom." There could be "no further doubt as to the 'fellow-traveling character' of the Socialist Party," wrote the American ambassador, who excoriated it in this fashion time and again.[68] Even so, the State Department insisted upon the advantages in "separating [the] non-Communist Left from [the] KKE" through a "public condemnation" of the rebellion. Svolos, of course, proved uncooperative and "would probably have to be arrested," Rankin reported. Eventually, the Greek government arrested his wife instead, claiming that an article she had written gave comfort to the rebels and called for a solution to the Greek civil war by a "policy of appeasement and reestablishment of democratic liberties." Svolos himself, dismissed from his teaching position at the University of Athens, assured embassy officials that his party sought political reconciliation rather than a Communist dictatorship, but they remained totally unconvinced.[69]

As Greek authorities accelerated their moves against the Socialist Party, U.S. officials either looked tactfully aside or assisted their actions. In early 1948, the Greek government arrested the editor and printer of the Socialist newspaper *Machi* for publishing an article that condemned wholesale executions of political prisoners. Citing the allegedly "extreme Marxist ideology" of the newspaper, Rankin claimed that "its political dialectic is for the most part indistinguishable from that of its suppressed [Communist] colleagues."[70] Although the State Department received protests against the continued incarceration of Mrs. Svolos from influential non-Communists—including French Socialist leader Leon Blum, American civil libertarian Roger Baldwin, and AFL president William Green—[71] Grady defended the action, arguing that the Greek government's record had been one of "remarkable leniency." The United States, he said, "should realize that [the] contradictory attitudes of urging Greece [to] vigorously fight Communist aggression on the one hand and on the other of decrying Greek attempts [to] control Communists behind the lines creates [an] atmosphere of uncertainty and confusion" and "encourage[s] fellow-traveling groups."[72] Nor was the U.S. embassy hostile to the Greek government's persistent denial of passports to Greek Socialist leaders to attend the conventions of fellow Socialist, Labor, and Social Democratic parties or of the Socialist International. Instead, it urged the State Department to press these parties to withdraw their invitations or to expel the Greek Socialists from the world Socialist movement. Grady reported in November 1948 that if the Socialist International could "be induced [to] disavow Svolos" and the Greek Socialists, "it might be worth while [to] persuade [the] Greeks [to] allow Svolos [to] participate in [the international] Congress. There would have to be [a] good prospect for public denunciation . . . however, before [the] Emb[assy] could effectively approach [the] Greek Govt [to] allow Svolos and [the] other reps [to] depart."[73]

Ironically, when the Socialist International did turn to the question of the Greek Socialist Party, its conclusions contradicted those of American officials. In May 1949, the world Socialist body adopted a report, written by Denis Healey of the British Labour Party and Victor Lareck of the Belgian Socialist Party, on the embattled Greek section. Although the Greek Socialist Party's attitude toward the civil war "has always been vague and equivocal," declared the report, the attitude of its leaders "has always been that of Left wing Socialists rather than fellow-travelers or crypto-Communists." Furthermore, "none of their political opponents . . . consider them to be crypto-Communists." It was "impossible" to estimate the Greek party's strength, noted the report, "since it has not been free to hold meetings over the last two years." Before that, however, it claimed some 15,000 members. The party's top labor leader, Dimitrios Stratis, was "a trade unionist of great personal integrity." As for the arrest of Mrs. Svolos, that had occurred "mainly in order to intimidate Svolos himself." The report concluded that the Greek Socialist Party was "the most representative Socialist organization" in Greece, and while its policies "may in the future leave much to be desired," it "cannot be considered as a fellow-traveling or crypto-Communist Party."[74] This analysis by an impeccably non-Communist—indeed, by 1949, anti-Communist— organization suggests that the uncompromising hostility of the Americans toward the only party of substance on Greece's non-Communist left owed less to the politics of the latter than to the political orientation of the former.

American officials also rejected the political leadership of a number of prominent Greek Liberals. Emmanuel Tsouderos, the wartime Prime Minister who had once been considered too close to the King, gradually became an advocate of amnesty, new elections, and a political solution to the civil war. In late 1948, Rankin reported disdainfully that Tsouderos was "out in left field" and had become an "appeaser." Naturally, he offered Greece "little in her search for effective leadership."[75] John Sofianopoulos, the Greek Foreign Minister in 1945–46, was another prominent politician who advocated broadening the government, granting amnesty, and arranging a political settlement of the war. In Rankin's eyes, this made him a "virtual if somewhat independent Soviet agent." Ambassador Grady labeled him a "fellow-traveler," and urged that he be kept from power. In early 1948, Rankin argued that the addition of Tsouderos, Sofianopoulos, or Svolos to the Greek government would destroy it by providing an "opening wedge" to the Russians.[76] Even more dangerous, from the embassy's standpoint, was the well-known newspaper publisher Demetrios Lambrakis, an unwavering partisan of the Liberal Party, especially its left wing. Although Lambrakis' advice had been rejected by Sophoulis when the latter formed a coalition with the Populists in September 1947, "there is no evidence that his interest and influence in the Liberal party has diminished," Rankin cautioned early the following year. "Given the views and influence of Lambrakis and the extreme orientation leftward of many Liberals . . . one cannot but have certain reservations" about depending upon the Liberal Party "to carry on the good fight." The embassy would "firmly discourage any broadening of the Government" to incorporate a "figure whose program is based on appeasement or any primarily political solution."[77]

Naturally, U.S. officials had little use for General Nicholas Plastiras, a former Prime Minister who emerged as a prominent advocate of political efforts to end the civil war. In November 1948, a group of Plastiras' followers sent U.N. President Herbert Evatt a telegram congratulating him for proposing that the civil war be halted by "measures of compromise." Grady, clearly irked by the move, suggested telling Evatt that the Plastiras group had "no public following in Greece" and that its "fellow-travelling character" was "becoming even more apparent." In a more detailed report containing a lengthy memorandum by Plastiras' followers, Rankin commented that it was "not difficult to understand why the General is popularly believed to have been 'captured' by fellow-travelers or worse, or why he has largely lost the prestige which otherwise might be accorded him as one of the 'grand old men' of Greek politics." The memorandum expounded, "in but thinly veiled language, the ideas which have become all too familiar from the mouthings of the Communists and their bedfellows."[78] In June 1949, when Plastiras told the embassy that he would like to visit Washington for conversations with U.S. officials, Grady conceded that the general was "not [a] Communist and probably not [a] conscious fellow-traveler"; nevertheless, "he is extremely politically naive and might be maneuvered into [a] position of front man by fellow-travelers." Soon afterward, Grady reported that the Greek government had denied Plastiras a passport and expressed his own relief that the general would not "be allowed to wander abroad." The good news from Grady crossed the telegram of Acting Secretary of

State James Webb, who told the ambassador to inform Plastiras' followers that, despite his "patriotic services to Greece
and anticommie record," the general could not be received
by high U.S. officials "since US policy aims at avoiding involvement in internal Grk politics." Having made this ritual
bow, Webb added that Plastiras should be urged to join the
"united front of all loyal Grks" in the "face [of the] common
commie peril."[79]

The problem with Liberals like Tsouderos, Sofianopoulos,
Lambrakis, and Plastiras was not that they were Communists
or even "fellow-travelers"; rather they were simply not as anti-
Communist as the Americans. As Griswold declared in a press
conference on May 20, 1948, U.S. officials did not believe
that there could be a political settlement of the civil war—or
at least none that would destroy what Webb termed the "commie polit[ical] influence and subversive mechanism in Greece."
A political settlement with the guerrillas, Rankin wrote, would
require "a promise of general elections carried out under a
government which would include, if not Communists, at least
certain champions of compromise and reconciliation between
the East and the West, such as Sofianopoulos or perhaps
Plastiras." Their introduction into the government "and a
renewed opportunity for the Communist and Communist-
front organizations . . . to carry on open as well as clandestine
propaganda and sabotage could be disastrous." There would
have to be "a long period of peace, relative economic stability,
and education before Communism is again permitted legal
existence in Greece." ("About one century," a State Department official scrawled in the margin.) Rankin concluded:
"Certainly not at present or in the immediate future can
Greece afford the disruption and treason that would ensue
from the reintroduction of the alien and subversive influence
of Communism."[80]

Here, then, was the real basis for the American concern
with Greek politics—what Rankin called "stamping out the
Communist revolt and influence in Greece."[81] The problem
was that, thanks to the wartime resistance and the postwar
reaction, Communism had become a major force in Greek

political life, with deep roots in the country's society, culture, and politics. Naturally, the Communists and their EAM sympathizers had no intention of being stamped out. Admittedly, left-wing violence had contributed to the militancy and popular appeal of the right and to a spreading disillusionment with those who had once been regarded as the heroes of the antifascist resistance. But many Greeks—and particularly many centrist politicians—were reluctant to pursue a bitter civil war among people who, however "subversive," were not "alien," but, unlike the Americans, Greek. To them, a political compromise—although not necessarily a Communist victory—seemed preferable to wholesale bloodshed and destruction. For this reason, American policymakers found their most consistent allies on the right of Greek politics, a region to which they sooner or later gravitated. This reliance on the right—tempered by the need for concessions to public opinion—deepened the determination of American officials to intervene in Greek politics, for it was far from certain that, in the course of normal parliamentary maneuvering, the right would emerge as the dominant element. Indeed, implicit in virtually all the secret communications of American policymakers was the assumption, unwritten but understood, that the Greeks could not be trusted with self-government.

5.
DEFENDING FREEDOM
1947–1949

Nearly every nation must choose between alternative ways of
life. . . . One way of life is . . . distinguished by free institutions
. . . guarantees of individual liberties, freedom of speech and
religion, and freedom from political oppression. . . . [The other]
relies upon terror and oppression, a controlled press and radio . . .
and the suppression of personal freedoms.

Harry Truman, March 12, 1947[1]

As Vandenberg and other congressional sympathizers with
the Truman administration's foreign policy had foreseen, promoting American intervention in Greece as a defense of freedom led easily to charges of hypocrisy. America's allies on the
Greek right—particularly within the armed forces and the
police—had little interest in civil liberties. Instead, they
tended to favor police state measures within the framework
of authoritarian institutions. Furthermore, since late 1946,
guerrilla activities had been growing in the mountains of
Greece. Amid alarming reports of troops ambushed and villages overrun, the Greek government was more inclined than
ever to abandon the liberal, positivist traditions of nineteenth-
century law and introduce newer concepts of twentieth-cen-
tury totalitarianism: ideological crimes, collective responsibility, and guilt by association. Nor did American officials
consider themselves bound by libertarian scruples. "We are
aware of the fact that in its efforts to combat the subversive
movement, there is a tendency on the part of certain elements
in the Greek Government to employ strong measures," Marshall wrote on July 11, 1947, in his instructions to Griswold.
"We should realize that stern and determined measures, although of course not excesses, may be necessary to effect the

136

termination of the activities of the guerrillas and their sup-porters as speedily as possible."[2]

In early 1947, "stern" measures were available in abun-dance. With the proclamation of the Truman Doctrine, Woodhouse wrote, "the government and its supporters ac-quired a new self-confidence, which often took ugly forms." In the countryside, right-wing mobs lynched prominent left-ists and the occupants of village prisons, while home guard units, anxious to claim the official bounty for the killing of "bandits," exhibited severed heads. From their mountain re-doubts, leftist guerrillas launched bloody retaliatory raids, fur-ther escalating the cycle of rural violence. Nor was the situ-ation calm in urban areas. On March 20, a member of the KKE's central committee was assassinated at noon on one of the principal streets in Salonika. Later that month, bands of armed men machine-gunned residents of that city's leftist districts. None of the murderers was apprehended.[3] The Greek government continued its prosecution of alleged sub-versives, increasing Greece's prison population by March 1 to more than 16,000, about twice its prewar size. Drawing on the loosely written Security Law of 1946, it also sent thousands of suspect persons and their families to remote island con-centration camps without trial or charge. George Polk, a CBS reporter, claimed that "anyone daring to criticize government policies was likely to be labelled 'Communist' and given a oneway ticket to a barren Aegean island." General Zervas, the none-too-scrupulous Minister of Public Order, notified MacVeagh that 7,238 Greeks had been exiled by the beginning of April. "No matter what the operations of the army," he confided to U.S. General William Livesay, "the main thing is to kill the Communists in the towns." Little wonder that Sophoulis publicly charged that the Greek government was "stifling civil liberties."[4]

In the spring of 1947, with congressional hearings on the Greek-Turkish aid program in progress, the State Department was caught in an uncomfortable situation. On April 11, writ-ing from Washington, MacVeagh complained to Prime Min-ister Maximos that American "public opinion is being constantly disturbed by reports of official toleration of rightist excesses and the application of security measures to non-subversive political opponents of the govt." State Department officials and "many others in authority realize fully . . . that drastic measures are necessary," MacVeagh explained, but "they are being embarrassed, and the success of the President's proposals is being imperilled, by the reports above mentioned." Presenting this note to Maximos, Keeley informed the latter than "more important than reassurance to the ambassador was to see [to it] that . . . observers, particularly foreign news correspondents," would file more favorable reports. Maximos promised to do his best.[5]

Cautioned by the Americans, Greek officials secured U.S. approval before their next major wave of arrests. On July 2, 1947—when, despite the simmering rebellion, the Communist Party remained legal, maneuvering for a cabinet reshuffle—Maximos questioned MacVeagh and General Livesay about taking immediate action against Communist leaders and organizers to prevent what he claimed would be escape abroad by some and major disruptions by others. In turn, the U.S. ambassador sounded out Secretary Marshall, who responded on July 3 that "we should not interpose objections." Marshall "assumed that [the] Greek Govt . . . would make clear that these leaders [were] . . . being arrested . . . for individual illegal acts or for participating in conspiracies or in organized subversive activities," thus avoiding damage to the "Greek case now under active discussion" in the U.N. Security Council. On receipt of this message, Maximos reassured the U.S. ambassador and authorized the action.[6] On July 9, at 2:00 A.M., the government's security forces began five days of nationwide arrests. At least 14,000 persons were rounded up and exiled, without trial, to the islands. Thanks to their superior intelligence network, most leading Communists escaped. But despite Marshall's caveats, thousands of persons were swept up in the raids who had no connection with the rebellion; among them were four employees of the British missions, one of them an English officer. As a result, by the end of July the small nation of Greece, with a population about the size of New York City's, had 36,622 persons under detention, about equally divided between prison and exile.[7]

British officials found the mass arrests of July 1947 considerably more disturbing than did their American counterparts. On July 14, the British chargé, Patrick Reilly, complained to MacVeagh that Greek authorities had "acted unwisely." While failing to do "any serious harm to the Communists," they "had damaged their position internationally at the worst possible moment." MacVeagh responded that he had "thought that the Greek Government contemplated arresting perhaps a dozen key men," but "supposed that the Greek Government's security information was so poor that they had to throw their net very wide to catch the right people." Four days later, Marshall informed the U.S. ambassador of British plans to press Greek officials to expedite screening and trials of those arrested, "to dissuade [the] Greek Govt from further indiscriminate arrests," and to see that "everything possible is done to mitigate [the] inevitable bad impression created abroad." When Marshall wondered if MacVeagh might want to address similar remarks to the Greek Foreign Office, the U.S. ambassador agreed to do so, albeit grudgingly. The Greek government, he insisted to Marshall, "cannot be blamed for [the] recent widespread preventive measures against [the] Communist menace, which is of a highly serious nature."[8] By contrast, the British seemed genuinely concerned about violations of individual liberties. British Ambassador Norton wrote ruefully that the "essence of deportation is detention without trial," and complained that the Foreign Office had never pressed for an end to this practice. Noting, with satisfaction, that a good proportion of exiles were being returned to their homes, another Foreign Office official remarked: "One can only ask oneself why they were ever removed."[9]

If American officials felt similar qualms, they did not lack the occasion to express them. To be sure, the Sophoulis government, which took office in September 1947, sought to institute less sweeping and repressive policies than its predecessors. By October, it had released 19,206 persons from their island detention camps. On the other hand, given the heightening rebellion, it continued to exile, imprison, and execute alleged subversives. Nor was Sophoulis totally able to control the Greek security forces, which had become a state within the state. According to Griswold, on December 10, 1947 the Prime Minister appealed to *him* to do something about the treatment of reserve officers. Out of 70 that had recently been called up for military service, 64 had been exiled to the islands. Sophoulis remarked sarcastically that if the proportion of Communists were this large, "the Communists and not the coalition should constitute the government."[10] To prepare for upcoming military operations against the guerrilla bands in the Peloponnesus, one Greek army general personally ordered the arrest of 4,300 local residents in late December 1948. Anticipating the protests of the center parties at the incarceration of many of their adherents, he cut the telephone wires to Athens to prevent word from reaching the capital before the arrested could be safely shipped off to concentration camps.[11] In May 1949, the U.S. consul general in Salonika reported another 2,800 arrests and deportations of "close relatives of Communists as well as suspected Communists carried out in northern Greece under Army orders." The exact number of "security" arrests by government authorities will probably never be known. But from July 1, 1947 to August 31, 1949, military courts-martial alone (which did not include trials under civil law or exile without trial) numbered 36,920.[12]

Once arrested, the accused often faced harsh measures and arbitrary treatment. Reporting on his visit to a combined civil-military prison in Salonika, the first commander of the U.S. Army Group in Greece described the conditions of persons arrested for the "display of a Communistic tendency." In each cell, measuring 15 by 25 feet, there were "twenty men . . . rolled in blankets lying on the bare earthen floor. Garbage attracting swarms of flies was piled a foot or more high . . . outside the cell rooms and the prevailing stench was nauseating." According to the officer accompanying him, these conditions "were not bad," by "Greek standards." The thousands of persons arrested in the Patras district reputedly received "very rough treatment," the U.S. consul wrote. An eyewitness saw one of the accused leaving his trial "heavily bandaged and hardly able to walk"; before his trial could be concluded, he had died. On other occasions, prisoners were dragged from their cells by government security forces and lynched.[13] If the accused received a trial—and survived it—he or she often fared relatively well. Of the 36,920 people court-martialed, 20,078 were acquitted. This fact, however, apparently owed something to the flimsiness of the charges. One former ECA official noted that he was called upon to testify in the trials of four people accused of crimes which had never occurred. Two, in fact, were accused of murdering him.[14]

Tens of thousands of Greeks never received trials but were simply banished to the grim island concentration camps. Although many died there of assorted privations, the camps were not designed as sites for extermination but as massive detention centers. To Makronissos, the chief detention island for men, the Athens government sent at least 30,000 persons, mostly conscripts considered of doubtful reliability (e.g., veterans of ELAS), for "reindoctrination." "When I remarked on the apparent wealth of artistic talent on Makronissos," reported a U.S. embassy official, the Greek military commander replied, "only half humorously, that all the young intellectuals in Greece had passed through this camp." Most of those interned on Makronissos were put through a lengthy program of political propaganda and coerced patriotism, together with physical and psychological pressure. Eventually, about 70 percent abjured Communism.[15] Many thousands of other Greeks passed varying lengths of time in exile on the islands of Ayios Efstratios, Ikaria, Larissa, Leros, Limnos, Trikkeri, Tripolis, and Zakynthos. As late as September 1949, Trikkeri alone housed 3,450 women, most of whom, reported Minor, had "close relatives in the guerrilla ranks." Detainees charged the Greek military authorities with harassment, torture, and occasional killings. The extent of such practices remains debatable, although not their occurrence. Exiles were sometimes released after screening, but the process was haphazard. On Ikaria, "the procedure of the investigation commissions is frankly farcical," the British chargé reported. "They were sent to Ikaria without any information about the great majority of the deportees and frequently asked the deportees themselves the reason for their arrest, of which the deportees were naturally usually ignorant."[16]

A British Police Mission report captured the flavor of exile life on Ayios Efstratios in August 1947. "Some 4,000 political offenders" existed on this "mass of bare, wind-swept volcanic rock," it noted. "There are 256 women (one with child at breast) and some hundreds of boys and girls. . . . Age is no bar, nor is physical disability. There is one old woman of over 80, one man is blind, several are crippled or partially paralysed. A great many are suffering from constitutional or chronic diseases; and an alarming number are in advanced stages of consumption." Currently, "at least 3,500 are without any form of shelter whatever." In addition there was "an acute shortage of drinking water" and "a very definite danger of typhoid," with washing possible only in the sea. What little food detainess could obtain was based "as much on their own money or on the funds supplied by their friends as on the Red Cross allowance." Commenting that there were "no sanitary arrangements" on the island except "one small latrine," the British Police Mission considered it a "wonder . . . that no epidemic has started." Although the commanding officer tried to segregate the prisoners by the seriousness of their offenses, he found this impossible, for he could obtain documents on only 100 of the detainees. Many claimed that they had no idea why they were arrested, for they had seen no warrant, order, or court. Others claimed that they had completed the statutory banishment of one year and should be released. The British Police Mission concluded that, "even if the various improvements contemplated and projected are carried out," the living conditions on the island would be "awful." It warned of "a catastrophe which may take any form."[17]

As before, exile and imprisonment operations proceeded with the general approval of American officials. To be sure, in November 1946, MacVeagh had told the King that "wives and children of fugitives should no longer be imprisoned and exiled as hostages" and had urged the Prime Minister to "amnesty all persons not guilty of actual crimes." But when the Greek government ignored this advice and the rebels escalated the revolt, U.S. officials accommodated themselves to the situation. "There has been a great deal of criticism of these camps" on Makronissos, Griswold cabled in November 1947, but "the report of the U.S. Army Group would indicate that the men are being well treated and that the objectives are being achieved." The following spring, attacking the "distorted picture" of Greece presented by the *New York Herald Tribune*, AMAG's chieftain publicly defended the Makronissos camps. The inmates, he insisted, merited incarceration (they "were found to have affiliations which cast grave doubt upon their loyalty to the state"), they were "well treated," and they merely received "indoctrination courses and other training."[18] Replying to the Greek government's inquiry about a new series of security arrests in March 1948, Rankin stated that he considered such arrests "quite necessary and justifiable as long as they were not of the 'mass' variety." Marshall approved Rankin's reply, suggesting only that the press be given background details "justifying" the arrests as they occurred, thus minimizing "unfavorable publicity." Despite the sweeping nature of the official crackdown, the following month Rankin commended what he called the "relatively modest scale upon which the Greek Government is taking legal action against these enemies of the State" and claimed that Greek judicial machinery afforded "reasonable protection to the individual—certainly as much as can be expected under present circumstances."[19]

In the context of the Greek civil war, American officials remained less concerned about defending civil liberties than about developing a good public relations program. Explaining that "much of the calumny to which the Greek Government has been subjected on the part of the international press has been the result of poor, inadequate publicity," the U.S. chargé expressed his confidence in new "press communiques to be issued by the Greek authorities explaining the details of the various executions." Early the following year, Rankin complained of the "alarming tendency . . . to play up . . . such ideas as that things are not going well, that the Greeks are acting badly and are hardly worth saving" and "that our aid is not being properly utilized." According to the U.S. chargé, "we can hardly do less than give Greece . . . the kind of support that the cheering section would give their football team if they truly desired victory." In June 1949, the counselor of the U.S. embassy, Harold Minor, reassured the State Department that criticism of widespread arrests and executions represented "a political weapon used by communists abroad to smear the activities and integrity of the Greek state." In general, he wrote, "there is little doubt that Greek justice has performed its function admirably under very difficult circumstances." The problem faced by Greece was not one "of 'rejuvenating' Greek justice or 'reforming' the army courts martial system, but rather, of ensuring the use of every available opportunity to combat communist propaganda."[20]

The Greek government's policy of executing political prisoners caused some of the most serious propaganda problems faced by American officials. During the civil war, the Greek judiciary pronounced thousands of politically linked death sentences, including 2,961 handed down by civil courts for participation in the December 1944 uprising and another 4,849 delivered by military court-martial for participation in the "third round" of 1946–49. From these two groups, an estimated 3,136 Greeks were actually executed (92 percent from the latter category) before the process came to a halt in September 1949.[21] Although U.S. officials professed satisfaction with the fairness of the Greek judicial system, the wisdom and compassion of the military courts, in particular, left much to be desired. Thanks to the Ministry of War's classification of Jehovah's Witnesses—the Protestant sect which preached the immorality of military service—as an "offshoot" of the KKE, the Greek military arrested hundreds of its members; many received severe sentences and some were executed.[22] Seventh Day Adventists faced similar difficulties, as did many persons whose "crimes" were highly questionable. A young man tending his tiny shop in Jannina when a woman sought to solicit funds for the families of exiled Communists received a death sentence for failing to report her to the security police. Even the State Department thought the punishment in this case "incredible"; on the other hand, its ability to act was hampered by the Greek military's practice of executing convicted persons within three days of the court-martial.[23]

American officials initially provided undeviating support for political executions. Although the Greek government complained to Washington of U.S. constraints in June 1947, MacVeagh retorted that these were "childish and petulant inaccuracies." The U.S. embassy had "never 'requested [the] Greek Government to suspend [the] execution of traitors.'" By early 1948, however, despite frequent executions of prisoners, the Greek government had run up a considerable backlog of death sentences, including almost all those dating from the December 1944 upheaval. According to Rankin, Christos Ladas, the Greek Minister of Justice, "courageously tackled the problem" by planning the execution of these persons in small groups in widely separated areas. Ladas hoped that this "would have a wholesome effect upon the guerrillas" and would at the same time "avoid unfavorable publicity." Rankin considered this an excellent idea. Although "some of those persons imprisoned and sentenced to death after the December 1944 rebellion may not have been at that time hardened Communists, it is unlikely that they have been able to resist the influence of Communist indoctrination organizations existing within most prisons." Marshall instructed the embassy in March 1948 that the State Department would not "interfere with [the] administration of Grk justice and fully understands [the] necessity for [a] firm policy toward [the] communists." Calling attention to the appearance of unfavorable stories about these plans in the American press, however, he warned that Greek authorities should "be prepared [to] offer [an] explanation . . . which will satisfy world public opinion."[24]

To the distress of American officials, world opinion did not coincide with their own. The widespread public executions, highlighted by newspaper stories and by the leftist assassination of Ladas on May 1, 1948, set off an international furor. In Norway, the ruling Labor Party denounced the mass executions as a "wave of terror," while the conservative opposition attacked them for violating the most elementary principles of justice. In Denmark, newspapers of every opinion assailed the policy of Greek authorities, and the government delivered a formal note of protest.[25] Winston Churchill himself complained about the executions to Queen Frederika and told the new Minister of Justice to "leave the killing of prisoners to the Bolshevists." From the British Foreign Office came word of Bevin's anger at the sudden execution of large numbers of persons linked to the 1944 events and of his belief that it might "throw the whole question [of] British policy re[garding] Greece into [the] melting pot again." Anxiously, Marshall instructed the U.S. embassy in Great Britain to emphasize the "relative moderation [of] Grk justice despite extreme Communist provocation" and the necessity to "at least minimize public evidence of differences . . . where strong British statements will be contrasted with US silence." Embarrassed by the uproar, the U.S. Secretary of State fell back on blaming the Communists for his difficulties. The Ladas assassination, he wrote on May 15, "was probably conceived as [a] diabolically clever, double-edged propaganda weapon." Greek authorities had "correctly" refused "to be intimidated," he noted, but should "avoid adding fuel to [the] propaganda flame" by first executing those "guilty of [the] most atrocious crimes and giving full publicity in each case."[26]

Stung by the international criticism, the State Department and elements in the Greek government began to retreat on the issue of political executions. In his dispatch of May 15, 1948, Marshall suggested that Greek authorities "might also give consideration to the possibility" that mass executions of those convicted for actions in December 1944 "might create grave political difficulties from [the] viewpoint [of] world opinion . . . which would more than offset any advantages from [the] point of view of maintaining law and order." That July, Rankin reported that the new Minister of Justice, George

Melas, opposed the continuation of executions along these lines, claiming "that this bloodshed and the hatred it engenders must be stopped." By contrast, the U.S. chargé bitterly objected to any change of course; instead, he argued that the Greek and U.S. governments should "proceed quietly along the lines laid down by Mr. Ladas." If a furor again developed, the Americans and the British should dig in "and prepare to take [propaganda] losses." This advice, however, had lost its savor in Washington. On August 6, 1948, Marshall notified the U.S. embassy: "We feel [that] Communist propaganda, uninformed reporting and certain Grk policies (particularly regarding executions and strikes) have succeeded in stigmatizing [the] Grk Govt in some sectors of world opinion." Consequently, he suggested that Greek court-martial policy "be re-examined with [a] view to reducing executions to [a] minimum." "Simple political expediency" required limiting executions pending the termination of the U.N. General Assembly meeting and postponing "for several months" any execution of those condemned for actions in December 1944.[27]

But the effort to narrow the scope of political executions ran afoul of the U.S. embassy. In a cable of August 21, 1948, Ambassador Grady insisted that such a policy would "play directly into Soviet hands" by validating outside criticism and preserving the Communist "'hard core' for [a] future armed attempt." The "US task," he maintained, was "to see that nothing prevents [the] Greeks from finishing [a] job well started or robs their victory of its effectiveness." Attacks on the Greek government's policy should be met "by positive presentation [of the] Greek position on its merits." Indeed, "Greek policy has been extremely lenient; fair trial is afforded, only those guilty of [the] most flagrant acts of open treason are condemned to death and [the] sentences of many of these are commuted to imprisonment." When protests erupted over the court-martial death sentence meted out to Manolis Glezos, a young man who had achieved wartime fame by tearing down the Nazi swastika from the Acropolis, Grady was unmoved. "Compassion might better be directed towards [the] suffering people of Greece," the ambassador noted, "particularly the thousands of young girls who have been ravished and the young boys who have been forced to fight and be killed in the guerrilla war."[28] Not even the attack on Jehovah's Witnesses ruffled his complacency. The embassy would make an "informal approach" to the Minister of War, he promised the uneasy State Department; but "our action and attitudes in this matter . . . should . . . be tempered by [the] degree to which this sect is proved to be under Communist domination."[29] In contrast to Grady, Acheson cabled that the State Department was "frankly shocked" at the execution of members of Jehovah's Witnesses. But with Grady unwilling to compromise, further State Department inclinations to temper the execution of political prisoners were brushed aside until the war's end.[30]

As Grady's remarks indicated, behind the U.S. support for political executions lay the determination of American and Greek officials to destroy the Greek Communist Party. Throughout 1946, in accordance with the Varkiza agreement, the KKE continued its role as a legal organization, engaged in the feverish maneuvering for advantage that characterized Athens politics. Although Zachariades ordered Markos to the mountains in the latter part of that year to give some structure to the nascent rural revolt, party leaders tarried in Athens, keeping more conventional political options open. The Athens government hesitated to proceed officially against the KKE, fearful of the adverse effects on international opinion. In the words of the director of the Greek anti-Communist intelligence network, the government preferred "entrusting" attacks upon the party "unofficially and secretly to individuals both within and without the government structure and to certain rightist organizations." Nevertheless, in August of that year, Thomas Karamessines, the top Central Intelligence Group operative at the U.S. embassy, reported on plans by the Greek general staff "to neutralize the KKE completely and effectively, even if it be necessary to declare the party illegal." Karamessines wondered "whether precipitate and ill-considered moves will not do more damage than good," but agreed "with the Staff's definition of the problem." MacVeagh considered his intelligence chief's advice "unexceptional."[31]

By 1947, with the rebellion gathering momentum, these plans reached fruition. In May, the British ambassador reported that members of the U.S. embassy had been discussing "the necessity" of outlawing the KKE. The British argued that this step would merely drive the Communists underground, but the Americans were impatient and ultimately prevailed. As Norton wrote, the U.S. embassy now encouraged the Greek goverment to "adopt sterner measures against the Communist Party." The American-authorized arrests of July 1947 followed, placing KKE leaders behind bars or inspiring them (and many others) to flee to the mountains. Subsequently, the rebel bands grew more fearsome, devastating isolated villages and cutting off large rural areas from official control. That December, with the rebellion in full sway, the Athens government passed a law formally dissolving the KKE, EAM, and all groups associated with them; seizing their assets; and making the expression of revolutionary ideas a crime subject to imprisonment. From the standpoint of American officials, this was a struggle to the death. "A cessation of hostilities in the immediate future would save the Communist cadre from destruction," Rankin warned in May 1948. "There must . . . be no leniency toward the confirmed agents of an alien and subversive influence."[32]

Keeping tabs on alleged Communists became a primary responsibility of the growing U.S. intelligence network in Greece. A few months following the December 1944 revolt, General Donovan, the OSS director, had instructed top OSS officials that henceforth the major target for intelligence operations in Greece would be Communist activity. Well aware of this, the KKE, as MacVeagh noted, instructed all party cells to "beware Brit[ish and] US . . . secret agents."[33] In 1946, the OSS was absorbed into the Central Intelligence Group, headed by Karamessines, the "special attaché" at the U.S. embassy who, according to the ambassador, maintained "working liaison with all Greek and British security offices as well as [a] sizeable US security file." By the fall of 1947, the embassy was coordinating its intelligence activities with the U.S. Army Group in Greece, AMAG, the FBI, the Greek Special Staff, the State Department, the British Troops Greece, and the British Military Mission. Within the U.S. embassy a "policy committee" directed intelligence operations after early 1947; it included the ambassador, the counselor, the economic counselor, the cultural attaché, the military attaché, and the naval attaché.[34] On July 2, 1947, the State Department instructed the embassy to begin submitting regular monthly dispatches on "Communist activities in Greece," focusing on party organization, recruitment, sources of funding, activities of leaders and "satellite" organizations, "infiltration of Communists into non-Communist groups," relations with foreign Communists, "activities in labor groups," and "anti-American propaganda." The embassy initially resisted this task because of understaffing, but it found the wherewithal to begin the reports that October.[35]

Although very little is known about American intelligence operations in Greece, they appear to have been widespread and of considerable importance. U.S. operatives filed reports on suspicious Greeks,[36] investigated U.S. personnel, and assisted Greek authorities in carrying out their mass deportations of alleged guerrilla sympathizers to island concentration camps. When New York City residents sought to hire members of Greece's left-wing maritime union to work on Israeli ships, the State Department's security division interdicted the attempt. When U.S. citizens wrote letters protesting death sentences in Greece, Griswold forwarded their names, addresses, and background details to the FBI "for the completion of its files."[37] In return, the FBI regularly sent the U.S. embassy reports on the "Communist" ties of Greek-American organizations.[38] To improve Greek intelligence work, Karamessines organized his Greek counterparts into KYP, the Greek central intelligence agency. After 1947, when the Central Intelligence Group became the basis of America's new Central Intelligence Agency, it was only a matter of time before the CIA organized a permanent abode for itself in

Greece. Karamessines established it in the late 1940s, probably in the spring of 1949, and it quickly grew into one of the most important CIA stations in Europe. It provided the United States with a window on the Balkans, the Mediterranean, and the Near East; at the same time, it served as the nerve center for the final phase of America's counterinsurgency campaign in Greece.[39]

The State Department faced a more dificult problem formulating a policy toward the non-Communist rebels, who constituted a substantial majority of the insurgent forces. They had joined the rebellion primarily because of sympathy with its professed aims, persecution by rightist vigilantes or government authorities, and conscription by guerrilla bands. To allay outside criticism of the Greek government and to undermine the guerrilla struggle, American officials sponsored a program of amnesty for those guerrillas who would lay down their arms. But few rebels availed themselves of it for, as Porter wrote, while the program "looked plausible on paper . . . the appointment of General Zervas as Minister of Public Order completely destroyed anyone's inclination to take" it "seriously." By May 1947, the failure of the amnesty program had acquired important ramifications, for the U.N. investigating commission was ready to recommend one supervised by the United Nations. U.S. officials feared that this would imply a rebuke to the Greek government and would remove the situation from their hands. Marshall thus notified the U.S. member of the commission that a U.N. recommendation on amnesty would not be acceptable and cabled MacVeagh that it was "essential that Greece should itself take [the] initiative on [the] amnesty question immediately." A Greek government announcement "should simply state its intention of requesting international observation in [the] very near future but not specify to whom that request will be made." According to Marshall, the "ultimate aim" of the State Department was:

1. To present [a] clear Greek record to world opinion;
2. To obtain [a] Greek initiative which might forestall S[ecurity]

C[ouncil] action on [a] Greek internal matter and S[ecurity] C[ouncil] criticism of [the] character of [the] Greek Govt.
3. To improve [the] Greek internal situation by effectively weakening [the] guerrilla movement.[40]

The Greek government, however, proved obdurate. Tsaldaris and the King objected that further talk of amnesty would undermine the morale of the Greek armed forces, encourage the rebel bands, and raise the possibility of Russian participation in international observation. Disgusted, MacVeagh thought that "Tsaldaris' stupidity was never more in evidence." After further American pressure, Prime Minister Maximos did proclaim the Greek government's "intention of requesting impartial foreign observers of one or more countries . . . to observe the fair and equitable treatment accorded anyone desirous to take advantage of the clemency of the state."[41] But no follow-up ensued.[42] In September 1947, the Sophoulis government did make what Keeley called a "sincere amnesty offer in contrast to [the] past half-hearted and poorly executed gestures." Yet Sophoulis refused international supervision, claiming that his past support for it had been purely "symbolic." Tsaldaris suggested that AMAG or the British serve as the amnesty guarantor. For a time, the U.S. government continued to suggest international observation. But on October 4, 1947, noting the reluctance of Tsaldaris "to take immediate steps for foreign supervision," Lovett instructed the U.S. embassy to drop the issue.[43]

In these circumstances, few guerrillas voluntarily surrendered,[44] and—after a two-month amnesty period—the Greek government's policy veered back to one of retribution for "bandit" actions. A typical propaganda leaflet, dropped by the Greek military in April 1948 on rebel territory, declared:

Bandits!
The time has come for you to pay. . . . By fire and iron I shall overshadow in reprisals all the crimes you have done. . . . You will pay for all. The revenge will be great and complete. . . .
Bandits!
Alas for you. For every house you have burned and for every Greek you have assassinated tens of you will be killed. . . . I foretell

you this because I have the power of our great country and our
great allies, Americans and British. . . .

> The High Military Commander
> of Peloponnesus

And, in fact, the treatment received by those who fell into
government hands could be quite vicious. According to a
February 1948 *New York Times* dispatch:

> Frenzied Greeks jeered, pelted and jabbed 121 captured guerrillas
> who were forced to march in an army victory parade through Sa-
> lonika's streets today.
>
> Had it not been for the display of modern war equipment, the
> spectacle might have come out of the Fourth Century B.C., when
> Alexander the Great sent back to Salonika . . . his conquered ene-
> mies chained to chariot wheels.
>
> A shrieking crowd estimated at more than 200,000 waited for
> hours to torment the captive rebels. . . .
>
> First came the grinning soldiers, mounting Bren guns, toting
> tommy guns, on foot, on motorcycles and trucks. . . .
>
> The guerrillas, weary from three days of fighting, straggled two
> and three abreast between army columns on each side of the street.
> They were pelted with rotten eggs, rolls of paper and bottles. Some
> Greeks armed with sharpened sticks broke through the soldier lines
> and prodded the rebels. The soldiers did not stop them.
>
> Leading the guerrillas was a woman, dressed in khaki. She
> marched proudly, without flinching. At her side were two men, the
> chins thrust out. Blood ran from a gash on one's forehead.
>
> Those behind looked more weary. The three-day battle in the
> mountains . . . showed on their muddy and blood-stained clothes,
> in their glazed eyes and bearded faces.
>
> . . . All who were capable of hobbling were pushed into the ranks
> for the two-mile parade. . . . There appeared little doubt they would
> be executed.

Most captured guerrillas were apparently tried by military
court-martial or put through the island "reindoctrination"
programs. Grady noted: "Guerrillas who surrender, especially
those who bring their arms with them, receive some prefer-
ential immediate treatment, but there is no set policy in this
regard."[45]

The collapse of American efforts to make amnesty programs

a success did not merely reflect the punitive drives of Greek authorities. With the Greek-Turkish aid program safely afloat and the U.N. investigation concluded, there was less need than in the past to attend to public relations. Moreover, key American officials, particularly in the U.S. embassy, agreed with the Greek authorities on the necessity of harsh measures. Only when the rebel forces were shattered and "deprived of hope and help," claimed Rankin in May 1948, should "surrendered guerrillas . . . be afforded an opportunity, through constructive labor . . . to earn their way back . . . to full citizenship and participation." Later that year, Grady argued that both the American and Greek governments "must resist those elements within their respective countries which . . . agitate for full political amnesty." Amnesty "may and perhaps should be granted" to those who could prove they were forcibly recruited by the rebels. But this should not be done "until after the state has successfully reasserted its dominance and then only in practice, not as a matter of stated policy." When the "bandit uprising has been quelled," the ambassador wrote the following year, the Greek government "may be able [to] apply measures of leniency on [a] large scale." But it remained to "be seen how many leaders, staff members and other persons there will be who cannot remain [in] Greece."[46]

When civil or military prosecution seemed inappropriate, Greek authorities turned to other means to attack dissidents or to undermine their influence. Within the Orthodox Church, political lines hardened perceptibly. In June 1947, an ecclesiastical court tried the Bishop of Kozani, a leader of the wartime resistance. Found guilty of "EAMism," he was defrocked. Meanwhile, the Greek government began political investigations of the civil service, with a legal centerpiece modeled, almost word for word, on President Truman's Loyalty Order of March 22, 1947. Commenting on the ensuing purge, Griswold noted that authorities in Athens were determined to "weed out all Communists and fellow travelers." Naturally, the Greek right applauded what one Populist journal (the mouthpiece of Tsaldaris) called this elimination of the "Slavo-Communist putrescence." Enthusiastic about the inception of their own struggle against domestic subversion, members of the Truman administration were not far behind. MacVeagh, in fact, complained to a congressional committee in early 1947 that "the fellow-travelers have probably increased quite a bit in the professional classes and the universities. The intelligentsia rather falls for the kind of propaganda the Communists put out."[47] Later that year, arguing that the Bishop of Kozani had "travelled without deviation along the Communist Party line," MacVeagh informed the State Department that he would not even acknowledge receipt of the prelate's letters.[48]

The Greek press became an important focus of official concern. In early 1947, freedom of the press prevailed in Athens, but the situation was far more constricted in the rural areas. During the mass arrests of July 1947, government authorities incarcerated the editors of northern Greece's Communist newspapers; shortly afterward, their newspapers were formally suppressed. On September 5, the Athens government suspended key provisions of the Greek constitution guaranteeing press freedom; henceforth, any newspaper could be shut down if it published unauthorized news of military action against the guerrillas, statements by insurgent forces, or comments unfavorable to the armed forces. That October, a court order closed down the KKE's *Rizospastis* and EAM's *Eleftheria Ellada*.[49] Meanwhile, the editor of *Rizospastis* received a six-year jail term for an article allegedly defaming the royal family, and the political editor of *Eleftheria Ellada* was arrested. Drawing on a new law which empowered the government to prohibit the publication of any new journals, the Greek Press Ministry refused permission to the KKE and EAM to publish newspapers in November.[50] The following month, when news of the Greek army's release of armed right-wing extremists appeared in the press, the editors of *Vima, Ethnos, Nea,* and *Eleftheria*—all Liberal journals—were hauled before an army court-martial. Distraught, Sophoulis complained to American officials about "these fascist measures," but claimed he was powerless to prevent them.[51] Indeed, military censorship of the Greek press continued for years. American officials apparently made no efforts to counteract these practices; instead, they authorized a number of them and concentrated on obtaining what they considered the proper content in the Greek press.[52]

It was not the Greek but the American press which particularly worried U.S. officials. "The American press should be an instrument of our foreign policy," Forrestal told Byrnes. To their regret, however, it was not. Ever since 1945, U.S. officials had been bewailing what MacVeagh called the "pro-EAM reporting of American correspondents." The "picture given of Greece" in *Time's* "propaganda," the ambassador complained in July 1946, "might well . . . have been lifted bodily from some issue of the Greek communist daily *Rizospastis*."[53] With the proclamation of the Truman Doctrine, American press dispatches from Greece assumed even greater significance. At a planning meeting that spring, Porter warned "that the importance of the non-Greek press could not be over-emphasized," for "publicity on the program might create an unfavorable impression in this country." McGhee reassured him that "many top officials" appreciated this fact; Harriman, for example, had "stated that a good account of our work in Greece in the U.S., utilizing the press, radio, and still and motion pictures, is of utmost importance." At his July 1947 meeting with top State, Navy, and Treasury Department officials before his departure for Greece, Griswold received specific instructions on "public relations." According to the minutes, "it was felt that great caution should be exercised by the Mission in its relations with the press, particularly in regard to dealing with newspapermen who were interested in the sensational side of the picture."[54]

The U.S. government went to considerable lengths to ensure a flow of favorable news about Greece to the American people. In the spring and summer of 1947, State Department officials participated in radio programs, met with journalists, placed articles in magazines, distributed press releases "to writers for magazines or radio use," developed "color material on members of the mission," held a luncheon for "top CBS commentators," and arranged for the appearance of favorable newspaper columns. Conversely, unflattering materials were weeded out. Alerted to a forthcoming critical story by Frank Gervasi, the Washington reporter for *Collier's*, Francis Russell of the State Department's Division of Public Affairs suggested to "one or two" close friends of the publisher that they inform him of the views of this "truculent Sicilian" and of the "questionable patriotism" of his article. In May 1948, Griswold wrote a lengthy piece for the *New York Herald Tribune* sharply criticizing the reporting of two of its correspondents (Homer Bigart and William Shirer) for "giving an uncertain over-all picture of Greece at a time when American public opinion should be positively informed on the subject." Later that year, the State Department succeeded in quashing a series of articles slated for the *New York Times* on U.S. embassy support for authoritarian political solutions.[55]

From the standpoint of U.S. officials, taming American newsmen in Greece was imperative. In July 1947, at Griswold's meeting with top American policymakers, Forrestal advised him to talk with the publishers of the *New York Times*, the *New York Herald Tribune*, and the Scripps-Howard papers, as well as with the heads of United Press and Associated Press, about the "left-wing or fellow-traveler writers serving the American press" in Greece and to "suggest . . . changes." Apparently, the State Department had few qualms about choosing the representatives of the news media for, only a few months earlier, Marshall solicited MacVeagh's advice on a "suitable" American newspaper correspondent to work in Athens for ABC. In November 1948, the Secretary of State spoke with the general manager of United Press about the dangers of appointing the *Christian Science Monitor's* correspondent, whom the State Department considered a leftist, the UP representative in Greece; as a result, U.S. officials were promised a "double breasted Americano."[56] Within Greece, the U.S. embassy brought what pressure it could on erring newsmen. At an "off the record" meeting in January 1948, Rankin lectured Homer Bigart on his alleged political indiscretions. The following month, the U.S. chargé instituted regular press conferences "to brief the correspondents on the Embassy and AMAG points of view." He wrote bitterly that "some means" had to be found "to instill in individual US correspondents a sense of responsibility concerning their reporting, either directly or through their publishers."[57]

Despite some gains, however, U.S. officials continued to find the news reported from Greece extremely objectionable. The "recent reporting" of *New York Herald Tribune* correspondent Seymour Freiden, wrote MacVeagh in August 1947, "though considerably improved over that of last year, has been consistently fault-finding in tone and plainly revealing of the author's hostility towards the present Greek Government." Although Robert Vermillion had "confined his most recent reporting from Greece for the United Press wire services mainly to Greek press handouts, his 'background' articles for the United Press itself and his attitude toward the present Greek regime have been openly and consistently critical." Other reporters had "gone further," including "the notorious Constantine Poulos," correspondent for the *Nation*. "The adventurous youngsters and elderly social misfits who largely represent the American press here are alike incapable of applying anything like sound knowledge or balanced judgment," MacVeagh complained. And yet, it remained crucial that "the journalists we support abroad be capable of representing us adequately and . . . create confidence both here and at home."[58] In February 1948, Rankin reported that the "embassy [was] increasingly concerned over [the] new wave [of] misrepresentation and vilification of Greeks and their Government in [the] US press." Could not the department bring the necessary pressure to bear upon "responsible publishers" to rectify the situation? Acknowledging the problem but reversing the solution, Marshall replied that "although [the] Dept [is] urgently considering local measures to present [the] US with better balanced reporting," the "most effective corrective action can be taken only in Greece since much material used by American correspondents clearly originates with American sources within Greece."[59]

After May 1948, the best-known American newsman in

Greece was undoubtedly George Polk, a CBS correspondent whose bound body was discovered that month floating in Salonika Bay. Like many other U.S. journalists, Polk had defended the idea of American intervention in Greece, while at the same time leveling persistent criticism at the reactionary policies of the Athens government.[60] Such criticism had infuriated the Greek right, as had his plan to interview Markos at rebel headquarters. According to Polk's widow, both the police and rightists had threatened him shortly before his death. Skeptical of the outcome of any investigation of Polk's murder by Greek authorities, the Overseas Writers Association initiated one of their own, headed by General Donovan. His chief investigator, Colonel James Kellis of the U.S. Air Force, originally accepted the version of events provided by the Greek police and approved by U.S. officials: that Communists had killed Polk. But, as Kellis later wrote: "I collected other information that contradicted the official investigation and reported to General Donovan that I believed there was an attempted right-wing cover-up." This created a serious dilemma. "Many of our officials here were concerned that if the extreme Right committed this murder and were discovered," it would "upset our aid program to Greece." Thus, Kellis found himself "between what I thought is the truth and our national and personal interest."[61]

Confronted with this choice, most U.S. and Greek officials placed a lower priority on truth. Rankin asked to meet with Kellis, telling him, "I don't see why you are breaking your back trying to uncover who killed this correspondent." According to Kellis, Rankin, the Greek police, and others "tried to impress on me the need to pin this murder on the Communists." When Kellis refused to be a party to such deception, Rankin informed Marshall on July 17 that the "Embassy believes [that the] sooner Kellis [is] removed from [the] scene the better." Within a few days, the Air Force recalled Kellis to Washington. No successor was appointed. Meanwhile, Donovan, ostensibly acting in a private capacity, worked closely with U.S. and Greek officials. Eventually, they produced what many of Polk's news colleagues considered a rigged trial, designed to prove a Communist plot to murder Polk. "It was a cover-up," recalled Marquis Childs; "a sham," observed Irving Gilman; "a whitewash," declared Alexander Kendrick. Dazed and dismayed by the proceedings, Polk's 19-year-old brother, William, asked Donovan bluntly if it were not important to get at the facts. "Why are you asking such difficult questions and making things so complicated?" the former intelligence chief retorted in exasperation. "Don't you understand we are in the middle of a war? You are a smart young man. . . . If you keep on, you will ruin your career."[62]

At least in part, the hostility and cynicism expressed by American officials toward the news media reflected frustration at their inability to mobilize the wholehearted support of American and world opinion behind U.S. policy. In late 1947, Cromie complained of the jaundiced view many Europeans held of the U.S. program. Early the following year, McGhee predicted that continued military aid for Greece would "elicit serious opposition both in Congress and among the public." Opinion analyses, he stated, showed that "the public has little understanding of: 1) The deterioration of the military situation . . . ; 2) the strategic importance of Greece in halting Communist expansion in the Near East; 3) the strategic importance of Greece in the protection of Near East petroleum resources." According to a State Department study done on September 30, 1948, although a majority of U.S. citizens did favor American aid to Greece, only 22 percent considered Greece a democracy, as compared to 45 percent who did not; among the college educated, the results were even more unfavorable.[63] Clearly the situation demanded attention. In September 1947, a meeting of American and British officials agreed on "the ineptness of Greek propaganda" and suggested specific remedies. That December, contending that "the value of propaganda as a weapon of war and politics should need no argument," the political section of the U.S. embassy called for "a concerted campaign . . . to arouse the people within Greece," to "break guerrilla morale," and to counteract "the widespread confusion of world opinion." The United

States "should develop the psychological warfare program already begun," Rankin added, and the Greeks, too, "must thus be taught to preach a dynamic doctrine of victory."[64]

The U.S. psychological warfare program apparently commenced in late 1948. Early the following year, Acheson reported on "steps . . . being taken to promote and assist an intensive Greek information program." The State Department was "supporting this project by providing funds and personnel, including experts in different media. Care will, of course, be exercised to keep [the] US role in [the] background." One such operation, suggested by Henderson as early as 1947, was the U.S. construction of a broadcasting station in Salonika to "cover the Balkans." According to the National Security Council, "nominally this station will be Greek-owned and operated."[65] Many other projects, some of them apparently linked to the CIA, remain secret.[66] In early March 1949, Ambassador Grady notified the State Department that he had appointed a "special morale group" consisting of Greek and American officials, the latter to "remain anonymous." Its first major activity involved the promotion of "Work and Victory Week," a propaganda venture suggested by the ambassador's wife. From March 20 to 25, Greece was convulsed by this mammoth political pageant; Church Day, Agriculture Day, Youth Day, and Labor and Industry Day drew millions of marching citizens ("virtually all Greeks participated," the ambassador proudly reported), as well as U.S. Navy and Marine units. Spyros Skouras, the movie magnate, coordinated parades and festivities in the United States and, according to Grady, "did much to bring about better understanding by the American people of the Greeks in their struggle to rehabilitate themselves."[67]

One of the uglier "psychological warfare" ventures in the Greek conflict involved the separation, sometimes coerced, of Greek children from their parents. During their retreats from contested territory in the winter of 1947–48, the guerrilla forces took with them thousands of local children, whom they relocated in refugee camps among Greece's Balkan Communist neighbors. The guerrillas claimed that the children had been evacuated, with their parents' consent, for their protection, while the government charged that the children had been kidnapped with the aim of intimidating government suporters. On March 10, 1948, Rankin reported that the "embassy believes that Markos' abduction of Greek children . . . is a major psychological blunder which we should exploit by [the] widest possible publication in [the] US and abroad." This issue, Rankin insisted a few weeks later, "can be turned into useful anti-Communist propaganda."[68] Griswold, on the other hand, hesitated. On March 23, he cabled that the reported child abduction was "proving unusually effective psychological warfare" against the government. In a panic, Greek authorities were themselves beginning the evacuation of thousands of children, sometimes forcibly, from rebel-held territory, a move which Griswold and other U.S. officials felt would tarnish the government cause, add to the financial burden of supporting refugees, and delay important military operations.[69] On April 24, Marshall secretly conceded that guerrilla propaganda was "deliberately exaggerating" rebel evacuation of children for its own ends and that the "majority" of children had "departed with [the] more or less willing consent [of the] Slavic minority or [their] communist parents."[70] However, despite the American understanding of the flimsiness of the "kidnapping" charge, as well as the double standard with which it was applied, the United States joined the Greek government in utilizing child abduction as a propaganda issue.[71] Eventually, about 43,000 children were evacuated from rebel territory (including some 15,000 by the government); many never returned.[72]

The forced evacuation of children was but one of the "emergency" measures employed by the Greek government against the guerrilla bands in the final period of the civil war. "Under American insistence," British Major Edgar O'Ballance noted, the authorities began "the systematic removal of whole sections of the population." This program "demarcated a 'front line' . . . prevented 'back infiltration' and . . . caused a blanket of silence to descend" upon the rebel-held countryside. By November 1947, Griswold reported, the army had forcibly evacuated 310,000 people to "safe areas."[73] Martial law, imposed on the Athens-Piraeus area in May 1948, was instituted throughout the country in November. BBC correspondent Kenneth Matthews recalled that it operated with "unprecedented severity. All previous mass arrests were exceeded by measures which now put thousands of known or suspected agents of the rebels behind the barbed wire of improvised concentration camps; death sentences were imposed and carried out without right of appeal."[74] From the outset, according to Grady, the Minister of Justice, Melas, "privately expressed [his] anxiety lest [George] Stratos [the Populist Minister of War], or more probably extremists hiding behind him, abuse martial law powers." But American officials welcomed the implementation of the emergency measures. "I sincerely hope that the appointment of General Papagos and the declaration of martial law will bring about a definite improvement," Marshall cabled King Paul on November 3. Two days later, Grady reported that, "though some abuses undoubtedly have and probably will occur, [the] administration of martial law has not so far been such in [the] Embassy's opinion as to justify extravagant fears." The Justice Minister's reaction was "exaggerated as usual," he maintained. "Properly administered, martial law may prove [an] effective and useful instrument."[75]

Only in the final months of the war, when the guerrilla defeat seemed imminent, did American policymakers begin a significant campaign to modify the Greek government's repressive policies. On August 16, 1949, Minor told the Prime Minister that his government "should announce favorable conditions for surrender and amnesty." One week later, he again spoke with the Prime Minister on the amnesty question, and suggested suspending executions as well. When the Prime Minister mentioned that the Greek government would probably be issuing a declaration announcing the end of executions for offenses connected with the post-1946 rebellion, Acheson responded that the State Department was "highly gratified" and fully endorsed the embassy's position. The Greek amnesty plan, announced to American officials on

August 26, involved the suspension of executions and the concentration of the remaining 16,000 exiles on Makronissos Island, where an "effort would be made to re-educate such persons in minimum time and return them to normal life." For the 18,000 remaining political prisoners, a tripartite program would be developed: (1) continued imprisonment for the leaders of the rebellion; (2) "screening and re-education on Makronissos" for those "who committed . . . serious offenses but are not regarded as leaders"; (3) immediate pardon for "those who committed offenses of small degree." The KKE would be permanently outlawed and all persons who had taken part in its activities or in the rebellion would "be deprived of political and civil rights for [a] limited period." Greeks outside the country would be barred forever from returning. The State Department immediately informed the Athens government of its "hearty approval" of this "constructive leniency program."[76] Under pressure from the armed forces, the Greek cabinet eventually put forward a noticeably harsher version, but the U.S government continued to urge restraint.[77]

The shift toward moderation, however, did not result from a sudden access of civil libertarian zeal. "Our view," Minor observed, is that "the Greeks themselves" should act on amnesty "in order [to] prevent further agitation for international control or supervision of some sort." As the United Nations was again scheduled to take up the Greek question, "timing was of [the] utmost importance." The Greek government, too, as Grady reported, drew up its program "to prevent international intervention [in] such internal affairs as [the] treatment [of the] guerrillas."[78] Indeed, both the State Department and the Greek government fought fiercely to avert any substantive U.N. recommendations on amnesty, leniency toward the rebels, or the suspension of executions. From the standpoint of American officials, it was imperative to imprison or exile permanently the leaders of the rebellion, to prevent the repatriation of the many thousands of refugees located in the Balkan Communist states, and to destroy the KKE. Arguing against U.N. action, Grady cabled that the Communists were "beaten finally by their own weapon and although innocents . . . were dragged along [the] bloody trail, I see no reason why, in mistaken confusion over these unfortunates, [the] real leaders should go unpunished." American and Greek officials did not want the fruits of military victory snatched from them by a broad U.N. plan for amnesty and reconciliation.[79]

Nor can it be said that the flurry of American concern for civil liberties in late 1949 had much impact upon the situation in Greece. The Athens government did end political executions on September 30, but it almost certainly would have done so anyway in light of the intense international pressure which culminated in a U.N. resolution on the subject the following month.[80] As for the tens of thousands of Greeks in prisons or concentration camps, their plight remained severe for years afterward. Although the Prime Minister told the press of his plans to surround "these boys and girls" with "an atmosphere calculated to encourage their tender souls," the reality was quite different. According to Minor, when political exiles were transferred to the military camp at Makronissos that October, they were set upon by the armed forces and systematically beaten for ten days. Of the 2,500 political detainees so treated, he wrote, "two or three were reported killed, thirty to fifty 'driven insane' and another one hundred or so 'critically wounded.'"[81] Asked during congressional hearings in June 1950 about the number of Greek political prisoners, the State Department reported that 23,000 persons remained incarcerated in Greece for "various security offenses"—16,000 after trials, 3,500 still "exiled temporarily" to Makronissos, and 3,500 with cases "still pending because of the overloaded Greek judicial system." As late as June 1952, Greek jails housed an estimated 11,000 political prisoners, nearly half sentenced to death or life imprisonment; thousands of other suspicious types remained incarcerated on the islands. Released after their nightmare of confinement, many thousands found their political rights and employment opportunities narrowly limited by government policy. At least 60,000 others remained abroad, barred from ever returning to their homeland.[82]

The dismal civil liberties record compiled by successive Greek governments resulted partly from the crisis atmosphere engendered by civil war and from their own authoritarian predilections, but it also owed much to U.S. policy. American officials had helped to install these governments and maintain them in power. In addition, they authorized or supported many of the "emergency" measures. At times, to be sure, they opposed particularly abhorrent policies, but largely from a need to placate world opinion. To write this is not to imply that the rebel movement was particularly scrupulous about civil liberties or that its actions always coincided with its professed principles. Nor is it to argue that U.S. officials had no respect at all for the ideal of individual freedom. Had they felt confident that stability and tough anti-Communist policies would prevail in Greece, U.S. officials might well have emphasized maintaining freedom of speech, freedom of the press, freedom of religion, and freedom of association. But in the context of Greece's postwar political upheaval, they lacked such confidence. Haunted by their fear of revolution and determined, at all costs, to destroy its constituency, American officials joined the Greek right in fostering policies of repression.

6.
THE ECONOMIC AID PROGRAM 1947–1949

We do not have either a broad understanding of the significance
and purpose of our work or any sort of a long range plan or
program to work toward. . . .
  We talk about "recovery" in a way . . . that conveys the idea
that we are trying to recreate an old order.

Clinton Golden, January 5, 1948[1]

From 1947 to 1949, Greece's deteriorating economic situation
greatly concerned American officials. Before the Second
World War, Greece was one of the most impoverished, underdeveloped nations in Europe. Agriculture, the source of live-
lihood for most Greeks, was hampered by the scarcity and
low fertility of arable land. Manufacturing was negligble, with
small-scale, inefficient production. The devastation of World
War II and the mismanagement of Greece by her postwar
rulers brought this fragile economy to a state near collapse,
immune to sizable transfusions of capital from UNRRA and
the British. Given their growing stake in Greece, American
officials became alarmed. In a message to Clayton of February
17, 1947, Paul Porter, head of the American Economic Mission, emphasized "the extreme gravity of the situation": severe
budgetary deficits, drastic inflation, the flight of capital overseas, and the inability of the right-wing government "to administer effectively the extensive reforms needed." With a
Communist-led revolution in progress, alleviating Greece's
bitter class and economic grievances seemed only reasonable
to Porter. He recalled "one ornate dinner when a leading
banker entertained me in his luxurious Athens apartment."
The financier, recently tried (and acquitted) as a Nazi collaborator, presented the visiting American dignitary with

"three liveried butlers, several magnificent wines," and a Romanoff princess "bedecked with rubies and diamonds." The contrast between these "extreme right Royalists of the political and commercial sphere" and "the starving children in the streets," Porter observed, "was simply too pat and cruel."[2] Other American officials, however, lacked Porter's egalitarian sensibilities. Consequently, it remained to be seen whether the U.S. aid program would be used to transform the Greek economic structure or merely to maintain it.

In preceding years, the Athens goverment's faltering efforts to revive the Greek economy had inspired scorn and dismay among American officials. The termination in August 1945 of the ambitious Varvaressos program of fiscal reform and price, wage, and commodity controls owed much to the preference of the Greek right for the painless alternative of foreign economic assistance. This fact was appreciated by U.S. authorities,[3] who took a cynical view of subsequent Greek aid and reparations requests. In June 1946, Rankin reported that too many Greeks had reached "the conclusion that the world owes Greece a living." With only the interest on the Greek reparations claim of $4 billion, he contended, "all Greeks could stop work, repair to the nearest coffee house and devote their full time to political dialectic!" That August, when the U.S. government rebuffed the request of a Greek delegation for U.S. economic aid, Acheson commented tartly that the encounter would produce a "good effect" if it convinced the Greek government that "any future US assistance will be greatly facilitated by [a] demonstration [of the] Greeks' ability to help themselves." Unfortunately, from the standpoint of Anglo-American officials, the prospects for such a demonstration appeared remote. Porter confided to his diary that "no Greek politician seems to have the courage or capacity to formulate a program containing the rudiments of basic economic policy." In early February 1947, Acheson declared gloomily that the Varvaressos measures constituted "in our opinion, the only constructive program that has been attempted in Greece since liberation."[4]

Porter's economic mission added significantly to the pressures for change. "In spite of $700,000,000 in foreign assist-ance," he wrote in his influential mission report of April 1, 1947, "Greece during the past two years has merely managed to survive. . . . No government has been able to develop an effective economic policy and to inaugurate necessary con-trols." Accordingly, the future appeared bleak. Without "sub-stantial foreign assistance" and "strong control measures" adopted by the Athens government, "another round of ex-treme inflation with all of its disastrous economic and political consequences is a certainty." Porter was particularly dismayed by the determination of the Athens government to cater to the cupidity of the small Greek upper class. There was a "wide disparity in the living standards and income throughout all Greece," he observed. "Profiteers, that is traders, speculators and black marketeers thrive in wealth and luxury, a problem with which no government has effectively dealt. At the same time, the masses of people live on bare subsistence." Porter believed that it was futile to expect recovery in these circum-stances. "No reconstruction and development can spring from the soil of political intrigue, corruption and exploitation," he noted in his diary; these were "hard generalities, but are really an understatement of Greece's present predicament."[5] In-deed, in Porter's opinion, the disintegration of the Greek economy followed logically from the shortsightedness and greed of the Athens oligarchy.[6]

Porter's economic report merely added official validation to common knowledge. By 1947, Greece's vivid class distinc-tions and blatant class rule had become a public scandal. Although most Greeks endured lives of terrible poverty and suffering, observed a British parliamentary delegation, "there is a small class of wealthy people" who "live in great luxury," "practically tax-free." In April 1947, *New York Times* corre-spondent Raymond Daniell wrote that "the shops are full of luxury goods, such as have not been seen in London since the war began, and all imported since liberation with bor-rowed funds, to be sold at inflated prices to the well-to-do." Journalists could not repress their incredulity at the life-style of the Greek upper class. "For the monied and irresponsible there is no lack of anything," commented Dana Adams Schmidt, another *New York Times* reporter. "Not far away the peasants are half-starved, but in the capital rich Athenians still get their pastries and whipped cream, their Scotch and their French wines, their nylons and American cigarettes." In the suburbs and at the beach, "delightful restaurants" abounded, he added; "there are tennis clubs, yacht clubs, night clubs." George Polk, with his customary disdain for Greek government policy, reported that, as "relief often impinges upon the money-making methods of the wealthy two per cent . . . official restrictions block as much philanthropic aid as possible." Large stocks of UNRRA supplies, formally destined to relieve the nation's mass misery, "are still lying unused in Greek warehouses."[7]

To many, the situation called for a reform program. In his mission report, Porter recommended instituting higher income levies, improving income tax enforcement, adopting measures to "prevent importers from making or retaining excessive profits," prohibiting the importation of luxury goods, taxing at least some of the profits of the Greek shipping industry, and promoting Greek exports. Although Porter did favor closer scrutiny of the government budget, he was far from fanatical on the point. Suggesting cutbacks in the large and inefficient civil service, he urged at the same time increasing its pay scale and improving its training. In addition, he advocated a limited range of price, wage, and rent controls; major reconstruction projects; and a far-reaching program of economic development. "Recovery only to the pre-war level of industrial activity would be inadequate if Greece is to become reasonably self-sufficient," he contended. With the Porter report and the State Department's own growing interest in offering alternatives to Communism (e.g., the Marshall Plan) as the backdrop, the Secretary of State adopted a liberal emphasis in his instructions for Griswold. "We are fully cognizant of the need for reform in Greek economic . . . life, and we believe that determined efforts should be made by the Mission to reconstruct the Greek economy on a basis that will do away as far as possible with corrupt practices and profiteering," he wrote. "We believe that the tax burden should be distributed equally, that labor and agriculture should be urged toward greater production, and that living standards should in general be raised."[8]

To execute this program and to cut through the anticipated resistance of Athens officials, American policymakers negotiated a series of extraordinary agreements with Greek authorities in the spring of 1947. In 1946, a British economic mission had placed individuals in Greek ministries for advisory purposes. But the American plan—suggested by Porter and implemented by the State Department—provided for the appointment of American experts with the power to enforce their recommendations.[9] Indeed, they could supervise programs and projects down to the smallest detail, securing compliance with their demands by withholding American aid. As McNeill noted, the 1947 agreements gave American representatives such wide authority that "the Greek government itself was thenceforth unable to take any important decision without their approval."[10] Thus, although the Truman Doctrine initially provided Greek authorities with a renewed sense of complacency,[11] the arrival of the new corps of American experts and administrators gradually altered the situation. By late September, AMAG had prepared an overall economic program for Sophoulis to announce over the radio. The following month, Griswold wrote confidently that, although Greek ministries were "extremely reluctant to surrender any part of their limited control over the economy," through "a firm, patient, and unyielding policy on all fronts, the Mission is gaining considerable ground." Observing the phenomenon, the British ambassador reported that "the Greeks already regard their new masters, the Americans, as harder than the old ones."[12]

Masters the Americans might be, but the direction of their economic program was soon in question. By the end of 1947, some 150 American economic and technical personnel, many with a very different political orientation from Porter's, had arrived in Greece. The two most powerful were Eugene Clay, an economist for the U.S. armed forces who was appointed chief economic adviser of AMAG, and Charles Coombs, a New York banker who became head of the Public Finance Division. Almost immediately, as Coombs recalled, there were "policy disagreements" and a "heated debate as to the relative essentiality of competing objectives." Although the Porter report provided clear guidelines for economic measures, a number of AMAG specialists regarded it with suspicion. "Little thought had been devoted to the formulation of . . . a balanced economic program prior to the actual arrival of the Griswold Mission," Coombs complained. Instead, "much attention had been centered upon the numerous shortcomings of Greek Government policy in the past and, in well rounded generalities, a host of reforms had been promised." At the U.S. embassy, which traditionally enjoyed excellent relations with the Greek upper classes and their right-wing spokesmen, the criticism was considerably more pointed. "I do not feel that we should attempt to use our aid to reform Greece or redistribute its wealth," the first secretary informed his superiors. "We should . . . build up . . . the pride and confidence of the Greek people in their own government, business, and banking institutions."[13]

American officials themselves often came from upper-class backgrounds or experienced social situations which proved unconducive to reformist zeal. Many were accustomed to a relatively comfortable existence, and could only be expected to defend the interests of the impoverished Greek masses (and remain indifferent to the influence of the Greek upper class) by some exercise of imagination or egalitarian political commitment. Dining with a U.S. embassy economic expert, Porter appraised him as a "lad with some independent resources," who maintained "an extraordinarily attractive villa" with "excellent" food and service. Not surprisingly, he leaned "towards support of the present government without too much concern for the economic condition of the peasants or the lower middle class." Americans "move about well-fed, with good clothes and expensive cars, in a country where poverty and tragedy are on all sides," a U.S. congressional study reported. There were "too many new automobiles being driven by chauffeurs, and too much pomp, circumstance and privilege" on the part of U.S. officials. By contrast, "everywhere in the city crowds milled around in rags and tatters." In addition, by September 1947, when most of AMAG's experts arrived, inflation had reached catastrophic proportions, lending what Coombs called a "crisis atmosphere" to the situation.[14] In this context, most U.S. advisers tended to devise more conservative solutions to the Greek economic dilemma than envisaged by Porter.

Inflation, of course, could be dealt with by a variety of measures, not all of them conservative. Sensitive to inflationary pressures, Varvaressos and Porter had championed price controls and rationing. During AMAG's existence, such measures were strongly advocated by the Labor Division, which considered controls on wages unfair and inequitable in the absence of controls on prices. But AMAG's leadership totally rejected this position. As Coombs recalled: "The cornerstone of the Mission program was a stabilization of the wage line." U.S. officials introduced an "incomes policy" in late 1947, and followed it up by bitter opposition to wage increases. For a time, strikes were banned on penalty of death.[15] Regulating prices and commodities, however, was quite another matter. "Owing largely to the ineffectiveness of the postwar Greek civil service," Griswold explained to the State Department in December 1947, "it was thought that premature efforts to impose a system of allocations, price controls, and rationing would jeopardize the prestige of the government and the Mission without any real prospect of success." This gave an apolitical cast to what was for some a conservative position, for Clay, only two weeks previously, had anchored his objections more deeply in classical economics. "The government structure is too weak and inefficient," Clay wrote, "and there is always the danger of destroying through too many controls one of the most important assets of Greece— which is the initiative and enterprise of the people."[16]

For Clay, as for most other AMAG officials, there was never any doubt about how to handle Greece's economic crisis. He

reported to Washington: "The most pressing problem confronting the Mission in early September was the establishment
of a satisfactorily balanced government budget."[17] Accom-
plishing this balancing act, however, was not quite so simple.
The Greek military received the largest share of government
expenditures, and this remained virtually sacrosanct. Even
on the civilian side, care of the hundreds of thousands of
wartime refugees constituted an enormous budgetary problem. Given the pitiful allotment of 15 cents a day per adult
(50 cents a day for a family with four children), there was not
much "fat" here to be cut. Still, in an effort to maximize
financial savings, U.S. officials did press Greek generals to
curtail their practice of forced evacuations.[18] Greece's civil
service, swollen by government patronage, was a more inviting target. In the fall of 1947, AMAG ordered the dismissal
of 15,000 of Greece's 80,000 public workers—without, however, raising the wages or improving the efficiency of the
remainder. The protests were immediate, even from the
Greek right. As Clinton Golden, director of AMAG's Labor
Division, wrote, "to lay off thousands with no other jobs in
sight and rapidly diminishing relief funds to take care of them
seems . . . a poor way of stemming communism." Eventually,
therefore, AMAG's attacks on the civil service subsided.[19] The
major slashes in public spending produced by what Golden
called the "budget balancers' brigade" occurred in funding for
relief and reconstruction—vulnerable areas which, ironically,
had served as the major public justification for the American
"aid" program.[20]

To cover the vast government outlays for the military and
the refugees, as well as to retain sufficient capital for reconstruction projects, the budget balancers pressed for dramatic
increases in taxation. On this subject, at least, the advice from
Porter and Marshall could hardly have been more explicit:
institute "direct" taxation (e.g., an income tax) to replace the
government's almost exclusive reliance upon "indirect" taxation (e.g., sales taxes), thus shifting most of Greece's tax
burden from the poor to the rich. Informed by the State
Department of plans to tax the wealthy, Harold Ickes, a sharp

critic of the U.S. program, retorted: "I will believe it when I see it."[21] His skepticism proved well-founded: on December 1, 1947, Clay reported that, "after detailed examination, the Mission decided that little if any possibility existed for an immediate shift from consumption to income taxation." This remained AMAG's position. Late the following year, Coombs stressed "the extreme difficulty . . . in adjusting taxation to ability to pay." Once again, the blame was placed on the inefficiency of the Greek civil service, which Coombs failed to mention was being dismantled at U.S. orders. "Foreign advisers have most reluctantly recognized," he declared, "that the administrative machinery of Greece is simply not up to the job of exacting the maximum contribution from the wealthier elements of the community in support of the military and recovery effort."[22]

Consequently, although Greek government tax receipts rose substantially under American pressure, the increment came about almost entirely as a result of indirect taxes. Raised by approximately 45 percent, these taxes constituted a major assault upon the living standards of the consuming poor. Clay estimated that the new tax structure confiscated one-third of the national income—a tremendous burden in a country so close to the margin of existence, and one which fell disproportionately upon those least able to pay. At the same time, this regressive tax structure left the rich free to dispose of their considerable income in unproductive and inflationary ways, most notably through speculation in the gold and commodity markets.[23] Modest efforts were made to introduce direct taxes as well, but the wealthy easily subverted these through false reporting or bribery. In 1949, when indirect taxes comprised but 17 percent of Great Britain's tax revenues, they accounted for 80 percent of state revenue in Greece. Between 1939 and 1951, the real income of Greece's commercial and industrial classes doubled; yet their contribution to Greece's tax revenues actually fell by half.[24]

Some of Greece's wealthiest citizens, the shipping magnates, were notorious for evading taxation. Although World War II brought about the destruction of most of the Greek merchant fleet, it was reconstituted after the United States made a gift of some 100 Liberty ships to the Athens government. The latter promptly sold them at cut rates to its wealthy clientele. These merchants, in turn, placed most of their new and very lucrative businesses under foreign flags and hoarded their vast profits in foreign banks, thus evading Greek taxes. Some of these mercantile millionaires resided in opulence in the fashionable Kolonaki section of Athens; others lived in great luxury in New York City, where they remained free of taxation by U.S. authorities as well through use of Greek diplomatic status. Griswold stated that he attempted to block the transfer of the vessels to Greek ownership without a previous agreement as to tax payment but was thwarted by the U.S. Maritime Commission. Another half-hearted AMAG effort to tap overseas shipping profits materialized in 1948, but had little effect. Cynical about the whole business, Griswold told a visiting congressman that, while "AMAG must interfere in the internal affairs of the Greek Government," the "existence of graft must be accepted as part of the system."[25]

In fairness to the Greek rich, it should be noted that they (and their spokesmen in the Athens government) generally opposed AMAG's emphasis on paring government expenditures and raising taxes;[26] they preferred to balance the budget through additional American aid and to fight inflation through the Greek government's sale of gold. During the repeated crises of the war and postwar period, those persons with sizable amounts of money had acquired the habit of protecting themselves against inflation by purchasing gold sovereigns. To prevent the price of sovereigns (and, it was thought, prices generally) from rising dramatically and to lower the quantity of drachmas in circulation, the Bank of Greece would periodically sell the gold coins. But U.S. State and Treasury Department officials doubted the efficacy of the process and believed that the widespread hoarding of gold represented a waste of investment capital and foreign exchange. Therefore, beginning in June 1947, U.S. authorities prohibited gold sales by the Bank of Greece, much to the distress of Greek officials.

AMAG wavered in November, however, and in January 1948 agreed to release $2 million in gold held by the Federal Reserve Bank in New York. Reluctantly, AMAG had concluded that gold sales might provide a respite in the inflationary cycle. At the same time, Griswold used release of the gold as a means of winning acceptance by Greek officials of further U.S. measures to curb inflation,[27] among them new banking and credit policies.[28]

With AMAG's major "reforms" in place, U.S. officials felt confident that the battle against inflation had been won, but such was not the case, at least for some time. Thanks to U.S. influence, Griswold reported in December 1947, controls had been established over government expenditures, wage levels, the exchange rate, and credit. He "hoped that control of these variables would be sufficient and that prices, production, and distribution might be left free to respond to the natural play of economic forces." But his optimism soon dissipated. In January 1948, he wrote that the "inflationary spiral continues unchecked"; AMAG's index showed that commodity prices had risen to 275 times those of the prewar period. On February 5, Rankin cabled that commodity prices were 51 percent higher than the preceding March, when the aid program was announced, and 33 percent above those at the end of September.[29] On March 10, commodity prices reached a new and dizzying height—306 times the prewar level. Although prices finally stabilized, even in some cases dipped, in mid-1948, the sluggish rate of recovery and the continued weakness of the drachma left the experts with the distressing sense that their harsh measures had had only a minimal impact on events. Rather than reassess their policies, however—for example, their failure to institute price or commodity controls—they seized upon more palatable if flimsier explanations. "Probably the most important error," wrote Coombs, "lay in the grant of excessive wage and salary increases."[30] The solution, then, lay not in altering the direction of U.S. economic policy but in pushing ahead with further austerity measures.

Given the long-awaited price stabilization, Coombs recalled, the spring and summer of 1948 promised to "bring about very substantial improvements in real wages and the general standard of living." A critical juncture had arrived, and the mission, he wrote, was

confronted with this basic policy issue: whether, first, to allow the natural downtrend of prices and resultant improvement of real wages to develop . . . or second, to utilize the opportunity afforded by a declining price level to embark upon a second phase of the reform program. . . . AMAG chose the second alternative of pushing ahead with other reform measures, generally of a cost-increasing nature, which offset the declining trend of free market prices. . . . The fruits of the earlier reform measures . . . were not permitted to run to seed in the form of higher real incomes and consumption but were rather utilized as a shock absorber for new taxes and other burdens upon the cost of living. Although no significant improvement in the standard of life was thus allowed to appear, the Greek economy was put upon a much more self-sustaining basis.

The new, budget-balancing measures referred to by Coombs were three in number: (1) a devaluation of the drachma; (2) a sharp increase in the cigarette tax; and (3) the elimination of the government's wheat subsidy, which heretofore had acted to lower the selling price of bread. Together, Coombs wrote, these measures "reduced the prospective budgetary deficit by 600 billion drachmae."[31]

The budget balancers awaited this campaign with keen anticipation. One of the Greek government's few gestures to the poor, the UNRRA-initiated wheat subsidy, particularly aroused their ire. "The government considers that it would be politically impossible to increase the price of rationed bread," Clay reported irritably on December 1, 1947. Nevertheless, "political difficulties will increase the longer the necessary price adjustment is delayed. The government should be required at an early date to face reality and to increase the price even to lower income groups sufficient to eliminate the subsidy." Clay noted that "milk raises a similar problem. . . . When UNRRA came . . . and found the degree of undernourishment which existed, they put in a free milk feeding program for everybody under 18 years." Greece was "far too poor a nation to ever be able to support such a program out of its own resources," Clay insisted. Accordingly, in January 1948, Griswold made the elimination of food subsidies one of the "reforms" to be enacted in return for AMAG's agreement to facilitate further gold sales and increases in military spending. He informed Sophoulis: "I am sure that the people of Greece will understand the necessity for an increase in the price of bread in order to enable the Government to finance an allout military campaign against the bandits and adequate care of the refugees." Sophoulis responded, however, that the only item in the American-imposed quid pro quo not acceptable to the Greek government was the elimination of the wheat subsidy. Allowing bread prices to rise by "four times and over," he observed, would cause "a social upheaval," as well as "very serious economic and social consequences." Faced with vigorous opposition, AMAG retreated grudgingly on this point.[32]

In the spring of 1948, however, AMAG renewed the struggle to eliminate the wheat subsidy and achieve a balanced budget. Confident that price stabilization would soften the impact of this budget cut, officials of the U.S. mission again pressed for agreement to it by the Greek government. They also championed the two other measures thought to be of budget-balancing significance: devaluating the drachma and sharply increasing cigarette taxes. Ironically, the U.S. pressure for budget economies came at precisely the moment when the State Department urged the Athens government to forgo sizable anticipated income. "To support and assist [the] present Ital[ian] Govt" in the 1948 elections, Lovett wrote in April, the State Department wanted the Greek government to announce "at [the] earliest possible date its desire to take [the] lead in proposing general renunciation [of] reparations from Italy." This must be "presented to [the] public as a positive contribution of a small but gallant nation, rather than a further sacrifice dictated by [the] Great Powers." Indeed, the move must "appear [to be] spontaneous" and to "receive [the] firm and enthusiastic support of [the] whole Greek Govt." From the standpoint of American officials, Greece could afford such Cold War largesse far better than it could giving bread and milk to the poor. Nevertheless, declining $100 million in reparations fell a bit beyond the limits of the Athens government's generosity. It did, however, accept the American demand to eliminate bread subsidies and to implement the other measures in the American package.[33]

Even U.S. officials conceded that most Greeks paid a stiff price for these and other American-sponsored fiscal measures. Each of the "reforms" of mid-1948 "added very substantially to the cost of living," Coombs admitted. Summing up the overall course of events from the vantage point of December 1948, he recalled: "Following a wage freeze in November 1947, customs duties were raised by 150%, the official dollar rate and import costs by 100%, the bread price by 80%, the turnover tax by 60%, and cigarette prices by 25%." Such policies "naturally aroused bitter and generalized resentment among the Greek public," which had learned to distrust promises of long-term improvement. He remarked: "The Greek peasant is considerably more concerned with the price of his daily bread than the state of repair of the Corinth Canal or Gorgopotamos Bridge." Like Coombs, most AMAG officials rejected measures for the improvement of living standards and opted, instead, for budget balancing and what he called "reliance upon the operation of competitive forces." AMAG had opposed "direct taxation, price and production controls, and general rationing," he stated, and its financial controls "reflected a severely classical approach." But the "harsh financial policy" of the U.S. mission, he insisted in its defense, had freed capital for reconstruction projects and had "secured a remarkably high degree of monetary and price stability."[34]

In other areas, such as foreign trade, American economic policies more closely resembled those advocated in the Porter report, but their results were not impressive. At American prodding, the Greek government established a Foreign Trade Administration, headed by an American, in October 1947. Attempting to narrow Greece's exceptionally unfavorable balance of payments, it carefully screened all applications for import licenses and worked to revive Greek exports.[35] By 1949, however, Greek exports had reached only 40 percent of their prewar value. Moreover, although exports rose steadily, so did imports, and the trade deficit actually widened. In 1950, when exports reached $90 million, imports hit a record $428 million. Other American programs contributed to these difficulties. Tobacco, for example, had provided Greece's most valuable export, with Germany as the largest purchaser. But although AMAG worked to restore Greek tobacco's position in the German market, the battle was finally won by U.S. tobacco companies.[36] In addition, for political reasons, Greek trade with nearby Eastern Europe collapsed and Greece became a leading customer of the United States. Since early 1946, the State Department had pressed for the establishment of a reciprocal trade treaty with the Greek government; in 1949, it secured its goal. Thus, despite AMAG's efforts to restrain imports, Greece became heavily dependent upon American products, which constituted about 30 percent of the import trade by the early 1950s.[37]

Had it possessed the will to do so, AMAG might have used its control of the Foreign Trade Administration to curb some of the most notorious abuses of the Greek oligarchy. Indeed, AMAG's top officials justified the creation of this government agency partly on the grounds of its ability to prevent the importation of nonessential luxury goods. By scrutinizing import licenses, the FTA probably made some headway along these lines. Yet, as C. A. Munkman, an official of the U.S. mission, observed, U.S. trade regulations left a "deliberate loophole." The exporter "was authorized to sell one-half of his foreign exchange for the best price he could get" as an inducement to expand exports. Thereafter, the purchaser "might use it to procure luxury or semiluxury items," such as automobiles, radios, and refrigerators. "Many Greeks and foreigners were extremely critical of this 'free' market," Munkman recalled, although he considered it a "safety valve" and a good means of encouraging Greek shipping magnates "to stay in or at least visit the homeland."[38] AMAG proved equally toothless when it came to dealing with speculators and monopolists who hoarded commodities as a means of inflating prices. In late 1948, for example, one group of promoters cornered the market in olive oil, a staple of Greek life, forcing up the price by 150 percent. Breaking the power of these groups would have taken government action, perhaps state trading ventures. But the Greek government had little interest in such action, while AMAG was determined, one of its reports noted, to restore trade "to commercial channels as rapidly as possible." These facts, combined with the absence of price controls, left postwar Greece a haven for speculators.[39]

Of all the American economic programs, the most successful were in the areas of reconstruction and public health. Under the direction of the U.S. Army Corps of Engineers and two private U.S. contractors, highways, bridges, railroads, harbor facilities, canals, and airfields in Greece were constructed or rebuilt. The highway program, which entailed the building of approximately 1,000 miles of first-class roads, was pressed vigorously, at least partly for military reasons. To counter the heavily armed and mechanized government army, the rebels specialized in mining and destroying roads and bridges. Conversely, AMAG and the Greek General Staff sought to open the isolated countryside to vehicular traffic. In the end, considerable progress was made by AMAG and the government, thus providing Greece with its first modern transportation network. In addition, the U.S. mission engaged in land reclamation, distributed farm equipment, instituted agricultural training programs, built schools and museums, imported insecticides, established health centers, and provided Greece with vital medical supplies. The battle against malaria, traditionally a scourge in Greece, was won by UNRRA and the British, but AMAG's Health Service consolidated and extended the earlier gains.[40] Had the devastation of civil war not accompanied such programs, their results would certainly have been more impressive. Even so, they softened some of life's grimmer features in Greece and provided a basis for the anticipated economic recovery.

Significantly, however, despite some progress in reconstruction and massive infusions of capital from the U.S. aid program, agricultural and industrial production in Greece failed to reach acceptable levels. Using 100 as the prewar index of agricultural productivity, the Economic Cooperation Administration estimated that, between 1947–48 and 1950–51, Greece moved from 86 to 93—a lower level than any other ECA nation except Austria. In mining, the record was even drearier. The index of Greek mineral production, which stood at 16 in 1947, rose to 20 in 1948 and fell back to 16 in 1949.[41] Greece's greatest progress came in the area of industrial production, which, according to ECA, rose from 64 in the first quarter of 1947 to 99 by the fourth quarter of 1949. Certainly, this represented an important advance. Even so, by this time the average recovery level for Marshall Plan recipients stood at 120, and Greece's recovery level fell below that of every other ECA nation except Germany. Britain's industrial recovery index, for example, then stood at 144, Denmark's at 152, Sweden's at 157. Worst of all, unlike these nations, Greece had not developed a significant manufacturing sector before World War II. Therefore, the restoration of the prewar level of industrial productivity meant only that Greece remained an underdeveloped, impoverished society. In 1953, four years after the civil war and during exceptionally fine weather conditions for agriculture, the average per capita income in Greece reached only $160.[42]

Average figures, of course, obscure the sharp contrast between poverty and wealth in Greece that remained untouched by government programs. By the end of the civil war, almost a tenth of Greece's population was awaiting resettlement in devastated villages, while a third was at least partially dependent upon state assistance programs. State aid to the poor, it might be added, was far from lavish. In October 1949, the U.S. consul at Salonika reported that "large numbers of refugees have been returned to their homes, some voluntarily and some against their wishes, and set down there without the means to plant new crops or, in general, to face the coming winter."[43] In subsequent years, most people who remained in Greece continued to live in the rural areas, where overall unemployment stood at 20 percent and underemployment considerably higher. "Family incomes," Munkman wrote in 1958, "may be as low as one hundred dollars per year." Meanwhile, other Greeks enjoyed lives of fantastic luxury. In 1949, Sophoulis conceded that he had been unable "to take the proper measures against the economic and political oligarchy of the country." General Van Fleet complained, wrote C. L. Sulzberger, that "the economic and social system . . . sometimes makes him feel like a Communist." Located in the midst of rich farmlands were mud shacks. "Where do the profits go?" Van Fleet demanded. "Greece is indeed a poor country," the journalist confided to his diary, "but there are too many rich people in it (or rich Greeks abroad who have milked it)."[44]

Even without redistributing wealth and income, U.S. officials might have alleviated poverty in Greece by sponsoring a major program for economic development. During 1947, such a program received its staunchest support from liberal figures outside regular State Department channels, among them Golden, Porter, and Chester Bowles (a former OPA director). The U.S. government, Golden complained to a friend, was "not talking about the possibility of making Greece anything but what she has always been—a poor country where most of the people grub a precarious living from the barren hillsides and narrow valleys." Golden thought that "harnessing the mountain streams in the north to develop electric power" and "increasing the flow of tourists to Greece" would stimulate new industries and employment opportunities. But by late 1947, Porter was out of the picture, Bowles's suggestions for a Near East development program had been politely but firmly rejected by Marshall, and Golden had decided that he was unable to work in Greece any longer.[45] Meanwhile the U.S. embassy, shorn of Ambassador Mac-Veagh but no less committed to a conservative approach, was preparing a counterattack on what it charged was AMAG's liberal bias. "The life blood of the Greek economy has been shut off for months and private initiative and enterprise smothered," claimed the first secretary in early 1948. "Instead of coming to Greece solely to help put Greek capital and private initiative back to work," AMAG seemed "determined to institute a paternalistic state-controlled economy."[46] Given such thinking, public investment in Greek economic growth was not high on the embassy agenda.

In 1948 and 1949, the conflict over economic development took a new form, largely thanks to congressional passage of the Marshall Plan. With U.S. economic aid to Greece brought under ECA supervision, American and Greek officials finally formulated a four year plan for economic recovery and growth. The actual policies of the Athens government, though, failed to meet Marshall Plan standards, and to the embassy's distress, ECA demanded action. In October 1948, the Deputy Director rejected the State Department's request for additional aid to Greece, commenting that "the Greek Government and its representatives . . . have persistently refused to cooperate wholeheartedly in the work of this organization." Meanwhile, the ECA director in Greece, John Nuveen, began to call attention to what he claimed was a deteriorating economic and political situation.[47] Grady and the embassy staff, however, refused to change course. Rather than channel U.S. aid funds toward ECA's ambitious development program, they persisted in allowing the Athens government to use them for military ventures or for daily operation of the government and the economy. At the same time, they continued to avoid championing a progressive tax policy that might have redirected the excess capital of the wealthy to public enterprises with a high productive potential.[48] Grady also fought to have Nuveen dismissed from his post and to force a drastic cut in the size of the ECA mission in Greece.[49]

Although Grady's conflict with ECA also had personal and political dimensions, it seems clear that he and his associates in the State Department disapproved of plans for industrial development in Greece. In August 1949, at a meeting of State Department officials, Grady joined with McGhee in opposing a massive ECA plan, drawn up with the assistance of a U.S. firm, for the development of Greece's hydroelectric power. According to the minutes, McGhee stated "the Greeks are not by temperament outstanding industrialists or large scale entrepreneurs"; hence "it would be a mistake . . . to attempt to apply in Greece the broad ECA formula of achieving economic viability by 1952." Grady added that "it would be artificial to attempt to transform Greece into an industrial nation." Instead, another look should be taken at "Greek

economic potentialities, including the population question."
Concurring with the ambassador, McGhee explained that
"it might be desirable to reduce the doses of American aid to
Greece, so that the Greek standard of living would gradually
be brought down to a level which the economy of the country
could support." This process of undeveloping Greece "would
have to be carried out gradually and very carefully to avoid
violent or unfavorable political reaction," he added, and
"would have to be accompanied by some plan for large scale
emigration." As Greece might not prove "a sound investment"
for American economic aid, "it might be necessary to regard
Greece as a 'holding operation' on the economic front."[50]

Eventually, this pessimistic appraisal of Greece's economic
potential prevailed. Even an official from ECA in Greece
reported to the State Department that he was " 'instinctively
opposed' to large-scale capital investment in Greece for in-
dustrialization." Greece was not a "proper" field for ECA
operations, he contended, as its problems were "not the same
as those of Western Europe." In practice, although U.S.
economic aid increased for a brief time, it continued to play
little role in stimulating industrial development. "Plans aimed
at the setting up of new industries," one specialist wrote,
"were still at an embryonic stage in 1952."[51] If the State Department frowned on public investment, however, it viewed
more traditional ventures by private capital with greater favor.
In September 1949, Jernegan reported that a Greek delegation, headed by the Minister of National Economy, was
scheduled to meet with leading U.S. bankers "in order to
obtain their views on the type of program and governmental
assurances likely to attract investors." The director of the
Greece, Turkey, and Iran division thought it "of course gratifying that the Greeks are beginning to think along these
lines." From Grady's standpoint, this was quite sufficient.
"The key to the situation here," he wrote in December 1949,
"is not to be too ambitious." With the war concluded, "our
problem now is economic," and it could be resolved satisfactorily "if we . . . cut our suit to the cloth we have. This means
getting the country revived without an attempt to remake
it."[52]

Even had American officials been determined to transform the Greek economy, their commitment to winning the war against the guerrillas placed severe constraints on what could be done. "The greatest obstacle to the reconstruction of Greece is the continuance of the civil war," Porter wrote in late 1947; "there can be no permanent solution . . . until the present military burden is reduced—until money and men are released for productive purposes." AMAG's chieftains also recognized the conflict inherent in the situation but, unlike Porter, tended to give top priority to the military. As Clay phrased it: "The Mission soon ascertained that there could be no hope for economic recovery until relative security could be reestablished." In September 1947, what he termed "the urgency of the military situation" led to a transfer of $9 million of U.S. aid funds from the economic to the military budget. That November, Griswold suggested diverting the large stocks of UNRRA supplies uncovered by AMAG investigation to the Greek armed forces. Although the State Department opposed this plan as a violation of the agreement between UNRRA and the Greek government,[53] it recognized the critical nature of the situation. On January 12, 1948, Marshall cabled Griswold that the "destruction [of the] guerrilla forces and [the] establishment of internal security . . . now have clearly assumed paramount importance" and should "take precedence over any portions [of the] present program which do not directly support them." In response, Griswold warned against a Communist victory "resulting from economic breakdown and [a] general popular rejection of [the] present political and social structure," but agreed "fully [with the] paramountcy [of the] restoration [of] internal security." AMAG, he maintained, "has not and will not prejudice military success by insistence upon economic programs and reform measures that do not directly or indirectly support [the] military effort."[54]

The consequences of this choice were soon apparent. Of the $300 million appropriated by Congress for the first year of the Greek aid program, the State Department had planned to provide 50 percent for the military, 48.5 percent for the economic program, and 1.5 percent for administration. But because of further diversions of U.S. aid, the actual funding for the first year shifted to 57.7 percent military and 41 percent economic aid.[55] Moreover, most U.S. aid formally designated as economic went for military-related purposes, such as refugee relief and construction projects of military utility. "Our economic policy," one U.S. officer reported happily to army headquarters, "is primarily directed toward the support of the military operations of the Greek Government."[56] Nor did the pattern shift in the latter part of the war. "No less than 80% of the drachma counterpart funds arising from the 1948–49 ECA grant for Greece—plus all tax revenues—must be earmarked for purposes other than economic recovery," Coombs reported at the end of 1948. There was a need for "cutting back ruthlessly upon every activity which does not serve the overriding necessity of restoring internal order." Subsequently, an ECA official told Congress: "We could not start a real economic development project until we had more security in Greece and that stage was not reached until 1950."[57]

The ECA administrator's testimony suggests a second key economic ramification of the war: its enormous wastefulness. The Athens government's armed forces employed approximately 250,000 people in war capacities (as compared to some 50,000 before World War II), and tens of thousands of others fought in the guerrilla ranks. The productive labor force was eroded still further by the flight of 700,000 refugees—nearly 10 percent of the population—from their homes and livelihoods. In addition, the war severely disrupted communication and transportation and led domestic and foreign capitalists, anxious to find a situation of greater security, to scrupulously avoid investments in Greece.[58] Finally, even an ambitious program of reconstruction could hardly compete with the war's deleterious effects. "During forty months of guerrilla warfare," one Greek cabinet minister recalled, "Greece suffered more destruction . . . than in . . . World War II." According to Greek government figures, $250 million of matériel (in 1948 prices) was wrecked beyond repair. If the value of homes damaged, the maintenance of refugees, and working hours lost are added, the figure rises to $1 billion. Little wonder that U.S. embassy officials privately conceded in early 1949 that "economically, while there has been some accomplishment, the line has hardly been held." As McNeill wrote: "The country as a whole was worse off in 1949 than it had been in 1944." On top of the disasters of the past, "the fresh damages of the guerrilla war had to be made good if Greece were to arrive at a . . . self-sustaining level."[59]

With the civil war at an end, however, American officials were inclined to regard the economic situation in Greece with less urgency. "Everything continues to go well—extremely well," Grady assured ECA director Paul Hoffman in November 1949; "Greece will not, like China, become a relief operation." The Greeks shared this "growing confidence," he told the State Department, and "want to take over government functions which have heretofore been carried on by Americans." Unfortunately, "while we are anxious to have them run their own affairs . . . there are a few points at which we must operate."[60] The following year, the U.S. ambassador informed Congress that Greece had received $2 billion in foreign assistance since liberation—about 75 percent from the United States—and had "made good use" of it. The U.S. program, he declared, was a "success." For Grady, at least, this was axiomatic. "History is on the side of free enterprise rather than on the side of collectivism," he assured a fashionable American luncheon gathering at the Grande Bretagne, the most luxurious hotel in Athens. "Collectivism . . . has within itself the seeds of its own destruction. . . . Capitalism, on the other hand, is bold and experimental, attributes upon which human progress must be based."[61]

Despite the encomiums of the U.S. ambassador, however, Greece's economic progress—stimulated by capitalism's "bold and experimental" ventures and by the highest level of per capita assistance granted any underdeveloped country since World War II[62]—remained far from impressive. Some gains had been made in reconstructing roads and harbors, improving health care, and slowing the disastrous inflationary spiral. Nevertheless, by 1949, the cost of living had risen to twenty times that of 1945 and the Greek currency had lost much of its value. Simultaneously, as an AMAG memorandum noted that November, there existed a "large measure of unemployment." Greece was "not only a poor country . . . but is likely to continue a poor country," with a "very low" standard of living compared to the nations of the West. Indeed, in fiscal 1951, of all NATO nations only Portugal had a lower per capita GNP than Greece. In March 1950, when Greece finally surpassed its miniscule industrial production of 1938, it had compiled a poorer recovery record than any NATO nation. That year, Grady admitted to Congress, the Greek government's revenues covered only 53 percent of its expenditures. Of the $400 million Greece spent abroad for civilian items, $250 million was financed by ECA assistance. Militarily, the situation was even worse. "Since she does not have the money to support her own defense forces," Grady added, "we must foot the bill." In 1954, one British specialist concluded: "Nobody can seriously suppose that if American aid were to be withdrawn now, Greece could avoid a total economic collapse."[63]

In fact, the aid program left but a slight imprint on the Greek economy. To be sure, the massive American funding and the overall direction of Greek economic affairs did prevent a total collapse. Yet American aid and supervision did little to reconstruct the shaky underpinnings of the Greek economy, to foster substantial economic growth, or to promote the general welfare. Instead, by turning to the familiar nostrums of free enterprise economics, American officials accomplished little beyond fortifying the privileged position of the Greek upper class within a context of economic underdevelopment. The diagnosis of the Americans "always has been the same," observed the Liberal newspaper *Eleftheria* in the spring of 1949: "great poverty; unscrupulous financial oligarchy; unethical and impractical political leaders." What, then, did the Americans do about this? "Absolutely nothing," claimed the journal. "Although they are severe critics, they are super-conservative when it comes to action."[64] Such a judgment may underestimate the American exercise of power, but not its direction. The major "reforms" introduced by U.S. officials were those preached by Adam Smith and the doyens of classical economics. And not surprisingly, these "reforms"—in conjunction with the American-sponsored war effort—left Greece virtually as impoverished, class-riven, and economically dependent as before the American experts arrived.

7.
TAMING THE GREEK LABOR MOVEMENT
1947–1949

[The] job here will not be conventional reporting but day by day
guiding, influencing, conciliating and, in effect, bullying several
elements in [the] Greek labor movement and some in [the] Govt
. . . while we work out a sound basis on which to develop here a
bona fide trade union movement, uncontrolled by Communists.
James H. Keeley, April 26, 1947[1]

Although the President's "Truman Doctrine" address of
March 12, 1947 did not refer to the Greek labor movement,
the future of that movement was very much on the minds of
prominent Americans. In secret State Department committee
meetings that April, the chief of the International Labor Division outlined plans for "bringing about labor stability in
Greece," while MacVeagh urged that "labor experts" be attached to the American Mission for Aid to Greece for "direction and supervision of the Greek labor movement." Marshall's instructions to Griswold, delivered on July 11, 1947,
illustrated the interests and concerns of American policymakers:

Careful attention should be given to the problem of the labor unions
in Greece. . . . Communist . . . control of the unions . . . would
create a situation likely to negate completely the work and objectives
of the Mission. Our aim is to encourage in Greece the development
of a free democratic labor movement concerned primarily with
genuine trade union objectives.[2]

Such concerns paralleled those of the leaders of the American
Federation of Labor. In late 1944, at the prodding of its leadership, the AFL established a Free Trade Union Committee

192

to build "free and democratic trade unions" in Europe, Asia, and Latin America as a means of challenging those purportedly under Communist leadership.[3] The problem for the AFL, as for the State Department, was what to do when "free trade unions" meant leftist ones. In these circumstances, a choice was inevitable, and neither the State Department nor the AFL hesitated to make it in Greece.

In the years before the arrival of the American mission, the history of the Greek labor movement was a stormy one, ridden with political turmoil and government intervention.[4] During World War II, Greek Communists sparked the formation of a trade union resistance organization, the Workers National Liberation Front (EEAM), with a leadership that reflected the general political orientation of the resistance movement: Costa Theos (Communist), Dimitrios Stratis (left Socialist), and John Kalomiris (right Socialist). According to C. M. Woodhouse, no admirer of the Greek left, EEAM "contained all that was best of organised labour in Greece. . . . There was a clear-cut division between collaborating puppets on the one hand and EEAM on the other." At the time of liberation, EEAM ousted its rivals and took control of the General Confederation of Labor (GSEE). However, the civil war of December 1944–January 1945 led the Greek government to purge the left-wing GSEE ledership and to appoint conservative labor officials to the federation's provisional executive. Deprived of power by administrative decree, the Communists sought to revive labor's popular front by establishing the Workers Anti-Fascist Organization (ERGAS) and appealing for support to the major international labor body, the World Federation of Trade Unions (WFTU). The Communists demanded trade union elections, while the Greek government tried to avoid them—both, apparently, certain that the left would emerge victorious. In June 1945, U.S. intelligence reported that a Greek Labor Ministry source considered "70 percent of organized labor leftist." Surveying the situation some years later, Hugh Seton-Watson concluded that it was "probable that the majority of workers throughout Greece at this time really preferred communist leadership."[5]

At the request of Greek unionists, representatives of the British Trades Union Congress (TUC) and the WFTU (to which the TUC was affiliated) journeyed to Greece in 1945 to work out a compromise between the feuding factions of the Greek labor movement. In December, meeting with the secretary of the WFTU, all factions agreed to procedures for trade union elections and to the convocation of a national GSEE congress on March 1, 1946, to choose the labor federation's executive. When ERGAS won the elections, however, leaders of labor's right wing, charging improper practices, boycotted the ensuing GSEE congress. Although WFTU observers certified that the "composition and conduct" of the congress were entirely appropriate and that its decisions expressed "the will of the working class of Greece," the right-wing leaders refused to accept this assessment or the minority of places reserved for them on the new GSEE executive. Instead, led by Fotis Makris—a former member of EEAM who had thrown in his lot with the Populist Party—they appealed to the Greek courts. Responding to their complaint in May 1946, the Council of State invalidated the ministerial decisions underpinning the GSEE elections. The Populist Minister of Labor, taking this as a green light for government action, demanded the resignation of the elected GSEE executive. When the latter refused to comply, he ordered the labor federation's offices and records seized, arranged for its leaders to be jailed, and appointed a new GSEE executive, under the control of Makris (now a Populist member of parliament) and his associates. Makris and his right-wing labor allies also began to receive direct financial support from industrialists and from the Populist government. Enraged, the ousted GSEE executive appealed to the WFTU, the TUC, and the courts. In October 1946, the latter ruled that, while the Minister of Labor could validly remove the elected (left-wing) GSEE executive from office, he lacked the authority to appoint a new one. This appeared to mean that the Greek labor movement lacked *any* recognized leadership.[6]

For British Foreign Secretary Bevin, a leader of the British Labour Party, these events were particularly embarrassing. One

Foreign Office official reported that the Greek government's removal of the elected GSEE executive "antagonized the WFTU . . . the TUC . . . organised labour everywhere, and a large body of His Majesty's Government's supporters." Anxious to resolve the Greek labor crisis, Bevin dispatched W. H. Braine, the British labor attaché in Rome, to Athens to negotiate an acceptable settlement. Braine met extensively with Greek leaders in the fall of 1946, and on November 2 signed an accord with Prime Minister Tsaldaris. The Braine-Tsaldaris agreement provided for the release of imprisoned labor leaders; the scheduling of new trade union elections under the supervision of Greek judges and international observers; and the appointment of a new GSEE provisional executive, consisting of 5 representatives from the Communist-led ERGAS, 2 Socialists (Stratis and Kalomiris), and 5 from the labor right-wing (EREP). According to a U.S. labor attaché, in a political showdown within the proposed GSEE executive, "the vote would have been six to six, since Stratis (Left-Socialist) had by now broken with the Communists, but still leaned leftward, while Kalomiris, moderate Socialist, had broken completely with the Communists and was now lining up with the Right." Initially, only the Socialists would accept the Braine-Tsaldaris formula. But after the WFTU urged compromise on both sides, ERGAS announced its acquiescence. The right, however, led by Makris, remained obdurate, while the government released only a small number of the imprisoned union leaders. Determined to overcome these last obstacles to a settlement, the British brought great pressure on the Populist government in the winter of 1946–47 to implement the Braine-Tsaldaris agreement.[7]

Into this volatile situation stepped Irving Brown, the European representative of the AFL's Free Trade Union Committee. Setting up shop in Brussels in 1946, Brown had been meeting frequently with anti-Communist union chiefs, U.S. officials, and European government leaders as part of the AFL's far-flung efforts to create anti-Communist labor bodies and to destroy the WFTU, which drew the AFL's ire because of Communist labor participation. In the United States, this campaign was underwritten by a $1 million fund, disbursed by Jay Lovestone, the AFL's chief foreign policy strategist. Once the secretary of the American Communist Party, Lovestone brought to the "free" labor movement, as Victor Reuther observed, "the working habits and undercover techniques that he learned in the highest [party] echelons." In early 1947, only the most rabidly anti-Communist labor movements welcomed the AFL's general orientation, and both America's Congress of Industrial Organizations (CIO) and Britain's TUC continued to participate in the WFTU, much to the disgust of AFL leaders.[8] Nevertheless, the overseas program of the AFL generated far greater sympathy within the State Department, which, given its growing commitment in Greece, fretted about the uncertain future of the Greek trade unions.[9] When Brown traveled to Athens in late February 1947 to examine the Braine-Tsaldaris agreement, he began a mission with important ramifications for U.S. foreign policy.

Brown was deeply disturbed by the situation he found in Greece. Before leaving Athens in early March 1947,[10] he discussed his impressions with officials at the American embassy, and six days later provided them with the first excerpts of his catalytic report. "Greece is the battlefield between east and west," he wrote. "Simple formulas creating unity in form and going through the motions of elections result not in a united trade union movement but in an instrument excellently set up for communist penetration and control." In Brown's opinion, the Braine-Tsaldaris agreement was particularly dangerous because: (1) it "proceeds upon the false assumption that the unity of a national organization . . . is necessarily desirable or possible at this stage of Greek development"; (2) "places faith in an election formula ignoring or failing to take into consideration the basic struggle between two diametrically opposed concepts in the labor movement"; and (3) it "continues the intervention of the WFTU when its pro-imperialist Russian role . . . is so clearly evident." In his communications with AFL and U.S. government officials, Brown urged the rejection of the Braine-Tsaldaris agreement, the promotion of measures to ameliorate the conditions of Greek workers, and the development of a center-right union bloc, which "can become the basis for a real trade union movement." He also recommended the immediate dispatch to Athens of a U.S. labor attaché thoroughly "acquainted with the history and background of world communism."[11]

With the appearance of Brown's report, American officials became alarmed. The United States had previously left the direction of Greek trade union affairs to the British, but the situation outlined by Brown seemed to call for American intervention. Citing Brown's warnings and the preference of Greek rightists for a separate labor organization, the U.S. embassy told the State Department on April 2, 1947 of its doubt "that [the] present is [a] propitious moment" for unification of the Greek labor movement and of its "fear that [the] zeal of British labor representatives . . . for [a] unified Greek labor movement at all costs can only play into the hands of disloyal Communists." The embassy urged the State Department either to press the British to drop plans for implementing the Braine-Tsaldaris agreement or to authorize the embassy to tell the Greek government "informally" that plans for unification should be scrapped. The embassy added that the right-wing Greek government "would welcome such [a] suggestion from [the] US."[12] Accordingly, on April 7, in Washington, Loy Henderson informed the British embassy that the State Department objected to the Braine-Tsaldaris agreement, for it would "give the Communists an opportunity to dominate the labor movement in Greece." Over the next two days, in London, the State Department made similar approaches to the Foreign Office and to Vincent Tewson, secretary of the TUC.[13]

The British, however, exhibited a somewhat more relaxed attitude than the Americans. Commenting on Brown's report, one Foreign Office diplomat noted that the AFL representative's opposition to the Braine-Tsaldaris agreement sprang from "a more extreme phobia against Communism than either British trades unionists or British Government representatives would evince." Furthermore, Brown did "not apparently realize that some effort had to be made to reach an agreed solution," unless the United States was "prepared to treat Greece as an area in a colonial stage of development." In Washington, the British claimed that Communists were not expected to control the GSEE provisional executive under the Braine-Tsaldaris agreement, and that the agreement had been drawn up under the assumption that they "would voluntarily abstain when they saw they could not dominate it."[14] Tewson provided a similar interpretation, claiming that, while unification would probably not succeed, "we must make an effort in order [to] convince [the] British labour movement we tried our best." Orme Sargent of the Foreign Office maintained that the presence on the provisional executive of "five Right Wing representatives should be sufficient to ensure that elections were reasonably fair," while M. S. Williams, acting head of the Southern Department, argued that, if free elections were held under the Braine-Tsaldaris formula, "the Communists are not likely to win out."[15]

American policymakers were not reassured. "The State Department felt strongly that the unification of the Greek trades union movement before American aid to Greece became effective would result in the Communists becoming firmly established," noted Sargent, while it "hoped that if things were left as they were until American aid for Greece had become effective the moderates would pluck up courage and would be able to secure control." Consequently, on April 11, Acheson instructed the embassy in Athens to inform the Greek Prime Minister that there should be "further study before decisions re[garding the] method of unifying unions and holding elections are reached. It would be unfortunate if precipitate action should be taken before [the] arrival [of] our mission in Greece."[16] Prime Minister Maximos, of course, was delighted with the American initiative, and confided to the Americans secret Greek government plans to establish a new GSEE provisional executive, composed of 10 rightists, 4 Communists, and 4 independents, "some of whom he thought might be persuaded to side with" the rightists. On

April 16, the State Department ordered Samuel Berger, the U.S. labor attaché in London, to go to Greece to evaluate the situation and to make "recommendations for [a] policy best suited to avert domination of [the] labor movement by elements which in our view would attempt to thwart [the] proposed US program in Greece."[17]

The major difference between American policymakers and their British counterparts was that the Americans were taking no chances of a Communist victory. Realizing that something was amiss, British diplomats in Athens met with U.S. embassy officials on April 16 in a final effort to salvage the Braine-Tsaldaris agreement. They contended that the agreement merely provided for trade union elections, and that even if the Communists emerged victorious, the situation would not be disastrous; non-Communist trade union members, they insisted, refused to follow Communist leaders into political strikes. However, they "made no impression," reported the British chargé, Patrick Reilly, for the Americans had "made up their minds" that Communist control of Greek unions "must be avoided at all costs." He added:

Mr. Keeley actually argued that if free elections would produce a Communist dominated executive it would be better to have none and in answer to the suggestion that this was hardly democratic, replied that . . . it was proper to protect them from electing Communists. Our argument that the latter were elected as trusted trade union leaders of long standing merely produced [the] reply that the sooner they were removed the better.

After close questioning by the British, the Americans finally revealed their secret *démarche* to the Greek government. Shocked at the tactics of American officials—which they now realized had destroyed their chances for implementing the Braine-Tsaldaris agreement—the British were also irritated by the American unwillingness "to run the slightest risk of a Communist victory" of any kind. Reilly informed the Foreign Office on April 17 that "at a time when the Americans were already having to lecture the Greeks about the undemocratic tendencies of their regime," it was paradoxical that "they should be urging the maintenance of the present trade union set-up, and should be prepared to admit that they would rather have no trade union elections than free elections that returned any Communists!"[18]

With the Braine-Tsaldaris formula scotched, the way lay open for a new settlement on terms more acceptable to the Americans. According to Reilly, "Keeley at first proposed that trades union elections should be forbidden until [the] general situation had improved . . . so that . . . workers would be less discontented and less likely to vote Communist." Keeley thought this "might take nine months to a year," but Berger and the British objected that "such a long ban on elections could not be justified." Eventually, it was agreed that Braine, Berger, and Tewson would try to work out an acceptable arrangement for elections and for the GSEE provisional executive. Berger reported to the State Department: "I did not see how a provisional executive could be composed on the basis of the representative strength of the various elements among the workers, since the Communists could clearly claim a majority on such a basis." Instead, "the formula had to be designed to keep the Communists in the minority, and yet must be one which could be defended before the court of bona fide world labor opinion." On April 29, Tewson, Berger, and Braine agreed on a 5-5-5 distribution of seats (the "Tewson formula") for left, center, and right, "in which the Communists could count on 5 possibly 6 votes, and the non-Communists 9."[19] The right, however, still refused to participate, with their refusal supported by U.S. officials. Indeed, the U.S. embassy demanded that Communists be *totally excluded* from participation in the GSEE provisional executive.[20]

The hard-line U.S. position on the Greek labor movement caused a sharp confrontation between the State Department and the British Foreign Office. Angered by American intervention,[21] Bevin dispatched a strong telegram to Marshall on May 5 and followed it up by an even stronger one the following day. "I am greatly disturbed about [Greek] trades union developments," he declared; they would have a deleterious impact "not only in Greece but even on Anglo–United States relations." If a GSEE executive "is established in Greece which is in no sense representative of the feelings of the Greek workers . . . the consequences will be very serious." Bevin complained that "American influence has been largely responsible for the repudiation of the Braine-Tsaldaris agreement by the Greek Government" and that "the political objections raised by your Embassy at Athens proved a stumbling block" to the Tewson formula.[22] Marshall replied that he did "not see how definitive steps toward [a] reconstituted General Confederation of Labor could be taken before next year since basic reforms are necessary. Meanwhile, it is hoped that the stabilizing influence of US aid will strengthen development of [the] kind of trade unions which both [the] US and UK desire in Greece." Even so, Marshall agreed not to object to "fair left-wing representation" on the GSEE provisional executive. Accordingly, he instructed the U.S. embassy in Athens:

We feel [the] matter has already progressed so far that insistence on our part that no Communists or pro-Communists be included in [the] provisional executive would make us vulnerable to charges of interfering [in the] internal affairs of Greek labor unions and give Communists [the] opportunity [to] strengthen sentiments of hostility to [the] Greek and American Govts in Brit[ish] labor circles. . . . Therefore, without abandoning our position that eventually [the] Greek trade union movement must purge itself of all Communist leaders . . . we are not now insisting that Communists or persons under Communist influence be excluded from [the] provisional executive provided [that a] majority of [the] executive is opposed to Communists.[23]

Anticipating Marshall's position, American and British officials in Greece had already begun working to build an invincible center-right majority. At the suggestion of Brown and Berger, they had been holding secret meetings since mid-May with center and right labor leaders to organize them into a formal bloc. The "task of organizing [the] bloc must, however, be handled carefully," MacVeagh cautioned, "to avoid [the] accusation [that the] US and UK governments [are] intervening in [the] internal affairs [of] Greece and [the] Greek

labor movement." To avoid the appearance of direct government participation, the AFL's Brown and the TUC's Tewson
were asked to return for the organizing work.[24] The British,
however, worried that too overt a center-right association
would lead to a leftist rejection of the Tewson formula. Brown,
on the other hand, insisted that the left be formally excluded
from any future executive and that the center-right bloc become the basis for a reconstituted Greek labor movement. In
late May, Brown and Braine became locked in a furious argument between exclusion and compromise, in which Brown
finally bolted from the room, declaring that he was going to
"get out of here." Berger took a middle course, arguing for
a center-right coalition as a means of overwhelming the left
and, ultimately, provoking its withdrawal. As he reported to
the State Department: "It was my hope that the Communists
would refuse to enter a provisional executive committee
which they could not dominate and . . . this proved correct."[25]

It proved correct, however, only after U.S., British, and
Greek government officials had circumscribed the power of
the left still further. In late May, after caucusing with leaders
of the center-right bloc, these officials agreed to modify the
Tewson formula in a fashion much to the advantage of the
right. Although ostensibly a 7-7-7 arrangement, it actually
provided for 6 seats to ERGAS, 1 to left-Socialists, 3 to right-
Socialists, and 11 to the right, thus giving the last a representation far in excess of its actual support within the Greek labor
movement.[26] Apologizing for even this measure of compromise with the left, MacVeagh notified Marshall on June 7
that it was necessary to accept the inclusion of "Communists
and fellow travellers" in the provisional executive to obtain
the support of the Socialists and Tewson and "thus avoid our
holding [the] bag"; the embassy, however, "agrees fully [that]
maneuvers from now on must be directed [to the] exclusion
[of the] Communists." U.S. success along these lines became
a certainty after Brown and the right insisted that the GSEE
forswear affiliation with the WFTU and accept future election
supervision by the AFL and CIO. On June 12, when the
Greek courts appointed a new GSEE provisional executive

in the line with the 7-7-7 formula, Costa Theos, the Communist labor leader, assailed it as a government maneuver to control the labor movement and announced that ERGAS would not accept its 6 allotted seats.[27] That July, the possibilities of compromise broke down entirely when the Greek government, as part of its overall crackdown upon the left, arrested Communist union officials, including three proposed ERGAS representatives on the GSEE executive.[28]

Although the British genuinely regretted the failure of compromise,[29] the Americans rejoiced at the outcome: a GSEE provisional executive, shorn of Communist participation, with 11 of its 15 members on the right. Berger reported to the State Department that the absence of Communists in the Greek labor confederation's leadership would make it "substantially easier to effect" future "purges" and to "wrest control from them in the coming elections." Moreover, "the recent arrests . . . will deprive ERGAS of its two foremost national leaders, and will weaken the Communists further." In spite of these gains, however, American officials were suspicious of Greek workers, for it was far from assured that they would elect the kind of leadership desired by the State Department. Therefore, Berger suggested on July 24 that "it would be unwise . . . to have elections for a national congress until there is certainty that the Communists will not emerge in control by virtue of their substantial influence over many local unions." Recent victories by non-Communists in local elections, he pointed out, occurred because EREP, the major right-wing group, was "demanding elections only in those unions where it thought there was a chance of defeating ERGAS." Hence, "until there is proof that the results of an election for a delegate conference will not produce a Communist majority," members of the GSEE provisional executive should be encouraged to bide their time, to "purge the fake unions, and to develop their united front." Meanwhile, American officials would continue their efforts to revamp the Greek labor movement.[30]

Since April 1947, the U.S. embassy in Athens had been

urging the appointment of a full-time labor attaché, preferably Irving Brown, to superintend Greek trade union matters, destroy Communist influence in the labor movement, and keep the center-right labor bloc together.[31] As a result of his other AFL commitments, Brown was not in a position to accept. Consequently, the State Department dispatched Berger on a temporary basis, later replacing him with a long-term foreign service appointee, Smith Simpson. Brown, however, was unimpressed by Simpson and—together with the embassy— called for the appointment of representatives of the U.S. labor movement to serve as labor advisers to AMAG, then in formation.[32] In July 1947, after negotiations with American labor leaders, the Labor Department, and Averell Harriman, the State Department announced the appointment of Clinton Golden, a professor at the Harvard Business School. Long active in the United Steelworkers of America, Golden had attended the March 1947 meetings between Acheson and top U.S. labor leaders and had shown his solid support for the Truman Doctrine. For his assistant, Golden chose Alan Strachan, the Washington representative of the United Auto Workers. Although both men were CIO members, and had once even been socialists, they were veterans of bitter fights against Communists in their own unions and, in line with the AFL's traditional orientation, had discarded class consciousness for job consciousness.[33]

By the time Golden and Strachan took up their duties in Athens in September 1947, the rightward course of Greek labor affairs, encouraged by American intervention, had become irresistible. With 11 seats out of 15 on the GSEE provisional executive, the right easily elected one of its leaders, John Patsantzis, to the top post, that of Secretary General. Meanwhile, Makris took control of the influential Athens labor center, while a close ally of his, Demetrios Theocharides, assumed power in Salonika. "Trade union administrations dominated by the Communists were ousted from office," recalled a U.S. government official, "some by ballot, others by force."[34] Centrist labor groups received much the same treatment. In the summer of 1947, when the government busied itself arresting and exiling left-wing labor leaders, it also arrested 45 Liberal trade unionists, while the right established its hegemony in Salonika through extensive fraud and violence. Centrist labor officials complained bitterly to the American embassy that "Theocharides and his followers do not hesitate to resort to pistols to enforce their demands." Beginning in late 1947, Makris, now lavishly funded by the Populist Party, purged 63 unions from his Athens labor center for alleged guerrilla sympathies—a move which apparently had more to do with his ruthless drive for power than anything else.[35] At the same time, the Greek government dissolved all trade unions affiliated with the Communist-led ERGAS and began to arrest and execute their leaders. On December 15, Tewson, speaking for the British TUC, warned Bevin that "the developments of the past few months are creating an indefensible position."[36]

American officials were also disturbed. Although they welcomed the elimination of Communist influence from the labor movement,[37] they feared that the continued stampede rightward would disrupt Greece's center-right labor bloc, turn moderate European and American labor organizations against American policy, and lead to the breakdown of U.S. control over Greek developments. Irving Brown warned AFL leaders of the need for "constant advice and guidance to the inexperienced Greek trade union leaders" as well as for "direct relationships with the State Department and the Greek mission to assist in developing policy." In Athens, American government officials worried that Greece's centrist labor leaders—moderate Socialists like Kalomiris and Laskaris or the leaders of the small Liberal trade unions—were either too weak or too prone to compromise with the Communists. Yet they also felt a measure of distaste for unscrupulous rightists like Makris and Theocharides. Eventually, they gravitated toward the more moderate spokesman of the labor right, Patsantzis, the GSEE Secretary General. Throughout the summer of 1947, Simpson worked closely with Patsantzis, accompanying him on tours, encouraging his faction within the GSEE, and cautioning him against extremist practices.

For a time, this strategy seemed to work. Not only did Patsantzis differentiate himself from Makris and Theocharides through more moderate policies, but he proved consistently willing to follow American leadership.[38]

Another reason for the U.S. support of Patsantzis was the assistance he provided toward negotiating an American-sponsored national wage agreement. Shortly after their arrival, Golden and Strachan turned their attention to the thorny issue of Greek wages. Thanks to the drastic inflation in wartime and postwar Greece, the wages of Greek workers lagged far behind the swiftly rising cost of living. On the other hand, determined to halt the upward price spiral, most American officials were opposed to future wage increases. Indeed, during a State Department planning meeting in April 1947, it was agreed to "press for a wage freeze in Greece," a position accepted by most U.S. officials in Athens.[39] Sympathetic to the plight of Greek workers and fearful that economic duress would drive them toward revolution, Golden and Strachan hoped to find a compromise through an incomes policy. When Greek workers, driven by desperation, threatened a general strike in October 1947, Golden succeeded in forcing through the establishment of "a national wage policy committee," in line with several paragraphs he inserted into a speech by the Greek Prime Minister. In subsequent negotiations between industry, labor, and the Greek government, the U.S. labor advisers managed to win agreement to a series of national wage guidelines. In about 10 percent of the cases, the guidelines increased worker take-home pay, but in the balance they merely clarified wage categories and rates and established the groundwork for subsequent wage adjustments, if based upon increased productivity, of up to 30 percent. Although this agreement could hardly be considered a major gain for Greek workers, particularly in the absence of any other measures to control inflation, Patsantzis and Kalomiris dutifully signed it on behalf of the GSEE.[40]

Jealous of Patsantzis's tightening grip on the GSEE leadership and convinced that he was being sidetracked by the Americans, Makris balked. The national wage agreement, he announced, represented a sellout to the industrialists, and his Athens labor center would organize a general strike in protest. To the disgust of American officials, who wanted to call Makris' bluff, Tsaldaris bailed out his Populist ally by promising that, if the followers of Makris did *not* strike, they would receive "special consideration" for wage increases. Through this maneuver, Golden noted, the "significance of the new freely negotiated collective agreement was diminished and the growing influence of Patsantzis was momentarily checked." The anger of American officials had barely subsided before Makris and Theocharides scheduled a special meeting of the GSEE provisional executive for mid-November. With the assistance of considerable funding from their rightist patrons, they planned to oust Patsantzis and Kalomiris while simultaneously installing themselves in absolute control of the Greek labor movement.[41]

The American response was swift and decisive. Informed of plans for this "rightist coup," the embassy frantically cabled Washington that "Makris and Theocharides (a) are not trade unionists; (b) are entirely political, being financed by one or more Rightist political parties; (c) have never made any pretense of working with Simpson [and] Golden and supporting [the] American program." Their victory would be a "severe blow" to American efforts in the labor arena. Marshall promptly replied that U.S. officials should impress upon Greek government leaders that the existing GSEE provisional executive represented the "only legitimate and defensible instrument" for the Greek labor movement, and that the success of "current intrigues" would jeopardize the entire American aid program.[42] In their meetings with Tsaldaris and the Greek Minister of Labor, American officials stressed these points, with Simpson adding that the withdrawal of Makris and Theocharides from the labor movement would be welcome. Deferring to American authority, Tsaldaris promised to whip his labor lieutenants into line. If Makris disobeyed, Tsaldaris declared, he would "arrest him."[43] Accordingly, when the GSEE provisional executive met on November 14, Patsantzis, Kalomiris, and the national wage agreement received a unanimous vote of confidence. Thereafter, Keeley reported that the Patsantzis forces would move to dismiss Makris and Theocharides from their GSEE posts and from their direction of the Athens and Salonika labor centers, with "supporting action" by the U.S. embassy and AMAG. "In seeking to exploit politically [the] wage situation and especially [the] collective agreements," noted Keeley, Makris "has stamped himself as [an] unreliable trade union leader." At the GSEE provisional executive meeting of December 5, Makris was dismissed from his post as a national secretary by a unanimous vote.[44]

But in December 1947, with Makris attempting to resurrect his power by threatening a strike of Athens banking and public utility employees, the situation took a new and dangerous direction. Early that month, while Griswold was out of town, his Special Assistant suggested an anti-strike law to the government's Cabinet Economic Policy Committee, apparently as a means of staving off the much feared inflationary wage increases.[45] Arguing that "the Americans want this law," Tsaldaris convinced his colleagues to pass legislation on December 6 banning strikes on penalty of death. In fact, the Populist leader had exaggerated the American desire for legislation this drastic; nevertheless, with the exception of the American labor advisers, few American officials exhibited much interest in modifying or repealing it.[46] They were merely concerned, Griswold noted, that "the political implications of the bill would have a seriously adverse effect on public opinion in the US and other countries." Therefore, they urged the Greek government to "issue a public statement interpreting the measure as a grant of power, necessary to have in time of war, which it did not intend to invoke except when essential to the public health, national security, or essential services of the state." On December 8, Tsaldaris issued the requisite statement.[47] And there the matter might have remained, had not the U.S. labor advisers instigated a public furor.

Golden, in particular, was enraged. "This legislation," he wrote, "violates every principle of democracy and human freedom and justifies all the charges of the Communists that this is a 'monarcho-fascist government.'" Reluctantly, he declared, he had "come to the conclusion that a receiver should be appointed for this bankrupt government and country. . . . All my work has been negated and there is little use in my remaining here longer."[48] Almost as disturbing were the attitudes of U.S. officials, who had "never" given the American labor advisers "the kind of acceptance and approval that should go along with our work"; few "felt that we were really needed or actually 'belonged.'"[49] Initially, Golden and Strachan considered resigning. Eventually, however, they decided to lead a fight against the legislation from within. Lacking any leverage in Athens, they drew on their contacts in the AFL and CIO hierarchy to launch a protest campaign. On December 16, as irate letters from U.S. labor leaders began pouring in, Golden gave Griswold an ultimatum: "Unless some steps can be taken to bring about the repeal of this legislation," he would resign.[50] Privately, Golden informed his friends that "my usefulness here is ended and no matter what the government decides to do, I feel that I should leave. There is no way in which I can rationalise their fool acts."[51]

These and related events caused a considerable stir among American policymakers. On December 23, Lovett notified Griswold that "considering all factors, including [the] vigorous reaction [of] American labor, we feel strong representations [are] warranted to achieve substantial modification" in the legislation. Furthermore, Golden's "resignation at this time would be [a] serious blow to AMAG prestige and future effectiveness." In Athens, American officials began a series of lengthy meetings with Greek government leaders to secure modifications of the penalties and limit the scope of the measure.[52] Golden, a participant in these discussions, was initially heartened by the cooperativeness of Prime Minister Sophoulis, who, he reported, "is way ahead of Tsaldaris and his Populist party and I think also somewhat to the left of some of our own people here!" But American representations made little headway, and on January 26, 1948, Sophoulis announced that the law would be retained without modification for the duration of the "emergency."[53] Three days later, speaking for the CIO, Philip Murray publicly blasted Greece's "vicious anti-labor law" as "typical of those passed by fascist governments everywhere in the world." CIO members, he announced, were "reaching the conclusion that the government of Greece could not have acted as it did . . . without at least the tolerance of the American Mission." Furthermore, Murray threatened that, unless the U.S. government issued a public protest against the anti-strike law, the CIO would withdraw its support from the Marshall Plan.[54] With CIO testimony in related congressional hearings scheduled to begin on February 3, the State Department was in no position to argue. "Urgent considerations," Marshall notified American officials in Athens, necessitated "definite assurance of [the law's] repeal or modification" by February 2.[55]

Things now fell into place, much to the satisfaction of Golden, Strachan, and American labor leaders. On February 1, Tsaldaris announced that the legislation would be repealed after the GSEE held its spring labor congress.[56] And, after further prodding by U.S. officials,[57] the Greek government did repeal the law, on May 7, 1948, by decree. Golden, meanwhile, had left Greece, having tendered his resignation on January 16. With his associates warning that a flamboyant resignation would simply help "Wallace and the commies," Golden kept silent in public about the reasons for his departure. Privately, however, he wrote that "there is just too much at stake to permit things to go on as they have in this setup." He and Strachan "could have been far more useful if some of our associates had been impressed in the first place with the importance of the labor and union factor in the whole situation." In Washington, Golden sought to convince American officials of the significance of overseas labor movements and, along the way, became the chief labor adviser in the European Recovery Program. Curiously, despite his disillusioning experience in Greece, he only dimly comprehended the fact that the hard-line American policy toward Greek workers owed less to disinterest than to distrust.[58]

With Golden's departure, Strachan and Simpson inherited the job of launching the "free" Greek labor movement through the long-awaited ninth GSEE Labor Congress—and a nasty job it was. To be sure, by early 1948, left-wing influence within the GSEE had been virtually eliminated; the Communists were in prison, in the hills, or in hiding, while Stratis' left-wing Socialists had withdrawn from the rightist-dominated GSEE. "Assisted by [the] Embassy and by AMAG," Rankin exulted, the "Greek labor situation has been saved from Communist control."[59] Nevertheless, the split between the Makris and Patsantzis factions within the GSEE continued to widen. Bolstered by an alliance with the right-wing General Zervas, the Makris forces expanded their ranks, attacked their rivals as "Communists and Bulgarians," and subjected them to beatings and assaults.[60] U.S. officials continued to condemn Makris and Theocharides as "reckless agitators," but Tsaldaris seemed determined to channel power and money to what he called "his" group.[61] With the congress scheduled to begin in late March 1948, the U.S. labor advisers sought to fund it through a $34,000 loan from American labor groups and to obtain some measure of recognition for it by securing fraternal delegates from the AFL, the CIO, and the TUC.[62] A loan of this magnitude, however, failed to materialize;[63] as a consequence, the Greek government declared Sunday, March 14, a workday and earmarked a portion of Greek workers' wages for the convention.[64] Securing fraternal delegates also proved a problem, for the TUC refused to send any and the CIO delegate bowed out as a result of illness. This left only the AFL's ubiquitous Irving Brown to add luster to the occasion.[65]

The GSEE Congress opened on March 28, 1948 in the Piraeus municipal theater, with some 1,500 delegates in attendance. It began well enough, from the Americans' standpoint, for the messages of welcome by Brown, Simpson, and Strachan drew prolonged applause. Immediately afterward, however, "bedlam broke loose," as the embassy reported. When Patsantzis proposed establishing a credentials committee heavily weighted to the advantage of his faction, Makris leaped on the stage and engaged in a shoving match with his rival amid growing pandemonium. At this point, Aristides

Dimitratos, once the neo-fascist Minister of Labor under the Metaxas dictatorship and now a Populist member of parliament, took the floor with a shrewdly demagogic speech.[66] In the following days, as the convention dissolved into bitter wrangling, name-calling, and fist- and chair-fights, forcing the police to intervene, Dimitratos—portraying himself as the only true friend of the workingman—moved increasingly to the fore. In a panic, Brown and Strachan worked desperately to reunite the Makris and Patsantzis factions and to head off the increasingly likely prospect of a Dimitratos victory. Brown warned that unless these factions cooperated, the AFL would wash its hands of the Greek labor movement. Strachan applied fierce pressure as well. Although the two rivals agreed to a compromise, it proved short-lived. The following day, Strachan noted, when Makris' followers were elected as the presiding officers, they "proceeded to go after Patsantzis with all the fury they could muster." Enraged, Patsantzis and his followers stormed out of the convention to hold their own. Once again, Dimitratos seized the floor and, in a speech which Strachan thought strikingly reminiscent of Hitler's, emerged as the most prominent figure on the troubled scene.[67]

For a time, the situation seemed beyond control. "We worked like beavers to try and get the Makris and Patsantzis factions together," reported Strachan. "There were now two dangers—one that the Patsantzis group would make a deal with Dimitratos, the other that there would be a split in the GSEE." Patsantzis and Kalomiris did, indeed, suggest electing Dimitratos GSEE Secretary General, as a means of defeating Makris.[68] Brown, however, told them that the AFL "would have nothing to do with such a character," for "the Communists would be given some substance to add to their propaganda about the 'fascist' nature of the Greek trade unions." Another alternative, suggested the Patsantzis faction, was "letting Makris have the GSEE" and "forming another labor movement," in alliance with the Stratis Socialists. But Strachan, in his own words, "took over and laid into them." He and Brown insisted that the Makris and Patsantzis forces accept an eight-point compromise program. Although Makris now dominated the rump GSEE convention, the Americans retained the power to compel his adherence, for AMAG had jurisdiction over payment of the workers' Sunday wages earmarked for funding the convention delegates. "It did not take two minutes for us to make up our minds," recalled Strachan; "no decision forthcoming from the Congress, no money."[69] But although the Patsantzis and Makris forces reunited in a single convention, the power struggle continued to rage. When Patsantzis produced a leaflet revealing that Makris had been accepting funding from the millionaire industrialist Bodossakis Athanassiadis, Makris conceded the veracity of the charge, but pointed out that Patsantzis had received his share of the spoils.[70]

Dimitratos, moreover, proved tougher than expected. After Tsaldaris tried, but failed, to subdue him, Strachan, as he recalled, "came to the point and told him that his election as Secretary-General would not be understood in America." Urging Dimitratos to "state publicly that he was not a candidate," Strachan promised to bring this "generous gesture to the attention of the American and British labor movements." Dimitratos, however, insisted that the Greek labor movement sorely needed his leadership and that he was sure that "the Americans did not approve the interference of the Govt in labor matters," for he "understood that we advocated free and democratic trade unions." "There he had me,"admitted Strachan. Indeed, Dimitratos almost had the secretary generalship as well, for the following day the Patsantzis forces threw in their lot with him. On the first ballot for the post, Dimitratos—capitalizing on the divisions in the battered labor movement—drew an absolute majority: 750 out of the 1,435 ballots cast. However, this fell slightly short of a majority of all registered delegates, the requirement for victory. And the next day, before the balloting could resume, the Populist Minister of Labor, having secured agreement from American officials, rammed through parliament a law to change the election rules. Hereafter, the Secretary General would be elected by the GSEE executive, which, in turn, would be elected at the convention by proportional representation. Claiming that he, the democratically elected leader of Greek labor, was the victim of government persecution, Dimitratos finally stalked out of the meeting, leaving the field to Makris and Patsantzis.[71]

The formal launching of the "free" Greek labor movement, then, proved less than a total success. Publicly, the Athens government proclaimed that it was "happy to remember that it did everything within its power to assist the working classes in holding the Congress and dealing with the agenda in complete liberty." Privately, the American assessment was less sanguine. Strachan informed Golden that he was "disappointed, of course," for "so little" had been accomplished. And yet, "if the movement is allowed to live in a free atmosphere for a few years," he was "sure that the genuine and responsible trade union leaders will take over the situation."[72] Even this hope was thwarted, however, for, with the new GSEE executive split virtually evenly between the Makris and Patsantzis forces, a two-month deadlock ensued over the election of the GSEE Secretary General. Finally, in June 1948, Lovett advised the embassy "to relax [the] pressure it is apparently exerting against [the] election [of] Makris," for there was "no reason to expect serious adverse reaction" to his victory and there was a need for the "earliest [possible] solution [of the] GSEE problem on [the] basis of [the] greatest possible unity [of the] non-Communist factions." Thereupon, the Greek Minister of Labor intervened to break the deadlock and facilitate the election of Makris.[73] Although the U.S. embassy promised to maintain "most cordial relations" with Makris and Theocharides, it reported its continuing belief that they "have worked for [the] perversion and frustration of the T[rade] U[nion] movement." Furthermore, the tumultuous GSEE congress and the victory of the Makris forces were widely viewed as a triumph for Greek government interference. Brown did not intend to give "a penny for the Greek trade unions," he informed Lovestone in disgust. Behind Makris, Dimitratos, and Theocharides "stood Tsaldaris, whose continued support of Makris and Theocharides is a very real factor in keeping the trade unions in a mess."[74]

Securely in power, Makris turned to making the General Confederation of Labor an instrument of his will. Between 1948 and 1950, as one U.S. official recalled, the GSEE leadership expelled unions "which it considered undesirable, while at the same time ordering other unions to exclude undesirable officials from membership or refuse membership to certain workers. Unions anxious to remain in the GSEE had to comply with its instructions." In Salonika, Makris' lieutenant, Theocharides, tightened his control of the local labor center through gunpoint intimidation and the denunciation of his rivals to the security police. Makris himself persisted in "taking advantage of the communist threat . . . to crush all opposition, whether communist or otherwise." Although the embassy worked diligently to patch up Makris' deteriorating relations with non-Communist labor groups, the leadership of the GSEE had become what the U.S. ambassador called "a tightly organized political-labor ring of a right-wing complexion," funded by Tsaldaris.[75] As a consequence, the left-Socialists of Stratis and the right-Socialists of Laskaris boycotted the GSEE, demanding guarantees of greater democracy. In 1950, the Laskaris group finally returned to the labor federation, but the Stratis group continued its nonparticipation, despite what one U.S. official called "the first" GSEE convention "that was *comparatively* democratic." The "intransigent ambition" of Makris "continues to cripple the labor movement," Simpson wrote gloomily.[76] Still, Makris remained the most powerful of the zealously anti-Communist labor leaders. In this context, U.S. support, though grudging, followed accordingly.

Indeed, American officials might have healed their rift with Makris entirely had he not been dangerously responsive to pressures from his desperate working class constituency. Determined to retain his union base against all challengers, whether leftist rivals or American administrators, Makris gradually emerged as an opportunistic champion of the impoverished Greek worker. By late 1947, as an International Labour Office report noted, the prices of essential items in Greece had risen more than 300 percent since 1939, with wages lagging far behind. One ECA official in Athens estimated that "the average worker here is getting about 75% less than a living wage."[77] In late 1947, the leaders of the GSEE had signed the rather modest national wage agreement only after receiving assurance that price controls would soon be instituted. Subsequently, however, although Golden and Greek labor leaders pressed hard for price controls and rationing on seven basic items—bread, olive oil, sugar, pulses, tomato paste, rice, and kerosene—AMAG never seriously considered such a program. In mid-1948, fully aware of mass working class discontent and the efforts of their leftist rivals to capitalize on it, the GSEE leadership demanded a wage increase equivalent to the increase in the cost of living since November 1947: 30 percent.[78] Appealing to U.S. officials and to his allies in the AFL, Makris claimed that "unless the Greek workers are assisted, they shall be sunk deeper into misery and become . . . certain prey to the Communist monster."[79]

American officials had already destroyed Communist influence in the trade unions, however, and were now far more concerned about controlling inflation. Therefore, they adopted a policy of undeviating hostility to wage increases. "The Government and the Mission are in complete agreement that the wage line must be held if runaway inflation is to be prevented," Griswold reported in March 1948. Later that month, he warned Sophoulis and Tsaldaris that "pressure for higher wages [must] be resisted," and had the Minister of Labor transmit this unwelcome news to GSEE leaders. In mid-June, Rankin reported that the "government and AMAG [are] adhering to their position [of] no wage increases,"[80] while in August the new U.S. ambassador, Henry Grady, told GSEE leaders that, although he sympathized "with their difficult situation," wage gains would be inflationary, and that only productivity increases would benefit the Greek economy and Greek workers. In reply, the union leaders "expressed deep appreciation [for] American aid and [an] intention to continue their cooperation," but insisted that Greek wages had dropped to 40 percent of their prewar purchasing power, that "many manufacturers and merchants [were] reaping excessive profits," and that the problem of increasing production should be solved by employers and the government, not by Greece's poorest people. Grady, however, remained implacable. On September 3 he issued a public statement reiterating that "the granting of a blanket wage increase at this time, or a general strike in support of such increases, would do irreparable damage to Greece."[81]

The opposition of U.S. officials to wage increases was not based on hostility to Greek workers, nor on a fear of Communism, but rather on a sincere commitment to a conservative economic approach. As one member of the U.S. mission recalled: "They saw the greatest good flowing to the Greek people from monetary stability and some degree of fiscal balance. The most vicious form of expropriation, they felt, was inflation." To combat inflation, they sought to limit wages and government spending. At the same time, as another U.S. official observed, "they lost no opportunity to attack . . . any system of controls in industry and commerce, and they could not tolerate the idea of any enterprise being run directly or indirectly by the government." Greek workers bitterly resented such policies, which cut drastically into their living standards and mobilized even their right-wing leaders in angry protest. U.S. officials, however, did not live as Greek workers and were therefore inclined to take a rather lofty, dispassionate view of labor's difficulties. Gardner Patterson, the American member of the Currency Committee of the Bank of Greece, recalled, with approval, that "the primary task was to lower the socially acceptable standard of living." Among most American officials, this sort of economic orthodoxy passed for superior wisdom.[82]

Such policies placed American officials and Greek labor on a collision course. In September 1948, Makris informed Secretary of State Marshall that the Greek government's compliance with AMAG's directives "condemned Greek workers to starvation and abolished their trade union rights." Determined to prevent the general strike which Makris threatened, American officials—with Marshall's authorization—bore down upon GSEE leaders and convinced them to accept a compromise. It confined the 30 percent wage raise to those workers who had not already received it and increased the minimum wage for women to only 55 cents a day.[83] Still smoldering, Ambassador Grady predicted that "Makris's recklessness will probably continue indefinitely," and he proved quite correct. In the spring of 1949, new strikes broke out, with Makris charging that official wage policy was "a provocation in view of the tragic situation of the working class." That December, despite escalating strikes and labor protests, as well as talk of forming a Greek labor party, Grady notified Washington that the U.S. mission was "reaffirming [its] position [on] holding [the] wage line."[84] Acheson replied that, even though the unrest was not Communist-inspired and the "GSEE's hand [was] to [a] large extent being forced by rank and file workers," the State Department was "seriously disturbed" by the situation. On the one hand, the department opposed wage increases, while, on the other, a GSEE failure "might result [in the] formation [of a] new polit[ical] bloc based on organized labor," which would "complicate forthcoming elections and could provide [a] vehicle for new Comm[unist] polit[ical] maneuvers." Grady reassured the State Department, however, that the "labor situation here is in no sense out of hand," for the strike wave was ebbing and U.S. policy had been "unequivocally enunciated to [the] Greek Government." Thus, "any Washington encouragement" given to the Greek labor movement "would do serious harm."[85]

Nor were the conflicts between the Greek labor movement and U.S. officials limited to wages. As one U.S. employee noted, all AMAG divisions except the Labor Division "had misgivings . . . about everything connected with the relief of workers, and were hostile to what they regarded as an overemphasis on security." With the exception of pensions, "they felt all benefits should be abolished to save the economy from being overburdened." Among these benefits were separation pay, Christmas and Easter bonuses, and paid holidays.[86] Even pensions constituted a serious source of friction. As a result of Golden's efforts, two U.S. experts were dispatched to Greece in the spring of 1948 to study the structure of the Greek social security system and "recommend measures for rendering it more efficient." The subsequent plans of Oscar Powell, an American appointed to administer the system, would have drastically reorganized it, eliminating some parts and centralizing the rest—"in the interest," an American official reported, "of sound financing and good administration."[87] The GSEE leadership, however, reacted furiously in 1949 to the American plans. Charging that Powell had refused to cooperate with workers' representatives, failed to understand the Greek people, and would destroy their decades-old social insurance funds, Makris appealed, unsuccessfully, to U.S. government and labor leaders to force the removal of the U.S. administrator. In December 1949, bringing the matter directly to the attention of Truman, Makris added bitterly, if cynically: "Workers . . . have been purposively ignored in all manifestations of the social and economic life of the country."[88]

Makris, of course, had considerably less to complain about than did his Communist counterparts. Accused of assisting or encouraging the guerrillas—a charge often applied quite loosely—Communist union chiefs were hauled before summary courts-martial and sentenced to prison or death. In February 1949, the Greek government executed Demetrios Paparigas, a former Secretary General of the GSEE.[89] Greek and American officials took particular interest in the prosecution of 97 leaders of the leftist Federation of Greek Maritime Unions (OENO). According to an embassy dispatch, "the arrest and exile to Icaria of the more dangerous leaders" occurred in the summer of 1947, but new sweeps continued for the following year. A 44-page secret report on the subject by Greek authorities, forwarded to Washington with the endorsement of the U.S. embassy, charged that the 6,800-member union had "created human monsters from vagabond elements, which were especially trained by it in criminal schools

where degeneration and inhumanity are engendered." It had
"strangled the economic interests of the sea-working world,
and sucks its blood through satanic propaganda." This "vo-
racious hyena"—led by a "gang of sadists, murderers, and
thieves"—"aims only at the realization of . . . anti-social and
anti-hellenic pursuits" and aimed to subjugate Greece "to the
enemy Slavic yoke." In November 1948, the Greek government sentenced 10 OENO leaders to death and others to long
terms of imprisonment.[90] Although the CIO and a number
of independent American unions protested against the executions of Greek labor leaders,[91] AFL and U.S. government
officials found nothing reprehensible about them. Matthew
Woll, head of the AFL's Free Trade Union Committee, told
AFL president William Green that "no affiliate of the A.F.
of L. should pay the slightest attention" to OENO's appeals.[92]

Although most anti-Communist operations of the U.S.
Central Intelligence Agency remain secret, some, at least,
appear to have affected Greek unions. Discussing CIA involvement with overseas labor movements, Victor Reuther
observed that "CIA funding was heaviest in Italy, France,
North Africa, and Greece." One key activity, later pointed to
with pride by CIA and AFL officials, involved the recruitment
of underworld gang members to attack workers who allegedly
obstructed the shipment of Marshall Plan and NATO supplies. Thomas Braden, the former chief of the CIA's "cultural"
activities, recalled that he provided the funding necessary for
Irving Brown "to pay off his strong-arm squads in Mediterranean ports, so that American supplies could be unloaded
against the opposition of Communist dock workers." Roy
Godson, a specialist on the AFL's foreign policy, has noted
that among these ports were those of Greece. Lovestone and
Brown frequently drew on the CIA for funding of their overseas ventures. But, as Braden remarked, "though Lovestone
wanted our money, he didn't want to tell us precisely how he
spent it." Therefore, the CIA finally "cut the [AFL] subsidy
down" and began using the surplus to fund its own ventures.[93]
Exactly what these entailed remains conjectural, but their
general orientation seems clear enough.

The consequences of American policies—exacerbated by an underdeveloped economy—were also evident. Noting that the standard of living of Greek workers was "no more than a fraction of its pre-war level," the International Labour Office claimed in a 1949 report that "the lack of a solid and united trade union movement is clearly one of the factors which explain this situation." At the end of 1950, the ECA reported, "workers in most Western European countries had regained or surpassed their prewar level of real earnings"; in Greece, however, "workers' standards of living were still dangerously low." In 1952, when a dozen eggs cost $1.20 in Athens, the average unskilled worker earned $1.25 a day. Greece also remained one of the few Marshall Plan nations with widespread unemployment and the virtual absence of a labor voice in government policy.[94] Pointing to "the weaknesses and backward development of the G.S.E.E.," Irving Brown stated in 1950 that U.S. government officials would have to work "as closely as possible with the G.S.E.E. leadership so that the latter can meet their problems with intelligence and understanding." This reversed the significance of the Greek trade union experience, though, for, as the ILO observed, there had been "one intervention after another by the government," and "it will be better for all concerned when the intervention of the government in the affairs of the trade unions can cease." Indeed, argued the ILO, "there should be a return to the principle of non-discrimination in union matters" and "to the principle that all workers, without distinction whatsoever, should enjoy freedom of association."[95]

Ironically, these were just the sort of principles that American officials supported in theory but subverted in practice. Aware of government domination of trade unions in Communist nations, U.S. policymakers, without hypocrisy, promised a "free labor movement" as a meaningful alternative. Nevertheless, given their determination to make a success of anti-Communism in Greece, this ideal received only occasional attention in day-to-day operations. Gradually, they curbed the independence of the Greek labor movement and undermined its vitality, reducing it to an enfeebled Cold War ally. In December 1949, the reformed GSEE became a founding member of the International Confederation of Free Trade Unions (ICFTU), the non-Communist rival to the WFTU. That month, in a BBC radio broadcast, Makris promised that ICFTU would "strike down Communism." At the Tenth GSEE Congress, the following year, the Greek labor federation exhibited the American flag and U.S. propaganda materials, fervently applauded the Korean War, and promised to expel all known Communists from union membership. On bread-and-butter issues, to be sure, even the right-wing leaders of the GSEE found themselves compelled, by pressure from a restless rank and file, to oppose American policy. But they met with little success. As one scholar of the Greek labor movement has noted, despite the GSEE's strikes and wage protests, it could make little headway on economic matters "because the Greek labor movement was not very effective."[96] Purged of leftist militants, crippled by factional divisions, led by cynical demagogues, and manipulated by industrialists and government officials, Greek trade unions lost their ability to defend working class interests.

8.
THE MILITARY SOLUTION
1947–1949

Senator PEPPER. I believe there was to be a military mission, you said, as part of our service that we are rendering to the Greek people.

Secretary ACHESON. I said that there probably would be some officers—you might call it a military mission—who would go to Greece for the purpose of seeing what was required . . . and to see that it got into the proper hands.

Hearings of the Senate Committee on Foreign Relations,
March 24, 1947[1]

Although President Truman presented the Greek-Turkish aid program as one devoted primarily to civilian assistance,[2] the military conflict acquired paramount importance. Military personnel ultimately constituted a sizable majority of U.S. advisers in Greece, just as military spending absorbed the bulk of U.S. assistance funds.[3] This contrast between rhetoric and reality reflected the fact that, initially, the Truman administration was optimistic about the outcome of the military struggle and determined to downplay controversial aspects of the program. Thus, although the relevant congressional legislation authorized U.S. military experts to exercise broad advisory functions, the War Department originally restricted the authority of the new U.S. Army Group in Greece (USAGG) to matters of supply. "It was believed at this time," notes the U.S. Army's secret history of the project, "that United States military assistance could be made effective simply by furnishing the Greek armed forces with what supplies and equipment they needed for the conduct of successful operations against the guerrillas." In addition, "no observers would be stationed with combat units in the field inasmuch as it was believed their presence there would give critics and opponents of the aid program an opportunity for accusing the United States of conducting military operations."[4] Thereafter, as the situation altered, U.S. policymakers gradually expanded the American military commitment until, at last, it became the dominant element of the American program in Greece.

In the spring of 1947, the Greek government's actual military position was shakier than it appeared. When the first components of USAGG arrived in Athens on May 24, the authorized strength of the Greek National Army (GNA) stood at 120,000 men (of whom 20,000 were designated as "temporary"); additional naval and air personnel brought the overall strength of the Greek armed forces to 168,000. The government also drew on thousands of armed civilians in the civil police and in right-wing "home guard" units and enjoyed the advantages attendant upon use of heavy military equipment from Great Britain and the United States. Yet the government's armed forces—and particularly its military leaders— were relatively ineffective. Many officers of the prewar period had either died in World War II, been separated from their professions for years, or been excluded from the armed forces because of past service in ELAS. Furthermore, among the army's rank and file, there was a noticeable unwillingness to fight. Often this was based on a distaste for the Athens government or on a simple desire for survival. At other times, it reflected the prestige still surrounding the Greek left thanks to its wartime resistance role. A U.S. Marine Corps colonel remarked ruefully: "It would take time for them to recognize . . . that the guerrillas no longer fought for Greece and freedom, but for the Kremlin and slavery." In late 1946, British intelligence reported that 25 percent of the GNA was considered unreliable.[5] Taking command of USAGG in June 1947, General William Livesay reported that no less than "7000 Communists" in the GNA were slated for "labor battalions . . . in an isolated spot." Eventually, with the help of U.S. military assistance, tens of thousands of army conscripts underwent what General Papagos termed "moral rehabilitation" in the Greek government's island concentration camps.[6]

On the rebel side, the situation was almost exactly reversed. Beginning operations in 1946 with only 2,500 troops, the self-styled Democratic Army maintained forces of only about 14,250 as late as April 1947. Eventually, their numbers stabilized at between 20,000 and 25,000, consisting almost entirely of light infantry, augmented by small numbers of widely dispersed anti-aircraft and field artillery pieces. The Democratic Army's relative weakness in numbers and matériel, however, was offset by several distinct advantages. Many of its officers had served with ELAS and were both deeply committed to their cause and skilled practitioners of guerrilla warfare. While more disparate, the rank and file of the Democratic Army—those dismissed by Greek and U.S. government officials as "bandits"—also constituted an effective fighting force. The most capable and highly motivated had fought in the wartime resistance or had received sanctuary and training in the Communist states to the north. Many others joined the rebels or were conscripted hastily; even so, while often deficient in military skills, they soon acquired a high morale.[7] According to the U.S. Army history of the conflict, guerrilla recruits "were drawn from all classes but came mainly from the peasant stock of northern Greece and the Communist laborers and white collar workers in the larger cities. Confirmed Communists constituted about 20% of the total strength." The small proportion of Communists in the Democratic Army apparently reflected the unwillingness or incapacity of many Greek Communists to embark on a military struggle, as well as the appeal of that struggle to a broader, nonparty constitutency. Indeed, despite the cautious policies of the KKE leadership and a popular longing for peace, by the spring of 1947 guerrilla bands had emerged even on the Aegean islands.[8]

Throughout 1946 and 1947, as a U.S. Army study noted, "the Communist forces maintained the initiative in the struggle for control of Greece." Drawing on classic guerrilla warfare tactics, the Democratic Army, commanded by the skilled and charismatic Markos Vafiadis, utilized Greece's extensive mountain ranges for base areas and evaded confrontation with superior forces or firepower. Lightly equipped and unimpeded by support services or territorial responsibilities, the rebels enjoyed excellent mobility and tactical flexibility. They concentrated their forces to attack isolated localities or thinly garrisoned towns and villages. When threatened by encirclement, the bands split into smaller units and regrouped elsewhere. Although the GNA conducted many minor "clearing operations" during this period, it met with little success. The bands proved too adroit at evading standup engagements, while the GNA returned quickly to a static defense of the major cities and towns.[9] Guerrilla raids, of course, also stirred up considerable resentment toward the insurgents. Even so, the rebellion was growing. In July 1947, the U.S. consul at Salonika reported glumly that "the situation between the Greek National Army and the andartes is a stalemate." Aware of the GNA's difficulties but confident of U.S. omnipotence, U.S. military officials remained optimistic. Conceding "the marked absence of a nationalistic spirit," armed forces "wherein the offensive spirit is lacking," and "a general decadence," Colonel Charles Lehner, Livesay's predecessor as USAGG commander, concluded that there was "nothing wrong with Greece that time, forceful U.S. guidance and American dollars will not correct."[10]

Fortified by these sanguine assumptions, U.S. military and diplomatic authorities initially resisted Greek government pressures for a military buildup. On April 29, 1947, a State Department planning committee resolved that "it would be undesirable to have any substantial increase in the Greek armed forces," at least until AMAG had a chance to investigate the situation. Jernegan noted the committee's "fear that an increase in the size of the armed forces would cut too deeply into funds available for economic development." Three days later, State Department officials reiterated this position at a SWNCC subcommittee meeting, where it won general acceptance. Even after AMAG's arrival in Athens,

Greek officials made little headway toward their goal of expanded military capability. On July 29, Tsaldaris complained to U.S. officials in Washington that both Griswold and Livesay refused to authorize a GNA of more than 120,000 men, while he considered a troop increase of 45,000 imperative. In response, Griswold and MacVeagh cabled from Athens on August 1 that the GNA was quite sufficient in size to defeat the insurgents; its difficulties, they emphasized, resulted from its own failures of strategy and command. Fully concurring with this appraisal, Livesay notified the War Department on August 13 that the GNA, "if properly and energetically utilized, is sufficient to decisively defeat the . . . bandits." In conversations with Greek military leaders, he observed, "I have repeatedly stressed . . . that . . . they should devote their planning to the best utilization of the funds available and not devote so much time to wishful thinking in an endeavor to obtain more. To date I have not been very successful except to convince them they cannot obtain more through me."[11]

But in the realm of military affairs—as in so many others— Greek officials could bring leverage to bear upon their American advisers thanks to the determination of the latter to defeat the rebels. General Livesay was the first to be pried loose from his recalcitrance. On August 21, 1947, he notified Griswold that despite his "belief that the Army at its present strength, properly and vigorously utilized, is sufficient to defeat the bandits," he had come to the conclusion that "the present strength Army is not going to be properly and vigorously utilized." Furthermore, "failure of the Army to suppress the bandits will be placed squarely on our shoulders for refusing the requested increases." In this context, he recommended that the "temporary" buildup of 20,000 in the GNA be made permanent and that an additional force of 10,000 soldiers be approved. In the following weeks, Griswold showed signs of approving this troop strength increase, although—according to embassy records—he wanted "to hold it over the head of the Cabinet to get compliance with our views on military leadership."[12] This proved impossible, however, because of the even more ambitious goals of the new cabinet. At a September 17 meeting of the Supreme National Defense Council, Sophoulis recommended raising GNA authorization by 30,000 (to 150,000 men) and replacing the right-wing home guard units with a 50,000-man National Defense Corps. U.S. officials objected strenuously but, as a compromise, authorized funding for a GNA increase of 10,000 troops. In October, this funding was rechanneled to a 21,000-man National Defense Corps (NDC). The reasoning was that, by garrisoning towns and villages, the NDC would free the GNA for offensive operations and thereby raise its effective combat strength.[13]

During 1947, British officials provided another source of irritation to Washington, for they seemed just as eager as their Greek counterparts to pass along military costs to the Americans. In 1947, approximately 14,000 British troops were stationed in Greece, in addition to the sizable British Military Mission, a body of 1,380 officers and enlisted men which trained the Greek army. When Bevin suggested retaining the British Military Mission "provided that the Greek government furnish food and accommodation," Marshall approved the arrangement on April 22. Having cut some of their military costs in Greece by transferring them, indirectly, to the U.S. aid program, the British effected further saving by reducing their troop strength. By July 30, only 5,000 British troops remained, and plans were announced to remove these last symbols of British military power in the following months. In Athens, a short-lived panic gripped American officials. "This astonishingly ill-timed decision," cabled MacVeagh, was "little short of catastrophic"; British troops supplied a "precious deterrent to [a] possible Slavic irruption" and occupation of northern Greece. Indeed, "perhaps no other action at [the] present moment could be better calculated to reinforce local Communist morale." From Griswold came word that British troop withdrawal would "make impossible the effective operation of AMAG," undermine the self-confidence of the Greek government, and raise the possibility of an "independent government based on Salonika." If the plan for British withdrawal were confirmed, he thought it should be offset by the dispatch of American troops, the organization of an

American training program, and the establishment of an American military command.[14]

In Washington, U.S. policymakers responded to the British troop withdrawal plan with indignation. On August 1, Marshall wired a strong protest to Bevin, inquiring as to the meaning of the action. To the top-echelon figures of the Truman administration, a fundamental shift in British foreign policy seemed in the offing. According to Forrestal, Harriman contended that the British decision on troop reduction "was influenced by the pressure from the extreme Left," and argued that "we should have to tell the British flatly that they would have small hope of getting additional help from the United States unless they faced up squarely to their problem, which essentially is that of inducing their people to go back to hard work"; Britain's "nationalization and socialization of industry could not be underwritten by Americans." At the U.S. cabinet meeting of August 8, Marshall "expressed sharp resentment of the British action," which he claimed was "obviously conditioned by political considerations at home." Asked for his views, Harriman again blamed it on "the extreme left-wingers" whom he denounced for reducing Britain's military strength and pressing "even more vigorously on nationalization of industry." He considered it "a serious question whether we should underwrite the stability of a government whose objectives seem to be moving further to the left." Somewhat more reflectively, Marshall cabled Lovett later that month that "our thorn-pulling operations on the British lion continue to be beset by her stubborn insistence on avoiding the garden path to wander in the thicket of purely local Labor Party misadventures. They are far too casual or free-handed in passing the buck of the international dilemma to [the] US."[15]

Faced with angry protests from Washington, as well as with the subtler pressures emanating from Britain's dependence on Marshall Plan assistance, Bevin sought to placate U.S. officialdom. On September 1, he spoke poignantly to the U.S. ambassador to Britain, Lewis Douglas, about the severe difficulties he had encountered within his party over demands for troop withdrawal, which he claimed had become irresistible. He suggested, Douglas reported, reviewing "the whole position in the Middle East . . . for the purpose of arriving at a 'gentlemen's understanding' in regard to a common policy and joint responsibility throughout the area." Although the State Department welcomed Bevin's proposal—which led to the Pentagon Talks of October 1947—it remained eager to have the British retain the burden of garrisoning the area and disturbed by the potential costs of new responsibilities to the United States.[16] As a result, U.S. pressure continued. On September 9, Bevin again complained, this time to Douglas and Loy Henderson, that "it would be just as difficult for the British Government to continue to maintain troops in Greece as it would be for the American Government to send troops to Greece." He did, however, agree to a postponement of the withdrawal date. In the ensuing months, both sides began to make concessions. To appease the Foreign Office, the State Department agreed to have the Greek government pick up additional expenses of the British Military Mission. Meanwhile, Bevin continued to postpone the British troop withdrawal. In the end, British troops remained in Greece until 1954.[17]

Despite the growing costs occasioned by Greek and British demands, the U.S. military supply program made an impressive debut in 1947. Early that year, the Greek armed forces acquired aircraft engines, training planes, landing and patrol craft, and mine sweepers under surplus property credits provided by the American government. In May, plans for arms shipments quickened with the arrival in Athens of advance contingents of USAGG. On June 10, 1947, USAGG sent the U.S. War Department its first requisition of supplies for the Greek armed forces. A U.S. Army history notes that, although it was necessary to acquire some British armaments to maintain the utility of material already in the hands of the GNA, "wherever possible, the USAGG drew upon surplus American stocks, which were available at a fraction of their original cost." These purchases facilitated the procurement of a volume of supplies far greater than that originally envisaged, thus enhancing the arms buildup and minimizing the political risks. On August 2, 1947, the first U.S. ship carrying a military cargo arrived at Piraeus. It was succeeded later that month by ten additional American vessels loaded with arms equipment, most notably motorized vehicles. By the end of the year, 174,000 long tons of military supplies, with a total value of $40 million, had been shipped to Greece under the U.S. aid program. "Greek troops are now fighting with our ammunition and subsisting on our supplies," George McGhee told a CBS radio audience. In addition, U.S. Army and Navy officers were distributing American military equipment to the Greek armed forces and training them in its use.[18]

The influx of American armaments, however, failed to halt the rebel advance. Guerrilla strength rose to 22,250 by the end of 1947; and an additional 5,000 rebels underwent training in the Communist states to the north. That October, the American consul in Salonika reported in dismay that, in northern Greece, sabotage had increased 60 percent and rebel recruitment 35 percent over the preceding month. Many of the new recruits were women, who eventually comprised about 20 percent of the Democratic Army.[19] Traveling by rail through government-held areas of Thrace that fall, U.S. Colonel Alan Miller reported an "ebb tide of civilian and military morale." His own train was stopped no less than fifteen times as a result of guerrilla action. By contrast, life in rebel-held territory was infused by growing confidence and revolutionary élan. One eyewitness account which reached the State Department contended that "the andartes ate well, were an optimistic lot, and danced and sang in the village square every evening." Although the guerrillas suffered heavy casualties in December 1947, when, at the behest of Zachariades, they made costly and futile attempts to seize a heavily fortified town as the capital of "Free Greece,"[20] there was little doubt that they held the initiative. "By the end of 1947," Major Edgar O'Ballance has claimed, "guerrilla tactics had the GNA tottering. It was over-extended, riddled with fifth columnists . . . and frustrated at every turn. . . . The Democratic Army held four-fifths of Greece, and Government supporters could not move far outside the towns in safety."[21]

Naturally, American officials grew increasingly alarmed. In August and September 1947, the State Department began contingency planning against the prospect of a rebel victory. Although the State Department assumed some measure of U.S. follow-up—including the establishment of a Greek exile government on the island of Crete and of American-directed guerrilla warfare on the mainland—the CIA, in subsequent studies, planned for a more decisive defeat with disastrous political and economic ramifications. Not only would there be a "profound psychological shock which would be felt around the world," a CIA study contended, but the United States would face "the possible loss of the petroleum resources of the Middle East (comprising 40 per cent of world reserves)."[22] On September 8, Marshall notified the U.S. embassy in London that "the situation has rapidly degenerated and Greece is seriously menaced." Griswold expressed his concurrence a week later, when he informed Marshall that the "increasing deterioration [of] conditions" necessitated "increased attention and effort to the military situation." Noting that Tsaldaris had expressed "deep concern over the whole situation in Greece," including the "deteriorating military situation," Keeley declared that "it is [the] Embassy's considered opinion that all elements [of the] situation should be immediately reviewed and coordinated and all necessary steps promptly taken." At a meeting of State Department and military officials on January 6, 1948, Marshall expressed his concern about the military situation and his determination to achieve a military victory. On January 12, he advised Griswold and the U.S. embassy that the "destruction [of the] guerrilla forces and [the] establishment [of] internal security . . . have clearly assumed paramount importance."[23]

In this context, the modest restraints exercised by U.S. officials upon troop strength increases were gradually abandoned. As late as November 28, 1947, Griswold still resisted Greek government pressures in this area, arguing that AMAG's economic program "could not be further reduced" to accommodate expansion of the Greek armed forces.[24] But on December 30, Lovett instructed the AMAG chieftain to authorize an increase in the GNA of 12,000 men (bringing it to 132,000) and an expansion of the National Defense Corps by 29,000 (bringing it to 50,000). In the spring of 1948, the U.S. government approved another "temporary" GNA increase, raising GNA numbers to 147,000—an increase which became permanent later that year. Meanwhile, the National Defense Corps, which was originally created to serve as a home guard, on a "minute man" basis, gradually abandoned this role and began operating as light infantry. Eventually, as one U.S. military analyst noted, its "status was undistinguishable from other units of the Army." At the same time, the right-wing home guard units, which the National Defense Corps had been designed to replace, continued their operations, armed, at British and American authorization, with American weapons. By November 1948, when the rebels numbered approximately 23,000, the Greek government's military establishment (not including home guard units) had reached 263,000. Even so, Greek military officials continued to press for a dramatic buildup.[25]

To most American officials, the success of the Greek armed forces depended less upon their size than upon their use in combat. Given what Livesay termed the "disinclination" of government troops "to come to grips with the bandits," their overwhelming numerical superiority had relatively little impact upon the military struggle. For this reason, American officials were anxious to increase the combat effectiveness of the Greek armed forces by placing them under U.S. command. In early September 1947, Cromie called attention to Livesay's claim "that he could clear up this situation with the present Greek Army within three months" and asked: "Why not let him try it?" "Operational control of the Greek Army," he noted, "is something I think we must come to."[26] On September 2, at a meeting in Athens, Griswold suggested to Henderson that Livesay be given personnel for planning and operational work, while MacVeagh added his opinion "that officers qualified in military planning should be obtained." This took the shape of a formal request two weeks later, when Griswold cabled the Secretary of State that the "time has

come when operational advice must be furnished [the] Greek
[armed] forces." As the British already maintained a sizable
military mission in Greece, Griswold thought they should be
approached first for "operational advice." But if the British
proved "unable or unwilling," he added, the United States
"should promptly furnish aid [of] this character." In this eventuality, he "urgently" recommended the "promptest despatch
[of] 125 to 200 American army officers for this purpose."[27]

This proposal to the State Department gained powerful
external support thanks to a special military mission to Greece
that same month, headed by U.S. Major General Stephen
Chamberlain. Fairly quickly, Chamberlain concluded that
foreign direction of the war was the only way to utilize the
GNA with any effectiveness. On September 29, 1947, he and
MacVeagh approached British officials in Athens about the
possibility of using their military officers to provide direct
operational advice. According to Ambassador Norton, when
"we replied that this was at present not allowed," Chamberlain
and MacVeagh "asked what we thought of the idea that
American officers should be attached to the Greek army for
this purpose. We replied that . . . this would be excellent."
The following day, with this groundwork laid, Prime Minister
Sophoulis requested authorization for General Livesay to advise the Greek government "on all phases of military matters."
Thus fortified, Griswold again pressed the State Department
to expand the role of the U.S. military mission to operational
advice; MacVeagh seconded this approach, adding a call for
what he termed "forward planning." Meanwhile, Chamberlain filed a report calling for the establishment of a Joint U.S.
Military Advisory and Planning Group in Greece (JUSMAPG)
to provide advice to the high-level staff of the Greek armed
forces and to place U.S. advisers with Greek military units.
Although the State Department delayed action until the U.N.
General Assembly had completed deliberations on the Greek
border question, it moved quickly thereafter, winning acceptance of Chamberlain's proposals by the end of 1947.[28]

Despite the controversy provoked in early 1947 by the military aid program, the State Department encountered sur-

prisingly little opposition to expanding the U.S. military role in Greece. The National Security Council approved Chamberlain's proposal on October 27 and the President signed it on November 3, 1947. Plans now moved forward for the dispatch of 90 U.S. officers and a somewhat smaller number of enlisted men, placed under AMAG jurisdiction, to provide operational advice to the Greek armed forces down to the division level. Only Congress provided an obstacle, albeit a minor one. At the time of congressional hearings on the Greek-Turkish aid program, Secretary of War Patterson had stated that the U.S. military mission would comprise no more than 40 officers and had promised to notify the chairmen of the Senate Foreign Relations Committee and the House Foreign Affairs Committee before expanding its size or scope. At Marshall's request, Secretary of the Army Kenneth Royall and two of his top generals made the necessary approaches to the legislators on November 10. According to General W. H. Arnold, although Congressman Eaton indicated his "wholehearted approval," Senator Vandenberg expressed his displeasure and "made the remark that if the Congress had been informed of our present intentions last May, there was a chance that the legislation would not have been passed." Indeed, Vandenberg declared that "he wanted to be advised in writing of our intentions and that he proposed to bring this up for discussion" at a meeting of his committee the following day. As usual, however, Vandenberg came to terms with the State Department. After Lovett discussed the issue with him at greater length, the Senator agreed to treat the matter as routine. Accordingly, on December 31, 1947, the secretaries of the armed forces officially established JUSMAPG.[29]

Meanwhile, U.S. officials initiated a search for more aggressive military leadership. Worried that Livesay failed to appreciate the seriousness of the Greek situation, the Army Department ordered him, in December 1947, to return to Washington for consultations. After meeting with the general, U.S. Army Chief of Staff Dwight Eisenhower and his aides began scouting around for a successor—in Marshall's words, "a more impressive personality at the head of the military contingent." In early January 1948, Eisenhower sent Marshall a list of five candidates for the post. Marshall's choice for JUSMAPG director, General James Van Fleet, had compiled an impressive combat record during World War II, which led to his rapid rise in the military hierarchy. Eisenhower described him as "definitely *not* the intellectual type," but "direct and forceful." On January 26, having obtained presidential approval, Marshall notified Griswold of Van Fleet's appointment. The Secretary of State thought that Livesay "should continue on the supply end," but the latter soon chose to return to the United States, contending that he had lost his effectiveness in the circumstances.[30]

The same recognition of the deteriorating military situation that prompted a new role for U.S. military advisers also released pressures for the dispatch of American combat forces. In mid-July 1947, President Truman directed Admiral William Leahy to consult with Secretary Forrestal on the possibility of sending the Mediterranean squadron to Greece, "with the purpose of having such a 'routine' visit exercise some deterrent effect on the activities of [the] guerrilla bands." Forrestal replied with alacrity that this could be arranged "at any time." In late August, John Foster Dulles, a member of the U.S. delegation to the United Nations, reported to Vandenberg that "the U.S. might go into the Assembly asking for a mandate to send troops into Greece to patrol the northern boundaries." Dulles considered this "a reckless thing to do and contrary to the spirit . . . of the Greek Assistance Act"; European nations, particularly, "would not want to be invited to back up what might appear to be a more or less private undeclared war between the U.S. and Russia, leading from what originally was a unilateral act of ours." In a meeting with State Department officials on the morning of August 28, he told them "that the future of [the] U.N. and perhaps the future of peace were at stake," and that he would not serve on the U.S. delegation in such circumstances. Although Lovett responded soothingly that "rumors re[garding] U.S. troops were largely unfounded," he stated that they "might have to protect U.S.

lives and property in Greece." Moreover, the Under Secretary thought that the United Nations might, "perhaps, indicate that if aggression continued, nations would be free to act" under Article 51, a provision of the U.N. charter granting nations the right of collective self-defense. According to Forrestal, on August 31 Lovett informed him that "in the event of further trouble in Greece" and Communist obstruction in the United Nations, "it was his plan to go to the General Assembly on the request of the Greek government under Article 51."[31]

In the winter of 1947–48, the question of committing U.S. combat forces came very close to receiving an affirmative response. On December 22, in a memo to the Secretary of State and other diplomatic officials, Henderson argued for the dispatch of U.S. combat troops to Greece, even in the absence of contingents from other nations, if the rebel government should attract troops or diplomatic recognition from Communist countries. "Greece is the test tube which the peoples of the whole world are watching," he wrote, "in order to ascertain whether the determination of the Western Powers to resist aggression equals that of international communism to acquire new territory and new bases."[32] At a meeting of middle-level military and diplomatic officials four days later, Henderson stated that U.S. forces, if they proved necessary in Greece, should be used—a position which won the backing of the Army's Assistant Chief of Staff. Kennan, on the other hand, expressed reluctance to commit American troops, contending that they might prove ineffective, that their future role in Greece remained unclear, and that the U.S. government was apparently unwilling to take an equally strong position elsewhere in the region. Although no decision was taken at this meeting, Henderson's position apparently prevailed in the following days. NSC 5—a draft produced on January 6 by the staff of the National Security Council with the assistance of representatives from State, Army, Navy, Air Force, and CIA—declared that "the United States should be prepared to send armed forces to Greece or elsewhere in the

Mediterranean . . . if it should become clear that the use of such forces is needed to prevent Greece from falling a victim to direct or indirect aggression."[33]

Gradually, however, a bureaucratic counterattack gathered strength. On January 10, 1948, the State Department's policy planning staff questioned "whether the dispatch of U.S. armed forces would necessarily be the most efficacious means of achieving the final objective and whether an advance decision to send troops, if things get worse in Greece, would be a sound and suitable way to express . . . [U.S.] determination." U.S. forces might be "the proper tool," it noted, "but we do not feel that we have, at the present time, an adequate basis on which to make this judgment." Marshall sided with the policy planning staff for, three days later, Lovett informed the National Security Council that the Secretary of State thought that NSC 5 "ought to be re-worked; that it dealt in too abstract terms with the dispatch of troops; and that it contained no adequate appraisal of the likely consequences." When another draft, NSC 5/1, appeared in early February, it was Henderson's turn to complain, for, as he wrote, it did "not contain a clear and definite statement that the United States should decide now that . . . it will send troops to Greece if necessary." NSC 5/2, adopted by the National Security Council on February 12 and subsequently approved by the President, represented a further defeat for the hard-liners, albeit one retaining some possibilities for military escalation. Warned by the Joint Chiefs of Staff that the dispatch of U.S. forces to Greece in sufficient numbers to be of consequence would necessitate a partial mobilization in the United States, the NSC called for no more than further studies of the use of U.S. military power in Greece. On the other hand, it did resolve that, in the event of Communist recognition of the rebel government, the United States would support a U.N. resolution that requested member states to aid Greece, with "extreme care . . . taken to insure that it does not preclude direct military assistance."[34]

As 1948 wore on, the idea of sending U.S. troops to Greece foundered irrevocably on political and strategic difficulties.

According to Henderson, Marshall secretly told the Senate Foreign Relations Committee "that while we might eventually consider sending a token force to Greece or B-26's to Athens, the difficulty lay in the fact that, under heavy Soviet pressure, such forces would either have to be 'backed up' or withdrawn 'ignominiously.'" Unfortunately, "it was necessary to conserve our very limited strength and apply it only where it was likely to be most effective." Questioned on the same subject, a U.S. Army general responded that, "from the strategic viewpoint," committing American forces to Greece would be "a 'mousetrap' operation." Although the NEA director continued to hope that this did not "absolutely preclude the possible use of force in some manner," a new blow was administered by NSC 5/3, with its news that the Joint Chiefs of Staff considered the dispatch of U.S. forces to Greece "militarily unsound."[35] NSC 5/4, adopted on June 3 and approved by the President on June 21, represented only a slight reworking of its predecessor, and concluded that "the United States should not now send armed forces to Greece as token forces or for military operations." The one loophole—a provision for reconsideration by November 1, 1948—was narrowed by a NSC resolution of January 10, 1949, which concluded that developments in the Greek situation had not been of sufficient consequence to justify sending U.S. armed forces.[36]

Although the U.S. military role in Greece stopped short of the combat phase, it reached sufficient proportions to undermine what remained of British influence. On December 11, 1947, Lovett instructed the U.S. embassy in London that, while the State Department desired the "closest possible collaboration between [the] US and Brit[ish] mil[itary] missions," this collaboration "must formally preserve (1) [the] US dominant role and (2) US ultimate freedom to determine advice to [the] Grk Govt independently of Brit[ain]."[37] The chiefs of the British and U.S. military missions formulated an agreement in January 1948 that defined the functions and relations of the two groups, with the Americans to advise on operations and logistics and the British to take charge of organization and training, but the agreement was never, as a U.S. Army history observes, "officially consummated." Subsequently, the Americans began to move into the training field, while the British attached themselves to GNA operations on the same basis as did the Americans.[38] In 1948, friction grew between military officials of the two nations, particularly with respect to the necessary size of the Greek armed forces. To maintain some influence over military affairs, the British pressed to integrate the two missions under Van Fleet's direction. However, arguing that integration "would pose problems of divided administrative and command responsibility," the U.S. Army helped scotch this plan later that year[39]—one additional sign of American hegemony in Greek affairs.

On a day-to-day working basis, however, American military officials continued their "special relationship" with the British. According to Livesay, in June 1947 he and his British counterpart "both agreed that we should work closely together and present a united front on ideas in connection with Greek aid." Minimizing rifts between the "great powers" would, after all, increase their leverage in dealing with those of lesser strength and, presumably, integrity. "One of the most important things before us is to convince the Greek Army and nation that we are one unit," Livesay instructed a group of American and British officers. "Be very careful what you say because this whole country is infested with Communists and misguided individuals who will distort what you say." To maximize security, the word "Henley" would be written on papers "not to be shown to the Greeks." As Livesay phrased it: "We will have no secrets from one another. . . . It is security from the Greeks I am talking about."[40]

Anglo-American officials found such unity useful in suppressing independent tendencies on the part of their Greek underlings. Sophoulis proved especially difficult for, upon taking office as Prime Minister, he sought to replace a number of rightist military commanders with republicans. At a meeting on September 6, 1947 of Henderson, the U.S. and British ambassadors, and Anglo-American military officials, it was agreed to oppose this move, "even to the extent of threatening to hold up supplies." Frustrated in his attempts to change the GNA high command, Sophoulis complained bitterly to a visiting U.S. congressional delegation later that month that the *andartes* would never surrender to rightist military officials who, in fact, were already becoming a "state within [the] state." In the economic field, the Americans "should not only control but should use the whip in view of what has transpired," the Prime Minister declared; "however, what is done in the military field is my business."[41] Anglo-American officials, though, did not agree. On October 3, at a meeting with the commander of the British military mission, Sophoulis again pressed for personnel changes, complaining that the Greek General Staff "had not kept him informed of what was happening" and that the commanding general of the GNA was inclined to flout the authority of the Prime Minister and the government. Again, however, he made no headway, for his foreign advisers continued to resist what they called "political interference" with the Greek armed forces.[42]

In 1948, when American officials reshuffled Greek military leadership, this "interference" failed to produce similar qualms. Balked repeatedly by the Populist Minister of War, Griswold demanded agreement from Sophoulis that, if his full cooperation could not be secured, "you will, if I inform you of the fact, promptly replace him."[43] Indeed, JUSMAPG and the British military mission were quite concerned in early 1948 about the GNA's chain of command. Not only did the chief of staff lack full control over subordinate commanders, but the government's Supreme National Defense Council (SNDC) occasionally ignored the advice of Anglo-American military officials. Consequently, on February 14, representatives of the American and British embassies and AMAG met with the Greek cabinet and presented an *aide-memoire* demanding concurrence on the following points, among others: (1) that the chief of AMAG and the directors of the U.S. and British military missions be present at all SNDC meetings; (2) that new powers be granted to the chief of staff; (3) that the cabinet either give unqualified support to the current chief of staff or immediately replace him; (4) that the government accept a "gentlemen's agreement" providing that Anglo-American military advice would either be promptly accepted or referred for action to a meeting of the ambassadors, the chief of AMAG, and the Prime Minister.[44] These provisions were quickly accepted by the Greek cabinet, which thereby lost considerable control over the progress of the war either to Greek military officials or to their American counterparts. The latter, of course, retained supreme authority. That summer, when top Greek military commanders were reshuffled, it was at the behest of Van Fleet.[45]

Indeed, by 1948, American military men were playing a far more active role in the conflict than was originally envisaged. When Van Fleet arrived in Athens on February 24 to take command, he was part of a major buildup of U.S. military personnel. By September 30, the membership of the U.S. Army, Navy, and Air Force contingents in Greece reached 450, comprising about two-thirds of AMAG's personnel. As a report to Congress noted, they worked with top Greek military officials on "overall strategic and tactical planning of operations against the guerrillas," supervised "the flow of military and naval equipment and supplies into Greece under the aid program," advised the Greek armed forces "on matters of supply and training," and gave "operational advice to the Greek Army down to the divisional level."[46] U.S. government statements emphasizing that U.S. officers did not participate in combat or command Greek troops underestimated their importance. Visiting GNA forward positions with Van Fleet that June, Sulzberger confided to his notebooks that the Americans "appear to be in charge of operations and there is not much disguising this fact, although everyone pretends it isn't so." U.S. officers accompanied Greek troops into battle, where they provided on-the-spot advice and, occasionally, were killed or wounded. At least three U.S. officers died in this fashion during the Greek civil war. Woodhouse wrote: "Both on the ground and in the air, American support was becoming increasingly active, and the theoretical line between advice, intelligence and combat was a narrow one."[47]

Asked by British officials in mid-February 1948 what he

would tell the Greeks when he arrived in Athens, Van Fleet replied unhesitatingly: "Get out and fight!" In military terms, this made good sense. When the general turned up in Athens later that month, the GNA was engaged once again in a static defense role, while the guerrillas operated with relative impunity throughout most of the countryside—raiding villages, forcing the surrender of occasional government military units, and establishing the rudiments of a rebel state in the mountains of the north. Particularly irksome to Americans was the fact that the Greek armed forces, so hesitant to take the field, now numbered 263,000 men (including 147,000 in the GNA), with impressive supplies of artillery, armor, and attack planes. By contrast, the rebels numbered 23,000 and had little artillery, no armor, and no aircraft.[48] Goaded into action by Van Fleet, the GNA began an offensive that April, commencing with a sweep through south-central Greece and then proceeding toward the guerrilla strongholds of the north. At the major guerrilla concentration, in the Grammos mountains, the Royal Hellenic Air Force used American napalm bombs for the first time on June 20.[49] After suffering heavy losses, the guerrillas conducted a masterful retreat from the Grammos into Albania. Shortly afterward, they reappeared at their stronghold in the mountains of Vitsi. Here they dug in and, from August 22 to September 14, despite vastly inferior numbers and firepower, held off the GNA and ultimately sent it reeling in retreat. In October, with winter snows settling in along the mountain slopes, the fighting came to a halt, leaving behind a swath of death and destruction.[50]

Thanks to the GNA's 1948 offensive, the rebel forces suffered their first serious losses. Throughout 1948, although Markos had argued strongly for the continuation of mobile guerrilla tactics, Zachariades and the majority of the KKE's political leadership had championed the use of the Democratic Army for a static defense of territory. In the summer of 1948, they prevailed. At Grammos and Vitsi, a heavy concentration of guerrilla forces held its ground tenaciously against vastly superior troop strength and armaments and, accordingly, suffered severe casualties. In the Grammos operation alone, an estimated 11,000 guerrillas were killed, wounded, or captured. For the year 1948, according to the Athens government, rebel casualties numbered 32,000. Substantial assistance from the Communist states to the north or a high degree of success with voluntary recruitment in Greece might have offset these losses, but neither materialized. Indeed, in the devastated, war-weary countryside, the guerrillas found it necessary to resort increasingly to conscription to replenish their ranks; in the cities, Communist activity declined so precipitously that the KKE leadership dismissed the Athens politburo for its failures. For the time being, the insurgents managed to maintain their fighting strength, high morale, and aggressiveness. And, in a protracted guerrilla struggle, this represented a kind of victory.[51] Nevertheless, it was unclear how long they could sustain this feat.

Ironically, however, the 1948 military offensive caused considerable consternation in Greek and American government circles. From their standpoint, the salient fact was that, despite the full use of superior numbers and firepower by the Greek armed forces, decisive victory remained elusive. The GNA sweep in south-central Greece had failed to trap the bulk of the region's rebel forces, who gradually filtered back to their mountain hideaways and even gained the initiative in the Peloponnese. More seriously, the rebel success at retreating into Albania, holding Vitsi, and, later, reoccupying the Grammos produced what even the usually optimistic State Department report to Congress conceded was "a bitter disappointment"—a "severe blow" to government morale. Secretly, the State Department's policy planning staff concluded that "the operations of the Greek armed forces . . . have not resulted . . . in any substantial reduction of the guerrilla threat. . . . The guerrillas are not militarily less active or efficient." In a pessimistic report filed that October, Van Fleet characterized guerrilla leadership, training, and morale as excellent. By contrast, he noted, the GNA, though "adequately fed, equipped and armed," showed serious weaknesses of training, command, and esprit de corps. These factors were epitomized during the inconclusive struggle at Vitsi. GNA units had thrown down their weapons and fled. Courts-martial and executions followed, while the commanding general resigned in disgrace. Van Fleet reported caustically that "everything that has been accomplished up there has been done by air and artillery."[52]

The difficult military situation inspired, characteristically, a new series of demands for the United States to increase Greek government troop strength and firepower. Even in early 1948, during a time of rising confidence, Athens officials had been pressing for a greatly expanded GNA[53] and for additional U.S. military equipment, including special incendiary bombs, flame throwers, and poison gas. But the State Department, hopeful that victory was in sight, countered with recommendations to reduce the size and cost of the Greek armed forces, while Van Fleet replied to Greek officials that napalm, rocket launchers, fighter planes, gunboats, and other U.S. weapons of war were already being delivered in abundance. In June 1948, Griswold reminded Greek officials that the creation of the 50,000-man National Defense Corps had been predicated upon promises to disband right-wing home guard units, which nonetheless continued their operations with 48,000 armed personnel.[54] After the stalling of the Grammos-Vitsi offensive, however, the Greek government, the British Military Mission, and JUSMAPG all called for dramatic increases in the strength of the Greek armed forces. Van Fleet submitted two proposed military budgets, with differing emphases, for the coming fiscal year. As compared to the current U.S. military expenditure in Greece of $150 million, Van Fleet's budgets required expenditures of $450 and $541 million respectively. Within the embassy, Rankin urged the ambassador to remind the State Department that "we are committed, morally and practically, to see Greece through at any cost." After all, he wrote, "this country is in effect our instrument . . . , one which we are shaping to use in the furtherance of our foreign policy. In speaking of Greek 'responsibilities' we must not forget that these are matters of detail; the overriding responsibilities are ours."[55]

But key American policymakers remained uneasy about

assuming unlimited liability for the Greek military. Ambassador Grady, for one, found Van Fleet's proposals exasperating. "Throughout its life," he wrote, "JUSMAPG, whenever threatened with stalemate, has sought to increase its mission by increasing [the] size and fire power of [the] Greek armed forces. . . . The key to success according to JUSMAPG thinking is always more: more men, more money and more equipment." On November 22, 1948, Grady informed the Secretary of State:

We have today in Greece an armed forces organization of 263,000 men, which is fed with American purchased daily rations . . . clothed in American purchased uniforms, equipped with American arms, transported by vehicles and pack animals supplied by America, and trained and advised in operations by American and British officers. Supporting [the] land army is heavy artillery, an air force and navy. This armed force . . . has been unable to make appreciable progress . . . against [a] bandit organization of some 25,000 men, fed with what they could steal or buy locally, clothed in remnants, armed with old weapons found in Greece or others supplied by their northern neighbors, transported on their own or their donkeys' legs, and trained by their own leaders. . . . The bandit land army is not backed by a single airplane, heavy gun or naval vessel. . . . It seems to me that we are not justified now in assuming we will obtain our objective through the use of the old method of increasing again the size and equipment of [the] armed forces.[56]

In Washington, U.S. officials—even within the Army—were inclined to agree. Eventually, Van Fleet was instructed to resubmit his budget request, with a ceiling of $200 million.[57] Although Greek officials continued to press for expanded U.S. military support, Washington's decision remained firm.[58]

Indeed, as a result of his tendency to ignore American diplomatic officials and to accommodate himself to the extravagant demands of the Athens government, Van Fleet found himself in serious difficulties. On July 26, 1948, Griswold formally recommended transferring Van Fleet elsewhere upon the conclusion of the Grammos offensive. Acknowledging that the JUSMAPG director had instilled as much offensive spirit into the GNA "as anyone possibly could," the

AMAG chieftain argued nonetheless that Van Fleet did "not have an interest in or an understanding of the financial and political problems in Greece." Furthermore, he lacked "the ability to take a firm stand against the pressure of Greek political leaders." Although the State Department failed to support Griswold's initiative, Van Fleet experienced additional trouble upon the arrival of the new ambassador, Henry Grady. In late 1948, President Truman informed Army Secretary Royall that "there's a good deal of feeling" within the State Department "that we ought probably to send somebody there . . . who gets along better with the other American officials and who does not just run a one-man show." Remarking that "I may have to choose between the ambassador . . . and Van Fleet," the President dispatched Royall to Greece to investigate the situation. Royall did not confer with Grady, who was in Washington, during his stay in Athens; instead, Van Fleet immediately took him in tow and delivered him to King Paul and Queen Frederika. The Queen, at her most charming, lauded the general and convinced the dazzled Army Secretary that Greece "couldn't get along without him." Upon returning to Washington, Royall recalled, he told the President: "Everything's all right in Greece. Just leave Van Fleet alone, and—ambassador or no ambassador—he'll win this war."[59]

In the winter of 1948–49, however, the war looked most unpromising. Disturbed by the situation, Marshall flew to Athens in October. Here he found what he termed "a rather depreciated state of morale" among U.S. and Greek government officials. "All were in agreement that what Greece lacked . . . was a spark of leadership," the Secretary of State noted; "the only trouble was that no one had any practical suggestion about the spark." Nevertheless, Marshall agreed with Grady that, in the circumstances, further increases in the size of the GNA would be far less efficacious than would its proper employment. This focused attention on the question of command. Among American and Greek officials, the idea had been gradually taking shape of centralizing Greek military authority in the hands of a "strong" commander-in-chief: General Papagos. When Marshall concurred with this assessment, Papagos was offered the position.[60] But Papagos set tough conditions for his acceptance, most notably: an increase in the GNA from 147,000 to 250,000 men and absolute freedom of military decision. As these conditions implied vast new U.S. military outlays and an end to JUSMAPG control of the Greek armed forces, U.S. officials found them totally unacceptable. Not until January 10 did Papagos and the Americans reach a compromise. The general would become commander-in-chief of the Greek armed forces, with new powers enabling him to replace corps commanders, institute martial law, and bypass the nation's civilian leadership. With this arrangement concluded, American officials took heart, at least initially.[61]

But the appointment of Papagos was not a panacea, and familiar patterns soon reasserted themselves. On January 26, 1949, JUSMAPG's assistant director felt called upon to assail the "dismal failure" of top GNA officers during three recent guerrilla attacks. "Practically all [GNA] commanders," he remarked, "invariably plead unfavorable weather, forbidding terrain, inadequate strength, and serious dangers to other vital areas, as a defense for their inertia and failures. Yet the inferior bandits continue to operate in the same weather and over the same terrain as must the GNA, with high success, in complete defiance of and with bold indifference to a greatly superior, better fed, better organized and better equipped GNA."[62] On February 5, Papagos informed the War Council (successor to the National Defense Council), as Grady noted, "that [the] size of [the] Greek Army was inadequate" and that he had accepted the position of commander-in-chief only upon assurances that the GNA would be increased to 250,000! Accordingly, he would call up conscripts and raise the salaries of Greek military officers above U.S. authorization levels; if balked, the general implied, he would resign. "In the vernacular," reported the irate U.S. ambassador, "he was telling us off." Irked by these events, the new NEA director, Joseph Satterthwaite, advised the Secretary of State that "the time has come for a final showdown with the Greek Government." The latter "must decide once and for all whether they are willing to accept U.S. assistance on the scale which it is possible for us to offer and whether they are prepared to make sincere attempts to use it effectively without any further attempts to . . . blackmail the United States." Although Acheson phrased these thoughts more tactfully in his subsequent dispatch to Athens, its import was much the same.[63]

The growing disgust of American officials with the incompetence and irresponsibility of the Greek government inspired modest attempts at reassessing the U.S. position in the winter of 1948–49; none, however, went very far. On January 4, the Acting Secretary of State warned the Greek ambassador that "the United States cannot carry Greece indefinitely. Unless it can be shown that the Greeks are doing all in their power to solve their internal problems, the United States may have to decide whether the money allotted to Greece might not be used to better advantage elsewhere." Nevertheless, this was an empty threat, for, as the Greek government well understood, U.S. officials, given their Cold War orientation, found the prospect of a rebel victory in Greece too horrifying to accept. Cessation of U.S. aid to Greece would be followed by a "virtually complete collapse . . . in a few months," warned the policy planning staff in late 1948. As a result, "the entire communist movement would be greatly encouraged and strengthened." A February 1949 study by the CIA made the point even more forcefully: "Any reduction of US aid might have [a] disastrous effect." These assumptions fed into NSC 42/1, adopted by the National Security Council on March 22, 1949 and approved by the President the following day. Noting that there had been an "examination of alternatives," it concluded that "U.S. security interests require the continuation of our Greek program."[64]

Only in the area of long-range planning did U.S. policymakers show signs of the discouragement that their Greek venture had inspired. In the spring of 1947, American officials had predicted strategic benefits to the United States from the Greek-Turkish aid program. But on November 24, 1948 the Joint Chiefs of Staff notified Forrestal, now Secretary of Defense, that "even with considerable military and economic assistance from the United States, Greece will in all probability never have the capability of successfully resisting those attacks in force which the USSR and/or her satellites could launch against her long northern frontier. Greek military spirit is now woefully lacking." Consequently, the United States should seek no more than "a Greek military establishment capable of maintaining internal security." Despite protests from hard-liners within the State Department, this policy prevailed.[65] When the Athens government inquired about the possibility of joining NATO, the State Department responded coolly. Asked to show support for Greece, Turkey, and Iran— all omitted from the North Atlantic Pact—the State Department would do no more than call attention to a speech by Marshall in which he talked of America's "interest" in their "security." The success of the Greek army, a subcommittee of the State-Army-Navy-Air Force Coordinating Committee (successor to SWNCC) concluded, must spring from a "renaissance . . . in the hearts and minds of a populace."[66] To those familiar with Greece's condition, the prospects were hardly reassuring.

Unexpectedly, however, the tide of battle in the Greek civil war shifted dramatically in 1949. Among the rebels, the losses sustained in the 1948 offensive had been more severe than officials in Athens or Washington realized. Furthermore, as American policymakers only dimly understood, by 1949 the insurgency was plagued with fierce political infighting, disoriented by changes in military tactics, and isolated from much of Greece's war-weary populace. Meanwhile, the Greek government's armed forces, now numbering 265,000, were thrown into battle by Papagos, who ordered no holds barred. Operating under martial law, army and police security forces interned thousands of alleged rebel sympathizers and suspected informers. A U.S. Army study noted that, in response to Van Fleet's demands for aggressive action, Papagos granted every officer "the authority to shoot on the spot anyone under his command who showed negligence or faintheartedness." At the same time, "JUSMAPG recommendations" to the Greek air force "resulted in successful use of napalm bombing against guerrilla concentrations and installations." Throughout the countryside of southern and central Greece, the initial locus of the government offensive, the GNA routed the rebel bands and decimated their remnants through relentless pursuit.[67]

The final, decisive battles of the civil war took place during August 1949 in the north. Here Zachariades had concentrated most of the guerrilla forces, in an apparent attempt to deal the GNA a sharp setback. At Vitsi, the government threw 50,000 troops against 7,700 rebels and, at Grammos, launched an assault of 25,000 troops upon the 4,700 defenders. In fierce engagements at these mountain redoubts, the government air force and artillery pounded rebel positions mercilessly. At Grammos, Greek war planes flew 826 sorties in six days, employing an estimated 250 tons of bombs, rockets, and napalm. The rebels fought back desperately, once again refusing to give ground despite overwhelming odds and once again sustaining heavy losses. This time, however, the result could hardly be in doubt. Unable to maintain the defense of Grammos and Vitsi at this terrible cost, thousands of the surviving rebel troops surrendered to government forces or retreated to the Balkan Communist states of the north, where they were disarmed and detained. On October 16, with the insurgency in disarray, the rebel leaders announced a "cease-fire." That November, Truman reported to Congress on the victory in Greece.[68]

The suddenness of the guerrilla collapse suggests that more was involved than the balance of military forces which, however unequal, was substantially the same at the outset of 1949 as it had been a year earlier.[69] Indeed, in September 1949, Grady estimated that, in addition to the 3,500 guerrillas still active in Greece, there were some 16,400 Greek rebels in Albania and Bulgaria. Though far more optimistic about the progress of the war in 1949 than he had been in 1948, Grady fully expected it to continue.[70] A major reason that it did not—stressed by Greek Communist officials as well as by American and British analysts—was Tito's defection from the cause of the insurgents. During 1949, the flow of military materials from Yugoslavia, formerly the most important source of external support to the rebels, gradually dried up. Furthermore, that July, Tito closed the Greek-Yugoslav border. This action quarantined 4,000 guerrilla effectives in his country and drove a wedge between the main concentration of rebel forces in northern Greece.[71] Another important factor was the KKE leadership's complete abandonment of guerrilla tactics for positional warfare. After November 1948, Zachariades and his supporters on the KKE central committee ousted Markos, reorganized the Democratic Army along conventional lines, launched attacks in strength on urban centers, and settled in at Grammos and Vitsi for a static defense. These moves, ostensibly designed for a series of hammer blows to the GNA and the Athens government, proved suicidal; they concentrated the lightly armed guerrilla forces in areas where they were virtually destroyed by the GNA's superior numbers and firepower.[72]

The greatest turnabout of 1949 occurred in morale. However few in numbers and poorly armed, the insurgents had always possessed an esprit de corps that compensated for their technical inferiority. As McNeill wrote: "They had a dream for the future to keep them warm on the mountain tops." By contrast, GNA conscripts were notable for their political alienation and unwillingness to fight. British Field Marshal Sir William Slim summed things up in early 1949 when he reported, gloomily, that "morale is, of course, the basic factor. If the belief of the Greek people in their cause and their will to victory were as great as that of the Communists, the war would be quickly won. But it is not." Nevertheless, throughout 1949, the morale of the government forces gradually rose, while that of the rebels plummeted. Van Fleet caught the drift of things, although not the meaning, when he wrote: "With the WILL TO WIN . . . this magnificent Greek Army, Navy, Air Force and Gendarmerie came alive and the international Communist gangsters began to run." Guerrilla recruitment ebbed disastrously. At the same time, the number of rebel surrenders dramatically increased and, as one U.S. military officer observed, "by July, probably the majority of the 18,500 guerrillas would have surrendered if given a chance."[73]

Among these factors, only morale owed much to the U.S. military aid program. This program, of course, had a considerable impact upon the war. By the end of 1949, the U.S. government had channeled $353.6 million worth of military aid to Greece,[74] including hundreds of warplanes and ships, 4,130 mortar and artillery pieces, 89,438 bombs and rockets, 159,922 small arms weapons, 7.7 million artillery and mortar rounds, and 455 million small arms rounds. Armed with this weaponry and directed by U.S. officers, Greek government forces succeeded in killing 36,839 insurgents ("nearer 50,000," according to a current Greek government official), capturing 20,128, and wounding many others. Within government ranks, the losses were considerably lighter: 14,356 killed, 30,476 wounded, and 4,617 missing.[75] This program, more than anything else, probably saved the Athens government from defeat. But few observers considered it the major cause of that government's victory. U.S. armament improvements "came too late to have any material effect during the war," one U.S. military analyst noted; "in all probability the war would have ended where it ended and when it ended had no changes in armament occurred." Woodhouse agreed. "The improvements introduced by . . . JUSMAPG," he wrote, "were not in the end decisive."[76] Indeed, if the dramatic insurgent collapse can be ascribed, in large part, to Tito's defection, the change in guerrilla tactics, and the decline in rebel morale, then it was rooted less in U.S. efforts—important as these were—than in the changes wrought by a realignment of Communist forces on the world scene. And it is within this international context that the full meaning of the Greek civil war, as well as the Cold War myopia of U.S. policymakers, becomes most evident.

9.
THE INTERNATIONAL DIMENSION 1947–1949

The problem in Greece is merely one of cessation of aggression and does not call for discussion or negotiation of any kind.
George F. Kennan, May 12, 1948[1]

In their awkward, often frustrated efforts to cope with the Greek civil war, American policymakers did not lose sight of that conflict's international dimension. Caught up in the worldwide political upheavals of the 1940s, they had grown accustomed to thinking in global terms. They assumed that the "enemy" had a grand, international plan; and revolutionaries, particularly leftist ones, danced on strings pulled in Moscow. Thus they applied to local events a Cold War political orthodoxy that left little room for national differences or idiosyncrasies. Marshall wrote to Lovett in the fall of 1948: "What is happening in Greece is merely an expression in keeping with the local circumstances of the general Soviet or Communist plot."[2] In actuality, the Greek insurrection had come under Communist direction, and external forces did play an influential role in it. But Washington officials failed to appreciate the curious fact that, despite the usual propaganda barrage from Moscow, Stalin was making serious efforts to halt the Greek conflict. And, conversely, they only dimly understood that the rebellion had its roots in the polarization of Greek politics and continued against enormous odds thanks to a combination of revolutionary fervor, stubborn nationalism, and aid from the Kremlin's foes. The result was that American policymakers, blinded by Cold War dogma, rejected important opportunities for compromise that might have ended the terrible bloodshed that engulfed Greek life.

254

Despite the American emphasis on Soviet responsibility for the civil war in Greece, no solid evidence emerged to indicate that the rebellion there was motivated (or even appreciably assisted) by Stalin's foreign policy. Admittedly, the U.N. Special Committee on the Balkans (UNSCOB) concluded repeatedly that Yugoslavia, Albania, and Bulgaria aided the rebels with sanctuary, supplies, and training. But the scattered locale of the rebellion, its roots in Greek politics, the tenuous ties between the Balkan states and the Soviet Union, and the limited extent of foreign aid from Communist sources call into question the idea of a Kremlin plot. According to Greek intelligence, most of the weapons used by the rebels came from non-Communist nations. Moreover, the relatively constant number of guerrillas under arms suggested to some U.S. military analysts a deliberate manpower ceiling, perhaps imposed by the paucity of external assistance.[3] "The extent of foreign support is difficult to estimate exactly," C. M. Woodhouse concluded in his comprehensive study of the Greek civil war. "Two things are certain, however: that the rebellion could not have continued without some foreign support; and that the KKE was disappointed with its scale." Even Americans close to events occasionally conceded the latter. In May 1948, a member of the Washington law firm representing the Athens government admitted to the State Department "that intelligence reports showed that Markos was not getting as much support as he desired from the Soviet satellites and that present indications were that general Kremlin policy was not to push for a Communist victory." It might also be noted that unlike American aid to the Athens government—which dwarfed external assistance to the rebels—Soviet aid was nonexistent, a point not contested by U.S. officials.[4]

Nevertheless, American policymakers persisted in defining the conflict in Greece as primarily a matter of Soviet aggression. In part, this was sincere enough, for U.S. officials failed to perceive any distinction between Soviet foreign policy and that of the Balkan Communist nations. It also, however, had useful propaganda aspects, for by magnifying the importance of foreign Communist intervention, American officials could offset criticism of their role and that of the the Athens government in the Greek civil war. Consequently, the State Department sought to focus world attention on outside support to the Greek rebels through the vehicle of the United Nations. In this venture, it proved largely successful. On October 21, 1947, drawing on its strength in the General Assembly, the U.S. government secured the establishment of UNSCOB, with a charge that concentrated its attention on the activities of the Balkan Communist nations. As before, the U.N. investigation was hardly impartial. Communist nations failed to participate in UNSCOB's operations. Furthermore, the State Department virtually wrote the UNSCOB report. On May 13, 1948, Marshall sent the U.S. delegation a detailed list of "conclusions" for UNSCOB to reach. As the Secretary of State noted, they were "framed so that desirable recommendations would flow naturally" from them. Shortly afterward, Marshall received word that, thanks to the efforts of U.S. officials, most delegations were "unobtrusively using [the] U.S. delegation drafts as [the] basis [of] their chapters." The indications were "that the report will conform to [the] pattern set by [the] US." Given this elaborate preparatory work, as well as the genuine meddling of the Balkan Communist nations in Greek affairs, new denunciations of Albanian, Bulgarian, and Yugoslavian assistance to the rebels followed in June and August 1948.[5]

At the same time, U.S. policymakers sought to prevent the United Nations from mediating the conflict. On February 3, 1948, the U.S. representative on UNSCOB reported an Australian government proposal "to seek [the] solution of [the] Greek problem through conciliation of [the] countries directly concerned in [the] present situation." It called for "cessation of support to Markos by [Greece's] northern neighbors in return for [a] Greek agreement on new internationally supervised elections, amnesty, participation of leftist elements in [the] government, reform of [the] labor laws, reduction of [the] armed forces, withdrawal of all foreign military instructors and advisors, and placing of economic aid to Greece under international administration." Two days later, Marshall informed Australian officials that "our views on [the] best means [toward a] solution [of the] Greek problem are substantially at variance. . . . It would be both unjust and unwise to call upon Greece to make concessions such as suggested." Defending the policies of the Athens government, he went on to caution that aid to Greece by an international body would encounter a "reluctance [by the] American Government and people [to] contribute huge sums of money without any control over their expenditure." Later that year, the delegations from Brazil, Pakistan, and Mexico joined the delegation from Australia in urging that UNSCOB move beyond its role of border surveillance to one of conciliation. To the dismay of the U.S. and Greek governments, the General Assembly president, Herbert Evatt of Australia, took the lead in conciliation attempts in late 1948 and 1949. In response, the U.S. Secretary of State criticized "conciliation gestures by UNSCOB, Evatt or anyone else" and contributed to the failure of the U.N. official's efforts.[6]

To support its charges of external aggression, the State Department claimed that foreign troops (other than British and American) were being readied for action in Greece. On August 9, 1947, Marshall notified U.S. missions to other Security Council members that they should inform these governments that "the US has reports from its own and other sources which provide reason to believe that preparations are being made for the use . . . of foreign armed forces on the pattern of the international brigades which served in the Spanish civil war." Actually, the U.S. ambassador in France had reported that, while it appeared that "some individual recruitment has taken place, there is no reason to believe thus far that it is on an important scale and is certainly not to be compared with that which took place during the Spanish civil war." From other non-Communist sources had come word that "stories of [an] international brigade have been persistently planted by Spanish Intelligence to encourage sympathy for Franco."[7] But the State Department clung doggedly to its allegation. When the British Foreign Office pointed out that it had never been able to confirm rumors of an international brigade, the U.S. representative responded that "its formation must be taken as a fact." From Moscow, the U.S. ambassador reported on August 30 that "an international brigade . . . is at least in [the] advance organizational stage, if not in actual being." Yet in Yugoslavia, the alleged assembly point for the putative international force, the U.S. embassy could discover no trace of it. In fact, the embassy could not understand why anyone would want to organize an international brigade, as "adequate Greek Communists" seemed available for the conflict. In any event, no international brigade materialized.[8]

To American officials, the dispatch of an international brigade to Greece would provide one means whereby foreign Communist parties would recognize the legitimacy of a rebel government. In the summer of 1947, of course, no formal alternative to the Athens government yet existed and the KKE was still operating as a legal political party. But American officials expected the worst. On July 17, when Markos issued a proclamation asking the termination of the growing violence by agreement, general amnesty, a revised government with leftist participation, and free elections, MacVeagh advised Washington that "none of these recent leftist proposals are to be taken seriously or considered as anything other than propaganda moves." According to the U.S. ambassador, they were "designed to confuse liberal and leftist opinion . . . and to provide advance justification for [the] eventual establishment of [a] rebel government." On September 5 and again on September 10, Markos communicated to the United Nations and to the world an offer of a cease-fire in return for the establishment of a coalition government that included EAM. Neither the Athens nor the U.S. government was interested in these offers; nor, apparently, was the KKE, which did not approve them. Meeting on September 12, the remnants of the KKE's central committee resolved to transfer the center of the party's activities to the hills and "to make the Democratic Army the force which will bring about in the shortest possible time the establishment of a Free Greece." Even so, while the conflict heightened in the fall of 1947, no rebel government appeared.[9]

The failure to establish a rebel government in the fall of

1947 may have resulted from the cool reception that Soviet leaders afforded rebel efforts. To be sure, in August 1947 the Soviet Union joined Yugoslavia in breaking diplomatic relations with the Athens government. Meanwhile, Soviet propaganda attacks increased. Nevertheless, when European Communist leaders organized the Cominform that fall, delegates from the KKE were conspicuously absent. "Many Communists wondered that no representative of the Greek Party was present," recalled Vladimir Dedijer, the Yugoslav journalist. But "bearing in mind the agreement on spheres of interest . . . it is easy to understand why Stalin did not invite the Greeks." Nor was this the only snub the Russians gave the KKE. As Vukmanovic-Tempo has revealed, despite Yugoslav efforts to win acknowledgment of the Greek struggle, "Soviet leaders did not allow the resolution of the first meeting of the Cominform to include a single sentence which might aid the people's revolutionary fight in Greece." "Not a word" appeared in the Cominform paper about Greek events, he added, and the Soviet Union failed to "organise any care for the refugees from Greece, or Greek children, or other aid." To the Yugoslavs, the lesson was clear enough. Vukmanovic-Tempo concluded, rhetorically: "Was that not all a consequence of the fact that the leadership of the Bolshevik Party had been against the revolutionary struggle of the Greek people from the outset?"[10]

What was clear to Communist leaders, however, remained obscure to American officials, unaccustomed to disputes among bona fide Reds. "At the time," recalled one member of the State Department, the establishment of the Cominform in Belgrade "seemed to Western observers to be open Soviet support of Yugoslavia in its part in the Communist/Slavic thrust at Greece." Lacking concrete evidence of Soviet mendacity in the eastern Mediterranean, Washington turned to subtler analyses that confirmed its policy of Cold War vigilance. "We do not believe [the] USSR wants war," Lovett conceded to the U.S. embassy in Turkey on October 10. "Soviet policy appears to be directed toward achievement of its aims through subversive activities of communist parties in various foreign countries and such other political, economic and psychological weapons as it finds available." Defending foreign nations against this sort of menace—devious, shifting, evanescent—inspired a state of constant anxiety. Symptomatically, the political section of the U.S. embassy in Athens warned: "The USSR and her satellites will not give up the initiative, but will on the contrary resort to any means necessary to thwart us."[11]

For these worried American officials, a critical moment arrived when, on December 24, 1947, the rebels at last announced the formation of the "first provisional democratic government of free Greece." Headed by Markos, the mountain-based government was a predominantly Communist affair with a radical program.[12] American officials anticipated rapid recognition and a surge of external support. To head these off, Lovett declared at a press conference on December 30 that recognition of the rebel government by any nation would "have serious implications" and "be clearly contrary to the principles of the UN Charter." Secretly, the State Department issued direct warnings to Albania, Bulgaria, and Yugoslavia; inaugurated a rapid military buildup in Greece; and prepared for the worst. "Almost certainly one or more of the satellites, and possibly the USSR, will recognize this 'free' Government," the National Security Council concluded on January 6, 1948. "The objective of such recognition will probably be to facilitate open military assistance."[13] With its eye on the dispatch of American troops—and at the very least a U.S. aircraft carrier—the Athens government echoed the American assessment four days later: "Recognition should be considered as certain."[14]

Once again, however, this faith in international Communist solidarity proved quite misplaced, for no countries, Communist or otherwise, recognized the rebel government. Even among American officials, the suspicion grew that something was amiss. From Moscow, the U.S. ambassador, Walter Bedell Smith, sent word on December 27, 1947 that, though the Soviet press featured dispatches from Belgrade on the establishment of the Markos government, "there has been neither editorial comment nor preliminary buildup beyond routine Tass reporting [of the] radio broadcasts [of the] Greek Democratic army and continued denigration [of the] Athens Government." Local observers, he contended, thought that the "USSR and others" were "holding off" recognition, "pending developments." On January 3, 1948, Ambassador Cavendish Cannon reported a "Yugoslav attitude of reluctance to make [a] definite decision on recognition of Markos." By January 12, Marshall had noticed the omission in the recent issue of the Cominform journal of "all but passing reference to the Markos regime." This was indicative, he informed U.S. missions, "of the present Soviet and satellite attitude in withholding a firm commitment on Markos in the face of their uncertainty regarding the reaction of the US." Drawing on its own intelligence sources, the Athens government also discerned the meaning of events. According to its spokesman in Washington, Zachariades had recently met in Moscow with Molotov, who told him "that the U.S.S.R. could take no further diplomatic steps at this time with regard to the Greek situation." Just as the Americans considered themselves responsible for the failure of Communist recognition to materialize, so Greek officials attributed it to a recent success of the Greek armed forces.[15]

Actually, Stalin probably deserved most of the credit. At the very least he tried to curb the ambitions of Balkan Communist leaders. In January 1948, Georgi Dimitrov, the Bulgarian Communist chief, told a press conference that, while the question of a Balkan federation was "premature," when it came of age "the nations of people's democracy, Romania, Bulgaria, Yugoslavia, Albania, Czechoslovakia, Poland, Hungary and Greece—mind you, and Greece!—will settle it." As Dedijer has noted, "the Kremlin reacted furiously to Dimitrov's statement." *Pravda* declared that "these countries require no questionable and fabricated federation"; instead, they should be "mobilizing and organizing internally." Dimitrov's gaffe, in conjunction with a wide-ranging series of treaties Yugoslavia concluded with the Communist nations of the Balkans, irritated Stalin so much that he summoned Yugoslav and Bulgarian leaders to Moscow.[16] At a meeting on February 10, Molotov brought up Dimitrov's recent statement about Balkan federation, whereupon Stalin interjected, "We see Comrade Dimitrov abandons himself fervently at press conferences; he does not mind his tongue. Whatever he says, whatever Tito says, is thought abroad to have been said with our knowledge." Crestfallen, the Bulgarian leader apologized: "It is true I was carried away at the press conference." Stalin, however, seemed determined to humiliate him. "You wanted to shine with new words," the Soviet dictator jeered; "that's all wrong, because such a federation is an impossibility." Abashed, Dimitrov groped for accommodation with the high priest of world Communism. "There is no essential difference between the foreign policy of Bulgaria and that of the Soviet Union," he protested. Angrily, Stalin retorted: "There are huge differences!"[17]

Brushing aside further attempts to deflect him from this line of argument, Stalin announced: "We called this meeting in order to discuss the differences in foreign policy between the Soviet Union on one side, and Bulgaria and Yugoslavia on the other." As in 1944–45, a KKE victory seemed likely to bolster Tito's hegemony in the Balkans, while at the same time angering the Western powers and thereby endangering Soviet holdings elsewhere in Eastern Europe. Accordingly, the Soviet dictator took a jaundiced view of the Greek uprising. "We do not agree with the Yugoslav comrades that they should help further the Greek partisans," he declared; "in this matter, we think that we are right and not the Yugoslavs." Indeed, he insisted that "the uprising in Greece has to fold up." Although Yugoslav Vice-Premier Eduard Kardelj responded that the Greek rebels might succeed "if foreign intervention does not grow and if serious political and military errors are not made," Stalin was implacable: "If, if! No, they have no prospect of success at all. What do you think, that Great Britain and the United States . . . will permit you to break their line of communication in the Mediterranean Sea! Nonsense. . . . The uprising in Greece must be stopped, and as quickly as possible." Others present mentioned the successes of the Chinese Communists, whom Stalin had also abandoned, but the Soviet dictator was adamant. "Greece is a different case," he insisted. "We should not hesitate, but let us put an end to the Greek uprising."[18]

The February 1948 confrontation with Yugoslav and Bulgarian officials was only the first round of Stalin's showdown with the leaders of Balkan Communism. Tito, the most independent, and therefore the most dangerous, came under increasing attack from Moscow in the following months. In mid-March, alleging local hostility and obstructionism, the Soviet government announced the withdrawal of all Russian military and civilian advisers from Yugoslavia. A fierce exchange of letters commenced between government leaders in Belgrade and Moscow, focusing on alleged doctrinal differences between their two Communist parties. Behind the obscure and tortuous rhetoric, it seems clear enough that Stalin sought to force Tito from power because of the latter's unwillingness to submit to the Kremlin line—an unwillingness which was exemplified by the Yugoslav leader's stubborn support of the Greek rebels. Unable to muster the necessary opposition to Tito within Yugoslavia, Stalin demanded that the Soviet-Yugoslav dispute be laid before his minions in the Cominform. Although the Yugoslavs refused to attend such a meeting, the Russians proceeded to organize the gathering in Bucharest. Here, on June 28, 1948, they pushed through a resolution which repeated their denunciations of Tito and expelled Yugoslavia from the international Communist body.[19]

In early 1948, as the conflict between the Soviet Union and Yugoslavia intensified, Stalin and his allies showed signs of scuttling the rebellion in Greece. On March 6, Bevin informed the U.S. ambassador in London of a report he had received indicating what he considered a softer Soviet approach to Greek affairs. That May, Albanian officials issued conciliatory statements, while their Bulgarian counterparts publicly pondered the reestablishment of diplomatic relations with the Athens government. A peace offensive seemed to be taking shape that June when, as Cannon noted, Zachariades returned to Greece "bearing Moscow's olive branch." Pointing to sudden Communist support for U.N. action in Greece, the U.S. ambassador called attention to a "new Stalinist strategy" championing "peace and freedom for smaller powers."[20] Later that month, shortly before Yugoslavia's expulsion from the Cominform, a Soviet diplomatic representative approached Greek Foreign Minister Tsaldaris and proposed the initiation of secret conversations between their governments for the settlement of outstanding disputes. Suspicious of Soviet motives, the American and British governments advised Tsaldaris to reject Moscow's overture. Nevertheless, the State Department and the Foreign Office took it quite seriously and spent two weeks formulating their response.[21]

Trapped in a situation that could only work to their disadvantage, KKE leaders also began to adapt to the new realities. On April 7, 1948, they proposed terms for settlement of the conflict to former Prime Minister Tsouderos, a leading advocate of conciliation. Although Sophoulis sharply rejected the idea of negotiations, new rebel peace offers materialized on May 31. Speaking over Democratic Army Radio, Markos proposed a cease-fire and announced a willingness to discuss "any proposal" which would "bring back peace to the country." The following day, Zachariades attested to the offer's legitimacy. In hindsight, even Greek government officials have conceded the probable sincerity of the rebels' offer. "The position of the KKE and its army was most delicate," Greece's former Minister of Defense has written, "for the quarrel was between the uncontested and authoritarian master of the 'Movement' and the one who was giving the actual unstinted support to the rebels. And it is thus quite probable that, seeing the approaching storm, the leaders of the rebellion sought a compromise settlement."[22] The growing disarray in the world Communist movement may also have played an important role in altering rebel military strategy. Guerrilla warfare, after all, necessitated a long, patient struggle. But if disaster loomed on the horizon, there would be greater reason to risk large-scale, decisive engagements.[23]

Whatever possibilities the Tito-Stalin dispute opened up for a negotiated settlement in Greece were decisively rejected by

American officials. On June 3, 1948, Henderson told a Greek journalist that the Markos peace proposals were valueless, for "there can be no compromise with Communism." A "permanent relaxation of Soviet expansionist policy could not be expected," he insisted, "since expansion was an integral part of Communist philosophy." The following day, Rankin cabled the Secretary of State that the Markos proposals should not be given "formal consideration." Noting that the "present gesture" might be a "prelude to [a] Soviet-sponsored move in [the] UN to intervene to stop hostilities in Greece," he hoped that the State Department would be "categorical in reaffirming that we are leading from strength not weakness and do not intend to be deterred from [a] firm course." On June 12, he warned that recent military victories "could be dissipated if we fall prey to Soviet and satellite endeavors to throw Greece off balance through [the] peace offensive." Such moves, he cautioned, "may well add up to a satellite effort to settle [the] Greek affair through [the] UN, leaving [the Greek] Communists unbroken to resume their campaign in Greece at [a] more propitious time." To the U.S. chargé, it was "essential" that the war effort "be terminated by the crushing defeat of [the] bandit forces and not through appeasement or conciliation." Seconding the embassy approach, Griswold cabled Marshall four days later that "there should be no contact between the Greek Government and the 'Markos government' bilaterally or on an international political level." The rebels must be given no alternative but surrender.[24]

Driven by this sort of bitter anti-Communism, American officials not only misjudged events in Greece during the first half of 1948 but remained largely ignorant of the growing conflict between the governments of the Soviet Union and of Yugoslavia. "Certainly none of us in Moscow expected a revolt in Communist ranks led by one so important and so well-trained as Tito," recalled the U.S. ambassador. "We in Moscow were surprised at the sudden dramatic announcement on June 28, 1948 that the Yugoslav Party had been expelled from the Cominform." Although accurate appraisals occasionally filtered through to the State Department, they were summarily rejected if they did not fit the official world view. On May 4, 1948, for example, the U.S. ambassador in Prague conveyed to Washington a report that the Cominform was "on [the] verge of . . . cutting loose from [the] Greek rebel movement" and that Tito felt "that his own and Yugoslavia's positions are too exposed and too closely tied to [the] Soviet Union's dictates." On May 11, Marshall replied authoritatively that he doubted that "international communism [would] decide [to] abandon [the] Greek venture," for "all signs point in [the] opposite direction." As to rumors of Tito's break with Stalin—already months in progress and about to assume irrevocable form—the American Secretary of State declared that "Tito does not differentiate between [the] aims of Yugo[slavia] and [the] Soviet Union of which, from [the] viewpoint [of] his personal allegiance, Yugo[slavia] already forms a part."[25]

During the last half of 1948, as the split between Tito and Stalin widened, it produced an extremely difficult situation for the rebel movement. On July 14, the Markos government again broadcast a peace appeal—without, however, stirring any interest among Greek and U.S. officials.[26] At the same time, the KKE avoided taking any public stand on the conflict between Moscow and Belgrade, thus becoming perhaps the only Communist party in the world to do so. Although the KKE central committee, at the insistence of Zachariades, voted in late July to endorse the Cominform's position, it acted in the greatest secrecy. To condemn Tito publicly risked depriving the rebels of their main external source of arms and food, as well as of Yugoslav bases and sanctuary. In addition, criticism of the Yugoslav leader would constitute a direct rebuke to the leadership of the large Slavo-Macedonian minority within the Democratic Army, which remained fiercely pro-Tito. On the other hand, to challenge Stalin meant isolation from world Communism and almost certain losses of Albanian and Bulgarian aid. For the time being, then, the rebels sought to insulate themselves from the division within the Communist movement. In December 1948, U.S. intelligence reported, a guerrilla representative conferred with top

Yugoslav officials in Belgrade, thanked them for assistance rendered despite the Cominform rift, and proposed increased political and military collaboration in the future.[27]

Meanwhile, terrible strains developed within the rebel leadership. Although the rank and file of the Democratic Army, only vaguely aware of the Tito-Stalin split, generally maintained a high morale, the situation differed dramatically at the top. The conflict sharpened between Zachariades, who remained loyal to Stalin, and Markos, who—out of either political affinity or strategic necessity—remained unwilling to break with Tito. Indeed, some Communist sources have maintained that, during the retreat from the Grammos in the summer of 1948, Zachariades tried to have Markos murdered. That November, in a pessimistic appraisal of the military situation, Markos criticized a strategy of sizable military engagements and called for a return to small-scale guerrilla warfare. Zachariades used the occasion to denounce this assessment as "opportunist" and "defeatist" and to obtain a vote of no-confidence in Markos from a majority of the KKE leadership. Markos continued for the next few months to command the Democratic Army officially, but effective power now passed to Zachariades.[28]

In the rapidly shifting circumstances of late 1948, Bulgarian and Albanian assistance to the rebellion, though significant, grew increasingly unreliable. American officials attributed the waning of Markos' star to the Cominform "peace offensive"[29] and, in part, this may have been correct. On July 23, Grady reported that, as a result of the new intra-Balkan tensions, Albania and Bulgaria had been hoarding military supplies destined for the insurgents. In addition, Albania suddenly refused entry to wounded guerrillas. Citing British intelligence reports that "Bulgaria is increasingly uncooperative towards [the] *andartes*," the U.S. consul in Salonika claimed that an "order has been given to stop building supply dumps in Bulgaria." In mid-August, the U.S. Secretary of the Army urged that "recent reports that the satellite countries have withdrawn support from Markos should receive careful scrutiny and continuing study."[30] Even so, with the expulsion of Tito from the

Cominform, a successful rebellion in Greece seemed more likely than before to secure long-time Bulgarian expansionist goals, most notably an outlet on the Aegean. Furthermore, stirring up Macedonian nationalism could potentially undermine Tito by splitting off from Yugoslavia its Macedonian republic of two million people. For these reasons, Bulgaria and Albania remained true to the rebellion, at least for the time being. But the portents were ominous for the insurgents. As the U.S. embassy noted, an article by Zachariades in the December 15, 1948 issue of the Cominform journal warned that the KKE "must produce results" in early 1949 or face the cessation of external assistance.[31]

Confronted with this intricate, volatile situation, American officials showed little understanding of the divisions between or within Communist movements, or of their meaning. The most perceptive, at the U.S. embassy in Belgrade, simply confessed their bafflement. "To what extent Yugoslav policies regarding Markos, Trieste, and Italian elections lagged behind or outran Soviet desires," they reported, "are unknown elements." Further from the scene, in Washington, the prevalent assumptions blocked any reassessment of the U.S. position. According to the State Department's policy planning staff, "the USSR undoubtedly counts on eventually exhausting Greek [and] U.S. morale, bringing about the cessation of U.S. aid and thereby winning Greece by default." Admittedly, the rebels were pressing for peace, but "there is . . . no indication and no reason to believe that the USSR would permit any political settlement with Greece which would not result in or pave the way for communist domination of the country." Beneath such apparently sophisticated analyses lay a simple faith in the efficacy of violence. Responding to Greek government urgings to press Albania to intern the retreating rebels, Lovett declared that "the only way to beat the guerrillas was by fighting and not by writing notes. Every effort should be made to wipe them out." The Under Secretary insisted that "the chief deterrent to further Albanian or other foreign aid to Markos would be vigorous prosecution of offensive military operations in Greece, just as the punishment of criminals in domestic society is the chief deterrent to crime."[32]

Of course, American and Greek government officials did recognize that Yugoslavia's break with the Soviet Union offered them new opportunities to disrupt the world Communist movement.[33] But because they believed Stalin to be the prime mover of the Greek rebellion, they assumed that, with a little Western economic aid as bait, Tito could easily be lured away from his close association with the insurgents. "The line which should be adhered to by representatives of the Department," Marshall wrote on July 1, 1948, is that the character of the Yugoslav regime would not "stand in the way of a normal development of economic relations between Yugoslavia and this country . . . provided Yugoslavia is willing to adopt a loyal and cooperative attitude in its international relationships." Later that month, he outlined the specifics, with an eye to Greece:

If Tito desires comprehensive trade treaties or [a] loan, Harriman would inform him that, while we will consider such [a] request, prior evidence [of] his good faith in regard [to] various aspects [of the] present Yugos[lav] policy, for example revision of Yugos[lavia's] position of aiding Markos, would be [the] condition's precedent.

The Athens government, too, grew fairly optimistic about Tito's conversion to a counterinsurgent position. "There is no other way out for him," it informed the State Department, "but an orientation becoming more and more definitive towards the West."[34]

In the latter half of 1948, Tito's position was indeed desperate; nonetheless, he continued to honor his commitments. "Yugoslavia was alone in the world," Dedijer recalled. "From the East came Stalin's anathema, from the West came misunderstanding and the old threats." Although Yugoslavia badly needed Western economic assistance, and did sign a trade agreement with the British in December, Belgrade's position remained intransigently revolutionary.[35] "Neither abroad nor at home has Tito attempted [a] compromise with non-Communist opinion," Cannon cabled on November 24; "his course apparently will be extreme Communist orthodoxy in [the] struggle against 'foreign imperialism and domestic reaction.'" Six days later, the State Department's policy planning staff informed the National Security Council that "Yugoslav material aid to the Greek guerrillas has apparently been somewhat reduced, owing to Yugoslavia's need to conserve its own resources." Nevertheless, the "Yugoslav policy of supporting the guerrillas remains unchanged, the movement of guerrilla reserves from Yugoslavia into Greece has been facilitated, and the guerrillas continue to enjoy great tactical advantage from the virtually unhindered use of Yugoslav territory." Observing that Yugoslav representatives "were the most fervent pleaders for Markos' cause" at the United Nations and that Yugoslav aid to the guerrillas "did not decrease by one bullet," a Greek Defense Minister concluded that Tito still hoped for a friendly neighbor to the south. According to Woodhouse, Tito probably began to lose interest in the rebellion in late 1947, but may have continued his support for it because of Stalin's very opposition.[36]

In early 1949, Stalin's contempt for the Greek rebellion became apparent even to U.S. officials, for a number of the rebellion's top leaders were removed in the interests of Cominform policy. At a meeting of the KKE central committee on January 29–30, somewhere in the Grammos, Zachariades led the Stalinists in a purge of Markos and other suspect officials from their posts in the KKE and in the "Free Greek government." Although the Markos ouster occurred ostensibly for reasons of "ill health," Zachariades accompanied it with vague denunciations of "opportunism" and "right deviationism." In addition, Zachariades and the new party leaders blamed the veterans of ELAS for difficulties encountered by the rebellion and systematically purged those Slavo-Macedonian leaders loyal to Tito.[37] American officials were divided on how to interpret these events. Some, particularly in Belgrade, viewed them as an attack upon "Titoism," with Markos as the Stalinists' arch-villain. Others, in Athens, considered the fall of Markos and the ascendancy of Zachariades further evidence of a shift in Cominform strategy from armed insurrection to political subversion. In either case, American, British, and Greek officials had good reason to rejoice, for the rebellion was being dismantled at the Kremlin's behest.[38]

This grew even more evident in February 1949, when Zachariades, on behalf of the KKE, endorsed the call by the Slavo-Macedonian component of the rebels for an autonomous Macedonia. Although Macedonian self-determination had once been a KKE position, it had been abandoned in 1936. Thereafter, the KKE had firmly resisted autonomist pressures from Greece's Macedonian minority and from Tito, who hoped to bring an independent Macedonia under his control. Instead, the Greek Communists argued for minority rights within the framework of a "democratic Greece." This proved a far more popular position among most Greeks who, Communist or not, tended to be nationalistic. Hence when the KKE suddenly revived its demand for Macedonian autonomy in 1949, the reason was transparent: Stalin wished to undermine Tito's control of Yugoslav Macedonia by stirring up Macedonian separatism. Admittedly, Macedonian autonomy would appeal to Slavo-Macedonians within the Democratic Army and would also strengthen the wavering support of Bulgaria, which, with Tito's expulsion from the Cominform, could expect to exercise hegemony over a new Macedonian state. But the KKE's endorsement of Macedonian autonomy, symbolized by the admission of two Slavo-Macedonians to the rebel government, represented a direct challenge to Tito as well as to the vast majority of Greeks. In the most telling fashion, Stalin and his henchmen had sacrificed the interests of the Greek rebellion to more pressing concerns of Soviet foreign policy.[39]

Within Greece, the response was devastating. "Here was an issue for which Greek soldiers were ready and willing to fight," recalled McNeill; meanwhile, among the insurgents, "morale cracked." In the government prisons, a flood of repentance declarations followed. The Minister of Public Order even printed a short form of the standard declaration for those who wished to renounce the KKE purely on the grounds of its Macedonian policy. That May, the U.S. embassy commented on "the disruptive effect the Macedonian issue has had on party membership and the difficulties its leaders have in finding an effective reply to the rumors that the KKE is 'selling Macedonia to the Bulgarians' and that the Communists 'are openly revealed as traitors.'"[40] From remnants of EAM, from the Socialist Party of Greece, and from unaffiliated individuals came bitter denunciations of the KKE's course of action. In July 1949, the U.S. consul in Salonika cited GNA intelligence reports that "andarte morale [is the] lowest since [the] start [of the] bandit movement." Even within the party leadership, the Macedonian stand caused serious divisions: some opposed it on nationalist grounds; others argued that it merely alienated the masses; and still others feared that it would mean a final break with Tito. Indeed, the disarray became so widespread that Zachariades beat a retreat into ambiguity and, eventually, withdrew support for the idea. But the stigma remained profound.[41]

In these circumstances, American officials grew more certain than ever that U.S. aid would pry Tito loose from his stubborn—indeed, from their standpoint, incomprehensible—attachment to the Greek rebels. On February 5, 1949, after talking with a member of the State Department's policy planning staff, C. L. Sulzberger noted that plans were afoot for American assistance to Tito and for an effort to close Yugoslavia's borders to supplies for the Greek rebels. Nine days later, when Under Secretary Webb inquired if the proposed assistance to Tito would be provided "on the basis of a quid pro quo," Hickerson replied that "that is the intention." Although the trade-off "would be mainly in the economic field," Satterthwaite "pointed out that it will not be too difficult for Tito to discontinue support for the guerrillas in Greece." On February 25, Acheson instructed Cannon in Belgrade to "constantly endeavor to exert as early as possible sufficient pressure on Tito to abandon assistance for the Greek guerrillas." At an opportune time, he added, Tito should "be made clearly [to] understand [that the] U.S. [is] not prepared to continue [to] make available goods or assist him [to] increase [the] level [of the] Yugo[slav] economy so long as his regime supports [the] insurrection." When Tito was "faced with [a] choice, his own vital interests will compel him to cease assistance." Although American influence along these lines appears to have been discreet, it could hardly have gone unrecognized. In a dispatch of May 26, 1949, Cannon informed Acheson of "our constant but informal pressure here" to block Yugoslav aid to the Greek insurgents.[42]

Once again, however, Tito rejected American blandishments. On March 22, 1949, nine months after Yugoslavia's expulsion from the Cominform, the National Security Council reported that "although guerrilla freedom of action within Yugoslavia is probably more closely supervised," the amount of Yugoslav aid to the rebels "appears to be on a par with that accorded prior to the break." From the standpoint of Greek and U.S. government officials, the one hopeful note sounded when, in February 1949, a Yugoslav agent initiated top secret contacts with the Athens government regarding negotiations for a possible Yugoslav-Greek entente. By April 21, however, no progress had been made in arranging the meeting.[43] That March and April, the royal Greek embassy informed the State Department, rebel forces traveled freely across the Yugoslav border; meanwhile, direct Yugoslav aid, although apparently less than in the past, continued to be "far from negligible." On May 12, Warren Austin reported that, in conciliation talks organized by the United Nations, the Yugoslav representative "was stronger even than [the] Alb[anian] rep[resentative] in insisting that Greece was entirely at fault." Some two weeks later, the U.S. representative on UNSCOB informed the State Department that Yugoslav aid to the rebels, "while channelized," had "definitely not ended." In late June 1949, a year after Tito's expulsion from the Cominform and nearly seventeen months after the inception of his dispute with Stalin, Yugoslavia continued to supply military equipment, sanctuary, and border transit to the Greek rebels.[44]

How should Tito's steadfast behavior be explained? Certainly, Yugoslav leaders were not naive. The purge of Markos caused serious distress within the Belgrade hierarchy, which viewed the action as an attack upon Greek "Titoism." In addition, Yugoslavia's party chiefs considered the KKE's new policy of self-determination for Macedonia an unfriendly one, designed to assist Stalin by undermining the Yugoslav state. Talking with Cannon that June, Kardelj and Deputy Foreign Minister Ales Bebler confessed ruefully that Yugoslavia "no longer has any friends in Greece."[45] On the other hand, Tito had no reason to like or even trust the Athens government, which symbolized just the sort of reactionary Balkan politics against which he had led his own revolution. Furthermore, Tito had long been a Communist militant, with close ties to the Greek rebellion. Perhaps he would be accepted back into the Communist movement (which, eventually, he was) or perhaps Markos would be reinstated (which also occurred, years later). Moreover, a sharp break with his past policies would lend substance to Stalin's charges of accommodation with capitalism and would place him at odds with the expansionist dreams of Yugoslav Macedonians, already the target of Kremlin policy. Consequently, despite some grumbling on the part of Yugoslav leaders—and U.S. officials did receive significant indications of dismay—Tito remained true to the Greek rebels through the first half of 1949.[46]

Tito's unwavering support of the insurgents contrasted with the policy of the Cominform nations, which stepped up their efforts in 1949 to secure an accommodation with the Greek and American governments—if possible at Tito's expense. In early February 1949, the Soviet chargé advised Tsaldaris, through the Foreign Minister's wife, that Greece should pursue a "firm" course in upholding its national interests. The following month, a member of the Bulgarian cabinet approached a Greek official in Berlin and suggested that their two nations join forces against Tito. Exhibiting a map of a partitioned southern Yugoslavia, he pointed out the section reserved for Greece.[47] Meanwhile, tiny Albania, geographically isolated from other Cominform nations by Yugoslavia and increasingly coveted by expansion-minded Greek and American officials,[48] also made accommodationist gestures. Along with the Bulgarian and Yugoslav governments, it sent negotiators that May to participate in U.N.-sponsored conciliation sessions designed to mend relations with Greece. At the same time, its government formally indicated a desire to discuss the establishment of diplomatic relations with the United States, on terms which it had previously rejected. Hickerson thought this particular move "made with Soviet consent and probably on Soviet suggestion."[49]

In retrospect, that seems quite possible. Throughout the first half of 1949, the Soviet Union veered toward a conciliatory foreign policy, stressing peaceful coexistence and the dangers of war. This soft-line approach, apparently designed to offset Soviet setbacks in the preceding years, acquired a clear orientation in the Balkans. On March 9, 1949, Cannon reported from Belgrade that "Yugoslavia has supplanted Greece as [the] immediate Communist objective [in] this part [of] Europe." Later that month, Kohler reached a similar conclusion from his vantage point as U.S. chargé in Moscow. "Liquidation [of] Tito [is] now [the] No. 1 Kremlin objective in [the] Balkans," he insisted, "to which Greek policy will be adapted as required."[50] On June 13, *Pravda* acknowledged the territorial integrity of Greece.[51]

The Kremlin's most dramatic move to end the Greek rebellion occurred in May 1949, when, in response to a U.S. initiative, it undertook direct negotiations on the subject with the Americans and the British. Although U.S. officials consistently rejected any peace discussions with the rebels or the Balkan Communist nations, they were certainly interested in ending the presumed Soviet support for the rebellion. Thus on March 21, 1949, Philip Jessup, U.S. representative to the United Nations, suggested to Russia's U.N. representative, Yakov Malik, that the great powers cooperate to settle the Greek conflict. "Is that an acute question between our two governments?" the Soviet official inquired. Jessup insisted that it was, and pointed to Soviet influence with Greece's Communist neighbors. Malik replied "with a laugh and with significant emphasis that they did have influence with *some* of them but not with all of them." On April 26, Dean Rusk, the Assistant Secretary of State for U.N. Affairs, again broached the possibility of great power action to end the Greek civil war. Reporting back on May 5, Gromyko, head of the Soviet U.N. delegation, stated that Moscow was ready to "discuss the matter in somewhat more concrete terms." Although U.S. officials hesitated to begin formal negotiations without Greek government participation, they were anxious to hear the Russian proposals; thus, "personal and unofficial" discussions ensued among the Americans, the British, and the Russians. Tactfully avoiding the question of the massive Anglo-American assistance to the Athens government, Gromyko called for the great powers to "use their influence" to bring about a settlement in Greece on the basis of a cease-fire, an amnesty, and the holding of parliamentary elections. During this conversation, Acheson reported, Gromyko "was unusually courteous and affable." American officials did not doubt Soviet sincerity in presenting these proposals,[52] which paralleled others made by the guerrillas that spring.[53]

Anglo-American officials, however, did not want to put these proposals into effect. For a time, they avoided making any reply to Gromyko. But in a meeting of May 14, they began to press their objections. Hector McNeil, the British representative, declared that they could not act "without the participation of the Greek government" and that "the northern frontier was the main issue." Rusk seconded McNeil's remarks, observing "that he was personally convinced that the real issue was the aid and assistance illegally furnished to the Greek insurgents across the northern Greek frontier." Somewhat taken aback, Gromyko responded that Russia stood ready to participate in a commission of the great powers to "control the border between Greece and its northern neighbors" and favored the removal of all foreign military assistance from Greece (including, presumably, that from Great Britain and the United States). At the same time, he would not drop the call for new parliamentary elections, which he now declared should proceed with great power supervision. In this fashion, the KKE might again secure a place in conventional Greek politics. Rusk summarized the two positions very well: "The Russians continued to emphasize an internal Greek problem. We and the British continued to emphasize the external Greek problem."[54]

Behind the State Department's decision to continue its claims of "external aggression" lay its determination to outlaw the KKE and other former constituents of EAM, to avoid international supervision of Greek elections, and to exploit the opportunities afforded by the Tito-Stalin rift and by the growing GNA military success. "On balance," noted a State Department memorandum, "we are in a strong bargaining position" and "the Russians are leading from weakness." When, on May 20, a Tass dispatch exposed the negotiations, American officials had already agreed that compromise was out of the question.[55] Although British pressures led to a brief reconsideration in late May and early June, a fierce blast from the Athens government and the American embassy scotched the prospects for further peace talks. Grady cabled on June 8 that "in the event of any further demarches by [the] USSR on the subject of Greece, we should hammer home the point that we find it utterly inconceivable that [the] Greeks should be expected to accord [to the] treacherous and brutal rebels [a] degree of leniency and freedom that [the] USSR and [its] satellites refuse as a matter of principle and doctrine to even their mildest critics."[56]

However intractable the American position, it could be sustained, after mid-1949, thanks to the collapse of the last significant foreign support for the rebellion. Threatened by the Cominform, denounced by the KKE, and (as Cannon reported), pressed "all spring" by U.S. officials "for [a] change in [its] Greek policy," the Yugoslav leadership finally moved to cut the rebels adrift. In late June 1949, during negotiations with the British for a loan, Tito indicated, at last, that Yugoslavia would close its frontier to the Greek insurgents and end its aid to them. Thereafter, the British prodded Tito to honor this commitment, as did the Americans, then in the process of developing their own aid program for Yugoslavia. On July 1, Acheson told the Yugoslav ambassador, Sava Kosanovic, just before his return to Belgrade for consultations, that the U.S. government considered the cessation of Yugoslav assistance to the guerrillas extremely important. Finally, on July 10, in a speech at Pola with Kosanovic at his elbow, Tito announced the "progressive closure" of Yugoslavia's frontier with Greece. He accused Greek Communist leaders of serving as tools of the Cominform campaign against Yugoslavia and predicted "fatal effects on the struggle for Greek liberation."[57]

American officials were overjoyed, and with good reason. Yugoslavia's defection deepened the divisions among the rebels and threatened to deprive them of their most important source of external support and sanctuary. Instructing Cannon to express U.S. satisfaction at Tito's Pola speech, Acheson urged him to "voice [the] hope that [the] announced policy of closing [the] frontier will in fact be implemented immed[iately]." It was "essential," added the Secretary of State, "that continuous pressure be exerted" for the new Yugoslav policy toward Greece "whenever [the] occasion arises for [the] discussion [of the] relationship between that policy and further western aid to Yugo[slavia]." Tito continued, for a time, to denounce the "monarcho-fascists" in Athens and to appeal to all Slavo-Macedonians and rank-and-file members of the KKE. Nevertheless, he closed the border on July 23, 1949 and began the dismantling of rebel camps and hospitals within his country. Zachariades responded by bitterly denouncing Yugoslavia's Communist leaders, accusing them of giving aid to Greek government troops and of plotting guerrilla defeat.[58] Such charges were inaccurate and unfair. Despite numerous obstacles, some erected by the KKE's own leaders, Yugoslav support for the rebellion had been lengthy and generous. "We . . . acted honestly," Vukmanovic-Tempo recalled. "We gave them everthing we could," but "Stalin ordered them to slander us. . . . When they refused to stop, we closed our borders." Or, as Kardelj put it: "If there is someone who bears moral-political responsibility for [the] difficulties with which [the] Greek democratic movement is faced, it is not Yugo[slavia]."[59]

Nor was the termination of Yugoslav support for the rebellion the only way in which Stalin's foreign policy, in the latter part of 1949, contributed to the guerrilla collapse. Stressing the new Soviet soft line on world affairs, Moscow continued to press for an end to the Greek civil war. The Russians "have already written off Greece," Kardelj informed American diplomats in early September.[60] That same month, the U.S. representative to UNSCOB reported that "Bulgaria . . . of late has displayed increasing signs of being fed up with [the] whole business." Meanwhile, Albania announced that it would disarm and intern all combatants entering its territory from Greece. Undergirding their disengagement from the rebellion lay Stalin's ruthless campaign against "Titoism." In Bulgaria, the secretary-general of the Communist party, Traicho Kostov, was expelled from the party in March, tried for treason in December, and then executed. Dimitrov, since Tito's heresy the most prominent figure in Balkan Communist affairs, traveled to Moscow that June and never returned. In Albania, General Koci Xoxe, the former deputy prime minister, was convicted in June of Titoism and executed later that month. Throughout Eastern Europe, neither Communist leaders nor followers were safe from the Kremlin's assault upon real or imagined opposition. According to Western estimates, Stalin initiated the purge of one-fourth the members of the East European Communist parties. Given the climate of fear, Bulgarian and Albanian officials had little incentive to indulge their ambitions in Greece.[61]

Heartened by these trends, as well as by GNA victories and the disintegration of rebel morale, American, British, and Greek government opinion grew increasingly intransigent. Among Greek civil and military leaders, especially, a clamor arose for seizing Albania. Responding to the Greek ambassador's pressure in late July 1949 for U.S. action against Albania, Grady retorted that, given U.S. recognition of that nation, "we can't land troops . . . or blockade its coasts." To this the Greek official responded knowingly that "State Department legal experts would always be able to find legal justification for such measures as we might wish to take," such as the establishment of "'international control' over Northern Epirus." Although U.S. and British officials generally sought to dampen expansionist fantasies over the following months,[62] they were not entirely immune to them. According to State Department records, at a meeting of September 14, in Washington, Bevin and Acheson agreed that they should "try to bring down" the Albanian government "when the occasion arises." "What government would replace [Enver] Hoxha if he is thrown out?" Bevin inquired; "are there any kings around that could be put in?" The Foreign Secretary "thought a person we could handle was needed." A U.S. official responded that "we had taken no decision with respect to a possible future government," as "the situation was still too fluid."[63] In these circumstances, of course, a compromise settlement with the rebels was beyond the realm of possibility. Opposing any moves toward "conciliation," Cannon claimed that "we should give not one inch" to projects that would transform the struggle from a military to a political one. From Moscow, the U.S. ambassador warned that "utmost vigilance should be exercised" lest conciliation efforts "afford [the] Soviets and [the] Greek Communists [an] entering wedge with which to turn their present military defeat into [an] eventual political victory."[64]

Such warnings, however, reversed the meaning of the Greek situation. In October 1949, when the insurgents abandoned their struggle, they still constituted a potentially dangerous military force; politically, though, the support for revolution—particularly from abroad—had largely evaporated. According to U.S. Army intelligence, while only 2,000 insurgents remained in Greece by November 1949, an estimated 12,000 combat-fit guerrillas were located in the Cominform countries to the north. Were these guerrillas to be reorganized and re-equipped, they could resume "a relatively large-scale campaign against the Greek Army."[65] But the political situation had shifted markedly. The morale of the guerrillas and their supporters had dropped sharply; conversely, the morale of the government and its supporters had reached a zenith. When the remnants of the Democratic Army crossed the borders into Albania, Bulgaria, and Yugoslavia, they received a chilly reception. Disarmed and detained, they now faced the sour discipline of the KKE's high command, among whom bitter feuds were already raging. "The available current information indicates that little or no effort is being made to revitalize the guerrilla organization," U.S. Army intelligence concluded. "The fact that Soviet policy in the Balkans at present seems preoccupied with Yugoslav defection, and the many reports of Greek guerrillas in Albania and Bulgaria being disarmed and of Greek 'refugees' being moved to Czechoslovakia, Hungary, Romania, and Poland, suggest that the Soviets will give a low priority to the Greek guerrillas." In this context, "the guerrillas can expect little or nothing in the way of outside support for the time being and will be extremely limited in their capabilities in Greece."[66]

Two weeks after the guerrilla "cease-fire," the journalist Constantine Poulos—citing the repeated Russian peace offensives, the purge of Markos, and the catastrophic campaign for Macedonian autonomy—concluded: "It was Moscow's decision which determined that the gallant Greek guerrilla movement was expendable."[67] As might be expected, the State Department adopted a radically different interpretation of events. On October 21, the American ambassador to the Soviet Union warned a U.S. diplomatic assemblage that Moscow had not "given up the cause of the Greek rebels. . . . The grand lines of Soviet policy remained the same," he insisted, and Russia would "take advantage of every chink in the armor of the non-Soviet world."[68] This faith in the Kremlin's revolutionary fidelity was echoed by the leadership of the KKE, now safely Stalinist, which announced on November 5 that the "basic fact in the outcome of the struggle was the treachery of Tito."[69] Given this agreement of the faithful on Cold War verities, the State Department failed to reexamine its assumptions; instead, it once again turned to the United Nations for a condemnation of the "internationally concerted Communist plot."[70] Only the Yugoslavs, in continued defiance of both great powers, remained unwilling to swallow this interpretation. In a pamphlet published in 1950 and presumably authorized by Tito, Vukmanovic-Tempo boasted of Yugoslavia's aid to the rebellion and charged that it was Moscow which had "no interest whatever" in a rebel victory.[71] This contention—borne out repeatedly in the 1940s by the realities of a complex international situation—gives a particularly tragic cast to the American government's implacable opposition to a negotiated settlement of the conflict.

10.
AFTERMATH
1950–1980

The death of democracy in Greece is not an isolated phenomenon; it is rather a single aspect of the spreading power of militarism and totalitarianism in the context of the competition between the United States and the Soviet Union. . . . Caught between these two powers, democracy is indeed at gunpoint.

> Andreas Papandreou, July 4, 1969[1]

The end of the civil war opened an era of new possibilities for Greece—one welcome from most political perspectives. In that grim conflict, an estimated 158,000 of Greece's 7.5 million people had been killed; 800,000 had become refugees (including up to 100,000 who fled to the Communist north); and many others had been crippled, wounded, or imprisoned.[2] Coming in the aftermath of World War II, the civil war completed the devastation of the Greek economy, bringing it to the verge of ruin. Nearly a third of the population was dependent on the state, in whole or in part, for its day-to-day survival. Others scratched out a miserable existence on their own. A British officer recalled:

Refugees returned . . . to a thin rocky soil which only frequent terracing could secure against the eroding rain, and to a life of physical labour which began at four or five in the morning and ended with dusk. Those who remained in the towns did so only to swell the numbers whose half-employment made a mock of unemployment figures: boys and men selling cigarettes, nuts, balloons, sponges, and countless other articles in the streets; small girls with old sad faces selling sprays of white scented jessamine in the restaurants moving silently from table to table.[3]

Even so, with the arrival of peace, the potential existed for considerable improvement in the fabric of Greek life. Eco-

nomic revival, social amelioration, and normal political pro-
cesses seemed, at last, on the agenda. After its ordeal of war
and destruction, the nation faced the long-postponed prospect of peaceful reconstruction under democratic auspices.
The only question remaining was: Would Greece's rightist
rulers and their American patrons allow it?

To Washington policymakers, Greece's internal needs,
though fully evident, were less important than its role as a
valuable pawn on the chessboard of international power politics. In the late 1940s, American plans for Greece emerged
in the midst of heightened concern for the security of the
Middle East. At the Pentagon Talks of fall 1947, British and
American officials sought to "review the whole position" in
the oil-rich region and to establish new policy guidelines. "Our
present thinking regarding the Middle East . . . goes far beyond" the "limited objectives" of the past, noted a State Department background paper. "We now take full cognizance
of the tremendous value of this area as a highway by sea,
land, and air between the East and the West; of its possession
of great mineral wealth; of its potentially rich agricultural
resources. We also realize the serious consequences which
would result if the rising nationalism of the peoples of the
Middle East should harden in a mould of hostility to the
West." Equally serious was the threat of Soviet expansion,
which "would have a disastrous effect not only on American
interests in the area but on our general position vis-à-vis the
Soviet Union." After reaching agreement with British officials, American leaders adopted a statement of policy, NSC
5/2, approved by the National Security Council on February
12, 1948. "The security of the Eastern Mediterranean and of
the Middle East is vital to the security of the United States,"
it declared. The security of this region "would be jeopardized
if the Soviet Union should succeed in its efforts to obtain
control of any one of the following countries: Italy, Greece,
Turkey, or Iran." As "it should be the policy of the United
States . . . to support the security of the Eastern Mediterranean and the Middle East," the United States "should assist
in maintaining the territorial integrity and political independ-

ence" of these countries, with "full use of its political, economic, and if necessary, military power."[4]

During the 1950s, as American corporations expanded their petroleum operations in the Middle East, anxiety continued to mount at possible Communist penetration of the area. "The Middle East is highly attractive and highly vulnerable" to "Communist aggression," a State Department background paper warned in September 1950. "Rupture of the flow of Middle East oil to normal markets or seizure of these resources from without or within would seriously affect U.S. and allied economic, political and strategic interests."[5] For Washington officials, maintaining the region's northern ramparts grew increasingly important. "Greece, Turkey and Iran constitute a barrier between the Soviet world on the one hand and the vital oil lands and strategic communications routes of the Middle East on the other," noted a key State Department memorandum at the end of that year. Accordingly, the United States should "assist in building a firm foundation for the continuation of anti-communist governments in the three countries"; "assist . . . in the maintenance of armed forces essential to assure internal security and . . . to resist foreign invasion"; and "continue to exert an active influence to prevent them from wavering in their determination to resist external pressures." Economic growth ranked as no more than a component of anti-Communist strategy. "Economic development is essential," the State Department maintained, "both in order to improve the abilities of these countries to maintain a military force appropriate to the present lack of international security and to develop a standard of living for the indigenous populations which will provide greater resistance to communist ideology and subversion."[6]

In February 1951, when the National Security Council formulated a new statement of American policy toward Greece, it adopted much the same approach. "The security of the Near East, and as a result the security interest of the United States, would be endangered if the USSR, directly or through any of its agents, obtained control of Greece," an NSC staff study concluded. "Western access to the oil of the area would be threatened, as well as U.S. communications and transportation facilities, and U.S. air and naval bases in the area." Expressing similar concerns, the National Security Council adopted NSC 103/1 on February 14, 1951. This policy statement proclaimed that it was "in the security interest of the United States that Greece not fall under communist domination." Toward this end, the United States would "promote the development of a stable democratic Greek government oriented to the West," "provide economic assistance and advice," and "lend appropriate support to the Greek military establishment." In turn, the Greek military would be used to maintain "internal security," repel or delay a Soviet-sponsored invasion, and bolster the southern flank of NATO.[7] Greece, in short, had considerable strategic significance for the United States and would be used accordingly in the Cold War.

But how American aims could best be attained was not immediately apparent in the new climate of post–civil war Greek politics. Hoping to find a strong, effective government to implement the ECA program, Ambassador Grady pressed for new elections in early 1950. The results of the elections, held on March 5, produced a surprise for Greek and American officials. In the aftermath of a bitter civil war that had virtually annihilated the left and elevated the right to positions of dominance in the parliament, cabinet, administrative apparatus, armed forces, and police, the Greek electorate handed the center and (to a lesser extent) the left a smashing victory, with 63 percent of the vote. The Populists (led by Tsaldaris), who had won 191 of the 250 seats in 1946, were reduced to 61, while the centrist parties (led by Plastiras, Venizelos, and Papandreou) captured 133. In addition, the leftist Democratic Front (led by Sofianopoulos and Svolos) garnered 22.[8] According to an agreement by the leaders of the center, published in the press, Plastiras would assume the post of Prime Minister. To the Greek right, and particularly to the palace and the officer corps, the prospect of a Plastiras government was particularly galling. Not only was the aging general a long-time opponent of the monarchy, but, during the campaign, he had called for social reform, amnesty for those charged with political crimes, and reduction of the armed forces. Unwilling to accept the mandate of the elections, the King offered Tsaldaris the opportunity to form a government. Predictably, however, the Populist leader failed to secure the necessary parliamentary support.[9]

Determined to exclude Plastiras from power and to stall for time until right-wing control of parliament could be restored, King Paul ran afoul of the U.S. embassy. In conversations later that month with Venizelos, the King urged the weak and ambitious Liberal Party leader to disavow his agreement with the other centrists and form a government of his own, tacitly supported by the right. Although Van Fleet, characteristically, backed this palace intrigue, Ambassador Grady strongly opposed it. On March 15, 1950, he told the King that "the center solution under Plastiras as Prime Minister was logical and reflected the will of the people as shown in the election." Any other alternative "would not be stable" and would inspire "a period of confusion." Indeed, "the by-passing of Plastiras" would ultimately "force him into the arms of Sofianopoulos and the result would be a strong leftist group which might ultimately take over political control of the country." Having received "assurances indirectly from Plastiras and others in the center group" that a strong army and a pro-American foreign policy would be maintained, Grady brushed aside the King's fears of Plastiras' alleged radicalism. The ambassador's position won the endorsement of Under Secretary Webb, who claimed that American public opinion would be "mystified and disturbed" by the King's plan, for Plastiras was clearly the election victor and had publicly pledged himself to uphold constitutional monarchy, work closely with the United States, and secure American aid.[10]

Shortly afterward, when the King ignored American pressures and installed a Venizelos government, the U.S. embassy quickly toppled it. On March 26, 1950, Grady spoke sharply to the new Prime Minister, challenging his ability to provide Greece with the "essential stability." In agreement with the ECA director and most of the top embassy staff, Grady sent Venizelos a letter, dated March 31, which he simultaneously released to the press. Calling attention to the "less than sat-isfactory performance of the Greek government," it declared that American funds for Greek programs would be halted until assurances were received of their proper use. Thus, it was "in the hands of the Greek government and the Greek Parliament to decide whether or not they wish to continue to receive American aid." To Acheson, Grady explained that "'gentle persuasion' does not seem to be effective with irre-sponsible politicians and stubborn monarchs." Naturally, the Greek government complained about this treatment to State Department officials in Washington; but it did not find much sympathy. According to the record of one meeting, "McGhee observed that he did not feel we were exercising any great pressure on the Greek government," but were "acting with exceptional restraint, considering the extent of American aid." Cromie "concurred," arguing "that Ambassador Grady's letter did not make any specific demands"; at the same time, he informed the Greek ambassador that the Venizelos cabinet "was not the kind of government which would be able to carry out the American aid program objectives." McGhee insisted that "this was obvious." Publicly and privately spurned by the Americans, Venizelos resigned on April 14. The next day, a Plastiras government took office, vowing its full cooperation with U.S. officials.[11]

The ascendancy of the center, however, came under im-mediate attack. Powerful forces, led by the palace, plotted feverishly to secure a right-wing alternative. As Grady pro-vided a serious obstacle, King Paul gave a lengthy interview to *U.S. News & World Report*, complaining about the am-bassador ("just criticizing everything and everybody") and the hard life of a modern monarch ("one continual worry"). Late that June, in an apparently unrelated development, the State Department transferred Grady to a new diplomatic assign-ment in Teheran.[12] Delighted at Grady's departure, the Greek right and its allies accelerated their efforts to remove Plastiras. On July 17, 1950, the day of his own departure from Greece, Van Fleet notified the State Department of the allegedly "dangerous" nature of the government in Athens. "Ever since the Plastiras govt was formed," he charged, "the Communists and fellow travellers have gradually regained their morale and influence and many are now in important positions." His recent field trips and discussions with Marshal Papagos "confirm many alarming moves by the Plastiras govt such as amnesty for dangerous war criminals and the relief of police and gendarmerie off[icer]s." It was "shocking," the U.S. military commander concluded, "that we support such a govt which permits red infiltration so soon after so much blood and money has been spent here to suppress Communist aggression." In another communication, the general contended that the State Department was backing a "traitor" and "turning Greece over to the Communists." Remarking that "Van Fleet's comments [were a] source [of] considerable concern" to the State Department, Acheson demanded an explanation from the U.S. embassy.[13]

Replying from Athens on July 19, 1950, the U.S. chargé, Harold Minor, sharply rebutted Van Fleet's "vague accusations," noting that terms like "Communist" were "used extremely loosely and freely by Greek rightists who tend [to] so identify anyone who disagrees with them"; nevertheless, he was clearly impatient with Plastiras and the Greek center for failing to meet American standards of anti-Communist militancy. The embassy had "taken corrective action" against moves by the Plastiras government "to undermine Papagos' position and our policy toward [the] Greek Army," Minor noted, and had been "concerned at [the] possibility of [the] appointment [of] dubious persons to key posts." It had also "forcefully warned" the Prime Minister's office "against any further clemency measures." The "crux of [the] matter," the uneasy chargé concluded, was that, at the time of the formation of the Plastiras government, the embassy did not object to plans to promote pacification, reconciliation, and unification of the nation around the tasks of reconstruction— "in a word, to take the road to peace." But though "these may still be Greece's internal needs," the "external situation has so drastically and dangerously altered" since the outbreak of the Korean War in late June, "that Greece now, like every other country, must give its first attention to [the] Communist menace." Therefore, "it is possible [that the] Plastiras government is not [the] best instrument to carry out this policy and may not be able to face up to altered external circumstances." Later that month, Minor reported that Plastiras desired increased economic assistance and liberalization of internal security measures—views which "indicated a lamentable lack of realism."[14]

Drawing similar conclusions, the State Department began to gravitate toward support of Marshal Papagos, now the darling of the right. "Plastiras' consistent record has been that of a patriotic non-communist Greek," McGhee informed the new American ambassador, John Peurifoy, on July 31, 1950. "He does tend, however, to be fuzzy-minded, impetuous and emotional in his traditional liberalism, and this led him to pursue a lax and sometimes rash policy towards the communists and fellow-travelers." As a result, the State Department was "considering whether . . . we should not support some stronger type of government, presumably headed by Marshal Papagos." On August 19, after Venizelos—again angling for the coveted post of Prime Minister—had withdrawn his support from the center government, Acheson notified the U.S. embassy that the "Dept believes any new govt under Plastiras" would "be undesirable." Accordingly, Venizelos now became Prime Minister, with rightist backing, and U.S. officials began developing a new political strategy. Webb informed the National Security Council the following month that, in Greece, "there are possibly new opportunities to be exploited; there are certainly new questions to be answered." Acheson, among others in the State Department, thought it "desirable . . . to use [the] strongest possible Emb[assy] influence" to substitute the "majority system" (actually, a district by district plurality arrangement) for proportional representation in Greek elections. This would help prevent "polarization" and lead to the development of a "stable Govt." Such plans were in line with those of the palace, which assumed that, when Papagos, the military hero of the civil war, at last made his political debut, a winner-take-all system would give him a huge victory.[15]

Arriving in Athens that September, Ambassador Peurifoy moved steadily, albeit with some difficulty, to place Greece's government in right-wing hands. Meeting with the King and Queen, he assured them of his cooperation and of U.S. support for the monarchy. In November 1950, the ambassador praised the King's plan to ask Papagos "to form and lead a Nationalist ticket" in forthcoming elections. This would have "immensely beneficial" consequences, he told the State Department, for "we will either have elections from which we are confident a really strong, able, and honest Papagos government will emerge," or the prospect would frighten other political leaders into cooperation with American officials.[16] In the spring of 1951, the general did enter Greek politics, although with less success than expected. A group of his associates attempted a military coup, which embarrassed the general. Later, a bitter personal quarrel erupted between Papagos and the King, seriously dividing the right. Soon, Peurifoy was complaining that "the King and little Queen are active as bees trying to prevent his election," thus "jeopardizing the whole structure here in Greece."[17] In September 1951, to the distress of American officials, the center again emerged victorious in national elections, restoring Plastiras as Prime Minister. Particularly worrisome to the Americans was the center's reform program and its plan to balance the budget by cutting military spending. U.S. officials thus adopted more forceful tactics in an effort to tilt the balance to the right. In March 1952, the embassy announced publicly its opposition to proportional representation in Greek elections and threatened a cutoff of American aid if it continued. Faced with this pressure, the center crumpled, accepting the American demand for a district by district plurality system. In the ensuing elections, held during November 1952, the Greek Rally party of Marshal Papagos, with 49 percent of the vote, captured 82 percent of the seats in parliament. To the intense satisfaction of American officials, the general had resurrected the right and governmental "stability."[18]

From 1952 to 1963, Greece was ruled by a succession of right-wing governments, in close partnership with the Americans. Their priorities were internal security, conservative economic programs, and military expansion. An advocate of "ruthless suppression," Papagos argued that "the fanatic and hardened incorrigibles must be prevented from spreading their poison," while "public education and psychological warfare must be used intensively in order to counteract Communist propaganda." Dominating parliament, the right also exercised power through the army and the monarchy, now, happily, reconciled with Papagos. Indeed, the American line of influence tended to run through the palace. As a leading scholar of Greek-American relations has noted, "American policy rested on the assumption that the king was the ultimate guarantor of political stability, military preparedness, and loyalty to the Western alliance."[19] When Papagos died in office in October 1955, Ambassador Peurifoy did not wait for the general's party to choose a successor, but went directly to the King and arranged for him to ask young Constantine Caramanlis to form a government. Previously, Caramanlis had been a figure of minor political importance, but he had won the admiration of the American embassy for his administrative efficiency. Thanks to a rigged electoral system, Caramanlis and his party, although usually outpolled by their opponents, garnered comfortable parliamentary majorities in subsequent elections. Combining ability, impeccable conservatism, and pro-American views, Caramanlis proved the ideal Prime Minister, from the embassy's viewpoint.[20]

Just as American officials had fostered the dominance of the right in Greek politics, so they promoted the development of sizable armed forces in the cause of "national security." Initially, to be sure, they took a quite different tack, for, with the end of the civil war, there seemed good reason to dismantle Greece's vast and expensive military machine. On October 3, 1949, noting that "the struggle is now primarily political and economic, rather than military," Grady urged the U.S. government "to strengthen the economy by relieving it of the drachmae burden of a large armed force." In line with the demands of U.S. officials, the Athens government began a program to reduce the Greek armed forces from their strength of 217,000 in late 1949 to 94,000 (including an 80,000-man GNA) by the end of 1950. Simultaneously, the U.S. military mission was to be cut from 538 to 129. But, as Webb noted, in mid-1950 this program was "arrested as a result of the Korean aggression and consequent Balkan uncertainties."[21] Thereafter, in accordance with the recommendations of the American military command in Greece, the U.S. Joint Chiefs of Staff authorized a Greek military establishment of some 164,000, including a 147,000-man GNA. Thus, Greece, although a small, underdeveloped nation, was soon maintaining an extraordinarily large and expensive military machine. In mid-1951, when Europe had an average of 12.6 men per thousand under arms, Greece had 21.6.[22]

American officials had ambitious plans for the Greek military. Initially dubious about the GNA's ability to resist an invasion from the north or even defeat the guerrillas, they had limited the mission of the Greek armed forces, until the rebel collapse, to the maintenance of "internal security." But on November 7, 1949, in a letter to the Department of the Army, Van Fleet "strongly" recommended "that we revise our thinking 'that Greece is not important militarily.'" Indeed, "Greece today is the keystone of the defense line from Western Europe to the Middle East." It could serve as "a secondary front of tremendous strategic value," providing for "Soviet diversion in the event of war." If the United States would only "eliminate fear" of the Russians, it could "win in the Balkans."[23] After the outbreak of the Korean War, Van Fleet's views attracted new adherents. "This Greek Army is a good investment and a going concern," reported his successor as JUSMAPG director in July 1950; "our policy for Greece viewed in the light of current events needs prompt and effective revision." State Department officials agreed. Noting the "considerable United States investment in the Greek armed forces," their "estimated high potential effectiveness," and the possibility that the Russians would resort to "satellite forces" in the Balkans, McGhee argued that "the Greek armed forces should be strengthened to enable them successfully to resist such satellite forces as are likely to be thrown against them." In NSC 103/1, adopted on February 14, 1951, the National Security Council resolved to aid the Greek military in "maintaining internal security," "repelling an attack by satellite forces," and "causing maximum practicable delay . . . to an attack involving direct Soviet participation." Finally, it would "press now for the inclusion of Greece as a full member of NATO."[24]

Greek participation in NATO formally integrated the Greek military machine with U.S. military policy. Ever since 1949, the American Joint Chiefs of Staff had incorporated the Greek armed forces into their battle plans. But NATO membership would legitimate this agreement and others by the Pentagon. Consequently, when the NATO pact was organized, as George Kennan recalled, he "stood alone . . . among those who had to do with its conclusion, in opposing the inclusion of Greece and Turkey." The objections came from Western European nations, who viewed Greek and Turkish participation as unnecessarily provocative.[25] In September 1950, therefore, the Joint Chiefs of Staff resolved that while it was desirable "to concert military planning and actions in the Mediterranean and the Near and Middle East with those already in progress in Western Europe," the inclusion of Greece and Turkey as full members of NATO might "adversely affect" treaty arrangements. For the time being, the JCS recommended "associate status" for the two Near East nations. In the spring of 1951, however, they contended that the time had arrived to admit Turkey and Greece as full members. Overcoming the remaining opposition, the U.S. government secured full membership for Greece in early 1952. The following fall, the Papagos government announced a bilateral agreement with Washington for the establishment of U.S. military bases in Greece. Formally, at least, these became NATO bases, just as a 400-member U.S. military mission supplied, equipped, trained, and planned strategy for the Greek armed forces under NATO's auspices. Practically, however, the Pentagon had acquired an important vested interest in Greece.[26]

Whatever the advantages of the swollen Greek military establishment, observers agreed that it constituted a serious burden for an impoverished people. Although U.S. military aid to Greece totaled about $1.4 billion by the end of 1961,[27] this compensated for only a fraction of the nation's losses or opportunities forgone. During the war in Korea, Greece sent a military contingent that suffered heavy casualties. For a nation desperately short of investment capital and chronically unable to balance its budget, the large annual outlay for the armed forces represented a major problem. According to a State Department pamphlet published in mid-1951, military spending that year accounted for 38 percent of the Greek budget—a percentage which remained roughly the same throughout the 1950s.[28] In fiscal 1952–53, for example, appropriations for the Greek security forces comprised at least 36 percent of state expenditures and 49 percent of the country's tax revenue. Even American officials recognized that the high cost of the Greek military establishment placed the Greek economy in an extremely difficult bind—although, of course, this did not dissuade them from championing it. "So long as present conditions of international tension continue," an NSC staff study concluded in 1951, "Greece will be required to make military expenditures which are in excess of those which could be supported by the Greek economy."[29]

Despite the heavy military burden, the Greek economy underwent some significant progress during the 1950s and early 1960s. In the new climate of peace that characterized the post–civil war decade, the nation's GNP grew at an average annual rate of 5.4 percent. Between 1938 and 1959, industrial production doubled, while agricultural output also increased substantially. By 1961, Greece's production of electric energy had reached almost ten times that of 1938. Two of the fastest-growing sectors of the Greek economy were tourism and the merchant marine. The number of tourists visiting Greece increased fivefold between 1938 and 1961. The Greek merchant fleet, virtually destroyed at the end of World War II, became one of the most important in the world— although, as a means of evading taxes, its millionaire owners kept most of it under foreign flags. In conjunction with the remittances of emigrants, these businesses eased Greece's otherwise severe balance of payments problem. If, in the early 1960s, Greece continued to be one of Europe's poorest countries, its economic situation had improved considerably since the nadir of the civil war.[30]

Nonetheless, serious structural weaknesses persisted. Despite Greece's limited arable land—estimated at about one-fourth the nation's surface—in 1961 more than half the labor force remained in agriculture, while 13 percent found employment in manufacturing. Investment in industry during this period declined markedly and, not surprisingly, the manufacturing sector remained stunted; in 1958, 85 percent of Greece's industrial plants employed five persons or less. When ranked by industrial output as a percentage of gross domestic product, Greece placed a bit ahead of India and a bit behind Argentina.[31] Externally, this meant that Greece's relationship to most of Europe and the United States followed the pattern typical of an underdeveloped nation. In 1960, manufactured and semimanufactured goods constituted only 10 percent of Greece's exports, but comprised 72 percent of its imports. Internally, Greece lacked the wherewithal to provide most of its citizens with a decent life. Unemployment and underemployment posed severe problems, while net per capita income reached only $353 by 1963—about a third of the level in EEC countries and a seventh of that in the United States.[32] Of course, not all of Greece's economic difficulties could be remedied easily by public policy. Even so, there existed considerable room for reform. As one U.S. study conceded, Greece had a "very uneven distribution of wealth"—a situation exacerbated during the 1950s, when wage and salary increases lagged considerably behind the rise of profits.[33] Pathetically weak, unions often lacked the ability to win wage gains or secure the enforcement of existing labor legislation.[34] Government social and economic policies further exaggerated inequalities—for example, by limiting expenditures on public education and continuing the reliance on an extremely inequitable tax system. So bleak was the prospect for the Greek lower classes that, between 1959 and 1963, almost a third of the Greek labor force emigrated in search of satisfactory employment.[35]

U.S. policy, formally encouraging economic growth, contributed in a number of ways to Greece's economic difficulties. The American economic aid program had initially been directed to making Greece economically self-supporting by 1952, but this goal grew increasingly unrealistic and unattractive in the late 1940s and early 1950s. Arguing that U.S. economic aid represented a waste of taxpayers' money and a handout to an undeserving nation, Grady, since late 1949, had urged its termination "at the earliest possible moment."[36] The Korean War and the accompanying arms race added yet another incentive to scuttle economic assistance. In his January 1951 budget message, President Truman declared: "Our program of economic aid to Europe must . . . be directed in support of the European military build-up, rather than to promoting further economic expansion." This attitude had immediate ramifications for Greece. That July, the State Department revealed that, henceforth, "a greater proportion of the funds" would "be devoted to purposes more related to defense," with "less emphasis . . . placed upon long-range economic development projects."[37] Subsequently, the bottom fell out of the U.S. program, as economic aid sank from $180 million (1951–52), to $81 million (1952–53), to $22 million (1953–54).[38]

"The net result was wholesale cancellation of programs, or at best a slowing down," a U.S. aid official recalled. "All social service construction, all work on roads, rails, ports, houses, hotels, museums, schools, stopped dead." Although the government continued its large electric power project, most agricultural improvement plans were canceled. In 1955, when a once-ambitious U.S. program of building hospitals and health centers came to an end, "practically none of the facilities planned or constructed was in operation." Indeed, this official observed, "Greece was literally spattered with works at all stages of completion, liberally plastered with such signs as 'Marshall Aid,' 'Gift of American People,' etc. until the Mission decided that diplomacy required that they be removed." Meanwhile, as U.S. economic assistance dwindled, U.S. officials pressed tough austerity measures on a reluctant Greek government. "The reorientation," an ECA advisor conceded, "was a bit rough. . . . We cut down the credit through Treasury representations. We succeeded in reducing investments and . . . in helping the government" to slash its budget.[39]

Furthermore, the priorities of U.S. advisers contributed to keeping Greece locked into its status as an underdeveloped nation. On paper, the Americans occasionally advocated economic reform measures: "development of light industry"; "restriction of imports to essential items"; "increasing the contribution of the Greek merchant marine"; and "shifting emphasis from indirect to direct taxation." In practice, however, they fostered the ascendancy of rightist parties, which simply ignored economic reforms and promoted their own concerns: preserving the class structure; leaving the oligarchy free to pursue easy profits and the easy life; and maintaining "internal security."[40] Moreover, under American pressure, the Greek government established regulations for trade and investment much to the advantage of foreign corporations. The latter—including such U.S. firms as Socony, Pan American, Trans World Airlines, American Export Lines, Caltex, and American Tobacco—thereby obtained a dominant position in the tiny Greek economy and directed it to their own interests. Although anxious to curtail U.S. public investment in Greece, the State Department welcomed the activities of the multinational corporations. "Every effort should be made to encourage further private investment in Greece," a State Department official told Congress in 1957. Noting that there already existed an investment guarantee program for Greece, which covered both expropriation and convertibility, he urged that these incentives be supplemented by advice to the Greek government "on steps it could take to make investment possibilities more attractive and better advertised." Throughout the 1950s and 1960s, foreign corporate involvement in the Greek economy did increase substantially, thus strengthening Greece's neocolonial relationship with industrially developed nations.[41]

Undergirding the rightist orientation of public policy lay a structure of fear and political repression unprecedented for a modern democratic nation. Although Greece's 1952 constitution contained provisions guaranteeing civil liberties, the Athens government continued the "emergency"measures of the civil war. Some of these provisions, such as the ones authorizing deportation and withdrawal of citizenship, had clauses limiting their applicability to the duration of the civil war, but until 1962, Greek courts gutted this limitation by ruling that the war had not "legally" ended. Consequently, large numbers of Greeks continued to be imprisoned, exiled, or denied employment on political grounds. Failure to vote in the 1946 elections, or perhaps having a suspect relative, provided sufficient cause for the police to deny an individual a Certificate of Social Belief, the prerequisite to public employment, attendance at a university, or even a driver's license.[42] Indeed, a secret network of military, police, and intelligence personnel exercised extraordinary power in every area of the nation's life. The Greek central intelligence agency, KYP, engaged in widespread wiretapping, mail tampering, and political surveillance—operations which extended to all government agencies, including the Prime Minister's office. Sometimes, the forces of repression moved openly, as when Dimitratos, returning to the Minister of Labor post he had once held under Metaxas, sought to smash the Greek labor movement. At other times, they operated in the shadows, as in the assassination of the popular parliamentary deputy, Grigoris Lambrakis.[43]

This emphasis upon "internal security" developed with full U.S. government support.[44] Contending that the "major dangers confronting Greece now come from within," Webb warned the embassy in May 1950 about the possible "recreation of commie org[anizations] and [the] capture of T[rade] U[nion]s and municipal govts by disguised commies." Thus, just as important as "reinforced police vigilance and careful screening of detainees before release" was ensuring that the Greeks would "clearly understand [the] commie design and learn [to] recognize commies and fellow travelers despite misleading labels." In Athens, Minor concurred on the desirability of "constant police vigilance" and secured the agreement of the palace on the "need to watch [the] trade union situation" and on the "dangers inherent in [the] forthcoming municipal election." To American officials, it was axiomatic that Greek Communists should be repressed and prevented from operating a legal party. In addition, they encouraged the widespread intelligence and police operations of Greek "security" agencies. Organized by the CIA, KYP continued to work closely with its parent agency on a variety of assignments and to be advised by U.S. personnel. Indeed, the CIA funded KYP directly, bypassing the regular budgetary channels of the Greek government.[45] One of the key targets of the CIA—and thus of KYP as well—was the Greek trade union movement. Together with the embassy's labor advisers, the AFL, and the Greek government, they helped to keep the GSEE under right-wing control and in its chronic state of debility.[46]

By the early 1960s, as a *Washington Post* reporter recalled, "Greece, more than any other country in Europe, had become an American Cold War protectorate." With all key policy decisions passing through American hands, the U.S. embassy, military mission, and CIA station became the true loci of power in Greece. Winning the approval of American officials was an important step in the advancement of Greek military officers, civil servants, intelligence operatives, bankers, and politicians, just as incurring their wrath would almost certainly prove disastrous. At a nod from the Americans, there would materialize cabinet posts, NATO training assignments, administrative promotions, sophisticated surveillance equipment, new and costly weapons, or simply lavish gifts and retainers. Dipping into the bottomless treasury of its secret funds, the CIA provided cooperative Greeks with airplanes, sports cars, tape recorders, and direct cash payments. In turn, the Greek elite shared its yachts, island vacations, and sumptuous dinner parties with its American benefactors. CIA director Allen Dulles was a sailing guest of the royal family, while the Athens CIA station provided the Queen with political briefings for her trips abroad, designed her itineraries, and furnished the palace with the latest gadgetry. A U.S. embassy official later remarked: "The CIA was in bed with the palace, the army, the Greek intelligence service, the rightist parties, the conservative business community, the establishment in general." Actually, the embassy adopted much the same orientation.[47] When a political issue emerged which threatened what American officials defined as U.S. interests—for example, when pressure developed in Greece to assert Greek jurisdiction over the strategically valuable island of Cyprus, then conveniently controlled by the British—this cozy arrangement could usually be counted upon to sidetrack it.[48]

But the Greek political climate was already beginning to shift. Dissatisfaction with the Athens government's right-wing policies grew throughout the 1950s and early 1960s. Meanwhile, a massive exodus from the countryside, originally inspired by the civil war and later continued by outward migration, widened horizons and shook traditional political loyalties. Although the Communists failed to experience a political comeback in the 1950s, a new left-wing political party, EDA, began to rally the discontented.[49] Others regrouped under the banner of the Center Union party, a centrist coalition put together in the late 1950s by George Papandreou. Together with his son Andreas, who returned to Greece after a career as an economist in the United States, the elder Papandreou fashioned a modern reform program for the Center Union. Riding a tide of public sentiment that had turned increasingly critical of authoritarian tactics, economic conservatism, and subservience to the United States, Papandreou launched an unrelenting campaign against the policies of the Caramanlis government and for new elections. When elections followed, in November 1963, the Center Union party, assisted by a split between Caramanlis and the palace, won a clear victory. Nevertheless, to avoid relying on EDA (and what the right would call "Communist support") to enact his reform program in parliament, Papandreou launched yet another campaign in the hope of securing a parliamentary majority. In February 1964, he met with unprecedented success, for the Center Union drew 53 percent of the vote—the largest percentage secured by any party in modern Greek history.[50]

The Center Union of George Papandreou, as his son recalled, was "committed to making Greece a modern European state." Determined to press forward with a domestic reform program, the Center Union government fostered free education at all levels, slackened controls on wages, and lightened the burden of agricultural debt. It also made the first serious efforts to dismantle the nation's police state apparatus by ending political intimidation in the countryside, transferring some of the more notorious right-wing officers out of key positions, and releasing all political prisoners detained since the civil war. In foreign policy, the Papandreou government remained committed to Greek participation in NATO but refused to accept a status of subservience. Its slogan was: "Allies, yes. Satellites, no." However, George Papandreou—unlike his son Andreas, who tended to be sharply critical of past policies and a rallying point for the left wing of the Center Union—was a battle-scarred veteran of Greek politics and preferred a cautious approach. Consequently, he took no more than modest steps to limit the power of the army and the prerogatives of King Constantine, Paul's successor. As a concession to both, he appointed a conservative member of the Center Union as Minister of Defense. In additon, he sought to retain satisfactory relations with the Americans.[51]

Prime Minister Papandreou's efforts, however, proved futile. As his son wrote, the government was soon embattled on "almost every policy front." The Center Union "clashed with the King over his prerogatives, especially over those related to the leadership of the armed forces"; it "clashed with the 'parallel government' of Greece, including the Americans, over the control" of KYP; "it clashed with the economic oligarchy of the country over a reformist and expansionist development policy, and with the large foreign investors who had obtained almost colonial terms." Finally, by emphasizing a more independent foreign policy, the Center Union ran afoul of the Americans. To Washington policymakers, both

Papandreous (and especially Andreas) were soon anathema. In 1964, when George Papandreou met with Lyndon Johnson in Washington, the atmosphere could hardly have been chillier. To make possible the establishment of NATO bases on Cyprus, now independent and nonaligned, the President demanded the adoption of the "Acheson plan," which entailed the partition of Cyprus between Greece and Turkey. Moreover, he threatened to withdraw NATO aid if Greece did not accept the plan. When Papandreou responded that, "in that case, Greece might have to rethink the advisability of belonging to NATO," Johnson retorted that "maybe Greece should rethink the value of a parliament which could not take the right decision." Later, the Greek ambassador remonstrated that "no Greek parliament could accept such a plan," only to have the American President explode:

Fuck your parliament and your constitution. America is an elephant, Cyprus is a flea. Greece is a flea. If these two fellows continue itching the elephant, they may just get whacked by the elephant's trunk, whacked good. . . . If your Prime Minister gives me talk about democracy, parliament and constitution, he, his parliament and his constitution may not last very long.

It was an instructive lesson on the relations between great and small powers. As an afterthought, the President added: "Don't forget to tell old Papa what's his name what I told you. . . .You hear?"[52]

Clearly, the situation was approaching a crisis. Within Greece, American officials freely vented the most hostile of sentiments toward the Center Union government and toward Andreas Papandreou, whom they viewed as the source of a spreading Communist infection within the body politic. In 1965, rumors flew about Athens of a military coup, backed by the Americans. One centrist general reported in disgust that the Americans "have had a rightwing caretaker in this property of theirs and were prepared to try a Liberal caretaker, but they will keep the Liberal only so long as he acts submissively like the old one." A turning point came when the Prime Minister sought to reorganize the Ministry of Defense.

The relevant minister resisted, backed by King Constantine. On July 15, in an unconstitutional move, the King forced the resignation of the Papandreou government. Thereafter, he attempted to split off members of the Center Union party and form a stable government of the right. Little could be done along these lines, however, for George Papandreou was determined to stand firm against further palace intrigues. As new elections approached, in 1967, the Papandreous waged a tumultuous campaign, demanding "basic alterations" in "the structure of power." Andreas Papandreou explained: "The King would have to learn to restrict himself to the constitutional limits of his authority; the Army would have to learn to obey the orders of the lawfully elected government; the Americans would have to learn that Greece belonged to the Greeks." Shortly before election day, it became apparent to observers that the Center Union would win an even more overwhelming victory than it had secured in 1964.[53] For defenders of the old order, the moment of truth had arrived.

On April 21, 1967, a band of military officers mobilized the armed forces and seized control of the Greek government. Their leader, Colonel George Papadopoulos, announced that they had acted to "save the nation from the precipice of communism"—a contention reinforced when King Constantine dutifully swore in the new regime. Imposing martial law, the right-wing junta closed down parliament, suspended the constitution, proscribed the political parties, gagged the press, placed labor unions under government control, purged the civil service, established strict censorship in the communications media and in the arts, and brought the entire society under intense police surveillance. In the months after its seizure of power, the junta imprisoned more than 40,000 people, some of whom it tortured hideously. What the colonels called the "new Christian civilization" had arrived, bringing with it a ban on long hair, miniskirts, and other modern trends and an emphasis on patriotism, obedience, religious education, and military government. At the same time, the junta encouraged large-scale foreign corporate investment and even presided over an economic boom. This did little to pacify the nation, however, for Greeks in all walks of life demonstrated a loathing for the new order, which many found redolent of fascism. When George Papandreou died in early November 1968, after having been imprisoned three times by the colonels, a crowd of 500,000 people lined his funeral route. In defiance of the regime's ban on political manifestations, they began chanting "down with tyranny" and "out with the junta." Characteristically, the police waded into the crowd, beating many and dragging others off to torture and imprisonment.[54]

The extent of American responsibility for the 1967 coup cannot be assessed with any exactitude, for the records and conversations leading to the event are still shrouded in secrecy; nevertheless, it is clear that American policy provided a vital ingredient without which the coup would not have occurred. Three of the top five conspirators in the coup were high-level officials of KYP who worked closely with their CIA counterparts. Among them was Papadopoulos, a right-wing military officer who had been on the CIA's payroll since 1952. Indeed, Papadopoulos was the chief liaison agent between KYP and the CIA. Furthermore, the conspirators used a NATO contingency plan, designed to eliminate internal "subversion" in the event of a Communist invasion, to implement their seizure of power. Yet, though there is good reason to believe that the CIA and perhaps the U.S. military mission were accomplices of the colonels, the nature of the coup apparently took the regular embassy staff and State Department officials in Washington by surprise. The reason was that the latter had pinned their hopes upon the generals' junta, a right-wing conspiratorial organization under the influence of the palace, which planned a coup in May. By acting in April, the colonels availed themselves of the groundwork laid by the King and the generals and, at the same time, placed themselves in the principal command positions. Even if—as seems unlikely—American officials did not formally authorize a coup, their fear of a Center Union election victory and unwillingness to oppose unconstitutional action to prevent it bolstered the determination of the conspirators. In addition, the conspirators had all been active in the civil war and in subsequent U.S. training programs—experiences which fostered their messianic notion that the armed forces were the saviors of the nation.[55]

The compatibility of the colonels' regime with U.S. policy quickly became evident. Although Western European governments condemned the dictatorship in the sharpest terms and sometimes gave secret funding to its opponents, Secretary of State Dean Rusk told the House Foreign Affairs Committee that, "except for our continuous moral support of King Constantine, there is nothing else we can do." Worried about public relations, the U.S. ambassador did inspire a short-lived embargo on U.S. shipments of heavy arms; secretly, however, they were resumed in 1968. In the fall of 1969, the National Security Council, chaired by Henry Kissinger, voted to restore full-scale assistance to the dictatorship, again on a secret basis. "Make it look as good as you can," President Richard Nixon told the new U.S. ambassador, "but the priority is military assistance." As a result, the U.S. government provided the junta with more military equipment during its first three years in power than it had supplied to its predecessor during a comparable period. Meanwhile, the U.S. government arranged for the homeporting of the U.S. Navy in Athens, lobbied against expulsion of Greece from the Council of Europe, and sent a steady procession of U.S. dignitaries to Athens to cement ties with the colonels. Among the latter were Secretary of Defense Melvin Laird, Secretary of Commerce Maurice Stans, NATO Commander General Andrew Goodpaster, and Vice-President Spiro Agnew. In 1972, Thomas Pappas, a Greek-American industrial tycoon with a $200 million empire in Greece and a position as vice-president of the Committee to Re-Elect the President, hosted a dinner in Athens for Stans, at which the Commerce Secretary read a tribute to the Papadopoulos regime from Nixon. "We in the United States Government," he stated, "particularly in American business, greatly appreciate the welcome that is given to American companies and the sense of security that the government of Greece is imparting to them." Delighted with these remarks, the controlled press displayed them prominently, including an observation by Stans that he had been asked by the President to convey his "warm love" to the junta.[56]

The story was exactly the same among those American officials who had played a crucial part in drafting the Truman Doctrine. They showed no scruples at subordinating its rhetoric of "free institutions" to Cold War desiderata. "American is a great power," Acheson privately told a former Greek official, irate at U.S. policy. "It is a role we could not have evaded. This role has its own logic. If we ignore such logic the world can either fall into anarchy or into the hands of Russia." Ironically, the former Secretary of State sounded remarkably like his counterparts in Moscow. "We just play the role history has thrust upon us," he insisted. "There was no realistic alternative to your colonels." Greece was "not ready for democracy." In public forums as well, American officials outlined their priorities. Testifying on May 17, 1968 before the Senate Foreign Relations Committee in behalf of U.S. military aid to the Athens regime, Secretary of Defense Clark Clifford stated bluntly: "The obligations imposed on us by the NATO alliance are far more important than the kind of government they have in Greece."[57] It was a position that contrasted starkly with the rhetoric, though not the policy, of twenty years before.

For American officials, of course, the crucial "lesson" provided by U.S. intervention in the Greek civil war was that it worked. Thus fortified, they faced the struggle for global hegemony with enhanced confidence. "Korea is the Greece of the Far East," Truman told an adviser shortly after fighting broke out in Asia. "If we are tough enough now, if we stand up to them like we did in Greece, they won't take any steps." Shortly afterward, calling attention to revolutionary struggles in Indochina and the Philippines, Acheson proposed to the National Security Council that it develop "effective means of anti-guerrilla warfare, utilizing the experience gained in jungle fighting during the war, in operations in Greece, in Korea, Malaya and elsewhere." Along the way, Washington officials received a boost from veterans of the Greek counterinsurgency campaign, who fanned out across the Third World.[58] In April 1950, confronting a leftist rebellion in the Philippines, the U.S. embassy recommended expanding the U.S. military mission's size and scope for "an operation similar to that which we carried out in Greece." That September, the Joint Chiefs of Staff reported on plans to strengthen the U.S. military contingent in the Philippines and "to pattern it generally after the United States Mission in Greece during the recent large-scale guerrilla activities." Outlining a $250 million "aid" program for the archipelago, the State Department's Dean Rusk assured uneasy members of the House Foreign Affairs Committee that "it would be a good deal like the U.S. operation in Greece."[59]

As American involvement deepened in Indochina, the Greek model helped to silence any doubts that might emerge about the wisdom of U.S. policy. Pointing to the faltering French effort to suppress the Vietminh, the U.S. chargé in Saigon observed in April 1950 that it "may eventually become necessary" for the U.S. government to "assume some responsibility" in Indochina, "as it did in Greece." The following month, he reported that "as in [the] case of Greece, [the] threat of spreading Communist political contagion East and West . . . should influence our action." Recommending the "limited use of US force," he envisaged "our going as far as we did in Greece and farther than was ever announced we could go. It is derivative of [the] Truman doctrine."[60] Dwight Eisenhower, succeeding Truman in the White House, concurred on the desirability of expanding the U.S. role in Indochina and also cited the U.S. experience in Greece. The return of the Democrats to power after 1961 merely continued the process. According to Theodore Sorensen, John Kennedy's speech writer and alter ego, the young President liked to compare the Vietnam War "to the long struggles against Communist guerrillas in Greece" and Asia. Lyndon Johnson recalled that when he became President, "President Truman gave me many good suggestions and wise counsel from his own experience. . . . He pledged his support for our efforts in Vietnam" and "told me he had faced the same problems of aggression—in Greece and Turkey and Korea." Defending his escalation of the war, Johnson repeatedly cited American intervention in Greece as one of his precedents. Behind the scenes, Walt Rostow, chairman of the State Department's policy planning council, assured Rusk that if new counter-insurgency measures were taken, "there is no reason we cannot win as clear a victory in South Viet-Nam as in Greece, Malaya, and the Philippines."[61]

The parallel drawn by American officials between the U.S. ventures in Greece and in Indochina was not entirely inappropriate, for in the mid-1970s, both collapsed. In Indochina, U.S. officials and their client governments finally lost their wars and fled ignominiously. In Greece, developments were more complex, but also resulted in a severe setback for American policy. Tacitly supported by Washington, the junta acted in July 1974 to overthrow the democratic, nonaligned government of Archbishop Makarios on Cyprus. But this action triggered a Turkish invasion of the island and the collapse of the junta. Democracy now returned to Greece, and with a strongly anti-American tone. Across the spectrum of Greek politics, a consensus developed on a number of previously forbidden items: maximum independence from great power control; elimination of the monarchy (voted 3 to 1 in a plebiscite); legalization of the Communist Party; and a firm stand against American designs on Cyprus. When a government headed by the conservative Constantine Caramanlis, once a strong supporter of American programs, was elected to office, it pursued a policy of independence from the United States and sponsored the withdrawal of Greece from the military side of NATO. His leading political competitor, Andreas Papandreou, head of the new Pan-Hellenic Socialist Movement, emerged as a critic of the United States and staunch advocate of nonaligned socialism. Although Communism showed no signs of making a comeback, Greek politics had shifted to the left. Even the conservatives had concluded that only by cutting loose from the leader of the "Free World" could Greece become a free nation.[62]

If, ultimately, American policy toward Greece proved a failure, it is only fair to consider the alternatives. Some recent scholars, though critical of American tactics, have suggested that without U.S. intervention in the 1940s, Greece would have become a dreary Soviet satellite on the order of Bulgaria. They admit that Stalin had little interest in Greek affairs but argue that the KKE, given its Stalinist orientation, probably would have ended up placing Greece at the service of the Kremlin.[63] This is an unpleasant possibility, but does it justify the intervention of a foreign nation to preclude it? After all, revolutions, civil wars, even elections, sometimes point toward developments which foreign powers dislike. Admittedly, after two catastrophic world wars, national sovereignty may be dated. Certainly, in the Cold War era, both the Soviet Union and the United States have widened their claims to serve as the final arbiters of the internal affairs of other nations. But in the absence of a consensus on the desirability of their assorted "Doctrines," as well as in the absence of a world government, has national independence—what Americans, when criticizing the colonialist practices of other nations, once championed as "self-determination"—become totally obsolete? Is the destiny of small nations simply to be determined by the rulers of the "great powers"? In a Greek controversy, was a Greek solution really out of the question?

Furthermore, would a Greek solution have led to such consequences? Bulgaria, to be sure, did become locked into the Soviet orbit, but Albania and Yugoslavia—whatever their other faults—did not. In addition, during the 1940s, the Greek left (for example, EAM) was not a pallid projection of Moscow's desires, carried forward by Red Army bayonets, but a powerful entity in its own right, with deep roots in Greek life. It is well to remember that the record of nations established through independent revolutionary struggles, even Communist ones (e.g., Yugoslavia, China, Cuba, and Vietnam), has not been one of subservience to Moscow's dictates. Quite possibly, Greece would have become a nation similar to (or perhaps aligned with) Yugoslavia. Apparently, this is what Tito assumed, at least until mid-1949. If Greece had followed the Yugoslav model, its domestic policy would have been that curious mixture of economic and cultural development programs, police state measures, and "workers' control" that has characterized that Balkan nation since the advent of Tito. However one evaluates this, a Yugoslav-style foreign policy—scrupulously nonaligned in world affairs—might well have been tolerable, even from the standpoint of the State Department.

Moreover, if British and American policy of the 1940s had been more tolerant of the left, according it the political influence which its popularity and important wartime role merited, it is not at all clear that the KKE would have chosen the path of revolution. All signs indicate that the party leadership made the decision for armed revolt as a last resort and that, as a KKE spokesman later conceded, "even many party functionaries and members did not agree with it." Recently, after decades of studying the Greek civil war, C.M. Woodhouse changed his mind and concluded that, if offered a reasonable opportunity, most of the left—including the KKE—might well have opted for parliamentary politics.[64] Resistance movements and Communist parties did so throughout much of Europe. Indeed, in scattered parts of Greece where compromise was tried—for example, on the island of Zante—the left did not take up arms.[65] Today, in the climate of tolerance that has emerged in Greece since the fall of the junta, two Communist parties exist in that land—one Moscow-oriented and the other "Eurocommunist." Both run candidates for office and accept conventional norms of democratic politics. Given some measure of acceptance, then, the Greek left of the 1940s might have followed the pattern of its counterparts in France and Italy, where Communist parties played an important and legitimate role. Or perhaps the case of Greece would have been unique. It is impossible to make such judgments with any degree of certainty.

What can be evaluated is the reality of American policy toward Greece: a sad story of intervention in the affairs of a foreign land, culminating in war, dictatorship, and alienation. Anxious about the security of U.S. petroleum resources in the Middle East, American policymakers had moved in the 1940s to strengthen the shaky Western position in Greece. In their opinion, this necessitated containing the Greek left, which, they assumed, was merely a creature of Soviet foreign policy. A tragic and bloody confrontation followed, reducing much of Greece to ruin, establishing the United States as the dominant power in Greek affairs, and inspiring a growing pattern of American overseas intervention. Given their single-minded focus on the threat from the left—during the civil war and in subsequent decades—American officials, despite their occasional reformist impulses, contributed to Greece's desperate political, social, and economic problems. Indeed, they helped to fasten upon Greece right-wing governments and policies which met badly the needs of an underdeveloped society. For a time, Washington sustained this feat within the framework of democratic institutions, albeit rather tattered and circumscribed ones. Eventually, however, American officials encouraged the establishment and maintenance of a right-wing military dictatorship as the only way to keep Greece in line with their aims. In short, the U.S. government treated Greece much as the Soviet Union treated its Eastern European satellites—as a piece of Cold War real estate. Little wonder, then, that American policy toward Greece ended in shambles. In the long run, subject peoples revolt against such treatment, and powers which play an imperial role should expect to inherit the consequences.

NOTES

1. CONTAINING THE WARTIME RESISTANCE

1. MacVeagh to Franklin D. Roosevelt, October 15, 1944, "MacVeagh (Greece)" folder, Box 54, PSF, (Franklin) Roosevelt papers.

2. Richard Clogg, *A Short History of Modern Greece*, pp. 93, 125; Christopher M. Woodhouse, *A Short History of Modern Greece*, pp. 138, 224; Stephen A. Larrabee, *Hellas Observed*, passim.

3. John A. Petropulos, *Politics and Statecraft*, passim; John Campbell and Philip Sherrard, *Modern Greece*, pp. 19–126; Theodore A. Couloumbis, et al., *Foreign Interference in Greek Politics*, pp. 15–73; Constantine Tsoucalas, *The Greek Tragedy*, pp. 15–35.

4. John S. Koliopoulos, *Greece and the British Connection*, pp. 1–168; Harry Cliadakis, "Le Régime de Metaxás," pp. 19–38 and "Political and Diplomatic Background," pp. 117–38; Bickham Sweet-Escott, *Greece: A Political and Economic Survey*, p. 8.

5. Elisabeth Barker, *British Policy in South-East Europe*, pp. 96–108; Koliopoulos, *Greece and the British Connection*, pp. 169–293; John O. Iatrides, *Revolt in Athens*, pp. 15–17.

6. Christopher M. Woodhouse, *The Struggle for Greece*, pp. 3–34, 76–77; Stefanos Sarafis, *Greek Resistance Army*, passim; D. M. Condit, *Case Study in Guerrilla War*, passim; Frank Smothers, et al., *Report on the Greeks*, pp. 19–20, 22–23; Henri Michel, *The Shadow War*, p. 214.

7. Christopher M. Woodhouse, *Apple of Discord*, pp. 146–47; L. S. Stavrianos, "The Greek National Liberation Front (EAM)," pp. 47–55; L. S. Stavrianos, *Greece*, pp. 64, 89; William H. McNeill, *The Greek Dilemma*, pp. 81–84.

8. Harold Macmillan, *The Blast of War*, p. 470; Office of Strategic Services, "The Greek Security Battalions" (May 18, 1944), R & A Report No. 2165, Box 2203, Foreign (Occupied) Areas Reports; OSS 65211 (March 12, 1944), OSS records; John Louis Hondros, "The German Occupation of Greece" (MS), pp. 110–12, 116–17.

9. Woodhouse, *Struggle for Greece*, pp. 29, 35, 44–45, 91–92, 103; Richard Clogg, "The Greek Government in Exile," p. 388; Floyd A. Spencer, *War and Postwar Greece*, p. 49; André Kédros, *La Résistance Grecque*, p. 173; Hondros, "The German Occupation of Greece" (MS), pp. 213–64; Extracts from War Diary, Army Group E, Doc. no. 65035/2, July 13, 26 and August 20, 1944, National Archives Publication T311, roll 180, frames 788 ff.

10. Reginald Leeper, *When Greek Meets Greek*, p. 29; Woodhouse, *Apple of Discord*, p. 52; Stavrianos, *Greece*, pp. 28–40.

11. Christopher M. Woodhouse, "Early British Contacts with the Greek Resistance"; Woodhouse, *Struggle for Greece*, pp. 25–26, 31–32, 42–43; E. C. W. Myers, *Greek Entanglement*, pp. 101–2, 108; Phyllis Auty and Richard Clogg, eds., *British Policy*, pp. 19, 117–18, 121–22, 134–37; Sarafis, *Greek Resistance Army*, pp. 62–63, 73.

12. Auty and Clogg, *British Policy*, pp. 275, 293; Sweet-Escott, *Greece*, p. 2.

13. Anthony Eden to Reginald Leeper, July 16, 1943, FO 371/37203, R6555, Foreign Office records (hereafter cited as FO records); Burton Berry to Secretary of State, July 14, 1943, 868.01/365, Department of State records (hereafter cited as SD records); Barker, *British Policy in South-East Europe*, pp. 152, 154–56; U.S. Department of State, *Foreign Relations of the United States, 1943* (hereafter cited as FR 1943), 4:131–32. In June, 1943, Churchill wrote peremptorily: "Why should his Kingship be called in question at this stage? He should go back as he left, as King and General." George II's unsavory connections with the dictatorship of the 1930s seem not to have overly bothered British officials, who retained considerable sympathy for Metaxas. Churchill's minute to Eden of June 15, 1943, FO 371/37203, R5552, FO records; Leeper, *When Greek Meets Greek*, pp. 10, 27–28.

14. Eden implies this in his published work, and his secret correspondence confirms it. Anthony Eden, *The Reckoning*, pp. 533–34; Eden's draft minute to Churchill of May 9, 1944, FO 371/43636, R7380, FO records.

15. Auty and Clogg, *British Policy*, pp. 12, 137; Woodhouse, *Apple of Discord*, pp. 73–74.

16. Myers, *Greek Entanglement*, p. 109; Woodhouse, *Struggle for Greece*, pp. 53–56; Auty and Clogg, *British Policy*, pp. 139–43, 147–66; Barker, *British Policy in South-East Europe*, pp. 164–66. On September 3, 1943, Churchill sent a telegram to George II, reading: "We are all looking forward to Your return to Greece at the Head of Your Army and remaining there until the will of the Greek people is expressed under conditions of tranquillity." Paul Alling to Wallace Murray and Adolf A. Berle, October 18, 1943, 868.01/402, SD records.

17. Winston Churchill, *Closing the Ring*, p. 538. Churchill noted that "this was the first suggestion that we might be forced to intervene in Greek internal affairs at the moment of liberation." *Ibid.*

18. *Ibid.*; C. J. C. Molony et al., *The Mediterranean and Middle East*, 5:570; Eden, *The Reckoning*, pp. 486–87. Noting the collapse of British plans for "eliminating the present E.A.M.-E.L.A.S. leaders," one Foreign Office official concluded glumly that "we now have to work for a united front." Britain was "compelled to support and collaborate with revolutionary elements such as Tito and the Communist leaders of E.A.M. because they alone are capable of keeping the Balkan pot boiling to the discomfiture

of the Germans." Orme Sargent to Reginald Leeper, January 6, 1944, FO 371/3210, R13883, FO records.

19. Churchill, *Closing the Ring*, pp. 539–44, 550; Stephen G. Xydis, *Greece and the Great Powers*, pp. 33–34; McNeill, *The Greek Dilemma*, p. 108; L. S. Stavrianos, "The Mutiny in the Greek Armed Forces"; Woodhouse, *Struggle for Greece*, pp. 78–80; *FR 1944*, 5:96–98. Apparently embarrassed by the mutinies, EAM condemned them as "mad actions of irresponsible persons." *FR 1944*, 5:108–10.

20. For Papandreou's bitter hostility to EAM, see George A. Papandreou, *The Third War*, pp. 15–26; Sarafis, *Greek Resistance Army*, pp. 50–51; *FR 1944* 5:102–3, 122; Woodhouse, *Apple of Discord*, pp. 194–95.

21. Churchill to Eden, May 28, 1944, FO 371/43731, R8331, FO records. One week earlier, Churchill assured Eden that the troops and armored car regiments he was sending to Greece "are not going there to fight Germans but only to keep order." In a paper submitted to the War Cabinet on June 7, 1944, Eden argued that "as regards Greece, we should have to set about now building up a regime which after the war would definitely look to Great Britain for support against Russian influence." Churchill's minute to Eden of May 21, 1944, FO 371/43714, R8563, FO records; Eden, *The Reckoning*, p. 534.

22. Churchill's minute to Eden of May 4, 1944, FO 371/43636, R7380, FO records; Winston Churchill, *Triumph and Tragedy*, pp. 72–73.

23. Xydis, *Greece and the Great Powers*, pp. 43–44; Stephen G. Xydis, "The Secret Anglo-Soviet Agreement," pp. 253–60.

24. Diary entry of August 21, 1944 in Charles Moran, *Churchill from the Diary of Lord Moran*, p. 185. See also Barker, *British Policy in South-East Europe*, p. 125.

25. *FR 1945*, 5:505. See also Churchill, *Triumph and Tragedy*, pp. 208–9, 238; *FR 1944*, 3:1327.

26. Churchill, *Triumph and Tragedy*, pp. 227–28. Churchill's and Stalin's thinking are explored in Churchill, *Triumph and Tragedy*, pp. 231–32, 234; *FR 1944*, 4:1014; Albert Resis, "The Churchill-Stalin Secret 'Percentages' Agreement," pp. 368–87.

27. Woodhouse, *Struggle for Greece*, p. 45. See also: Vojtech Mastny, "Spheres of Influence and Soviet War Aims," pp. 91–92.

28. Minute by Denis Laskey of December 24, 1943, FO 371/37210, R13620, FO records; *FR 1944*, 5:84–86. Citing Soviet delay, Xydis reaches an opposite conclusion on Moscow's intentions. Xydis, "The Secret Anglo-Soviet Agreement," pp. 251-52.

29. U.S. Army Counter Intelligence Corps memo, March 17, 1944, "800 USAFIME Reports" folder, Box 2479, Athens post records.

30. *FR 1944*, 5:95, 99–101; Office of Strategic Services, "The Interests and Policies of the Major Allies in Greece" (June 2, 1944), R & A Report no. 2205, SD records.

31. Milovan Djilas, *Wartime*, p. 437; Stephen E. Palmer, Jr. and Robert R. King, *Yugoslav Communism*, p. 91; Michel, *The Shadow War*, p. 343; Vojtech Mastny, "Soviet War Aims at the Moscow and Teheran Conferences," pp. 485, 497.

32. Svetozar Vukmanovic-Tempo, *How and Why*, p. 86; Barker, *British Policy in South-East Europe*, pp. 188–92.

33. Paul Shoup, *Communism and the Yugoslav National Question*, pp. 84–86, 145–50; Palmer and King, *Yugoslav Communism*, pp. 117–18; Walter R. Roberts, *Tito, Mihailovic and the Allies*, p. 251; Barker, *British Policy in South-East Europe*, pp. 196–201; Kirk to Secretary of State, January 23, 1945, 868.00/1-2345, SD records; OSS XL53541 (March 1, 1945), OSS records. A somewhat different account, stressing Vukmanovic-Tempo's revolutionary zeal and the Central Committee's opposition to the "Balkan command," is offered in Djilas, *Wartime*, p. 350.

34. Sarafis, *Greek Resistance Army*, p. 223.

35. #32308 (July 28, 1944), Pericles Mission records; Harold Shantz to Secretary of State, July 28, 1944, 868.01/7-2844, SD records; Sterling Larrabee to Kollender, July 26, 1944 and Memorandum from Pericles, July 28, 1944, "800 G.S." folder, Box 2478, Athens post records; William J. Donovan to Roosevelt, July 27, 1944 and July 28, 1944, Box 168, PSF, Roosevelt papers.

36. Sarafis, *Greek Resistance Army*, p. 225; #32308 (August 20, 1944), Pericles Mission records; OSS L45704 (September 9, 1944), OSS records; Edgar O'Ballance, *The Greek Civil War*, p. 78; Vojtech Mastny, *Russia's Road to the Cold War*, p. 205.

37. #32308 (August 1, 1944), Pericles Mission records; Harold Shantz to Secretary of State, August 16, 1944, "800 G.S." folder, Box 2479, Athens post records; McNeill, *The Greek Dilemma*, p. 121; Hondros, "German Occupation of Greece" (MS), p. 321. Conversely, some non-Communists, like Sarafis, seemed quite willing to seize power. Spencer, *War and Postwar Greece*, pp. 73–74.

38. Xydis, *Greece and the Great Powers*, pp. 50–51. The Caserta agreement of September 26, 1944 is reprinted in Iatrides, *Revolt in Athens*, pp. 311–13.

39. Minute by Eden of September 20, 1944, FO 371/43693, R15286, FO records. Leeper reported that November: "There is no evidence of Soviet Mission seeking to play any political role. Colonel Woodhouse has seen a good deal of Colonel Popov and is continuing to do so in Athens. He likes him personally and assures me that Popov is grinding no political axe and is profoundly sceptical of anything that ELAS tells him. A junior member of the Russian Mission observed to a British officer in Macedonia in a confidential moment the other day, that although Russia had no interest in Greece, he was very much puzzled by one thing—why had the British put up with this rabble for so long?" Papandreou, "who would be the first to be suspicious of Soviet Russia if there were any grounds for it, has on

several occasions lately emphasized how disappointed the Communists are by the Soviet Government's lack of interest in them." Noting how "gratifying" it was that the Russian officers "take such a realistic view," one British official suggested "thanking the Soviet Government for their adherence to the understanding reached at Moscow that we should play the lead in Greece." Another observed: "I don't think we can accuse the Russians of not abiding by the bargain." Leeper to Foreign Office, November 21, 1944 and minutes by Denis Laskey of November 22, 1944 and by G. L. Clutton of November 23, 1944, FO 371/43772, R18966, FO records.

40. Woodhouse, *Struggle for Greece*, pp. 97–99, 101–2 and *Apple of Discord*, p. 211; Hondros, "The German Occupation of Greece" (MS) p. 322; Hugh Seton-Watson, *The East European Revolution*, p. 318; Sweet-Escott, *Greece*, p. 40.

41. Vukmanovic-Tempo, *How and Why*, pp. 41–42. American intelligence reported that EAM publications of this period had a "moderate" tone. Yugoslav militants, too, thought that "a social-democratic, agreement-monger line of approaching the solution of the question of power had won the day." OSS, "Political and Economic Outlook of the EAM on the Eve of the Greek Crisis" (January 5, 1945), R & A Report no. 2821, SD records; Vukmanovic-Tempo, *How and Why*, pp. 48–49.

42. *FR 1944*, 5:140.

43. Kirk to Secretary of State, October 5, 1944, "848 Greece" folder, Box 621, Caserta post records; Eden, *The Reckoning*, pp. 566, 569–70. Woodhouse maintains that three weeks after the Germans left Athens, "neither side had formed any aggressive intentions, but each suspected the other." Woodhouse, *Struggle for Greece*, p. 111.

44. Churchill, *Triumph and Tragedy*, pp. 286–87. See also Spencer, *War and Postwar Greece*, p. 72.

45. Churchill's minute to Eden of November 28, 1944, FO 371/43697, R19672, FO records; Barker, *British Policy in South-East Europe*, p. 169.

46. For very different appraisals of Roosevelt's sympathies, see Stavrianos, *Greece*, p. 184; Stephen Rousseas, *Death of a Democracy*, p. 77; Elliott Roosevelt, *As He Saw It*, pp. 222–23; OSS, "The Greek Political Crisis" (December 4, 1944), R & A Report no. 2752, SD records.

47. Berle to Roosevelt, March 12, 1943, "Roosevelt, F. D.—1943" folder, Box 67, Berle papers; Welles to Roosevelt, March 15, 1943 and Roosevelt, "Memorandum for the Under Secretary of State" (March 17, 1943), "OF 206 (1943)" folder, Box 206, OF file, Roosevelt papers.

48. E. Warner to Pierson Dixon, June 15, 1943, FO 371/37235, R5422, FO records.

49. *FR 1943*, 4:142–43.

50. *Ibid.*, pp. 147–48; U.S. Department of State, *Foreign Relations of the United States: The Conferences at Washington and Quebec*, pp. 932–34, 1044–47; Cordell Hull, *Memoirs*, 2:1240.

51. U.S. Department of State, *Foreign Relations of the United States:*

The Conferences at Cairo and Tehran, pp. 850–52; Woodhouse, *Struggle for Greece,* pp. 73–74; *FR 1943,* 4:158–60.

52. Henry Maitland Wilson, *Eight Years Overseas,* p. 187. On October 22, 1943, Roosevelt complained to Churchill: "In both Yugoslavia and Greece the guerrilla forces appear to be engaged largely in fighting each other." Francis Loewenheim, et al., eds., *Roosevelt and Churchill,* pp. 384–85.

53. MacVeagh diary, December 3, 1943; Roosevelt to MacVeagh, January 15, 1944, "MacVeagh (Greece)" folder, Box 54, PSF, Roosevelt papers.

54. MacVeagh diary, December 7 and 8, 1943 and March 15, 1944; Eden, *The Reckoning,* pp. 498–99; *FR 1943,* 4:157–58; MacVeagh to Roosevelt, December 13, 1943, "MacVeagh (Greece)" folder, Box 54, PSF, Roosevelt papers. George II later claimed, rather implausibly, that Roosevelt became so angry that he rose from his chair and walked a few steps. Cyrus L. Sulzberger, *A Long Row of Candles,* p. 335.

55. Woodhouse, *Struggle for Greece,* pp. 73–75; Roosevelt to MacVeagh, January 15, 1944, "MacVeagh (Greece)" folder, Box 54, PSF, Roosevelt papers.

56. *FR 1944,* 5:98–99; MacVeagh to Secretary of State, May 8, 1944, 868.01/538, SD records. The British Foreign Secretary wrote to the British ambassador in May 1944: "The President has told the Prime Minister that our policy towards Greece has his full support." Eden to Leeper, May 28, 1944, FO 371/43731, R8331, FO records.

57. *FR 1944,* 5:132–34; MacVeagh diary, August 24, 1944.

58. Murray to Secretary of State, June 3, 1942, 868.001G 291/102, SD records.

59. Murray and Foy Kohler, Memorandum of December 29, 1942, 868.01/333-1/4, SD records.

60. Kohler, Memorandum of January 15, 1943, 868.01/333-1/4, SD records.

61. *FR 1943,* 4:126–27. See also *ibid.,* pp. 133–34.

62. Berle, "Relations with the Greek Government in Exile and Possible Reoccupation of Greek Territory" (August 25, 1943), 868.01/379, SD records; Beatrice Bishop Berle and Travis B. Jacobs, eds., *Navigating the Rapids,* p. 445; *FR 1943,* 4:149. The British ambassador in Washington reported that "the people in the State Department, and particularly Mr. Berle, never hid from their American contacts . . . that they do not agree with our support of the King." Halifax to Foreign Office, September 9, 1944, FO 371/43692, R14265, FO records.

63. *FR 1943,* 4:141. For other signs of State Department disaffection from the Churchill-Roosevelt policy toward Greece, see *ibid.,* p. 150; Hull to Roosevelt, September 2, 1944, "Greece, 1943–45" folder, Box 54, PSF, Roosevelt papers; MacVeagh diary, July 13 and 14 and August 15, 1944.

64. John O. Iatrides, ed., *Ambassador MacVeagh Reports,* pp. vii, 3–9; MacVeagh diary, December 5, 1943; MacVeagh to Roosevelt, February 17,

1944, "MacVeagh (Greece)" folder, Box 54, PSF, Roosevelt papers. See also MacVeagh to Secretary of State, June 13, 1944, 868.01/596, SD records; MacVeagh diary, February 9, May 9, May 12, May 29 and June 28, 1944; MacVeagh, "Memorandum" (c. December 1943), "Greece, 1943–45" folder, Box 54, PSF, Roosevelt papers.

65. MacVeagh diary, April 3 and 29, 1944; MacVeagh to Roosevelt, May 15, 1944. "MacVeagh (Greece)" folder, Box 54, PSF, Roosevelt papers. See also MacVeagh diary, June 28, 1944; FR 1944, 5:95–96; MacVeagh to Roosevelt, October 15, 1944, "MacVeagh (Greece)" folder, Box 54, PSF, Roosevelt papers.

66. MacVeagh diary, September 9, 1944; MacVeagh, "Report on Greece and Yugoslavia" (August, 1944), "Naval Aide's File A-14" folder, Box 163, MR files, Roosevelt papers. It should be noted that MacVeagh generally distrusted the British and particularly his British counterpart, Reginald Leeper, whom MacVeagh considered suspiciously "Jewish." Leeper, MacVeagh wrote, "has some un-English qualities, like a love for bargaining and indirection, which make . . . me think he may very well have some Jewish blood." MacVeagh diary, October 24, 1944.

67. MacVeagh diary, December 18, 1943, August 3 and 31, 1944; F. Noel-Baker, "Memorandum" (August 11, 1944), FO 371/43734, R13834, FO records.

68. MacVeagh diary, November 5, 1944. Discussing the Balkans with C. L. Sulzberger, MacVeagh contended that "Germany may rise again . . . but it is more likely that the threat will come from Russia next time, and it is chiefly against such an eventuality that we must be alive today." MacVeagh diary, September 22, 1944. See also FR 1944, 5:85–86, 136–37; MacVeagh diary, September 9 and October 28, 1944.

69. Anthony Cave Brown, ed., The Secret War Report, pp. 256–58; James G. Kellis, "The Development of U.S. National Intelligence," pp. 91–92; OSS L46149 (September 13, 1944) and Moses Hadas and Jay S. Seeley to William L. Langer, June 15, 1944, OSS XL1000, OSS records; Moses Hadas to William Langer, September 7, 1944, Box 2, Records Relating to the Cairo Outpost, R & A Branch, OSS records; OSS, "The Interests and Policies of the Major Allies in Greece" (June 2, 1944), R & A Report No. 2205, SD records; R. Harris Smith, OSS, pp. 127–28.

70. George Vournas to James Barnes, October 19, 1943, "Greece" folder, Box 156, Hopkins papers.

71. "Periodical Intelligence Summary No. 28 Up to 16th August 1944," FO 371/43691, R13725, FO records. See also Colin Gubbins, "SOE/OSS Relations" (November 25, 1943), WO 201 1598, War Office records.

72. Donovan, "Memorandum for the Secretary of State" (July 17, 1944), 868.01/7-1744, SD records. See also Donovan, "Memorandum for the President" (July 18, 1944), "OSS Reports, July 1944" folder, Box 168, PSF, Roosevelt papers; D. Talbot Rice to A. R. Dew, July 22, 1944, FO 371/43714, R11658, FO records.

73. Leeper to Foreign Office, September 3, 1944, FO 371/43691, R13843 and J. M. Martin To P. J. Dixon, September 26, 1944, FO 371/43692, R14265, FO records.

74. George C. Vournas to author, February 17, 1978; Jay S. Seeley to author, March 2, 1978; L. S. Stavrianos to author, February 24, 1978; Brown, *The Secret War Report*, pp. 260–61; Smith, OSS, p. 350. Among the favorable assessments of EAM, see, for example, OSS L43800 (August 15, 1944), OSS L46149 (September 13, 1944), and OSS L50938 (December 23, 1944), OSS records.

75. OSS, "Communist-Led Organizations Within the Free Greek Forces" (August 6, 1943), R & A Report no. 1062, SD records. Among the unfavorable assessments of EAM, see, for example, OSS, "Resistance in Greece and Its Relation to Allied Policy" (January 25, 1944), R & A Report no. 1741, SD records; OSS L40837 (July 14, 1944) and OSS 109050 (December 19, 1944), OSS records; Charles Edson to Robert Wolff, December 11, 1943, Box 2, Records Relating to the Cairo Outpost, 1944–47, R & A Branch, OSS records.

76. Donovan to Roosevelt, October 25, 1943, Box 167, PSF, Roosevelt papers. Other indications that the OSS leadership viewed the Greek left with apprehension can be found in MacVeagh diary, January 19 and September 11, 1944; Jay S. Seeley to author, March 2, 1978; Brown, *The Secret War Report*, pp. 260–61.

77. Carl Devoe, "Report on Pericles Mission" (August 25, 1944), #32308, Pericles Mission records.

78. Halifax to Foreign Office, September 9, 1944, FO 371/43692, R14265, FO records.

79. *FR 1944*, 5:112–15, 117–18; Hull, *Memoirs*, 2:1451–52. Actually, after Hull's initial rejection, Churchill wrote directly to Roosevelt, but the latter channeled the message back to the State Department for a reply which, predictably, was negative. With his second message to Roosevelt, on June 11, Churchill managed to bypass the State Department. Hull, *Memoirs* 2:1453–54.

80. *FR 1944*, 5:118–19; Hull, *Memoirs*, 2:1454–56; Edward R. Stettinius Jr., *Roosevelt and the Russians*, pp. 11–13. When MacVeagh complained about the arrangement to Hull the following month, the Secretary of State replied: "That wasn't our fault, it came from across the street." MacVeagh diary, July 11, 1944.

81. Sulzberger, *A Long Row of Candles*, p. 241; Eden, *The Reckoning*, p. 533; MacVeagh diary, June 24, 26, and 27, 1944; A. R. Dew's minute of June 26, 1944, FO 371/43768, R10012, FO records.

82. USSR, Ministry of Foreign Affairs, *Correspondence During the Great Patriotic War*, 1:235–36, 238; Churchill, *Triumph and Tragedy*, pp. 80–81; Orme Sargent's minute of July 6, 1944 and Eden's minute of July 7, 1944, FO 371/43636, R10483, FO records; *FR 1944*, 5:128–31. Churchill asked: "Does this mean that all we had settled with the Russians now goes down

through the pedantic interference of the United States?" Eden responded: "I fear that it is just what it does mean." Churchill's minute to Eden of July 10, 1944 and Eden's marginal comments of the same date, FO 371/ 43636, R10483, FO records.

83. Murray to Secretary of State, September 30, 1944, 868.01/9-2844, SD records. Averell Harriman reported to Roosevelt from Moscow that when the British ambassador mentioned the proposed British landings in Greece, "Stalin commented 'Good. It's high time.'" Harriman to Roosevelt, September 25, 1944, Box 11, MR files, Roosevelt papers.

84. At the insistence of the State Department's Charles Bohlen, Roosevelt's expression of hopes for the meeting's success was intercepted and a section was inserted demanding the presence of U.S. Ambassador Harriman. But Roosevelt later congratulated Stalin and Churchill on the meeting's successful outcome. Charles E. Bohlen, "Memorandum for the Hon. Harry L. Hopkins" (October 3, 1944) and Roosevelt to Harriman, October 4, 1944, "Book 9: Churchill in Moscow" folder, Box 335, Hopkins papers; Lynn Etheridge Davis, *The Cold War Begins*, p. 157; Robert Dallek, *Franklin D. Roosevelt and American Foreign Policy*, p. 479.

85. Herbert Feis, *Seen from E.A.*, pp. 95–101; Bernard Brodie, *Foreign Oil and American Security*, p. 3; "Petroleum—United States Foreign Policy" folder, Box 85, Hull papers. The argument of this section is developed at length in Thomas G. Paterson, *Soviet-American Confrontation*, ch. 9.

86. Herbert Feis, *Petroleum and American Foreign Policy*, pp. 14–15, 19, 36; Raymond F. Mikesell and Hollis B. Chenery, *Arabian Oil*, pp. 14–15; Feis, *Seen from E.A.*, pp. 93, 95–101.

87. Navy Department memorandum of March 13, 1944, Box 22, Forrestal papers; "Statements Made by Senator Truman (April, 1945)," Box 10, Rosenman papers.

88. Feis, *Seen from E.A.*, pp. 102–3; Herbert Feis, "Memorandum for the President" (June 14, 1943), Box 85, Hull papers.

89. Navy Department memorandum of March 13, 1944, Box 22, Forrestal papers; Feis, *Petroleum and American Foreign Policy*, p. 27; Howard M. Sachar, *Europe Leaves the Middle East*, pp. 394–95.

90. John A. Loftus, "Middle East Oil," pp. 22–23; George Lenczowski, *Oil and State in the Middle East*, pp. 15–17; Robert Engler, *The Politics of Oil*, p. 66.

91. Mikesell and Chenery, *Arabian Oil*, p. 53; FR 1945, 8:45. See also Phillip J. Baram, *The Department of State in the Middle East*, pp. 207–9.

92. Engler, *The Politics of Oil*, pp. 199, 249–50; Feis, *Seen from E.A.*, pp. 111–33; Benjamin Shwadran, *The Middle East, Oil, and the Great Powers*, pp. 310–15, 320–32; Gerald D. Nash, *United States Oil Policy*, pp. 172–75.

93. Engler, *The Politics of Oil*, p. 201; Nash, *United States Oil Policy*, p. 171.

94. "Middle East Oil" folder, Box 22, Forrestal papers; Xydis, *Greece and the Great Powers*, pp. 78–79.

95. *FR 1944*, 3:101–3. See also Feis, *Seen from E.A.*, pp. 104–6; Sachar, *Europe Leaves the Middle East*, p. 497.

96. Langer to Harry S. Aldrich, October 23, 1944, Box 1, Records Relating to the Cairo Outpost, R & A Branch, OSS records; Berle to Policy Committee, September 26, 1944, "State Department Policy Committee (Jan–Sept '44)" folder, Box 70, Berle papers. See also Alexander Kirk to Herbert Feis, December 4, 1952, Box 20, Feis papers.

97. Herbert Feis, "Order in Oil," p. 619. Feis noted that "our interest is in free and full development of, and access to, the oil and other resources of the Middle East." Feis, *Petroleum and American Foreign Policy*, p. iv.

98. *FR 1945*, 8:34–39, 51–54; Baram, *The Department of State in the Middle East*, pp. 106–15; Walter Laqueur, *The Struggle for the Middle East*, pp. 5–9.

99. Feis, *Seen from E.A.*, pp. 156–82; Mikesell and Chenery, *Arabian Oil*, pp. 95–97; Lenczowski, *Oil and State in the Middle East*, pp. 169–72; Nash, *United States Oil Policy*, pp. 176–78; Engler, *The Politics of Oil*, pp. 252–53.

100. Feis, *Seen from E.A.*, pp. 180–83; *FR 1945*, 8:54. See also Ickes to Truman, October 11, 1945, "OF 56 (1945–48)" folder, Box 270, Official File, Truman papers.

101. Bruce R. Kuniholm, *The Origins of the Cold War in the Near East*, pp. xv–xxi, 3–5, 73–129; MacVeagh diary, October 25 and November 10, 1944.

102. As an alternative, EAM proposed reconstituting the army, with numerical parity maintained between EAM and anti-EAM components. EAM's motives in the December confrontation have been seriously disputed, but the most painstaking, objective research thus far has concluded that the resistance organization was acting defensively. See, for example, Iatrides, *Revolt in Athens*, pp. 152–85; Woodhouse, *Struggle for Greece*, pp. 112–24. EAM documents, captured by the British, also lead to the conclusion that EAM leaders sincerely feared the establishment of a rightist dictatorship. See the documents enclosed in MacVeagh to Secretary of State, January 22, 1945, "800-Balkan Political Groups" folder, Box 2480, Athens post records.

103. In a bitter message to Papandreou of November 28, 1944, Churchill accused the Greek Prime Minister of "slipping more and more hopelessly into the grip of E.A.M." He added: "My agreement with Marshal Stalin has been faithfully maintained by the Soviets. I hope you will arouse yourself before we have to say goodbye and your country slithers into ruin." At Eden's suggestion, this message was not sent directly to Papandreou but was given to Leeper, to be used at his discretion. Apparently, it was used. On November 30, Leeper reported to Eden that, when the royalist army arrived in Athens, EAM "tried to demobilise" it. "Papandreou refused,

backed by General Scobie and me. They then tried infiltration. . . . Papandreou weakened. General Scobie and I, reinforced by telegrams from the Prime Minister and you, refused to permit this. Papandreou accepted our advice and stood firm." Churchill to Papandreou, November 28, 1944 and Eden to Churchill, November 28, 1944, FO 371/43697, R19672 and Leeper to Foreign Office, November 30, 1944, FO 371/43697, R19719, FO records.

104. Woodhouse, *Struggle for Greece*, pp. 126–28; *FR 1944*, 5:141–42, 144; Churchill to Leeper, December 5, 1944, FO 371/43736, R19933, FO records. For the most detailed account of the police attack upon the demonstration, see Lars Baerentzen, "The Demonstration in Syntagma Square."

105. Churchill, *Triumph and Tragedy*, pp. 288–91; Churchill to Scobie, December 5, 1944, FO 371/43736, R19933, FO records.

106. See, for example, Macmillan, *The Blast of War*, p. 504; Churchill, *Triumph and Tragedy*, p. 296; Churchill to Hopkins, December 10, 1944, "Book 10: Growing Crises in Greece" folder, Box 337, Hopkins papers.

107. Leeper, *When Greek Meets Greek*, pp. 112–13; Woodhouse, *Apple of Discord*, p. 218. See also Leeper to Foreign Office, December 5, 1944, FO 371/43772, R20054, FO records.

108. Macmillan, *The Blast of War*, p. 501; Robert E. Sherwood, *Roosevelt and Hopkins*, p. 838.

109. Sherwood, *Roosevelt and Hopkins*, pp. 838–39; Loewenheim et al., *Roosevelt and Churchill*, pp. 60–61; Eden to Halifax, December 6, 1944, FO 371/43697, R20178, FO records; Churchill to Hopkins, December 9, 1944, "Book 10: Growing Crises in Greece" folder, Box 337, Hopkins papers.

110. Kohler to MacVeagh, February 17, 1945, 868.00/2-1745, SD records. The U.S. ambassador in Great Britain reported: "Whether we wanted it so or not Stettinius's statement, which was directed at British action in Italy, was generally understood to include the Greek situation." Stettinius's personal "Record" of early December also indicates that the State Department was considerably less interested in the Greek crisis than in its Italian counterpart. John G. Winant to Hopkins, December 11, 1944, "Book 10: Growing Crises in Greece" folder, Box 337, Hopkins papers; U.S. Department of State, *Foreign Relations of the United States: The Conferences at Malta and Yalta*, pp. 429–43.

111. Sherwood, *Roosevelt and Hopkins*, pp. 837–38; Halifax to Foreign Office, December 7, 1944, FO 371/43697, R20239 and December 11, 1944, FO 371/38551, AN4618, FO records.

112. Stettinius to American embassy, London, December 6, 1944, "Warm Springs, Dec. 9–18, 1944" folder, Box 20, MR files, Roosevelt papers; Henry L. Stimson diary, December 19, 1944; Halifax to Foreign Office, December 7, 1944, FO 371/43697, R20239, FO records; Thomas M. Campbell and George C. Herring, eds., *The Diaries of Edward R. Stettinius, Jr.*, pp. 191–92, 231–32.

113. Kohler and Baxter, "Memorandum for the President" (December

6, 1944), 868.00/12-644, SD records; Leeper to Foreign Office, December 4, 1944, FO 371/43691, R20053 and December 13, 1944, FO 371/43698, R20778, FO records.

114. MacVeagh diary, December 4, 1944; *FR 1944*, 5:142–43, 158.

115. MacVeagh to Roosevelt, December 8, 1944 and Murray to Secretary of State, December 18, 1944, 868.00/12-1844, SD records. MacVeagh confided to his diary that "the winner of this battle royal here is likely to be . . . the small Communist Party, which has so well played its hand, and into whose hand the British have perfectly played." MacVeagh thought Communists had "precipitated the present crisis." A month later, MacVeagh told Roosevelt that the upheaval had been "fathered by international communism." MacVeagh diary, December 7, 1944; MacVeagh to Roosevelt, January 15, 1945, "MacVeagh (Greece)" folder, Box 54, PSF, Roosevelt papers.

116. James MacGregor Burns, *Roosevelt*, p. 538.

117. Macmillan, *The Blast of War*, p. 510; Woodhouse, *Struggle for Greece*, p. 128; Churchill, *Triumph and Tragedy*, p. 296; Joseph Davies, "Journal," December 6, 9, and 18, 1944, Box 15, Joseph Davies papers.

118. Cominch and CNO (Ernest King) to Com 8th Fleet, December 8 and 9, 1944, "Despatches of American LSTs" folder, Box 88, MR files, Roosevelt papers; Admiral Somerville to Chiefs of Staff, December 9, 1944, FO 371/43698, R20593, FO records; Foy Kohler, "Memorandum of Conversation" (December 9, 1944), 868.00/12-944, SD records; Sherwood, *Roosevelt and Hopkins*, pp. 840–42. For U.S. military fears that British troop withdrawals were weakening the Italian front, see McNarney to War Department, December 9, 1944, "Despatches of American LSTs" folder, Box 88, MR files, Roosevelt papers.

119. *FR 1944*, 5:150–51, 154–55; Churchill to Hopkins, December 16, 1944, "Book 10: Growing Crises in Greece" folder, Box 337, Hopkins papers; *Congressional Record*, 79th Cong., 1st sess., January 6, 1945, 91:69; Churchill, *Triumph and Tragedy*, p. 296; Dallek, *Franklin D. Roosevelt*, pp. 504–6.

120. Churchill, *Triumph and Tragedy*, pp. 293, 713; Macmillan, *The Blast of War*, p. 523; *FR 1945*, 5:505. British officials did not blame the Russians for the outbreak of fighting in December. See, for example, Leeper, *When Greek Meets Greek*, p. xvi; Woodhouse, *Apple of Discord*, pp. 113, 115; Macmillan, *The Blast of War*, p. 503.

121. Papandreou, *The Third War*, p. 38.

122. Kenneth Matthews, *Memories of a Mountain War*, p. 89; McNeill, Report of the Assistant Military Attaché (December 26, 1944), "121-MA Reports" folder, Box 2478, Athens post records; MacVeagh to Secretary of State, June 1, 1945, 868.00/6-145, SD records. See also McNeill, *The Greek Dilemma*, p. 121.

123. OSS L53539 (February 11, 1945) and OSS L53690 (February 15, 1945), OSS records; "A.I.S. Weekly Reports No. 18, 11–17 February, 1945," FO 371/48259, R4187, FO records.

124. U.S. Department of State, *Conferences at Malta and Yalta*, pp. 782, 849; Stettinius, *Roosevelt and the Russians*, p. 244.

125. Moran, *Churchill*, p. 250. See also Mastny, *Russia's Road to the Cold War*, p. 231.

126. MacVeagh to Secretary of State, February 27, 1945, "800-Communist Activity" folder, Box 2480, Athens post records.

127. MacVeagh to Secretary of State, January 23, 1945, 868.00/1-2345, SD records. See also Shoup, *Communism and the Yugoslav National Question*, p. 150.

128. Edward R. Stettinius, Jr., "Special Information for the President" (December 15, 1944), Box 95, Roosevelt papers; Kirk to Secretary of State, January 7, 1945, 868.00/1-745 and MacVeagh to Secretary of State, January 10, 1945, 868.00/1-1045, SD records; Xydis, *Greece and the Great Powers*, p. 64.

129. OSS L53539 (February 11, 1945), OSS 119589 (March 6, 1945) and OSS L51964 (January 24, 1945), OSS records. Yugoslav hostility to British intervention, as well as Tito's caution in the context of great power displeasure, is discussed in Djilas, *Wartime*, p. 426.

130. Kirk to Secretary of State, December 22, 1944, 868.00/12-2244, SD records.

131. Eden, *The Reckoning*, p. 577; Macmillan, *The Blast of War*, p. 506.

132. Churchill, *Triumph and Tragedy*, pp. 308–10; FR 1944, 5:156–60; Eden, *The Reckoning*, pp. 577–79; Macmillan, *The Blast of War*, p. 518.

133. See, for example: FR 1944, 5:148–49, 156–58; Leeper to Foreign Office, December 13, 1944, FO 371/43698, R20779, FO records.

134. Churchill, *Triumph and Tragedy*, pp. 311, 313–14; Eden, *The Reckoning*, pp. 581–82. Having made this discovery, the British proceeded to blame others for their previous blindness. On January 11, 1945, Macmillan entered in his diary: "On thinking over events in Greece, I . . . feel that— in addition . . . to the Communist plotters . . . —the King of the Hellenes is the real villain of the piece. Far back at Cairo in the winter of 1943 he twisted and turned." As a result, the republican/monarchist split widened, and "the tragic side of this division is that it disunites the bourgeois parties instead of letting them come together in opposition to Marxism and revolution." Macmillan, *The Blast of War*, pp. 532–33.

135. FR 1944, 5:173–75, 177–78.

136. EAM did not turn in all its weapons. On the other hand, it surrendered considerably more arms than was stipulated at Varkiza and disbanded its military forces. Sarafis, *Greek Resistance Army*, p. 278; Woodhouse, *Struggle for Greece*, p. 104; McNeill, *The Greek Dilemma*, p. 163.

137. For a discussion of the Varkiza agreement and its text, see Iatrides, *Revolt in Athens*, pp. 247–51, 320–24.

138. Iatrides, *Revolt in Athens*, p. 250; Woodhouse, *The Struggle for Greece*, pp. 129–30, 133, 135.

139. Halifax to Foreign Office, April 24, 1945, FO 371/48411, R7396 and

Leeper to Foreign Office, April 17, 1945, FO 371/48266, R6914, FO records; Macmillan, *The Blast of War*, pp. 552-53.

140. Leeper to Orme Sargent, April 1, 1945 and minute by Denis Laskey of April 17, 1945, FO 371/48266, R6868, FO records.

141. *FR 1945*, 8:203-8; Minutes by W. G. Hayter and Eden of March 22, 1945, FO 371/48264, R6104, Alexander Cadogan's minute to Churchill of April 14, 1945, and Churchill's to Cadogan of April 15, 1945, FO 371/48266, R6957, Macmillan to Eden, April 18, 1945, FO 371/48266, R6972, FO records; MacVeagh diary, April 23, 1945.

142. MacVeagh to Secretary of State, August 2, 1945, 868.00/8-245, SD records. Two days later, MacVeagh reiterated: "Chief local significance British elections danger Labor government accept EAM . . . 'democratic' pretensions face value." MacVeagh to Secretary of State, August 4, 1945, 868.00/8-445, SD records.

143. Harold Caccia to Bevin, August 9, 1945, FO 371/48276, R13415, FO records.

144. Eugene J. Meehan, *The British Left Wing*, pp. 68-69; Sachar, *Europe Leaves the Middle East*, pp. 407-8; Bevin, "Greece" (May, 1946), FO 371/58694, R8301, FO records. See also Xydis, *Greece and the Great Powers*, p. 126; Clement Attlee, *Twilight of Empire*, pp. 175-76.

145. *FR 1945*, 8:135, 162-63; Attlee to Regent of Greece, August 1, 1945, FO 371/48276, R13007, FO records.

146. *FR 1945*, 8:122; Woodhouse, *Apple of Discord*, pp. 256-57; McNeill, *The Greek Dilemma*, pp. 163-68. For additional material on what Sweet-Escott called "something of a white terror," see Sweet-Escott, *Greece*, pp. 43-44; Woodhouse, *Apple of Discord*, pp. 96-97, 228-29; *FR 1945*, 8:114, 116-18; MacVeagh to Secretary of State, March 16, 1945, 868.00/3-1645, April 20, 1945, 868.00/4-2045, May 22, 1945, 868.00/5-2245, and June 27, 1945, 868.00/6-2745, SD records; Geoffrey Chandler, *The Divided Land*, pp. 83-84, 98; Woodhouse, *Struggle for Greece*, pp. 145, 147; George D. Kousoulas, *Revolution and Defeat*, pp. 225-26; Rousseas, *Death of a Democracy*, pp. 73-74; OSS L55752 (April 19, 1945), OSS records. Even before the outbreak of fighting in December, Greece's prewar fascist leadership was conspiring to regroup behind British power. The British would help Greece "to create a 'right' political life with the King at the head," predicted Constantine Maniadakis, the former Minister of Public Security under Metaxas. Therefore, "we must all return as soon as possible and organise ourselves, because the future belongs to us." Maniadakis to Ambrose Ziffos, November 18, 1944, FO 371/48257, R3546, FO records. Maniadakis regained public office in the 1950s.

147. *FR 1945*, 8:116-18; National Liberation Front (EAM), *White Book*, pp. 121-34; Woodhouse, *Struggle for Greece*, pp. 140-41.

148. Charles F. Edson to MacVeagh, February 14, 1945, enclosure in MacVeagh to Secretary of State, February 15, 1945, 868.00/2-1545, SD records; McNeill, *The Greek Dilemma*, pp. 59-61; Woodhouse, *Struggle*

for Greece, pp. 13–14; Spencer, *War and Postwar Greece*, pp. 89–90; O'Ballance, *The Greek Civil War*, pp. 110, 114–15.

149. Woodhouse, *Struggle for Greece*, pp. 151–52; OSS XL15580 (July 25, 1945), OSS records; Evangelos Averoff-Tossizza, *By Fire and Axe*, p. 155; Jerome Sperling to MacVeagh, July 2, 1945, enclosure in MacVeagh to Secretary of State, July 6, 1945, 868.00/7-645, SD records. Zachariades told the press in June 1945: "The Communist Party of Greece never did stand for social revolution," but "has always striven, as it does today, to gain the support of the majority of the nation." Vukmanovic-Tempo observed disdainfully: "If this is not social-democratic reformism, we simply do not know what social-democratic reformism is." Vukmanovic-Tempo, *How and Why*, pp. 32–33.

150. Dominique Eudes, *The Kapetanios*, pp. 234–40; Kédros, *La Résistance Grecque*, p. 518; O'Ballance, *The Greek Civil War*, pp. 113, 115–16.

151. Milovan Djilas, *The New Class*, p. 197; Djilas, *Wartime*, p. 437; MacVeagh to Secretary of State, June 1, 1945, 868.00/6-145, SD records.

152. USSR, Ministry of Foreign Affairs, *Correspondence*, 1:331.

153. U.S. Department of State, *Foreign Relations of the United States: The Conference of Berlin*, 2:150–53, 525, 1592; James F. Byrnes, *Speaking Frankly*, p. 75. See also Mastny, *Russia's Road to the Cold War*, p. 301. Byrnes recalled: "Whenever the Soviets were faced with an issue that annoyed them or placed them on the defensive it was standard operating procedure for them to gather up a sheaf of British and American press reports from Greece and launch a counterattack." *Speaking Frankly*, pp. 73–74.

154. Xydis, *Greece and the Great Powers*, p. 95; Shoup, *Communism and the Yugoslav National Question*, pp. 150, 157.

155. *FR 1945*, 8:115–16.

156. U.S. Department of State, *The Conference of Berlin*, 1:671–72; MacVeagh to Secretary of State, August 1, 1945, "871 Confidential" folder, Box 2480, Athens post records.

157. MacVeagh to Secretary of State, July 25, 1945, "848-UNRRA" folder, Box 2480, Athens post records. On another occasion, he wrote: "How impossible these Greeks are, hypersensitive, ego-centric, and likeable, all in one, like children!" Although a bit sobered by the events of December 1944, MacVeagh still referred in his diplomatic dispatches to "the generally childlike and impressionable character of the Greeks." MacVeagh diary, May 4, 1944; MacVeagh to Secretary of State, December 28, 1944, 868.00/12-2844, SD records.

158. MacVeagh to Secretary of State, May 15, 1945, 868.00/5-1545 and March 16, 1945, 868.00/3-1645, SD records. For additional evidence of MacVeagh's tendency to blame the left for rightist terror, see: *FR 1945*, 8:116–18.

159. OSS 109078 (December 18, 1944), OSS records; MacVeagh to Secretary of State, July 28, 1946, 868.00/7-2846, SD records.

160. The strange kinship with the United States felt throughout the world by the wartime left is discussed in Franz Schurmann, *The Logic of World Power*, pp. 72–76. Its flimsy basis is noted in Michel, *The Shadow War*, pp. 56–59. For the naive faith of EAM adherents in America, see Constantine Poulos, "Rule Britannia," pp. 772–74; Smith, *OSS*, p. 128; Sarafis, *Greek Resistance Army*, pp. 113, 124–25; McNeill, *The Greek Dilemma*, pp. 142, 212.

2. THE GATHERING CRISIS

1. Loy W. Henderson, "Foreign Policies," p. 595. Henderson called the attention of the author to this speech and stressed its importance as an indication of the State Department's concern about Mideast oil. Personal interview with Loy Henderson, January 13, 1976, Washington, D.C.

2. Woodhouse, *Struggle for Greece*, pp. 163–65 and *Apple of Discord*, pp. 246–47; Heinz Richter, *Griechenland*, pp. 566–94; Chandler, *The Divided Land*, pp. 104–5, 108–9; Couloumbis et al., *Foreign Interference*, p. 114; Tsoucalas, *Greek Tragedy*, p. 94.

3. Stephen G. Xydis, "Greece and the Yalta Declaration," p. 12; *FR 1945*, 8:116–17, 257–58; David Balfour (Washington) to Foreign Office, August 1, 1945, FO 371/48276, R13041, FO records; Byrnes to American embassy (Athens), September 1, 1945, 868.00/8-2845, SD records.

4. Moses Hadas to William Langer, November 2, 1945, OSS XL2426, OSS records; L. S. Stavrianos, "Vacuum in Greece"; *FR 1945*, 8:178–79.

5. Chandler, *The Divided Land*, p. 124; Spencer, *War and Postwar Greece*, p. 91; McNeill, *The Greek Dilemma*, p. 185.

6. MacVeagh to Byrnes, December 23, 1945, 868.00/12-2345, and John L. McCrea to Chief, Foreign Activity Correlation, Liaison War and Navy, Department of State, December 28, 1945, 868.00/12-2345, SD records.

7. *FR 1945*, 8:286. A week later, MacVeagh warned that if the Sophoulis government fell, the State Department would "realize that under existing conditions in Britain, any succeeding Greek Govt. would almost certainly be still further Left." *Ibid.*, p. 297

8. Woodhouse, *Apple of Discord*, pp. 228–29; McNeill, *The Greek Dilemma*, pp. 187–88; Sweet-Escott, *Greece*, p. 50; Stavrianos, *Greece*, pp. 164–65, 174; Leeper to Bevin, February 11, 1946, FO 371/58674, R 2233, FO records; William H. McNeill, "The Stability of the Greek Government," enclosure in MacVeagh to Secretary of State, January 19, 1946, 868.00/1-1946, SD records.

9. Minute by W. S. Warner of February 23, 1946, FO 371/58676, R2713, FO records.

10. *FR 1944*, 5:145; MacVeagh to Secretary of State, December 27, 1944, "P" Project records; U.S. Department of State, *The Conference of Berlin*, 1:659, 663–64.

11. Foreign Office to British embassy (Washington), June 27, 1945, FO 371/48272, R10729, FO records; *FR 1945*, 8:126–31.

12. Minute by D. Howard of June 26, 1945, FO 371/48272, R10729, FO records; U.S. Department of State, *The Conference of Berlin*, 2:1043–44; *FR 1945*, 8:126, 156–57; John Campbell, "The Greek Civil War," p. 45.

13. Trefor E. Evans, ed., *The Killearn Diaries*, p. 340; Harold Caccia to Foreign Office, July 7, 1945, FO 371/48274, R11561, Minute by Churchill to Foreign Office, July 7, 1945, FO 371/48274, R11515, Foreign Office to British embassy (Athens), November 23, 1945, FO 371/48286, R19908 and Churchill to Bevin, November 27, 1945, FO 371/48287, R20548, FO records.

14. *FR 1945*, 8:150–51, 157; Halifax to Foreign Office, July 6, 1945, FO 371/48274, R11516 and Pierson Dixon to Orme Sargent, September 16, 1945, FO 371/48280, R16292, FO records.

15. *FR 1945*, 8:136–37; Bevin, "Draft Telegram to Prime Minister of South Africa" (September, 1945), FO 371/48280, R15919, FO records.

16. The story of the U.S. component of the observation group is told in Lawrence G. Byrnes, "History of the United States Section Military, Allied Mission to Observe the Greek Elections" (MS).

17. *FR 1945*, 8:170; MacVeagh to Secretary of State, October 6, 1945, 868.00/10-645, SD records; Sweet-Escott, *Greece*, p. 47.

18. Chandler, *The Divided Land*, p. 103.

19. MacVeagh to Secretary of State, January 17, 1946, 868.00/1-1746, SD records.

20. *FR 1945*, 8:185–91; Karl Rankin to Secretary of State, February 14, 1946, 868.00/2-1446, SD records.

21. Sophoulis' comments were transmitted in Constantine Rendis to Bevin, February 15, 1946, FO 371/58675, R2633, FO records. For additional efforts by Sophoulis government to secure postponement, see Rankin to Secretary of State, March 6, 1946, 868.00/3-646 and March 19, 1946, 868.00/3-1946, SD records; *FR 1945*, 8:191; *FR 1946*, 7:115–16.

22. Bevin to Leeper, February 8, 1946, FO 371/58673, R1905 and Leeper to Foreign Office, February 17, 1946, FO 371/58675, R2520, FO records. See also *FR 1946*, 7:117–18; Cabinet meeting of March 11, 1946, Cabinet records.

23. Stavrianos, *Greece*, pp. 166–67; Tsoucalas, *Greek Tragedy*, p. 96; Woodhouse, *Apple of Discord*, pp. 262-63; Leeper to Foreign Office, February 21, 1946, FO 371/58676, R2771, FO records; Averoff-Tossizza, *By Fire and Axe*, p. 164.

24. *FR 1946*, 7:119, "Digest of the Dinner on the Greek Elections in Honor of the Hon. James Grafton Rogers" (May 9, 1946), Records of Meetings, vol. 12, Council on Foreign Relations records.

25. Bevin hoped that U.S. support for the British position would "tilt the scale and once there was a break, the whole of the Opposition Front might cave in with the result that the Communists would be the only party who would in fact abstain." *FR 1946*, 7:124–25.

26. *Ibid.*, p. 126; Acheson to U.S. embassy, Athens and Rankin to Secretary of State, March 29, 1946, 868.00/3-2946, SD records. For earlier

evidence of U.S. pressure against postponement, see *FR 1945*, 8:192; *FR 1946*, 7:97, 117, 121–22.

27. Minute by W. G. Hayter of February 21, 1946, FO 371/58676, R3032, FO records; *FR 1946*, 7:119. For other evidence of British preference for a centrist victory, see Norton to Bevin, June 6, 1946, FO 371/58696, R9040, FO records.

28. Philip Jordan, "Greece in Purgatory," pp. 624–25; *New York Herald Tribune*, March 23, 1946. A U.S. intelligence agent reported that "it is very easy" to obtain fraudulent voting booklets. Indeed, "eight booklets are now in the files of our office in Athens." Local right-wing leaders "are able to procure as many duplicate and triplicate booklets as their trusted friends may require." OSS XL22822 (October 22, 1945), OSS records. See also MacVeagh to Secretary of State, October 2, 1945, 868.00/10-245, SD records.

29. Years later, Leeper maintained that "in 1946, 25 percent was generally considered by their opponents to be the voting strength of EAM." Yet, in February 1946, he was reporting to the Foreign Office: "The general calculation, with which I am told that EAM agree, is that under the proportional system the latter will secure 100 seats out of 300, that the Centre will lose heavily, and that the Right will emerge as the strongest party, but without an absolute majority." The U.S. chargé, Karl Rankin, was inclined to agree with rightist estimates that the left's voting strength was about 33 percent. He predicted (incorrectly) that EAM would "not reject the opportunity" of electing "a sizable and 'troublesome' delegation" to the Greek legislature. Leeper, *When Greek Meets Greek*, p. xxi; Leeper to Foreign Office, February 19, 1946, FO 371/58675, R2628, FO records; Rankin to Secretary of State, February 14, 1946, 868.00/2-1446, SD records.

30. Woodhouse, *Struggle for Greece*, pp. 169–72; Xydis, *Greece and the Great Powers*, pp. 181–82; Lincoln Bloomfield and Amelia Leiss, *Controlling Small Wars*, p. 158; Kousoulas, *Revolution and Defeat*, pp. 233–34.

31. The Allied mission claimed that abstentions constituted only 40 percent of the electorate, for "the total registration figures are . . . inaccurate and misleading." If so, this undermines the contention of the left and other observers that most Greeks eligible to vote did not do so, but supports its argument that the election registers were inaccurate. The mission also alleged that only 9.3 percent of the electorate abstained for political reasons. (This allegation apparently reflected the mission's rather naive assumption that, after a decade of tyranny and violence, people threatened by rightist terror were willing to broach their leftist motives to strangers.) Most other British and American observers thought the figure of 9.3 percent much too small. The new British ambassador, Sir Clifford Norton, put leftist abstention at 30 percent. Indeed, even the Allied mission, somewhat inconsistently, claimed that had there not been a boycott, the left could have elected 20 to 25 percent of the legislature and "might have prevented" the right from obtaining an absolute majority. Consequently, it is difficult to un-

derstand how the mission could have termed the results—an overwhelmingly right-wing Chamber of Deputies—"a true and valid verdict of the Greek people." It is considerably easier to understand why the State Department welcomed the mission's report. U.S. Department of State, *Report of the Allied Mission to Observe the Greek Elections*, passim; "Statement of the Allied Mission for Observing the Greek Elections"; Sweet-Escott, *Greece*, p. 52; Chandler, *The Divided Land*, p. 133; Norton to Foreign Office, April 6, 1946, FO 371/58684, R5434, FO records; *FR 1946*, 7:135; McNeill, *The Greek Dilemma*, p. 194.

32. T.H.K. to W. Witman, July 9, 1946, "850.3 Capital" folder, Box 2482, Athens post records. The author of this memo, Thomas Karamessines, was a U.S. intelligence agent who became the top CIA operative in Greece and, eventually, the director of the CIA's covert operations bureau.

33. Seton-Watson, *The East European Revolution*, pp. 324–25; Sweet-Escott, *Greece*, pp. 53–54; *FR 1946*, 7:159–60, 186, 261–62; Chandler, *The Divided Land*, pp. 154–57; Sarafis, *Greek Resistance Army*, pp. xvi–xvii; O'Ballance, *The Greek Civil War*, pp. 118–19; *New York Herald Tribune*, September 17, 1946; Richter, *Griechenland*, p. 588.

34. *Report of the British Parliamentary Delegation*, pp. 4–5. The British mission added: "Although it is unlawful to bear arms this law is only enforced against members of the Left." *Ibid.*

35. MacVeagh to Secretary of State, July 28, 1946, 868.00/7-2846 and August 10, 1946, 868.00/8-1046, SD records; *FR 1946*, 7:187. In the northern Peloponnesus, MacVeagh reported, "leading Leftists have fled from [their] homes and democratic activity on [the] part of both Liberals and Leftists is at a standstill since this produces instant threats of destruction . . . or death." MacVeagh to Secretary of State, August 28, 1946, 868.00/8-2846, SD records.

36. MacVeagh to Secretary of State, October 9, 1946, "P" Project records; MacVeagh to Secretary of State, July 31, 1946, 868.00/7-3146, SD records. See also "Digest of the Dinner on the Greek Elections in Honor of the Hon. James Grafton Rogers" (May 9, 1946), Records of Meetings, vol. 12, Council on Foreign Relations records.

37. U.S. Department of State, *Greece: Policy and Information Statement* (July 15, 1946), p. 2, Byrnes papers; *FR 1946*, 7:137; Minute by Pierson Dixon of April 5, 1946, FO 371/58687, R6045, FO records.

38. *FR 1946*, 7:148–49; Paraphrase of telegram from the United Kingdom Delegation at Paris to the Foreign Office, April 26, 1946, 868.00/5-346, SD records; Cabinet meeting of May 20, 1946, Cabinet records.

39. "I have searched my conscience to see whether there is any alternative to the support of this Right Wing Government," Norton informed London that May. "I am convinced that there is not." In June, another Foreign Office official declared that "there is at present no reasonable or obvious possible alternative to a Populist Government." Furthermore, "the King himself, to judge by departmental reports, would be likely to exercise

a sensible and moderating influence on the Populist Party if he returned to Greece." The contempt felt by the Foreign Office for the Greek Left and Center—and for Greeks in general—is revealed in a dispatch from Norton that October: "Almost all Greeks are extremists by nature, and this failing . . . is clearly ineradicable. Moreover, the 'harmless non-Communist Left,' which itself suffers from the national failing, has provoked the rough and ready methods of the authorities by its manifest subservience to the KKE on almost every controversial issue of policy. (This applies also, in some measure, even to the so-called 'Centre,' i.e. the Sophoulis Liberals)." He concluded that Greece is "a country which is irremediably corrupt." Norton to C.F.A. Warner, May 13, 1946, FO 371/58694, R8479, Minute by W. G. Hayter of June 24, 1946, FO 371/58696, R9040 and Norton to Bevin, October 2, 1946, FO 371/58710, R14870, FO records. See also Foreign Office to British embassy (Washington), October 28, 1946, FO 371/58710, R14984 and Norton to Sargent, November 18, 1946 and Sargent to Norton, December 17, 1946, FO 371/58715, R17040, FO records.

40. Xydis, *Greece and the Great Powers*, pp. 212–13; U.S. Department of State, *The Conference of Berlin*, 1:652.

41. *FR 1946*, 7:131–32; MacVeagh to Loy Henderson, April 23, 1946, 711.68/4-2346, SD records.

42. United Kingdom Delegation to the Conference of Foreign Ministers at Paris to Foreign Office, April 27, 1946, FO 371/58687, R6382, FO records.

43. Norton to Bevin, May 19, 1946, FO 371/58692, R7716 and May 20, 1946, FO 371/58692, R7810, FO records. Sophoulis maintained that he had consented to early elections because of Bevin's promise to postpone a plebiscite until at least 1948. Spencer, *War and Postwar Greece*, p. 97.

44. *FR 1946*, 7:162; MacVeagh to Secretary of State, August 16, 1946, 869.00/8-1646, SD records. See also William Gwynn to Secretary of State, July 16, 1946, 868.00/7-1646 and MacVeagh to Secretary of State, August 19, 1946, 868.00/8-1946, SD records.

45. *FR 1946*, 7:204–7, 237.

46. William H. McNeill, "Incipient Split in the Greek Communist Party" (May 21, 1946), "820.02 (Confidential)" folder, Box 2482, Athens post records; Kousoulas, *Revolution and Defeat*, pp. 234–35.

47. Woodhouse, *Struggle for Greece*, pp. 142–43, 173–77; Kousoulas, *Revolution and Defeat*, p. 240; Eudes, *The Kapetanios*, pp. 250–69.

48. Woodhouse, *Struggle for Greece*, pp. 182–83; Tsoucalas, *Greek Tragedy*, pp. 102–4; Woodhouse, "The Revolution in Its Historical Context," pp. 8–9; Eudes, *The Kapetanios*, pp. 265–74; MacVeagh to Secretary of State, July 28, 1946, 868.00/7-2846, SD records. According to Vukmanovic-Tempo, the Yugoslav militant, the 1946–49 struggle "was organized by rank-and-file members and junior officers of the Greek Communist Party, against the wishes of the leadership." Recent scholarship has suggested that Zachariades sought a more aggressive course in the summer of 1946, but that his orders were sabotaged by less enthusiastic members of the central

committee. In 1964, a KKE leader claimed that, although the central committee had opted for armed struggle in February 1946, it did not begin to prepare for it until fifteen months later. "The policy of the Party leadership at this time," he maintained, "was clearly contradictory and vacillating." Vukmanovic-Tempo, *How and Why*, pp. 48, 65; Ole L. Smith, "A Turning Point in the Greek Civil War"; Zizis Zografos, "Some Lessons of the Civil War in Greece," pp. 45–46.

49. *FR 1946*, 7:233–34, 238–39; Xydis, *Greece and the Great Powers*, pp. 400–5; MacVeagh to Secretary of State, November 2, 1946, 868.00/11-246 and November 4, 1946, 868.00/11-446, SD records.

50. *FR 1946*, 7:271; *FR 1947*, 5:4–5, 9–11, 13.

51. *FR 1946*, 7:239; MacVeagh to Secretary of State, November 15, 1946, 868.00/11-1546 and December 11, 1946, 868.00/12-1146, SD records.

52. *FR 1947*, 5:10–11.

53. U.S. Department of State, *Greece: Policy and Information Statement* (July 15, 1946), p. 2, Byrnes papers; MacVeagh to Secretary of State, June 1, 1945, 868.00/6-145, SD records.

54. Xydis, *Greece and the Great Powers*, pp. 198, 272-73, 380-82; Inverchapel to Foreign Office, October 25, 1946, FO 371/58712, R15743, FO records.

55. *FR 1945*, 8:209.

56. George Woodbridge, *UNRRA*, 2:94–137, As late as the summer of 1946, UNRRA goods were being "hawked about the streets and sold in the shops," noted the British parliamentary delegation. "There seems to be a grave deficiency in the law in respect to these matters." *Report of the British Parliamentary Delegation*, p. 12.

57. Woodhouse, *Struggle for Greece*, p. 146; Unsigned to Secretary of State, September 3, 1945, 868.00/9-345 and MacVeagh to Secretary of State, September 4, 1945, 868.00/9-445, SD records.

58. *FR 1945*, 8:246–49.

59. *Ibid.*, p. 215.

60. *Ibid.*, pp. 235, 252–53. See also Xydis, *Greece and the Great Powers*, p. 146.

61. *FR 1945*, 8:210, 268–69, 284–88; MacVeagh to Secretary of State, January 11, 1946, 868.51/1-1146, SD records.

62. MacVeagh to Secretary of State, October 26, 1945, 868.51/10-2645, SD records. See also *FR 1945*, 8:223.

63. *FR 1945*, 8:263–65. The War Department also rejected any U.S. military obligation in Greece, and argued that the Greek problem was more "internal than external." Robert P. Patterson to Secretary of State, November 10, 1945, 868.00/11-1045, SD records.

64. *FR 1945*, 8:267, 272; Halifax to Foreign Office, December 22, 1945, FO 371/48289, R21406, FO records.

65. *FR 1945*, 8:290–92, 299; Michael Wright to Douglas Howard, December 27, 1945, FO 371/58719, R239, FO records.

66. William O. Baxter, "Greek Economic-Financial Situation: Chronology" (January 10, 1946), 868.51/1-1046, SD records.

67. MacVeagh to Secretary of State, December 14, 1945, 868.51/12-1445 and January 11, 1946, 868.51/1-1146, SD records; Leeper to Foreign Office, December 15, 1945, FO 371/48288, R20990, FO records; FR 1945, 8:298.

68. U.S. Department of State, "Memorandum of the Press and Radio News Conference, Friday, January 11, 1946," folder 556, Byrnes papers. See also "$25,000,000 Loan to Greek Government."

69. Byrnes to Herbert Lehman, March 22, 1946, Special File 110, Lehman papers; William H. McNeill, Greece: American Aid in Action, p. 24; FR 1946, 7:188–89. British observers had already reached this conclusion. Discussing Greek leaders, one British official wrote: "They are not now concerned to remedy the situation with as little delay as possible, but to let it deteriorate until, as they hope, we feel obliged to give them everything they care to ask for." Minute by M. S. Williams of January 7, 1946, FO 371/58719, R202, FO records. See also Report of the British Parliamentary Delegation, p. 14.

70. FR 1946, 7:165, 169–73.

71. Ibid., pp. 175, 177–78; Sulzberger, A Long Row of Candles, p. 316. Tsaldaris, recalled Acheson, "was a weak, pleasant, but silly man." At Paris, he "asked us for six billion in economic aid. Mr. Byrnes and I struggled without much success to focus his interest on more possible and essential achievements." Dean Acheson, Present at the Creation, p. 199.

72. Henry A. Wallace oral history interview, pp. 3913-14, 4816, 5071–72.

73. Cabinet Meeting of July 8, 1946, Cabinet records; Xydis, Greece and the Great Powers, pp. 242–43; FR 1946, 7:184.

74. FR 1946, 7:187–88, 190–91, 201; Acheson to American embassy (London), July 13, 1946, 868.51/7-1346, SD records; William H. Taylor and Edward H. Foley to John W. Snyder, August 7, 1946, "Greece—general, 1946–49" folder, Snyder papers. The State Department's Economic Division reported: "One of the chief reasons why Greece cannot use additional funds is that no attempt has been made to put its economy on a sound basis. Its fiscal system is chaotic; its main source of revenue is from the sale of UNRRA goods and excise taxes. The Greeks do not believe in income taxes, and believe taxation to be inflationary. They have made no attempt at putting into effect controls which are necessary to rehabilitate their economy. . . . Gold is sold on the open market. The Government permits the earnings of shippers to be kept in banks outside of Greece. The Greek economy could not absorb the [proposed] $175 million if it were given to them." F. Lincoln and P. B. Nortman to Norman Ness and Sumner, August 20, 1946, 868.51/8-2046, SD records.

75. FR 1946, 7:232.

76. Ibid., pp. 223–24.

77. "Note of Interview between Mr. A. V. Alexander and Mr. Byrnes on Tuesday, October 15th, 1946" and Foreign Office to British embassy (Washington), October 24, 1946, FO 371/58658, R15570, FO records.

78. *Ibid.*; Havlik to Ness, McGuire, and Lincoln, August 21, 1946, 868.51/ 8-2146, SD records; Joseph Marion Jones, *The Fifteen Weeks*, pp. 75–76.

79. Byrnes to Clayton, October 1, 1946, enclosure in Clayton to Acheson, October 8, 1946, 868.00/10-846, SD records; Inverchapel to Foreign Office, October 31, 1946, FO 371/58658, R15942, FO records.

80. G.A.L. to Lauris Norstad, October 25, 1946, P & O 092 TS, Case 84, Plans and Operations Division, Army General Staff records; MacVeagh to Henderson, October 19, 1946, 868.00/10-1946, SD records; *FR 1946*, 7:237.

81. *FR 1946*, 7:240–41.

82. U.S. Department of State, *Greece: Policy and Information Statement* (July 15, 1946), pp. 10–11, 14, Byrnes papers.

83. *FR 1946*, 7:226–27; Lincoln to Colonel Bonesteel, December 6, 1946, 868.00/12-646, SD records.

84. The following argument is developed at length in Paterson, *Soviet-American Confrontation*, ch. 9; Kuniholm, *Origins of the Cold War in the Near East*, passim.

85. *FR 1946*, 7:1–5, 8–9, 45–46.

86. Chester W. Nimitz to James Forrestal, July 23, 1946, "Russia" folder, Box 15, Clifford papers.

87. Lincoln to Bonesteel, December 6, 1946, 868.00/12–646, SD records.

88. Clark Clifford, "American Relations With the Soviet Union" (September 24, 1946), pp. 12, 63, "Foreign Relations—Russia 1946 Report" folder, Box 63, Elsey papers.

89. Jones, *The Fifteen Weeks*, p. 11; Robert P. Patterson to Truman, July 27, 1946, "Russia" folder, Box 15, Clifford papers.

90. For additional evidence on this point, see Jones, *The Fifteen Weeks*, pp. 46–85; Acheson, *Present at the Creation*, pp. 194–96; Chiefs of Staff Committee, "Assistance to Greece and Turkey" (October 27, 1946), FO 371/58658, R15933, FO records.

91. James F. Byrnes, *All In One Lifetime*, p. 351; Walter Millis, ed., *The Forrestal Diaries* p. 141; Attlee, *Twilight of Empire*, p. 163.

92. Arnold A. Rogow, *James Forrestal*, p. 179; Xydis, *Greece and the Great Powers*, pp. 180, 186–87.

93. Forrestal diaries, September 30, 1946.

94. *FR 1946*, 7:827–29; John L. Gaddis, *The United States and the Origins of the Cold War*, p. 336; Kuniholm, *Origins of the Cold War in the Near East*, pp. 359–61.

95. The quotations are from Forrestal's record of the meeting. Forrestal diaries, August 15, 1946; Jones, *The Fifteen Weeks*, p. 63; Harry S. Truman, *Years of Trial and Hope*, pp. 96–97.

96. Gaddis, *The United States and the Origins of the Cold War*, p. 336; *FR 1946*, 7:857–58; Stephen Xydis, "The Truman Doctrine in Perspective," p. 248.

97. Acheson made this remark to Truman, Bevin, and French Foreign Minister Robert Schuman in April 1949. *FR 1949*, 3:174–75.

98. *FR 1946*, 7:225; James McCormack, Jr., "U.S. Security Interests in Greece" (September 5, 1946), Box 89, State-War-Navy Coordinating Committee records (hereafter cited as SWNCC records).

99. *FR 1946*, 7:209–13; Forrestal diaries, September 25, 1946.

100. *FR 1946*, 7:235–36, 240–44, 255, 262–63; Minute by C.F.A. Warner of October 20, 1946, FO 371/58712, R15733, FO records.

101. Xydis, *Greece and the Great Powers*, p. 130. See also U.S. House of Representatives, Committee on International Relations, *Military Assistance Programs*, Part 2, p. 312; D. George Kousoulas, "The Truman Doctrine and the Stalin-Tito Rift," pp. 428–30.

102. Xydis, *Greece and the Great Powers*, pp. 163–66; Xydis, "The Secret Anglo-Soviet Agreement," pp. 270–71; Campbell, "The Greek Civil War," p. 45; Campbell and Herring, *The Diaries of Edward R. Stettinius, Jr.*, pp. 448–49; "Report From London to the Office of Public Affairs," pp. 233–34.

103. Clark Kerr to Foreign Office, January 23, 1946, FO 371/58735, R1118 and Roberts to Foreign Office, February 8, 1946, FO 371/58735, R2142, FO records. A British official contended: "One can only draw the conclusion that their visit was not a great success." A high-level KKE leader who did meet with top Soviet officials that January was told that the KKE should scuttle any plans for rebellion and should participate in electoral politics. Minute by A. D. Smyth of February 13, 1946, FO 371/58735, R2142, FO records; Kousoulas, "The Truman Doctrine and the Stalin-Tito Rift," p. 428.

104. Roger Allen to W. G. Hayter, July 30, 1946, FO 371/58735, R11493 and Foreign Office to British Embassy, Athens, September 8, 1946, FO 371/58735, R12752, FO records; Xydis, *Greece and the Great Powers*, p. 302; Woodhouse, *Struggle for Greece*, p. 192.

105. Woodhouse, *Struggle for Greece*, pp. 158–61, 181–82; Evangelos Kofos, *Nationalism and Communism in Macedonia*, pp. 152, 166–69; Seton-Watson, *The East European Revolution*, p. 325; Palmer and King, *Yugoslav Communism*, pp. 128–29; Campbell, "The Greek Civil War," pp. 41–42; Stavro Skendi, "Albania Within the Slav Orbit"; Shoup, *Communism and the Yugoslav National Question*, pp. 133–34, 157–58; *FR 1946*, 7:229.

106. For massive evidence on these points, see FO 371/48388, FO 371/48389, FO 371/48390, FO 371/58615, FO 371/58869, and FO 371/58870, FO records. See also John O. Iatrides, *Balkan Triangle*, pp. 56–57. "So far from representing Stalin's will," notes Louis Halle, this "represented the degree to which the area over which he could make his will effective was limited." Louis J. Halle, *The Cold War as History*, p. 86.

107. Stavrianos, *Greece*, pp. 7–8; Kédros, *La Résistance Grecque*, p. 520; Couloumbis et al., *Foreign Interference*, p. 116; O'Ballance, *The Greek Civil War*, p. 131; Marshall D. Shulman, *Stalin's Foreign Policy Reappraised*, pp. 72, 283. A leading scholarly authority on Tito's Yugoslavia has written: "On their own initiative the Yugoslavs had started to give considerable help to

the Greek communist rebels. This was an embarrassment to Stalin. . . .
True though it was, no one in the west would believe that Yugoslav support
for the Greek rebels was Tito's independent policy." Phyllis Auty, *Tito: A
Biography*, p. 251.

108. Vladimir Dedijer, *The Battle Stalin Lost*, pp. 269–70; Vukmanovic-
Tempo, *How and Why*, p. 3. These and similar claims by the Yugoslavs
were made, of course, after the Tito-Stalin split of 1948, and it is probable
that they were intended, at least partly, to win some degree of respect
within Communist parties outside the Soviet Union for Yugoslavia's Marxist integrity. The modest gains within these circles, however, could hardly
be expected to compensate for the losses they would incur within the ranks
of Western policymakers who, by this time, constituted Yugoslavia's major
foreign support. Therefore, it would be unwise to dismiss such statements
as sheer propaganda.

109. Milovan Djilas, *Conversations with Stalin*, pp. 131–32, 182–83. See
also Halle, *The Cold War as History*, pp. 85, 231; Roberts, *Tito, Mihailovic
and the Allies*, pp. 324–25; Iatrides, *Balkan Triangle*, pp. 42–44.

110. Woodhouse, *Struggle for Greece*, p. 191.

111. Xydis, *Greece and the Great Powers*, pp. 442–43; Byrnes, *Speaking
Frankly*, p. 303; *FR 1946*, 7:284–85.

112. Campbell, "The Greek Civil War," pp. 49–53; Djilas, *Conversations
with Stalin*, pp. 131–32; Xydis, *Greece and the Great Powers*, pp. 442–43;
Averoff–Tossizza, *By Fire and Axe*, p. 198. Acknowledging the "reversal
of Soviet policy in the Security Council," Xydis is hard put to account for
it but finally concludes that it represented a Russian attempt "to forestall
as much as possible" U.S. intervention in Greece. This is an imaginative
explanation, but ultimately tautological. Xydis, "The Truman Doctrine in
Perspective," pp. 250, 252 and "America, Britain, and the USSR in the
Greek Arena," pp. 594–95.

113. Mikesell and Chenery, *Arabian Oil*, pp. 27, 177, 182; Loftus, "Middle East Oil," p. 29.

114. Brodie, *Foreign Oil and American Security*, p. 20; Max W. Ball,
"Report on the Oil Situation" (February 15, 1948), "Of 56 (1945–48)" folder,
Box 270, Official File, Truman papers; Mikesell and Chenery, *Arabian Oil*,
p. 29; Engler, *The Politics of Oil*, p. 67.

115. Mikesell and Chenery, *Arabian Oil*, pp. 34, 180; Max W. Ball,
"Report on the Oil Situation" (February 15, 1948), "OF 56 (1945–48)" folder,
Box 270, Official File, Truman papers; Peter R. Odell, *Oil and World Power*,
p. 33.

116. Loftus, "Middle East Oil," p. 28; Sachar, *Europe Leaves the Middle
East*, p. 395.

117. Isaiah Frank, "Private U.S. Foreign Investment in Materials" (August 2, 1951), "Chronological" folder, President's Materials Policy Commission records; "Statement by Eugene Holman, President, Standard Oil
Company (N.J.) Before the House Interstate and Foreign Commerce Com-

mittee" (July 9, 1947), "OF 56 (1945–48)" folder, Box 270, Official File, Truman papers; Mikesell and Chenery, *Arabian Oil*, p. 70.

118. *FR 1945*, 8:57–59.

119. *Ibid.*, pp. 61–63; Loftus, "Middle East Oil," pp. 17, 20–21; Engler, *The Politics of Oil*, pp. 72–73; *FR 1946*, 7:29–30, 41–43, 48–49; Lenczowski, *Oil and State*, pp. 154–59.

120. Loftus, "Middle East Oil," p. 21; *FR 1947*, 5:630.

121. *FR 1946*, 7:26, 32–34, 39. See also *FR 1947*, 5:657–59.

122. Woodhouse, *Apple of Discord*, p. 275; *FR 1947*, 5:629–31, 634–35; Loftus, "Middle East Oil," p. 22; Lenczowski, *Oil and State*, pp. 18–19; Mikesell and Chenery, *Arabian Oil*, p. 43.

123. "Oil in Peace and War, Opening Statement by Ralph K. Davies, Deputy Petroleum Administrator for War, Before the U.S. Senate Special Committee to Investigate Petroleum Resources" (November 28, 1945), Box 9, Ralph K. Davies papers. See also the other statements by Davies in this file.

124. See, for example, Wilcox to Clayton, January 29, 1946, "Petroleum" folder, Box 5, Clayton-Thorp office files; Forrestal diaries, August 13, 1946; *FR 1946*, 7:4; "The Foreign Economic Policy of the United States: Address by William L. Clayton" (November 13, 1946), Box 42, Clayton papers (Truman).

125. Henderson, "Foreign Policies," p. 595.

126. Minutes of SWNCC subcommittee for the Middle East, September 7, 1945, Box 89, SWNCC records.

127. *FR 1946*, 7:28. See also *ibid.*, pp. 6–7.

128. Henderson, "Foreign Policies," p. 594; Joint Chiefs of Staff, "Memorandum for the President" (July 26, 1946), "Russia" folder, Box 15, Clifford papers; Clifford, *American Relations With the Soviet Union* (September 24, 1946), p. 63, "Foreign Relations—Russia 1946 Report" folder, Box 63, Elsey papers.

129. Murray to Secretary of State, March 11, 1946, "Foreign Relations—Russia 1946 Report" folder, Box 63, Elsey papers; Truman, *Years of Trial and Hope*, p. 95. See also Robert Patterson to Truman, July 27, 1946, "Russia" folder, Box 15, Clifford papers; George V. Allen, unpublished memoirs, p. 130, Box 1, Allen papers.

130. In retrospect, most scholars believe that the Kremlin did not accord the Middle East a prominent place in its political thinking until the mid-1950s. See, for example, Walter Z. Laqueur, *The Soviet Union and the Middle East*, pp. 136–39.

131. MacVeagh's views are indicated above. Henderson's long-time anti-Soviet attitude is outlined in K. Tolley, "Memorandum for Captain Smedberg" (February 26, 1946), Box 24, Forrestal papers; Daniel Yergin, *Shattered Peace*, pp. 26–27, 30–31, 38–39, 152, 180, 186. Acheson's development as a Cold Warrior is described in: Lloyd C. Gardner, *Architects of Illusion*, pp. 202–17; David McLellan, *Dean Acheson*, p. 115.

132. See, for example, Roger Makins to Christopher Warner, November 19, 1946, FO 371/58658, R15942, FO records; Richard N. Gardner, *Sterling-Dollar Diplomacy*, pp. 299–300.

133. Acheson, *Present at the Creation*, p. 213; McLellan, *Dean Acheson*, pp. 96–97; Halle, *The Cold War as History*, pp. 115–16; Jones, *The Fifteen Weeks*, pp. 100–1, 105–7, 112–13.

134. See, for example, Forrestal diaries, January 21, 1947; Rogow, *James Forrestal*, p. 178; Jones, *The Fifteen Weeks*, pp. 118–19.

135. According to Xydis, who interviewed a member of the delegation, Constantine Caramanlis (currently President of Greece), Acheson "showed considerable understanding of the communist threat. He warned them, however, against taking a similar line when they conferred with . . . Henry Wallace." Xydis, "The Truman Doctrine in Perspective," p. 248.

136. Minutes of Cabinet Meeting of June 3, 1946, C.M. (46) 54 and Minutes of Cabinet Meeting of July 8, 1946, C.M. (46) 66, Cabinet records.

137. Hector McNeil to Orme Sargent, November 29, 1946, FO 371/58716, R17463 and Minute of December 2, 1946 by M. S. Williams, FO 371/58659, R17594, FO records.

138. C.O.S. (46) 277 (0), November 13, 1946, "Turkey and Greece—Anglo-American Assistance," FO 371/53658, R15933, McNeil to Bevin, December 4, 1946, FO 371/53659, R17594, Bevin to McNeil, December 5, 1946, and McNeil to Sargent, December 9, 1946, FO 371/58659, R17720, FO records.

139. Norton to Foreign Office, November 13, 1946 and Foreign Office to Athens, November 15, 1946, FO 371/58732, R16478, FO records; Xydis, *Greece and the Great Powers*, p. 463.

140. See, for example, M. S. Williams, "Draft Brief for Secretary of State" (December 19, 1946), FO 371/58659, R18501, FO records.

141. Ernest Bevin, "Policy Towards Greece and Turkey" (January 25, 1947), C.P. (47) 34, Cabinet records.

142. Minutes of Cabinet Meeting of January 30, 1947, C.M. (47) 14, Cabinet records.

143. Foreign Office to Athens, February 3, 1947, FO 371/67032, R1819, FO records. See also M. S. Williams, "Assistance for Greece" (February 5, 1947), FO 371/67032, R2439, FO records.

144. Dalton to Attlee, February 11, 1947, FO 371/67032, R2443 and Dalton to Bevin, February 13, 1947, FO 371/67032, R2440, FO records.

145. Minutes by M. S. Williams and C.F.A. Warner of February 14, 1947, FO 371/67032, R1900 and Bevin to Dalton, February 15, 1947, FO 371/67032, R2440, FO records.

146. Minute by Bevin of February 18, 1947, FO 371/67032, R2442, FO records. Dalton confirmed this interpretation of the meeting's outcome in his diary, although, rather ungenerously, he ascribed it to some last-minute confusion on the part of the Foreign Secretary. The Foreign Office, it

seems, had not only opposed sending Treasury's blunt aid cutoff message to Washington (through the British ambassador, Lord Inverchapel) but had fretted that relaying it to Athens (through Norton) would cause the Greek government to collapse. Thereafter, at the crucial meeting of February 18 between the Chancellor and the Foreign Secretary, Dalton said that "I wanted firm instructions sent both to Norton and Lord I., but I was quite prepared to do a deal." He was "willing that N. should be allowed to hold his hand, provided we sent Lord I. into action at Washington." According to Dalton, Bevin replied, "not perhaps quite realising what he was agreeing to, 'Well, that's quite fair.'" The result, Dalton recalled, was the dispatch of "a stiff Treasury draft" to Washington. Dalton diary, March 14, 1947.

147. Attlee, *Twilight of Empire*, p. 172. See also Hugh Dalton, *High Tide and After*, pp. 206–7; Dalton diary, March 14, 1947; Francis Williams, *Ernest Bevin*, pp. 263–64; Xydis, "The Truman Doctrine in Perspective," p. 257.

148. Norton to Foreign Office, November 13, 1946, FO 371/58732, R16478, FO records; *FR 1946*, 7:286–88; *FR 1947*, 5:2; "Memorandum of Conversation" (December 21, 1946), 868.51/12-2146, SD records; Xydis, *Greece and the Great Powers*, pp. 443–53.

149. Byrnes, *All In One Lifetime*, pp. 384–85; Inverchapel to Foreign Office, February 19, 1947, FO 371/67000, R2375, FO records; *FR 1946*, 7:278; Economic Mission to Greece, "Terms of Reference," Henderson to Acheson, November 12, 1946, and Rountree to Porter, January 10, 1947, "American Economic Mission to Greece—Correspondence and Memoranda (1946–47)" folder, Porter papers.

150. Byrnes, "Memorandum for the President" (December 20, 1946), 868.00/12-2046, SD records; *FR 1946*, 7:278–79, 282–83.

151. *FR 1947*, 5:16–17, 24, 26–28. See also *ibid.*, pp. 38–39; Truman, *Years of Trial and Hope*, p. 99; Porter diary, February 20, 1947, "Diary (February 1947)" folder, Porter papers.

152. *FR 1947*, 5:29–31; Acheson, *Present at the Creation*, p. 217; Jones, *The Fifteen Weeks*, p. 131.

153. Acheson, *Present at the Creation*, pp. 217–18; *FR 1947*, 5:32–35; Truman, *Years of Trial and Hope*, pp. 99–100; Jones, *The Fifteen Weeks*, p. 132.

154. *FR 1947*, 5:45, 50–51, 68; Forrestal diaries, February 24, 1947.

155. *FR 1947*, 5:44–45; Jones, *The Fifteen Weeks*, pp. 130, 133–34; Acheson, *Present at the Creation*, pp. 217–18; Henry S. Villard, *Affairs at State*, pp. 87–88. For additional indications of the crucial importance of Acheson and Henderson at this time, see George F. Kennan, *Memoirs*, pp. 313–14; "Interview with Norman Ness" (November 7, 1958), p. 6, "Marshall Plan Project" folder, Box 1, Garwood papers.

156. Acheson, *Present at the Creation*, pp. 218–19; Jones, *The Fifteen Weeks*, pp. 19, 38; *FR 1947*, 5:57; Acheson to Secretary of War, March 5, 1947, Box 1, Jones papers; McLellan, *Dean Acheson*, p. 115.

157. George Elsey Oral History interview, p. 354. On Truman's lack of hesitation, see also Truman, *Years of Trial and Hope*, pp. 100–1; Tom Connally, *My Name is Tom Connally*, p. 317.

158. Xydis, "The Truman Doctrine in Perspective," p. 253; Jones, *The Fifteen Weeks*, p. 160.

159. Apparently, Porter's cable was never sent. Porter to Truman, March 3, 1947, "American Economic Mission to Greece—Correspondence and Memoranda (1946–47)" folder, Porter papers; MacVeagh to Henderson, March 6, 1947, 868.00/3-647 and MacVeagh to Secretary of State, March 12, 1947, 868.50 PORTER/3-1247, SD records; Norton to Foreign Office, March 6, 1947, FO 371/67034, R3055, FO records. See also Porter to Acheson, April 22, 1947, 868.20/4-2247, SD records; Yergin, *Shattered Peace*, p. 288.

3. THE TRUMAN DOCTRINE

1. Jones to William Benton, February 26, 1947, Box 1, Jones papers.

2. Jones, "The Drafting of the President's Message of March 12, 1947," Box 1, Jones papers. See also *FR 1949*, 3:174; Truman, *Years of Trial and Hope*, p. 103; Truman to Edwin W. Pauley, April 3, 1947, PSF Subject File, Truman papers.

3. Surveying the public response to the September 1946 conflict between Truman and Wallace over foreign policy, a Gallup poll found that respondents supported Wallace's position by 78 percent to 16 percent. In subsequent months, anti-Soviet feeling assumed greater proportions. Nevertheless, according to a State Department study, in February 1947 more than 70 percent of the country opposed a "get tough with Russia" policy. Lawrence S. Wittner, *Cold War America*, p. 30; Alonzo L. Hamby, *Beyond the New Deal*, pp. 155, 175–77; Jones, *The Fifteen Weeks*, pp. 89–91; Herbert S. Parmet, *The Democrats*, p. 71; Yergin, *Shattered Peace*, p. 283.

4. William L. Clayton, "Memorandum" (March 5, 1947), "Confidential Marshall Plan Memos" folder, Box 42, Clayton papers (Truman); *FR 1947*, 5:47. See also Jones to Benton, February 26, 1947, Box 1, Jones papers.

5. Truman, *Years of Trial and Hope*, p. 103; *FR 1947*, 5:60–62; Arthur H. Vandenberg, Jr., *The Private Papers of Senator Vandenberg*, p. 338.

6. Acheson, *Present at the Creation*, p. 219; "JMJ notes on Acheson's presentation to Dep't working group, Feb. 28" and Jones, "The Drafting of the President's Message to Congress on the Greek Situation" (March 12, 1947), Box 1, Jones papers.

7. Jones, "The Drafting of the President's Message to Congress on the Greek Situation" (March 12, 1947), Box 1, Jones papers; Truman, *Years of Trial and Hope*, pp. 103–4. Although Truman claimed that "there was no voice of dissent," one participant recalled a less mellifluous reception. Connally, *My Name Is Tom Connally*, p. 318. See also Jones, *The Fifteen Weeks*, p. 142.

8. "JMJ notes on Acheson's presentation to Dep't working group, Feb.

28," Box 1, Jones papers; William D. Leahy diary, February 27, 1947, Leahy papers; Bert Cochran, *Harry Truman and the Crisis Presidency*, p. 187; Susan M. Hartmann, *Truman and the 80th Congress*, p. 57.

9. Acheson, *Present at the Creation*, pp. 221–22; Vandenberg to Bennett, March 5, 1947, Box 2, Vandenberg papers. See also Vandenberg to Richard W. Grace, March 7, 1947, Box 3, Vandenberg papers. Scholars of varying persuasions have suggested that the Truman administration was less phobic about the presumed threat of Communism than its rhetoric implied. Richard Freeland has contended that the administration merely used anti-Communism as the cover for an expansionist foreign policy. John Gaddis has maintained that the shift to global anti-Communism occurred only with the onset of the Korean War. Truman's Greek policy, Gaddis has argued, represented no more than an attempt to restore the European balance of power. See, for example, Richard M. Freeland, *The Truman Doctrine and the Origins of McCarthyism*, passim; John L. Gaddis, "Was the Truman Doctrine a Real Turning Point?" Both arguments have some merit, for it does appear that the administration used anti-Communism to sell its foreign policy and that the anti-Communism of government policymakers heightened in fervor in subsequent years. Nevertheless, by emphasizing these points, scholars neglect the significance of a crucial factor: the fear of Communist advances on a global basis.

10. "SWNCC Subcommittee on Foreign Policy Information Meeting, 2/28/47" and Jones, "The Drafting of the President's Message to Congress on the Greek Situation" (March 12, 1947), Box 1, Jones papers; Acheson, *Present at the Creation*, p. 220.

11. Forrestal diaries, March 3–5, 1947; Rogow, *James Forrestal*, pp. 335–36; *FR 1947*, 5:89–90.

12. See, for example, "SWNCC Subcommittee on Foreign Policy Information Meeting, 2/28/47," Box 1, Jones papers; Jones, *The Fifteen Weeks*, p. 130.

13. Although Xydis has claimed that Henderson and Economou-Gouras prepared the final draft, this appears to exaggerate the Greek role. According to Orme Sargent of the British Foreign Office, the Greek ambassador to Great Britain told him that Henderson "had dictated" the draft to Economou-Gouras. Joseph Jones recalled that "the message was drafted in the State Department and suggested to the Greek government." Acheson's memoirs deal rather delicately with the Greek aid request, but the meaning is unmistakable: "Greece was in the position of a semiconscious patient on the critical list where relatives and physicians had been discussing whether his life could be saved. The hour had come for the patient to be heard from. On March 3, with the support of kind friends and their guidance of a feeble hand, the Greek Government wrote asking for the help." Xydis, *Greece and the Great Powers*, pp. 478–79; Minute by Sargent of March 3, 1947, FO 371/67034, R2999, FO records; Jones, *The Fifteen Weeks*, p. 77; Acheson, *Present at the Creation*, p. 221.

14. *FR 1947*, 5:69–71, 87; Economou-Gouras to Marshall, March 3, 1947, 868.00/3-347, SD records; "Aid to Greece and Turkey," p. 827. Only later that year did some congressmen realize—and complain—that the Greek government's aid request was drafted by the Truman administration. By then, however, it was too late to do anything about it. George Bender to John Taber, September 2, 1947 and Taber to Bender, September 10, 1947, Box 42, Taber papers.

15. Acheson, *Present at the Creation*, pp. 220–21; *FR 1947*, 5:80.

16. Norton to Foreign Office, March 1, 1947, FO 371/67001, R2810 and Inverchapel to Foreign Office, March 6, 1947, FO 371/67034, R3038, FO records.

17. Truman, *Years of Trial and Hope*, pp. 104–5; *FR 1947*, 5:97–100; Leahy diary, March 7, 1947, Leahy papers; Forrestal diaries, March 7, 1947. For what may be the text of Forrestal's remarks, see: "Statement by James Forrestal" (February 27, 1947), Box 125, Forrestal papers.

18. *FR 1947*, 5:98, 116; Forrestal diaries, March 8, 1947; Truman, *Years of Trial and Hope*, p. 105; Mary Margaret Davies, "The Role of the American Trade Union Representatives in the Aid to Greece Program" (MS), pp. 175–77. For a further indication of the administration's efforts to cultivate business leaders, see "Digest of the Meeting of March 13, 1947," "British Foreign Policy," vol. 14, tab A, Records of Groups, Council on Foreign Relations records.

19. Forrestal, "Memorandum to Secretary Snyder re: Names of Publishers" (March 12, 1947) and Forrestal to Paul C. Smith, March 19, 1947, Box 91, Forrestal papers; "Excerpts from a telephone conversation between Forrestal and James Reston of the *New York Times*, 13 March 1947," Box 1, Jones papers.

20. *Public Papers of the Presidents: Harry S. Truman, 1947*, pp. 167–72. According to Acheson, both he and Clayton "spent considerable time" on this address. Gregory W. Sand, "Clifford and Truman" (MS), p. 197. For other indications that the administration was (in the words of Joseph Jones) "virtually obsessed" with easing world trade barriers, see "Address by the Hon. Willard L. Thorp, Asst. Sec. of State for Economic Affairs, before the American Institute of Mining and Metallurgical Engineers" (March 18, 1947) and "Address by the Hon. Willard L. Thorp, Asst. Sec. of State for Economic Affairs, before the Women's Action Committee" (March 27, 1947), Box 1, Jones papers; Jones, *The Fifteen Weeks*, pp. 91–99.

21. "Excerpts from telephone conversation between Forrestal and Paul Shields, 20 March 1947," Box 91, Forrestal papers. Forrestal was remarkably consistent in his concerns, and said much the same thing to non-businessmen. See, for example, "Minutes of Informal Press Interview Held by Secretary Forrestal, 28 February 1947," Box 8, Forrestal papers; Forrestal diaries, May 2, 1947.

22. "Extract from a Monthly Review for Period Ended 31st May [1947], Compiled by the South African Charge d'Affaires, Athens," FO 371/67042,

R8838, FO records. For the fear of Joseph Jones that, if Greece and other unstable areas collapsed, the United States could not "possibly avoid a depression far greater than that of 1929–32," see Jones to Benton, February 26, 1947, Box 1, Jones papers.

23. Jones, *The Fifteen Weeks*, p. 146; *FR 1947*, 5:121–22; "JMJ notes on Acheson's presentation to Dep't working group, Feb. 28," Box 1, Jones papers.

24. "SWNCC Subcommittee on Foreign Policy Information Meeting, 2/28/27," Box 1, Jones papers; Jones, *The Fifteen Weeks*, pp. 150–51.

25. Jones, *The Fifteen Weeks*, pp. 185–86; "SWNCC Subcommittee on Foreign Policy Information Meeting, 2/28/47," Box 1, Jones papers; Robert H. Ferrell, *George C. Marshall*, pp. 77–78.

26. *FR 1947*, 5:85; Halle, *The Cold War as History*, pp. 120–21. Actually, it was not until March 3 that the "democracy" approach was formally approved by SWNCC. Prior to that, Russell remained unsure of "how to couch the existing world conflict, i.e., whether as a conflict between U.S. and Russia, between free enterprise and socialism, between capitalism and communism, or however." *FR 1947*, 5:76–78, 123.

27. Jones, *The Fifteen Weeks*, p. 143; Truman, *Years of Trial and Hope*, p. 105; "JMJ notes on Acheson's presentation to Dep't working group, Feb. 28," and "The Drafting of the President's Message to Congress on the Greek Situation" (March 12, 1947), Box 1, Jones papers.

28. Jones, *The Fifteen Weeks*, pp. 156–57; "Draft of March 10, 1947," "Truman Doctrine Speech, 3/12/47" folder, Box 17, Elsey papers. Secretly, of course, American policymakers continued to talk in just these terms. At the SWNCC subcommittee meeting of February 28, 1947, General Arnold stated: "If Greece falls, Soviet pressure on Turkey will be irresistible. If Greece and Turkey should fall, the Eastern Mediterranean, with its oil supplies, would be untenable." "JMJ notes on Acheson's presentation to Dep't working group, Feb. 28," Box 1, Jones papers.

29. *FR 1947*, 5:66; Jones, *The Fifteen Weeks*, p. 110.

30. Charles E. Bohlen, *The Transformation of American Foreign Policy*, pp. 86–87 and *Witness to History*, p. 261. See also Elsey to Clifford, March 7, 1947, "Speech to Congress on Greece, 3/12/47" folder, Clifford papers; John M. Vorys to "Jim," March 29, 1947, Box 19, Vorys papers.

31. Jones, *The Fifteen Weeks*, pp. 155, 162, 176; Kennan, *Memoirs*, pp. 314–15, 319–22; Ferrell, *George C. Marshall*, p. 84; Acheson, *Present at the Creation*, p. 221. See also *FR 1947*, 3:229–30.

32. *Public Papers of the Presidents: Harry S. Truman*, 1947, pp. 176–79.

33. Truman, *Years of Trial and Hope*, p. 106; Ferrell, *George C. Marshall*, p. 83.

34. Jones, *The Fifteen Weeks*, pp. 174–75; Thomas G. Paterson, "The Dissent of Senator Claude Pepper," William C. Pratt, "Senator Glen H. Taylor: Questioning American Unilateralism," and Henry W. Berger, "Sen-

ator Robert A. Taft Dissents from Military Escalation," (in Paterson, ed., *Cold War Critics*), pp. 128–30, 148–51, 177–78; Claude Pepper to Harold Ickes, April 7, 1947, Box 58, Ickes papers. Another Senator wrote to Truman that his proposal for military aid made it "hard to avoid the conclusion that we would be taking the first step toward the beginning of World War III." Joseph C. O'Mahoney to Truman, March 10, 1947, "OF 386 (1947)" folder, Official File, Truman papers. For Pepper's general dismay at American foreign policy, see Pepper to Thomas G. Corcoran, October 4, 1946, Folder 627, Byrnes papers.

35. See, for example, Ferrell, *George C. Marshall*, p. 90; Byrnes, *Speaking Frankly*, pp. 299–300, 302; Forrestal diaries, April 4, 1947; Dulles to Paul Hutchinson, June 24, 1947 and Dulles to Arthur H. Vandenberg, July 21, 1947, Dulles papers.

36. See the reports for March 19 and 22, April 2 and 22, and May 8, 1947 entitled "Editorial Reaction to Current Issues," prepared by the Division of Press Intelligence, Office of Government Reports, PSF Subject File, Truman papers.

37. Barton J. Bernstein, "Walter Lippmann and the Early Cold War," pp. 39–40; Wittner, *Cold War America*, p. 34; *Washington Post*, March 18, 1947. For a devastating attack on the administration's policy in Greece by journalist Arthur Krock, see *New York Times*, April 1, 1947.

38. *Washington Post*, March 28, 1947; Elmo Roper, "Public Opinion Survey of Reactions to President Truman's Proposal Regarding Greece and Turkey" (n.d.) and Roper, "A Study of What People Say in Describing Their Reactions Toward the Truman Proposal for Aid to Greece and Turkey" (April 1947), Confidential File, Truman papers; "Evaluation of the Current Opinion Situation on Greek-Turkish Problem" (March 26, 1947), Box 380, Lot 54D202, Francis H. Russell files, SD records; Jones, *The Fifteen Weeks*, p. 179. For further evidence of considerable public resistance to U.S. intervention in Greece, see "Greek and Turkish Loan" folders, Boxes 177–78, Connally papers.

39. "The Shape of Things," *Nation* (March 15, 1947), 164:289; Freda Kirchwey, "Manifest Destiny, 1947." Even before the President's address, but after news of the British aid requests had reached the press, the *Nation* asked: "Has not the war and its aftermath proved, in Greece and elsewhere, that the old imperialist techniques are bankrupt?" "The Shape of Things," *Nation* (March 8, 1947), 164:261.

40. James G. Patton to Harry S. Truman, March 26, 1947, "Greece and Turkey (1947), OF 426" folder, Official File, Truman papers; U.S. Senate, Committee on Foreign Relations, *Assistance to Greece and Turkey: Hearings*, pp. 94–95; Mark Solomon, "Black Critics of Colonialism and the Cold War," pp. 219–20.

41. U.S. House of Representatives, Committee on Foreign Affairs, *Assistance to Greece and Turkey: Hearings*, p. 236. Cadbury's testimony re-

portedly "rocked" the House Foreign Affairs Committee. James Read to Clarence Pickett, April 3, 1947, Box 16, Friends Committee on National Legislation records.

42. Opposition to the Truman Doctrine by PCA and other liberal spokesmen is discussed in Hamby, *Beyond the New Deal*, pp. 176–78; Norman D. Markowitz, *The Rise and Fall of the People's Century*, p. 234; McGeorge Bundy, ed., *The Pattern of Responsibility*, p. 42.

43. Markowitz, *The Rise and Fall of the People's Century*, pp. 235–41; *New York Times*, April 1, 1947; Henry Wallace oral history interview, pp. 5071–72. For a hostile account of the Madison Square Garden rally, which drew upon Elliott Roosevelt and other New Deal symbols, see Chester Kerr to Wilson Wyatt and Leon Henderson, n.d., Acheson papers.

44. Senate Committee on Foreign Relations, *Assistance to Greece and Turkey*, pp. 134–41. LaGuardia contended that "there is a distinct governing class in Greece, and that governing class is not ready for democracy." *Ibid.*, p. 134.

45. Joseph P. Lash, *Eleanor: The Years Alone*, pp. 86–88; Eleanor Roosevelt to Truman, April 17, 1947, "Harry S. Truman, 1945–48" folder, Box 4560, Eleanor Roosevelt papers; Mary Welek Atwell, "Eleanor Roosevelt and the Cold War Consensus," pp. 103–6.

46. Gallman to Secretary of State, March 13, 1947, PSF Subject File, Truman papers; *New York Times*, April 12, 1947.

47. Meehan, *The British Left Wing*, p. 107; Harold J. Laski, "Britain Without Empire," p. 356.

48. See, for example, *New York Times*, March 13, 1947; Caffery to Secretary of State, March 13, 1947, Cabot to Secretary of State, March 14, 1947, Dunn to Secretary of State, March 16, 1947, and Berry to Secretary of State, March 19, 1947, PSF Subject File, Truman papers; William T. Stone, "Memorandum for Mr. Hickerson" (April 15, 1947), 768.00/4-1547, SD records.

49. Minute by D. J. McCarthy of April 15, 1947, FO 371/67040, R5536 and J. E. Coulson to G. A. Wallinger, August 6, 1947, FO 371/67072, R11108, FO records; Harrison to Secretary of State, March 14, 1947, PSF Subject File, Truman papers. Nearly two years later, the U.S. ambassador in Oslo was still complaining that Norwegians "do not seem to appreciate the basic issues involved" in the Greek conflict. Even the Norwegian Foreign Minister, who publicly praised U.S. policy, told him privately: "What a pity that we have to support such a government as exists in Greece." Acheson responded glumly that "misunderstanding of [the] Greek problem and US objectives in Greece exists also in Sweden and Denmark." Villard to Secretary of State, December 21, 1948 and Acheson to Villard, February 8, 1949, 868.00/12-2148, SD records.

50. MacVeagh to Secretary of State, March 5, 1947, 868.00/3-547 and March 17, 1947, 868.00/3-1747, SD records; Raymond Daniell, "Symptom and Tragedy of Our Time," p. 61; Rousseas, *Death of a Democracy*, pp.

80–81; MacVeagh to Secretary of State, March 13, 1947, PSF Subject File, Truman papers.

51. In fact, according to Porter, in late February 1947 an EAM representative met with him and "indicated that he would submit an economic program if we were interested." MacVeagh to Secretary of State, March 11, 1947, 868.00/3-1147, SD records; Porter diary, February 25, 1947, "Diary (February 1947)" folder, Porter papers.

52. Margaret Carlyle, ed., *Documents on International Affairs*, pp. 7–10; M. Peterson to Foreign Office, March 23, 1947, FO 371/67037, R4074, FO records; U.S. Senate, Committee on Foreign Relations, *Legislative Origins of the Truman Doctrine*, p. 98. One specialist on Soviet policy has noted: "The Truman Doctrine . . . did not unduly disturb the Kremlin. . . . It was not seen by the Kremlin as a threat. Stalin did not even mention the Doctrine in his chat with [Harold] Stassen." Adam Ulam, *Stalin*, p. 657. See also Jones, *The Fifteen Weeks*, p. 223; Alexander Kendrick, "Moscow Conference Report," p. 7.

53. *New York Times*, April 1, 1947.

54. House Committee on International Relations, *Military Assistance Programs*, pp. 309, 321–24, 336; Senate Committee on Foreign Relations, *Legislative Origins of the Truman Doctrine*, pp. 40, 57, 66, 84, 95, 131–32, 134.

55. Senate Committee on Foreign Relations, *Legislative Origins of the Truman Doctrine*, pp. 91–92, 98, 125.

56. Inverchapel to Foreign Office, April 12, 1947, FO 371/67040, R4989, FO records; *FR 1947*, 5:274–75.

57. Senate Committee on Foreign Relations, *Legislative Origins of the Truman Doctrine*, pp. 36–39, 41, 45, 47, 69; House Committee on International Relations, *Military Assistance Programs*, pp. 318, 320, 325, 341–42.

58. Senate Committee on Foreign Relations, *Legislative Origins of the Truman Doctrine*, pp. 42–43; Frederick J. Dobney, ed., *Selected Papers of Will Clayton*, pp. 190–91.

59. House Committee on International Relations, *Military Assistance Programs*, pp. 330, 349–50, 404–5; House Committee on Foreign Affairs, *Assistance to Greece and Turkey*, pp. 22–23, 108.

60. Senate Committee on Foreign Relations, *Legislative Origins of the Truman Doctrine*, pp. 17, 21, 94–95, 141–42, 186–90; House Committee on International Relations, *Military Assistance Programs*, pp. 336–37; *FR 1947*, 5:120.

61. Connally, *My Name Is Tom Connally*, p. 319; Hartmann, *Truman and the 80th Congress*, p. 63; Vandenberg, *Private Papers*, pp. 351–52; Press release of speech by Kenneth Wherry, Box 16, Wherry papers; William Langer to Vandenberg, March 21, 1947 and to T. E. Savageau, April 15, 1947, Box 178, Langer papers.

62. House Committee on International Relations, *Military Assistance Programs*, pp. 309, 436–38; Senate Committee on Foreign Relations, *Leg-

islative Origins of the Truman Doctrine, p. 67; Henry P. Fletcher to Robert A. Taft, March 9, 1947, Box 690, Taft papers; Francis Case, Reply to Telegram from the *Huron Daily Plainsman,* Drawer 34, Case papers (Dakota Wesleyan); Senate Committee on Foreign Relations, *Assistance to Greece and Turkey,* p. 7.

63. International Outlook," p. 109; House Committee on Foreign Affairs, *Assistance to Greece and Turkey,* pp. 14–16; Bevin (Moscow) to Attlee (Foreign Office), March 27, 1947, FO 371/67038, R4231, FO records; Senate Committee on Foreign Relations, *Legislative Origins of the Truman Doctrine,* p. 22. Even the President's adviser, Admiral William Leahy, failed to see a clear-cut distinction between the situations in China and Greece. Leahy diary, February 27, 1947, Leahy papers.

64. *FR 1947,* 3:229–30; Jones, *The Fifteen Weeks,* pp. 191–96.

65. Senate Committee on Foreign Relations, *Legislative Origins of the Truman Doctrine,* pp 101–2, 106, 111, 126, 129; *Congressional Record* (April 15, 1947), p. 3393.

66. House Committee on International Relations, *Military Assistance Programs,* p. 310; *Washington Post,* March 28, 1947. For difficulties on this score with influential figures, see, for example, Eleanor Roosevelt to Acheson, March 26, 1947, Box 3745, Eleanor Roosevelt papers; John B. Bennett to Vandenberg, March 3, 1947, Box 2, Vandenberg papers; Richard B. Scandrett, Jr. to Taft, March 13, 1947, Box 690, Taft papers.

67. House Committee on International Relations, *Military Assistance Programs,* pp. 310–11; House Committee on Foreign Affairs, *Assistance to Greece and Turkey,* pp. 4–5; Senate Committee on Foreign Relations, *Assistance to Greece and Turkey,* p. 37.

68. Senate Committee on Foreign Relations, *Legislative Origins of the Truman Doctrine,* p. 224; Connally, *My Name Is Tom Connally,* p. 319; Vandenberg, *Private Papers,* pp. 344–46.

69. Elmo Roper, "Public Opinion Survey of Reactions to President Truman's Proposal Regarding Greece and Turkey" (n.d.) and Earl Newsom to John R. Steelman, April 10, 1947, Confidential File, Truman papers; Forrestal diaries, April 4, 1947; Acheson *Present at the Creation,* pp. 223–24.

70. Behind closed doors, Vandenberg was quite clear about his motives. "I am not directing my suggestion to any thought that we are going to get any aid out of the United Nations," he declared. Unfortunately, "we cannot just say it. The people will not believe us." The United States was "engaged now in an ideological contest with the Russians," and "we have to use all of our available ideological resources." Ironically, then, despite Vandenberg's insistence upon "realism," he drew upon the "United Nations" in much the same way the State Department drew upon "democracy": as a propaganda cloak behind which anti-Communist intervention could be implemented. Senate Committee on Foreign Relations, *Legislative Origins of the Truman Doctrine,* pp. 14–16, 23–24, 126–28, 143, 169–70, 173–75, 196–97; Acheson, *Present At the Creation,* p. 224.

71. Elmo Roper, "A Study of What People Say in Describing Their Reactions Toward the Truman Doctrine" (April 1947), p. 16, Confidential File, Truman papers. Of those Americans who liked something about the Truman Doctrine, 42.2 percent of the wealthiest named its "firm stand against Russian aggression and the spread of Communism," as compared to 22.6 percent of the poorest. The responses were almost exactly reversed when these two groups named plans to "help people in need." *Ibid.*, p. 18.

72. "Oil," p. 83; "The Great Oil Deals," pp. 138–43, 175–82; "Washington Outlook," p. 5; "New Diplomacy, New Business," p. 16; W. E. Knox to Truman, March 27, 1947, "OF 386 (1947)" folder, Official File, Truman papers; Acheson, *Present at the Creation*, p. 224. See also "Excerpts from a telephone conversation between James V. Forrestal and Reese H. Taylor, 25 March 1947," Box 91, Forrestal papers.

73. Forrestal to Thomas B. Holcomb, March 1, 1947, Box 125, Forrestal papers.

74. See, for example, Jones, *The Fifteen Weeks*, pp. 163, 174; *New York Times*, March 7, 1947.

75. "Excerpts from a telephone conversation between James V. Forrestal and Rep. Carl Vinson of Ga., 13 March 1947," "Speech to Congress on Greece, 3/12/47" folder, Clifford papers; "Statement of Senator Robert A. Taft on Greek and Turkish Loan," Box 556, Taft papers; Ronald Radosh, *Prophets on the Right*, pp. 156–59; Joe Martin, *My First Fifty Years in Politics*, p. 193.

76. Francis Case to Harry Truman, May 10, 1947, "Greece and Turkey (1947), OF 426" folder, Official File, Truman papers; Senate Committee on Foreign Relations, *Legislative Origins of the Truman Doctrine*, pp. 46, 131, 137, 142; Vandenberg, *Private Papers*, p. 344.

77. Hartmann, *Truman and the 80th Congress*, pp. 69–70; House Committee on International Relations, Military Assistance Programs, pp. 311–12. Some of the most prominent critics of the Truman Doctrine, like Walter Lippmann, ended up supporting the Greek-Turkish aid bill. Lippmann to Robert Patterson, May 2, 1947, Box 20, Patterson papers.

78. Mary Sperling McAuliffe, *Crisis on the Left*, pp. 23–27; Markowitz, *Rise and Fall of the People's Century*, p. 235.

79. Thomas G. Paterson, "Presidential Foreign Policy, Public Opinion, and Congress: The Truman Years." For some suggestions on the impact of World War II upon popular thinking about war and peace, see Lawrence S. Wittner, *Rebels Against War*, ch. 4.

80. In the House, the one member of the American Labor Party voted against the legislation. For further discussion of the opposition to the bill on the left and the right, see Jasper Bell to Wyman Wickersham, May 12, 1947, folder 575, Bell papers.

81. *Public Papers of the Presidents: Harry S. Truman 1947*, pp. 254–55. The text of the legislation is printed in: "Passage of Bill Authorizing Assistance to Greece and Turkey," pp. 1070–73.

82. Campbell, "The Greek Civil War," pp. 54–55; Jones, *The Fifteen Weeks*, pp. 159–61; Senate Committee on Foreign Relations, *Legislative Origins of the Truman Doctrine*, p. 139; George Elsey oral history interview, pp. 358–59.

83. Truman stated: "We have considered how the United Nations might assist in this crisis. But the situation is an urgent one requiring immediate action, and the United Nations and its related organizations are not in a position to extend help of the kind that is required." This cryptic comment was clarified by Acheson a week later when, secretly, he told Patterson and Forrestal "that we might as well face the fact that [the] UN will not settle problems of this type and that it is impossible for the UN to intervene in cases involving subversive movements." *Public Papers of the Presidents: Harry S. Truman 1947*, p. 177; FR 1947, 5:126–27.

84. Jones, *The Fifteen Weeks*, p. 184. Austin's two addresses are printed in: "Aid to Greece and Turkey," pp. 857–65. The originals are found in the Austin papers.

85. FR 1947, 5:841, 846–48, 862–63.

86. U.S. Department of State, *The United Nations and the Problem of Greece*, pp. 52–72; C. E. Black, "Greece and the United Nations," p. 557; Woodhouse, *Struggle for Greece*, pp. 197–98, 204. Woodhouse noted "the ultimate division of the UN Commission between two points of view, both of which contained truth. It was certainly true that the Greek Government had brought trouble on its own head by its domestic policy; it was also true that the Governments of Albania, Yugoslavia and Bulgaria were seeking by encroachment and intrigue to expand their frontiers southwards. Which of these truths was logically prior was as unascertainable . . . as the relative priority of hen and egg." Woodhouse, *Apple of Discord*, p. 271.

87. FR 1949, 6:273–74.

88. FR 1947, 5:173–74, 837, 867–68, 870.

89. "If we respond to these [Greek and Turkish] requests, we cannot be said to be intervening in the affairs of Greece and Turkey," the Senate Foreign Relations Committee reported to Congress. "The Committee is assured that the greatest care will be taken to avoid taking any action which could be regarded as an infringement on the sovereignty of either country." House Committee on International Relations, *Military Assistance Programs*, p. 429; Senate Committee on Foreign Relations, *Legislative Origins of the Truman Doctrine*, p. 220. See also, Senate Committee on Foreign Relations, *Assistance to Greece and Turkey*, p. 44.

90. "SWNCC Subcommittee on Foreign Policy Information Meeting, 2/28/47," Box, 1, Jones papers. See also, Marshall to American embassy (Athens), February 28, 1947, "American Economic Mission to Greece— Correspondence and Memoranda (1946–47)" folder, Porter papers.

91. Xydís, *Greece and the Great Powers*, pp. 479–80, 483; Xydís, "The Truman Doctrine in Perspective," p. 254; Couloumbis et al., *Foreign Interference in Greek Politics*, p. 116.

92. *FR 1947*, 5:89–90, 93; Porter to Acheson, April 22, 1947, 868.20/4-2247, SD records.

93. House Committee on International Relations, *Military Assistance Programs*, pp. 354, 412–14; Dobney, ed., *Selected Papers of Will Clayton*, p. 194; Senate Committee on Foreign Relations, *Legislative Origins of the Truman Doctrine*, pp. 75, 82. Joseph Jones recalled: "The word intervention was never used . . . in explaining to the congressional committees how American aid to Greece would be administered. But their administrative plans . . . added up to intervention on a massive scale." Jones, *The Fifteen Weeks*, p. 77.

94. Marshall to American embassy, Athens, May 27, 1947, 868.00/5-2747, SD records.

95. *FR 1947*, 5:170–71, 175–76, 182–88, 204; A. N. Overby to Willard Thorp, May 21, 1947 and John W. Snyder to Clark Clifford, May 23, 1947, Confidential File, Truman papers; Elsey to Clifford, May 23, 1947 and Elsey, "Comments on State-Treasury," "Foreign Aid-Truman Doctrine (Greece-Turkey)" folder, Elsey papers.

96. Truman to Griswold, June 5, 1947 and accompanying White House notes, Confidential File, Truman papers; Patterson to Truman, November 14, 1946, Box 19, Patterson papers; Acheson, "Memorandum for the President" (April 2, 1947), 868.00/4-247, SD records.

97. "Speech of the Honorable Dwight Griswold on the Governors' Round Up Program on Blue Network, April 13, 1945," "PPF 405" folder, President's Personal File, Truman papers.

4. CONTROLLING GREEK POLITICS

1. Monthly Report to the Secretary of State from the Chief of the American Mission for Aid to Greece" (September 15, 1947), 868.20/9-1947, SD records.

2. Campbell and Sherrard, *Modern Greece*, pp. 85–160; D. George Kousoulas, *Modern Greece: Profile of a Nation*, pp. 23–169; Clogg, *A Short History of Modern Greece*, pp. 75–132.

3. "Report on Greece, address by George C. McGhee, Coordinator for Aid to Greece and Turkey, broadcast over CBS, October 15, 1947," Box 1, Jones papers; U.S. Department of State, *First Report to Congress on Assistance to Greece and Turkey*, p. 2; Davies, "The Role of the American Trade Union Representatives" (MS), p. 191; Woodhouse, *Struggle for Greece*, p. 235.

4. *FR 1947*, 5:215–16; Forrestal diaries, July 9, 1947.

5. *FR 1947*, 5:221–22, 224.

6. MacVeagh to Secretary of State, May 7, 1947, 868.00/5-747, SD records; *FR 1947*, 5:178. This disdain for Tsaldaris was widespread among American officials. U.S. intelligence reported: "A wealthy, highly ambitious man, Tsaldaris is described as being jealous of his power, selfish, conceited and completely unrealistic in his evaluation of United States' attitudes and

the needs of his country." Marshall replied to MacVeagh that "we are well aware" that any replacement of Maximos by Tsaldaris as Prime Minister "would be most unfortunate." Office of Intelligence Research, "Biographic Reports on Members of the Greek Cabinet Appointed September 8, 1947" (October 14, 1947), OIR Report no. 4531, P&O 350.05, Plans and Operations Division, Army General Staff records; *FR 1947*, 5:182.

7. Norton to Foreign Office, May 8, 1947, FO 371/67003, R6476 and Bevin (Paris) to Foreign Office, July 2, 1947, FO 371/67145, R11452, FO records.

8. MacVeagh to Karamessines, March 26, 1947, 868.00/3-2447 and Keeley to Secretary of State, March 31, 1947, 868.00/3-3147, SD records; Irving Brown, "Confidential Report on Greece, France, and England" (July 7, 1947), Box 17, Thorne papers. Still in Greece at the time, Porter told MacVeagh that the new government was "not a true coalition but a reshuffling of the rightist groups." He confided to his diary that "it is quite obvious to anyone who looks at the policies of this group that it is not representative in the democratic sense, has no program and merely wants to continue to buy time." Porter diary, February 19, 1947, "Diary (February 1947)" folder, Porter papers.

9. O'Ballance, *The Greek Civil War*, pp. 131, 135, 142–43; Woodhouse, *Struggle for Greece*, p. 208; McNeill, *Greece*, pp. 36–37.

10. Tsoucalas, *Greek Tragedy*, p. 101; O'Ballance, *The Greek Civil War*, pp. 144–45; Keeley to Secretary of State, April 24, 1947, 868.00/4-2447, SD records. See also Averoff-Tossizza, *By Fire and Axe*, pp. 204–5, 212–13.

11. *FR 1947*, 5:240; MacVeagh to Secretary of State, July 15, 1947, 868.00/ 7-1547, SD records; McNeill, *Greece*, pp. 35–36.

12. MacVeagh to Secretary of State, July 15, 1947, 868.00/7-1547, SD records; *FR 1947*, 5:231–32.

13. *FR 1947*, 5:243–44, 251, 300; MacVeagh to Secretary of State, July 25, 1947, 868.00/7-2547, SD records.

14. McNeill, *Greece*, pp. 36–37; *FR 1947*, 5:237–40, 303–4.

15. These practices, as well as the overall military struggle, are discussed at greater length in chapters 5 and 8. For a picture of the conflict through the eyes of an anguished observer, see Kazantzakis, *The Fratricides*, passim.

16. *FR 1947*, 5:264, 280, 295–96, 303. The State Department concurred on the necessity for a center-right coalition. *Ibid.*, p. 297; Villard to Armour, August 6, 1947, 868.01/8-647, SD records.

17. *FR 1947*, 5:253–54, 286, 309–13; MacVeagh to Secretary of State, August 21, 1947, 868.00/8-2147, SD records; Iatrides, *Ambassador MacVeagh Reports*, p. 722.

18. *FR 1947*, 5:318; Reilly to Foreign Office, August 28, 1947, FO 371/ 67007, R11830 and August 30, 1947, FO 371/67007, R11914, FO records. A copy of the memorandum, which summarized Griswold's August 25 warning, is contained in MacVeagh to Secretary of State, September 2, 1947, 868.002/9-247, SD records. Endorsed by Griswold and delivered to

Tsaldaris, it declared that "a less broad government . . . is inadmissible." If such a government were formed, construction work "will be suspended, while importation of supplies (not food supplies) will be limited until the final evolution of the situation has become apparent." In addition, "no intervention will be allowed" to maintain the value of the Greek currency, for its fluctuation "must be due to purely political reasons." Griswold discussed his role in detail in "Monthly Report to the Secretary of State from the Chief of the American Mission for Aid to Greece" (September 15, 1947), 868.20/9-1947, SD records.

19. *FR 1947*, 5:319; MacVeagh to Secretary of State, September 2, 1947, 868.002/9-247, SD records; Reilly to Wallinger, August 30, 1947, FO 371/ 67097, R12771, FO records.

20. Clark to Secretary of State, August 30, 1947, 868.01/8-3047 and "Monthly Report to the Secretary of State from the Chief of the American Mission for Aid to Greece" (September 15, 1947), 868.20/9-1947, SD records; Reilly to Foreign Office, August 29, 1947, FO 371/67007, R11883, FO records; *FR 1947*, 5:368–69.

21. *FR 1947*, 5:324–25; Leonard J. Cromie, "Memorandum of Conversation" (September 1, 1947), "800 Greece (Conf.)" folder and Cromie, "Memorandum of Conversations" (September 3, 1947), "800" folder, Box 2483, Athens post records. "It is not the American intention . . . to support a one-sided centrist solution of the Greek governmental problem," MacVeagh assured Washington. At the same time, he planned to leave "to the Greeks themselves the actual setting up of their Government or at least the luxury of thinking that such action is their own." Meanwhile, though, the British ambassador reported: "Henderson is anxious not to appear as a sort of *deus ex machina*, but of course he is up to the neck in this wasp's nest." MacVeagh to Secretary of State, September 2, 1947, 868.002/9-247, SD records; Norton to Foreign Office, September 4, 1947, FO 371/67007, R12204, FO records. See also Horace H. Smith to Henderson, September 1, 1947, 711.68/9-147, SD records.

22. Cromie, "Memorandum of Conversations" (September 3, 1947) and S. Calligas, "Memorandum of Conversation" (September 4, 1947), "800" folder, Box 2483, Athens post records. These memos are also enclosed in Keeley to Secretary of State, September 16, 1947, 111.75/9-1647, SD records.

23. S. Calligas, "Memorandum of Conversation" (September 4, 1947), Harold B. Minor, "Memorandum of Conversation" (September 4, 1947) and S. C., "Outline of Conversation" (September 5, 1947), "800" folder, Box 2483, Athens post records; Minutes of the meeting of Tuesday, 9th September 1947, FO 371/67046, R12491, FO records. See also MacVeagh to Secretary of State, September 6, 1947, 868.00/9-647 and Keeley to Secretary of State, September 16, 1947, 111.75/9-1647, SD records.

24. Grady to Secretary of State, October 27, 1948, 868.00/10-2748, SD records; *FR 1947*, 5:333–34.

25. Stavrianos, *Greece*, pp. 188, 197; Sweet-Escott, *Greece*, p. 77; Averoff-Tossizza, *By Fire and Axe*, p. 231.

26. Minutes by David Balfour of September 2, 1947, FO 371/67007, R11885, September 9, 1947, FO 371/67007, R12273 and of September 10–11, 1947, FO 371/67007, R12325, FO records; Office of Intelligence Research, "Biographic Reports on Members of Greek Cabinet Appointed September 8, 1947" (October 14, 1947), OIR Report no. 4531, P & O 350.05, P & O Division, Army General Staff records. For further indications of Sophoulis's retreat from his earlier positions, see *New York Times*, September 5, 1947.

27. *New York Times*, December 4, 1947; Stavrianos, *Greece*, p. 189.

28. *FR 1948*, 4:112, 137; Rankin to Secretary of State, February 16, 1948, 868.00/2-1648 and Cromie to NEA, December 8, 1948, 868.00/12-848, SD records.

29. *FR 1947*, 5:355; Lovett to American embassy (Athens), December 2, 1947, 868.00/12-247, Keeley to Secretary of State, December 3, 1947, 868.00/12-347, Rankin to Secretary of State, December 18, 1947, 868.00/12-1847, Griswold to Secretary of State, December 22, 1947, 868.00/12-2247, Griswold to Secretary of State, December 26, 1947, 868.00/12-2647, Rankin to Secretary of State, January 8, 1948, 868.00/1-848, and Harold B. Minor to Secretary of State, May 4, 1948, 868.00/5-448, SD records.

30. Griswold to Secretary of State, June 17, 1948, 868.00/6-1748 and July 9, 1948, 868.00/7-948, U.S. Military Attaché to Secretary of State, August 20, 1948, 868.00/8-2048 and Minor to Secretary of State, August 17, 1949, 868.00/8-1749, SD records.

31. The Populist leader to whom this suggestion was addressed replied that this might be dangerous, since it was always advisable to have a "reliable opposition." Thus, if the Populists lost, "one knows that the 'opposition,' say the Liberals, will not really change things very much." Cromie, "Memorandum of Conversation" (November 29, 1949), 868.00/11-2949, SD records.

32. Paul Porter, "Wanted: A Miracle in Greece," p. 106. As Porter's article appeared in print only two weeks after the creation of the Sophoulis government, he may have been referring to its predecessors. On the other hand, many of the figures and interests discussed by Porter retained power under Sophoulis. Indeed, U.S. intelligence reported that "Athanassiades Bodossakis, the leading industrialist of Greece, supports Sophoulis strongly and is reliably reported to supply him with party funds." Office of Intelligence Research, "Biographic Reports on Members of the Greek Cabinet Appointed September 8, 1947" (October 14, 1947), OIR Report no. 4531, P & O 350.05, P & O Division, Army General Staff records.

33. Howard K. Smith, *The State of Europe*, pp. 225, 238; Matthews, *Memories of a Mountain War*, pp. 247–48.

34. *FR 1948*, 4:48; Norton to Bevin, November 18, 1947, FO 371/67011, R15294, FO records. See also Woodhouse, *Struggle for Greece*, p. 236.

35. Davies, "The Role of the American Trade Union Representatives"

(MS), pp. 223, 235; "Monthly Report of the Chief of AMAG to the Secretary of State" (October 15, 1947), Box 7, SD Committees records. In late 1948, an ECA official noted: "The Greek political parties have . . . come to identify their country's interests with those of the U.S. as closely as if Greece were a forty-ninth state." Charles E. Coombs, "The Greek Problem," enclosure in E. T. Dickinson, Jr. to John Nuveen, December 20, 1948, "800 Greece-Secret" folder, Box 2485, Athens post records.

36. *FR 1948*, 4:88; Griswold to McGhee, March 3, 1948, 868.00/3-348 and Rankin to Secretary of State, February 22, 1948, 868.00/2-2148, SD records.

37. *New York Times*, November 21, 1947; personal interview with Loy Henderson, January 13, 1976; Iatrides, *Ambassador MacVeagh Reports*, pp. 725–28; Cromie to NEA, December 8, 1948, 868.00/12-848, SD records; Henry F. Grady, "Adventures in Diplomacy," p. 197, Box 5, Grady papers; *FR 1947*, 5:370–71, 378–79, 398.

38. *FR 1947*, 5:393–94, 400, 404–7, 411–13, 416–17; Iatrides, *Ambassador MacVeagh Reports*, pp. 728–33; John O. Iatrides, "Greece and the Origins of the Cold War," p. 251; personal interview with Loy Henderson, January 13, 1976; *FR 1948*, 4:14, 88–91.

39. Griswold to McGhee, January 12, 1948, 868.00/1-1248 and January 22, 1948, 868.00/1-2248 and Griswold to Henderson, July 7, 1948, 868.00/7-748, SD records; Marshall, "Memorandum for the President" (May 10, 1948) with enclosures and Grady to Secretary of State, Confidential File, Truman papers; Grady, "Adventures in Diplomacy," p. 198, Box 5, Grady papers.

40. Matthews, *Memories of a Mountain War*, pp. 155–56; Kédros, *La Résistance Grecque*, p. 521; Norton to Bevin, May 6, 1947, FO 371/67124, R6059, FO records.

41. Keeley to Secretary of State, April 3, 1947, 868.001 PAUL/4-347, SD records; George Polk, "Greece Puts Us to the Test," p. 534; Sulzberger, *A Long Row of Candles*, p. 391. For Frederika's ability to charm U.S. officials, see also Rankin to Secretary of State, May 22, 1948, 868.0011/5-2248, SD records.

42. Rankin to Secretary of State, February 5, 1948, 868.00/2-548 and Keeley to Secretary of State, April 3, 1947, 868.001 PAUL/4-347, SD records; Rankin, "Memorandum of Conversation" (January 13, 1948), Box 2485, Athens post records.

43. Abbot Low Moffat, "Memorandum of Conversation" (February 10, 1948), 868.20/2-1848, SD records; Rankin, "Memorandum of Conversation" (February 6, 1948), "800.1 (Secret)" folder, Box 2486, Athens post records. The Queen's version of what Henderson told her during the September cabinet crisis may well be doubted. Even so, it is noteworthy that, according to the British ambassador, Tsaldaris "said that he had been much disturbed by an American suggestion made to the King that, if other solutions failed, the King should invite someone from outside Parliament to pick the best

government he could." Tsaldaris claimed that "such an arrangement . . . cut at the true foundations of democracy and was only a veiled dictatorship." Norton to Foreign Office, September 8, 1947, FO 371/67007, R12374, FO records.

44. Raymond Daniell, "Where the 'Cold War' Is Shooting War," p. 32; Grady to Secretary of State, July 23, 1948, 868.20/7-2348, SD records.

45. Colonel Charles R. Lehner to Director, Plans and Operations Division, Department of the Army, October 30, 1947, P & O 091 Greece, Section IV, Case 52, P & O Division, Army General Staff records; McGhee to Marshall, February 24, 1948, 868.00/2-2448, SD records.

46. Van Fleet to Grady, October 9, 1948, P & O 091 Greece TS, Section IV, Case 40, P & O Division, Army General Staff records. See also Paul H. Nitze to W. McWilliams, November 30, 1948 and Under Secretary to Marshall, December 1, 1948, "PPS 44" folder, Box 2, Policy Planning Staff records; James A. Van Fleet, "How We Won in Greece," p. 390.

47. FR 1948, 4:170.

48. Ibid., pp. 176–77, 183; FR 1949, 6:234.

49. FR 1948, 4:186–87; Rankin to Secretary of State, November 26, 1948, 868.00/11-2648. Grady claimed that he took this position based upon a State Department memo; however, neither the editors of the Foreign Relations series nor I have been able to locate it.

50. FR 1948, 4:187.

51. Rankin to Secretary of State, December 1, 1948, 868.00/12-148, Cromie to NEA, December 8, 1948, 868.00/12-848 and Rankin to Secretary of State, December 22, 1948, 868.20/12-2248, SD records. Rankin's doubts were based upon skepticism as to the efficacy of the Papagos "solution." He argued that if a Papagos-Markezinis government "should obtain [a] majority vote under [the] threat of dissolving [the] Chamber [of Deputies], there is still no real assurance that it would be more efficient than predecessor governments. [The] only certainties are that [the] government machinery would be disorganized for some time . . . that most of those Greek cabinet members and other high officials who have cooperated closely with America would be dropped . . . and that [the] alienation of [the] major parties and their leaders could be expected [to] result [in] dictatorial methods to offset [the] lack [of] political support." Therefore, he favored efforts to broaden the Sophoulis-Tsaldaris government "as long as possible." Rankin to Secretary of State, December 22, 1948, 868.20/12-2248, SD records.

52. FR 1949, 6:233–35, 237; Sulzberger, A Long Row of Candles, pp. 428–30. See also William Rountree to McGhee, January 14, 1949, 868.00/1-1449, SD records.

53. Grady to Harriman, January 12, 1949, 868.00/1-1749 and Grady to Secretary of State, January 14, 1949, 868.00/1-1449, SD records; FR 1949, 6:240n.

54. Grady to Secretary of State, January 18, 1949, 868.01/1-1849, and

Rankin to Secretary of State, March 8, 1949, 868.00/3-849, SD records; Grady to McGhee, January 22, 1949, "Greece—Correspondence, 1946–1951" folder, Box 3, Grady papers.

55. *FR 1949*, 6:237–38; Sulzberger, *A Long Row of Candles*, pp. 429–31; Hoffman to Harriman and Nuveen, December 25, 1948, "Greece—Correspondence, 1946–1951" folder, Box 3, Grady papers.

56. Sulzberger, *A Long Row of Candles*, pp. 430–31. The head of ECA's labor division in Greece also reported that Harriman was critical of Grady during his visit. Alan Strachan to Clinton Golden, July 24, 1949, Box 1, Golden papers.

57. *FR 1949*, 6:238n; Grady to McGhee, January 17, 1949, "Greece—Correspondence, 1946–1951" folder, Box 3, Grady papers. For other illustrations of Grady's concern about the actions of the two ECA officials at the time, see *FR 1949*, 6:256–57; Grady to Lovett, January 14, 1949, Grady to McGhee, January 22, 1949, and "Memorandum for Burton Berry" (n.d.), "Greece—Correspondence, 1946–1951" folder, Box 3, Grady papers.

58. Grady, "Adventures in Diplomacy," pp. 200–2, Box 5, Grady papers.

59. Sweet-Escott, *Greece*, p. 77: Rankin to Secretary of State, March 8, 1949, 868.00/3-849, SD records; *FR 1949*, 6:241; Helen Zotos Journal, January 16, 1949, Box 4, Zotos papers. American officials used the threat of a Markezinis dictatorship to frighten Greek political leaders into forming a government. See, for example, Cromie to Satterthwaite, Hare, Jernegan, and Baxter, January 5, 1949, 868.00/1-549, SD records.

60. Woodhouse, *Struggle for Greece*, p. 267; Sweet-Escott, *Greece*, pp. 77–78; Gayn, "Democracy's Distant Cousin," p. 15; Rankin to Secretary of State, January 27, 1949, "350-Greece (Secret)" folder, Box 2488, Athens post records.

61. *FR 1949*, 6:245; Harriman to Acheson, February 28, 1949 and Acheson to Harriman, March 15, 1949, Acheson papers.

62. *FR 1949*, 6:295–96; Seton-Watson, *The East European Revolution*, p. 328.

63. *FR 1949*, 6:309–12, 314–15, 318, 458–59; Sweet-Escott, *Greece*, pp. 78–79; Grady to McGhee, December 23, 1949, 868.20/12-2349, SD records. The royal family, it should be noted, remained fervent supporters of Markezinis, who was cleared by the courts of the currency charges. In August 1949, Frederika told Minor that she continued to regard Markezinis as the "hope of Greece." Grady to Secretary of State, August 23, 1949, 868.00/8-2349, SD records.

64. McNeill, *The Greek Dilemma*, pp. 55–56; Rankin to Secretary of State, January 28, 1948, 868.00/1-2848, SD records.

65. *FR 1947*, 5:102–3, 182; "Notes for Conversation with Monsieur Tsaldaris" (August 16, 1947), FO 371/67145, R11452, FO records. See also Minutes by G. A. Wallinger of August 18, 1947 and by D. J. McCarthy of August 6, 1947, FO 371/67006, R10677, FO records.

66. "Summary of conversation, August 28 [1947], between Ambassador

MacVeagh and General Zervas," enclosure in American embassy (Athens) to Secretary of State, September 2, 1947, "Sept. 1947" folder, "P" Project records; Reilly to Foreign Office, August 29, 1947, FO 371/67007, R11883, FO records. MacVeagh, however, advised Maximos that "in the last resort he should accept him." *Ibid.*

67. Rankin to Secretary of State, January 28, 1948, 868.00/1-2848, Smith Simpson to Secretary of State, October 11, 1948, 868.00/10–1148, and Lovett to American embassy (Athens), November 17, 1948, 868.00/10-1148, SD records. In one such reevaluation, Van Fleet observed that Zervas "desires to set himself up as the supreme military commander or military dictator." And while Greece "requires a strong government, headed by a strong leader," Van Fleet doubted that Zervas was the appropriate individual. Van Fleet to Grady, December 31, 1948, 868.00/2-1949, SD records.

68. MacVeagh to Secretary of State, June 23, 1947, 868.00/6-2347 and Rankin to Secretary of State, June 21, 1948, 868.00/6-2148, SD records; *FR 1947*, 5:226.

69. *FR 1947*, 5:477; Rankin to Secretary of State, December 31, 1947, 868.00/12–3147, June 21, 1948, 868.00/6-2148, July 3, 1948, 868.00/7-348, and July 9, 1948, 868.00/7-948, SD records.

70. Rankin to Secretary of State, March 18, 1948, 868.00/3-1848 and June 21, 1948, 868.00/6-2148, and Douglas to Secretary of State, August 11, 1949, 868.00/8-1149, SD records.

71. Caffery to Secretary of State, June 21, 1948, 868.00/6-2148, Roger Baldwin to Acheson, May 17, 1949, 868.00/5-1749 and May 31, 1949, 868.00/5-3149, and William Green to Acheson, November 9, 1949, 868.00/11-949, SD records.

72. Grady to Secretary of State, November 13, 1948, 868.00/11-1348, SD records. For further State Department justifications of the arrest of Mrs. Svolos, see William O. Baxter to Baldwin, June 3, 1949, 868.00/5-1749 and Cleon O. Swayzee to Green, December 14, 1949, 868.00/11-949, SD records.

73. Rankin to State Department, June 21, 1948, 868.00/6-2148, SD records; Grady to Secretary of State, November 20, 1948, "800S (Secret)" folder, Box 2485, Athens post records.

74. Herbert Weiner to Secretary of State, June 8, 1949, 868.00/6-849, SD records.

75. Keeley to Secretary of State, March 19, 1947, 868.00/3-1947 and Rankin to Secretary of State, November 18, 1948, 868.00/11-1848, SD records.

76. *FR 1947*, 5:22–23; Baxter, "Memorandum of Conversation" (May 8, 1947), 868.00/5-847, Rankin to Secretary of State, January 4, 1948, 868.00/1-448 and Grady to Secretary of State, June 3, 1948, 868.00/6-349, SD records.

77. Rankin to Secretary of State, February 16, 1948, 868.00/2-1648, SD records.

78. Grady to Secretary of State, November 8, 1948, 868.00/11-848 and Rankin to Secretary of State, November 9, 1948, 868.00/11-948, SD records. The memorandum was actually rather moderate in orientation. "Our movement disavows the Communist rebellion," it declared. It also criticized rightist persecution, however, and called for a sincere amnesty, the restoration of civil liberties, and new elections. *Ibid.*

79. Grady to Secretary of State, June 3, 1949, 868.00/6-349 and June 6, 1949, 868.00/6-649 and James Webb to American embassy (Athens), June 9, 1949, 868.00/6-349, SD records.

80. *New York Times*, May 21, 1948; Webb to American embassy (Athens), June 9, 1949, 868.00/6-349 and Rankin to Secretary of State, May 15, 1948, 868.00/5-1548, SD records.

81. Rankin to Secretary of State, May 15, 1948, 868.00/5-1548, SD records.

5. DEFENDING FREEDOM

1. *Public Papers of the Presidents: Harry S. Truman, 1947*, pp. 178–79.

2. Nicos C. Alivizatos, "The 'Emergency' Regime and Civil Liberties" (MS), pp. 1–10; *FR 1947*, 5:221.

3. Woodhouse, *Struggle for Greece*, p. 202; Averoff-Tossizza, *By Fire and Axe*, p. 218; O'Ballance, *Greek Civil War*, pp. 136–37; MacVeagh to Secretary of State, March 22, 1947, 868.00/3-2247, Keeley to Secretary of State, March 24, 1947, 868.00/3-2447, and Raleigh A. Gibson to Secretary of State, April 2, 1947, 868.00/4-247, SD records; C.P.M. to Warner, November 14, 1947, FO 371/67011, R15110, FO records.

4. British Police Mission Report for March 1947, FO 371/67131, R6057, FO records; Polk, "Greece Puts Us to the Test," p. 534; MacVeagh to Secretary of State, May 11, 1947, 868.00/5-1149, SD records; William G. Livesay diary, July 1, 1947, Livesay papers; Raymond Daniell, "Symptom and Tragedy of Our Time," p. 60.

5. *FR 1947*, 5:142–43; Keeley to Secretary of State, April 14, 1947, 868.00/4-1447, SD records.

6. Livesay diary, July 2, 1947, Livesay papers; *FR 1947*, 5:208–9, 211, 217.

7. *FR 1947*, 5:232, 240; MacVeagh to Secretary of State, August 6, 1947, 868.00/8-647, SD records; Reilly to Foreign Office, July 25, 1947, FO 371/67006, R10231 and British Police Mission Report for July 1947, FO 371/67131, R11762, FO records.

8. Reilly to Foreign Office, July 14, 1947, FO 371/67006, R10227, FO records; *FR 1947*, 5:244–45, 250, 260–61.

9. Norton to Warner, December 19, 1947, FO 371/67061, R16942 and Minutes by David Balfour of August 15, 1947, FO 371/67006, R10952 and of September 4, 1947, FO 371/67007, R12110, RO records.

10. British Police Mission Report for October 1947, FO 371/67131,

R16183, FO records; *FR 1947*, 5:471; Moffat, "Memorandum of Conversation" (December 10, 1947), 868.00/1-348, SD records.

11. Woodhouse, *Struggle for Greece*, p. 259; Rankin to Secretary of State, December 30, 1948, 868.00/12-3048 and December 31, 1948, 868.00/12-3148, SD records; Averoff-Tossizza, *By Fire and Axe*, pp. 311–12.

12. Gibson to Secretary of State, May 14, 1949, 868.00/5-1449 and R. G. Memminger to State Department, November 9, 1949, 868.00/11-949, SD records.

13. Charles R. Lehner to Director, Plans and Operations Division, Department of the Army, October 30, 1947, P & O 091 Greece, Section IV, Case 52, P & O Division, Army General Staff records; L. Pittman Springs to Secretary of State, February, 11, 1949, 868.00/2-1149, SD records. The lynching of prisoners is discussed in "Monthly Report of the Chief of AMAG to the Secretary of State" (May 15, 1948), Box 7, SD Committees records.

14. Memminger to State Department, November 9, 1949, 868.00/11-949, SD records; Christos Jecchinis, *Trade Unionism in Greece*, p. 193.

15. Woodhouse, *Struggle for Greece*, p. 215; O'Ballance, *The Greek Civil War*, p. 169; Chandler, *The Divided Land*, pp. 204–7; Sweet-Escott, *Greece*, p. 75; Kousoulas, *Revolution and Defeat*, p. 258; Miner to Memminger, August 9, 1949, 868.00/8-1949, SD records.

16. Miner to Memminger, August 9, 1949, 868.00/8-1949 and Minor to Secretary of State, June 27, 1949, 868.00/6-2749, September 10, 1949, 868.00/9-1049 and December 5, 1949, 868.00/12-549, SD records; Eudes, *The Kapetanios*, pp. 301–2, 315–16, 357–58; Aphrodite Mavroede, "Makronisos Journal"; Reilly to Bevin, September 4, 1947, FO 371/67007, R12018, FO records.

17. British Police Mission, "Report on Living Conditions of Deportees on Ayios Efstratios" (August 15, 1947), FO 371/67007, R12018, FO records.

18. *FR 1946*, 7:61–62; "Monthly Report of the Chief of AMAG to the Secretary of State" (November 15, 1947), Box 7, SD Committees records; *New York Herald Tribune*, May 2, 1948. For other indications of U.S. government complacency about the camps, see Minor to Secretary of State, June 27, 1949, 868.00/6-2749 and Miner to Memminger, August 9, 1949, 868.00/8-1949, SD records; House Committee on International Relations, *Military Assistance Programs*, pp. 84–85.

19. *FR 1948*, 4:58–59; Rankin to Secretary of State, April 8, 1948, 868.00/4-848, SD records.

20. Rankin to Secretary of State, April 8, 1948, 868.00/4-848 and February 4, 1949, 868.00/2-449 and Minor to Secretary of State, June 27, 1949, 868.00/6-2749, SD records.

21. Rankin to Secretary of State, May 15, 1948, 868.00/5-1548, Minor to Secretary of State, August 18, 1949, 868.00/8-1949, Grady to Secretary of State, September 15, 1949, 868.00/9-1549 and Memminger to Department of State, November 9, 1949, 868.00/11-949, SD records.

22. An official of the U.S. branch of Jehovah's Witnesses charged in

March 1949 that some 600 Jehovah's Witnesses had been arrested in Greece during the preceding year, frequently during sermons or group Bible study. Jail terms for members of such congregations ranged up to fifteen years. In addition, Jehovah's Witnesses drafted into the armed forces were tortured and executed. Two months later, the State Department conceded that two Jehovah's Witnesses had been executed and five others sentenced to death. Grady to Secretary of State, February 24, 1949, 868.00/2-2449, Grant Suiter to Acheson, March 18, 1949, 868.00/3-1849, and Derward Sandifer to Eleanor Roosevelt, May 27, 1949, 868.00/4-849, SD records.

23. Rankin to Secretary of State, April 30, 1948, 868.00/4-3048, Carlyle B. Haynes to Eleanor Roosevelt, 868.00/5-448 and Springs to Secretary of State, September 22, 1948 and Lovett to Springs, October 1, 1948, 868.00/9-2248, SD records.

24. *FR 1947*, 5:196–97, 203; Rankin to Secretary of State, March 17, 1948, 868.00/3-1748 and July 14, 1948, 868.00/7-1448, SD records; *FR 1948*, 4:59–60. For further State Department and AMAG justifications of the Ladas policy see *FR 1948*, 4:74–75; *New York Herald Tribune*, May 2, 1948.

25. Sweet-Escott, *Greece*, p. 73; O'Ballance, *The Greek Civil War*, p. 168; Bay to Secretary of State, May 8, 1948, 868.00/5-848 and Marvel to Secretary of State, May 11, 1948, 868.00/5-1148, SD records.

26. Sulzberger, *A Long Row of Candles*, p. 392; Douglas to Secretary of State, May 5, 1948, 868.00/5-548 and Rankin to Secretary of State, July 14, 1948, 868.00/7-1448, SD records; *FR 1948*, 4:82–83, 86.

27. *FR 1948*, 4:86–87, 118–20; Rankin to Secretary of State, July 14, 1948, 868.00/7-1448, SD records.

28. According to Grady, the crime of Glezos and his companions was "conspiring together to leave Greece on [a] Communist Party mission designed [to] further [the] cause of [the] rebellion." During the trial, Rankin noted, the defense lawyer portrayed Glezos as a consistent nationalist rather than as a Communist. The prosecutor, however, responded: "The defendant, having brought down the flag of the Germans from the Acropolis, not only did not act patriotically, but on the contrary by his act added to the difficulties of the Greek people." *FR 1948*, 4:139–41; Hondros, "German Occupation of Greece" (MS), p. 140; Rankin to Secretary of State, December 23, 1948, 868.00/12-2348 and Grady to Secretary of State, March 14, 1949, 868.00/3-1449, SD records.

29. Grady to Secretary of State, February 24, 1949, 868.00/2-2449, SD records; *FR 1949*, 6:259–60.

30. Baxter, "Memorandum of Conversation" (December 20, 1948) and Baxter to Jernegan, December 22, 1948, 868.00/12-2048, SD records.

31. MacVeagh to Secretary of State, January 28, 1947, "P" Project records; MacVeagh to Secretary of State, August 10, 1946, 868.00/8-1046, SD records.

32. Norton to Bevin, May 10, 1947, FO 371/67003, R6344 and November 18, 1947, FO 371/67011, R15294, FO records; Matthews, *Memories of a*

Mountain War, p. 169; Seton-Watson, *The East European Revolution,* p. 327; Sweet-Escott, *Greece,* p. 72; Woodhouse, *Apple of Discord,* p. 279; text of law entitled "For the Security of the State, of the Regime, of the Social Order, and for the Protection of Civil Liberties," 868.00/1-248 and Rankin to Secretary of State, May 15, 1948, 868.00/5-1548, SD records.

33. Smith, OSS, pp. 128–29; MacVeagh to Secretary of State, May 24, 1945, 868.5045/5-2445, SD records.

34. MacVeagh to Secretary of State, May 28, 1947, 868.00/5-2847, SD records; Major General S. J. Chamberlain, "The Greek Situation," P & O 091 Greece TS (October 24, 1947), P & O Division, Army General Staff records; MacVeagh to Keeley, February 27, 1947, "820.02 (Secret)" folder, Athens post records.

35. S. Morris to Officer in Charge of American Mission, Athens, July 2, 1947, 868.00B/7-247, Henderson to MacVeagh, September 30, 1947, 868.00B/9-3047, and Keeley to Henderson, October 8, 1947, 868.00B/10-847, SD records.

36. See, for example, Lester Houck to Jack Neal, October 24, 1946, 868.00B/10-2446, SD records; Karamessines to Consul-General, May 27, 1945, "711.5 Civil Prisoners" folder, Box 2479, Athens post records; MacVeagh to Secretary of State, September 26, 1946, "P" Project records.

37. Woodhouse, *Struggle for Greece,* pp. 261, 305; D. L. Nicholson to Jernegan, June 14, 1949, 868.5043/6-1449 and Griswold to Secretary of State, July 29, 1948, 868.00/7-2948, SD records.

38. See, for example, J. Edgar Hoover to Frederick B. Lyon, June 4, 1945, 868.01/6-445, October 5, 1945, 868.01/10-545, and December 14, 1945, 868.01/12-1445, SD records.

39. *Washington Post,* January 7, 1976; Yiannis Roubatis and Karen Wynn, "CIA Operations in Greece." I have been unable to determine precisely when Karamessines left the U.S. embassy staff for the new CIA headquarters. The monthly reports on Communist activities ended with the following message from the State Department, which may indicate his departure: "It is believed that owing to changed conditions, the Embassy is no longer in a position to obtain the desired information in sufficient quantity and with sufficient regularity to justify the continuation of regular monthly reports." The *New York Times* reported that Karamessines worked for the CIA in Athens in 1947 and 1948 and served as station chief from 1951 to 1953. T. M. Nordbeck to Officer in Charge of the American Mission, Athens, June 20, 1949, 868.00B/5-1149, SD records; *New York Times,* August 2, 1974.

40. Porter, "Wanted: A Miracle in Greece," p. 107; *FR 1947,* 5:160–61, 169–70, 840, 842.

41. *FR 1947,* 5:170, 174–75; MacVeagh to Secretary of State, May 7, 1947, 868.00/5-747, SD records.

42. In late June 1947, the Greek government declared that "any public discussion concerning further amnesty measures at present would be highly

detrimental, as it would cause the morale of the bands' leadership to rise." Shortly afterward, the British noted that the U.S. government considered it an "inopportune moment to raise the question of the amnesty" and would take no action on the subject of foreign observers. Royal Greek embassy, Memorandum of June 30, 1947, 868.00/6-3047, SD records; Balfour to Foreign Office, July 14, 1947, FO371/67004, R9633, FO records.

43. *FR 1947*, 5:343–44, 348–49, 359. Woodhouse has argued that the Sophoulis amnesty "was offered as a sop to liberal opinion." Sophoulis, however, later claimed that he "had believed that provided there was assurance of no rightist excesses the amnesty would be effective." Woodhouse, *Struggle for Greece*, p. 216; Moffat, "Memorandum of Conversation" (May 15, 1948), 868.00/5-1748, SD records.

44. Foreign Office to Washington, October 10, 1947, FO 371/67046, R13576 and Norton to Bevin, November 18, 1947, FO 371/67011, R15294, FO records; Gibson to Secretary of State, October 9, 1947, 868.00/10-947 and Weekly Report of the American Mission for Aid to Greece (October 29, 1947), 868.00/10-3047, SD records.

45. Springs to Secretary of State, April 29, 1948, 868.00/4-2948 and Grady to Secretary of State, August 19, 1948, 868.00/8-1948, SD records; *New York Times*, February 13, 1948. The Salonika events are confirmed in "Guerrillas on Parade."

46. Rankin to Secretary of State, May 15, 1948, 868.00/5-1548 and Grady to Secretary of State, May 27, 1949, 868.00/5-2749, SD records; *FR 1948*, 4:141.

47. At this point in MacVeagh's testimony, right-wing Congressman William Colmer interjected: "That is true in this country as well." The ambassador replied: "That is right." MacVeagh to Secretary of State, June 30, 1947, 868.00/6-3047, Rankin to Secretary of State, January 15, 1948, 868.00/1-1548 and May 10, 1948, 868.00/5-1048. SD records; "Monthly Report of the Chief of AMAG to the Secretary of State" (January 15, 1948), Box 7, SD Committees records; Alivizatos, "The 'Emergency' Regime and Civil Liberties" (MS), p. 9; House Committee on International Relations, *Military Assistance Programs*, p. 341.

48. MacVeagh to Secretary of State, June 30, 1947, 868.00/6-3047, SD records.

49. Lascelles to Warner, January 14, 1947, FO 371/67047B, R1048 and Norton to Foreign Office, September 7, 1947, FO 371/67107, R12272, FO records; Gibson to Secretary of State, September 4, 1947, 868.00/9-447 and Keeley to Secretary of State, November 3, 1947, 868.00/11-347, SD records; John Dimakis, "The Greek Press," p. 231.

50. Keeley to Secretary of State, October 31, 1947, 868.00/10-3147 and November 11, 1947, 868.00/11-1047, SD records; Norton to Bevin, November 18, 1947, FO 371/67011, R15294, FO records.

51. An AMAG official present recalled that Sophoulis had denounced the army action as "almost pure fascism." "Memorandum of Conversation"

(December 23, 1947), 868.00/1-348, "Memorandum of Conversation" (December 24, 1947), 868.00/12-3147, and Rankin to Secretary of State, January 8, 1948, 868.00/1-848, SD records; Golden to Charlton Ogburn, December 23, 1947, Box 1, Golden papers; *New York Times*, December 24, 1947.

52. *FR 1949*, 6:444; O'Ballance, *The Greek Civil War*, p. 155; Burton Y. Berry to the Chief of AMAG, October 23, 1948, "891 (Secret)" folder, Athens post records.

53. Xydis, *Greece and the Great Powers*, p. 596; MacVeagh to Secretary of State, August 1, 1945, "871 Confidential" folder, Box 2480, Athens post records; MacVeagh to Secretary of State, July 31, 1946, 868.00/7-3146, SD records. See also "Digest of the Dinner on the Greek Elections in Honor of the Hon. James Grafton Rogers" (May 9, 1946), Records of Meetings, vol. 12, Council on Foreign Relations records.

54. Minutes of the Interim Greece-Turkey Assistance Committee meeting of April 25, 1947, Box 7, SD Committees records; *FR 1947*, 5:216.

55. Carter to Russell, August 4, 1947, 868.00/8-447, Russell to General Hilldring, March 20, 1947, 868.00/3-2047, and Baxter, "Memorandum of Conversation" (December 23, 1948), 868.00/12-2348, SD records; *New York Herald Tribune*, May 2, 1948.

56. Forrestal diaries, July 9, 1947; *FR 1947*, 5:216; Marshall to American embassy, Athens, May 6, 1947, 811.91268/5-647, SD records; Grady to Secretary of State, November 23, 1948 and Marshall to American embassy, Athens, November 24, 1948, "891 Press (Conf)" folder, Athens post records.

57. Rankin, "Memorandum of Conversation" (January 22, 1948), "891 (Secret)" folder, Athens post records; Rankin to Secretary of State, February 18, 1948, 868.00/2-1848 and "Memorandum of Conversation" (February 20, 1948), 868.00/2-2048, SD records.

58. MacVeagh claimed that American correspondents in Greece were "problem children in need of careful nursing." MacVeagh to Secretary of State, August 11, 1947, 811.91268/8-1147, SD records. See also MacVeagh to Secretary of State, July 28, 1947, 868.00/7-2847, SD records.

59. Rankin to Secretary of State, February 18, 1948 and Marshall to American embassy, Athens, February 27, 1948, 868.00/2-1848, SD records.

60. See, for example, Polk, "Greece Puts Us to the Test," pp. 529–36. Journalistic support for the left was largely a figment of the official imagination. A *New York Times* correspondent noted: "Objective American newspaper men are unpopular in the official set. Some Americans who are hardly able to distinguish a Marxist from a macaroon have been startled to discover that in Athens they are labeled Communists." Dana Adams Schmidt, "The Modern Tragedy in Ancient Greece," p. 20. See also Zotos Journal, passim, Zotos papers.

61. Yiannis P. Roubatis and Elias Vlanton, "Who Killed George Polk?" pp. 13–16; *New York Times*, May 1 and September 17, 1977; Matthews, *Memories of a Mountain War*, pp. 184–92.

62. *New York Times*, September 17, 1977; Roubatis and Vlanton, "Who

Killed George Polk?" pp. 16–32; Harrison Salisbury, "On an Unsolved Mystery"; Grady to Secretary of State, July 24, 1948, 868.00/7-2448, SD records. William Polk served on the State Department's Policy Planning Council from 1961 to 1964 and subsequently became president of the Adlai Stevenson Institute of the University of Chicago. Kellis worked as director of the CIA's Operations Division from 1950 to 1954 and later became a business executive. Both continued to insist that the U.S. handling of the Polk case was a travesty of justice. And, in 1977, the Polk case began to unravel. The only individual jailed for the murder charged that he had "confessed" under torture; another individual condemned to death *in absentia* volunteered to return for a new trial; and the only physical evidence was challenged as a fabrication. Roubatis and Vlanton, "Who Killed George Polk?" passim; *New York Times,* January 20 and May 1, 1977.

63. Enclosure in Keeley to Secretary of State, December 2, 1947, 868.00/ 12-247 and Jernegan to Satterthwaite, October 22, 1948, 868.00/10-2248, SD records; McGhee to Carter, February 3, 1948, 72A6248, Lot 54D202, Box 380, Francis H. Russell files, SD records.

64. Meeting of September 9, 1947, FO 371/67046, R12491, FO records; *FR 1947,* 5:448; Rankin to Secretary of State, February 4, 1949, 868.00/2-449, SD records. See also *FR 1948,* 4:177–78; Minor, "Memorandum of Conversation," enclosure in Keeley to Secretary of State, September 16, 1947, 111.75/9-1647, SD records.

65. Acheson to Villard, February 8, 1949, 868.00/12-2148, SD records; Meeting of September 9, 1947, FO 371/67046, R12491, FO records; *FR 1949,* 6:275; Zotos Journal, July 22, 1948, Zotos papers.

66. For some discussion of covert operations, see Damon, "Memorandum of Conversation" (April 12, 1949), 868.00/4-1248, SD records.

67. Grady to State Department, March 10, 1949, 868.00/3-1049 and George W. Edman to Secretary of State, April 2, 1949, 868.00/4-249, SD records; "Greece—Work and Victory Week" folder, Box 1 and Grady, "Adventures in Diplomacy," pp. 213–15, Box 5, Grady papers; *FR 1949,* 6:284. Speeches for the occasion by Acheson and Truman are reprinted in "Work and Victory Demonstration in Greece," p. 433.

68. Woodhouse, *Struggle for Greece,* pp. 208–9; Couloumbis et al., *Foreign Interference,* p. 118; Rankin to Secretary of State, March 10, 1948, 868.00/3-1048 and April 3, 1948, 868.00/4-348, SD records. For Rankin's determination to use the issue for propaganda purposes, see also Rankin to Secretary of State, April 4, 1948, 868.00/4-448, SD records.

69. Griswold to Secretary of State, March 23, 1948, 868.00/3-2348, SD records. For additional evidence of the Greek government's own child abduction program, and of U.S. efforts to limit it, see Baxter, "Memorandum of Conversation" (March 24, 1948), 868.504/3-2448 and Rankin to Secretary of State, April 9, 1948, 868.00/4-948, SD records; "Monthly Report of the Chief of AMAG to the Secretary of State" (April 15, 1948), pp. 3, 62, Box 7, SD Committees records.

70. On April 9, Griswold informed the State Department of AMAG's "belief that relatively few children have in fact been kidnapped by the guerrillas" and that "such children as may have been exhibited in the satellite countries as refugees are children of the guerrillas or their supporters." In August, the State Department reported that "there is inadequate evidence . . . that any substantial number of children were forcibly taken" by the guerrillas. Marshall to American Legation, Bern, April 29, 1948, 868.00/4-2448 and Griswold to Secretary of State, April 9, 1948, 501.BB BALKANS/4-948, SD records; FR 1948, 4:254.

71. See, for example, Matthews, Memories of a Mountain War, pp. 176–82; Carlyle, ed., Documents on International Affairs, pp. 326–29; House Committee on International Relations, Military Assistance Programs, p. 79; Averoff-Tossizza, By Fire and Axe, pp. 261, 269; "Discussion of the Greek Case in the General Assembly," p. 816; FR 1950, 5:413.

72. On November 27, 1948, the U.N. General Assembly adopted a resolution urging that the children be returned from other Balkan states in cases where "their father or mother or . . . their closest relative express a wish to this effect." Although the U.N. estimated that 28,000 children were brought to the Balkan states during the civil war, the International Red Cross reported that, by early 1951, requests for only 10,344 children had been received. The Greek government soon dropped the issue, fearing that the children would return from Eastern Europe as zealous Communists. Sweet-Escott, Greece, p. 71; Woodhouse, Struggle for Greece, p. 249; O'Ballance, The Greek Civil War, p. 169; André Fontaine, History of the Cold War, p. 295.

73. O'Ballance, Greek Civil War, p. 215; Van Fleet, "How We Won in Greece," p. 390; McNeill, Greece, p. 40; Averoff-Tossizza, By Fire and Axe, p. 216; FR 1947, 5:402–3.

74. Rankin to Secretary of State, May 4, 1948, 868.00/5-448, SD records; Sweet-Escott, Greece, p. 72; Matthews, Memories of a Mountain War, pp. 262–63.

75. Grady to Secretary of State, November 5, 1948, 868.00/11-548, SD records; FR 1948, 4:183. For other indications of U.S. support, see U.S. Military Attaché, Athens to Secretary of State, November 4, 1948, 868.00/ 11-448, SD records.

76. FR 1949, 6:388; Acheson to American embassy, Athens and Grady to Secretary of State, August 26, 1949, 868.00/8-2649 and Acheson to American embassy, Athens, September 19, 1949, 868.00/9-649, SD records.

77. FR 1949, 6:424–25, 428; Grady to Secretary of State, September 22, 1949, 868.00/9-2249 and September 28, 1949, 868.00/9-2849, SD records.

78. FR 1949, 6:388, 420. For further evidence that these measures were designed to forestall U.N. action, see Grady to Secretary of State, August 26, 1949, 868.00/8-2649 and Acheson to American embassy, Athens, September 19, 1949, 868.00/9-649, SD records; FR 1949, 6:424–25. Truman, on the other hand, apparently felt a sincere sense of disgust at the Greek

government's policies. According to Acting Secretary of State James Webb, Truman believed "it is necessary for us to restrain the Government and take whatever steps are necessary to prevent the wholesale slaughter of prisoners. . . . He feels that the Greek Government has been unnecessarily brutal in punitive measures and that we have some responsibility to restrain these." Truman made these observations on September 26, however, more than a month after the State Department initiative had begun. *FR 1949*, 6:427–28.

79. *FR 1949*, 6:419–21, 450–51; Cromie to Benjamin Cohen, October 22, 1949, 868.00/10-2249 and Acheson to Certain American Diplomatic and Consular Officers, November 17, 1949, 868.00B/11-1749, SD records.

80. See, for example, *FR 1949*, 6:451–52, 468–69; David K. E. Bruce to Secretary of State, November 9, 1949, 851.00/11-949, SD records.

81. Sulzberger, *A Long Row of Candles*, p. 469; Minor to Secretary of State, December 5, 1949, 868.00/12-549, SD records; Chandler, *The Divided Land*, pp. 204–7. For two very different pictures of life in the postwar detention camps, see Basil Davidson, "Markronessos"; London *Times*, November 17, 1949.

82. House Committee on International Relations, *Military Assistance Programs*, p. 199; R. V. Burks, *The Dynamics of Communism in Eastern Europe*, pp. 22–23; David Horowitz, *The Free World Colossus*, pp. 193–94; Kousoulas, *Revolution and Defeat*, p. 284. One Greek government official has recently claimed that civilians who fled to the north from 1947 to 1949 numbered 76,965. Averoff-Tossizza, *By Fire and Axe*, pp. 351–52.

6. THE ECONOMIC AID PROGRAM

1. Golden to William L. Batt, January 5, 1948, Box 1, Golden papers. At the time, Golden was director of AMAG's Labor Division. His background and activities are discussed in chapter 7.

2. Campbell and Sherrard, *Modern Greece*, p. 299; Wray O. Candilis, *The Economy of Greece*, p. 41; *FR 1947*, 5:17–22; Porter, "Wanted: A Miracle in Greece," p. 106; Porter diary, January 24 and 25, 1947, Porter papers.

3. C. A. Coombs, "The First Annual Program for Greece: Review of OEEC Recommendations," pp. 42–49, "Mission to Greece, General" folder, Box 3, Iverson papers; Rankin to MacVeagh, August 22, 1945, "860-Confidential" folder, Box 2480, Athens post records.

4. Rankin to Secretary of State, June 19, 1946, "851 Financial Conditions" folder and Acheson to American embassy, Athens, August 14, 1946, "850 Economic Matters" folder, Box 2482 Athens post records; Coombs, "The First Annual Program for Greece," pp. 49–57, "Mission to Greece General" folder, Box 3, Iverson papers; Porter diary, January 23, 1947, Porter papers; Acheson, "Memorandom of Conversation" (February 6, 1947), 868.00/2-647, SD records. For additional evidence of U.S. impatience at Greek economic policy, see MacVeagh to Secretary of State, October 26, 1945, "851 Conf." folder, Box 2480, Athens post records; U.S. Depart-

ment of State, "Greece: Policy and Information Statement" (July 15, 1946), pp. 3–4, Byrnes papers; Porter diary, January 20, 22, and 25 and February 6, 8, 17, 20 and 27, 1947, Porter papers.

5. American Economic Mission to Greece, "Summary and Recommendations of the Report" (April 1, 1947), passim, Box 6, SD Committees records; Porter diary, February 27, 1947, Porter papers. A greatly abbreviated version of the report, which lacks the flavor of the original, is found in *FR 1947*, 5:136–37.

6. *FR 1947*, 5:18–22; Porter to Acheson, April 22, 1947, 868.20/4-2247, SD records; Porter diary, January 20 and 26 and February 10, 1947, Porter papers; Yergin, *Shattered Peace*, pp. 287–88.

7. *Report of the British Parliamentary Delegation*, p. 13; Daniell, "Symptom and Tragedy," p. 7; Schmidt, "The Modern Tragedy in Ancient Greece," p. 9; Polk, "Greece Puts Us to the Test," pp. 530–33. See also Allen D. Fields, "Kolonaki and the Others."

8. American Economic Mission to Greece, "Summary and Recommendations of the Report" (April 1, 1947), pp. 13–21, Box 6, SD Committees records; *FR 1947*, 5:222. For the significance to the State Department of Porter's report, see Acheson to Porter, May 3, 1947, "American Economic Mission to Greece—Correspondence and Memoranda (1946–47)" folder, Porter papers.

9. Porter to Secretary of State, March 7, 1947, "American Economic Mission to Greece—Correspondence and Memoranda (1946–47)" folder, Porter papers; British embassy (Washington, D.C.) to Foreign Office, April 11, 1947, FO 371/67119, R5211 and "Final Report of the British Economic Mission to Greece, 10th July 1947," FO 371/67102, R10370, FO records; Stavrianos, *Greece*, p. 186; American Economic Mission to Greece, "Summary and Recommendations of the Report," pp. 23–28, Box 6, SD Committees records.

10. On April 12, 1948, Lovett informed ECA chieftain Paul Hoffman that the U.S. agreements with the Greek government "provide for economic measures and controls by the American Mission considerably beyond those contemplated under the ERP legislation." Another U.S. official recalled that "each major field of aid was the subject of a formal agreement. . . . Specific project agreements were made covering each major item or class of smaller items. . . . These agreements specified objects, intentions, conditions, procedure of administration, and funds required." McNeill, *Greece*, p. 35; *FR 1948*, 4:76; C. A. Munkman, *American Aid to Greece*, p. 72. See also *FR 1948*, 4:202.

11. Coombs, "The First Annual Program for Greece," pp. 57–59, "Mission to Greece, General" folder, Box 3, Iverson papers; Porter, "Wanted: A Miracle in Greece," p. 106; Porter to MacVeagh, March 15, 1947, "American Economic Mission to Greece—Correspondence and Memoranda (1946–47)" folder, Porter papers.

12. Griswold to Secretary of State, September 30, 1947, 868.00/9-3047, SD records; "Monthly Report of the Chief of AMAG to the Secretary of State" (October 15, 1947), Box 7, SD Committees records; Norton to Bevin, November 18, 1947, FO 371/67011, R15294, FO records. In late 1947, Acheson stated bluntly: "It was necessary to interfere in their internal affairs in order to get them straightened out." Yergin, *Shattered Peace*, p. 292.

13. U.S. Department of State, *Second Report to Congress on Assistance to Greece and Turkey: For the Period Ended December 31, 1947*, p. 1; Davies, "The Role of the American Trade Union Representatives" (MS), p. 194; Coombs, "The First Annual Program for Greece," pp. 61–62, "Mission to Greece, General" folder, Box 3, Iverson papers; Horace Smith to Rankin and H. Lawrence Groves, January 29, 1948, "851 AMAG" folder, Box 2486, Athens post records; C. Lloyd Bailey, "Memorandum on Greek-Turkish Aid Program," Box 16, Friends Committee on National Legislation records.

14. Porter diary, January 24, 1947, Porter papers; *Congressional Record Appendix* (April 9, 1949), 95:A2162; "A Factual Summary Concerning the American Mission for Aid to Greece" (June 15, 1948), p. 17 and Coombs, "The First Annual Program for Greece," pp. 58–62, "Mission to Greece, General" folder, Box 3, Iverson papers.

15. Davies, "The Role of the American Trade Union Representatives" (MS), pp. 335–36; Coombs, "The First Annual Program for Greece," p. 63 and "A Factual Summary Concerning the American Mission for Aid to Greece" (June 15, 1948), pp. 17–18, "Mission to Greece, General" folder, Box 3, Iverson papers. For a detailed discussion of U.S. efforts to hold the wage line in Greece, see chapter 7.

16. "Monthly Report of the Chief of AMAG to the Secretary of State" (December 15, 1947), and Eugene Clay, "Report of the Economic Adviser of the American Mission for Aid to Greece on the Economic and Financial Condition of Greece" (December 1, 1947), Box 7, SD Committees records.

17. Clay, "Report of the Economic Adviser of the American Mission for Aid to Greece" (December 1, 1947), Box 7, SD Committees records. For AMAG's undeviating focus upon balancing the budget, see also Griswold to Secretary of State, January 7, 1948, 868.00/1-748 and Griswold to Henderson, April 17, 1948, 868.00/4-1748, SD records; Norton to Bevin, November 18, 1947, FO 371/67011, R15294, FO records; Golden to William L. Batt, January 5, 1948, Box 1, Golden papers.

18. Candilis, *The Economy of Greece*, pp. 74–75; "Monthly Report of the Chief of AMAG to the Secretary of State" (October 15, 1947, November 15, 1947, and April 15, 1948), Box 7, SD Committees records; *FR 1947*, 5:307. The massive nature of the refugee problem is discussed in: Harry N. Howard, "The Refugee Problem in Greece."

19. Michael Mark Amen, *American Foreign Policy in Greece*, p. 116; "Monthly Report of the Chief of AMAG to the Secretary of State" (October 15, 1947 and January 15, 1948), Box 7, SD Committees records; U.S. De-

partment of State, *Fourth Report to Congress on Assistance to Greece and Turkey: For the Period Ended June 30, 1948*, p. 8; Golden to Charles Tyroler, November 2, 1947, Box 2, Golden papers.

20. Clay, "Report of the Economic Adviser of the American Mission for Aid to Greece" (December 1, 1947), Box 7, SD Committees records; Golden to William L. Batt, January 5, 1948, Box 1, Golden papers; Coombs, "The First Annual Program for Greece," p. 60, "Mission to Greece, General" folder, Box 3, Iverson papers.

21. American Economic Mission to Greece, "Summary and Recommendations of the Report" (April 1, 1947), pp. 13–14, Box 6, SD Committees records; *FR 1947*, 5:222; Ickes to McGhee, November 29, 1947, 868.00/11-2947, SD records.

22. In a report written for the Greek government in early 1952, Varvaressos noted: "Our foreign economic advisers, although repeatedly stressing the inadequate participation of the wealthier classes to [alleviating] the tax burden of the country, have paid insufficient attention to the possibilities of increasing receipts from direct taxation and have concentrated most of their efforts on the expansion of revenues from indirect taxation." Clay, "Report of the Economic Adviser of the American Mission for Aid to Greece" (December 1, 1947), Box 7, SD Committees records; Coombs, "The Greek Problem," enclosure in E. T. Dickinson, Jr. to John Nuveen, December 20, 1948, "800 Greece-Secret" folder, Box 2485, Athens post records; Kyriakos Varvaressos, *Report on the Greek Economic Problem*, p. 63.

23. "The fiscal policy of the country," noted Varvaressos, "consists in imposing practically the whole burden of taxation on the poorer classes." He estimated that the effective rate of taxation on the incomes of the business and professional classes averaged only 4.2 percent. Coombs, "The First Annual Program for Greece," p. 68, "Mission to Greece, General" folder, Box 3, Iverson papers; Clay, "Report of the Economic Adviser of the American Mission for Aid to Greece" (December 1, 1947), Box 7, SD Committees records; John Coppock to anonymous, January 8, 1949, enclosure in Walter Salant to Paul A. Porter, February 21, 1949, "American Economic Mission to Greece—Correspondence and Memoranda (1949–71)" folder, Porter papers; Varvaressos, *Report on the Greek Economic Problem*, pp. 54, 62.

24. U.S. Department of State, *Fourth Report to Congress on Assistance to Greece and Turkey*, p. 8; Smith, *The State of Europe*, p. 227; Sweet-Escott, *Greece*, p. 160; McNeill, *The Greek Dilemma*, p. 228; Candilis, *The Economy of Greece*, p. 75; Munkman, *American Aid to Greece*, p. 70; Varvaressos, *Report on the Greek Economic Problem*, pp. 42, 50–51.

25. "Memorandum of Conversation" (October 23, 1947), "Sept., 1947" folder, "P" Project records; Polk, "Greece Puts Us to the Test," p. 533; Seton-Watson, *The East European Revolution*, p. 334; Sweet-Escott,

Greece, p. 151; Amen, *American Foreign Policy in Greece*, p. 120; Harry Vaughan to Stanley Woodward, December 3, 1948, Confidential File, Truman papers.

26. See, for example, Keeley to Secretary of State, November 11, 1947, 868.00/11-1147, SD records; Coombs, "The Greek Problem," enclosure in Dickinson to Nuveen, December 20, 1948, "800 Greece-Secret" folder, Box 2485, Athens post records.

27. Candilis, *The Economy of Greece*, pp. 76, 78; *FR 1947*, 5:481; Ness to Porter, February 13, 1947, and Clayton and Ness to Porter, February 13, 1947 and February 26, 1947, "American Economic Mission to Greece—Correspondence and Memoranda (1946–47)" folder, Porter papers; Eugene Clay, "Background Report," Box 5 and Clay, "Report of the Economic Adviser of the American Mission for Aid to Greece" (December 1, 1947) and "Monthly Report of the Chief of AMAG to the Secretary of State" (March 15, 1948), Box 7, SD Committees records; Griswold to Secretary of State, January 21, 1948, 868.5151/1-2148, SD records; U.S. Department of State, *Third Report to Congress on Assistance to Greece and Turkey: For the Period Ended March 31, 1948*, pp. 7–10.

28. For a detailed discussion of banking and credit issues in Greece, see Paul Atkins, "Notes on the Activities of Paul M. Atkins as Banking and Foreign Exchange Specialist of the American Mission for Aid to Greece, July 21 to December 13, 1947," Box 10, Atkins papers.

29. "Monthly Report of the Chief of AMAG to the Secretary of State" (December 15, 1947 and January 15, 1948), Box 7, SD Committees records; Rankin to Secretary of State, February 5, 1948, 868.00/2-548, SD records. For somewhat different figures, but a similar trend, see Dimitrios Delivanis and William Cleveland, *Greek Monetary Developments*, pp. 192, 195.

30. A Factual Summary Concerning the American Mission for Aid to Greece" (June 15, 1948), p. 18 and Coombs, "The First Annual Program for Greece," p. 75, "Mission to Greece, General" folder, Box 3, Iverson papers; "Monthly Report of the Chief of AMAG to the Secretary of State" (June 15, 1948), Box 7, SD Committees records; U.S. Department of State, *Fourth Report to Congress on Assistance to Greece and Turkey*, p. 1.

31. Coombs, "The First Annual Program for Greece," pp. 80–81, "Mission to Greece, General" folder, Box 3, Iverson papers.

32. Clay, "Report of the Economic Adviser of the American Mission for Aid to Greece" (December 1, 1947), Box 7, SD Committees records; Griswold to Secretary of State, January 7, 1948, 868.00/1-748, January 14, 1948, 868.00/1-1448 and February 4, 1948, 868.00/2-448, SD records. Uncertain of American funding, Porter had also favored eliminating the milk program, although he conceded that it was "one of UNRRA's most successful activities" and expressed his hope that "the Greek Government would find ways and means of continuing this program with such private help as might be forthcoming." Porter diary, February 3, 4, and 8, 1947, Porter papers.

33. Coombs, "The First Annual Program for Greece," pp. 81–82, "Mission to Greece, General" folder, Box 3, Iverson papers; FR 1948, 4:68–70; FR 1948, 3:434.

34. Coombs, "The First Annual Program for Greece," pp. 75, 81, 89, "Mission to Greece, General" folder, Box 3, Iverson papers; Coombs, "The Greek Problem," enclosure in Dickinson to Nuveen, December 20, 1948, "800 Greece-Secret" folder, Box 2485, Athens post records; Davies, "The Role of the American Trade Union Representatives" (MS), pp. 28–29.

35. Clay, "Background Report," Box 5, SD Committees records; Weekly Report of the American Mission for Aid to Greece (October 29, 1947), 868.00/10-3047, SD records; Norton to Bevin, November 18, 1947, FO 371/67011, R15294, FO records.

36. Stavrianos, Greece, p. 212; Sweet-Escott, Greece, pp. 145, 184; Munkman, American Aid to Greece, pp. 50, 58; Seton-Watson, The East European Revolution, p. 334; "Monthly Report of the Chief of AMAG to the Secretary of State" (May 15, 1948), Box 7, SD Committees records; Coombs, "The Greek Problem," enclosure in Dickinson to Nuveen, December 20, 1948, "800 Greece" folder, Box 2485, Athens post records.

37. Before World War II, American products constituted 7.6 percent of Greece's imports. Department of State, "Memorandum of the Press and Radio News Conference, Friday, January 25, 1946," Folder 556, Byrnes papers; Anonymous to MacVeagh, December 13, 1946, 711.682/12-1346, Lampton Berry to R. G. Barnes, August 10, 1948, 711.68/7-3048, Jack K. McFall to Secretary of State, May 14, 1949, 711.682/5-1449 and Winthrop G. Brown to Grady, June 20, 1949, 711.682/5-1449, SD records; Sweet-Escott, Greece, p. 149; Amen, American Foreign Policy in Greece, p. 176.

38. Clay, "Background Report," Box 5, SD Committees records; Coombs, "The First Annual Program for Greece," p. 74, "Mission to Greece, General" folder, Box 3, Iverson papers; Munkman, American Aid to Greece, pp. 58–61.

39. Seton-Watson, The East European Revolution, p. 332; Alexander Kendrick, "Greece's Ultimate Solution," p. 15; Mark Gayn, "Democracy's Distant Cousin," p. 16; Chandler, The Divided Land, p. 208; Candilis, The Economy of Greece, p. 44; "A Factual Summary Concerning the American Mission for Aid to Greece" (June 15, 1948), p. 4, "Mission to Greece, General" folder, Box 3, Iverson papers; Varvaressos, Report on the Greek Economic Problem, p. 17.

40. "A Factual Summary Concerning the American Mission for Aid to Greece" (June 15, 1948), pp. 6–10, 14–15, "Mission to Greece, General" folder, Box 3, Iverson papers; "U.S. Completes Reconstruction of Greek Transportation System"; Munkman, American Aid to Greece, pp. 57, 175, 199–200; Stavrianos, Greece, p. 192; U.S. Department of State, First Report to Congress on Assistance to Greece and Turkey, p. 3 and Fourth Report to Congress on Assistance to Greece and Turkey, pp. 13–18.

41. Economic Cooperation Administration, Eleventh Report to Congress

of the Economic Cooperation Administration: For the Quarter Ended December 31, 1950, p. 10; Candilis, The Economy of Greece, p. 66; McNeill, Greece, p. 54.

42. By June 30, 1951, when Greece's industrial productivity index reached 130, this remained the poorest recovery of any ECA nation with the exception of West Germany. Economic Cooperation Administration, Third Report to Congress of the Economic Cooperation Administration: For the Quarter Ended December 31, 1948, p. 126; Economic Cooperation Administration, Seventh Report to Congress of the Economic Cooperation Administration: For the Quarter Ended December 31, 1949, p. 19; Munkman, American Aid to Greece, p. 70; Economic Cooperation Administration, Thirteenth Report to Congress of the Economic Cooperation Administration: For the Quarter Ended June 30, 1951, p. 17.

43. Committee for Economic Development, Economic Development Issues: Greece, Israel, Taiwan, Thailand, p. 33; McNeill, Greece, p. 40; Douglas Flood to Secretary of State, October 18, 1949, 868.00/10-1849, SD records.

44. According to a leading study of the Marshall Plan, the standard of living of Greek workers remained "dangerously low" at the end of 1950. "It was clear that the benefits of increased economic activity did not automatically 'trickle down' to wage earners and farmers—especially in countries where free labor movements were weak and where economic stratification was reinforced by fiscal policies, legislation, and custom." In 1952, Varvaressos reported to the Greek government that, if the increase in industrial production "had improved the general standard of living, the poorer classes would not be worse off today than they were before the war." He argued that "the striking inequalities which prevail in the distribution of income . . . are not seriously denied by anyone." Candilis, The Economy of Greece, p. 80; Munkman, American Aid to Greece, pp. 49, 52; New York Times, January 18, 1949; Sulzberger, A Long Row of Candles, p. 501; Harry B. Price, The Marshall Plan and Its Meaning, pp. 141–42; Varvaressos, Report on the Greek Economic Problem, pp. 43, 157.

45. American Economic Mission to Greece, "Summary and Recommendations of the Report" (April 1, 1947), pp. 18–21, Box 6, SD Committees records; Marshall to Bowles, July 15, 1947, Box 41, Bowles papers; Golden to William L. Batt, January 5, 1948, Box 1, Golden papers; Davies, "The Role of the American Trade Union Representatives" (MS), p. 27.

46. Horace C. Smith to Rankin and H. Lawrence Groves, January 29, 1948, "851 AMAG" folder, Box 2486, Athens post records.

47. Once ECA arrived in Greece, a U.S. official recalled, "the Mission became slanted toward recovery and development. Mission personnel were impatient that so little was being done toward Marshall Plan objectives. They believed that work toward them could be carried forward in spite of chaotic conditions and that constructive work would help build Greek morale and be a factor in winning the war." Candilis, The Economy of

Greece, p. 43; Lovett to Hoffman, October 6, 1948, 840.50 RECOVERY/
10-648, Howard Bruce to Lovett, October 15, 1948, 840.50 RECOVERY/
10-1548, and Lovett to American Embassy, Athens, October 23, 1948,
868.00/10-2348, SD records; Francis F. Lincoln, *United States' Aid to
Greece*, p. 86.

48. By the end of 1949, only two industrial projects, totaling $10.5 mil-
lion, had been approved in Greece by ECA and funds had been neither
expended nor even authorized for them. Committee for Economic Development, *Economic Development Issues*, pp. 70–71; Candilis, *The Economy of Greece*, pp. 44, 52–53; McNeill, *Greece*, pp. 47–48; Rountree to
McGhee, January 14, 1949, "Greece—Correspondence, 1946–1951" folder,
Box 3, Grady papers; John Coppock to anonymous, January 8, 1949, enclosure in Walter Salant to Paul A. Porter, February 21, 1949, "American
Economic Mission to Greece—Correspondence and Memoranda (1949–71)"
folder, Porter papers; Amen, *American Foreign Policy in Greece*, pp. 161,
163.

49. McGhee to Lovett, November 9, 1948, 868.00/7-948, SD records;
Acheson to Grady, February 8, 1949, Grady to Acheson, February 11, 1949
and Grady, "Memorandum for Burton Berry" (n.d.), "Greece—Correspondence, 1946–1951" folder, Box 3 and Grady, "Memorandum" (March
31, 1949), Box 1, Grady papers.

50. The U.S. government ultimately approved an electric power program
for Greece; however, it was a much smaller one than originally proposed,
with its general managers drawn from the American corporation. Cromie,
"Memorandum of Conversation" (August 4, 1949), 868.6463/8-449, SD records; Lincoln, *United States' Aid to Greece*, pp. 91, 113–14. For other
evidence of U.S. government concern about Greece's "overpopulation,"
see *FR 1949*, 6:270.

51. Cromie, "Memorandum of Conversation" (August 12, 1949), 868.50/
8-1249, SD records; McNeill, *Greece*, pp. 47–48; Candilis, *The Economy of
Greece*, p. 81. For additional objections to an economic development pro-
gram, even within ECA, see Coombs, "The Greek Problem," enclosure in
Dickinson to Nuveen, December 20, 1948, "800 Greece" folder, Box 2485,
Athens post records.

52. The proposal for an electric power program, it should be noted,
suggested public ownership, and this feature attracted considerable criticism from some American officials. According to one member of the U.S.
aid program, they "believed that with so much United States aid going to
Greece an American utility company should own and operate the power
system." Ultimately, however, when the system was built, it was on a
publicly owned basis, in accordance with the desire of the Greek government. Jernegan to McGhee, September 15, 1949, 868.002/9-1549, SD records; Grady to Herbert Elliston, December 30, 1949, "E-Misc" folder, Box
1, Grady papers; Lincoln, *United States' Aid to Greece*, p. 91.

53. Porter, "Wanted: A Miracle in Greece," p. 14; Clay, "Background

Report," Box 5, SD Committees records; Griswold to Secretary of State, November 15, 1947 and Lovett to American embassy, Athens, November 19, 1947, 868.00/11-1547, SD records.

54. FR 1948, 4:26–28. See also U.S. Department of State, Second Report to Congress on Assistance to Greece and Turkey, pp. 11–12.

55. From the spring of 1947 to June 1948, the reconstruction and agricultural program allocations were cut by more than half, the public health program allocation was cut by nearly half, and the training program approached abolition. Only the military and consumer import programs grew. U.S. Department of State, Second Report to Congress on Assistance to Greece and Turkey, p. 8; FR 1948, 4:76–77; FR 1949, 6:272–73; Amen, American Foreign Policy in Greece, p. 135.

56. Candilis, The Economy of Greece, p. 67; U.S. Department of State, Fifth Report to Congress on Assistance to Greece and Turkey: For the Period Ended September 30, 1948, pp. 8–9; C.V.R.S. to General Wedemeyer, October 22, 1948, P & O 091 Greece, Section X, P & O Division, Army General Staff records.

57. Discussing ECA, one U.S. aid official recalled: "Circumstances forced it, as they had forced AMAG, to give priority to the support of the military, though the real purpose of the Marshall Plan was reconstruction." Coombs, "The Greek Problem," enclosure in Dickinson to Nuveen, December 20, 1948, "800 Greece" folder, Box 2485, Athens post records; House Committee on International Relations, Military Assistance Programs, p. 81; Lincoln, United States' Aid to Greece, p. 66. See also Coombs, "The First Annual Program for Greece," p. 2, "Mission to Greece, General" folder, Box 3, Iverson papers.

58. Discussing these items, Coombs acknowledged that the guerrilla war was a "major rathole." Coombs, "The Greek Problem," enclosure in Dickinson to Nuveen, December 20, 1948, "800 Greece" folder, Box 2485, Athens post records.

59. Averoff-Tossizza, By Fire and Axe, pp. 3, 356; FR 1949, 6:242; McNeill, Greece, pp. 45–46.

60. Grady to Hoffman, November 7, 1949, "Appointment—Ambassador to Greece" folder and Grady to Burton Berry, November 9, 1949, "B-Miscellaneous" folder, Box 1, Grady papers.

61. House Committee on International Relations, Military Assistance Programs, p. 190; "Text of Ambassador Grady's Talk Before Propeller Club" (January 26, 1950), "Press Releases and Clippings" folder, Box 4, Grady papers. For similar figures and optimism on the results of the U.S. aid program, see Harold F. Alderfer, "Greece and the West Today" (April 1951), "Mission to Greece, General" folder, Box 3, Iverson papers.

62. Xydis, Greece and the Great Powers, p. 533; Munkman, American Aid to Greece, p. vii.

63. Evaluating the situation some three decades later, McNeill wrote: "Greece was as impoverished in 1949 as it had been in 1944. Ports and

roads had been built; otherwise, long-range productive investment had been postponed. Economic aid had mainly gone into feeding the refugees and meeting the budget deficits." Woodhouse, *Struggle for Greece*, p. 266; John W. Gunter, "Economic Principles of Greek Reconstruction and Development" (November 23, 1949), "Mission to Greece, General" folder, Box 3, Iverson papers; House Committee on International Relations, *Military Assistance Programs*, pp. 190, 194; Sweet-Escott, *Greece*, p. 162; William H. McNeill, *The Metamorphosis of Greece Since World War II*, p. 90.

64. Although American officials conceded, secretly, that they had not been particularly effective as reformers, Greek observers were considerably more caustic. A U.S. National Security Council staff study concluded in early 1951: "Efforts of the United States to promote enactment and implementation of legislation designed to distribute equitably the incidence of taxation, to improve the efficiency of Greek fiscal and administrative procedures, and to free the Greek economy from monopolistic and stultifying practices have been only partially successful." The following year, Varvaressos was considerably sharper in his report to the Greek government: "One of the most discouraging phenomena of the last five years has been the unwillingness of the State to make use of the many and effective means at its disposal in order to force businessmen to comply with the laws and with the essential requirements of society, and the wholly erroneous impression which it has given that it is powerless in the face of the immunity which these persons enjoy." Minor to Secretary of State, April 20, 1949, 868.00/4-2049, SD records; NSC 103, NSC records; Varvaressos, *Report on the Greek Economic Problem*, p. 105.

7. TAMING THE GREEK LABOR MOVEMENT

1. Keeley to Secretary of State, April 26, 1947, 868.5043/4-2647, SD records. As Counselor of the U.S. Embassy in Athens, Keeley was then directing it in the absence of MacVeagh and Rankin.

2. Minutes of the Interim Greece-Turkey Assistance Committee meeting of April 23, 1947, Box 7, SD Committees records; *FR 1947*, 5:223–24.

3. Godson, *American Labor and European Politics*, pp. 36–41, 66–70, 105–6; Philip Taft, *Defending Freedom*, pp. 68–70.

4. For a balanced history of the Greek labor movement through the mid-1940s, see Jecchinis, *Trade Unionism in Greece*, pp. 11–57. A Greek trade unionist, Jecchinis subsequently served as an employee of ECA in Greece.

5. *Ibid.*, pp. 62–66, 78, 89; Woodhouse, *Apple of Discord*, pp. 32–33; Woodhouse, *Struggle for Greece*, pp. 115, 149, 152–53; OSS Dispatch of June 14, 1945 from Athens, Box 2, R & A Branch, Records Relating to the Cairo Outpost, OSS records; Rountree to Porter, February 7, 1947, "American Economic Mission to Greece—Correspondence and Memoranda (1946–47)" folder, Porter papers; Seton-Watson, *The East European Revolution*, p. 333.

6. International Labour Office, *Labour Problems in Greece*, pp. 225–28,

234–47; Jecchinis, *Trade Unionism in Greece*, pp. 78–87, 93–95, 100–2; Woodhouse, *Apple of Discord*, p. 269; Woodhouse, *Struggle for Greece*, pp. 177–78; Rankin to Secretary of State, March 3, 1946, 868.00/3-346, SD records. For detailed information on government and business funding of Makris, see E. Peck to W. J. Hull, October 22, 1946, FO 371/58713, R15893, FO records; Davies, "The Role of the American Trade Union Representatives" (MS), p. 254. Almost all contemporary observers, including the Americans, described Makris and his allies as right-wing. Those labor leaders called centrists were often moderate Socialists or Liberals, while those characterized as leftists were either KKE members or other types of Marxists and Marxist-Leninists.

7. M. S. Williams to A. J. D. Winnifrith, April 11, 1947, FO 371/67057, R3901, FO records; Samuel Berger, "Report on the Greek Trade Union Problem" (July 24, 1947), "850.4" folder, Box 2484, Athens post records; Holland to Reams, May 28, 1947, 868.504/5-2847, SD records; ILO, *Labour Problems in Greece*, pp. 248–50; Jecchinis, *Trade Unionism in Greece*, pp. 102–3. Although Stratis and Kalomiris served on the ERGAS-dominated GSEE executive in 1946, neither was affiliated with ERGAS and neither supported the Communist-led guerrilla war. Labelling Theos "a Moscow trained Communist" and Makris a "stooge [of the] industrialists," MacVeagh characterized Kalomiris and Stratis as "moderate" and "probably most representative [of the] better labor elements." MacVeagh to Secretary of State, October 9, 1945, 868.5043/10-945, SD records. See also Kalomiris to Bevin, May 15, 1946, FO 371/58693, R7926, FO records.

8. Godson, *American Labor and European Politics*, pp. 7, 36–41; Ronald Radosh, *American Labor and United States Foreign Policy*, pp. 307–10; Victor Reuther, *The Brothers Reuther*, p. 423; Peter Weiler, "The United States, International Labor, and the Cold War," pp. 1–7. The CIO and the TUC, which played a major role in founding the WFTU in 1945, withdrew from it in 1949.

9. For the general agreement between the State Department and American leaders, particularly from the AFL, upon the necessity of an anti-Communist program in Greece, see Michael Ross to Philip Murray, March 20, 1947, Box 8, Golden papers. The State Department's hostility to the WFTU is reported in John Henniker to M. S. Williams, April 23, 1947, FO 371/67058, R5704, FO records.

10. According to MacVeagh, Brown departed from Athens on March 5, ten days after he arrived. MacVeagh to Secretary of State, March 5, 1947, 868.5043/3–447, SD records.

11. Holland to Reams, May 28, 1947, 868.504/5-2847, SD records; Irving Brown, "Report and Recommendations on the Crisis in Greece" (n.d.), Brown papers. A slightly different version of the same report in enclosed in George M. Abbott to Keeley, April 1, 1947, "850.4" folder, Box 2484, Athens post records.

12. Samuel Berger, "Report on the Greek Trade Union Problem" (July

24, 1947), "850.4" folder, Box 2484, Athens post records; Keeley to Secretary of State, April 2, 1947, 868.5043/4-247, SD records.

13. Baxter, "Memorandum of Conversation" (April 7, 1947), 868.5043/4-747, SD records; Inverchapel to Foreign Office, April 9, 1947, FO 371/67057, R4829, FO records; Lewis Douglas to Secretary of State, April 8, 1947, 868.5043/4–847 and April 9, 1947, 868.5043/4–947, and Keeley to Secretary of State, April 10, 1947, 868.00/4-1047, SD records.

14. Minute by D. J. McCarthy of May 7, 1947, FO 371/67058, R5899, FO records; Baxter, "Memorandum of Conversation" (April 7, 1947), 868.5043/4-747, SD records.

15. Douglas to Secretary of State, April 8, 1947, 868.5043/4-847 and April 9, 1947, 868.5043/4-947, SD records; Sargent to British embassy (Athens), April 11, 1947, FO 371/67057, R4829, FO records.

16. Sargent to British embassy (Athens), April 11, 1947, FO 371/67057, R4829, FO records; Acheson to American embassy (Athens), April 11, 1947, 868.504/4-497 and Acheson to American embassy (Moscow), April 11, 1947, 868.504/4-1147, SD records. For the actual message to the Greek government, delivered on April 12, 1947, see the enclosure with American embassy (Athens) to Secretary of State, May 9, 1947, 868.504/5-947, SD records.

17. Keeley to Secretary of State, April 18, 1947, 868.00/4-1847 and Acheson to Berger, April 16, 1947, 868.5043/4-1647, SD records. Before leaving for Greece, Berger conferred extensively with Foreign Office and TUC officials and read Brown's report and British correspondence on the subject. He remained in Greece from April 21 to June 2. Berger, "Report on the Greek Trade Union Problem" (July 24, 1947), "850.4" folder, Box 2484, Athens post records.

18. Reilly to Sargent, April 16, 1947, FO 371/67057, R5292 and April 17, 1947, FO 371/67057, R5521 and Reilly to Warner, April 17, 1947, FO 371/67057, R5590, FO records.

19. Norton to Foreign Office, April 25, 1947, FO 371/67057, R5673, FO records; Berger, "Report on the Greek Trade Union Problem" (July 24, 1947), "850.4" folder, Box 2484, Athens post records.

20. Norton to Foreign Office, May 1, 1947, FO 371/67058, R5893, "Greek Trade Union Question—21st April to 3rd May, 1947," FO 371/67058, R6378, Norton to Foreign Office, May 4, 1947, FO 371/67058, R6053, FO records. By May 1, however, the U.S. embassy had softened its terms somewhat to a GSEE provisional executive in which "the Communists should be placed in absolute minority with an overwhelming majority of non-Communists opposed to them." Norton to Foreign Office, May 2, 1947, FO 371/67058, R6052, FO records.

21. Bevin wrote that the "intervention by U.S.A. on this matter may well cause an explosion in the House and damage the whole U.S.-U.K. relations. . . . I cannot see why we should be treated like this after handling Greece all this time." Undated minute (probably May 2, 1947) by Ernest Bevin, FO 371/67058, R6317, FO records.

22. Bevin to Inverchapel, May 5, 1947, 868.5043/5-547 and Inverchapel to Marshall, May 6, 1947, 868.5043/5-647, SD records; Bevin to Inverchapel, May 6, 1947, FO 371/67058, R6085, FO records.

23. Inverchapel to Foreign Office, May 16, 1947, FO 371/67059, R6715, FO records; Marshall to American embassy (Athens), May 21, 1947, 868.5043/5-647 and June 3, 1947, 868.5043/5-2247, SD records.

24. MacVeagh to Secretary of State, May 12, 1947, 868.5043/5-1247 and May 14, 1947, 868.5043/5-1447, and Achilles to Secretary of State, May 17, 1947, 868.5043/5-1747, SD records; Inverchapel to Foreign Office, May 13, 1947 and Hector McNeil to Tewson, May 19, 1947, FO 371/67058, R6404, FO records.

25. Minutes by M. S. Williams of May 16 and 19, 1947, and by C. F. A. Warner of May 19, 1947, FO 371/67058, R6404, Foreign Office to British embassy (Athens), May 22, 1947, FO 371/67059, R6690, W. H. Braine to G. Myrrdin-Evans, June 1, 1947, FO 371/67060, R7854, FO records; Berger, "Report on the Greek Trade Union Problem" (July 24, 1947), "850.4" folder, Box 2484, Athens post records.

26. Norton to Foreign Office, June 6, 1947, FO 371/67059, R7675, FO records; Berger, "Report on the Greek Trade Union Problem" (July 24, 1947), "850.4" folder, Box 2484, Athens post records. The facade of 7-7-7 division was maintained by giving Makris and his right-wing allies 4 of the 7 center seats. Smith Simpson, "Developments in the Greek Trade Union Movement" (October 7, 1947), "Sept. 1947" folder, "P" Project records; D. Alan Strachan to Victor Reuther, February 25, 1949, Box 36, Cope papers.

27. MacVeagh to Secretary of State, June 5, 1947, 868.5043/6-547, June 7, 1947, 868.5043/6-747, June 12, 1947, 868.00/6-1247, SD records; Norton to Foreign Office, June 4, 1947, FO 371/67059, R7533 and Bevin to Norton, June 4, 1947, FO 371/67059, R7570, FO records; James Carey to Cope, n.d., Box 17, Cope papers; Sweet-Escott, *Greece*, p. 141.

28. Reilly to Foreign Office, July 11, 1947, and Hector McNeil to Tewson, July 18, 1947, FO 371/67060, R9486, FO records.

29. As late as mid-August 1947, they were still pressing Tsaldaris to release leftist trade union leaders and to implement the most recent agreement. See, for example, "Notes for Conversation with Monsieur Tsaldaris" (August 16, 1947), FO 371/67145, R11452, FO records.

30. Reilly to Foreign Office, July 11, 1947, FO 371/67060, R9486 and Southern Department to Chancery (Athens), October 31, 1947, FO 371/67061, R13515, FO records; Berger, "Report on the Greek Trade Union Problem" (July 24, 1947), "850.4" folder, Box 2484, Athens post records; Keeley to Secretary of State, October 10, 1947, 868.504/10-1047, SD records.

31. Keeley to Secretary of State, April 18, 1947, 868.00/4-1847 and April 26, 1947, 868.5043/4-2647, SD records.

32. MacVeagh to Secretary of State, June 6, 1947, 868.00/6-647 and June 7, 1947, 868.5043/6-747, and Caffery to Secretary of State, June 23, 1947, 868.504/6-2347, SD records; Taft, *Defending Freedom*, pp. 172–73; Irving

Brown, "Confidential Report on Greece, France, and England" (July 7, 1947), Box 17, Thorne papers.

33. Marshall to Caffery, July 2, 1947, 868.504/6-2347, SD records; "Summary of the International Activities of the Department of Labor, Fiscal 1947," Box 355, Labor Department records; Davies, "The Role of the American Trade Union Representatives" (MS), pp. 22–24, 203–14; Michael Ross to Philip Murray, March 20, 1947, Box 8, Golden papers. For a detailed examination of Golden's views, as well as copies of some of the Golden letters cited elsewhere, see Thomas R. Brooks, *Clint*, passim.

34. Jecchinis, *Trade Unionism in Greece*, pp. 110–11; Chancery to Southern Department, September 26, 1947, FO 371/67061, R13515, FO records; Smith Simpson, "Developments in the Greek Trade Union Movement" (October 7, 1947), "Sept. 1947" folder, Box 2139, "P" Project records. Strachan later wrote: "The Communists were purged from the trade unions and labor centers in not too ceremonious a fashion I suspect. It would be my judgment that some Left-wingers suffered in this purge. Unfortunately, many of the Left-wingers, although not Communists, had been associated with them so closely that it was hard to distinguish them from party members. Although I do not condone such measures, I realize that when feelings run high, as they certainly did in this case, there is no middle course. The result is frequently one which cannot stand the scrutiny of close observation. This is exactly what happened in the Greek trade union movement." Strachan to Victor Reuther, February 25, 1949, Box 36, Cope papers.

35. MacVeagh to Secretary of State, August 27, 1947, 868.00/8-2747, Rankin to Secretary of State, December 29, 1947, 868.5043/12-2947, and Keeley to Secretary of State, October 16, 1947, 868.5045/10-1647, SD records; Davies, "The Role of the American Trade Union Representatives" (MS), p. 395.

36. ILO, *Labour Problems in Greece*, pp. 261–62; Tewson to Bevin, December 15, 1947, FO 371/67061, R17041, FO records.

37. See, for example, Keeley to Secretary of State, October 10, 1947, 868.504/10-1047 and 868.5043/10-1047, SD records.

38. Smith Simpson, "Developments in the Greek Trade Union Movement" (October 7, 1947) and Smith Simpson, "Confidential Biographic Data on John Patsantzis" (June 1947), "P" Project records; Irving Brown, "Report to International Labor Committee" (November 10, 1947), Box 17, Thorne papers; Davies, "The Role of the American Trade Union Representatives" (MS), p. 359. The British embassy took an even more mordant view of the Greece's non-Communist labor officials: "Most of the 'leaders of standing' are not reputable trade union leaders at all. They are political cheap-jacks, who exploit the working classes of Greece for personal, political, and financial gain." Chancery to Southern Department, September 26, 1947, FO 371/67061, R13515, FO records.

39. *Report of the British Parliamentary Delegation*, p. 12; Minutes of the Interim Greece-Turkey Assistance Committee meeting of April 25, 1947,

Box 7, SD Committees records; MacVeagh to Secretary of State, July 3, 1947, 868.5043/7-347, SD records; Davies, "The Role of the American Trade Union Representatives" (MS), pp. 25-26.

40. Golden to David A. Morse, November 19, 1947 and Golden to Meyer Bernstein, October 28, 1947, Box 1, Golden papers; Jecchinis, *Trade Unionism in Greece*, p. 113; Clay, "Report of the Economic Adviser of AMAG" (December 1, 1947), Box 7, SD Committees records. Both Golden and the ILO later observed that the small wage gains made under the agreement were quickly nullified by rising prices. Golden to Marion Hedges, January 23, 1948, Box 1, Golden papers; ILO, *Labour Problems in Greece*, p. 45.

41. Golden to Meyer Bernstein, November 9, 1947 and Golden to David A. Morse, November 19, 1947, Box 1, Golden papers; Davies, "The Role of the American Trade Union Representatives" (MS) pp. 358–61; Jecchinis, *Trade Unionism in Greece*, p. 114; Keeley to Secretary of State, November 11, 1947, 868.00/11-1147, SD records.

42. Keeley to Secretary of State, November 11, 1947, 868.00/11-1147 and Marshall to U.S. embassy (Athens), November 14, 1947, 868.5043/11-1047, SD records.

43. Smith Simpson, "Memorandum of Conversation" (November 12, 1947), 868.5043/11-2647, SD records; Davies, "The Role of the American Trade Union Representatives" (MS), pp. 361-62; Norton to Foreign Office, November 15, 1947, FO 371/67061, R15220, FO records; Golden to Morse, November 19, 1947, Box 1, Golden papers.

44. Keeley to Secretary of State, November 18, 1947, 868.5045/11-1847, November 20, 1947, 868.5045/11-2047 and December 8, 1947, 868.00/12-847, SD records.

45. The role of Griswold's Special Assistant has been documented by Margaret Mary Davies, who worked at the time in AMAG's labor division and later conducted a series of interviews on the subject for her doctoral dissertation. Davies, "The Role of the American Trade Union Representatives" (MS), pp. 366–73. Although Davies declines to name the individual, scattered evidence and the process of elimination point to the conclusion that it was probably Geoffrey May. See, for example, Golden to Meyer Bernstein, December 21, 1947, Box 1, Golden papers; Golden to David Morse, December 16, 1947, 868.00/12-2347, SD records; Brooks, *Clint*, pp. 289–90.

46. Keeley to Secretary of State, December 10, 1947, 868.5045/12-1047, SD records; Golden to Charlton Ogburn, December 23, 1947, Box 1 and Golden to Joseph Scanlon, January 29, 1948, Box 9, Golden papers; Davies, "The Role of the American Trade Union Representatives" (MS), p. 379.

47. "Monthly Report of the Chief of AMAG to the Secretary of State" (December 15, 1947), Box 7, SD Committees records; Rankin to Secretary of State, December 23, 1947, 868.5045/12-2347, SD records.

48. Golden to David A. Morse, December 26, 1947, Box 11 and Golden to Charlton Ogburn, December 23, 1947, Box 1, Golden papers. See also

Dora Golden to Meyer Bernstein, December 19 and 23, 1947, Box 1, Golden papers.

49. Golden to Philip M. Kaiser, December 7, 1947, Box 11, Golden papers. See also Golden to Joseph Scanlon, January 29, 1948, Box 9 and Golden to Meyer Bernstein, December 21, 1947, Box 1, Golden papers.

50. Davies, "The Role of the American Trade Union Representatives" (MS), pp. 380–82; Golden to Joseph Scanlon, January 29, 1948, Box 9, Golden papers; Golden to Griswold, December 16, 1947, 868.00/12-2347, SD records; Strachan to Victor Reuther, February 25, 1949, Box 36, Cope papers. Among the protest letters written at the time, see Matthew Woll to Sophoulis, December 16, 1947 and Woll to Golden and Lovett, n.d., 868.504/12-1647, SD records.

51. Golden to Morse, December 16, 1947, 868.00/12-2347, SD records.

52. Lovett to Griswold, December 23, 1947, 868.5045/12-1949, Griswold, "Memorandum of Conversation" (December 23, 1947), 868.00/1-348, and "Memorandum of Conversation" (December 24, 1947), 868.00/12-3147, SD records; Golden to Morse, December 26, 1947, Box 11, Golden papers.

53. Golden to Morse, December 29, 1947, Box 11, Golden papers; Marshall to American embassy (Athens), January 30, 1948, 868.5045/1-2648, SD records.

54. Murray's statement was in the form of a letter to Marshall of January 29, 1948, which he released to the press the following day. Philip Murray to Marshall, January 29, 1948, 868.5045/1-2948, SD records; CIO press release of January 30, 1948, Box 1, Golden papers. For additional evidence of behind-the-scenes labor lobbying along these lines, see A. F. Whitney to Marshall, January 14, 1948, 868.00/1-1448 and Marshall to American embassy (Athens), January 14, 1948, 868.5045/1-1448, SD records; Jay Lovestone to Golden, December 30, 1947, Box 2, Golden papers.

55. Marshall to American embassy (Athens), January 30, 1948, 868.5045/1-2948, SD records. See also Henderson to Marshall and Henderson to Lovett, January 30, 1948, 868.5045/1-2948, SD records.

56. Letters were immediately dispatched to the leaders of the AFL and CIO, William Green and Philip Murray, informing them of this. Henderson to Marshall, February 2, 1948, 868.5045/1-2948, SD records. For the actual letter, see Marshall to Murray, February 2, 1948, Box 19, Cope papers.

57. See, for example, Marshall to American embassy (Athens), March 24, 1948, 868.00/3-2048, Baxter, "Memorandum of Conversation" (March 24, 1948), 868.504/3-2448, and "Memorandum of Conversation" (March 26, 1948), 868.00/4-748, SD records.

58. Golden to Griswold, January 16, 1948, Box 1, Meyer Bernstein to Golden, January 27, 1948, Box 3, and Golden to Philip M. Kaiser , January 24, 1948, Box 11, Golden papers; Davies, "The Role of the American Trade Union Representatives" (MS), pp. 389-92; Brooks, *Clint*, pp. 315–18. In December 1947 Golden was arguing that "quite a different concept of responsibilities and even attitudes must be developed . . . on the part of

the State Department, this, and other future Missions." But by the follow-ing February, the critical edge was blunted somewhat, replaced by a desire to "do everything to enlist the cooperation of the labor movements in the democratic countries" in ERP's "application and administration." Golden to Meyer Bernstein, December 21, 1947, Box 1 and Golden to E. J. Lever, February 22, 1948, Box 9, Golden papers.

59. Jecchinis, *Trade Unionism in Greece*, pp. 115–16; Stratis to American Federation of Labor, August 1, 1948, Box 17, Thorne papers; Rankin to Secretary of State, February 18, 1948, 868.5043/2-1848, SD records.

60. Rankin to Secretary of State, January 14, 1948, 868.00/1-1448, Feb-ruary 16, 1948, 868.00/2-1648, and March 24, 1948, 868.5043/3-2448, SD records.

61. Rankin to Secretary of State, January 19, 1948, 868.00/1-1948 and January 22, 1948 with enclosures, 868.5043/1-2248, SD records.

62. Golden to Frank Fenton, January 24, 1948, Box 2, Golden to Van A. Bittner and Elmer Cope, January 26, 1948 and Murray to Golden, February 16, 1948, Box 3, Golden papers; Minutes of Meeting of Committee on International Labor Relations, February 19, 1948, Box 17, Thorne pa-pers; Rankin to Secretary of State, March 30, 1948, 868.5043/3-3048, SD records.

63. Under pressure from the State Department, Lovestone's Free Trade Union Committee agreed to make a loan of $2,000. Other U.S. funding, perhaps from the CIA, may have been provided as well. Lovett to American embassy (Athens), March 31, 1948, 868.5043/3-2748 and Simpson to Thomas W. Holland, March 31, 1948, 868.504/3-3148, SD records. See also Taft, *Defending Freedom*, p. 174.

64. Jecchinis, *Trade Unionism in Greece*, p. 115; Davies, "The Role of the American Trade Union Representatives" (MS), pp. 407–8.

65. Douglas to Secretary of State, February 24, 1948, 868.5043/2-2448, Rankin to Secretary of State, March 3, 1948, 868.00/3-248 and March 17, 1948, 868.5043/3-1748, and Marshall to American embassy, February 17, 1948, 868.00/1-1948, SD records; "Monthly Report of the Chief of AMAG to the Secretary of State" (March 15, 1948), Box 7, SD Committees records.

66. Strachan to Golden, April 11, 1948, Box 8, Golden papers; Rankin to Secretary of State, March 29, 1948, 868.5043/3-2948, SD records. During World War II, Dimitratos was expelled from the cabinet by the King as one of the worst of the old Metaxas group. At the same time, he was investigated by the FBI for his contacts with fascist elements in Greece. Frederick B. Lyon to J. Edgar Hoover, September 19, 1942, 868.002/28L, SD records.

67. Rankin to Secretary of State, April 2, 1948, 868.5043/4-248, April 4, 1948, 868.5043/4-448 and May 5, 1948, 868.5043/5-548, and Irving Brown, "Report on the Greek Labor Convention," 868.504/4-2248, SD records; Strachan to Golden, April 11, 1948, Box 8, Golden papers; Jecchinis, *Trade Unionism in Greece*, p. 116; Davies, "The Role of the American Trade Union Representatives" (MS), pp. 418–19.

68. Strachan to Golden, April 11, 1948, Box 8, Golden papers. Rankin attributed this to what he described as the tendency of Greeks to be "one of the most undependable and unstable of peoples. . . . The fact that a certain amount of guile and craftiness is a part of the Greek's nature reinforces this tendency." Rankin to Secretary of State, May 5, 1948, 868.5043/5-548, SD records.

69. Brown, "Report on the Greek Labor Convention," 868.504/4-2248, SD records; Strachan to Golden, April 11, 1948, Box 8, Golden papers; Davies, "The Role of the American Trade Union Representatives" (MS), pp. 421–25. "With this ace in the hole we both felt we could do some realistic bargaining," wrote Strachan. "Fortunately for everyone, this side of the Congress has not been discovered by the press." Strachan to Golden, April 11, 1948, Box 8, Golden papers.

70. Strachan to Golden, April 11, 1948, Box 8, Golden papers; Davies, "The Role of the American Trade Union Representatives" (MS) pp. 420–21. During the convention, Makris and Theocharides continued to receive funds from wealthy industrialists through the assistance of Tsaldaris. Rankin to Secretary of State, April 3, 1948, 868.00/4–348, SD records.

71. Strachan to Golden, April 11, 1948, Box 8, Golden papers; Davies, "The Role of the American Trade Union Representatives" (MS), pp. 423–34; Jecchinis, *Trade Unionism in Greece*, p. 117; Rankin to Secretary of State, April 7, 1948, 868.5043/4-748, SD records.

72. ILO, *Labour Problems in Greece*, p. 349; Strachan to Golden, April 11, 1948, Box 8, Golden papers.

73. Jecchinis, *Trade Unionism in Greece*, pp. 118–19; Lovett to American embassy (Athens), June 2, 1948, 868.5043/5-2048 and Rankin to Secretary of State, June 9, 1948, 868.5043/6-948, SD records; Davies, "The Role of the American Trade Union Representatives" (MS), p. 436.

74. Rankin to Secretary of State, June 4, 1948, 868.5043/6-448 and Brown, "Report on the Greek Labor Convention," 868.504/4-2248, SD records; Jecchinis, *Trade Unionism in Greece*, p. 119.

75. Jecchinis, *Trade Unionism in Greece*, pp. 122–23; Grady to Secretary of State, January 24, 1949, 868.504/1-2449 and Douglas Flood to Secretary of State, December 2, 1949, 868.5043/12-249, SD records.

76. ILO, *Labour Problems in Greece*, p. 378; Rankin to Secretary of State, August 30, 1948, Box 2486, Athens post records; Jecchinis, *Trade Unionism in Greece*, pp. 135–45.

77. ILO, *Labour Problems in Greece*, p. 37; Sweet-Escott, *Greece*, p. 131; "Excerpt from letter received from Joe Heath, Economic Cooperation Administration, Mission to Greece" (n.d.), "Convention file 1948," Green papers.

78. Davies, "The Role of the American Trade Union Representatives" (MS), pp. 440–41; Jecchinis, *Trade Unionism in Greece*, pp. 124, 126; Cromie to Satterthwaite et al., January 5, 1949, 868.00/1-549, SD records; U.S. Department of State, *Fourth Report to Congress on Assistance to Greece and Turkey: For the Period Ended June 30, 1948*, p. 30.

79. Makris to Marshall, October 7, 1948 and Makris to William Green, December 3 and 10, 1948, "Convention file 1948," Green papers.

80. Monthly Report of the Chief of AMAG to the Secretary of State, March 15, 1948, Box 7, SD Committees records; Griswold, "Memorandum of Conversation" (March 26, 1948), 868.00/4-748, Rankin to Secretary of State, March 27, 1948, 868.00/3-2748 and June 17, 1948, 868.5043/6-1748, SD records. In the same report where he remarked that 71 percent of family expenditures in Athens went for food, the chief of the U.S. mission noted that AMAG had "recommended that the Government resist demands for higher wages and salaries." "Monthly Report of the Chief of AMAG to the Secretary of State" (May 15, 1948), Box 7, SD Committees records.

81. Grady to Secretary of State, August 27, 1948, "850.4 CONF" folder, Box 2486, Athens post records; Grady to Secretary of State, September 3, 1948, 868.5045/9-348, SD records; "Ambassador Henry F. Grady Outlines American Mission's Labor Policy" (September 3, 1948), "Press Releases and Clippings" folder, Box 4, Grady papers. See also Chief, ECA, Mission to Greece to D. Helmis, December 27, 1948, 868.00/1-749, SD records.

82. Davies, "The Role of the American Trade Union Representatives" (MS), pp. 334–35; Jecchinis, *Trade Unionism in Greece*, p. 128; Strachan to Golden, November 27, 1949, Box 1, Golden Papers. For another casual dismissal of plans for "social improvement," see Coombs, "The Greek Problem," enclosure in Dickinson to Nuveen, December 20, 1948, "800 Greece" folder, Box 2485, Athens post records.

83. Marshall to American embassy (Athens), September 14, 1948, 868.5043/9-748, SD records; Jecchinis, *Trade Unionism in Greece*, pp. 126–27; Woodhouse, *Struggle for Greece*, pp. 233–34.

84. Grady to Secretary of State, September 24, 1948, 868.5045/9-2448, December 3, 1949, 868.5045/12-349, December 5, 1949, 868.504/12-549, December 8, 1949, 868.5045/12-849, December 10, 1949, 868.5045/12-1049, SD records; Seton-Watson, *The East European Revolution*, p. 334.

85. Acheson to American embassy (Athens), December 8, 1949, 868.5041/12-849 and Grady to Secretary of State, December 13, 1949, 868.5041/12-1349, SD records.

86. Jecchinis, *Trade Unionism in Greece*, pp. 125, 128.

87. "International Labor Activities of the Department of Labor, December, 1947," Box 360, Labor Department records; Strachan to Thorne, June 7, 1948, Box 16, Thorne papers; Bert Jewell to William Green, March 8, 1949, "Convention file 1948," Green papers.

88. Miner to Secretary of State, October 4, 1949, 868.5042/10-449, Minor to Secretary of State, October 22, 1949, 868.5042/10-2249, Makris to Truman, December 1, 1949, 868.5042/12-149, Grady to Secretary of State, December 5, 1949, 868.504/12-549, SD records, Strachan to Golden, November 27, 1949, Box 1, Golden papers.

89. Tobin to Baxter, December 21, 1948, 868.00/12-2148, SD records; John Demelis to William Green, February 28, 1949, "Convention file 1948," Green papers.

90. Minor to Secretary of State, September 27, 1948 and enclosure, 868.5043/9-2748 and Leonard Cowles to James Wolfe, January 18, 1949, 868.00/12-848, SD records; Zotos Journal, February 3, 1949, Zotos papers. Thanks to pressure from the United Nations and from Liberal deputies in the Greek parliament, the Greek government eventually suspended the executions. Woodhouse, *Struggle for Greece*, p. 245.

91. See, for example, A. F. Whitney to Willard Thorpe, May 5, 1948, 868.00/5-548, SD records; Lovett to American embassy (Paris), October 21, 1948, Box 2486, Athens post records. The State Department estimated that it received about three hundred messages from American unions and locals protesting against executions of Greek labor leaders; about half were in response to the OENO trial. At its 1948 national convention, the CIO voted to "condemn the execution of trade union officials, in Greece and other countries." Tobin to Baxter, December 21, 1948, 868.00/12-2148, SD records.

92. See, for example, Golden to Donald Henderson, January 21, 1948, Box 17, Cope papers; Joe Heath to George Delaney, October 14, 1949, Woll to Green, October 24, 1949 and Frank X. Martell to Green, February 8, 1950, "Convention file 1949," Green papers. Woll, it should be noted, was referring to the broad array of difficulties OENO faced from Greek and American government persecution, rather than to the death sentences per se. Unlike the CIO, however, the AFL remained conspicuously silent on the latter point.

93. Reuther, *The Brothers Reuther*, p. 412; Thomas W. Braden, "I'm Glad the CIA Is 'Immoral' "; Godson, *American Labor and European Politics*, pp. 120–21; Radosh, *American Labor and United States Foreign Policy*, p. 323.

94. ILO, *Labour Problems in Greece*, pp. 208, 297; Economic Cooperation Administration, *Eleventh Report to Congress of the Economic Cooperation Administration*, p. 18; Spencer, *War and Postwar Greece*, p. 142; Zolotas, *Monetary Equilibrium*, pp. 146–47; Economic Cooperation Administration, *Seventh Report to Congress of the Economic Cooperation Administration*, p. 31.

95. Surveying the situation, a leading scholar of modern Greece wrote: "Under the watchful eye of American advisers . . . trade unions were placed once again under state control." ILO, *Labour Problems in Greece*, pp. 303, 321; Irving Brown and Elmer Cope, "Report on Greece" (c. January 1950), "Convention file 1949," Green papers; John O. Iatrides, "American Attitudes Toward the Political System of Postwar Greece," p. 66.

96. Varvaressos reached a similar conclusion in 1952: "In Greece, the trade union movement is not sufficiently developed to be able to protect effectively the interests of the working class." Davies, "The Role of the American Trade Union Representatives" (MS), p. 400; Jecchinis, *Trade Unionism in Greece*, pp. 129, 135–45; Makris to William Green, September 16, 1949, "Convention file 1949," Green papers; Sweet-Escott, *Greece*, p. 141; Varvaressos, *Report on the Greek Economic Problem*, p. 109.

8. THE MILITARY SOLUTION

1. Senate Committee on Foreign Relations, *Assistance to Greece and Turkey: Hearings*, p. 43.

2. See, for example, his address to Congress of March 12, 1947. *Public Papers of the Presidents: Harry S. Truman, 1947*, p. 179.

3. On May 31, 1948, AMAG had 571 American employees, of whom 388 served with the Army and Navy groups. By August 1949, the U.S. aid program employed some 1,000 Americans, more than 600 of them from the armed forces. American Mission for Aid to Greece, "A Factual Summary Concerning the American Mission for Aid to Greece" (June 15, 1948), p. 20, "Mission to Greece, General" folder, Box 3, Iverson papers; Charilaos G. Lagoudakis, "Greece (1946–1949)," p. 513. The shift to using most U.S. aid funds for the military program is discussed in chapter 6.

4. U.S. Army Historical Division, "History of the United States Army Group (Greece): Volume I—Prelude," pp. 74–76, Army General Staff records.

5. U.S. Army Historical Division, "Brief History USAGG, Procurement, 24 May 47–31 Aug 49," p. 12 and Charles R. Lehner to Director, P & O Division, October 30, 1947, P & O 091 Greece, Section IV, Case 52, P & O Division, Army General Staff records; J. C. Murray, "The Anti-Bandit War: Part III," pp. 54–57; MacVeagh to Secretary of State, October 25, 1946, 868.20/10–2546, SD records.

6. Livesay diary, June 20, 1947, Livesay papers; Alexander Papagos, "Guerrilla Warfare," p. 236. This program of "moral rehabilitation" is discussed in chapter 5.

7. J. C. Murray, "The Anti-Bandit War: Part I," p. 18, "The Anti-Bandit War: Part II," pp. 51–52, and "The Anti-Bandit War: Part III," pp. 50–52. The State Department claimed that the rebels were "fanatically led by Communists who have recruited many hardened criminals, and who have forced loyal Greeks into their service by threats against them or their families." General Van Fleet characterized the rebels as "international bandits," whose "leaders are all notorious criminals." McNeill, however, provides a less diabolical picture: "When two or three organizers came to a new district, and invited the boys of the poor hill villages to take up arms, they regularly found twenty or thirty young fellows—below draft age and therefore staying idly and discontentedly at home—who were willing to follow them. With such a core, it was possible to conscript others. . . . The army filled its ranks by conscription only slightly better organized, so that accident often determined on which side a particular individual fought." U.S. Department of State, *First Report to Congress on Assistance to Greece and Turkey*, p. 12; Zotos Journal, November 28, 1948, Zotos papers; McNeill, *Greece*, pp. 38–39. For Greek and British views on the reasons for enlistment in guerrilla ranks, see Averoff-Tossizza, *By Fire and Axe*, p. 201; *London Times*, July 15, 1947.

8. U.S. Army Historical Division, "History JUSMAPG—Greece, January 1, 1948–March 25, 1949," p. 16, Army General Staff records; Averoff-

Tossizza, *By Fire and Axe*, pp. 223, 359–60; Bloomfield and Leiss, *Controlling Small Wars*, pp. 170–72.

9. U.S. Army Historical Division, "History JUSMAPG—Greece, January 1, 1948–March 25, 1949," p. 40, Army General Staff records; Vukmanovic-Tempo, *How and Why*, p. 76; Murray, "The Anti-Bandit War: Part I," pp. 17–18 and "The Anti-Bandit War: Part II," pp. 51–52; Gibson to Secretary of State, September 2, 1947, 868.00/9-247, SD records; Papagos, "Guerrilla Warfare," pp. 233–36.

10. Gibson to Secretary of State, June 28, 1947, 868.00/6-2847 and July 3, 1947, 868.00/7-347, SD records; Lehner to Director, P & O Division, Department of the Army, October 30, 1947, P & O 091 Greece, Section IV, Case 52, P & O Division, Army General Staff records.

11. Jernegan to Villard, April 30, 1947 and Minutes of the SWNCC subcommittee for the Near and Middle East, May 1, 1947, Box 89, SWNCC records; *FR 1947*, 5:265-66, 270-71, 273; Livesay to Lauris Norstad, August 13, 1947, P & O 091 Greece TS, Case 3 Part I, P & O Division, Army General Staff records. See also *FR 1947*, 5:152–53; Livesay diary, July 4 and August 8, 1947, Livesay Papers; Villard to Armour, August 6, 1947, 868.01/8-647, SD records.

12. Livesay to Griswold, August 21, 1947, P & O 091 Greece TS, Case 3, Part I, P & O Division, Army General Staff records; Livesay diary, August 22 and September 10, 1947, Livesay papers; Minor, "Memorandum of Conversation" (September 2, 1947), enclosure in Keeley to Secretary of State, September 16, 1947, 111.75/9-1647, SD records; Record of meeting of September 9, 1947, FO 371/67046, R12491, FO records.

13. Livesay to Griswold, September 18 and 19, 1947, P & O 091 Greece TS, Case 7, P & O Division, Army General Staff records; "Memorandum of Conversation" (September 18, 1947), 868.00/9-2647, SD records; U.S. Army Historical Division, "Brief History of USAGG, Procurement, 24 May 47–31 Aug 49," p. 13, Army General Staff records; *FR 1947*, 5:390, 396–98.

14. *FR 1947*, 5:116–17, 149, 268, 276–80.

15. Forrestal diaries, August 4 and 8, 1947; *FR 1947*, 5:273–75, 313.

16. According to a State Department background paper for the Pentagon Talks, "the British realize their inability to implement their political and economic policy in the Middle East without American help but they hope that such cooperation on our part will not preclude their retention of a certain special position in the area. The question is whether the British would be prepared in consideration for such assistance to maintain primary military responsibility for the area and whether the type of political and economic cooperation which they desire would fall within our current capabilities and policies." *FR 1947*, 5:322–23, 513.

17. *FR 1947*, 5:399–400, 424, 497; Xydis, *Greece and the Great Powers*, p. 539.

18. *FR 1947*, 5:135, 321, 526; U.S. Army Historical Division, "Brief History USAGG, Procurement, 24 May 47–31 Aug 49," pp. 9–15, Army Gen-

eral Staff records; U.S. Department of State, *Second Report to Congress on Assistance to Greece and Turkey*, p. 9; McGhee, "Report on Greece," address broadcast on October 15, 1947, Box 1, Jones papers.

19. U.S. Army Historical Division, "History JUSMAPG—Greece, January 1, 1948–March 25, 1949," p. 18, Army General Staff records; Gibson to Secretary of State, October 25, 1947, 868.00/10-2547, SD records; O'Ballance, *The Greek Civil War*, p. 151.

20. *FR 1947*, 5:336; Katherine W. Bracken to Secretary of State, May 28, 1947, 868.00/5-2847, SD records; Woodhouse, *Struggle for Greece*, pp. 211–12.

21. O'Ballance, *The Greek Civil War*, p. 218. See also Gibson to Secretary of State, September 13, 1947, 868.00/9-1347, SD records; Dana Adams Schmidt, "The Front in Greece Is Everywhere," p. 12.

22. Forrestal diaries, August 31, 1947; "Report by Policy Planning Staff on United States Policy in the Event of the Establishment of Communist Power in Greece" (September 18, 1947), PPS 8, Box 1, Policy Planning Staff records; Central Intelligence Agency, "Possible Consequences of Communist Control of Greece in the Absence of US Counteraction" (February 9, 1948), CIA records.

23. *FR 1947*, 5:331, 337–38, 424–27, 439; Benjamin F. Taylor to McGhee, January 23, 1948, 868.20/1-2348, SD records; *FR 1948*, 4:26.

24. *FR 1947*, 5:428. See also *ibid.*, p. 481; Henderson, "Memorandum of Conversation" (December 22, 1947), 868.01/12-2247, SD records.

25. *FR 1947*, 5:478–79; U.S. Department of State, *Third Report to Congress on Assistance to Greece and Turkey*, p. 5; Murray, "The Anti-Bandit War: Part I," pp. 21–22; U.S. Army Historical Division, "History JUSMAPG—Greece, January 1, 1948–March 25, 1949," p. 116, Army General Staff records; *FR 1948*, 4:189.

26. Livesay diary, September 10, 1947, Livesay papers; Cromie to Henderson, September 2, 1947, 711.68/9-247, SD records; U.S. Army Historical Division, "Brief History USAGG, Procurement, 24 May 47–31 Aug 49," p. 14, Army General Staff records.

27. Minor, "Memorandum of Conversation" (September 2, 1947), enclosure in Keeley to Secretary of State, September 16, 1947, 111.75/9-1647, SD records; *FR 1947*, 5:339.

28. Norton to Foreign Office, October 1, 1947, FO 371/67151, R13362, FO records; *FR 1947*, 5:356, 361–63, 367, 375–78, 384–86; Amen, *American Foreign Policy in Greece*, pp. 181–82.

29. *FR 1947*, 5:362, 391–93, 399–400, 480; Marshall to Royall, November 7, 1947, 868.20 MISSIONS/11-447, SD records; W. H. Arnold, "Conversation with Senator Vandenberg" (November 13, 1947), P & O 091 Greece TS, Case 3, Part I, P & O Division, Army General Staff records.

30. Anonymous, "Conversation of General Arnold with Mr. Henderson" (c. December 1947), P & O 091 Greece, Section VI, Case 58 and A. C. Wedemeyer to Dwight Eisenhower, February 6, 1948, P & O 091 Greece

TS, Case 3, P & O Division, Army General Staff records; Eisenhower to Marshall, January 7, 1948, 868.00/1-748, SD records; *FR 1948*, 4:36–37. According to Van Fleet, Queen Frederika played a major role in convincing Marshall to appoint him: "He had met Her Majesty in London, where they were both present for the wedding of Princess Elizabeth and Prince Philip of Greece. It was during a very busy day when General Marshall was prevailed upon to give Her Majesty an appointment of some fifteen minutes. It didn't take too long for Frederika to convince the General of the importance of the interview and, as it turned out, General Marshall cancelled two hours of appointments to listen to the pleas of the Queen. . . . In the Queen's words, she wanted, at once, a combat general, not a supply sergeant!" Van Fleet, "How We Won in Greece," p. 388.

31. Leahy diary, July 16, 1947, Leahy papers; Dulles to Lovett, August 25, 1947, Dulles to Vandenberg, August 28, 1947, and memorandum of conversation on August 28, 1947 by Dulles (misdated August 28, 1948), Dulles papers; Forrestal diaries, August 31, 1947.

32. *FR 1947*, 5:458–61. The complete version is found in P & O 091 Greece TS, Section II, Case 14, P & O Division, Army General Staff records. See also *FR 1948*, 4:9–13.

33. *FR 1947*, 5:466–69; T. W. Parker to Wedemeyer, December 29, 1947, P & O 091 Greece TS, Case 9, P & O Division, Army General Staff records; *FR 1948*, 4:5.

34. *FR 1948*, 4:21–25, 27–28, 39–41, 50–51; Forrestal diaries, February 12, 1948.

35. *FR 1948*, 4:64–65, 93–95. See also JCS 1826/6 (17 February 1948), CCS 092 Greece (12/30/47), Section 1 and JCS 1856 (26 March 1948), 311 Middle East & Near East Area (1/13/48), Joint Chiefs of Staff records.

36. *FR 1948*, 4:101; *FR 1949*, 6:235–36. NSC 5/4 can be found in the President's Secretary's File, Truman papers. It contains a section on CIA estimates omitted from the version of NSC 5/3 printed in *FR 1948*, 4:93–95.

37. *FR 1947*, 5:452. See also Eisenhower to General Morgan, December 4, 1947, "SWNCC 091—GREECE Miscellaneous" folder, Box 76, SWNCC records.

38. U.S. Army Historical Division, "Brief History JUSMAPG, 1 January 1948 to 31 August 1949," pp. 2–3 and "History JUSMAPG—Greece, January 1, 1948–March 25, 1949," pp. 53–54, Army General Staff records; Griswold to Secretary of State, February 19, 1948, 868.20 MISSION/2-1948, SD records.

39. Van Fleet, "How We Won in Greece," p. 390; Forrestal diaries, November 13, 1948; Wedemeyer to Templar, July 27, 1948, P & O 091 Greece TS, Section IV, Case 32, P & O Division, Army General Staff records.

40. Livesay diary, June 24, 1947 and Livesay's address of January 16, 1948, Livesay papers.

41. Norton to Foreign Office, September 8, 1947 and Minute by David Balfour of September 10, 1947, FO 371/67007, R12350, FO records; MacVeagh to Secretary of State, September 6, 1947, 868.00/9-647, Keeley to Secretary of State, September 21, 1947, 868.00/9-2147 and September 24, 1947, 868.00/9-2447, SD records.

42. Livesay diary, September 30 and October 6, 1947, Livesay papers; Rawlins, "Record of Conversation Between Commander, BMM(G) and Prime Minister, Mr. Sophoulis" (October 3, 1947), 868.00/10-2847 and "Memorandum of Conversation" (December 24, 1947), 868.00/12-3147, SD records.

43. Griswold to Secretary of State, January 7, 1948, 868.00/1-748, January 9, 1948, 868.00/1-948, and January 14, 1948, 868.00/1-1448, SD records.

44. U.S. Army Historical Division, "History JUSMAPG—Greece, January 1, 1948–March 25, 1949," pp. 54–59, Army General Staff records; Rankin to Secretary of State, February 19, 1948, 868.00/2-1948, SD records.

45. Monthly Report of the Chief of AMAG to the Secretary of State" (March 15, 1948), p. 2, Box 7, SD Committees records; O'Ballance, *The Greek Civil War*, p. 166; *New York Times*, July 29 and August 3, 1948.

46. U.S. Department of State, *Fourth Report to Congress on Assistance to Greece and Turkey*, pp. 5–6; U.S. Department of State, *Third Report to Congress on Assistance to Greece and Turkey*, pp. 3–4; Edwin P. Curtin, "American Advisory Group Aids Greece in War on Guerrillas," p. 11.

47. Sulzberger, *A Long Row of Candles*, p. 394; Frederick H. Loomis, "Report From Greece," p. 5; U.S. Army Historical Division, "History JUSMAPG—Greece, January 1, 1948–March 25, 1949," p. 89, Army General Staff records; Zotos Journal, February 11, 1949, Zotos papers; Woodhouse, *Struggle for Greece*, p. 260–61.

48. Douglas to Secretary of State, February 19, 1948, 868.00/2-1948, SD records; U.S. Army Historical Division, "Brief History JUSMAPG, 1 January 1948 to 31 August 1949," pp. 4–6, Army General Staff records; "A Factual Summary Concerning the American Mission for Aid to Greece" (June 15, 1948), pp. 3–4, "Mission to Greece, General" folder, Box 3, Iverson papers; O'Ballance, *Greek Civil War*, p. 167.

49. Discussing the employment of the "fire bomb (Napalm), hitherto not used in operations against [the] bandits," Griswold foresaw the only drawback as one of public relations. He wrote that month: "We must expect propaganda agencies of Communist countries to seize upon this fact to charge that use of [the] fire bomb is unethical. . . . [The] principal propaganda broadside will be directed against [the] United States, stressing that [the] fire bomb was made in America and used in Greece according to [the] plans of [the] American Army." Griswold thought it "vital that we be prepared for such propaganda by offensive propaganda of our own coordinated with GNA military operational plans." Murray, "The Anti-Bandit War: Part I," p. 18; U.S. Army Historical Division, "History JUSMAPG—Greece,

January 1, 1948–March 25, 1949," p. 90, Army General Staff records; Averoff-Tossizza, *By Fire and Axe*, p. 286; Yergin, *Shattered Peace*, p. 293; Zotos Journal, June 21, 1948, Zotos papers; *FR 1948*, 4:107.

50. U.S. Army Historical Division, "Brief History JUSMAPG, 1 January 1948 to 31 August 1949," pp. 14–15, Army General Staff records; O'Ballance, *The Greek Civil War*, pp. 171–73, 176; Averoff-Tossizza, *By Fire and Axe*, pp. 295–98.

51. Woodhouse, *Struggle for Greece*, pp. 231–33; U.S. Army Historical Division, "History of the United States Army Group (Greece): Volume II—Fiscal Year 1948," p. 2, Army General Staff records; Murray, "The Anti-Bandit War: Part II," pp. 52–55; O'Ballance, *The Greek Civil War*, p. 177; *FR 1948*, 4:198–99.

52. Averoff-Tossizza, *By Fire and Axe*, pp. 290–91, 295–98; *FR 1948*, 4:196, 206; Van Fleet to Anonymous, October 1, 1948 and Van Fleet to Wedemeyer, October 25, 1948, P & O 091 Greece TS, Section V, Case 40, P & O Division, Army General Staff records; Woodhouse, *Struggle for Greece*, 242–44, 257–58; *FR 1949*, 6:232. See also Van Fleet to Grady, October 8, 1948, "D-Misc." folder, Box 1, Grady papers; Baxter, "Memorandum of Conversation" (November 24, 1948), 868.00/11-2448, SD records; Pagagos, "Guerrilla Warfare," p. 238.

53. Berry, "Memorandum" (March 22, 1948), enclosure in Griswold to Secretary of State, March 24, 1948, 868.00/3-2448, SD records; U.S. Army Historical Division, "History JUSMAPG—Greece, January 1, 1948–March 25, 1949," pp. 82–83, Army General Staff records; Hanson Baldwin to Alexis Kyrou, January 15, 1948, Series I, Box 6, Baldwin papers.

54. U.S. Army Historical Division, "History JUSMAPG—Greece, January 1, 1948–March 25, 1949," pp. 92–93, Army General Staff records; *FR 1948*, 4:125–29, 135–36; Griswold to Secretary of State, July 1, 1948, 868.00/7-148, SD records.

55. Marcy, "Greek Government Memorandum Concerning Increases in Armed Forces" (October 1, 1948), 868.00/10-148, SD records; Van Fleet to Grady, October 7, 1948, P & O 091 Greece TS, Section IV, Case 40 and Maddocks to Deputy Chief of Staff, December 14, 1948, P & O 091 Greece TS, Section V, Case 36, P & O Division, Army General Staff records; Rankin to Grady, October 22, 1948, "820 Greek Army (Secret)" folder, Box 2486, Athens post records.

56. *FR 1948*, 4:187–90. See also *ibid.*, pp. 168–69; Grady to Secretary of State, December 7, 1948, 868.20/12-748, SD records; Grady to Kenneth de Courcy, October 16, 1948, "D-Misc." folder, Box 1, Grady papers.

57. *FR 1948*, 4:178, 193–94; Maddocks to Deputy Chief of Staff, December 14, 1948 and Maddocks to Van Fleet, December 9, 1948, P & O 091 Greece TS, Section V, Case 36, P & O Division, Army General Staff records; U.S. Army Historical Division, "History of the United States Army Group (Greece): Volume II—Fiscal Year 1948," p. 17, Army General Staff records.

58. Minor, "Transmitting Copy of Letter from Greek Government Regarding Increases in Greek Army" (December 9, 1948), 868.20/12-948, Royal Greek embassy to State Department, December 13, 1948, 868.20/12-1348, Royall to Secretary of State, January 11, 1949, 868.20/1-1149, and Grady to Secretary of State, April 2, 1949, 868.20/4-249, SD records.

59. Griswold to Secretary of State, July 26, 1948 and McGhee to Secretary of State, August 13, 1948, 868.00/7-2648, SD records; Kenneth C. Royall oral history interview, pp. 181–93.

60. FR 1948, 4:162–64, 166, 198, 204; Grady to Secretary of State, October 26, 1948, 868.20/10-2648 and William H. Draper, Jr. to Lovett, 868.20/12-2448, SD records; Grady, "Adventures in Diplomacy," pp. 202–3, Box 5, Grady papers.

61. Maddocks to Sievers, January 25, 1949 and Van Fleet to Maddocks, January 29, 1949, P & O 091 Greece, Section I, Case 10, P & O Division, Army General Staff records; FR 1949, 6:248–49; Woodhouse, Struggle for Greece, pp. 246–47.

62. Reuben E. Jenkins to T. Kitrilakis, January 26, 1949 and Van Fleet to Papagos, January 26, 1949, "GEOG L—Greece 370.02" folder, "Civil War in Greece" materials, Army Department records.

63. FR 1949, 6:246–49; Satterthwaite to Secretary of State, February 8, 1949, 868.20/2-849, SD records; U.S. Army Historical Division, "History JUSMAPG—Greece, January 1, 1948–March 25, 1949," p. 123, Army General Staff records.

64. FR 1949, 6:231–32, 278; FR 1948, 4:196; Central Intelligence Agency, "Effects of a U.S. Foreign Military Aid Program" (February 24, 1949), CIA records.

65. FR 1947, 3:217–18; FR 1948, 4:191–92; Cromie to Jernegan, November 24, 1948, 868.00/11-2448, SD records; Near and Middle East Subcommittee, "Memorandum for the State-Army-Navy-Air Force Coordinating Committee" (December 15, 1948), Box 89, SWNCC records.

66. FR 1948, 4:215; FR 1948, 5:259; FR 1949, 4:243–44, 270; Subcommittee for Rearmament, "Memorandum for the State-Army-Navy-Air Force Coordinating Committee" (December 27, 1948), Box 134, SWNCC records.

67. U.S. Department of State, Seventh Report to Congress on Assistance to Greece and Turkey, pp. 4–12; U.S. Army Historical Division, "History JUSMAPG—Greece, January 1, 1948–March 25, 1949," p. 126 and U.S. Army Historical Division, "Brief History, JUSMAPG, January 1, 1948 to December 31, 1949," p. 19, Army General Staff records.

68. Woodhouse, Struggle for Greece, pp. 261, 277–78, 285; Theodossios Papathanasiades, "The Bandits' Last Stand in Greece," pp. 23–31; Murray, "The Anti-Bandit War: Part V," p. 52; U.S. Department of State, Eighth Report to Congress on Assistance to Greece and Turkey, pp. 1–8.

69. Indeed, according to the Greek General Staff, between January 1948 and January 1949 the guerrilla strength in Greece actually grew from 22,350

to 24,090. Some years later, a member of the General Staff contended that, in January 1949, the rebels, "with an excellent informer and intelligence network throughout the country, had the initiative." He noted that "the guerrilla domination was so complete, that movement throughout the country was still limited to armed convoys 1 or 2 days a week in certain areas. . . . Sabotage of waterworks, industrial plants, roads, and railroads were practically daily occurrences." U.S. Army Historical Division, "Brief History JUSMAPG, 1 January 1948 to 31 August 1949," p. 26, Army General Staff records; Papathanasiades, "The Bandits' Last Stand," p. 22.

70. The State Department later claimed that "25,000 or 29,000" Greek guerrillas retreated to Albania and Bulgaria at the end of the war. Even if some of these people were noncombatants, the remainder constituted a potentially effective guerrilla force. Grady to Secretary of State, September 10, 1949, 868.00/9-1049, SD records; House Committee on International Relations, *Military Assistance Programs*, p. 84.

71. Kousoulas, *Revolution and Defeat*, p. 271; Woodhouse, *Struggle for Greece*, p. 276; Campbell, "The Greek Civil War," p. 44; Seton-Watson, *The East European Revolution*, p. 328; McNeill, *Greece*, p. 42; Murray, "The Anti-Bandit War: Part I." pp. 14-15, 19 and "The Anti-Bandit War: Part IV," p. 60. Van Fleet alone has challenged the importance of Tito's defection. Given the general's self-interest in magnifying the significance of U.S. military efforts, it is hardly surprising that he would do so. Van Fleet, "How We Won in Greece," p. 391.

72. O'Ballance, *The Greek Civil War*, pp. 179-81, 216; Averoff-Tossizza, *By Fire and Axe*, p. 253; Edward R. Wainhouse, "Guerrilla War in Greece," p. 24.

73. McNeill, *Greece*, p. 41; "Report on Greece by C.I.G.S." (March 18, 1949), 868.20/3-3149, SD records; Woodhouse, *Struggle for Greece*, p. 267; Murray, "The Anti-Bandit War: Part III," p. 53 and "The Anti-Bandit War: Part I," p. 20; Van Fleet, "How We Won in Greece," p. 390.

74. This figure is drawn from a U.S. Army history of the conflict. Specific data are virtually impossible to obtain, for actual expenditures in a given period do not necessarily match congressional allocations (in this case, $388.1 million). One recent authority, after extensive research, has concluded that total direct American military spending in Greece during this time fell somewhere between $345.5 million and $428 million. U.S. Army Historical Division, "Brief History, USAGG, Procurement, 24 May 1947 to December 31, 1949," p. 35, Army General Staff records; Amen, *American Foreign Policy in Greece*, p. 166.

75. U.S. Army Historical Division, "Brief History, USAGG, Procurement, 24 May 1947 to December 31, 1949," p. 38, Army General Staff records; Averoff-Tossizza, *By Fire and Axe*, p. 355; Lionel C. McGarr to N. L. Anscheutz, October 3, 1949, 868.00/10-349, SD records; Curtin, "American Advisory Group." pp. 10-11; Lincoln, *United States' Aid to Greece*, pp. 64-65.

76. Murray, "The Anti-Bandit War: Part II," pp. 57–58; Woodhouse, *Struggle for Greece*, p. 238. See also Murray, "The Anti-Bandit War: Part I," pp. 14–15.

9. THE INTERNATIONAL DIMENSION

1. Kennan to Secretary of State, May 12, 1948, Box 33, Policy Planning Staff records.

2. *FR 1948*, 4:164.

3. Most of the rebel arms were British, Italian, and German. U.S. Department of State, *Fourth Report to Congress on Assistance to Greece and Turkey*, p. 7; Smith, *The State of Europe*, p. 237; "Organization of the Bandit Army" (December 15, 1948), "GEOG L Greece 370.64" folder, "Civil War in Greece" materials, Army Department records; O'Ballance, *Greek Civil War*, p. 163; Murray, "The Anti-Bandit War: Part I," p. 18.

4. Woodhouse, *Struggle for Greece*, pp. 225–26; Robert McClintock, "Memorandum of Conversation" (May 7, 1948), 501.BB BALKANS/5-748, SD records. The law firm was that of Covington, Burling, Rublee, Acheson and Shorb. See also *FR 1948*, 4:93–94; Lagoudakis, "Greece (1946–1949)," p. 506.

5. C. E. Black, "Greece and the United Nations," p. 564; Campbell, "The Greek Civil War," p. 56; *FR 1948*, 4:245–46; Parsons to Secretary of State, May 21, 1948, 501.BB BALKANS/5-2048, SD records; "Balkan Commission Reports."

6. *FR 1948*, 4:225–28, 234, 243; Campbell, "The Greek Civil War," pp. 58–59; *FR 1949*, 6:258, 294, 299, 333–35; Kofos, *Nationalism and Communism in Macedonia*, p. 174; American embassy (Athens), "Transmitting Translation of Telegram from Under Secretary for Foreign Affairs" (June 1, 1949), 868.00/6-149, SD records; Woodhouse, *Struggle for Greece*, p. 272. It should be noted that, for reasons unrelated to the Greek conflict, American officials intensely disliked Evatt, the Australian Minister for External Affairs. Evatt, on the other hand, consistently sought a closer relationship with the United States. Joseph M. Siracusa and Glen St. John Barclay, "Australia, the United States, and the Cold War," pp. 39–47.

7. *FR 1947*, 5:880–81; Caffery to Secretary of State, July 15, 1947, 851.00/7-1547 and Marshall to U.S. Delegation to the United Nations, July 16, 1947, 868.00/7-1647, SD records.

8. Minute of August 12, 1947 by Warner, FO 371/67072, R11169, FO records; Smith to Secretary of State, August 30, 1947, 868.01/8-3047 and Cavendish Cannon to Secretary of State, August 28, 1947, 868.00/8-2847, SD records; Bloomfield and Leiss, *Controlling Small Wars*, p. 168.

9. *FR 1947*, 5:245–46; Llewellyn Thompson to Hickerson, September 2, 1947, 868.01/8-3047, SD records; Woodhouse, *Struggle for Greece* , pp. 216–17.

10. Woodhouse, *Struggle for Greece*, pp. 210–11; Dedijer, *Tito*, 292–93; Vukmanovic-Tempo, *How and Why*, pp. 6, 82.

11. Lincoln, *United States' Aid to Greece*, p. 41; FR 1947, 5:364, 443. See also FR 1947, 5:529; Forrestal diaries, November 7, 1947; Bonesteel to Lovett, August 15, 1947, 868.00/8-1547, SD records.

12. Carlyle, ed., *Documents on International Affairs, 1947–1948*, pp. 322–23; Woodhouse, *Struggle for Greece*, p. 218; FR 1947, 5:462–63.

13. Lovett to American embassy, Athens, December 27, 1947, 868.01/ 12-2647, SD records; FR 1947, 5:471–74, 478; Carlyle, ed., *Documents on International Affairs, 1947–1948*, pp. 323–24; FR 1948, 4:3; Sweet-Escott, *Greece*, p. 65.

14. FR 1947, 5:366–67, 465, 469; Vassili Dendramis to Henderson, January 10, 1948, 868.01/1-1048, SD records.

15. FR 1947, 5:470; FR 1948, 4:1055–56; Marshall to Certain American Missions, January 12, 1948, Box 2485, Athens post records; Baxter, "Memorandum of Conversation" (February 4, 1948), 868.00/2-448, SD records. On May 25, 1948, the National Security Council noted that "satellite aid to Markos has been on a lesser scale than apparent preparations would have supported." FR 1948, 4:93–94.

16. Dedijer, *Tito*, pp. 313–14; Iatrides, *Balkan Triangle*, p. 22; Woodhouse, *Struggle for Greece*, pp. 228–30.

17. Dedijer, *Tito*, pp. 316–17; Kousoulas, "The Truman Doctrine and the Stalin-Tito Rift," pp. 430–32. See also FR 1948, 4:1082.

18. Dedijer, *Tito*, pp. 318–22; Dedijer, *The Battle Stalin Lost*, pp. 68–69; Djilas, *Conversations with Stalin*, pp. 181–82; Kousoulas, "The Truman Doctrine and the Stalin-Tito Rift," p. 431.

19. Kousoulas, "The Truman Doctrine and the Stalin-Tito Rift," pp. 433–36; Carlyle, ed., *Documents on International Affairs, 1947–1948*, pp. 348–406; Woodhouse, *Struggle for Greece*, pp. 250–52.

20. FR 1948, 3:844; Cannon to Secretary of State, June 8, 1948, "800 Free Greek Govt SECRET" folder, Box 2485, Athens post records.

21. FR 1948, 4:115, 117, 120–21, 129; Douglas to Secretary of State, July 28, 1948 and Satterthwaite to Lovett, July 29, 1948, 868.00/7-2848 and Jernegan to Lovett, August 10, 1948, 868.00/8-1048, SD records.

22. Rankin to Secretary of State, April 7, 1948, 868.00/4-748, SD records; FR 1948, 4:80–81; Carlyle, ed., *Documents on International Affairs, 1947–1948*, pp. 324–25; O'Ballance, *The Greek Civil War*, p. 170; Averoff-Tossizza, *By Fire and Axe*, pp. 267–69.

23. For a more extensive discussion of this shift in military strategy, see chapter 8.

24. Henderson, "Memorandum of Conversation" (June 3, 1948), 868.00/ 6-348, SD records; FR 1948, 4:101–2, 106–8. Greek government leaders did, in fact, announce that the only alternatives open to the "bandits" were unconditional surrender or "extermination by arms." Rankin to Secretary of State, June 3, 1948, 868.00/6-348 and July 15, 1948, 868.00/7-1548, SD records.

25. Iatrides, *Balkan Triangle*, pp. 23–24; Walter Bedell Smith, *My Three Years in Moscow*, p. 203; Laurence Steinhardt to Secretary of State, May

4, 1948 and Marshall to American embassy (Prague), May 11, 1948, 868.00/ 5-448, SD records. Cannon later maintained that the U.S. embassy in Belgrade alerted the State Department to the Tito-Stalin split on June 5, 1948. Digest of the Meeting of September 23, 1948: Cavendish Cannon, "Marshall Tito's Relations with Moscow," Records of Meetings, vol. 14, Council on Foreign Relations records.

26. Carlyle, ed., *Documents on International Affairs, 1947–1948*, pp. 325–26.

27. Averoff-Tossizza, *By Fire and Axe*, p. 277; Burks, *Dynamics of Communism*, pp. 102–3; Woodhouse, *Struggle for Greece*, pp. 253–54; Eudes, *The Kapetanios*, p. 325; Edward C. Kennelly to Chief of Mission, July 30, 1948, Box 2483, Athens post records; Baldwin to Secretary of State, December 18, 1948, 868.00/12-1848, SD records.

28. Woodhouse, *Struggle for Greece*, pp. 244, 254–55; Eudes, *The Kapetanios*, pp. 327–38; Averoff-Tossizza, *By Fire and Axe*, pp. 317–21.

29. See, for example, Reams to Secretary of State, July 15, 1948, "800 Free Greek Govt SECRET" folder and Grady to Secretary of State, August 13, 1948, "800 Russia SECRET" folder, Box 2485, Athens post records; Rankin to Secretary of State, July 14, 1948, 868.00/7-1448, SD records.

30. Grady to Secretary of State, July 23, 1948, "800 c/800 Yugo SECRET" folder, Box 2485, Athens post records; Gibson to Secretary of State, July 25, 1948, 868.00/7-2548, SD records; *FR 1948*, 4:134.

31. Seton-Watson, *The East European Revolution*, pp. 356–58; Lagoudàkis, "Greece (1946–1949)," p. 508; Minor to Secretary of State, May 4, 1949, 868.00/5-449, SD records.

32. *FR 1948*, 4:122–23, 155, 207, 1090. See also *Ibid.*, pp. 118, 1104.

33. Their reluctance to aid Yugoslavia, however, is highlighted in Lorraine M. Lees, "The American Decision to Assist Tito."

34. NSC 18 (July 6, 1948), NSC records; *FR 1948*, 4:1094; Cromie, "Memorandum of Conversation" (August 30, 1948) and Royal Greek embassy (Washington) to Secretary of State, August 30, 1948, 868.00/8-3048 and Grady to Secretary of State, September 17, 1948, 868.00/9-1748, SD records.

35. Dedijer, *Tito Speaks*, p. 375; Iatrides, *Balkan Triangle*, p. 27; Kousoulas, "The Truman Doctrine and the Stalin-Tito Rift," p. 436; Reams to Secretary of State, September 8, 1948, "800 Free Greek Govt (Secret)" folder, Box 2485, Athens post records.

36. *FR 1948*, 4:207, 1115; Averoff-Tossizza, *By Fire and Axe*, pp. 277–78; Woodhouse, *Struggle for Greece*, pp. 230–31, 253. For a more expansionist explanation of Tito's motives, see Palmer and King, *Yugoslav Communism*, pp. 129–30.

37. *FR 1949*, 6:250; Woodhouse, *Struggle for Greece*, pp. 262–63; Gayn, "Democracy's Distant Cousin," p. 17; Spencer, *War and Postwar Greece*, p. 117; Grady to Secretary of State, February 9, 1949, 868.00/2-949, SD records.

38. Greek government officials attributed Markos' ouster to the Tito-

Cominform rift and predicted that it would damage insurgent morale, for Markos has "great prestige among the rebels." *FR 1949*, 6:250–52; Acheson to Certain American Diplomatic Missions, February 18, 1949, 868.00/2-1849, Grady to Secretary of State, February 24, 1949, 868.00/2-2449, and Directors for European Affairs and Near East and African Affairs to Webb and Acheson, March 2, 1949, 868.00/2-1649, SD records; Zotos Journal, February 5, 1949, Zotos papers.

39. Kofos, *Nationalism and Communism in Macedonia*, pp. 175–76, 179; Shoup, *Communism and the Yugoslav National Question*, pp. 158–62; Woodhouse, *Struggle for Greece*, pp. 253–54, 264; Burks, *Dynamics of Communism*, p. 103; Palmer and King, *Yugoslav Communism*, p. 127; Grady to Secretary of State, March 3, 1949, 868.00/3-349, Cannon to Secretary of State, March 4, 1949, 868.00/3-449, Rankin to Secretary of State, March 23, 1949, 868.00/3-2349 and Cannon to Secretary of State, April 12, 1949, 868.00/4-1249, SD records.

40. McNeill, *Greece*, pp. 43–44; Burks, *Dynamics of Communism*, p. 103; Minor to Secretary of State, May 16, 1949, 868.00/5-1649, SD records. See also *FR 1949*, 6:286; U.S. Department of State, *Seventh Report to Congress on Assistance to Greece and Turkey*, p. 2.

41. Averoff-Tossizza, *By Fire and Axe*, p. 335; Gibson to Secretary of State, July 30, 1949, 868.00/7-3049, SD records; Kofos, *Nationalism and Communism in Macedonia*, p. 182; Shoup, *Communism and the Yugoslav National Question*, pp. 161–62; Palmer and King, *Yugoslav Communism*, pp. 129–30.

42. Sulzberger, *A Long Row of Candles*, p. 433; *FR 1949*, 5:864, 873–74, 895–96. See also *FR 1949*, 6:360.

43. *FR 1949*, 6:267–68, 276; Grady to Secretary of State, February 18, 1949, 868.00/2-1849 and Douglas to Secretary of State, March 18, 1949, 868.00/3-1849, SD records.

44. Cromie, "Memorandum of Conversation" (June 22, 1949), 868.00/6-2249, SD records; *FR 1949*, 6:316–17, 340.

45. *FR 1949*, 6:265; Woodhouse, *Struggle for Greece*, p. 263; Baldwin to Secretary of State, February 21, 1949, 868.00/2-2149 and Cromie, "Memorandum of Conversation" (June 22, 1949), 868.00/6-2249, SD records; *FR 1949*, 5:897.

46. Seton-Watson, *The East European Revolution*, pp. 358–59; Acheson to American embassy (Athens), March 9 and June 27, 1949, "350 Yugo (Secret)" folder and Cannon to American embassy (Athens), April 26, 1949, "320 Greece-Yugo (Secret)" folder, Box 2488, Athens post records; *FR 1949*, 5:897; Cannon to Secretary of State, August 4, 1949, 868.00/8-449, SD records.

47. Grady to Secretary of State, February 8, 1949, 868.00/2-849, SD records; *FR 1949*, 6:268. For Bulgaria's mixed attitude toward the rebellion, see Kousoulas, "The Truman Doctrine and the Stalin-Tito Rift," pp. 436–37.

48. In September 1948, a GNA general not only ordered the shelling of

Albania but dispatched an infantry company into that country to over-whelm Albanian detachments who, he claimed, were assisting the rebels. On April 1, 1949, the Greek ambassador proposed to State Department officials that, in the event of Cominform action to overthrow Tito, the Western powers should organize "a naval operation . . . to storm Albania" and occupy it. That same day, Grady cabled the State Department that it would be "inadvisable" for the Athens government to renounce its claim to Northern Epirus. "Consideration should be given Albania's strategic location," he added, and the U.S. government "should not take any step which could be represented as indicating even tacit approval [of the] com-plete absorption [of] Albania into [the] Eastern satellite system." Averoff-Tossizza, *By Fire and Axe*, p. 249; FR 1949, 6:287–89.

49. Woodhouse, *Struggle for Greece*, p. 272; FR 1949, 5:302.

50. Shulman, *Stalin's Foreign Policy Reappraised*, passim; Cannon to Secretary of State, March 9, 1949, 868.00/3-949 and Kohler to Secretary of State, March 28, 1949, 868.00/3-2849, SD records.

51. Woodhouse, *Struggle for Greece*, p. 274.

52. FR 1949, 3:703; FR 1949, 6:303–309; Acheson to American embassy (Athens), May 19, 1949, 868.00/5-1849, SD records; Kennan, "Notes for Secretary's Meeting" (May 20, 1949), Box 33, Policy Planning Staff records; "Frontier Violations Basic Issue in Greek Situation."

53. On May 3, 1949, the rebels put forward a similar peace proposal—their twenty-first since 1946. O'Ballance, *The Greek Civil War*, p. 191; Harry Howard to Cromie and Baxter, May 4, 1949, 868.00/5-449, SD records; Shulman, *Stalin's Foreign Policy Reappraised*, pp. 71–72; Minutes of the Policy Planning Staff Meeting of May 9, 1949, Box 32, Policy Planning Staff records.

54. FR 1949, 6:320–22, 330–33; Satterthwaite to Rusk, May 9, 1949, 868.00/5-949, Rusk, "Memorandum of Conversation" (May 16, 1949), 868.00/5-1649, Satterthwaite to Secretary of State, May 17, 1949, 868.00/5-1749, Acheson to American embassy (Athens), May 19, 1949, 868.00/5-1859 and Cromie, "Memorandum for the President" (May 19, 1949), 868.00/5-1949, SD records.

55. FR 1949, 6:326–29, 356; Cromie to Satterthwaite, Jernegan, and Bax-ter, May 17, 1949, 868.00/5-1749 and Acheson to American embassy (Ath-ens), May 19, 1949, 868.00/5-1849, SD records.

56. FR 1949, 6:337, 344–56; Webb to American embassy (Paris), May 26, 1949, PSF Subject File, Truman papers; American embassy (Athens), "Transmitting Translation of Telegram from Under Secretary of Foreign Affairs" (June 1, 1949), 868.00/6-149, SD records.

57. FR 1949, 5:904; FR 1949, 6:363–64, 368; Iatrides, *Balkan Triangle*, pp. 59–60.

58. FR 1949, 6:369–70; Iatrides, *Balkan Triangle*, p. 63; Woodhouse, *Struggle for Greece*, pp. 273–74; Kofos, *Nationalism and Communism in Macedonia*, p. 185.

59. Dedijer, *The Battle Stalin Lost*, pp. 269–70; Cannon to American

embassy (Athens), July 24, 1949, "320 Greece-Yugo (Conf)" folder, Box 2488, Athens post records; *The Greek Partisans Accuse*, passim.

60. Cannon to American embassy (Athens), September 8, 1949, "320 Greece-Yugo (Secret)" folder, Box 2488, Athens post records. For similar assessments, see Minutes of the Policy Planning Staff Meeting of September 14, 1949, Box 32, Policy Planning Staff records; Jernegan, "Memorandum of Conversation" (October 21, 1949), 868.00/10-2149, SD records.

61. *FR 1949*, 6:393, 397; Shulman, *Stalin's Foreign Policy Reappraised*, pp. 37–38; Woodhouse, *Struggle for Greece*, pp. 264–65, 272–73.

62. *FR 1949*, 6:373–75, 381–86, 425–26; Minor to Secretary of State, August 8, 1949, 868.00/8-849 and Grady to Secretary of State, September 14, 1949 and Jernegan, "Greece" (September 14, 1949), 868.00/9-1449, SD records.

63. In late 1949, according to Kim Philby, then a Soviet agent within the British intelligence hierarchy, American and British officials attempted to overthrow the Albanian government and to establish a successor linked to the West. The venture, however, proved a fiasco. *FR 1949*, 6:414–15; Kim Philby, *My Silent War*, pp. 194–98.

64. The royalist newspaper *Kathimerini* greeted Truman's seventh statement to Congress on Greek aid as follows: "Truman agrees with the Greek view that there is no room for experiments in appeasement. There is only a peace imposed by arms." *FR 1949*, 6:417, 426; Minor to Secretary of State, August 6, 1949, 868.00/8-649, SD records.

65. The U.S. ambassador to the Soviet Union declared in December 1949 that "Greek rebel forces of 10,000" were in Communist territory. They constituted a "latent military threat which [the] Soviets can always reorganize rapidly for action inside Greek borders." The following March, Under Secretary of State Webb claimed that "combat-fit guerrilla reserves outside Greece may total as high as 25,000." Intelligence Division, General Staff, U.S. Army to Director of Intelligence, November 7, 1949. P & O 091 Greece, Section III, Case 58, P & O Division, Army General Staff records; *FR 1949*, 6:467; *FR 1950*, 5:343.

66. Woodhouse, *Struggle for Greece*, pp. 271, 284–85; O'Ballance, *The Greek Civil War*, pp. 200–1; Intelligence Division, General Staff, U.S. Army to Director of Intelligence, November 7, 1949, P & O 091 Greece, Section III, Case 58, P & O Division, Army General Staff records.

67. Constantine Poulos, "Greece: Betrayal as Usual," p. 412. For more recent assessments with similar conclusions, see Woodhouse, *Struggle for Greece*, p. 289; Eudes, *The Kapetanios*, passim; House Committee on International Relations, *Military Assistance Programs*, pp. 312–14.

68. *FR 1949*, 4:477. But for indications that some State Department officials thought that Stalin had abandoned the Greek rebels, at least temporarily, see McGhee to Grady, November 8, 1949, 868.20/10-1549 and Cromie, "Memorandum of Conversation" (December 21, 1949). 711.68/12-2149, SD records.

69. In later years, when Soviet-Yugoslav relations thawed, the party line shifted. Writing about the civil war in 1964, a KKE spokesman did not mention Tito at all. Instead, he blamed the defeat of the rebellion upon British and American "imperialists," Greek "reactionaries," and the "Left sectarian policy of the [KKE] leadership at the time." Grady to Secretary of State, November 8, 1949, 868.00/11-849, SD records; Zizis Zografos, "Some Lessons of the Civil War in Greece."

70. "Discussion of the Greek Case in the General Assembly"; *Documents on American Foreign Relations, January 1–December 31, 1949*, pp. 664–66.

71. Vukmanovic-Tempo, *How and Why*, p. 92; Woodhouse, *Struggle for Greece*, p. 275. For further Yugoslav denunciations of Soviet betrayal in Greece, see *Borba*, August 10, 1949, quoted in Cannon to Secretary of State, August 12, 1949, 868.00/8-1249, SD records; *The Greek Partisans Accuse*, passim.

10. AFTERMATH

1. Andreas Papandreou, *Democracy at Gunpoint*, p. 11.

2. The figures cited by various authorities differ widely. Estimating the number killed, the Greek government claimed about 40,000 combatants (mostly rebels), the U.S. government claimed 75,000, and Anglo-American observers claimed 158,000. Given the large number of unrecorded civilian deaths, the last figure does not seem unreasonable. The number of refugees finding shelter within Greece has been estimated at from 700,000 to 750,000, while the number that fled abroad has been put at from 50,000 to 100,000. See, for example, Xydis, *Greece and the Great Powers*, p. 541; Woodhouse, *Struggle for Greece*, pp. 285–86; O'Ballance, *The Greek Civil War*, pp. 192, 202; Tsoucalas, *Greek Tragedy*, p. 114; Chandler, *The Divided Land*, pp. 195–96; Couloumbis et al., *Foreign Interference*, p. 117; Foreign Operations Administration, *Greece* (1954), "Mission to Greece, General" folder, Box 3, Iverson papers.

3. As late as the beginning of 1952, Greece's per capita income stood at $130. Howard S. Ellis et al., *Industrial Capital in Greek Development*, pp. 233–34; Papandreou, *Democracy at Gunpoint*, p. 2; Chandler, *The Divided Land*, p. 210; Varvaressos, *Report on the Greek Economic Problem*, p. 3.

4. *FR 1947*, 5:513–14, 563–64, 575, 623; *FR 1948*, 4:47. The idea that Greece, Turkey, Iran, and Italy constituted a defensive wall for Anglo-American oil interests in the Mideast was repeated numerous times during this period by American officials. On September 5, 1947, for example, Secretary of War Royall and Secretary of the Navy Forrestal, commenting on the consequences of Greece going Communist, predicted a "drastically adverse effect. Forces friendly to, if not under the domination of, the USSR would be on the Mediterranean. . . . Access by the United States and Great Britain to the petroleum products of the Middle East, which are essential to their economic welfare and military potential, would be jeopardized." *FR 1947*, 5:328.

5. Engler, *The Politics of Oil*, pp. 65–79, 182–266; Louis L. Gerson, *John Foster Dulles*, pp. 241–300; Herbert S. Parmet, pp. 470–87, 493–94, 531–33; Walter LaFeber, *America, Russia, and the Cold War*, pp. 188–98, 205–206; *FR 1950*, 5:9–121.

6. A State Department memorandum of February 8, 1951 declared that Greece, Turkey, Iran, and Yugoslavia constituted "the shield of the Middle East." *FR 1950*, 5:254–58; *FR 1951*, 1:46.

7. These interests continued to be the primary ones of American officials. In 1957, for example, a State Department spokesman told a congressional committee that "Communist control of Greece would threaten the entire Middle East." He explained that "the strategic location of Greece . . . its tie-in with Turkey, forming a defensive tier to the north, its membership in and contribution to NATO, and its strategic position in relation to Communist ambitions and activities in the Middle East . . . are considered by United States officials in Greece to be the most important factors behind United States security interests in that country." NSC 103 and NSC 103/1, NSC records; U.S. Senate, Special Committee to Study the Foreign Aid Program, *Greece, Turkey, and Iran*, pp. 13–14.

8. McNeill, *Greece*, pp. 61–62; Grady, Adventures in Diplomacy," pp. 207–8, "Chapter 12—Adventures in Diplomacy" folder, Box 5, Grady papers; Jean Meynaud, *Les Forces Politiques en Grèce* p. 486; Seton-Watson, *The East European Revolution*, pp. 328–29; Woodhouse, *Struggle for Greece*, p. 287; Stavrianos, *Greece*, pp. 217–18.

9. Grady, "Adventures in Diplomacy," p. 207, "Chapter 12—Adventures in Diplomacy" folder, Box 5, Grady papers; John Coppock to Paul A. Porter, April 9, 1950, "American Economic Mission to Greece—Correspondence and Memoranda (1949–71)" folder, Porter papers; Papandreou, *Democracy at Gunpoint*, pp. 84–85.

10. Coppock to Porter, April 9, 1950, "American Economic to Greece—Correspondence and Memoranda (1949–71)" folder, Porter papers; Grady to Herbert Elliston, April 6, 1950, "E-Misc." folder, Box 1, Grady Papers; *FR 1950*, 5:345–48; House Committee on International Relations, *Military Assistance Programs*, p. 88.

11. *FR 1950*, 5:351–52, 354, 356–57, 359–61, 364–69; Maurice Goldbloom, "United States Policy in Post-War Greece," p. 230; McNeill, *Greece*, p. 62. The following month, still fuming at the "capriciousness and manifest incompetence" of Venizelos, Webb suggested that the embassy "work towards" the "removal of Venizelos as Liberal Leader by his own Party." *FR 1950*, 5:375–76.

12. Although some writers have suggested that Grady's difficulties with the King led to his dismissal, Grady's unpublished memoirs and correspondence, while quite hostile to Paul and Frederika, do not indicate it. Moreover, in January 1950, Grady had already suggested that he be relieved of his Greek assignment. Grady, "Adventures in Diplomacy," pp. 210–12, "Chapter 12—Adventures in Diplomacy" folder, Box 5 and Grady to

McGhee, January 20, 1950, "Appointment—Ambassador to Greece" folder, Box 1, Grady papers; "An interview with King Paul of Greece," pp. 28, 31.

13. According to Grady, "Van Fleet has, in effect, joined the conspirators." He identified the latter as "the Rightists, centering around the Palace." *Ethnikos Kiryx*, June 25, 1950, "Appointment—Ambassador to Greece" folder, and Grady to Minor, July 28, 1950, "Iran—Amb. Assignment to" folder, Box 1, Grady papers; FR 1950, 5:380, 396.

14. Although Minor's dispatch of July 19, 1950 suggested the Korean War as a turning point in the American appraisal of Plastiras, the embassy had long given disparaging reports to Washington about his potential use by Communists. Indeed Minor had written one such report in December 1949. FR 1950, 5:380–82, 386–87; Grady to Secretary of State, November 8, 1948, 868.00/11-948 and Minor to Secretary of State, December 16, 1949, 868.00/12-1649, SD records.

15. FR 1950, 5:395–97, 399–402, 415–17; Goldbloom, "United States Policy in Post-War Greece," pp. 230–31.

16. FR 1950, 5:416–17, 432–33; Iatrides, "American Attitudes Toward the Political System of Postwar Greece," p. 65; McNeill, *Greece*, p. 75.

17. Although Peurifoy and Grady had been estranged because of differing attitudes toward the King, both diplomats now rallied behind the candidacy of Papagos. Grady to Peurifoy, November 9, 1950, Peurifoy to Rountree, March 16, 1951, Peurifoy to Grady, August 23, 1951 and Grady to Peurifoy, September 6, 1951, "P—Misc." folder, Box 1, Grady papers.

18. Theodore A. Couloumbis, *Greek Political Reaction to American and NATO Influences*, pp. 53–55, 61–69; Iatrides, "American Attitudes Toward the Political System of Postwar Greece, pp. 68–69; Sweet-Escott, *Greece*, p. 84; Spencer, *War and Postwar Greece*, p. 142; Sulzberger, *A Long Row of Candles*, p. 790; McNeill, *Greece*, p. 76. For additional indications of the strong American opposition to proportional representation in Greece, see FR 1950, 5:259; Rountree to Grady, July 10, 1951, "R—Misc." folder, Box 1, Grady papers.

19. Foreign Operations Administration, *Greece* (1954), "Mission to Greece, General" folder, Box 3, Iverson papers; Papagos, "Guerilla Warfare," p. 241; Couloumbis, *Greek Political Reaction to American and NATO Influences*, pp. 5, 194–96; Nicos P. Mouzelis, *Modern Greece*, pp. 117–18; Iatrides, "American Attitudes Toward the Political System of Postwar Greece," p. 67.

20. Laurence Stern, *The Wrong Horse*, p. 17; Couloumbis, *Greek Political Reaction to American and NATO Influences*, pp. 97–109; Goldbloom, "United States Policy in Post-War Greece," p. 233; Papandreou, *Democracy at Gunpoint*, pp. 93–98; Rousseas, *The Death of a Democracy*, pp. 88–90.

21. FR 1949, 6:431–32, 436; FR 1950, 5:335–38; 343, 411; House Committee on International Relations, *Military Assistance Programs*, p. 80; Chief of Staff, U.S. Army to Anonymous, n.d., P & O 091 Greece TS, Section III, Case 25 and Charles L. Bolte to Chief of Staff, U.S. Army, P

& O 091 Greece TS, Section I, Case 1/5, P & O Division, Army General Staff records.

22. *FR 1950*, 5:406, 621; U.S. Army Historical Division, "Command Report—Joint US Military Aid Greece, 1951," Army General Staff records; Sweet-Escott, *Greece*, p. 158.

23. Actually, Van Fleet was not sanguine about Greece's fortunes in the event of such a conflict. Three days later, he wrote that Greece would be "part of a cover plan. I recognize that Greece cannot be held in the event of war with Russia, and therefore, it represents a considerable liability to have it. . . . According to the Commander, British Mediterranean Fleet, Greece would be of greater strategic value to the West if she were entirely under the sea. But during peace time Greece is of tremendous strategic value to the US" as a "diversion of Soviet strength." NSC 103, NSC records; *FR 1949*, 6:455; Van Fleet to Department of the Army, November 7 and 10, 1949, P & O 091 Greece TS, Section II, Case 22/1, P & O Division, Army General Staff records.

24. *FR 1950*, 5:387–89, 398–99; NSC 103/1, NSC records.

25. 381 Greece (6-20-49), Combined Chiefs of Staff records; George F. Kennan, *The Cloud of Danger*, pp. 114–15; Goldbloom, "United States Policy in Post-War Greece," p. 233; Couloumbis, *Greek Political Reaction to American and NATO Influence*, p. 45.

26. *FR 1950*, 5:1306–9; Omar Bradley to Secretary of Defense, May 22, 1951, JCS 1704/51, CCS 092 GREECE (12-30-47), Combined Chiefs of Staff records; Couloumbis, *Greek Political Reaction to American and NATO Influence*, pp. 33, 77; Goldbloom, "United States Policy in Post-War Greece," p. 233; Senate Special Committee to Study the Foreign Aid Program, *Greece, Turkey, and Iran*, p. 20.

27. Different authorities provide different figures, a fact which may reflect the secrecy of some military aid or the difficulty in classifying it. None, however, differ substantially. See, for example, Lincoln, *United States' Aid to Greece*, p. 184; George Coutsoumaris et al., *Analysis and Assessment of the Economic Effects of the U.S. PL 480 Program in Greece*, pp. 19–20; Xydis, "The Truman Doctrine in Perspective," p. 240; Committee for Economic Development, *Economic Development Issues*, p. 44.

28. Again, the figures cited by authorities vary, in this case from 30 to 52.8 percent. *FR 1950*, 5:435–36; U.S. Department of State, "Strength for Free Europe: Contributions of Our North Atlantic Allies" (July 1951), "Mission to Greece, General" folder, Box 3, Iverson papers; Munkman, *American Aid to Greece*, pp. 71–72; Couloumbis, *Greek Political Reaction to American and NATO Influence*, p. 37; "Greece's Defense Burden," p. 464.

29. Sweet-Escott, *Greece*, p. 158; NSC 103, NSC records. See also Varvaressos, *Report on the Greek Economic Problem*, pp. 31–32.

30. Dimitrios A. Germidis and Maria Negreponti-Delivanis, *Industrialisation, Employment, and Income in Greece*, p. 22; Coutsoumaris et al.,

Analysis and Assessment, p. 26; Mouzelis, *Modern Greece*, p. 25; McNeill, *Greece*, p. 3 and *The Metamorphosis of Greece*, pp. 90–107, 160–68.

31. Coutsoumaris et al., *Analysis and Assessment*, pp. 26–28; Howard S. Ellis et al., *Industrial Capital in Greek Development*, pp. 19, 26, 46, 106; George Coutsoumaris, *The Morphology of Greek Industry*, pp. 36, 248; Xenophon Zolotas, *Monetary Equilibrium*, p. 32.

32. Germidis and Negreponti-Delivanis, *Industrialisation, Employment, and Income*, p. 30; Zolotas, *Monetary Equilibrium*, pp. 27, 120–22; Mouzelis, *Modern Greece*, pp. 27–28; Sweet-Escott, *Greece*, p. 135; Munkman, *American Aid to Greece*, pp. 150–51.

33. U.S. Senate Special Committee to Study the Foreign Aid Program, *Greece, Turkey, and Iran*, p. 16; Varvaressos, *Report on the Greek Economic Problem*, pp. 90–92; Jean Crockett, *Consumer Expenditures and Incomes in Greece*, p. 99; Zolotas, *Monetary Equilibrium*, pp. 143–44.

34. Alec P. Alexander, *Greek Industrialists*, p. 117; Irving Brown, "Report on Greece" (May 4, 1951), enclosure in Green to Brown, "1950 Convention File," Box 18, Green papers.

35. Zolotas, *Monetary Equilibrium*, pp. 106–13, 187–91; Germidis and Negreponti-Delivanis, *Industrialisation, Employment, and Income*, pp. 162, 191, 195; Jecchinis, *Trade Unionism in Greece*, pp. 159–61.

36. Grady, "Adventures in Diplomacy," p. 213, "Chapter 12—Adventures in Diplomacy" folder, Box 5 and Grady to Rountree, March 6, 1951, Grady to Paul Porter, March 24, 1951, and Grady to Peurifoy, April 27, 1951, "P—Misc." folder, Box 1, Grady papers.

37. Lincoln, *United States' Aid to Greece*, pp. 105–6, 125; McNeill, *Greece*, pp. 64–66; Candilis, *The Economy of Greece*, p. 53; Rountree to Grady, July 10, 1951, "R—Misc." folder, Box 1, Grady papers.

38. Committee for Economic Development, *Economic Development Issues*, p. 37; Lincoln, *United States' Aid to Greece*, pp. 165, 184.

39. Munkman, *American Aid to Greece*, pp. 77–79, 109, 118, 130, 179–81, 184; Price, *The Marshall Plan and Its Meaning*, p. 279.

40. In 1965, the director of the Bank of Greece conceded: "It would appear that a substantial part of business profits has been devoted to luxury consumption." *FR 1950*, 5:262; Zolotas, *Monetary Equilibrium*, p. 150.

41. *FR 1950*, 5:261; Iatrides, "American Attitudes Toward the Political System of Postwar Greece," p. 69; Stavros B. Thomadakis, "Notes on Greek-American Economic Relations"; U.S. Senate Special Committee to Study the Foreign Aid Program, *Greece, Turkey, and Iran*, pp. 14, 16, 22.

42. Alivizatos, "The 'Emergency' Regime and Civil Liberties, 1946–1949" (MS), pp. 10–12; Papandreou, *Democracy at Gunpoint*, pp. 4, 62–63; John A. Katris, *Eyewitness in Greece*, pp. 77–80.

43. Iatrides, "American Attitudes Toward the Political System of Postwar Greece," pp. 66–67; Jecchinis, *Trade Unionism in Greece*, pp. 159–61; Nicolas Svoronos, *Histoire de la Grèce Moderne*, pp. 116–17, 119–20.

44. Acheson, particularly, brushed aside criticism that Greece was not

particularly democratic. "Of course, they do not have exactly the same kind of institutions that we do," he told the Advertising Council in February 1950. "The only question that we should ask is whether they are determined to protect their independence against Communist aggression." Bundy, ed., *The Pattern of Responsibility*, p. 143.

45. FR 1950, 5:267, 369–73; Lagoudakis to Cromie, November 16, 1949, 868.00/11-1649, SD records; Stern, *The Wrong Horse*, p. 18; *New York Times*, August 2, 1974; Katris, *Eyewitness in Greece*, pp. 44–45.

46. FR 1950, 5:259; Papandreou, *Democracy at Gunpoint*, p. 103; Jecchinis, *Trade Unionism in Greece*, pp. 151–52; Makris to Green, January 17, 1950, Green to Brown, February 15, 1950, Brown to Green, April 25, 1950, and Green to Oldenbroek, May 1, 1950, "1949 convention file," Green papers.

47. Stern, *The Wrong Horse*, pp. 13–14, 16; McNeill, *Greece*, pp. 67–68; Price, *The Marshall Plan and Its Meaning*, pp. 314, 319; Couloumbis et al., *Foreign Interference*, pp. 122–27; Papandreou, *Democracy at Gunpoint*, pp. 102–4; Iatrides, "American Attitudes Toward the Political System of Postwar Greece," p. 69; Adamantia Pollis, "United States Foreign Policy Towards Authoritarian Regimes in the Mediterranean," pp. 35, 41–42.

48. For the cavalier U.S. dismissal of Greek claims to Cyprus during the 1950s, see Van Coufoudakis, "United States Foreign Policy and the Cyprus Question," pp. 107–10; FR 1950, 5:234, 260; George V. Allen oral history interview, pp. 55–57.

49. Woodhouse, *Struggle for Greece*, p. 288; McNeill, *Greece*, p. 199; Mouzelis, *Modern Greece*, pp. 125–26; Irwin T. Sanders, *Rainbow in the Rock*, pp. 294–325.

50. Iatrides, "American Attitudes Toward the Political System of Postwar Greece," p. 70; Theodore A. Couloumbis, "Defining Greek Foreign Policy Objectives," pp. 25–26; George K. Zaharopoulos, "The Monarchy and Politics in Modern Greece," pp. 205–6; Papandreou, *Democracy at Gunpoint*, pp. 5–7.

51. Jean Meynaud, *Rapport sur L'Abolition de la Démocratie en Grèce*, pp. 17–18; Papandreou, *Democracy at Gunpoint*. pp. 117–20; George Frangos and Peter Schwab, eds., *Greece Under the Junta*, p. 8; Svoronos, *Histoire de la Grèce Moderne*, pp. 120–22; Rousseas, *The Death of a Democracy*, pp. 21–22.

52. Johnson's remarks were related by the Greek ambassador to another Greek diplomatic official, Philip Deane (Gigantes). Papandreou, *Democracy at Gunpoint*, p. 7; Katris, *Eyewitness in Greece*, p. 45; Iatrides, "American Attitudes Toward the Political System of Postwar Greece," p. 70; Stern, *The Wrong Horse*, pp. 25–30; Philip Deane, *I Should Have Died*, pp. 96, 112–14. See also Theodore A. Couloumbis, "Post World War II Greece," pp. 298–301.

53. Deane, *I Should Have Died*, pp. 92–94, 109–10; Zaharopoulos, "The

Monarchy and Politics," pp. 207–8; Meynaud, *Rapport sur L'Abolition de la Démocratie*, pp. 18–51; Papandreou, *Democracy at Gunpoint*, pp. viii–ix, 9; Stern, *The Wrong Horse*, p. 35; Rousseas, *The Death of a Democracy*, pp. 26–32.

54. Ronald Steel, *Imperialists and Other Heroes*, pp. 189–92; Frangos and Schwab, eds., *Greece Under the Junta*, pp. 15–30, 57–59, 77–78, 95–97; Papandreou, *Democracy at Gunpoint*, pp. 26, 319–22; Xydis, "The Truman Doctrine in Perspective," p. 240; S. Victor Papacosma, *The Military in Greek Politics*, pp. 186–87; Mouzelis, *Modern Greece*, pp. 129–30.

55. Stern, *The Wrong Horse*, pp. 12–13, 19, 35–46; Papandreou, *Democracy at Gunpoint*, pp. 10–11, 23–24, 226–30; Frangos and Schwab, eds., *Greece Under the Junta*, p. 13; Iatrides, "American Attitudes Toward the Political System of Postwar Greece," p. 71; Deane, *I Should Have Died*, p. 126; *New York Times*, August 2, 1974; Rousseas, *The Death of a Democracy*, pp. 58–62, 92–99; George Zaharopoulos, "Politics and the Army in Post-War Greece," p. 33; *Washington Post*, May 15, 1967.

56. Frangos and Schwab, eds., *Greece Under the Junta*, pp. 30–31, 125–30; Stern, *The Wrong Horse*, pp. 7, 47–68, 72; Couloumbis, "Defining Greek Foreign Policy Objectives," p. 26; Couloumbis et al., *Foreign Interference*, pp. 135–39; Steel, *Imperialists and Other Heroes*, p. 205; Iatrides, "American Attitudes Toward the Political System of Postwar Greece," p. 71; Pollis, "United States Foreign Policy Towards Authoritarian Regimes," p. 42.

57. Deane, *I Should Have Died*, pp. 122–24; Papandreou, *Democracy at Gunpoint*, p. 327.

58. They were especially active in Taiwan, Vietnam, and the Philippines, where their services were in considerable demand. As early as April 1950, the U.S. chargé in the Philippines recommended the assignment to the U.S. military mission of "a substantial number of officers having actual experience in guerrilla and anti-guerrilla operations," among them personnel with "experience in the recent operations in Greece." Another rising star in the "national security" firmament was Thomas Karamessines, the CIA's station chief in Athens, who became director of the agency's covert operations on a global basis. Barton Bernstein, "American Intervention in the Korean Civil War," p. 8; Acheson to James S. Lay, Jr., October 26, 1950, NSC 90, NSC records; *FR 1951*, 1:82–85; Sanders, *Rainbow in the Rock*, p. 306; *FR 1950*, 6:1437; *Washington Post*, January 7, 1976.

59. In January 1951, a U.S. Army representative on the State Department's Southeast Asia Aid Policy Committee recommended "dispatch of U.S. personnel to the combat-team level, as in Greece." He explained that "the experience in Greece had shown how useful this effort can be." *FR 1950*, 6:1437, 1488, 1490–91: *FR 1951*, 6:10.

60. The Greece-Vietnam parallel was drawn by other American officials as well. In January 1950, for example, noting Soviet recognition of Ho Chi

Minh's government in Indochina, the U.S. ambassador in France predicted that "we may soon be faced with [a] situation similar to that formerly prevailing in Greece." *FR 1950*, 6:705, 710, 778, 803–4.

61. Kuniholm, *The Origins of the Cold War in the Near East*, pp. 419–20; Theodore Sorensen, *Kennedy*, pp. 660–61; Lyndon B. Johnson, *The Vantage Point*, pp. 31, 422; *New York Times*, February 24, 1966; Neil Sheehan et al., *The Pentagon Papers*, pp. 447–48. See also *New York Times*, April 3, 1963; *The Pentagon Papers: The Senator Gravel Edition*, 3:715–16.

62. U.S. Senate, Committee on Foreign Relations, *Greece and Cyprus*, passim; Stern, *The Wrong Horse*, pp. 112–15, 125–46, 158, 160; Couloumbis, "Defining Greek Foreign Policy Objectives," pp. 26–43; John O. Iatrides, "Reviewing American Policy Toward Greece," p. 15; Theodore A. Couloumbis, "A New Model for Greek-American Relations," p. 199.

63. See, for example, Yergin, *Shattered Peace*, p. 295; Iatrides, "Greece and the Origins of the Cold War," p. 249.

64. Once a participant in many of the events in question, Woodhouse is currently a leading scholar of modern Greece and director of the Royal Institute of International Affairs. Iatrides, "American Attitudes Toward the Political System of Postwar Greece," p. 72; Zografos, "Some Lessons of the Civil War," pp. 44–45; Auty and Clogg, eds., *British Policy*, p. 144.

65. Zante, an island of 436 square kilometers, 75 percent of it mountainous, then had a population of 42,148. It contained numerous leftists, some of them KKE members, who could have participated in the revolt, had they chosen to do so. But peace reigned on Zante, for, in late 1947, the island's political leaders worked out an agreement guaranteeing all persons full individual and political rights. This agreement was broken in early 1949, when the Greek government's armed forces arrested 52 "alleged communists and fellow travellers" on the island and shipped them off to the concentration camp at Makronissos. Springs to Secretary of State, December 20, 1947, 868.00/12-2047 and February 18, 1949, 868.00B/2-1849, SD records.

BIBLIOGRAPHY

MANUSCRIPT COLLECTIONS

Dean Acheson papers. Harry S. Truman Library. Independence, Mo.

George V. Allen papers. Truman Library.

Joseph and Stewart Alsop papers. Library of Congress. Washington, D.C.

Army General Staff records. National Archives. Washington, D.C.

Athens post records. Washington National Records Center. Suitland, Md.

Paul Atkins papers. Yale University Library. New Haven, Conn.

Warren R. Austin papers. University of Vermont Library. Burlington, Vt.

Hanson Baldwin papers. Yale University Library.

Jasper Bell papers. University of Missouri Library. Columbia, Mo.

Adolf A. Berle, Jr. papers. Franklin D. Roosevelt Library. Hyde Park, N.Y.

Chester Bowles papers. Yale University Library.

Irving Brown papers. AFL-CIO Library. Washington, D.C.

James F. Byrnes papers. Clemson University Library. Clemson, S.C.

Cabinet records. Public Record Office. London, England.

Francis H. Case papers. Dakota Wesleyan University Library. Mitchell, S.D.

Francis H. Case papers. Truman Library.

Caserta post records. Washington National Records Center.

Central Intelligence Agency records. National Archives.

William L. Clayton papers. Rice University Library. Houston, Texas.

William L. Clayton papers. Truman Library.

William L. Clayton and Willard Thorp office files. Truman Library.

Clark M. Clifford files. Truman Library.

Clark M. Clifford papers. Truman Library.

Combined Chiefs of Staff (Joint Chiefs of Staff) records. National Archives.

Tom Connally papers. Library of Congress.

Elmer Cope papers. Ohio Historical Society. Columbus, Ohio.

Council on Foreign Relations records. Council on Foreign Relations. New York, N.Y.

Oscar Cox papers. Roosevelt Library.

Hugh Dalton diary. London School of Economics. London, England.

Joseph D. Davies papers. Library of Congress.

Ralph K. Davies papers. Truman Library.

Department of the Air Force records. National Archives.

Department of the Army records. Office of the Chief of Military History. Washington, D.C.

Department of Labor records. National Archives.

Department of State records. (SD records.) National Archives.

Department of State Committees records. (SD Committees records.) National Archives.

John Foster Dulles papers. Princeton University Library. Princeton, N.J.

George M. Elsey papers. Truman Library.

Herbert Feis papers. Library of Congress.

Foreign (Occupied) Areas Reports, Adjutant General's Office. Washington National Records Center.

Foreign Office records. (FO records.) Public Record Office, London.

James V. Forrestal diaries. Princeton University Library.

James V. Forrestal papers. Princeton University Library.

Friends Committee on National Legislation records. Swarthmore College Peace Collection. Swarthmore, Pa.

Ellen Clayton Garwood papers. Truman Library.

Clinton S. Golden papers. Pennsylvania State University Library. University Park, Pa.

Henry F. Grady papers. Truman Library.

William Green papers. State Historical Society of Wisconsin. Madison, Wisc.

Harry Hopkins papers. Roosevelt Library.

Cordell Hull papers. Library of Congress.

Harold Ickes papers. Library of Congress.

Kenneth R. Iverson papers. Truman Library.

Joseph M. Jones papers. Truman Library.

William Langer papers. University of North Dakota Library. Grand Forks, N.D.

William D. Leahy papers. Library of Congress.

Herbert H. Lehman papers. Columbia University Library. New York, N.Y.

William G. Livesay papers. U.S. Army Military History Research Collection. Carlisle Barracks, Pa.

Lincoln MacVeagh diary. In the possession of Professor John Iatrides. Cheshire, Conn.

National Security Council records. (NSC records.) National Archives.

Office of Strategic Services records. National Archives.

Robert P. Patterson papers. Library of Congress.

"P" Project, State Department file, 1944–47, Intelligence Division, Army General Staff records. ("P" Project records.) Washington National Records Center.

Pericles Mission records. Central Intelligence Agency. Washington, D.C.

Policy Planning Staff records. National Archives.

Paul A. Porter papers. Truman Library.

President's Committee on Foreign Aid records. Truman Library.

President's Materials Policy Commission records. Truman Library.

Eleanor Roosevelt papers. Roosevelt Library.

Franklin D. Roosevelt papers. (Official File [OF], Map Room Files [MR], and President's Secretary's File [PSF].) Roosevelt Library.

Samuel Rosenman papers. Truman Library.

John W. Snyder papers. Truman Library.

Sidney Souers papers. Truman Library.

State-Army-Air Force Coordinating Committee (State-War-Navy Coordinating Committee) records. (SWNCC records.) National Archives.

Edward R. Stettinius, Jr. papers. University of Virginia Library. Charlottesville, Va.

Henry L. Stimson diary. Yale University Library.

John Taber papers. Cornell University Library. Ithaca, N.Y.

Robert A. Taft papers. Library of Congress.

Florence Thorne papers. State Historical Society of Wisconsin.

Harry S. Truman papers. Truman Library.

Arthur H. Vandenberg papers. University of Michigan Library. Ann Arbor, Michigan.

John M. Vorys papers. Ohio Historical Society.

War Office records. Public Record Office, London.

Kenneth Wherry papers. State Historical Society of Nebraska. Lincoln, Nebraska.

Helen Zotos papers. State Historical Society of Wisconsin.

ORAL HISTORY INTERVIEWS

George V. Allen. Columbia University Oral History Collection.

Anthony Bernaris. Truman Library.

William L. Clayton. Columbia University Oral History Collection.

Constantinos A. Doxiadis. Truman Library.

George M. Elsey. Truman Library.

Loy Henderson. Columbia University Oral History Collection.

Marx Leva. Truman Library.

Kenneth C. Royall, Sr. Columbia University Oral History Collection.

Constantine Tsaldaris. Truman Library.

Henry A. Wallace. Columbia University Oral History Collection.

PERSONAL COMMUNICATIONS

Charles A. Coombs. Letter to the author, September 5, 1979.

Costa G. Couvaras. Letter to the author, February 20, 1978.

Loy Henderson. Personal interview, January 13, 1976.

Harry N. Howard. Letter to the author, October 1, 1979.

John B. Howard. Letters to the author, August 28 and September 10, 1979.

John D. Jernegan. Letter to the author, August 23, 1979.

Allen C. Miller II. Letter to the author, November 18, 1979.

Jay S. Seeley. Letter to the author, March 2, 1978.

L. S. Stavrianos. Letter to the author, February 24, 1978.
Henry S. Villard. Letter to the author, September 5, 1979.
George C. Vournas. Letter to the author, February 17, 1978.
James E. Webb. Letter to the author, August 29, 1979.

OTHER UNPUBLISHED MATERIAL

Alivizatos, Nicos C. "The 'Emergency' Regime and Civil Liberties, 1946–1949." Paper delivered at the 1978 convention of the Modern Greek Studies Association.

Byrnes, Laurence G. "History of the United States Section Military, Allied Mission to Observe the Greek Elections (AMFOGE) 25 October 1945–18 April 1946." Office of the Chief of Military History, Department of the Army.

Davies, Margaret Mary. "The Role of the American Trade Union Representatives in the Aid to Greece Program, 1947–1948." Ph.D. dissertation, University of Washington, 1960.

Gardner, Hugh. "Civil War in Greece, 1945–49." Incomplete draft manuscript. Office of the Chief of Military History, Department of the Army.

Hondros, John Louis. "The German Occupation of Greece, 1941–1944." Ph.D. dissertation, Vanderbilt University, 1969.

Iatrides, John O. "The Greek Experience with the Truman Doctrine: Review and Assessment." Paper delivered at the 1977 convention of the International Studies Association.

—— "From Liberation to Civil War: The United States and Greece, 1944–46." Paper delivered at the 1975 convention of the American Historical Association.

—— "The Truman Doctrine: The Beginning of United States Penetration in Greece." Paper delivered at the 1975 Conference on United States Policy Toward Greece and Cyprus, American University.

Kellis, James G. "The Development of U.S. National Intelligence, 1941–1961." Ph.D. dissertation, Georgetown University, 1963.

Pedersen, James H. "Focal Point of Conflict: The United States and Greece, 1943–1947." Ph.D. dissertation, University of Michigan, 1974.

Sand, Gregory W. "Clifford and Truman: A Study in Foreign Policy and National Security, 1945–49." Ph.D. dissertation, Saint Louis University, 1972.

Wittner, Lawrence S. "American Policy Toward Greece, 1943–1947: Prelude to the Truman Doctrine." Paper delivered at the 1978 convention of the Organization of American Historians.

—— "American Policy Toward Greece, 1944–1949." Paper delivered at the 1978 convention of the Modern Greek Studies Association.

OFFICIAL PUBLICATIONS

Documents on American Foreign Relations, January 1—December 31, 1949. Princeton, N.J.: Princeton University Press, 1950.

Economic Cooperation Administration. *Third Report to Congress of the Economic Cooperation Administration: For the Quarter Ended December 31, 1948.* Washington, D.C.: U.S. Government Printing Office, 1949.

—— *Seventh Report to Congress of the Economic Cooperation Administration: For the Quarter Ended December 31, 1949.* Washington, D.C.: U.S. Government Printing Office, 1950.

—— *Eleventh Report to Congress of the Economic Cooperation Administration: For the Quarter Ended December 31, 1950.* Washington, D.C.: U.S. Government Printing Office, 1951.

—— *Thirteenth Report to Congress of the Economic Cooperation Administration: For the Quarter Ended June 30, 1951.* Washington, D.C.: U.S. Government Printing Office, 1951.

The Greek Partisans Accuse. New York: Yugoslav Information Center, 1950.

International Labour Office. *Labour Problems in Greece: Report of the Mission of the International Labour Office to Greece (October-November 1947).* Geneva: International Labour Office, 1949.

National Liberation Front (E.A.M.). *White Book, May 1944—March 1945.* New York: Greek American Council, 1945.

The Pentagon Papers: The Senator Gravel Edition. 4 vols. Boston: Beacon Press, 1975.

Public Papers of the Presidents: Harry S. Truman, 1947. Washington, D.C.: U.S. Government Printing Office, 1963.

Report of the British Parliamentary Delegation to Greece, August, 1946. London: His Majesty's Stationery Office, 1947.

Sheehan, Neil, et al., eds. *The Pentagon Papers: As Published by the New York Times.* New York: Bantam Books, 1971.

Union of Soviet Socialist Republics. Ministry of Foreign Affairs. *Correspondence Between the Chairman of the Council of Ministers of the U.S.S.R. and the Presidents of the U.S.A. and the Prime Ministers of Great Britain During the Great Patriotic War of 1941-1945.* 2 vols. Moscow: Foreign Languages Publishing House, 1957.

U.S. Congress. *Congressional Record.* 78th through 81st Congresses.

U.S. Department of State. *Department of State Bulletin.* Vols. 8–21 (1943–1949).

—— *Report to Congress on Assistance to Greece and Turkey:* Quarterly pamphlets, 1947–49. Washington, D.C.: U.S. Government Printing Office, 1947–49.

—— *Foreign Relations of the United States* (FR). Annual volumes, 1943–51. Washington, D.C.: U.S. Government Printing Office, 1964–79.

—— *Foreign Relations of the United States: The Conference at Quebec, 1944.* Washington, D.C.: U.S. Government Printing Office, 1972.

—— *Foreign Relations of the United States: The Conference of Berlin (The Potsdam Conference), 1945.* 2 vols. Washington, D.C.: U.S. Government Printing Office, 1960.

—— *Foreign Relations of the United States: The Conferences at Cairo and*

Tehran, 1943. Washington, D.C.: U.S. Government Printing Office, 1961.

—— *Foreign Relations of the United States: The Conferences at Malta and Yalta, 1945.* Washington, D.C.: U.S. Government Printing Office, 1955.

—— *Foreign Relations of the United States: The Conferences at Washington and Quebec, 1943.* Washington, D.C.: U.S. Government Printing Office, 1970.

—— *Problems of Greece, Korea, and Palestine.* Washington, D.C.: U.S. Government Printing Office, 1949.

—— *Report of the Allied Mission to Observe the Greek Elections.* Washington, D.C.: U.S. Government Printing Office, 1946.

—— *The United Nations and the Problem of Greece.* Washington, D.C.: U.S. Government Printing Office, 1947.

U.S. Department of State and Senate Committee on Foreign Relations. *A Decade of American Foreign Policy: Basic Documents, 1941–1949.* Washington, D.C.: U.S. Government Printing Office, 1950.

U.S. House of Representatives, Committee on Foreign Affairs. *Assistance to Greece and Turkey: Hearings.* 80th Cong., 1st sess. Washington, D.C.: U.S. Government Printing Office, 1947.

U.S. House of Representatives, Committee on International Relations. *Military Assistance Programs.* Part 2. Historical Series, Vol. 6. Washington, D.C.: U.S. Government Printing Office, 1976.

U.S. Senate, Committee on Foreign Relations. *Assistance to Greece and Turkey: Hearings.* 80th Cong., 1st sess. Washington, D.C.: U.S. Government Printing Office, 1947.

—— *Greece and Cyprus, 1975: A Report by Senator Claiborne Pell.* 94th Cong., 1st sess. Washington, D.C.: U.S. Government Printing Office, 1975.

—— *Legislative Origins of the Truman Doctrine: Hearings Held in Executive Session . . . on S. 938, A Bill to Provide for Assistance to Greece and Turkey.* 80th Cong., 1st sess. Washington, D.C.: U.S. Government Printing Office, 1973.

U.S. Senate, Special Committee to Study the Foreign Aid Program. *Greece, Turkey, and Iran: Report on United States Foreign Assistance Programs by Former Ambassador Norman Armour.* 85th Cong., 1st sess. Washington, D.C.: U.S. Government Printing Office, 1957.

Varvaressos, Kyriakos. *Report on the Greek Economic Problem.* Washington, D.C.: n.p., 1952.

BOOKS AND ARTICLES

Acheson, Dean. *Present at the Creation: My Years in the State Department.* New York: Norton, 1969.

Agee, Philip. "The American Factor in Greece: Old and New." In Philip Agee and Louis Wolf, eds., *Dirty Work: The CIA in Western Europe*, pp. 157–64. Secaucus, N.J.: Lyle Stuart, 1978.

"Aid to Greece and Turkey." *Department of State Bulletin Supplement* (May 4, 1947), 16:827–909.

Alexander, Alec P. *Greek Industrialists: An Economic and Social Analysis.* Athens: Center of Planning and Economic Research, 1964.

Amen, Michael Mark. *American Foreign Policy in Greece, 1944–1949: Economic, Military, and Institutional Aspects.* Frankfurt: Peter Lang, 1978.

"An Interview with King Paul of Greece." *U.S. News & World Report* (April 21, 1950), 28:28–31.

Attlee, Clement. *Twilight of Empire: Memoirs of Prime Minister Clement Attlee.* New York: A. S. Barnes, 1962.

Atwell, Mary Welek. "Eleanor Roosevelt and the Cold War Consensus." *Diplomatic History* (Winter 1979), 3:99–113.

Auty, Phyllis. *Tito: A Biography.* New York: McGraw-Hill, 1970.

—— and Richard B. Clogg, eds. *British Policy Towards Wartime Resistance in Yugoslavia and Greece.* London: Macmillan, 1975.

Averoff-Tossizza, Evangelos. *By Fire and Axe: The Communist Party and the Civil War in Greece, 1944–1949.* New Rochelle, N.Y.: Caratzas, 1978.

Baerentzen, Lars. "The Demonstration in Syntagma Square on Sunday the 3rd of December, 1944." *Scandinavian Studies in Modern Greek* (1978), no. 2, pp. 3–52.

"Balkan Commission Reports." *Department of State Bulletin* (August 22, 1948), 19:238.

"Balkan States Discuss Greek Dispute." *Department of State Bulletin* (November 21, 1948), 19:637.

Baram, Phillip J. *The Department of State in the Middle East, 1919–1945.* Philadelphia: University of Pennsylvania Press, 1978.

Barker, Elisabeth. *British Policy in South-East Europe in the Second World War.* London: Macmillan, 1976.

Barnet, Richard J. *Intervention and Revolution: The United States in the Third World.* New York: World, 1968.

Berger, Henry W. "Senator Robert A. Taft Dissents from Military Escalation." In Thomas G. Paterson, ed., *Cold War Critics: Alternatives to American Foreign Policy in the Truman Years*, pp. 167–204. Chicago: Quadrangle, 1971.

Bernstein, Barton J. "American Intervention in the Korean Civil War: Part II." *Foreign Service Journal* (February, 1977), 54:8–11, 33–34.

—— "Walter Lippmann and the Early Cold War." In Thomas G. Paterson, ed., *Cold War Critics: Alternatives to American Foreign Policy in the Truman Years*, pp. 18–53. Chicago: Quadrangle, 1971.

Berle, Beatrice Bishop, and Travis B. Jacobs, eds. *Navigating the Rapids, 1918–1971: From the Papers of Adolf A. Berle.* New York: Harcourt Brace Jovanovich, 1973.

Black, C. E. "Greece and the United Nations." *Political Science Quarterly*, (December 1948), 63:551–68.

Bloomfield, Lincoln P., and Amelia C. Leiss. *Controlling Small Wars: A Strategy for the 1970's*. New York: Knopf, 1969.

Bohlen, Charles E. *The Transformation of American Foreign Policy*. New York: Norton, 1969.

—— *Witness to History, 1929–1969*. New York: Norton, 1973.

Braden, Thomas W. "I'm Glad the CIA Is 'Immoral.'" *Saturday Evening Post* (May 20, 1967), pp. 10–12.

Brodie, Bernard. *Foreign Oil and American Security*. New Haven, Conn.: Yale Institute of International Studies, 1947.

Brooks, Thomas R. *Clint: A Biography of a Labor Intellectual*. New York: Atheneum, 1978.

Brown, Anthony Cave, ed. *The Secret War Report of the OSS*. New York: Berkley Medallion, 1976.

Brown, James William. "Greece: Obsessed With the Junta." *Nation* (March 20, 1976), 222:334–36.

Bundy, McGeorge, ed. *The Pattern of Responsibility*. Boston: Houghton Mifflin, 1952.

Burks, R.V. *The Dynamics of Communism in Eastern Europe*. Princeton, N.J.: Princeton University Press, 1961.

Burns, James MacGregor. *Roosevelt: The Soldier of Freedom*. New York: Harcourt Brace Jovanovich, 1970.

Byrnes, James F. *All In One Lifetime*. New York: Harper & Bros., 1958.

—— *Speaking Frankly*. New York: Harper & Bros., 1947.

Campbell, John. "The Greek Civil War." In Evan Luard, ed., *The International Regulation of Civil Wars*, pp. 37–64. New York: New York University Press, 1972.

—— and Philip Sherrard. *Modern Greece*. New York: Praeger, 1968.

Campbell, Thomas M., and George C. Herring, eds. *The Diaries of Edward R. Stettinius, Jr., 1943–1946*. New York: Franklin Watts, 1975.

Candilis, Wray O. *The Economy of Greece, 1944–66: Efforts for Stability and Development*. New York: Praeger, 1968.

Carlyle, Margaret, ed. *Documents on International Affairs, 1947–1948*. London: Royal Institute of International Affairs, 1952.

Chandler, Geoffrey. *The Divided Land: An Anglo-Greek Tragedy*. London: Macmillan, 1959.

Churchill, Winston. *Closing the Ring*. Vol. 5 of *The Second World War*. Boston: Houghton Mifflin, 1951.

—— *Triumph and Tragedy*. Vol. 6 of *The Second World War*. Boston: Houghton Mifflin, 1953.

"The Churchill Tragedy." *New Republic* (December 18, 1944), 111:819–21.

Cliadakis, Harry. "The Political and Diplomatic Background to the Metaxas Dictatorship." *Journal of Contemporary History* (1979), 14:117–38.

—— "Le Régime de Metaxás et la Deuxième Guerre Mondiale." *Revue D'Histoire de la Deuxième Guerre Mondiale* (July 1977), no. 107, pp. 19–38.

Clogg, Richard. "The Greek Government in Exile, 1941–44." *International History Review* (July 1979), 1:376–98.

—— *A Short History of Modern Greece.* Cambridge: Cambridge University Press, 1979.

Cochran, Bert. *Harry Truman and the Crisis Presidency.* New York: Funk & Wagnalls, 1973.

Coles, Harry L., and Albert K. Weinberg. *Civil Affairs: Soldier Become Governors.* (*United States Army in World War II: Special Studies*) Washington, D.C.: Office of the Chief of Military History, 1964.

Committee for Economic Development. *Economic Development Issues: Greece, Israel, Taiwan, Thailand.* New York: Committee for Economic Development, 1968.

Condit, D. M. *Case Study in Guerrilla War: Greece During World War II.* Washington: Department of the Army, 1961.

Connally, Tom. *My Name Is Tom Connally.* New York: Crowell, 1954.

Coufoudakis, Van. "United States Foreign Policy and the Cyprus Question." In Theodore A. Couloumbis and Sallie M. Hicks, eds. *U.S. Foreign Policy Toward Greece and Cyprus: The Clash of Principle and Pragmatism,* pp. 106–38. Washington, D.C.: Center for Mediterranean Studies and the American Hellenic Institute, 1975.

Couloumbis, Theodore A. "Defining Greek Foreign Policy Objectives." In Theodore A. Couloumbis and John O. Iatrides, eds., *Greek-American Relations: A Critical Review,* pp. 21–47. New York: Pella, 1980.

—— *Greek Political Reaction to American and NATO Influences.* New Haven, Conn.: Yale University Press, 1966.

—— "A New Model for Greek-American Relations: From Dependence to Interdependence." In Theodore A. Couloumbis and John O. Iatrides, eds., *Greek-American Relations: A Critical Review,* pp. 197–206. New York: Pella, 1980.

—— "Post World War II Greece: A Political Review." *East European Quarterly* (Fall 1973), 7:285–310.

—— , John A. Petropulos, and Harry J. Psomiades. *Foreign Interference in Greek Politics: An Historical Perspective.* New York: Pella, 1976.

Coutsoumaris, George. *The Morphology of Greek Industry: A Study in Industrial Development.* Athens: Center of Economic Research, 1963.

—— , et al. *Analysis and Assessment of the Economic Effects of the U.S. PL 480 Program in Greece.* Athens: Center of Planning and Economic Research, 1965.

Crockett, Jean. *Consumer Expenditures and Incomes In Greece.* Athens: Center of Planning and Economic Research, 1967.

Curtin, Edwin P. "American Advisory Group Aids Greece in War on Guerrillas." *Armed Cavalry Journal* (January–February 1949), 58:8–11, 34.

Dallek, Robert. *Franklin D. Roosevelt and American Foreign Policy, 1932–1945.* New York: Oxford University Press, 1979.

Dalton, Hugh. *High Tide and After: Memoirs, 1945–1960*. London: Frederick Muller, 1962.

Daniell, Raymond. "Sympton and Tragedy of Our Time." *New York Times Magazine* (April 6, 1947), pp. 7, 59–61.

—— "Where the 'Cold War' Is Shooting War." *New York Times Magazine* (February 15, 1948), pp. 12, 32.

Davidson, Basil. "Makronessos." *New Statesman and Nation* (January 7, 1950), 39:4–5.

Davis, Lynn Etheridge. *The Cold War Begins: Soviet-American Conflict over Eastern Europe*. Princeton, N.J.: Princeton University Press, 1974.

Deane, Philip. *I Should Have Died*. New York: Atheneum, 1977.

Dedijer, Vladimir. *The Battle Stalin Lost: Memoirs of Yugoslavia, 1948–1953*. New York: Viking Press, 1971.

—— *Tito*. New York: Simon & Schuster, 1953.

—— *Tito Speaks: His Self Portrait and Struggle with Stalin*. London: Weidenfeld & Nicolson, 1953.

Delivanis, Dimitrios, and William Cleveland. *Greek Monetary Developments, 1939–1948*. Bloomington: Indiana University Press, 1949.

Djilas, Milovan. *Conversations with Stalin*. New York: Harcourt, Brace & World, 1962.

—— *The New Class: An Analysis of the Communist System*. New York: Praeger, 1972.

—— *Wartime*. New York: Harcourt Brace Jovanovich, 1979.

Dimakis, John "The Greek Press." In John T. A. Koumoulides, ed., *Greece in Transition: Essays in the History of Modern Greece*, pp. 209–35. London: Zeno, 1977.

"Discussion of the Greek Case in the General Assembly." *Department of State Bulletin* (November 28, 1949), 21:813–16.

"Discussion of the Greek Situation." *Department of State Bulletin* (November 21, 1949), 21:779–83.

Dobney, Frederick J., ed. *Selected Papers of Will Clayton*. Baltimore: Johns Hopkins University Press, 1971.

Eden, Anthony. *The Reckoning*. Vol. 3 of *The Memoirs of Anthony Eden*. Boston: Houghton Mifflin, 1965.

Ellis, Howard S. et al. *Industrial Capital in Greek Development*. Athens: Center of Economic Research, 1964.

Engler, Robert. *The Politics of Oil: A Study of Private Power and Democratic Directions*. Chicago: University of Chicago Press, 1967.

Eudes, Dominique. *The Kapetanios: Partisans and Civil War in Greece, 1943–1949*. New York: Monthly Review Press, 1972.

Evans, Trefor E., ed. *The Killearn Diaries, 1934–1946*. London: Sidgwick & Jackson, 1972.

Feis, Herbert. "Order in Oil." *Foreign Affairs* (July 1944), 22:616–26.

—— *Petroleum and American Foreign Policy*. Stanford, Calif.: Stanford University, 1944.

—— *Seen from E. A.: Three International Episodes.* New York: Knopf, 1947.

Ferrell, Robert H. *George C. Marshall.* Vol. 15 of *The American Secretaries of State and Their Diplomacy.* New York: Cooper Square, 1966.

Fields, Allen D. "Kolonaki and the Others." *Nation* (March 29, 1947), 164:358–59.

Fitzsimons, M. A. *The Foreign Policy of the British Labour Government, 1945–1951.* Notre Dame, Ind.: University of Notre Dame Press, 1953.

Fontaine, André. *History of the Cold War: From the October Revolution to the Korean War.* New York: Random House, 1970.

Foot, Michael. *Aneurin Bevan: A Biography.* Vol. 1. *1897–1945.* New York: Atheneum, 1963.

Frangos, George, and Peter Schwab, eds. *Greece Under the Junta.* New York: Facts on File, 1973.

Freeland, Richard M. *The Truman Doctrine and the Origins of McCarthyism: Foreign Policy, Domestic Politics, and Internal Security, 1946–1948.* New York: Knopf, 1972.

"Frontier Violations Basic Issue in Greek Situation." *Department of State Bulletin* (May 29, 1949), 20:696–97.

Gaddis, John Lewis. *The United States and the Origins of the Cold War, 1941–1947.* New York: Columbia University Press, 1975.

—— "Was the Truman Doctrine a Real Turning Point?" *Foreign Affairs* (January 1974), 52:386–402.

Gardner, Hugh H. *Guerrilla and Counterguerrilla Warfare in Greece, 1941–1945.* Washington, D.C.: Office of the Chief of Military History, Department of the Army, 1962.

Gardner, Lloyd C. *Architects of Illusion: Men and Ideas in American Foreign Policy, 1941–1949.* Chicago: Quadrangle, 1972.

Gardner, Richard N. *Sterling-Dollar Diplomacy: The Origins and the Prospects of Our International Economic Order.* New York: McGraw-Hill, 1969.

Garwood, Ellen Clayton. *Will Clayton: A Short Biography.* Austin: University of Texas Press, 1958.

Gayn, Mark. "Democracy's Distant Cousin." *New Republic* (April 4, 1949), 120:15–18.

Germidis, Dimitrios A., and Maria Negreponti-Delivanis. *Industrialisation, Employment, and Income in Greece: A Case Study.* Paris: Organisation for Economic Co-operation and Development, 1975.

Gerson, Louis L. *John Foster Dulles.* Vol. 17 of *The American Secretaries of State and Their Diplomacy.* New York: Cooper Square, 1967.

Godson, Roy. *American Labor and European Politics: The AFL as a Transnational Force.* New York: Crane, Russak, 1976.

Goldbloom, Maurice. "United States Policy in Post-War Greece." In Richard Clogg and George Yannopoulos, eds., *Greece Under Military Rule,* pp. 228–54. New York: Basic Books, 1972.

"The Great Oil Deals." *Fortune* (May 1947), 35:138–43, 175–82.

"Greece's Defense Burden." *Economist* (November 15, 1952), p. 464.

"Greek Citizens of Soviet Origin Deported to Soviet Central Asia." *Department of State Bulletin* (October 31, 1949), 21:670.

"Guerrillas on Parade." *Newsweek* (February 23, 1948), pp. 35–36.

Halle, Louis J. *The Cold War as History*. New York: Harper & Row, 1967.

Hamby, Alonzo L. *Beyond the New Deal: Harry S. Truman and American Liberalism*. New York: Columbia University Press, 1973.

Harriman, W. Averell, and Elie Abel. *Special Envoy to Churchill and Stalin, 1941–1946*. New York: Random House, 1975.

Hartmann, Susan M. *Truman and the 80th Congress*. Columbia: University of Missouri Press, 1971.

Henderson, Loy W. "Foreign Policies: Their Formulation and Enforcement." *Department of State Bulletin* (September 29, 1946), 15:590–96.

Horowitz, David. *The Free World Colossus: A Critique of American Foreign Policy in the Cold War*. New York: Hill & Wang, 1965.

Howard, Harry N. "The Refugee Problem in Greece." *Department of State Bulletin* (March 7, 1948), 18:291–93.

Hull, Cordell. *The Memoirs of Cordell Hull*. 2 vols. New York: Macmillan, 1948.

Hurewitz, J. C. *Middle East Dilemmas: The Background of United States Policy*. New York: Harper & Bros., 1953.

Iatrides, John O., ed. *Ambassador MacVeagh Reports: Greece, 1933–1947*. Princeton, N.J.: Princeton University Press, 1980.

—— "American Attitudes Toward the Political System of Postwar Greece." In Theodore A. Couloumbis and John O. Iatrides, eds., *Greek-American Relations: A Critical Review*, pp. 49–73. New York: Pella, 1980.

—— *Balkan Triangle: Birth and Decline of an Alliance Across Ideological Boundaries*. The Hague: Mouton, 1968.

—— "Greece and the Origins of the Cold War." In John T. A. Koumoulides, ed., *Greece in Transition: Essays in the History of Modern Greece*, pp. 236–51. London: Zeno, 1977.

—— "Reviewing American Policy Toward Greece: The Modern Cassandras." In Theodore Couloumbis and John O. Iatrides, eds., *Greek-American Relations: A Critical Review*, pp. 11–20. New York: Pella, 1980.

—— *Revolt in Athens: The Greek Communist "Second Round," 1944–1945*. Princeton, N.J.: Princeton University Press, 1972.

—— "United States' Attitudes Toward Greece During World War II." In *Essays in Memory of Basil Laourdas*, pp. 599–625. Thessaloniki, 1975.

"International Outlook." *Business Week* (March 15, 1947), pp. 109–10.

Jecchinis, Christos. *Beyond Olympus*. London: George G. Harrap, 1960.

—— *Trade Unionism in Greece: A Study in Political Paternalism*. Chicago: Labor Education Division, Roosevelt University, 1967.

Johnson, Lyndon Baines. *The Vantage Point: Perspectives of the Presidency, 1963–1969*. New York: Holt, Rinehart & Winston, 1974.

Jones, Joseph Marion. *The Fifteen Weeks.* New York: Harcourt, Brace & World, 1964.

Jordan, Philip. "Greece in Purgatory." *Nation* (December 8, 1945), 161:624–26.

Katris, John A. *Eyewitness in Greece: The Colonels Come to Power.* St. Louis, Mo.: New Critics Press, 1971.

Kazantzakis, Nikos. *The Fratricides.* Trans. by Athena Gianakas Dallas. New York: Simon & Schuster, 1964.

Kédros, André. *La Résistance Grecque (1940–1944).* Paris: Robert Laffont, 1966.

Kendrick, Alexander. "Greece's Ultimate Solution." *New Republic* (March 7, 1949), 120:14–17.

—— "Moscow Conference Report." *New Republic* (March 24, 1947), 116:7.

Kennan, George F. *The Cloud of Danger: Current Realities of American Foreign Policy.* Boston: Little, Brown, 1977.

—— *Memoirs: 1925–1950.* Boston: Little, Brown, 1967.

Kirchwey, Freda. "Manifest Destiny, 1947." *Nation* (March 22, 1947), 164:317–19.

Kofos, Evangelos. *Nationalism and Communism in Macedonia.* Thessaloniki: Institute for Balkan Studies, 1964.

Koliopoulos, John S. *Greece and the British Connection, 1935–1941.* London: Oxford University Press, 1977.

Kolko, Gabriel. *The Politics of War: The World and United States Foreign Policy, 1943–1945.* New York: Random House, 1970.

Kolko, Joyce, and Gabriel Kolko. *The Limits of Power: The World and United States Foreign Policy, 1945–1954.* New York: Harper & Row, 1972.

Kousoulas, D. George. *Modern Greece: Profile of a Nation.* New York: Scribner's, 1974.

—— *Revolution and Defeat: The Story of the Greek Communist Party.* London: Oxford University Press, 1965.

—— "The Truman Doctrine and the Stalin-Tito Rift: A Reappraisal." *South Atlantic Quarterly* (Summer 1973), 72:427–39.

Krock, Arthur. *Memoirs: Sixty Years on the Firing Line.* New York: Funk & Wagnalls, 1968.

Kuniholm, Bruce R. *The Origins of the Cold War in the Near East: Great Power Conflict and Diplomacy in Iran, Turkey, and Greece.* Princeton, N.J.: Princeton University Press, 1980.

LaFeber, Walter. *America, Russia, and the Cold War, 1945–1971.* New York: Wiley, 1972.

Lagoudakis, Charilaos G. "Greece (1946–1949)." In D. M. Condit et al., eds. *The Experience in Europe and the Middle East,* pp. 497–527. Vol. 2 of *Challenge and Response in Internal Conflict.* Washington, D.C.: American University, 1967.

Laqueur, Walter Z. *The Soviet Union and the Middle East.* New York: Praeger, 1959.

—— *The Struggle for the Middle East: The Soviet Union in the Mediterranean, 1958–1968.* New York: Macmillan, 1969.

Larrabee, Stephen A. *Hellas Observed: The American Experience of Greece, 1775–1865.* New York: New York University Press, 1957.

Lash, Joseph P. *Eleanor: The Years Alone.* New York: New American Library, 1973.

Laski, Harold J. "Britain Without Empire." *Nation* (March 29, 1947), 164:353–56.

Leeper, Reginald. *When Greek Meets Greek.* London: Chatto & Windus, 1950.

Lees, Lorraine M. "The American Decision to Assist Tito, 1948–1949." *Diplomatic History* (Fall 1978), 2:407–22.

Legg, Keith R. *Politics in Modern Greece.* Stanford, Calif.: Stanford University Press, 1969.

Lenczowski, George. *Oil and State in the Middle East.* Ithaca, N.Y.: Cornell University Press, 1960.

Lincoln, Francis F. *United States' Aid to Greece, 1947–1962.* Germantown, Tenn.: Professional Seminars, 1975.

Loewenheim, Francis L., Harold D. Langley, and Manfred Jonas, eds. *Roosevelt and Churchill: Their Secret Wartime Correspondence.* New York: Saturday Review Press, 1975.

Loftus, John A. "Middle East Oil: The Pattern of Control." *Middle East Journal* (January 1948), 2:17–32.

Loomis, Frederick H. "Report From Greece." *Military Review* (April 1950), 30:3–9.

McAuliffe, Mary Sperling. *Crisis on the Left: Cold War Politics and American Liberals, 1947–1954.* Amherst: University of Massachusetts, 1978.

McLellan, David S. *Dean Acheson: The State Department Years.* New York: Dodd, Mead, 1976.

Macmillan, Harold. *The Blast of War, 1939–1945.* New York: Harper & Row, 1967.

McNeill, William H. "Dilemmas of Modernization in Greece." *Balkan Studies* (1967), 8:305–16.

—— *Greece: American Aid in Action, 1947–1956.* New York: Twentieth Century Fund, 1957.

—— *The Greek Dilemma: War and Aftermath.* London: Victor Gollancz, 1947.

—— *The Metamorphosis of Greece Since World War II.* Chicago: University of Chicago Press, 1978.

—— "The Outbreak of Fighting in Athens, December 1944." *American Slavic and East European Review* (1949), 8:252–61.

Markowitz, Norman D. *The Rise and Fall of the People's Century: Henry A. Wallace and American Liberalism, 1941–1948.* New York: Free Press, 1973.

Martin, Joe. *My First Fifty Years in Politics: As Told to Robert J. Donovan.* New York: McGraw-Hill, 1960.

Mastny, Vojtech. *Russia's Road to the Cold War: Diplomacy, Warfare, and the Politics of Communism, 1941–1945.* New York: Columbia University Press, 1979.

—— "Soviet War Aims at the Moscow and Teheran Conferences of 1943." *Journal of Modern History* (September 1975), 47:481–504.

—— "Spheres of Influence and Soviet War Aims in 1943." In Sylvia Sinanian et al., *Eastern Europe in the 1970s*, pp. 87–107. New York: Praeger, 1972.

Matthews, Kenneth. *Memories of a Mountain War: Greece, 1944–1949.* London: Longman, 1972.

Mavroede, Aphrodite. "Makronisos Journal." *Journal of the Hellenic Diaspora* (Fall 1978), 5:115–28.

Meehan, Eugene J. *The British Left Wing and Foreign Policy.* New Brunswick, N.J.: Rutgers University Press, 1960.

Meynaud, Jean. *Les Forces Politiques en Grèce.* Lausanne: Études de Science Politique, 1965.

—— *Rapport Sur L'Abolition de la Démocratie en Grèce.* Montreal: Études de Science Politique, 1967.

Michel, Henri. *The Shadow War: European Resistance, 1939–1945.* New York: Harper & Row, 1972.

Mikesell, Raymond F., and Hollis B. Chenery. *Arabian Oil: America's Stake in the Middle East.* Chapel Hill: University of North Carolina Press, 1949.

Millis, Walter, ed. *The Forrestal Diaries.* New York: Viking, 1951.

Molony, C. J. C. et al. *The Mediterranean and Middle East.* Vol. 5. Part of *History of the Second World War*, James Butler, ed. London: Her Majesty's Stationery Office, 1973.

Moran, Charles. *Churchill Taken from the Diary of Lord Moran: The Struggle for Survival, 1940–1965.* Boston: Houghton Mifflin, 1966.

Moss, W. Stanley. *A War of Shadows.* New York: Macmillan, 1952.

Mouzelis, Nicos P. *Modern Greece: Facets of Underdevelopment.* London: Macmillan, 1978.

Munkman, C. A. *American Aid to Greece: A Report on the First Ten Years.* New York: Praeger, 1958.

Murphy, Robert. *Diplomat Among Warriors.* Garden City, N.Y.: Doubleday, 1964.

Murray, J. C. "The Anti-Bandit War: Part I." *Marine Corps Gazette* (January 1954), 38:14–23.

—— "The Anti-Bandit War: Part II." *Marine Corps Gazette* (February 1954), 38:50–59.

—— "The Anti-Bandit War: Part III." *Marine Corps Gazette* (March 1954), 38:48–57.

—— "The Anti-Bandit War: Part IV." *Marine Corps Gazette* (April 1954), 38:52–60.

—— "The Anti-Bandit War: Part V." *Marine Corps Gazette* (May 1954), 38:52–58.

Myers, E. C. W. *Greek Entanglement*. London: Rupert Hart-Davis, 1955.

Nash, Gerald D. *United States Oil Policy, 1890–1964*. Pittsburgh: University of Pittsburgh Press, 1968.

"New Diplomacy, New Business." *Business Week* (March 22, 1947), pp. 15–16.

New York Times, 1943–1980.

O'Ballance, Edgar. *The Greek Civil War, 1944–1949*. New York: Praeger, 1966.

Odell, Peter R. *Oil and World Power: Background to the Oil Crisis*. Baltimore, Md.: Penguin, 1975.

"Oil." *Time* (March 24, 1947), 49:83–90.

Palmer, Stephen E., Jr., and Robert R. King. *Yugoslav Communism and the Macedonian Question*. Hamden, Conn.: Archon, 1971.

Papacosma, S. Victor. *The Military in Greek Politics: The 1909 Coup D'Etat*. Kent, Ohio: Kent State University Press, 1977.

Papagos, Alexander. "Guerrilla Warfare." In Franklin M. Osanka, ed., *Modern Guerrilla Warfare: Fighting Communist Guerrilla Movements, 1941–1961*, pp. 228–42. Glencoe, N.Y.: Free Press, 1963.

Papandreou, Andreas. *Democracy at Gunpoint: The Greek Front*. Garden City, N.Y.: Doubleday, 1970.

Papandreou, George A. *The Third War*. Athens: Hellenic, 1949.

Papandreou, Margaret. *Nightmare in Athens*. Englewood Cliffs, N.J.: Prentice-Hall, 1970.

Papathanasiades, Theodossios. "The Bandits' Last Stand in Greece." *Military Review* (February 1951), 31:22–31.

Parmet, Herbert S. *The Democrats: The Years After FDR*. New York: Macmillan, 1976.

—— *Eisenhower and the American Crusades*. New York: Macmillan, 1972.

"Passage of Bill Authorizing Assistance to Greece and Turkey." *Department of State Bulletin* (June 1, 1947), 16:1070–73.

Paterson, Thomas G. "The Dissent of Senator Claude Pepper." In Thomas G. Paterson, ed., *Cold War Critics: Alternatives to American Foreign Policy in the Truman Years*, pp. 114–39. Chicago: Quadrangle, 1971.

—— "Presidential Foreign Policy, Public Opinion, and Congress: The Truman Years." *Diplomatic History* (Winter 1979), 3:1–18.

—— *Soviet-American Confrontation: Postwar Reconstruction and the Origins of the Cold War*. Baltimore, Md.: John Hopkins University Press, 1973.

Petropulos, John A. *Politics and Statecraft in the Kingdom of Greece, 1833–1843*. Princeton, N.J.: Princeton University Press, 1968.

Philby, Kim. *My Silent War*. New York: Grove Press, 1968.

Polk, George. "Greece Puts Us to the Test." *Harper's* (December 1947), 195:529–36.

Pollis, Adamantia. "United States Foreign Policy Towards Authoritarian Regimes in the Mediterranean." *Millennium* (Spring 1975), 4:28–51.

Porter, Paul. "Wanted: A Miracle in Greece," *Collier's* (September 20, 1947), 120:14–15, 106–7.

Poulos, Constantine. "Greece: Betrayal as Usual." *Nation* (October 29, 1949), 169:411–13.

—— "Greek Tragedy, 1945." *Nation* (November 3, 1945), 161:450–52.

—— "The Lesson of Greece." *Nation* (March 27, 1948), 166:343–45.

—— "Report from Athens." *New Republic* (March 17, 1947), 116:26–27.

—— "Rule Britannia." *Nation* (December 23, 1944), 159:772–74.

Powers, Richard J. "Containment: From Greece to Vietnam—and Back?" *Western Political Quarterly* (December 1969), 22:846–61.

Pratt, William C. "Senator Glen H. Taylor: Questioning American Unilateralism." In Thomas G. Paterson ed., *Cold War Critics: Alternatives to American Foreign Policy in the Truman Years*, pp. 140–66. Chicago: Quadrangle, 1971.

Price, Harry Bayard. *The Marshall Plan and Its Meaning.* Ithaca, N.Y.: Cornell University Press, 1955.

Radosh, Ronald. *American Labor and United States Foreign Policy.* New York: Random House, 1970.

—— *Prophets on the Right: Profiles of Conservative Critics of American Globalism.* New York: Simon & Schuster, 1975.

——, and Leonard P. Liggio. "Henry A. Wallace and the Open Door." In Thomas G. Paterson, ed., *Cold War Critics: Alternatives to American Foreign Policy in the Truman Years*, pp. 76–113. Chicago: Quadrangle, 1971.

"Report from London to the Office of Public Affairs, Department of State." *Department of State Bulletin* (February 17, 1946), 14:233–36.

Resis, Albert. "The Churchill-Stalin Secret 'Percentages' Agreement on the Balkans, Moscow, October 1944." *American Historical Review* (April 1978), 83:368–87.

Reuther, Victor. *The Brothers Reuther: And the Story of the UAW.* Boston: Houghton Mifflin, 1976.

Richter, Heinz. *Griechenland zwischen Revolution und Konterrevolution (1936–1946).* Frankfurt: Europäische Verlagsanstalt, 1973.

Roberts, Walter R. *Tito, Mihailovic, and the Allies, 1941–1945.* New Brunswick, N.J.: Rutgers University Press, 1973.

Rogow, Arnold A. *James Forrestal: A Study of Personality, Politics, and Policy.* New York: Macmillan, 1963.

Roosevelt, Elliott. *As He Saw It.* New York: Duell, Sloan, and Pearce, 1946.

Roubatis, Yiannis, and Karen Wynn. "CIA Operations in Greece." In Philip Agee and Louis Wolf, eds., *Dirty Work: The CIA in Western Europe*, pp. 147–56. Secaucus, N.J.: Lyle Stuart, 1978.

Roubatis, Yiannis P., and Elias Vlanton. "Who Killed George Polk?" *More* (May 1977), 7:12–32.

Rousseas, Stephen. *The Death of a Democracy: Greece and the American Conscience.* New York: Grove Press, 1968.

Sachar, Howard M. *Europe Leaves the Middle East, 1936–1954.* New York: Knopf, 1972.

Salisbury, Harrison. "On an Unsolved Mystery." *Progressive* (May 1977), 41:24–25.

Sanders, Irwin T. *Rainbow in the Rock: The People of Rural Greece.* Cambridge, Mass.: Harvard University Press, 1962.

Sarafis, Stefanos. *Greek Resistance Army: The Story of ELAS.* London: Birch Books, 1951.

Schmidt, Dana Adams. "The Front in Greece Is Everywhere." *New York Times Magazine* (December 7, 1947), pp. 12–13, 52–55.

—— "The Modern Tragedy in Ancient Greece." *New York Times Magazine* (August 24, 1947), pp. 9, 20–21.

Schurmann, Franz. *The Logic of World Power: An Inquiry into the Origins, Currents, and Contradictions of World Politics.* New York: Pantheon, 1974.

Seton-Watson, Hugh. *The East European Revolution.* London: Methuen, 1956.

"The Shape of Things." *Nation* (March 8, 1947), 164:261.

"The Shape of Things," *Nation* (March 15, 1947), 164:289.

Sherwood, Robert E. *Roosevelt and Hopkins: An Intimate History.* New York: Harper & Bros., 1948.

Shoup, Paul. *Communism and the Yugoslav National Question.* New York: Columbia University Press, 1968.

Shulman, Marshall D. *Stalin's Foreign Policy Reappraised.* New York: Atheneum, 1966.

Shwadran, Benjamin. *The Middle East, Oil, and the Great Powers.* New York: Praeger, 1955.

Siracusa, Joseph M. and Glen St. John Barclay. "Australia, the United States, and the Cold War, 1945–51: From V-J Day to ANZUS." *Diplomatic History* (Winter 1981), 5:39–52.

Skendi, Stavro. "Albania Within the Slav Orbit: Advent to Power of the Communist Party." *Political Science Quarterly* (1948), 63:257–74.

Smith, Howard K. *The State of Europe.* New York: Knopf, 1951.

Smith, Ole L. "A Turning Point in the Greek Civil War, 1945–1949." *Scandinavian Studies in Modern Greek* (1979), no. 3, pp. 35–46.

Smith, R. Harris. *OSS: The Secret History of America's First Central Intelligence Agency.* New York: Dell, 1973.

Smith, Walter Bedell. *My Three Years in Moscow.* Philadelphia: Lippincott, 1950.

Smothers, Frank, William Hardy McNeill, and Elizabeth Darbishire

McNeill. *Report on the Greeks.* New York: Twentieth Century Fund, 1948.

Solberg, Carl. *Oil Power.* New York: New American Library, 1976.

Solomon, Mark. "Black Critics of Colonialism and the Cold War." In Thomas G. Paterson, ed., *Cold War Critics: Alternatives to American Foreign Policy in the Truman Years,* pp. 205–39. Chicago: Quadrangle, 1971.

Sorensen, Theodore C. *Kennedy.* New York: Harper & Row, 1965.

Speer, Albert. *Inside the Third Reich: Memoirs by Albert Speer.* Trans. by Richard and Clara Winston. New York: Macmillan, 1970.

Spencer, Floyd A. *War and Postwar Greece: An Analysis Based on Greek Writings.* Washington, D.C.: Library of Congress, 1952.

"Statement of the Allied Mission for Observing the Greek Elections." *Department of State Bulletin* (April 21, 1946), 14:671–73.

Stavrianos, L. S. *Greece: American Dilemma and Opportunity.* Chicago: Henry Regnery, 1952.

—— "The Greek National Liberation Front (EAM): A Study in Resistance Organization and Administration." *Journal of Modern History* (March 1952), 24:42–55.

—— "The Immediate Origins of the Battle of Athens." *American Slavic and East European Review* (1949), 8:237–51.

—— "The Mutiny in the Greek Armed Forces, April 1944." *American Slavic and East European Review* (1950), 9:302–11.

—— "The United States and Greece: The Truman Doctrine in Historical Perspective." In Dwight E. Lee and George E. McReynolds, eds., *Essays in History and International Relations,* pp. 36–59. Worcester, Mass.: Clark University, 1949.

—— "Vacuum in Greece." *New Republic* (December 24, 1945), 113:863–65.

Steel, Ronald. *Imperialists and Other Heroes: A Chronicle of the American Empire.* New York: Random House, 1975.

Stern, Laurence. *The Wrong Horse: The Politics of Intervention and the Failure of American Diplomacy.* New York: Quadrangle, 1977.

Stettinius, Edward R., Jr. *Roosevelt and the Russians: The Yalta Conference.* Garden City, N.Y.: Doubleday, 1949.

Suits, Daniel B. *An Econometric Model of the Greek Economy.* Athens: Center of Economic Research, 1964.

Sulzberger, Cyrus L. *A Long Row of Candles: Memoirs and Diaries, 1934–1954.* New York: Macmillan, 1969.

Svoronos, Nicolas. *Histoire de la Grèce Moderne.* Paris: Presses Universitaires de France, 1972.

Sweet-Escott, Bickham. *Greece: A Political and Economic Survey, 1939–1953.* London: Royal Institute of International Affairs, 1954.

Taft, Philip. *Defending Freedom: American Labor and Foreign Affairs.* Los Angeles: Nash, 1973.

Thomadakis, Stavros B. "Notes on Greek-American Economic Relations." In Theodore A Couloumbis and John O. Iatrides, eds., *Greek-American Relations: A Critical Review*, pp. 75–89. New York: Pella, 1980.

Truman, Harry S. *Memoirs*. Vol. 2. *Years of Trial and Hope*. Garden City, N.Y.: Doubleday, 1956.

"The Truman Doctrine." *New Republic* (March 24, 1947), 116:5–6.

Tsou, Tang. *America's Failure in China, 1941–1950*. Chicago: University of Chicago Press, 1963.

Tsoucalas, Constantine. *The Greek Tragedy*. Baltimore, Md.: Penguin, 1969.

"25,000,000 Loan to Greek Government." *Department of State Bulletin* (January 20, 1946), 14:78–79.

Ulam, Adam B. *Stalin: The Man and His Era*. New York: Viking, 1973.

—— *Titoism and the Cominform*. Cambridge, Mass.: Harvard University Press, 1952.

"U.S. Completes Reconstruction of Greek Transportation System." *Department of State Bulletin* (June 26, 1949), 20:826–27.

"U.S. Position on Problems Confronting Fourth General Assembly." *Department of State Bulletin* (October 3, 1949), 21:489–90.

Vandenberg, Arthur H., Jr., ed. *The Private Papers of Senator Vandenberg*. Boston: Houghton Mifflin, 1952.

Van Fleet, James A. "How We Won in Greece." *Balkan Studies* (1967), 8:387–93.

Villard, Henry Serrano. *Affairs at State*. New York: Crowell, 1965.

Vlavianos, Basil. "Behind the Greek 'Mutiny.'" *Nation* (May 13, 1944), 158:566–68.

Vukmanovic-Tempo, Svetozar. *How and Why the People's Liberation Struggle of Greece Met With Defeat*. London: Merritt & Hatcher, 1950.

Wainhouse, Edward R. "Guerrilla War in Greece, 1946–49: A Case Study." *Military Review* (June 1957), 37:17–25.

Warlimont, Walter. *Inside Hitler's Headquarters, 1939–45*. New York: Praeger, 1964.

"Washington Outlook." *Business Week* (March 8, 1947), pp. 5–6.

Washington Post, 1943–1980.

"Washington Wire." *New Republic* (March 10, 1947), 116:11.

Weiler, Peter. "The United States, International Labor, and the Cold War: The Breakup of the World Federation of Trade Unions." *Diplomatic History* (Winter 1981), 5:1–22.

"Who's Where." In Philip Agee and Louis Wolf, eds., *Dirty Work: The CIA in Western Europe*, pp. 717–34. Secaucus, N.J.: Lyle Stuart, 1978.

Williams, Francis. *Ernest Bevin: Portrait of a Great Englishman*. London: Hutchinson, 1952.

Wilson, Henry Maitland. *Eight Years Overseas, 1939–1947*. London: Hutchinson, 1950.

Wittner, Lawrence S. "American Policy Toward Greece During World War II." *Diplomatic History* (Spring 1979), 3:129–49.

—— *Cold War America: From Hiroshima to Watergate.* New York: Holt, Rinehart & Winston, 1978.

—— *Rebels Against War: The American Peace Movement, 1941–1960.* New York: Columbia University Press, 1969.

—— "The Truman Doctrine and the Defense of Freedom." *Diplomatic History* (Spring 1980), 4:161–87.

Woodbridge, George. *UNRRA: The History of the United Nations Relief and Rehabilitation Administration.* 2 vols. New York: Columbia University Press, 1950.

Woodhouse, Christopher M. *Apple of Discord: A Survey of Recent Greek Politics in Their International Setting.* London: Hutchinson, 1948.

—— "Early British Contacts with the Greek Resistance in 1942." *Balkan Studies* (1971), 12:347–63.

—— "The 'Revolution' in Its Historical Context." In Richard Clogg and George Yannopoulos, eds., *Greece Under Military Rule*, pp. 1–16. New York: Basic Books, 1972.

—— *A Short History of Modern Greece.* New York: Praeger, 1968.

—— *The Struggle for Greece, 1941–1949.* London: Hart-Davis, MacGibbon, 1976.

Woodward, Llewellyn. *British Foreign Policy in the Second World War.* Vol. 3. From *History of the Second World War.* London: Her Majesty's Stationery Office, 1971.

"Work and Victory Demonstration in Greece." *Department of State Bulletin* (April 3, 1949), 20:433.

Xydis, Stephen G. "America, Britain, and the USSR in the Greek Arena, 1944–1947." *Political Science Quarterly* (December 1963), 78:581–96.

—— *Greece and the Great Powers, 1944–1947: Prelude to the "Truman Doctrine."* Thessaloniki: Institute for Balkan Studies, 1963.

—— "Greece and the Yalta Declaration." *American Slavic and East European Review* (1961), 20:6–24.

—— "The Secret Anglo-Soviet Agreement on the Balkans of October 9, 1944." *Journal of Central European Affairs* (October, 1955), 15:248–71.

—— "The Truman Doctrine in Perspective." *Balkan Studies* (1967), 8:239–62.

Yergin, Daniel. *Shattered Peace: The Origins of the Cold War and the National Security State.* Boston: Houghton Mifflin, 1977.

Zaharopoulos, George. "The Monarchy and Politics in Modern Greece." In John T. A. Koumoulides, ed., *Greece in Transition: Essays in the History of Modern Greece*, pp. 190–208. London: Zeno, 1977.

—— "Politics and the Army in Post-War Greece." In Richard Clogg and George Yannopoulos, eds., *Greece Under Military Rule*, pp. 17–35. New York: Basic Books, 1972.

Zografos, Zizis. "Some Lessons of the Civil War in Greece." *World Marxist Review* (November 1964), 7:43–50.

Zolotas, Xenophon. *Monetary Equilibrium and Economic Development: With Special Reference to the Experience of Greece, 1950–1963.* Princeton, N.J.: Princeton University Press, 1965.

INDEX

Acheson, Dean: on plebiscite concerning monarchy, 44; on economic assistance, 50–51; on Soviet pressure on Turkey, 55–56; on Red Line Agreement, 61; on Soviet Union, 63; on need to assist Greece, 67–72, 100–1; and drafting of Truman Doctrine, 78–79; and Eleanor Roosevelt, 82; before congressional hearings, 85–90, 223; and United Nations, 91, 350n83; on Gromyko proposal, 97; on "Papagos solution," 128; on government repression of opposition, 148, 405n44; and Griswold, 170–71; on Braine-Tsaldaris agreement, 198–200; on labor unrest, 218; on Papagos' demands for larger Greek army, 248–49; on aid to Tito, 272–73; and Tito's break with guerrillas, 278; on possible action against Albanian government, 280; and Van Fleet, 289; on Plastiras, Papagos, and electoral system, 290; on Cyprus ("Acheson plan"), 303; on intervention and Papadopoulos junta, 307; on Tsaldaris, 334n7
Aegean Sea, 268
Agnew, Spiro, 306
Agricultural policy, 302
Agricultural production, 182–83
Albania: and Italy, 2; spreading influence of Soviet Union in, 36; Greek exiles and guerrillas in, 45, 58, 96, 243–44, 251, 255, 266–68, 280, 394n70; Greek territorial claims on, 47, 58, 279, 398n48; question of recognizing Democratic Government, 260; and possible Balkan federation, 261; and Soviet efforts to end Greek

rebellion, 263; and collapse of Greek rebellion, 274–75, 279–81; postwar relationship to Soviet Union, 310
Alexander, A. V., 52
American Broadcasting Corporation (ABC), 157
American Economic Mission, 167
American Export Lines, 298
American Federation of Labor (AFL): and Brown, 106–7, 205; establishes Free Trade Union Committee, 192–93; and WFTU, 195–96, 202; and anti-strike law, 209; and GSEE, 211–12; on government repression of opposition, 220, 386n91
American Mission for Aid to Greece (AMAG): and public opinion, 104–5; rift with U.S. embassy and dissolution of, 117–19; intelligence activities of, 150; and amnesty program, 152; and economic program for Sophoulis government, 171; on wage and price controls, food subsidies, and public health and reconstruction, 173, 179–80, 182–84, 216–19; on economic impact of civil war, 187; and armed forces, 232–33; *see also* Griswold, Dwight
American Tobacco Company, 298
Americans for Democratic Action, 94
Amnesty program, 151–54, 163–64, 362n42
Anderson, Clinton, 75, 101
Anglo-American Petroleum Agreement, 21–22, 62
Anglo-American policy differences: over oil, 20–21; over labor movement, 197–203, 378n20
Anglo-Iranian Oil Company, 61

CONTEMPORARY AMERICAN HISTORY SERIES
WILLIAM E. LEUCHTENBURG, GENERAL EDITOR